**From the Library of**

*Bernard and Muriel Frank*

HARRY C. TREXLER
LIBRARY

Gift of

Dr. & Mrs. Bernard
Frank

MUHLENBERG
COLLEGE

# American Jewish Year Book

# American Jewish Year Book 1989

VOLUME 89

Prepared by THE AMERICAN JEWISH COMMITTEE

Editor
DAVID SINGER

Associate Editor
RUTH R. SELDIN

THE AMERICAN JEWISH COMMITTEE
NEW YORK
THE JEWISH PUBLICATION SOCIETY
PHILADELPHIA

COPYRIGHT © 1989 BY THE AMERICAN JEWISH COMMITTEE
AND THE JEWISH PUBLICATION SOCIETY

*All rights reserved. No part of this book may be reproduced in any form without permission in writing from the publisher, except by a reviewer who may quote brief passages in a review to be printed in a magazine or newspaper.*

ISBN 0-8276-0351-7

*Library of Congress Catalogue Number: 99-4040*

PRINTED IN THE UNITED STATES OF AMERICA
BY THE HADDON CRAFTSMEN, INC., SCRANTON, PA.

# Preface

Two special articles in this volume are devoted to the American Jewish community, specifically, to the enormous changes that have taken place in the social and religious spheres just in the last two decades. In "The Impact of Feminism on American Jewish Life," Sylvia Barack Fishman uses sociodemographic data from a variety of sources to document the radical transformation of Jewish women's lives as a result of the feminist movement. She also traces the entry of women into public religious roles, reviews the ideological debate surrounding Jewish feminism, and discusses the implications of this social revolution for the Jewish family and the Jewish community.

Jack Wertheimer's "Recent Trends in American Judaism" takes a close look at developments in the Orthodox, Conservative, Reform, and Reconstructionist movements since the late 1960s, including demographic data, changes in liturgy, and responses to intermarriage and other social forces. The author also discusses the rise of the *havurah* movement and other new forms of religious expression.

Regular articles on Jewish life in the United States are Earl Raab's "Intergroup Relations," Lawrence Grossman's "Jewish Communal Affairs," and "The United States, Israel, and the Middle East," by Kenneth Jacobson. The article on Jewish population in the United States is by Barry A. Kosmin, Paul Ritterband, and Jeffrey Scheckner, of the North American Jewish Data Bank.

Events in Israel are covered extensively by Ralph Mandel. This year's reports on Jewish life around the world include updates on Brazil and Argentina, by David Schers and Shlomo Slutzky. Estimates for world Jewish population are provided by researchers at the Hebrew University of Jerusalem.

Carefully compiled directories of national Jewish organizations, periodicals, and federations and welfare funds, as well as religious calendars and obituary notices, round out the 1989 AMERICAN JEWISH YEAR BOOK.

We are grateful to Murray Pearson and Michele Anish for their proofreading efforts and to Diane Hodges for compiling the index. We also acknowledge the assistance of many colleagues at the American Jewish Committee, especially Cyma M. Horowitz, director of the Blaustein Library, Lotte Zajac, and all our other co-workers in Information and Research Services.

THE EDITORS

# Contributors

HENRIETTE BOAS: journalist, Amsterdam, Holland.

Y. MICHAL BODEMANN: associate professor, sociology, University of Toronto, Canada; visiting professor, Freie Universität, Berlin, West Germany.

SERGIO DELLAPERGOLA: director, Division of Jewish Demography and Statistics, Institute of Contemporary Jewry, Hebrew University of Jerusalem, Israel.

SIMONETTA DELLA SETA: Jerusalem correspondent, *Il Giornale* (Italy); researcher, Hebrew University of Jerusalem, Israel.

SYLVIA BARACK FISHMAN: research associate, Cohen Center for Modern Jewish Studies, Brandeis University; teaching associate, Brown University program in Judaic studies.

ZVI GITELMAN: professor, political science, University of Michigan.

LAWRENCE GROSSMAN: director of publications, American Jewish Committee.

NELLY HANSSON: researcher in political science and sociology, Paris, France.

KENNETH JACOBSON: director, Middle Eastern Affairs, Anti-Defamation League of B'nai B'rith.

LIONEL E. KOCHAN: Oxford Center for Post-Graduate Hebrew Studies, England.

MIRIAM KOCHAN: writer, translator, Oxford, England.

BARRY A. KOSMIN: director, North American Jewish Data Bank, Graduate School, City University of New York.

RALPH MANDEL: journalist, translator, Jerusalem, Israel.

ROBIN OSTOW: Solomon Ludwig Steinheim Institut für Deutsch-jüdische Geschichte, Duisburg, West Germany.

EARL RAAB: executive director emeritus, San Francisco Jewish Community Relations Council.

PAUL RITTERBAND: professor, sociology and Jewish studies, City College and the Graduate School, City University of New York.

viii / CONTRIBUTORS

JEFFREY SCHECKNER: administrator, North American Jewish Data Bank, Graduate School, City University of New York.

DAVID SCHERS: researcher, educational adviser, School of Education, Tel Aviv University, Israel.

U.O. SCHMELZ: professor emeritus, Jewish demography, Institute of Contemporary Jewry, Hebrew University of Jerusalem, Israel.

SHLOMO SLUTZKY: sociologist, journalist, Tel Aviv, Israel.

HAROLD M. WALLER: associate professor, political science, McGill University, Montreal, Canada; director, Canadian Center for Jewish Community Studies.

JACK WERTHEIMER: Joseph and Martha Mendelson Associate Professor of American Jewish History, Jewish Theological Seminary of America.

# Contents

PREFACE v
CONTRIBUTORS vii

## SPECIAL ARTICLES

The Impact of Feminism on American Jewish Life  *Sylvia Barack Fishman*  3
Recent Trends in American Judaism  *Jack Wertheimer*  63

## UNITED STATES

CIVIC AND POLITICAL
Intergroup Relations  *Earl Raab*  165
The United States, Israel, and the Middle East  *Kenneth Jacobson*  186

COMMUNAL
Jewish Communal Affairs  *Lawrence Grossman*  212

DEMOGRAPHIC
Jewish Population in the United States, 1988  *Barry A. Kosmin, Paul Ritterband, and Jeffrey Scheckner*  233

## OTHER COUNTRIES

| | | |
|---|---|---|
| CANADA | Harold M. Waller | 255 |

LATIN AMERICA

| | | |
|---|---|---|
| Argentina | David Schers and Shlomo Slutzky | 270 |
| Brazil | David Schers and Shlomo Slutzky | 282 |

WESTERN EUROPE

| | | |
|---|---|---|
| Great Britain | Lionel and Miriam Kochan | 290 |
| France | Nelly Hansson | 303 |
| The Netherlands | Henriette Boas | 315 |
| Italy | Simonetta Della Seta | 324 |

CENTRAL EUROPE

| | | |
|---|---|---|
| Federal Republic of Germany | Y. Michal Bodemann | 336 |
| German Democratic Republic | Robin Ostow | 349 |

EASTERN EUROPE

| | | |
|---|---|---|
| Soviet Union | Zvi Gitelman | 353 |
| Soviet Bloc Nations | Zvi Gitelman | 361 |

| | | |
|---|---|---|
| ISRAEL | Ralph Mandel | 366 |
| WORLD JEWISH POPULATION, 1986 | U.O. Schmelz and Sergio DellaPergola | 433 |

## DIRECTORIES, LISTS, AND OBITUARIES

NATIONAL JEWISH ORGANIZATIONS

| | |
|---|---|
| United States | 445 |
| Canada | 491 |

JEWISH FEDERATIONS, WELFARE FUNDS,
COMMUNITY COUNCILS
United States 494
Canada 505

JEWISH PERIODICALS
United States 506
Canada 514

OBITUARIES: UNITED STATES 515

SUMMARY JEWISH CALENDAR,
5749–5753 (Sept. 1988–Aug. 1993) 528

CONDENSED MONTHLY CALENDAR,
1988–1990 (5748–5751) 530

SELECTED ARTICLES OF INTEREST IN RECENT VOLUMES
OF THE AMERICAN JEWISH YEAR BOOK 557

INDEX 561

# Special Articles

# The Impact of Feminism on American Jewish Life

by Sylvia Barack Fishman

*Introduction*

THE LIVES OF JEWS in the United States—like the lives of most Americans—have been radically transformed by 20 years of feminism. Some of these changes have been effected by the larger feminist movement and some by a specifically Jewish feminist effort. Thus, while many feminist celebrities, such as Betty Friedan and Bella Abzug, are Jews, the focus of their feminism has not been specifically Jewish in nature; they have profoundly changed the behavior and attitudes of American Jews as Americans and not as Jews. Pioneers of the contemporary Jewish feminist movement, on the other hand—women such as Rachel Adler, Paula Hyman, and Aviva Cantor—are primarily recognizable within the Jewish sphere. They and many other Jewish feminists have significantly altered the character of Jewish religious, intellectual, cultural, and communal life in the United States.

In the stormy late 1960s and early 1970s, when the rising stars of contemporary American feminism were publicly denounced from synagogue pulpits as aberrant and destructive, feminist attitudes and goals seemed revolutionary. Today, however, many general feminist and Jewish feminist attitudes and goals have been absorbed and domesticated within the public lives of mainstream American Jewry. Female rabbis and cantors have been trained, ordained, and graduated from Reform, Reconstructionist, and now Conservative seminaries, and are becoming accepted as part of the American Jewish religious scene. Life-cycle events for females, such as the *"Shalom Bat"* and Bat Mitzvah ceremonies, are commonplace. Women's organizations which a short time ago expressed ambivalence about the impact of feminism on their ranks now officially espouse feminist goals.[1]

---

[1]The Women's Division of the Council of Jewish Federations, for example, a group which seems to epitomize commitment to establishment values and communal survival, featured a number of feminist figures at its 1987 General Assembly in Miami. Enthusiastically calling themselves "feminists," officers of the Women's Division gave a platform to Amira Dotan, an Israeli female brigadier general; Alice Shalvi, founder of the Israel Women's Network; Susan Weidman Schneider, editor of *Lilith* magazine; and other highly identified feminists.

In their private lives as well, American Jews demonstrate the impact of feminism. American Jewish women, historically a highly educated group, are even more highly educated today. Moreover, their educational achievements are by and large directed into occupational goals, rather than following the open-ended liberal arts and sciences mode that typified female higher education in the 1950s and 1960s. Partially because they are pursuing educational and career objectives, American Jewish women today marry later and bear children later than they did 25 years ago, and they are far more likely than married Jewish women in the past to continue working outside the home after they marry and bear children. The late-forming, dual-career family has become the norm in many American Jewish communities.

At the same time that feminism has become a mainstream phenomenon, important feminists have pulled back from the radicalism of their original positions. Most celebrated, perhaps, is Betty Friedan, who in *The Second Stage*[2] reevaluated family and voluntaristic activity as desirable goals for women. Many feminists have responded to the anti-Jewish bias of some strands of feminism not only with articulate denunciations but also with personal rediscovery of, and commitment to, more intensive Jewish experience, as Letty Cottin Pogrebin, editor of *Ms.* magazine testifies.[3] A number of recent appealing novels about strong, intelligent, accomplished—and yet passionate and vulnerable—Jewish women have also helped to deradicalize the face of Jewish feminism. Indeed, left-wing militant feminists have angrily denounced this mainstreaming of feminism with the claim that bourgeois hierarchies have coopted the movement.

The gap between establishment American Judaism and contemporary American feminism seems to have narrowed. A quasi-feminist stance appears to be *de rigueur* in large parts of the American Jewish community. However, the extent of substantive influence exerted by both general and Jewish feminism on American Jewish communal, organizational, religious, and familial life has yet to be examined. It is the purpose of this article to survey the impact of both types of feminism on key spheres of American Jewish life.

It is important to note at the outset that neither general nor Jewish feminism was created in a vacuum and neither exerts its influence in a vacuum; factors other than feminism have also been at work in effecting transformations. Feminist emphasis on career achievement and individual fulfillment is part of a general cultural focus on the individual, rather than on familial or communal values. Feminist critiques of religious texts, in-

---

[2]Betty Friedan, *The Second Stage* (New York, 1981).
[3]Letty Cottin Pogrebin, "Anti-Semitism in the Women's Movement: A Jewish Feminist's Disturbing Account," *Ms.*, June 1982, pp. 145–49.

the enemy. The patriarchal family was pictured as a repressive cultural institution which served to restrict women to the domestic domain. As Gloria Steinem explained, the "demystified" origin and purpose of marriage was "to restrict the freedom of the mother—at least long enough to determine paternity." Men promoted religious and societal restrictions of female sexuality so that they might control "the most basic means of production—the means of reproduction."[6] Shulamith Firestone found even gestation and childbirth a barbarous process that served no useful purpose except to enslave women.[7]

Numerous articles and books explored contemporary feminist issues. A wide variety of organizational subgroups formed, with the purpose of translating feminist insights into social change. The largest, the National Organization of Women (NOW), concentrated on economic issues, such as promoting legislation to prevent discrimination against women in the marketplace through the Equal Rights Amendment (ERA). Other groups, such as Women Against Pornography, called attention to, and actively opposed, pornographic literature and films, which they characterized as hostile to women; they worked to reduce rape and other overt violence against women, sponsoring marches to "Take Back the Night." Smaller, more extreme groups, such as the Society for Cutting Up Men (SCUM) and No More Nice Girls, were openly antimale, recommending either independent or lesbian life-styles. Together, these feminist groups comprised a movement devoted to nothing less than the radical transformation of the position of women in the United States.

*Jewish Feminism*

In the late 1960s and early 1970s, a feminist movement with a specifically Jewish focus became distinct from generalized feminism. Jewish women began to examine the inequities and forms of oppression in Jewish life and, at the same time, to explore Judaism as a culture and religion from a feminist perspective. The critique of Judaism came from various quarters and focused on a range of issues. Some of these actually paralleled the broader feminist agenda; others addressed specific Jewish concerns. In the former category were attacks on Judaism for its part in relegating women to inferior status and to narrowly prescribed roles, at home and in the wider world. These attacks were often voiced by early activists in the general feminist movement, who also happened to be Jews. Thus, Vivian Gornick,

---

[6]Gloria Steinem, "Humanism and the Second Wave of Feminism," *The Humanist,* May/June 1987, pp. 11–15, 49.
[7]Shulamith Firestone, *The Dialectic of Sex* (New York, 1971).

in an article entitled "Woman as Outsider," characterized traditional Jewish relationships between the sexes as hateful and repressive, in a description that was fairly representative of certain strands within feminist thought:

> In the fierce unjoyousness of Hebraism, especially, woman is a living symbol of the obstacles God puts in man's way as man strives to make himself more godly and less manly. . . . These structures are not a thing of some barbaric past, they are a living part of the detail of many contemporary lives. Today, on the Lower East Side of New York, the streets are filled with darkly brooding men whose eyes are averted from the faces of passing women, and who walk three feet ahead of their bewigged and silent wives. If a woman should enter a rabbinical study on Grand Street today, her direct gaze would be met by lowered eyelids; she would stand before the holy man, the seeker of wisdom, the worshipper of the spirit, and she would have to say to herself:

> Why, in this room I am a pariah, a Yahoo. If the rabbi should but look upon my face, vile hot desire would enter his being and endanger the salvation of his sacred soul. . . . So he has made a bargain with God and constructed a religion in which I am all matter and *he* is all spirit. I am (yet!) the human sacrifice offered up for his salvation.[8]

Jewish family values were denounced, with the family depicted as a woman's prison, echoing views expressed in the general feminist movement. Jewish communal attitudes came under attack as well. The female volunteer, in particular, was denigrated as a mere pawn, an unpaid slave laborer who made it possible for paid male organizational employees to achieve their goals.[9] Not only did male communal professionals exploit the labor of female volunteers, feminists charged, but even male volunteers were culpable: male, but not female, volunteers had the opportunity to rise through the ranks to decision-making positions of prestige and power, while women were contained in low-ranking, powerless organizational ghettos.[10] Furthermore, those women who did enter Jewish communal work professionally were kept in the most subordinate, least lucrative slots, while male Jewish communal professionals rose into executive posts.

The religious realm gave rise to a number of specifically Jewish issues. Jewish divorce law, for example, and women's role in communal worship were two that received wide public attention. To Jewish feminists, they exemplified women's unequal status and cried out for immediate correction. Involvement with these pressing matters was accompanied by, and some-

---

[8]Vivian Gornick, "Woman as Outsider," *Women in Sexist Society: Studies in Power and Powerlessness*, ed. Vivian Gornick and Barbara K. Moran (New York, 1971), pp. 70–84.

[9]See, for example, Doris B. Gold, "Women and Voluntarism," in Gornick and Moran, eds., *Women in Sexist Society*, pp. 384–400; Paula Hyman, "The Volunteer Organizations: Vanguard or Rear Guard?" *Lilith*, no. 5, 1978, pp. 17–22; and Amy Stone, "The Locked Cabinet," *Lilith*, no. 2, Winter 1976–77, pp. 17–21.

[10]Aviva Cantor, "The Missing Ingredients—Power and Influence in the Jewish Community," *Present Tense*, Spring 1984, pp. 8–12.

times evolved into, deeper and broader consideration of women's place in Jewish history, law, and culture, past and present. The growth of the Jewish feminist movement was aided by certain developments in the broader society. The period of the late 1960s and early 1970s was one in which Jewish consciousness and pride were at a high in certain circles—particularly on college campuses—and in which challenges to authority were the norm among American middle-class young adults, especially among Jewish youth. Educated young Jews were actively exploring and challenging their heritage—but Jewish women found that their particular concerns were not being adequately addressed. Articles began to appear by women who were fluent in Jewish source materials, addressing specifically Jewish problems from a feminist perspective. Two early articles that sparked Jewish feminist thought were Trude Weiss-Rosmarin's "The Unfreedom of Jewish Women,"[11] which focused on the "unfairness of Jewish marriage laws to divorced and abandoned women," and Rachel Adler's "The Jew Who Wasn't There,"[12] which contrasted male and female models of traditional Jewish piety. Adler's article appeared in a special issue of *Davka* magazine—a counterculture publication—that included a variety of feminist articles.

By late 1971, Jewish women's prayer and study groups were being formed. Women from the New York Havurah (one of the new coed, communal worship-and-study groups that developed on college campuses) joined together with like-minded friends to explore the status of women in Jewish law. Eventually this group evolved into Ezrat Nashim (a double-entendre that refers to the area in the synagogue traditionally reserved for women but that also means, literally, "the help of women"), a particularly influential, albeit small, organization. Committed to equality for women within Judaism, Ezrat Nashim comprised primarily Conservative women, many of whom had attended the Hebrew-speaking Conservative Ramah camps. Their appearance at the convention of the Conservative Rabbinical Assembly in 1972—the same year that the Reform movement voted to admit women to its rabbinical program—was an important initiating step in the process of influencing Conservative leaders to consider admitting women to the Conservative rabbinical program.[13] Jewish feminism went from a small, localized effort to a broader, more diverse operation at the first national Jewish women's conference in 1973, organized by the North Amer-

---

[11]Trude Weiss-Rosmarin, "The Unfreedom of Jewish Women," *Jewish Spectator,* Oct. 1970, pp. 2–6.
[12]Rachel Adler, "The Jew Who Wasn't There," *Davka*, Summer 1971, pp. 6–11.
[13]Steven Martin Cohen, "American Jewish Feminism: A Study in Conflicts and Compromises," *American Behavioral Scientist,* Mar.-Apr. 1980, pp. 519–58.

ican Jewish Students' Network. Drawing more than 500 women of varied educational levels and religious backgrounds from throughout North America, the conference spawned new groups, regional and local conferences, and a National Women's Speakers' Bureau.[14]

The ideas and issues percolating within the formative Jewish feminist movement were published and widely circulated in a special issue of *Response* magazine, called *The Jewish Woman: An Anthology*.[15] Edited by Elizabeth Koltun, the 192-page issue included 30 articles and a bibliography. Many of the authors contributing to this issue became key figures in Jewish feminism: Judith Hauptman (Talmud), Paula Hyman and Judith Plaskow Goldenberg (women in rabbinic literature and law), Martha Ackelsberg (religious and social change), Aviva Cantor Zuckoff and Jacqueline K. Levine (communal issues), Marcia Falk (biblical poetics), Charlotte Baum (American Jewish history), Rachel Adler (women in Jewish law and culture), and others. The work was later revised for book publication by Schocken Books, and included additional articles by other Jewish feminist thinkers, among them Arlene Agus (women's rituals), Blu Greenberg (feminist exploration within a traditional context), and Sonya Michel (American Jewish literature).[16]

A second National Conference on Jewish Women and Men in 1974 also drew hundreds of participants and gave birth to the Jewish Feminist Organization (JFO), which was committed to promoting the equality of Jewish women in all areas of Jewish life. The JFO survived only a short time, however, and was succeeded by a more limited New York Jewish Women's Center, which was active from approximately 1975 to 1977.

The autumn of 1974 also saw the publication of a special issue of *Conservative Judaism*, which explored topics connected to "Women and Change in Jewish Law." Among the articles was one that became a hallmark of Jewish antifeminism. In it, psychiatrist Mortimer Ostow characterized Jewish feminism as an attempt to obliterate "the visible differences between men and women" and a possible encouragement of "trans-sexual fantasies." Even if this were not a conscious or unconscious aim of Jewish feminists, Ostow warned, the end result of fully empowering women within public Judaism would be to emasculate Jewish men, producing a society where women dominated the synagogue but suffered frustration in the bedroom as a result.[17] Ostow's article evoked a flood of profeminist responses from

---

[14]Martha Ackelsberg, "Introduction," in *The Jewish Woman: An Anthology*, ed. Elizabeth Koltun, special issue of *Response* magazine, 1973, pp. 7–9.
[15]Ibid.
[16]Elizabeth Koltun, ed., *The Jewish Woman: New Perspectives* (New York, 1976).
[17]Mortimer Ostow, "Women and Change in Jewish Law," *Conservative Judaism*, Fall 1974, pp. 5–12.

both men and women, which were gathered together in a second special issue of *Conservative Judaism*, titled "Women and Change in Jewish Law: Responses to the Fall 1974 Symposium." In a detailed statement leading off the collection, Arthur Green answered Ostow's objections to Jewish feminism point by point, noting that "the gentleness of a loving mother-God might serve as a good counter-balance to the sometimes overbearing austerity of God as father, king and judge. Mother Rachel, Mother Zion, and widowed Jerusalem have done much to add to the warmth of our spiritual heritage."[18]

Although Reform Judaism had no theological barriers to the ordination of women, it was not until 1972 that the first female Reform rabbi, Sally Priesand, was ordained. It would be another decade before the first female Conservative rabbi, Amy Eilberg, would be ordained at the Jewish Theological Seminary (in 1985) and two women would be named to tenured positions in Judaica: Paula Hyman to a chair in Jewish Studies at Yale, and Judith Hauptman as associate professor of Talmud at JTS (both in 1986).

The development and growth of Jewish feminism in the interim have been documented in a variety of publications. One striking piece of evidence for the legitimation of Jewish feminism by the Jewish intellectual and organization establishments was the appearance in the 1977 *American Jewish Year Book* of a special article, "The Movement for Equal Rights for Women in American Jewry." In this piece, Anne Lapidus Lerner captured the atmosphere of hopeful ferment that pervaded many Jewish religious and communal arenas.

A unique product of Jewish feminism is a glossy magazine, *Lilith*, which was created to explore religious, political, communal, and personal aspects of Jewish life through the eyes of Jewish feminism. The premier issue, published in 1976, featured a photograph of a woman wearing *tefillin* and an interview with Betty Friedan. Although *Lilith*, which operates on a shoestring, has appeared on a somewhat irregular basis, each issue has a wide readership, especially among highly identified Jewish women. In addition, many books and anthologies have gathered and disseminated Jewish feminist thought. Among the most comprehensive, Baum, Hyman, and Michel's *The Jewish Woman in America* [19] utilizes historical, sociological, and literary sources to trace the odyssey of Jewish women in American Jewish life. Susannah Heschel's anthology *On Being a Jewish Feminist*[20] explores and updates these issues, with a special emphasis on "creating a

---

[18]Arthur Green, "Women and Change in Jewish Law: Responses to the Fall 1974 Symposium," *Conservative Judaism,* Spring 1975, pp. 35–56.
[19]Charlotte Baum, Paula Hyman, and Sonya Michel, *The Jewish Woman in America* (New York, 1976).
[20]Susannah Heschel, ed., *On Being a Jewish Feminist: A Reader* (New York, 1983).

feminist theology of Judaism." The Biblio Press has published several extensive bibliographies listing materials relating to Jewish feminism,[21] and Susan Weidman Schneider, editor of *Lilith*, compiled a broad-based practical compendium of Jewish feminist resource materials, including hundreds of names and addresses, as well as useful summaries and discussions, in *Jewish and Female*.[22]

The growth of Jewish feminism was helped, ironically, by the presence of anti-Semitism within the ranks of the general feminist movement. The anti-Semitism emerged on several fronts. The first was political and came as a tidal wave of anti-Israel criticism at a series of international women's conferences. Listening with horror to the repeated condemnation of "Zionist oppression," Jewish participants learned that even among women they could feel like outsiders.[23]

On the religious front, some Christian feminist theologians asserted that Christianity had been ruined by Judaism, with Jewish patriarchalism sullying what would otherwise have been a purely egalitarian Christianity. Just as Protestant thinkers once blamed the Old Testament for infusing values of vengeance and carnality into Christianity, feminist theologians managed to ascribe the strikingly misogynist and antisexual attitudes of some of the Gospels to "a concession to Judaism" or "an unavoidable contamination" by "the sexism of first century Palestinian Judaism." Consequently, Jewish feminist scholars sometimes felt chastened in their approach to classical Jewish texts, in the apprehension that their critiques might "be misunderstood or even misappropriated as providing further proof to Christian feminists for their negation of Judaism."[24]

A third form of anti-Semitism sought to deny Jewish women their own sense of group identity. A professor of American history and women's studies recalls that at a conference on women's issues, which included talks on the black female experience, the Hispanic female experience, and the Irish Catholic female experience, the conference organizer insisted, "Jewish women are just white middle class women. There is nothing that differentiates them from the ruling majority. There is no reason to treat them as a specialized minority or to devote any of our time to their particular experi-

---

[21]Biblio Press, Fresh Meadows, New York.
[22]Susan Weidman Schneider, *Jewish and Female: Choices and Changes in Our Lives Today* (New York, 1984).
[23]See, for example, Friedan, *The Second Stage*, pp. 162–66; Pogrebin, "Anti-Semitism in the Women's Movement"; and Annette Daum, "Anti-Semitism in the Women's Movement," *Pioneer Woman*, Sept.–Oct. 1983, pp. 11–13, 22–24.
[24]Susannah Heschel, "Current Issues in Jewish Feminist Theology," *Christian-Jewish Relations* 19, no. 2, 1986, pp. 23–32. See also Judith Plaskow, "Blaming Jews for Inventing Patriarchy," and Annette Daum, "Blaming Jews for the Death of the Goddess," *Lilith*, no. 7, 1980, pp. 11–12, 12–13.

ence." As Ellen Umansky comments, "By the early 1970s, it seemed to many that they were embraced as women but scorned as Jews." In reaction to the pressure that they either repudiate their Judaism or at least keep silent about it, Umansky notes that "many Jewish feminists, especially secular feminists, began to assert their Jewishness, vigorously, forcefully, and with pride." Jewish feminism, Umansky adds, "emerged as a means of asserting both *Jewish* visibility within the feminist movement and *feminist* consciousness within the U.S. Jewish community."[25]

The goals of Jewish feminism—as distinct from general feminism—as Cohen[26] points out, can be divided roughly into "communal" and "spiritual" areas. Although communally oriented Jewish feminists have been most interested in gaining access to seats of decision making and power, the spiritualists have worked for development in the areas of ritual, law, liturgy, and religious education. However, it should be noted that the division between religious and communal feminist agendas is not always clear, and in fact the two areas often impinge upon and affect each other.

Similarly, while the themes of contemporary American feminism and Jewish feminism are distinct, within the lives of American Jews they often overlap. Thus, a particular Jewish woman, sensitized by the ubiquitousness of feminist values in society, may work toward both occupational development and fuller participation in public Jewish prayer and ritual. Within her life, these enterprises may be linked emotionally and intellectually. The particular blend of feminism and Jewish feminism found in the United States today is a unique American hybrid, which does not exist in exactly the same form among any other contemporary Jewish population.

## Feminism and Family

Probably no single aspect of feminism has aroused as much anxiety and debate as its possible impact on "the Jewish family," long regarded as the foundation of Jewish continuity and strength. Even within the Jewish feminist world, lines have been sharply drawn over this issue. At one end of the ideological spectrum, Martha Ackelsberg asserts that "the nuclear family as we know it is not, in itself, central to the continuity of Judaism: it is instead, simply one possible set of relationships through which young people may be born, nurtured, and prepared for membership in the Jewish community, and adults may find opportunities for companionship and intimacy. Once we realize that there are other means to achieve those same

---

[25]Ellen M. Umansky, "Females, Feminists, and Feminism: A Review of Recent Literature on Jewish Feminism and a Creation of a Feminist Judaism," *Feminist Studies* 14, Summer 1988, pp. 349–65.
[26]Cohen, "American Jewish Feminism," p. 529.

ends, and that even 'undermining the family' need not necessarily threaten Jewish survival, the path is open to think about alternatives to the nuclear family."[27] Ackelsberg urges the Jewish community to accept and encourage a number of alternative household styles. Individuals can contribute to the survival of the Jewish community through many pathways, she maintains, not only by having children. "Heterosexual nuclear families are not the only contexts in which people can or do covenant, nor are they the only units in or through which people may express love, or long-term care and commitment," Ackelsberg insists.[28]

In an exchange with Ackelsberg in *Sh'ma*, Susan Handelman disputes the claim that Jewish vitality is separable from traditional normative Jewish family life. Reaching back to Genesis, with its poignant preoccupation with matchmaking, marriage, and procreation, Handelman posits that the Jewish family was the primary and most enduring institution of Judaism. The family not only educated the young and supported Jewish institutions, it was the embodiment of Jewish values. To speak of Judaism without the primacy of the traditional Jewish family, Handelman suggests, is to commit an irreparable violence upon both the religion and the culture.[29]

Other female Jewish intellectuals are wary of feminist agendas, especially as they seem to endanger Jewish values. Thus, Marie Syrkin states that Jewish women who eschew motherhood are maiming themselves and the Jewish community. She feels they should revise their values and recognize that, on a personal level, "some forms of achievement can be gained only through the loss of a vital aspect of womanhood." On a communal level, she warns that the feminist agenda may directly conflict with the survival of the Jewish people: "Insofar as feminism liberates women from traditional roles and encourages life-styles antithetical to procreation and the fostering of the family, feminist ideology affects the Jewish future."[30]

Lucy Dawidowicz states her case against the "new Amazons . . . of women's liberation" even more firmly. She dismisses most strands of Jewish feminism as "a kind of ideological *sh'atnez*, the mixture of wool and linen prohibited in Jewish law." Unlike "Jewish women of achievement" in the past, who were "animated as much by passion to Jewish commitment as by personal ambition," she argues, most contemporary Jewish feminists "are merely an adjunct of the worldwide feminist movement." Indeed, according

---

[27]Martha A. Ackelsberg, "Families and the Jewish Community: A Feminist Perspective," *Response* 14, no. 4, Spring 1985, pp. 5–19, 18.
[28]Martha A. Ackelsberg, "Family or Community? A Response," *Sh'ma*, Mar. 20, 1987.
[29]Susan Handelman, "Family: A Religiously Mandated Ideal," ibid.
[30]Marie Syrkin, "Does Feminism Clash with Jewish National Need?" *Midstream*, June/July 1985, pp. 8–12.

to Dawidowicz, "only the most Jewishly committed feminists seem even to be aware of the incompatibilities between some objectives of the feminist movement and the Jewish communal need for stability, security, and survival."[31]

The normative Jewish family may indeed be a threatened institution, but it is not threatened exclusively by feminism. Other, equally important factors include: a cultural ethos that stresses individual achievement and pleasure; materialistic expectations that elevate the perceived standard of what a "middle-class" life-style comprises; a tightening economic market requiring dual incomes to maintain middle-class life-styles; the sexual revolution; and patterns of chronological polarization that split families by sending adolescents to far-off university campuses and grandparents to the Sunbelt.

## Attitudinal Change

Whether the forecasts of doom concerning the Jewish family have merit or not, only future historians will be able to assess. What is clear at this point is that, in keeping with their general well-documented tendency to hold liberal social attitudes, Jews have warmly embraced the feminist idea. In a 1985 study of Jewish and non-Jewish women, conducted by Sid Groeneman for B'nai B'rith Women, non-Jewish and Jewish women were compared on a composite scale that measured attitudes toward "feminism, or . . . the modern version of women's roles and rights." Nearly half of Jewish women surveyed scored "high" on this scale, compared to only 16 percent of non-Jewish women. Several attitudes displayed by Jewish women can be construed as indicating a major change from traditional Jewish attitudes toward the family. Thus, 60 percent or more of Jewish women disagreed with the following statements: (1) "A marriage without any children will normally be incomplete and less satisfying"; (2) "When both parents work, the children are more likely to get into trouble"; (3) "Most women are happiest when making a home and caring for children." An overwhelming 91 percent of Jewish women—compared to 56 percent of non-Jewish women—agreed that "every woman who wants an abortion ought to be able to have one."[32]

Furthermore, the goals that these Jewish women had for their daughters indicated that feminist values were being passed to the next generation.

---

[31] Lucy S. Dawidowicz, "Does Judaism Need Feminism?" *Midstream,* Apr. 1986, pp. 39–40.
[32] Sid Groeneman, "Beliefs and Values of American Jewish Women," a report by Market Facts, Inc., presented to the International Organization of B'nai B'rith Women, 1985, pp. 30–31. The data were drawn from 956 questionnaires roughly divided between Jewish and non-Jewish informants. Ages of the women who completed the questionnaires were 59 percent ages 25 to 44, 41 percent ages 45 to 64. The study presents dramatic documentation of the transformation of values among American Jewish women under age 45.

Only 22 percent of Jewish women had family-oriented goals for their daughters, such as wanting their daughters to "have a good family, husband, marriage, children," or being "loving, caring, good parents." In contrast, 69 percent of Jewish women wanted their daughters to have qualities that would help them function successfully in the world, such as being "independent, self-reliant, self-sufficient, self-supportive, determined, ambitious, intelligent, knowledgeable, talented, skillful and creative."[33]

The study also found its sample of Jewish women to be far more liberal than non-Jewish women in attitudes toward premarital and extramarital sex. More than three-quarters of Jewish women said that sex before marriage was acceptable, while fewer than half of non-Jewish women approved of premarital sex. Perhaps even more startling, given Jewish religious and cultural prohibitions against adultery, 28 percent of Jewish women said they "could envision situations when sex with someone other than one's spouse is not wrong," compared to only 12 percent of the non-Jewish sample.[34]

Lesbianism remains a force in the Jewish feminist movement, as in the general feminist movement. Anne Lerner notes "the degree to which lesbianism, in particular, has become an accepted fact of life" at the Reconstructionist Rabbinical College.[35] Evelyn Torton Beck, in her anthology *Nice Jewish Girls*, describes the painful encounters of Jewish lesbians with anti-Semitism among lesbian feminists, but also offers testimony to the creative force and Jewish pride of some lesbian Jewish women.[36]

## DEMOGRAPHIC CHANGES IN THE LIVES OF AMERICAN JEWISH WOMEN

The true impact of feminism and related social forces can be seen in the daily lives of American Jewish women, men, and children. During the past 20 years, dramatic changes have taken place in patterns of American Jewish family formation and in the educational and occupational profile of American Jews. Areas of change in the lives of American Jewish women that have been substantively influenced by feminism include later marriage and childbirth, higher levels of education and occupational achievement, and changed patterns in labor-force participation.

---

[33]Ibid., pp. 38–40.
[34]Ibid., pp. 23–24.
[35]Anne Lapidus Lerner, "Judaism and Feminism: The Unfinished Agenda," *Judaism,* Spring 1987, pp. 167–73.
[36]Evelyn Torton Beck, *Nice Jewish Girls: A Lesbian Anthology* (New York, 1982). See also Batya Bauman, "Women-identified Women in Male-identified Judaism," in Heschel, ed., *On Being a Jewish Feminist*, pp. 88–95.

THE IMPACT OF FEMINISM / 17

## Changes in Life-Cycle Patterns[37]

Few statistics more strikingly illustrate cultural change than the figures on marital status among American Jews (table 1). Twenty years ago the National Jewish Population Study found that four out of five American Jewish households consisted of married couples, the great majority of whom either had or expected to have two or more children. At that time, the percentage of Jewish singles was far below the percentage of singles in the general U.S. population: only 6 percent of American Jewish adults had never been married, compared to 16 percent singles in the 1970 U.S. Census data. In contrast, in the 1980s, the proportion of Jewish singles equals or exceeds that of the general population in many cities: about one-fifth of Jewish adults in most U.S. cities have never been married. Furthermore, the

---

[37]All nationwide figures for the American Jewish population in 1970 are derived from the National Jewish Population Study. Data from individual city studies are drawn from the following city studies completed in the 1980s, including: Gary A. Tobin, *A Demographic Study of the Jewish Community of Atlantic County* (Jan.1986); Gary A. Tobin, *Jewish Population Study of Greater Baltimore* (July 1986); Sherry Israel, *Boston's Jewish Community: The 1985 CJP Demographic Study* (May 1987); Policy Research Corporation, *Chicago Jewish Population Study* (1982); Population Research Committee, *Survey of Cleveland's Jewish Population, 1981* (1981); Allied Jewish Federation of Denver, *The Denver Jewish Population Study* (1981); Gary A. Tobin, Robert C. Levy, and Samuel H. Asher, *A Demographic Study of the Jewish Community of Greater Kansas City* (Summer 1986); Bruce A. Phillips, *Los Angeles Jewish Community Survey Overview for Regional Planning* (1980); Michael Rappeport and Gary A. Tobin, *A Population Study of the Jewish Community of MetroWest, New Jersey* (1986); Ira M. Sheskin, *Population Study of the Greater Miami Jewish Community* (1982); Bruce A. Phillips, *The Milwaukee Jewish Population Study* (1984); Lois Geer, *The Jewish Community of Greater Minneapolis 1981 Population Study* (1981); Paul Ritterband and Steven M. Cohen, *The 1981 Greater New York Jewish Population Survey* (1981); William L. Yancey and Ira Goldstein, *The Jewish Population of the Greater Philadelphia Area* (Philadelphia: Institute for Public Policy Studies, Social Science Data Library, Temple University, 1984); Bruce A. Phillips and William S. Aron, *The Greater Phoenix Jewish Population Study* (1983–1984); Jane Berkey and Saul Weisberg, United Federation of Greater Pittsburgh, *Survey of Greater Pittsburgh's Jewish Population* (1984); Gary A. Tobin and Sylvia Barack Fishman, *A Population Study of the Jewish Community of Rochester, New York* (forthcoming); Lois Geer, *1981 Population Study of the St. Paul Jewish Community* (1981); Gary A. Tobin and Sharon Sassler, *San Francisco Bay Area Population Study* (1988); Gary A. Tobin, *A Demographic and Attitudinal Study of the Jewish Community of St. Louis* (1982); Gary A. Tobin, Joseph Waksberg, and Janet Greenblatt, *A Demographic Study of the Jewish Community of Greater Washington D.C.* (1984); Gary A. Tobin and Sylvia Barack Fishman, *A Population Study of the Jewish Community of Worcester* (Sept. 1987). Percentages in this paper have been rounded from .5 to the next highest number. Data were collected through a variety of sampling methodologies to reach both affiliated and nonaffiliated Jews, with a strong emphasis on random-digit-dialing telephone interviews. Much of the data presented here is taken from published studies; in these cases the studies are cited. Some information has been taken directly from complete data files from Jewish population studies made available to the Cohen Center for Modern Jewish Studies. References to this data simply refer to the particular community.

percentage of divorced Jewish households has risen from 6 percent in 1970 to double or triple that figure in some cities. Even though the Jewish divorce rate is not higher than the national average, it is far higher than the previous Jewish divorce rate: in Boston, for example, the 5-percent divorce rate of 1985 is five times higher than the 1965 divorce rate of 1 percent. The percentage of American Jewish households consisting of married couples has dropped to two-thirds, as has the overall married-couple rate in the 1980 census data.

American Jewish women are marrying later and beginning their families later. Often, the age at which the first child is born is substantially later than the age of first marriage. In a common scenario, a woman who marries at age 28 may postpone bearing her first child until age 34 in order to finish her professional training and establish her career. In Baltimore, among the 87 percent of Jewish women ages 45 to 64 who had children, one-third gave birth to their first child before age 22 and another one-half gave birth between ages 23 and 29. Thus, for mothers ages 45 to 64, four out of five had given birth to their first child before they reached age 30. In contrast, for women currently ages 25 to 34, only half had ever given birth. While some analysts are sanguine about the effect of delayed childbirth on Jewish population growth,[38] others warn that postponing childbearing will, on average, mean smaller American Jewish families.[39]

There are several reasons why families may not achieve their expected

---

[38]Calvin Goldscheider is the foremost proponent of the idea that expected family size, rather than the current number of children per family, reveals the actual completed family size that will be achieved by a given cohort. According to this view, delayed marriage and childbirth among a group can mean they have very few children during a certain period but will bear them later and fulfill their family-size expectations. Goldscheider states: "Expected fertility measures show a very high aggregate prediction for actual fertility. That has been the case particularly for Jews . . . who plan and attain their family size desires with extreme accuracy." Calvin Goldscheider, *Jewish Continuity and Change: Emerging Patterns in America* (Bloomington, Ind., 1986), pp. 92-94.

[39]U.O. Schmelz and S. DellaPergola argue strongly against the so-called optimistic position. See "Demographic Consequences of U.S. Population Trends," AJYB 1983, vol. 83, pp.148-59, 154. As noted in Gary A. Tobin and Alvin Chenkin, "Recent Jewish Community Population Studies: A Roundup," AJYB 1985, vol. 85, pp. 154-78, 162-63, the most striking evidence of the lowered Jewish fertility rate is the declining number of young people in the American Jewish population. Nearly one-third of the Jewish population was under 20 years old in the 1970 National Jewish Population Study, but in the post-1980 individual city studies only between one-fifth and one-quarter of American Jews were 19 years of age or younger. The figures for individual cities are as follows: New York—23 percent age 19 and under; Washington, D.C.—23 percent age 17 and under; St. Paul—21 percent age 19 and under; Minneapolis—27 percent age 19 and under; Milwaukee—24 percent age 17 and under; Rochester—24 percent age 19 and under; Pittsburgh—22 percent age 19 and under; Phoenix—25 percent age 17 and under; Philadelphia—17 percent age 15 and under; Nashville—28 percent age 19 and under; Miami—20 percent age 19 and under; Denver—21 percent age 17 and under; Los Angeles—20 percent age 17 and under.

TABLE 1. MARITAL STATUS OF CONTEMPORARY JEWISH POPULATIONS IN U. S. CITIES, COMPARED TO 1980 U.S. CENSUS, 1970 NJPS, AND 1970 U.S. CENSUS (PERCENT)

| Location | Year Study Completed | Married | Single | Widowed | Divorced |
|---|---|---|---|---|---|
| Atlantic City | 1985 | 67 | 13 | 13 | 6 |
| Boston | 1985 | 61 | 29 | 4 | 5 |
| Baltimore | 1985 | 68 | 19 | 9 | 5 |
| Chicago | 1982 | 65 | 23 | 6 | 6 |
| Cleveland | 1981 | 69 | 11 | 13 | 8 |
| Denver | 1981 | 64 | 23 | 4 | 9 |
| Kansas City | 1985 | 70 | 17 | 7 | 5 |
| Los Angeles | 1979 | 57 | 17 | 12 | 14 |
| Miami | 1982 | 61 | 7 | 23 | 8 |
| Milwaukee | 1983 | 67 | 14 | 9 | 10 |
| Minneapolis | 1981 | 66 | 22 | 7 | 5 |
| Nashville | 1982 | 70 | 17 | 8 | 5 |
| New York | 1981 | 65 | 15 | 11 | 9 |
| Phoenix | 1983 | 63 | 18 | 9 | 10 |
| Richmond | 1983 | 67 | 14 | 12 | 7 |
| Rochester | 1987 | 68 | 23 | 6 | 3 |
| St. Louis | 1982 | 68 | 9 | 17 | 6 |
| St. Paul | 1981 | 66 | 20 | 11 | 3 |
| San Francisco | 1988 | 69 | 19 | 4 | 7 |
| Washington, D.C. | 1983 | 61 | 27 | 4 | 7 |
| Worcester | 1987 | 69 | 14 | —18— | |
| U.S. Census | 1980 | 67 | 19 | 8 | 6 |
| NJPS | 1970 | 78 | 6 | 10 | 5 |
| U.S. Census | 1970 | 72 | 16 | 9 | 3 |

*Source:* See text footnote 37.

family size. First, where family size expectations are maintained, biological problems such as infertility are far more frequent as the age of the primipara (first-time mother) rises. Furthermore, the rate of fetal abnormalities rises along with age of the mother, sometimes further discouraging later childbirth. In addition, as numerous older first-time mothers have testified, the disruptive effect of children on an established dual-career household can serve as an effective motivation for limiting family size; sometimes expected family size is revised downward in response to the emotional and logistical difficulties that follow the birth of a first child. Finally, some employers actively discourage the birth of more than one child.

In addition to its effect on population size, the postponement of marriage and family formation may have a deleterious effect on synagogue and Jewish organizational affiliation. As part of a long-standing pattern of American Jewish life, the great majority of Jews do not join synagogues and organizations until they have married and had children. This life-cycle effect, in addition to the time constraints suffered by dual-career couples, seems to be one reason for diminished proportions of American Jewish women being actively involved in Jewish institutions.

Feminist goals may also lead to stress within marriage, and thus to divorce. Noticing that a surprisingly high proportion of divorced women in the general population had master's degrees, researchers analyzed the relationship between higher education and marital history. They found that women who obtained their master's degrees before marriage were not more likely than average to be divorced, whereas women who obtained their master's degrees after marriage were far more likely than average to be divorced. The researchers hypothesized that marriages which from their inception included a woman already in a professional role were psychologically adjusted to weather the pressures of two careers far better than those which began with more conventionally divided gender roles, and later switched course.[40]

No study has been published analyzing Jewish populations in this way, but data on the relationship between educational levels and marital status among Jewish women indicate that there may be a correlation between educational achievement and divorce. Among Jewish women in Baltimore, 32 percent of divorced women had master's degrees, compared to 7 percent of singles, 15 percent of married women with children at home, and 22 percent of married women with grown children. In Boston, among women ages 35 to 45, 9 percent of married women had master's degrees compared to 26 percent of divorced women in that age group. Unfortunately, the population studies do not reveal the date of degree completion, so we do not know what proportion of the divorced women's M.A.s were obtained before, during, or after their marriages. It is not possible, therefore, to establish a causal relationship between the educational achievement of Jewish women and divorce.

---

[40]Sharon K. Houseknecht, Suzanne Vaughan, and Anne S. Macke, "Marital Disruption Among Professional Women: The Timing of Career and Family Events," *Social Problems,* Feb. 1984, pp. 273–83.

## Educational and Occupational Achievement

Another area of American Jewish life clearly influenced by feminism is the freedom of educational and occupational opportunity that American Jewish women now enjoy. Jewish women ages 25 through 34 are far more likely than women over age 55 to complete their bachelor's degrees and to obtain postgraduate degrees, as shown in table 2, which uses data from MetroWest (Essex and Morris counties), New Jersey. However, while MetroWest Jewish women ages 25 to 34 are about as likely as men to complete bachelor's degrees and to obtain master's degrees, men are still over three times as likely as women to complete medical, dental, legal, and doctoral degrees.

Impressionistic evidence indicates that Jewish women are currently enrolling in large numbers in professional programs, and data on the career plans of Jewish college women also show that the aspirations of young Jewish females have changed. Charles Silberman reports that a "1980 national survey of first-year college students taken by the American Council on Education found that 9 percent of Jewish women were planning to be lawyers—up from 2 percent in 1969. The proportion planning a career in business management increased by the same amount, and the number planning to be doctors tripled, from 2 percent to 6 percent. In this same period the number of Jewish women planning to be elementary school teachers dropped . . . from 18 percent in 1969 to six percent in 1980; those choosing secondary school teaching plummeted from 12 percent to only one per-

TABLE 2. SECULAR EDUCATION OF JEWS IN METROWEST, N.J.,[a] BY SEX AND AGE (PERCENT)

| Education Completed | 25–34 F/M | 35–44 F/M | 45–54 F/M | 55–64 F/M | 65+ F/M |
|---|---|---|---|---|---|
| H.S. or less | 16/15 | 15/10 | 24/14 | 42/18 | 63/39 |
| B.A. | 56/50 | 53/38 | 50/42 | 37/45 | 27/37 |
| M.A. | 24/23 | 27/26 | 23/23 | 18/21 | 7/15 |
| D.D.S., M.D., Atty. | 3/11 | 3/18 | [b]/12 | 1/10 | 2/ 6 |
| Ph.D. | 1/ 2 | 2/10 | 3/ 9 | 2/ 6 | 2/ 3 |
| Total % | 100/101 | 100/102 | 100/100 | 100/100 | 101/100 |

*Source:* See text footnote 37.
[a]MetroWest data from Essex and Morris counties, New Jersey.
[b]Indicates less than 1%.
(N = 1,477 males, 1,623 females)
Totals above or below 100% due to rounding of numbers.

cent."[41] Data collected during the next decade will indicate whether the gap between male and female completion of professional degrees will continue to narrow.

Just as educational data show that Jewish women are achieving more than in the past, occupational data on American Jewish women show some areas of movement. Table 3, reporting the occupations of currently employed Jewish men and women in MetroWest, New Jersey, illustrates the advancement of women into medicine, law, engineering, and science, as well as into executive positions. Still, while women in the younger groups are twice as likely to be employed in those fields as women in the older groups, Jewish men are still far more likely than Jewish women to be doctors, lawyers, or engineers.

Jewish women ages 35 to 44 are twice as likely to be physicians or attorneys as are women ages 55 to 64—but Jewish men ages 35 to 44 are more than four times as likely as Jewish women to be practicing those professions. Women have increasingly been moving into engineering and the sciences, going from 2 percent in the 45 to 54 age group to 4 percent in the 25 to 34 age group, while men engineers and scientists from ages 25 to 54 have remained at a stable 8 percent.

Jewish women ages 35 to 64 are outnumbered by men three to one in managerial positions; however, women ages 25 to 34 almost equal men in these positions. Younger Jewish women are far more likely to be executives and far less likely to be clerical or administrative support workers. The percentage of managers and administrators doubles in the younger group: 22 percent of women ages 25 to 34, compared to 11 percent of the women ages 35 to 54. Seventeen percent of women ages 25 to 34 are employed as clerical workers, compared to 28 percent of women ages 45 to 54 and 38 percent of women ages 55 to 64.

Data from Washington, D.C. (see table 4) illustrate the occupational shifts that are most pronounced in those communities offering broad employment possibilities to women. In Washington, Jewish women ages 25 to 34 show a strong shift toward law as a professional career choice. However, while the percentage of Washington Jewish women practicing law has increased tenfold from the oldest to the youngest groups, Jewish men are still more than twice as likely to practice law, even in the youngest group.[42] (While Washington is unique in its atypically large demand for attorneys

---

[41]Charles Silberman, *A Certain People: American Jews and Their Lives Today* (New York, 1985), p.123.
[42]Nine percent of women ages 25 to 34 are attorneys, compared to 1 percent of women ages 45 to 54. It should be noted that the practice of law among younger Jewish men has increased substantially also: 23 percent of men ages 25 to 34 are lawyers or judges, compared to 13 percent ages 45 to 54.

TABLE 3. OCCUPATIONS OF CURRENTLY EMPLOYED JEWS IN METROWEST, N.J.,[a] BY SEX AND AGE (PERCENT)

| Occupations | 25–34 F/M | 35–44 F/M | 45–54 F/M | 55–64 F/M |
|---|---|---|---|---|
| M.D., D.D.S., etc. | 1/ 6 | 2/ 9 | 1/ 8 | 1/ 8 |
| Atty., judge | 2/ 7 | 2/11 | [b]/ 8 | [b]/ 4 |
| Engineer, scientist | 4/ 8 | 4/ 8 | 2/ 8 | 1/10 |
| Teacher, soc. worker | 14/ 1 | 30/ 4 | 19/ 4 | 20/ 3 |
| College prof. | [b]/ 1 | 1/ 3 | 2/ 1 | 1/ 1 |
| Writer, artist | 5/ 4 | 3/ 1 | 7/ 1 | 2/ 3 |
| Allied health | 9/ 4 | 6/ 1 | 7/ 2 | 7/ 2 |
| Manager, admin. | 22/25 | 11/30 | 11/33 | 9/29 |
| Technical, sales | 22/27 | 19/24 | 21/26 | 16/29 |
| Clerical | 17/ 3 | 20/ 2 | 28/ [b] | 38/ 2 |
| Service | 4/14 | 2/ 7 | 2/ 6 | 3/ 9 |
| Total % | 100/100 | 100/100 | 100/97 | 98/100 |

Source: See text footnote 37.
[a]MetroWest data from Essex and Morris counties, New Jersey.
[b]Indicates less than 1%.
(N = 1,388 males, 1,427 females)
Totals above or below 100% due to rounding of numbers.

in government-related positions, the growth of law as the career of choice for Jewish women has been noted in many law schools and many Jewish communities.)

The practice of medicine, college teaching, writing, and artistic work is highest among women ages 35 to 44. While the data cited by Silberman indicate that teaching and social work are losing their appeal for young Jewish women, this is not the case in Washington. The percentage in these traditionally "female" fields climbs from older to younger working women, with 18 percent of Washington Jewish women ages 35 to 44 working as teachers or social workers. The percentage of Washington Jewish women involved in clerical work has diminished, but not radically: about one-fifth of Washington Jewish women ages 25 to 34 are clerical or administrative support staff.

As a city which offers broad occupational opportunities for women, Washington may dramatize some new trends in career movement. In the large metropolitan areas, especially on either coast, Jewish women are edging away from professional fields that are relatively weak in terms of

TABLE 4. OCCUPATIONS OF CURRENTLY EMPLOYED JEWS IN WASHINGTON, D.C., BY SEX AND AGE (PERCENT)

| Occupations | 25–34 F/M | 35–44 F/M | 45–54 F/M | 55–64 F/M |
|---|---|---|---|---|
| M.D., D.D.S., etc. | 2/ 7 | 4/ 8 | 1/ 7 | 3/ 4 |
| Atty., judge | 9/23 | 4/24 | 1/13 | 1/ 8 |
| Engineer, scientist | 3/11 | 4/12 | 2/21 | 5/16 |
| Teacher, soc. worker | 16/ 3 | 18/ 2 | 18/ 2 | 13/ 4 |
| College prof. | 3/ 4 | 3/ 5 | 2/ 8 | 3/ 4 |
| Writer, artist | 8/ 7 | 9/ 4 | 4/ 4 | 4/ 3 |
| Allied health | 8/ 2 | 4/ 1 | 3/ 4 | 3/ 1 |
| Manager, admin. | 20/16 | 19/28 | 24/28 | 20/31 |
| Technical, sales | 10/16 | 9/10 | 17/ 9 | 14/20 |
| Clerical | 16/ 6 | 20/ 2 | 24/ 2 | 29/ 2 |
| Service | 4/ 5 | 5/ 4 | 4/ 4 | 4/ 5 |
| Total % | 99/100 | 99/100 | 100/102 | 99/98 |

Source: See text footnote 37.
(N = 1,159 males, 998 females)
Totals above or below 100% due to rounding of numbers.

financial and status rewards and into fields that offer larger salaries. In most Midwestern and smaller cities, on the other hand, these new career trends among Jewish women have not yet had much statistical impact; in those areas, Jewish female professionals still cluster in the lowest paid fields—teaching and social work. Thus, among working Jewish women in Pittsburgh, 21 percent are social workers or teachers, while 4 percent are physicians, dentists, attorneys, or engineers. In Minneapolis, 16 percent of working Jewish women are social workers or teachers—more than five times the percentage in more lucrative professions. Denver has a relatively high proportion—almost 12 percent—of female doctors, lawyers, and engineers, partially because of the exceptionally high percentage of female engineers (8 percent, compared to 9 percent male engineers). In contrast, in Minneapolis, only 3 percent of Jewish women are doctors, lawyers, or engineers, compared to 17 percent of Jewish men; in Pittsburgh, the ratio is 4 percent women to 20 percent men; and in St. Louis, the ratio is 2 percent women to 17 percent men.

## Labor-Force Participation

In 1957, only 12 percent of Jewish women with children under six worked outside the home, compared to 18 percent of white Protestants. As recently as 15 years ago it was still true that Jewish women were likely to work until they became pregnant with their first child, and then to drop out of the labor force until their youngest child was about junior-high-school age. Barry Chiswick has suggested that the high occupational achievement level of Jewish men may owe a great deal to Jewish women who provided an environment of family stability.[43]

The labor-force participation of Jewish women today departs radically from patterns of the recent past. In most cities the majority of Jewish mothers continue to work, at least part-time, even when their children are quite young. This phenomenon can be examined in two ways: by looking at age group and by looking at family type. An examination of changes among age groups is useful, because it permits comparison with earlier data. Thus, in the 1975 Boston study, the labor-force participation of Jewish women dipped lower than that of any other white ethnic group during the childbearing years. Among women ages 30 to 39, the number of working Boston Jewish women in 1975 fell to 42 percent, compared to about half of white Protestant, Irish Catholic, and Italian Catholic mothers. Past age 40, the percentage of Boston Jewish women at work soared higher than that of any other subgroup, with almost three-quarters of Jewish women in the labor force.[44]

Data from the 1985 demographic study of the Boston Jewish population show a very different picture, as seen in table 5. The majority of Jewish women in every age group except for those over 65 are working, and the younger the age group the more likely they are to be employed. Only about one-third of Boston Jewish women in the two age groups most likely to have young or school-age families—ages 30 to 39 and 40 to 49—are not employed.

If we examine the working-mother phenomenon from a life-cycle vantage point, the present high rate of labor-force participation by Jewish mothers with even the youngest children emerges unequivocally. Table 6 compares the employment patterns of mothers of preschool children in ten cities. In Boston, Baltimore, San Francisco, and Washington, three out of every five Jewish mothers of preschool children are employed.

Perceived economic need is probably the single most significant factor affecting the proportion of Jewish women who work outside the home. As

---

[43] Barry R. Chiswick, "The Labor Market Status of American Jews: Patterns and Determinants," AJYB 1985, vol. 85, pp. 131–53.
[44] Goldscheider, *Jewish Continuity and Change*, pp. 125–34.

TABLE 5. EMPLOYMENT STATUS OF BOSTON JEWISH WOMEN, 1985, BY AGE (PERCENT)

| Ages | Not Employed | Employed Full-Time | Employed Part-Time |
|---|---|---|---|
| 18–29 | 15 | 65 | 19 |
| 30–39 | 28 | 38 | 34 |
| 40–49 | 35 | 45 | 19 |
| 50–64 | 43 | 33 | 25 |
| 65+ | 94 | 3 | 2 |

Source: Adapted from *1985 CJP Demographic Study*, p. 25.

has been widely demonstrated among the general American population, for middle-class families today, two incomes are often needed in order to attain and maintain a middle-class standard of living: that is, purchase of a single-family home in a desirable location, relatively new automobiles and major

TABLE 6. LABOR-FORCE PARTICIPATION OF JEWISH MOTHERS OF CHILDREN UNDER 6, COMPARED TO 1986 U.S. CENSUS (PERCENT)

| Cities | Full-Time | Part-Time | Homemaker | Other |
|---|---|---|---|---|
| Boston | 29 | 36 | 33 | 2 |
| Baltimore | 27 | 38 | 35 | 1 |
| Kansas City | 28 | 21 | 44 | 7 |
| MetroWest | 22 | 26 | 49 | 4 |
| Milwaukee | 18 | 32 | 36 | 14 |
| Philadelphia | 23 | 14 | 59 | 3 |
| Pittsburgh | 29 | 25 | 42 | 4 |
| Phoenix | 26 | 21 | 50 | 3 |
| Rochester | 22 | 32 | 42 | 4 |
| San Francisco | 36 | 25 | 31 | 8 |
| Washington | 34 | 30 | 30 | 6 |
| Worcester | 15 | 34 | 51 | 1 |
| U.S. Census | —54— | | | |

Source: Adapted from Gabriel Berger and Lawrence Sternberg, *Jewish Child-Care: A Challenge and an Opportunity* (Cohen Center for Modern Jewish Studies, Brandeis University, *Research Report* No. 3, Nov. 1988), p. 20.

appliances, and attractive educational options for one's children, including college and possibly private school and/or graduate school. It is also true that perceptions of what constitutes a middle-class life-style have been significantly revised upward, so that more income is needed by "middle-class" families. These factors are especially significant for American Jewish families, which have traditionally had a strong ethic of providing their children with "everything."[45]

However, in addition to economic need, employment opportunities, job preparation, and social pressure are equally important factors in the labor-force participation of Jewish women. Younger Jewish women are more likely than their mothers to have used their schooling to prepare for specific careers, and they are often less willing to let those careers lie fallow while they become full-time homemakers. Younger women are also more likely to be surrounded by peers who urge them to work, rather than to become homemakers. By and large, women over 50 received their schooling at a time when most Jewish women did not work after marriage unless there was dire financial need. Consequently, even women who completed college often had no specific career preparation; the liberal arts degree was used as a kind of intellectual finishing school. Moreover, a wife's working might indicate that her husband was an inadequate provider; therefore even women who were trained as teachers or librarians sometimes hesitated to return to the job market. Furthermore, according to David Reisman, 20 years ago a woman who successfully combined career and family life was likely to be greeted with "shrewish and vindictive" envy by her peers, rather than admiration or a spirit of live and let live.[46]

The great majority of middle-aged and older Jewish women, therefore, have worked only part-time or not at all for many years. Their daughters, on the other hand, have matured with an ethos that is more likely to make the homemaker feel defensive. Among women 40 and under, especially those who live in cities with a strongly career-oriented atmosphere, even women with young children often complain that they are made to feel inadequate if they are not pursuing careers at the same time that they are raising their families.

---

[45]Marshall Sklare states the matter well: " . . . [H]e offers the child what are sometimes termed the 'advantages' or, in common American-Jewish parlance 'everything,' as in the expression: 'they gave their son everything.' 'Everything' means the best of everything from the necessities to the luxuries: it includes clothing, medical attention, entertainment, vacations, schools, and myriad other items." Marshall Sklare, *America's Jews* (New York, 1971), p. 88.
[46]David Reisman, "Two Generations," *Daedalus*, Spring 1984, 711–35.

## Personal and Communal Implications of Demographic Change

As we have seen, substantial proportions of today's American Jewish households no longer fit the classic pattern of a working, highly educated husband living with a nonemployed, somewhat less educated wife and their several mutual children. Better education and career aspirations for women, later marriage and later childbirth, smaller families, rising rates of divorce, and widespread labor-force participation of Jewish mothers have changed the demographic profile of the American Jewish family. These changes have serious implications for individuals, who are confronted by difficult lifestyle decisions. They have also challenged the organized Jewish community to evaluate and make adjustments to new demographic realities.

It should be noted that although this discussion places the concept of "working mother" in a contemporary feminist context, the attempt at fusion of the two roles has long historical antecedents in the Jewish family. European and immigrant Jewish women often had a "characteristic aggressiveness and marketplace activism"[47] which they saw as an intrinsic part of their commitment to family and to society at large. Jewish women worked long hours at the sewing machine; they took in boarders; they ran grocery stores to help support their families. They also took active and often dangerous roles in union organizations because they believed that they could help better society. At the same time, connections between work and family were the norm in many traditional Jewish families.

For Jewish couples who married before the impact of women's liberation, there was almost always a commitment to the primacy of the family. They did not wonder whether or not to have children, and postponement of the first child was likely to depend on the father's career—as many couples waited until the conclusion of a residency or other professional training—rather than the mother's. Today, however, there are no *a priori* commitments to marriage and family, or to traditional gender roles. A 1985 survey found that only one-third of Jewish women believe that home-centered women make better mothers than women who work outside the home; while close to one-half of non-Jewish women think that employed women are less effective mothers and that children are more likely to get into trouble when both parents work.[48]

Couples now deciding to have children face an entirely different set of psychological barriers from those in the past. Rather than worrying about family or communal disapproval if working mothers decide to continue working, many are anxious about employer and peer-group disapproval if

---

[47]Hasia Diner, "Jewish Immigrant Women in Urban America," unpublished paper for the Mary I. Bunting Institute, Radcliffe College.
[48]Groeneman, "Beliefs and Values of American Jewish Women."

they curtail their working hours and career advancement to make time for child care. Contemporary values, which emphasize holding a stimulating job, personal development and growth, and experiencing the pleasures of an open and vital society, make the decision to have children a difficult one. Young women who have devoted many years to higher education and professional training and then to establishing careers are torn by conflicting desires. As they edge into their 30s and beyond, many long for a child but worry that the limitations imposed by pregnancies and maternity leaves will stunt their professional growth. Most are less willing than earlier working women to fall back temporarily to part-time or free-lance work and to risk jeopardizing career advancement.[49] In Baltimore, for example, more than half of the married women who haven't yet had children are professionals, compared to one-third of the women with children at home and fewer than one-quarter of women with grown children.

Again, it is important to remember that women alone are not responsible for these decisions: many potential fathers too are concerned that children will change a very pleasant dual-career life-style by limiting their freedoms, diminishing their financial status, and imposing on them a portion of child-care and family-related household tasks.[50]

The changes that have taken place in attitudes and life-style have certainly not met with universal acceptance. Some critics warn that feminism has introduced attitudes and behaviors that may be destructive, in both the short and the long run, to the survival of the Jewish people in the United States. Others regard feminist agendas as a litany of immature demands. If Jewish women want to work and have children, claim these critics, they are making the decision and ought to be willing to shoulder the responsibilities themselves.

Blu Greenberg, a modern Orthodox feminist, is torn between desire for feminist advancement and fears for the physical survival of the Jewish community. Although she has written and spoken widely on behalf of feminist agendas, especially within traditional religious realms, she points out that "by delaying childbirth from the 20s to the 30s, we lose an entire generation every three decades. Career counseling with the Jewish people's needs in mind," she suggests, "would temper feminist claims with Jewish ones; it would enable couples to consider more seriously the option of having children first and then moving on to dual careers."[51]

---

[49]Fertility decisions by career couples have been a favorite topic for the media. Among many articles, see Darrell Sifford, "Couples Agonize Over Parenthood," *Boston Globe*, Apr. 24, 1980; Nan Robertson, "Job VS Baby: A Dilemma Persists," *New York Times*, Nov. 18, 1982.

[50]Nadine Brozan, "New Marriage Roles Make Men Ambivalent About Fatherhood," *New York Times*, May 30, 1980.

[51]Blu Greenberg, "Feminism and Jewish Survival," in *On Women and Judaism: A View from Tradition* (Philadelphia, 1981), pp. 151–69, 164.

Both Midge Decter and Ruth Wisse see the conflict between career and family as basically an individual, rather than a communal problem. They assert that individual women can deal with career/family conflicts through strength of character and good planning. Decter portrays "the liberated woman" as a spoiled child of the sixties, who does not have enough common sense and self-discipline to know "that marriage is not a psychic relationship but a transaction, in which a man forgoes the operations of his blind boyhood lust, and agrees to undertake the support and protection of a family, and receives in exchange the ease and comforts of home." Decter notes wryly that "if a woman opts to have both marriage and a career, she will put herself in the way of certain inevitable practical difficulties, the managing of which will on the other hand also widen her options for gratification."[52]

Wisse shares Decter's jaundiced view of the *angst* that some feminists report when they think about juggling career and familial responsibilities. She tells modern mothers to be more firm in urging their daughters to marry and have children at the biologically appropriate time. If daughters speak of careers, perhaps mothers should answer as Wisse's mother did: "*Bay yidn zaynen nishto kayn nones*"—"We Jews have no nuns." Furthermore, she has nothing but scorn for women who do not appreciate the blessings of the conventional marriage: "Happy is the woman whose husband is prepared to carry the economic burden of the family during at least her child-rearing years, and those who have enjoyed such protective blessings are nothing short of wicked when, explicitly or implicitly, they contrive to destroy the fragile contract that promotes them."[53]

On the other side of the spectrum are Jewish communal leaders and thinkers who either approve of the feminist agenda and think it should be supported in Jewish life, and/or who take a pragmatic approach to the landscape of American Jewish family life as it exists today. Paula Hyman castigates Jewish community leaders who seem to value women more for their reproductive value than for the contribution which they *as individuals* can make to the Jewish community.[54]

In reality, while some women reject traditional family life in the single-minded pursuit of a career, many Jewish women today do indeed feel their familial and professional interests to be organically related. It is these women who are most likely to state that their traditional orientation helps them to balance dual responsibilities. Sheila Kamerman points out that in the past even working women "shaped and fitted their work around their

---

[52]Midge Decter, *The Liberated Woman and Other Americans* (New York, 1971), p. 94.
[53]Ruth Wisse, "Living with Women's Lib," *Commentary*, Aug. 1988, pp. 40–46.
[54]Ben Gallob, "Leader Flays Appeal for Larger Families," *Jewish Advocate* (Boston), Sept. 20, 1979, quoting recent issue of *Sh'ma*.

families and their family responsibilities while men have shaped and fitted their families around their work and job demands. Some of the tensions now emerging are a consequence of some women adopting men's attitudes and behavior, while others are insisting that some modification is required of both men and women if the goal is for individual, family and child well-being."[55]

Some observers feel that regardless of one's approval or disapproval of feminism, it is incumbent on Jewish communal organizations to work to accommodate new life-styles, rather than to judge them, to exhort against them, or to hope they will go away. Gladys Rosen points out that the near-demise of the extended family opens the way for communal involvement in support for dual-career families: "There is a desperate need for universal Jewish day care for preschoolers and expanded opportunities for day school education which would enable mothers to work while offering enriched Jewish education to their children."[56] Rela Geffen Monson notes that in terms of support, the relationship of Jewish institutions and the Jewish family has actually been reversed: the family is becoming "the recipient of community services rather than their support." This reordering offers Jewish communal organizations and institutions the opportunity to assist in transmission of values to the children of the new American Jewish family, she urges.[57]

Shirley Frank suggests that a number of broad attitudinal and practical changes by the Jewish community are needed to support Jewish families. Jewish community leaders who say they want larger Jewish families ought to champion expanded after-school Jewish programs which incorporate Hebrew school curricula with recreational programming, she says. They ought to make sure that every community has attractive Jewish day-care programs. Every synagogue service, every adult educational program, every Jewish social event ought to automatically offer good child-care provisions. Children should be seen as a welcome part of Jewish life by the very people who urge women to have more children—and then "openly discriminate against" or "ostracize" families with "restless small children or wailing infants."[58]

---

[55]Sheila B. Kamerman, *Being Jewish and Being American: A Family Policy Perspective on the U.S. Social Policy Agenda and the Jewish Communal Policy Agenda*, a paper prepared for the American Jewish Committee's Task Force on Family Policy, Feb. 1981, p. 23.
[56]Gladys Rosen, "The Impact of the Women's Movement on the Jewish Family," *Judaism*, Spring 1979, p. 167.
[57]Rela Geffen Monson, "Implications of Changing Roles of Men and Women for the Delivery of Services," *Journal of Jewish Communal Service* 63, no. 4, Summer 1987, pp. 302–10.
[58]Shirley Frank, "The Population Panic: Why Jewish Leaders Want Jewish Women to Be Fruitful and Multiply," *Lilith*, no. 4, Fall/Winter 1977/78, pp. 13–17, 17.

Despite the problems associated with balancing the demands of family and career, many of those who are doing it find that the blend leads to general feelings of happiness, satisfaction, and fulfillment. The great majority of Jewish career women with large families in Kuzmack and Salomon's study (Washington, D.C., 1980) were pleased with their lives on both a personal and a professional level. Almost 85 percent felt they were "successful" or "very successful" at child rearing; three-quarters described themselves as personally "extremely satisfied" or "very much satisfied"; and over 80 percent said they were "successful" or "very successful" at work.[59]

When considering the challenges faced by dual-career Jewish families and the Jewish communities they live in, it is important to note that feminism is often practically combined with deep emotional ties to Jewish values. While some have attempted to identify the dual-career couple with an assimilationist, "egalitarian" family model,[60] many of the women who aspire to combine work and motherhood are more committed Jewishly than either men or stay-at-home mothers.[61] Dual-career couples are an important, even predominant, group among young and middle-aged cohorts in every Jewish denomination. Kuzmack and Salomon's study showed that the great majority of such women are deeply committed to Jewish life. All but six of the women belonged to synagogues, three-quarters sent their children to religious schools, and more than half marked the Sabbath with some form of observance.

Although the Washington women said that their Jewish values and lifestyles enhanced familial devotion, stability, and structure, and increased the family's ability to weather dual-career stresses and strains, they felt that the local Jewish community was sadly failing Jewish dual-career families. They voiced the complaint that "the Jewish community is urging us to have more children, but it isn't willing to help us meet the cost." The area of largest dissatisfaction was that of day care and Jewish education. "Mothers of young children . . . complained bitterly about the lack of Jewish day care centers. 'Children should be raised in a Jewish environment, and day-care is part of that,' " said one. Others complained that Hebrew schools, day schools, and Jewish camps were unwilling to lower tuition fees for large Jewish families unless their income was very low. Jewish organizations, they felt, retained the attitude that Jewish women should have more children

---

[59]Linda Gordon Kuzmack and George Salomon, *Working and Mothering: A Study of 97 Jewish Career Women with Three or More Children*, National Jewish Family Center, American Jewish Committee, 1980, p. 23.

[60]Norman Linzer, *The Jewish Family: Authority and Tradition in Modern Perspective* (New York, 1984).

[61]Abraham D. Lavendar, "Jewish College Women: Future Leaders of the Jewish Community," *Journal of Ethnic Studies* 52, Summer 1976, pp. 81–90.

*and* that Jewish women should bear the financial and psychological burden of raising those children.[62]

While Jewish women were taught for centuries that the home was their proper sphere of influence, American Jewish women today energetically pursue educational and occupational accomplishment as well. At the same time, many American Jewish women reject the notion that they are uniquely responsible for the well-being of their households; rather, they seek to share responsibility for that sphere with husbands, paid household help, and family-support institutions.

Despite the skepticism of both male and female critics of the feminist agenda, the influence of feminism on the educational and occupational lives of American Jewish women seems to be growing, rather than weakening. As a result, feminism is having a major impact not only on the family but on another cornerstone of Jewish society as well—Jewish communal organizations.

## CHANGES IN COMMUNAL LIFE AND ORGANIZATIONAL BEHAVIOR

### The Feminist Critique of Voluntarism

Jewish communal and organizational life, like other spheres of Jewish life in America, has been strikingly affected by feminism. Women have penetrated former male bastions of power as volunteers in Jewish organizations and have worked for equity as professional Jewish communal workers. Not least, Jewish organizations have become more aware of the needs of contemporary American Jewish women, men, and children in changing households. Voluntarism fit well into the lives of American Jewish women, especially in the years after World War II. In the 1950s, the typical American Jewish woman was better educated and more leisured than her Gentile counterpart. Jewish women had two or three children as compared to a rate of three to four children for non-Jews, and they spaced their children carefully, beginning childbearing later and finishing earlier than non-Jewish women. The majority of American Jewish children were in school by the time their mothers reached their late thirties.

Articulate and well educated, many Jewish women poured their energies into communal work. Volunteer communal work earned familial and communal approval. It was seen as an extension of the role of the nurturing Jewish mother and drew on the long tradition of the Jewish

---
[62]Ibid., pp. 19–21.

woman as a giver of charity and a doer of good deeds. Jewish women and the organizations they served thrived together: voluntarism gave women the opportunity to use their intelligence, organizational ability, and talents in challenging projects; communal organizations on local, national, and international levels were enabled to complete major projects because Jewish women treated volunteer work with dedication and seriousness.

However, in the 1960s and 1970s female voluntarism came under the critical scrutiny of the feminist movement. To feminist critics, voluntarism was a subterfuge, an escape from the emptiness of the homemaker's existence. Doris Gold, for one, lambasted a system that exploited "more than 13 million volunteers who 'work' for no pay at all—a virtual underground of antlike burrowers in our social welfare institutions." Calling female voluntarism "pseudowork," Gold wondered "why have trained, educated, 'aware' women opted for voluntarism, instead of structured work or creativity, during or after childrearing years?"[63]

In "The Sheltered Workshop," Aviva Cantor asserted that Jewish organizational work was nothing more than "a placebo," or "a distorted form of occupational therapy," designed to keep Jewish women "busy with trivia and involved with a lot of time-consuming social activities."[64]

For many Jewish feminists, the issue is not so much that the volunteers are not paid—male volunteers, after all, are unpaid as well—as that female volunteers have been systematically cut off from opportunities for decision making and power. One vivid symbol of institutional resistance to change is the UJA's policy of sexual exclusiveness in its local leadership cabinets and its prestigious National Young Leadership Cabinet, which grooms future leaders of federations. Because only men are allowed in many local cabinets and in the national cabinet, feminists charge that they serve the function of perpetuating an anti-egalitarian bias. UJA leaders cite "intense male camaraderie" as a primary reason for excluding women from the cabinet: it has been claimed that men in leadership positions bond together in intense personal and idealistic relationships, and that women would disrupt male bonding; and it has been feared that the presence of women in the pressured and deeply involved atmosphere of weekend retreats and working weekends would entice men into extramarital relationships. The national UJA leadership has so far withstood pressure to change its policy and to admit women to its most effective structure for molding future leaders.[65]

Jewish women who have attained positions of power in Jewish organiza-

---

[63]Gold, "Women and Voluntarism," pp. 384–400.
[64]Aviva Cantor, "The Sheltered Workshop," *Lilith*, no. 5, 1978, pp. 20–21.
[65]Stone, "The Locked Cabinet," pp. 17–21.

tions have joined in the critique. Although, unlike many feminist critics, they do not find organizational activities worthless per se, they say that women have been consciously excluded from opportunities for power. One of the first to voice distress publicly over inequities in the Jewish communal world was Jacqueline Levine, then vice-president of the Council of Jewish Federations and Welfare Funds (CJF). Stating that she had frequently been included as "the only—and therefore the token—female representative" in Jewish communal leadership settings, Levine cited leadership figures as they existed in 1972: in three of the top ten cities, 13 percent of the combined boards of directors and 16 percent of the persons serving on federation committees were women. The percentages of women involved were somewhat larger in the medium-size and smaller cities.[66]

From a feminist standpoint, the situation has improved in the past decade and a half, but is still far from equitable. Women now comprise between one-quarter to one-fifth of federation board members, executive committee members, and campaign cabinet members. Women have been federation presidents in Baltimore, Boston, Dallas, Houston, Los Angeles, Milwaukee, New York, Omaha, Toledo, and San Jose. Shoshana Cardin has served as the first female president of CJF. The percentage of women on the boards of federations and federation-funded agencies rose from 14 percent in 1972 to 40 percent in the mid-1980s.[67] According to a 1987 JWB study, women comprise one-third of all Jewish community-center board members.[68] Ironically, perhaps, as Chaim Waxman observes, among Jewish women's organizations, where it might be expected that all chief executive officers would be women, a substantial number of male directors are to be found.[69]

## The Contemporary Jewish Female Volunteer

The Jewish population studies conducted in more than 20 U.S. cities since 1980 give us figures on the current percentage of American Jewish women who volunteer for Jewish causes. Testimony by Jewish communal leaders, organizational records, and anecdotal evidence indicate that 25 years ago the percentage of American Jewish women who volunteered for Jewish causes was much higher. However, we lack sufficient comparable data from the past to state this as a firm fact.

---

[66]Jacqueline K. Levine, "The Changing Role of Women in the Jewish Community," *Response*, Summer 1973, pp. 59–65. This is an edited text of an address to the 1972 General Assembly of the Council of Jewish Federations and Welfare Funds.

[67]Reena Sigman Friedman, "The Volunteer Sphere," *Lilith*, no. 14, Winter/Spring 1985–86, p. 9.

[68]Edward Kagen, *A Profile of JCC Leadership* (New York, 1987).

[69]Chaim I. Waxman, "The Impact of Feminism on American Jewish Communal Institutions," *Journal of Jewish Communal Service*, Fall 1980, pp. 73–79.

Jewish women are more likely than non-Jewish women to volunteer for certain kinds of organizations. According to one targeted study, Jewish women are ten times more likely than non-Jewish women to volunteer for ethnic causes, such as B'nai B'rith (compared to NAACP and Polish Women's Alliance, among non-Jewish populations), by a margin of 39 percent to 3 percent. Although Jewish women are substantially less likely to volunteer for a church or synagogue group than are non-Jewish women (59 percent of Jewish women compared to 69 percent of non-Jewish women), the synagogue group remains the single activity most likely to attract Jewish women. Among nonsectarian causes that attract Jewish women, high on the list are business and professional activities, which draw the membership of 28 percent of Jewish women but only 16 percent of non-Jewish women. This may be related to the relatively high rate of careerism among Jewish women. Jewish women are also far more likely to volunteer time for cultural activities, civic and public affairs, and feminist causes.[70]

No research has yet been published analyzing the Jewish organizational behavior of a large sample of American Jewish women. However, several studies both of the general population and of Jewish women have focused on specific groups of active volunteers. These studies give some indication of the demographic factors that correlate most closely with a propensity to volunteer.

The factors motivating Jewish women to volunteer may be somewhat different from those motivating women in the general population. Among the latter, research indicates an inverse correlation between careerism and voluntarism. A study of a Midwestern population found that women who were highly educated but were married to men who disapproved of their working outside the home were the group most likely to participate in volunteer work. The portrait of the typical volunteer in this nonsectarian study revealed a woman younger than 45, well educated, and satisfied with her traditional marriage.[71] In contrast, several leadership studies of active Jewish women volunteers suggest that many Jewish women who volunteer are labor-force participants. The "Council of Jewish Federations Women's Division Leadership Survey,"[72] a 1987 profile of CJF Women's Division

---

[70]Groeneman, "Beliefs and Values of American Jewish Women," pp. 11–12.

[71]Vicki R. Schram and Marilyn M. Dunsing, "Influences on Married Women's Volunteer Work Participation," *Journal of Consumer Research* 7, Mar. 1981, pp. 372–79. Data from this study are part of the Quality of Life Survey 1976–77. The data are drawn from interviews with 228 homemakers in Champaign-Urbana, Illinois, originally contacted through random sampling in the 1970–71 Survey of Life Styles of Families. Only married women under age 65 with children and husbands were included in this study.

[72]Gary A. Tobin and Sylvia Barack Fishman, "CJF Women's Division Leadership Survey Executive Summary," Cohen Center for Modern Jewish Studies, Brandeis University. The data for this study were gathered from 130 completed questionnaires, which were distributed

activists, showed that well over half of those with school-age children, ages 6 to 17, worked outside the home.

Household income seems to be positively related to volunteer activity, especially in leadership positions. Annual household income among the CJF Women's Division leaders in the sample was $135,000 for women ages 35 to 44 and $171,000 for women ages 45 to 64. Both average incomes are approximately two to three times higher than average incomes for Jewish families in those age brackets.

Ninety-four percent of the Women's Division leadership sample were currently married. Like most American Jewish women, they were highly educated: 62 percent of the respondents had B.A.s, 24 percent M.A.s, and 3 percent doctorates, medical, dentistry, or law degrees.

The Women's Division volunteers in the sample tended to be more traditional than other American Jewish women, both in terms of family formation patterns and in terms of religious observance. Respondents in the study averaged about three children each in their households, compared to about two children typical of all American Jewish households. Likewise, respondents were far more likely to mark the Sabbath and Jewish holidays with some observance.

Similarly, a study of Jewish women volunteers in Dallas[73] revealed a group of affluent, highly educated, fairly traditional women. The group was far more likely than average to maintain Jewish observances such as lighting Sabbath candles, fasting on Yom Kippur, eating only matzah and no bread on Passover, and to belong to a synagogue. Like the Women's Division leadership, the annual household income of Dallas Jewish leadership is relatively high: over one-third of the group enjoyed a household income of over $100,000 and another one-quarter had a household income of between $75,000 and $100,000.

The Dallas study seems to illustrate a disparity between behaviors and attitudes toward feminism that may be peculiar to Southern Jewish populations, which are more likely to be influenced by cultural prescriptions of traditional feminine roles. While more than half of the group worked outside the home, almost two-thirds said they perceived themselves as "home-

---

to Women's Division leaders during and after the 1986 CJF General Assembly. Respondents represented a diverse group from federations throughout the United States.

[73]The Dallas study of Jewish leadership was conducted during the spring of 1981 by mailing survey questionnaires to board officers and committee heads in Jewish organizations. Ninety-three women responded; they included leaders in the Federation, Jewish Family Services, Jewish Vocational Counseling Service, Jewish Community Center, Home for Jewish Aged, American Jewish Committee, American Jewish Congress, B'nai B'rith Anti-Defamation League, and all temples and synagogues. Jeffrey Becker Schwamm, "Recruitment of the Best: A Study of Why Dallas Jewish Women Leaders Volunteer," *Journal of Jewish Communal Service* 60, no. 3, Spring 1984, pp. 214–21.

makers," 40 percent said they perceived themselves as "career women," and only 36 percent said they perceived themselves as "feminists." Despite this reluctance to identify themselves as feminists, when asked about incentives to volunteer in Jewish communal organizations, two-thirds of the Dallas volunteers said that "dealing with problems which are challenging" was "very important." More than half named "intellectual stimulation" and "self-actualization and personal growth" as "very important." Thus, even in some highly traditional Jewish environments where women are loathe to identify themselves as feminists, mainstream Jewish women have tended to internalize feminist perspectives.

## Volunteers, Employed Women, and Jewish Communal Responses

Money is a factor in voluntarism for obvious reasons, but also for some that are not so obvious. The authors of the Dallas study comment that "transportation, convenience of meeting location, and alternative child-care arrangements represent no problem to almost all the respondents." Many less affluent Jewish women who combine careers and motherhood, however, have indicated that transportation, convenience of location, and alternative child-care arrangements are crucial issues indeed. A university professor participating in a panel discussion on "American Jewish Women and the World of Work" described her difficulties in chauffeuring her six-year-old from Jewish nursery school in the morning to nonsectarian day care in the afternoon. "After a day of working and driving back and forth," she commented, "I can't imagine a Jewish communal cause which would be interesting or important enough to drag me out of the house to start driving around for more child care."[74]

Conflict between labor-force participants and homemakers adds another, troubled dimension to the impact of feminism on the Jewish communal realm. Jewish mothers who do not work outside the home sometimes express hurt that the contemporary Jewish community does not assign them adequate status. Homemakers may feel that career women expect them to carry an unfair share of volunteer work, yet look down on them because of their apparent lack of ambition and skills. Still, Zena Smith Blau points out that although fewer Jewish women today are willing to throw themselves heart and soul into the many Jewish communal organizations that have flourished on the free talents, intelligence, and time of Jewish wives, volunteerism among Jewish women remains significantly higher than among high-status Protestant and nonreligious women. Blau speculates that the traditional emphasis on community work in Jewish families may have

---

[74]Ileana Gans, panelist commenting at the Conference on Jewish Culture in the South: Past, Present, and Future, Asheville, North Carolina, Apr. 1988.

contributed to Jewish marital stability: the optional social interactions and ego-gratification derived from communal work refreshed the marital bond and relieved stress.[75]

Some women use their volunteer work as a basis for vocational retraining after their children are grown and become career women after all.[76] However, others find that their volunteer activities and "life experience" do not gain them much ground in the job market, and that they must retrain themselves to gain occupational skills and credentials.[77] Other Jewish homemakers devote considerable time and energy to self-development, enrolling in classes of all kinds, partially in an effort to demonstrate to themselves that they are just as accomplished as their salaried sisters. These women also may be less willing than women in the past to volunteer, because they perceive the call to voluntarism as a form of exploitation of their nonemployed status.

It cannot be stressed enough that feminism has affected the voluntaristic activity of Jewish men as well as Jewish women. This is especially true in dual-career families. For couples who are under intense pressure during the working hours, evenings and weekends become a haven not easily abandoned for communal causes. Furthermore, when dual-career couples decide to have children, they are often extremely "professional" about the concept of "quality time" with their children. Volunteer activities which cut into these times are sometimes perceived as diminishing, rather than enhancing, the social aspects of their lives. This new generation of Jewish parents is often repelled, rather than attracted, by the segregated structure of synagogue brotherhoods and sisterhoods and federation women's divisions and leadership cabinets.

## *The Professional Jewish Communal Worker*

Feminism has affected Jewish communal life not only through its volunteers but through its professionals as well. Jewish communal service is a field increasingly populated by women; the 1988 enrollment of the Hornstein Program in Jewish Communal Service at Brandeis University, for example, consisted of 26 women and 11 men. Still, despite the presence of qualified women in the field, many of whom hold graduate degrees and many of whom have more seniority than the men they work with, very few

---

[75]Zena Smith Blau, "A Comparative Study of Jewish and Non-Jewish Families in the Context of Changing American Family Life," prepared for the American Jewish Committee Consultation on the Jewish Family and Jewish Identity, 1972.

[76]John Corry, "Mrs. Lieberman of Baltimore: The Life and Times of an Organization Lady," *Harper's*, Feb. 1971, pp. 92–95.

[77]Schneider, *Jewish and Female*, pp. 482–84.

women are promoted to executive positions. One recent article noted that "a 1981 survey of over 2000 professional staff in 273 agencies, conducted by the Conference of Jewish Communal Service (CJCS), indicated that although women constituted over half (58 percent) of the total staff, they made up only 8 percent of executive directors and assistant directors. A great majority of professional women (92 percent) were in the two lower job categories: 32 percent as supervisors and 60 percent line staff."[78]

Those who do achieve executive positions frequently earn salaries far lower than those of their male colleagues. Thus, a report by the Jewish Welfare Board in 1984 noted that 112 men were employed as executive directors, compared with 4 women, and that the average male director earned $51,500 while the average female director earned $44,250. In a similar 1984 CJF report, among the 80 male executive directors, the average salary was $53,179, while among the 8 female executive directors the average salary was $25,294.[79] Some of the reasons cited for not promoting women are the same as those given in the nonsectarian world: women are reluctant to relocate; women get married and pregnant and are therefore unreliable employees. Other reasons are peculiar to the world of Jewish communal service. It is a constant struggle to find high-caliber persons interested in the field, therefore attention cannot be "wasted" on efforts for equal opportunities for women; if women flood the executive strata of Jewish communal service, salaries in the field will automatically be depressed.[80]

Few wealthy female volunteers who have risen to power have worked to substantively improve the situation for female professionals in Jewish communal service. Moreover, some powerful female professionals have been loathe to rock the boat in order to benefit the female line workers below. Jacqueline Levine asserts that "too often those who have been accepted, or co-opted, or have 'made it,' don't look any farther than their own inclusion."[81] Many Jewish agencies have published statements and formed commissions to promote affirmative action, including the American Jewish Committee, the American Jewish Congress, the Anti-Defamation League of B'nai B'rith, the National Jewish Community Relations Advisory Council, the Council of Jewish Federations on a national level, as well as many on local levels. However, as many observers have commented, acknowledging and studying the problems have not always led to equity even within those organizations themselves.

[78]Reena Sigman Friedman, "The Professional Sphere," *Lilith*, no. 14, Fall/Winter 1985–86, p. 11.
[79]Debby Friss, "Room at the Top?" *Hadassah Magazine*, Jan. 1987, pp. 20–23.
[80]Ibid.
[81]Levine, "Changing Role," p. 60.

Interestingly, both men and women in power have indicated that feminist goals in the Jewish communal world will be achieved when women learn to be more aggressive in furthering their own cause. Thus, Irving Bernstein, former UJA executive, discussing the underrepresentation of women on the National Executive Committee and Campaign Cabinet of the national UJA, states that women's progress is impeded by women's discomfort with the idea that they must forcefully assert themselves and their views, even in the face of opposition.[82] Naomi Levine, former executive director of the American Jewish Congress, urges women to study job descriptions, salaries, and promotions, and to take legal action where necessary to eliminate discrimination.[83] Anne Wolfe, who served as national staff director of the American Jewish Committee's committee on the role of women, says that "nice conferences" change little; "a much more revolutionary push by women" is needed to achieve feminist goals.[84]

Despite feminist progress in many areas—and despite the apparent mainstreaming of feminist attitudes within many national Jewish organizations—the relationship between Jewish communal life and feminist goals is still troubled. Feminism has brought new conflicts into Jewish communal life and has exacerbated older ones. However, it also presents the Jewish communal world with the opportunity to utilize more fully the skills of American Jewish women, both as volunteers and as professional workers for the Jewish community.

## FEMINISM AND JEWISH RELIGIOUS MOVEMENTS

### The Feminist Critique of Judaism

More than in any previous period of Jewish history, women today have made themselves central to the public functioning of religious life. This has led to sharp conflict, with opponents arguing that feminist efforts in this area will undermine normative Judaism. The evidence is, however, that feminist interest in Jewish prayer, study, ritual, and life-cycle celebrations has been marked by high creativity, and that as feminists have explored Jewish religious life, they have often demonstrated a renewed commitment to Judaism. Feminists argue that they have involved Jewish women in their Judaic heritage on an egalitarian basis for the first time in Jewish history:

---

[82]Steven M. Cohen, Susan Dessel, Michael Pelavin, "The Changing (?) Role of Women in Jewish Communal Affairs," in Koltun, ed., *The Jewish Woman*, pp. 193–200.
[83]Cantor, "The Missing Ingredients," p. 12.
[84]Ibid.

that they have empowered Jewish women to acquire the intellectual tools needed to deal competently with Jewish source materials and texts, as well as the liturgical skills which make them equal partners with men in prayer; that they have examined Jewish source materials from a female-centered, rather than a male-centered perspective; and that they have created rituals and midrashim which deal specifically with the feminine experience of Jewish life cycles, history, and culture. According to feminists, Jewish women are at last gaining the opportunity to explore their own spirituality.

Some aspects of this creative renewal—such as Jewish life-cycle celebrations for females—affect huge numbers of American Jewish women; other aspects—such as female ordination and the practice by women of traditionally male-focused rituals—directly affect only highly committed and involved women. However, even women who are not directly involved in the more intensive forms of Jewish feminist spirituality may be indirectly shaped by an environment in which women have increasingly become public Jews.

It is of course ironic that at a time when most American Jewish men seem to be drawing away from Jewish ritual, and few men worship regularly with *tallit* and *tefillin*, some Jewish women have been exploring these and other traditionally male modes of religious expression. While fewer Jewish men are attracted to the rabbinate, partially because restrictive codes barring them from other professions have almost disappeared, increasing numbers of Jewish women have been entering the field, first in the Reform (1972) and Reconstructionist (1975) branches and later in the Conservative (1985) denomination. Among the masses of American Jewish boys and girls, the education of Jewish females has drawn close to approximating the education of Jewish males.

For most of Jewish history, the role of women within Judaism was shaped by rabbinic law (Halakhah). Although this body of law prescribed behavior for Jewish women, they were not involved in the formal discussion or decision-making processes—they were passive recipients of a nonrepresentative system.[85]

---

[85]Blu Greenberg summarizes the laws and concepts which most determined a Jewish woman's role thus: "Talmudic law spelled out every facet of the law as it applied to the woman. She was exempt from those positive commandments that must be performed at specific times, such as wearing the *tzitzit* and *tefillin*, reciting the *Shema*, and the three complete daily prayer services (Kiddushin 29a; Eruvin 96b; Berakhot 20a-b; Menahot 43a). She was exempt also from certain commandments that were not time specific (Eruvin 96b). In various communal or group events, she could be a participant-observer but had no equal status in performance of ritual. This held true for the mitzvah of *sukkah*, the celebration of *simhat bet ha-sho'evah*, the redemption of the firstborn, inclusion in the minyan for grace after meals, and reading the Torah at the communal prayer service (Sukkah 2:18, 53a; Kiddushin 34a; Megillah 47b, 23a)." Greenberg, *On Women and Judaism*, pp. 62–63.

According to some Jewish feminist scholars, such as Rachel Biale, the Halakhah has not excluded Jewish women nearly as much as the folk cultures that have surrounded it. It was folk culture, not postbiblical Jewish law, for example, that perpetuated the notion of menstrual contamination and made menstruating women feel unwelcome in synagogues in certain European Jewish communities. Contrary to popular opinion, Biale suggests, "the law may have preceded common practice in what to the contemporary eye are liberal, compassionate attitudes toward women."[86] Most feminist scholars of Judaism, however, would be inclined to agree with Judith Plaskow's view[87] that the Halakhah contains much that is objectionable because it has been male-centered from its inception. Even at Mount Sinai, she points out, Moses addresses the community as though it were composed exclusively of men. This exclusion is deeply troubling to feminists because biblical memory is an active force in the spiritual lives of Jews. Plaskow maintains that the issue of female exclusion extends into, and is exacerbated by, later developments in Halakhah, as expounded through the Talmud, its commentators, and the responsa literature. Because "Halakhah is formulated by men in a patriarchal culture," she asserts, it defines the normative Jewish experience as the experience of men. According to Plaskow, "Feminism questions any definition of 'normative' Judaism that excludes women's experience."

Jewish feminists involved with religious issues can be divided between those who feel bound by Jewish law and those who do not. The former have been careful to maintain all ritual requirements incumbent upon Orthodox women, while working to effect change within the law itself. The latter feel that rabbinic law can be treated as a flexible guide to practice rather than as a rigid set of demands. They have worked for behavioral change within Jewish religious life, urging women to take on religious duties and roles previously proscribed to women, even if those duties and roles are prohibited by traditional law. Both types of Jewish feminists have sought to revitalize traditional modes of religious expression for women, as well as to create new rituals and liturgies.

## American Jewish Life-Cycle Celebrations

In the past, ritual responses to the birth of a girl were pallid. The father was one of several men in the synagogue called to make a blessing on the

---

[86]Rachel Biale, *Women and Jewish Law: An Exploration of Women's Issues in Halakhic Sources* (New York, 1984), p. 7.
[87]Judith Plaskow, "Standing Again at Sinai: Jewish Memory from a Feminist Perspective," *Tikkun* 1, no. 2, 1987, pp. 28–34; idem, "Halakhah as a Feminist Issue," *Melton Journal*, Fall 1987, pp. 3–5.

Torah, and there he would recite a prayer for the health of mother and child and name his daughter. Some families would also mark the occasion by serving simple refreshments after Sabbath services, but no talk was given and no songs were sung, nor was the infant herself brought to the synagogue. As recently as 25 years ago, a lavish *kiddush* for a girl could arouse sarcastic commentary: "You're doing all this for a girl?" Today, however, an elaborate *kiddush* is expected for the birth of a daughter, even in strictly Orthodox circles. Moreover, neglected customs have been revived and new customs have arisen to give both mother and daughter the opportunity to mark these momentous events. In some synagogues, women who have just given birth recite *birkat hagomel* aloud during the Torah-reading portion of the Sabbath service, thanking God for the deliverance from danger, rather than leaving such thanksgiving to the father's proxy recital. The once unknown ceremony of *"Shalom Bat,"* welcoming a daughter, has become ubiquitous in Jewishly knowledgeable communities. In the home or synagogue, with mother and daughter present, friends gather to listen to talks, eat, sing, and celebrate together. Some parents compose new prayers for the occasion; others make use of printed materials that have been written and disseminated in liberal Orthodox, Conservative, Reform, and Reconstructionist circles.[88]

Reconstructionist founder Mordecai Kaplan, who was also closely associated for many years with the Jewish Theological Seminary, may have been the first to suggest the concept of Bat Mitzvah,[89] and Conservative Judaism made popular the actual celebration of this event. At first, few families chose to celebrate the Bat Mitzvah,[90] and many Conservative synagogues limited the celebration to less problematic Friday-night services, when the Torah is not read. By the late 1980s, however, most Conservative and almost all Reform congregations had made Bat Mitzvah and Bar Mitzvah ceremonies virtually identical, including calling girls to the Torah.

For women who missed having a Bat Mitzvah in their youth, such a celebration at a later stage in life provides the opportunity for both a renewed commitment to Judaism and a feminist assertion of personhood. One recent adult Bat Mitzvah states, "In the midst of our Jewish lives, there was a void—something that was not quite okay for us. One of us said she wanted to stand where her husband and four children stood and read a *haftarah* from the same bimah. Two of us are making up for being denied

---

[88]For a listing of printed materials on *Shalom Bat* ceremonies, see Schneider, *Jewish and Female*, pp. 121–29.

[89]Carole Kessner, "Kaplan on Women in Jewish Life," *Reconstructionist*, July-Aug. 1981, pp. 38–44.

[90]Marshall Sklare, *Conservative Judaism: An American Religious Movement* (New York, 1972), pp.154–55.

this chance years ago when we were told in our shuls there was no such thing as girls being bat mitzvah."[91] These ceremonies involve women ranging in age from young adulthood to old age and are a regular feature in many Conservative and Reform congregations.

Orthodox practitioners have slowly responded to the pressure to celebrate a girl's religious majority. Some congregations have established a format for celebrating Bat Mitzvah on Sunday morning or Shabbat afternoon at a special *se'udah sh'lishit*, the traditional festive "third meal." At these occasions the girl typically delivers a *d'var torah*, a homiletic address illustrating her familiarity with biblical texts, marking the seriousness of the occasion. Other congregations leave the mode of celebration up to the discretion of the child and her parents. These celebrations have become commonplace in many Orthodox circles, with families sometimes traveling great distances to be at a Bat Mitzvah, just as they would for a Bar Mitzvah. Much feminist commentary on this phenomenon has tended to concentrate on the disparity between limited Orthodox forms of Bat Mitzvah, on the one hand, and egalitarian Conservative and Reform modes of Bat Mitzvah, on the other. This, however, misses the point that Orthodoxy has in fact traveled a farther road than the Conservative, Reform, and Reconstructionist branches in breaking away from previously prevailing norms.

## Synagogue Participation and Ritual Observance by Women

The diversity of congregational attitudes toward female participation in synagogue services is illustrated in a 1978 study that evaluated questionnaires filled out by the rabbis of 470 congregations of different sizes, drawn from different branches of the American Jewish religious community and distributed among the several geographic areas of the United States.[92] Investigators Daniel Elazar and Rela Monson found that mixed seating and women leading the congregation in English readings were almost universal among Reform and Conservative congregations. Almost all Reform congregations counted women toward a *minyan* (required prayer quorum) and allowed them to chant the service; slightly less than half the Conservative congregations did so; and none of the Orthodox. Nearly all Reform congregations and about half of Conservative congregations honored women with *aliyot* to the Torah, while none of the Orthodox congregations did. Women gave sermons in almost all Reform congregations, more than three-quarters of Conservative congregations, and 7 percent of Orthodox congregations.

---

[91]Susan Gilman, "Bat Mitzvah Ceremonies Not Just Kid Stuff," *Queens Jewish Week* (New York), May 27, 1988.

[92]Daniel J. Elazar and Rela Geffen Monson, *The Evolving Role of Women in the Ritual of the American Synagogue* (Philadelphia and Jerusalem, 1978).

Most Reform congregations and almost two-thirds of Conservative congregations had women opening the ark and chanting *kiddush* and *havdalah*, but only 2 percent of Orthodox congregations did similarly. As these data were gathered in the late 1970s, and before the Conservative movement's landmark decision to ordain female rabbis, we can safely assume that considerable movement has taken place in most Conservative congregations to increase egalitarian practices.

Egalitarian attitudes toward prayer become especially important to women who wish to say *kaddish* daily for departed loved ones. Traditional synagogues are the most likely to have daily prayers—and they are also the most likely to be unwilling to count women for a *minyan*, posing a serious problem for the would-be female *kaddish* reciter. Greta Weiner recalls entering one Conservative synagogue, only to be pushed to the back of the chapel by a man who insisted that her presence would be "disruptive to the men trying to pray." Refusing to count her and her teenage daughter for the *minyan*, the congregation that evening had only nine men and did not include the *kaddish* in its prayers.[93]

The egalitarian prayer model is championed outside established synagogues in many *havurot*. *Havurot*—prayer and study groups which often involve relatively small numbers of fairly knowledgeable and/or committed Jews—have a participatory and egalitarian ethos. They have been the locus of much creative ferment in the American Jewish community, ferment which has often filtered out and eventually influenced more established synagogues and temples. Because *havurot* have no rabbis, cantors, or other professionals to lead services, read from the Torah, deliver sermons, and teach classes, and rely on group members to undertake these responsibilities, they have been pioneers in providing opportunities to women in these areas.

The expansion of female participation in worship takes place not only in an egalitarian context but in an all-female setting as well. In all-female prayer groups, women have the opportunity to lead prayers and read the Torah, and in general to be active participants in a ritual sphere in which for millennia they were nonessential auxiliaries. Even in all-female groups, however, conflicts arise between Orthodox and non-Orthodox women. While some non-Orthodox women welcome the all-female context so that they can read, lead, and pray without the potentially intimidating presence of men, Orthodox women need the all-female format because they will only perform in this way if men are not present. Furthermore, many Orthodox women will not recite the approximately 20 percent of the prayer service reserved for a quorum of ten men unless they receive permission to do so from a recognized male rabbinical *posek* (person recognized as a competent

---

[93]Greta Weiner, "The Mourning Minyan," *Lilith*, no. 7, 1980, pp. 27–28.

formulator of Jewish law). As Steven Cohen notes, feminist religious styles "are predominantly determined by differences in approach to Jewish life rather than by differences in approach to feminism."[94]

Prayer is far from a new concept for women in the Orthodox Jewish world. According to Maimonides and other classical rabbinical commentators, women are required to pray daily, although they are excused from the time restrictions for prayer and are not counted as part of a *minyan*. Consequently, in the past, numerous Orthodox European women prayed daily in their homes, as do many contemporary Orthodox American women. Nor is group prayer by women per se controversial, as it is a regular occurrence in many Orthodox girls' yeshivahs. Two new phenomena have infuriated some Orthodox rabbis, however: women choosing to pray separately, rather than being relegated to separation by men; and women carrying and reading from Torah scrolls.

In the words of one participant, Rivkeh Haut, "Reading from a *sefer torah* is at the heart of every women's prayer service. The Torah is carried about the room, so that every woman present may reach out and kiss it. The entire Torah portion for that week is read. This Torah reading is the basic innovation of women's *tefillah* [prayer] groups."[95] Orthodox Jewish women of all ages have reported being moved to tears the first time they looked into a Torah scroll as part of a women's prayer group. "I never realized how much I was excluded from—or how much it meant to me," said one Boston grandmother.

Despite the cautious respect with which Orthodox women approached this activity, some Orthodox leaders launched vigorous campaigns against female group prayer. Thus, in 1985 Rabbi Louis Bernstein, then president of the Rabbinical Council of America, invited five Yeshiva University Talmud professors to issue a responsum on the appropriateness of female *minyanim*, this despite the fact that the prayer groups scrupulously avoided identifying themselves as such. The resulting one-page responsum prohibited women's *minyanim* as a "falsification of Torah," a "deviation," and a product of the "licentiousness" of feminism. The responsum, condemned by more moderate modern Orthodox figures for its startling, undocumented brevity and blatant lack of halakhic objectivity,[96] was followed by a more scholarly but no less inflammatory 17-page article by Rabbi Hershel Schacter.[97] When some of the rabbis involved were interviewed by the popular Jewish press, their remarks underscored the personal and political

---
[94]Cohen, "American Jewish Feminism," pp. 530–31.
[95]Rivkeh Haut, "From Women: Piety Not Rebellion," *Sh'ma*, May 17, 1985, pp. 110–12.
[96]See, for example, David Singer, "A Failure of Halachic 'Objectivity,'" *Sh'ma*, May 17, 1985, pp. 108–10.
[97]See Michael Chernick, "In Support of Women's Prayer Groups," *Sh'ma*, May 17, 1985, pp. 105–08, for a discussion of Schacter's article in Yeshiva University's journal *Beit Yitzhak*, Mar. 1985.

nature of their "halakhic" ruling. "What are they doing it for? A psychological lift? It has no halakhic meaning. If they want to get their kicks there are other ways to get it," said one, under cover of anonymity. Bernstein dismissed the importance of Orthodox women's spiritual explorations by stating, "They [the rabbis] don't owe the women anything."[98]

Despite the negative reaction among key elements of Orthodox leadership, women's prayer groups continue to flourish in many cities. Even in areas where women's prayer groups do not meet on a regular basis, they meet for special occasions, such as Simhat Torah. They have become a popular locus for Orthodox Bat Mitzvahs, since they offer girls the opportunity to read from the Torah and recite the *haftarah*, the reading from Prophets.

The impact of feminism on Orthodox women's observance can be seen in other phenomena as well, such as the pressure that exists in many communities to construct an *eruv*. The *eruv*, a Sabbath boundary marker, transforms a given area from a public realm to a private realm, according to talmudic law, thus making it halakhically acceptable to carry objects on the Sabbath—and to push a baby carriage as well. Prof. Nahum Sarna suggests that when Orthodox communities assumed that young women would simply remain home with their children until they could walk to the synagogue, few communities went to the trouble of setting up and maintaining an *eruv*. Today, however, far larger proportions of Orthodox women assume that their proper place is in the synagogue on the Sabbath morning, even after they have attained the life-cycle stage of motherhood. Consequently, notes Sarna, construction of an *eruv* has become a high communal priority in areas where large numbers of young Orthodox couples have settled.[99]

*Jewish Education*

It is difficult to overestimate the importance of Jewish education in helping women to advance significantly within the religious sphere. In Judaism, no activity is more revered than study; study confers status on the individual and makes possible the mastery of the basic Jewish sources. For most of Jewish history, study was an activity available to women only on the rudimentary level and in informal contexts. Widespread formal Jewish education for women is a relatively recent phenomenon.[100]

---

[98]Larry Cohler, "Orthodox Rabbis' Responsa Condemns Women's Prayer Groups," *Long Island Jewish World*, Feb. 15–21, 1985.
[99]Nahum Sarna, personal conversation, Sept. 1988.
[100]Deborah R. Weissman, "Education of Jewish Women," *Encyclopedia Judaica Year Book, 1988* (Jerusalem, 1988), pp. 29–36.

The slow, cumulative growth of Jewish education for women is linked to the process of Emancipation and acculturation to Western society. In Germany, where the Jewish community was profoundly affected by the ideals of the Haskalah (Jewish Enlightenment), both the burgeoning Reform movement and the enlightened neo-Orthodox movement of Samson Raphael Hirsch sponsored formal Jewish education for girls. In Eastern Europe, where the Jewish community proved more resistant to Westernization, such schooling came somewhat later. After World War I, some secular Jewish schools, both Yiddishist and Hebraist, provided formal education for girls. Most importantly, Sara Schnirer[101] established the Bais Yaakov movement, which revolutionized Jewish education for girls in the Orthodox world. Schnirer's educational work won the support of such leading Orthodox figures as the Hafetz Hayyim and the Belzer Rebbe, who pointed out that women receiving sophisticated secular education but rudimentary Jewish education were likely to abandon Orthodoxy. Today, intensive Jewish education of girls is widely accepted by all Orthodox elements as an absolute necessity. In day schools ranging from Satmar's Bais Rochel system, which eliminates the 12th grade to make sure its graduates cannot attend college, to coeducational Orthodox schools such as Ramaz in New York and Maimonides in Boston, which provide outstanding secular education and teach both boys and girls Talmud, a rigorous Jewish education for girls has become an undisputed Orthodox communal priority. During the past decade, it has also become increasingly popular for Orthodox young women to spend a year of religious study in an Israeli yeshivah between high school and college.

Young American Jewish women today are far more likely than their grandmothers were to receive some formal Jewish education (see table 7).[102] In MetroWest, New Jersey (Essex and Morris counties), only 56 percent of women over age 65 had received some formal Jewish education, compared to 80 percent of girls ages 14 to 17. Additionally, data *not* included in table 7 show that among American Jewish women over age 55, the Orthodox women are the most likely to have received some formal Jewish education

---

[101]The daughter of a Belzer Hassid, Sarah Schnirer was born in 1883 and received minimal Jewish education as a child, but pursued her education on her own and later with neo-Orthodox teachers in Vienna. She returned to Krakow determined to "rescue Judaism for the new generation" by providing intensive Jewish education for girls in an Orthodox setting. In 1917 she opened a school with 25 girls; the school expanded rapidly and new branches were established. In 1937–1938, 35,585 girls were enrolled in 248 Bais Yaakov schools in Poland alone. See Menachem M. Brayer, *The Jewish Woman in Rabbinic Literature*, vol. 2 (Hoboken, N.J.: Ktav, 1986), pp. 79–80.

[102]This discussion draws upon Sylvia Barack Fishman, *Learning About Learning: Insights on Contemporary Jewish Education from Jewish Population Studies*, Cohen Center for Modern Jewish Studies, Brandeis University, 1987, pp. 25–29.

and the nonobservant and the "just Jewish" the least likely.[103] Sunday School education for girls is most frequent in the Reform movement, while Orthodox girls are most likely to be exposed to day schools, private tutors, Yiddish schools, and the like.

## Ordination

In 1972, Hebrew Union College, the Reform seminary, ordained Sally Priesand as the first female rabbi. Since then, the school has ordained well over 100 women. Over one-third of the entering rabbinic class in 1986 was female. Still, most Reform congregations continue to express a preference for a male primary rabbi; women rabbis are far more likely to find employment as assistant rabbis, chaplains, and Hillel directors.[104]

Now that the earliest female Reform rabbis have attained some seniority within the movement, it remains to be seen if they will also attain rabbinical posts with the prestige and salaries commensurate with their status.

Female Reform cantors have found much more widespread acceptance and have obtained employment in many prestigious congregations. In 1986 the entire entering class of cantors at Hebrew Union College was composed of women. Halakhically, women cantors pose as many problems as women rabbis (although the problems are somewhat different), and there is no halakhic difference between a primary rabbi and an assistant rabbi. Therefore, the bias against women primary rabbis but in favor of women cantors and assistant rabbis would appear to be cultural. Clearly, despite assumptions of full egalitarianism, a substantial number of Reform congregants seem content to relegate female clergy to subordinate positions.

The struggle within the Jewish Theological Seminary in moving toward Conservative ordination of women provides a well-documented case study of the evolution of women's role within American Judaism. The way toward considering such an idea was opened by the votes first to give women *aliyot* (1955) and later to count women for a *minyan* (1973) by the Rabbinical Assembly's Committee on Jewish Law and Standards. During the late 1970s, there was strong pressure within the Conservative movement to change the Seminary's policy and to begin to ordain women as Conservative rabbis. Seminary chancellor Gerson D. Cohen and Rabbi Wolfe Kelman,

---

[103]"Just Jewish" refers to respondents in the Jewish population studies who did not define themselves by any wing of Judaism, i.e., Orthodox, Conservative, Reform, Reconstructionist, or Traditional, but said instead that they were "just Jewish." In addition, some population studies categorize people by the number of Jewish rituals they observe, independent of their denominational identification, as "highly observant," "moderately observant," "low-observant," and "nonobservant." "Other" (generally a very small percentile) refers to people who do not currently define themselves as Jewish.

[104]I am grateful to Rabbi Sanford Seltzer for a conversation clarifying many of these issues.

TABLE 7. FORMAL JEWISH EDUCATION OF JEWS IN METROWEST, N.J.,[a] BY AGE, SEX, AND DENOMINATION (PERCENT)

### Age and Sex

|  | 0–5 M/F | 6–13 M/F | 14–17 M/F | 18–24 M/F | 25–34 M/F | 35–44 M/F | 45–54 M/F | 55–64 M/F | 65–74 M/F | 75+ M/F |
|---|---|---|---|---|---|---|---|---|---|---|
| Total ever received Jewish education | 33/39 | 85/80 | 88/80 | 89/79 | 82/64 | 89/63 | 89/63 | 87/55 | 85/56 | 90/58 |
| Total received no Jewish education | 65/58 | 13/18 | 12/20 | 11/20 | 18/33 | 10/35 | 9/34 | 11/43 | 13/39 | 8/41 |

### Denomination and Sex

|  | Orthodox All | Orthodox M | Orthodox F | Conservative All | Conservative M | Conservative F | Reform All | Reform M | Reform F | Just Jewish All | Just Jewish M | Just Jewish F | Other All | Other M | Other F |
|---|---|---|---|---|---|---|---|---|---|---|---|---|---|---|---|
| Total ever received formal Jewish education | 81 | 89 | 73 | 78 | 88 | 69 | 75 | 84 | 66 | 51 | 63 | 39 | 61 | 74 | 48 |
| Total received no Jewish education | 18 | 10 | 26 | 19 | 10 | 28 | 24 | 15 | 33 | 48 | 36 | 59 | 35 | 25 | 47 |

*Source:* Sylvia Barack Fishman, *Learning About Learning: Insights on Contemporary Jewish Education from Jewish Population Studies* (Cohen Center for Modern Jewish Studies, Brandeis University, 1987), pp. 26, 27.
[a]MetroWest data from Essex and Morris counties, New Jersey.

executive vice-president of the Rabbinical Assembly, were strongly in favor of the change, as were many younger pulpit rabbis. At the annual convention of the Rabbinical Assembly in May 1977, the majority of rabbis voted to ask for the formation of an interdisciplinary commission "to study all aspects of the role of women as spiritual leaders in the Conservative Movement." The final report of the commission, presented in 1979, minimized both halakhic difficulties and the strength of feeling of dissenting rabbis. It stated that it would be morally wrong for the Conservative movement to continue to deny ordination to qualified women. A majority of Conservative congregations, said the commission, were ready to accept female rabbis, as were three-quarters of current rabbinical students. The commission strongly recommended "that the Rabbinical School of The Jewish Theological Seminary of America revise its admission procedures to allow for applications from female candidates and the processing thereof for the purpose of admission to the ordination program on a basis equal to that maintained heretofore only for males," and that the Seminary "educate the community" properly "so as to insure as smooth and as harmonious an adjustment to the new policy as possible."[105]

The commission's premises and recommendations were opposed by several older and senior Seminary professors who themselves had studied at Orthodox yeshivahs and were committed to traditional halakhic Judaism. At the Seminary chapel, for example, men and women were seated separately, despite the long-standing and accepted Conservative custom of mixed pews, and despite the majority opinion of the Rabbinical Assembly's Law Committee permitting the counting of women as part of the *minyan* for public worship, issued in 1973. The ordination of women was also opposed by a substantial group of Conservative pulpit rabbis.

Shortly after the commission report appeared, Charles Liebman, then a visiting professor at the Jewish Theological Seminary, and Saul Shapiro, an active Conservative layman and a senior planner with IBM, prepared *A Survey of the Conservative Movement and Some of Its Religious Attitudes*,[106] for the Biennial Convention of the United Synagogue of America in November 1979. Liebman and Shapiro divided the Conservative laity into a large group that had little if any commitment to the halakhic process and a small, loyal core that took Halakhah seriously. Liebman and Shapiro suggested

---

[105] *Final Report of the Commission for the Study of the Ordination of Women as Rabbis*, Jan. 30, 1979. Signed by Gerson D. Cohen, Victor Goodhill, Marion Siner Gordon, Rivkah Harris, Milton Himmelfarb, Francine Klagsbrun, Fishel A. Perlmutter, Harry M. Plotkin, Norman Redlich, Seymour Siegel, and Gordon Tucker.

[106] Charles S. Liebman and Saul Shapiro, *A Survey of the Conservative Movement and Some of Its Religious Attitudes*, sponsored by the Jewish Theological Seminary of America in cooperation with the United Synagogue of America, Sept. 1979.

that the traditional minority might well represent Conservative Judaism's best chance for a viable and vital future, but warned that it could be alienated from the Conservative movement if female rabbis were ordained by the Jewish Theological Seminary.

Liebman and Shapiro's view did not deflect the agenda of the pro-ordination factions. A group of women who wanted to become Conservative rabbis were already studying at the Jewish Theological Seminary. On December 6, 1979, they sent a letter to members of the faculty, in which they said:

....We are seriously committed to Jewish scholarship and to the study of Jewish texts. Although some of our specific practices vary, we are all observant women who are committed to the halachic system.

We wish to serve the Jewish community as professionals in a variety of educational and leadership capacities. We are interested in teaching, writing, organizing, counseling and leading congregations. Although we realize that these tasks can be performed by people who are not rabbis, we desire to receive rabbinical training, and the title "rabbi," because we feel that with this authority we can be most effective in the Jewish community. We believe that our efforts are sorely needed and that there are many communities where we would be fully accepted and could accomplish much towards furthering a greater commitment to Jewish life.

We are fully aware that there are a number of complicated halachic issues related to Jewish women. We feel that these issues should be addressed carefully, directly and within the scope of the halachic process. This process, however, should not delay the admission of women to the Rabbinic School. We wish above all to learn and to serve God through our work in the Jewish community.[107]

In December 1979, the faculty senate of JTS voted 25 to 18 to table the question of ordination. In the spring of 1980, Gerson Cohen announced the initiation of a new academic program for women, which would be parallel to the rabbinic program but would sidestep the emotional issue of ordination. In May 1980, however, the Rabbinical Assembly voted 156 to 115 supporting women's ordination. Although the entire senior faculty of the Seminary's department of Talmud continued to oppose ordination, as did a large minority of pulpit rabbis, in October 1983, the Seminary faculty voted 34 to 8 to admit women to the rabbinical program. The first women entered the rabbinical school in September 1984; the class included 18 women and 21 men. Amy Eilberg, already an advanced student, was the first woman to receive Conservative ordination, graduating in 1985.

The Orthodox movement could hardly remain untouched by all this, despite the denunciations of leading Orthodox figures. Indeed, a few Orthodox rabbis responded positively to feminist ferment within the Conservative movement, suggesting that something similar might eventually happen in

---

[107]Signed by Debra S. Cantor, Nina Beth Cardin, Stephanie Dickstein, Nina Bieber Feinstein, Sharon Fliss, Carol Glass, and Beth Polebaum.

the Orthodox community. Rabbi Avraham Weiss stated: "There are aspects of the rabbinate such as public testimony, involvement in a bet din and leading a public liturgical service that women may not, according to Jewish law, be involved in. However there are aspects of the rabbinate—the teaching of Torah and counseling—in which women can fully participate on the same level as men. . . .a new title must be created for women to serve this purpose."[108] Blu Greenberg went one step further. In an article entitled "Will There Be Orthodox Women Rabbis?" she answered in the affirmative:

> Will it happen in my lifetime? I am optimistic. At this moment in history, I am well aware that the Orthodox community would not accept a woman as a rabbi. Yet we are moving towards a unique moment in history. More than any other, the Orthodox community has widely educated its women in Torah studies. Thus, though it rejects the formal entry of women into rabbinic studies, *de facto*, through the broad sweep of day school, yeshiva high school education and beyond, it has ushered them, as a whole community, into the learning enterprise. At the very same moment in time, Reform, Reconstructionist, and Conservative Judaism are providing us with models of women as rabbis. At some point in the not-too-distant future, I believe, the two will intersect: more learned women in the Orthodox community and the model of women in leadership positions in the other denominations. When that happens, history will take us where it takes us. That holds much promise for the likes of me.[109]

## Feminist Ritual, Midrash, and Liturgy

Jewish feminists concerned with religious issues have urged the inclusion of female experience and female images of the divine in Jewish ritual, midrash, and liturgy.

At the radical end of the spectrum are those who seek to discover and recreate "goddess spirituality." The popular Jewish press reported that a student at the Reconstructionist Rabbinical College, Jane Litman, was building small goddesses and ostensibly worshiping them. Litman denied this, saying that the goddess episode was misinterpreted by "name-callers who seek to halt the forward march of social justice." She stated that "most liberal Jews accept that images of God are psycho-social symbols, not descriptions of any tangible reality," and insisted that "women's images of the Deity must be given the same credence as men's." Several other feminists came to Litman's defense, including novelist E. M. Broner, who argued that goddess worship was a way of gaining access to a deity which

---

[108]Quoted in "First Woman Set for Conservative Ordination Looks to Future," *Jewish Week* (New York), Mar. 1, 1985.
[109]Blu Greenberg, "Will There Be Orthodox Women Rabbis?" *Judaism*, Winter 1984, pp. 23–33.

"Judaism had expunged." Such creative exploration, said Broner, put "women on the cutting edge of Judaism, making us stretch."[110]

Most Jewish feminists seeking to develop female-oriented rituals recoil from incorporating goddesses into Judaism. Ellen Umansky, for one, urges exploration that is mindful of both Jewish tradition and the spiritual needs of Jewish women.[111] Arlene Agus states bluntly, "Worship of other deities is simply not a legitimate route for Jews to take." Agus notes that there are several "continuums" in Jewish feminist thinking, and that most seek to build and expand, rather than to totally transform, normative Judaism.[112]

Many Jewish feminists are interested in revisions of the liturgy that incorporate feminine attributes of the godhead and references to the matriarchs. Traditional Jewish prayers, Umansky points out, refer repeatedly to God in male imagery and continually recall the interaction of God with male biblical figures. She argues that if "Jewish women are not subordinate and if their relationship with God is every bit as intimate as the relationship of men, then let us change the liturgy to reflect this awareness." She goes on:

> How many times can I praise God as the Shield of Abraham or the Shield of Our Fathers without feeling that if He left out our mothers, surely He must be leaving out me. . . . The image that dances before me is of a male God who blesses His sons, those human beings (our fathers) who were truly created in His image. To Jewish medieval mystics, God was not simply a King and a Father but also Shechinah, She-Who-Dwells-Within. The Shechinah represented the feminine element of the Divine. It was She who went into exile with the people of Israel, She who wept over their sorrows, She they yearned to embrace. The Kabbalists, then, knew God as Mother and Father, Queen and King. Might we not incorporate these insights into our worship service?[113]

Jewish feminists have also worked to create rituals which express women's spirituality within the context of Jewish tradition. Agus[114] describes the Jewish feminist attraction to the celebration of Rosh Hodesh, the festival of the New Moon, which "traditionally held unique significance for women perhaps dating back as far as the Biblical period." The Rosh Hodesh celebration is appealing to tradition-minded yet creative feminists, says Agus, precisely because "it offers unlimited opportunities for exploration of feminine spiritual qualities and experimentation with ritual, all within the

---

[110]"Can a Reconstructionist Rabbi Go Too Far?" *Baltimore Jewish Times*, Mar. 27, 1988. Jane R. Litman, "Can Judaism Respond to Feminist Criticism?" *Baltimore Jewish Times*, Apr. 24, 1987.
[111]Prof. Ellen Umansky, telephone conversation, Sept. 1988.
[112]Arlene Agus, telephone conversation, Sept. 1988.
[113]Ellen Umansky, "(Re)Imaging the Divine," *Response*, no. 13, Fall/Winter 1982, pp. 110–19.
[114]Arlene Agus, "This Month Is for You: Observing Rosh Hodesh as a Woman's Holiday," in Koltun, ed., *The Jewish Woman*, pp. 84–93.

framework of an ancient tradition which has survived up to the present day." In the Rosh Hodesh ceremonies suggested by Agus, women wear new clothes, give charity, recite prayers, poems, and a special *kiddush*, recite *sheheheyanu* (thanksgiving prayer) at the eating of new fruits, have a festive meal featuring round and egg-based foods, and include the prayers said on festivals, *shir hama'alot* and *ya'aleh veyavo,* in the grace after meals.

The Passover Seder has provided another opportunity for creative feminist spirituality. In describing the evolution of the first of her feminist Haggadahs, Aviva Cantor deals with both the strengths and the limitations of feminist transformations of Jewish ritual. She states:

> I rewrote the Haggadah, first taking care of the minor changes: making God "ruler of the universe" instead of "king," adding the names of Jacob's wives to the Exodus narrative, and changing "four sons" to "four daughters." The major change was to utilize the four-cups ritual and to dedicate each cup of wine to the struggle of Jewish women in a particular period. The Haggadah's aim was to provide connecting links between Jewish women of the past and us here in the present. A great deal of material came from Jewish legends and historical sources, some only recently discovered.

Although the feminist Seder experience was quite enjoyable for the participants, Cantor reports, she missed the heterogeneity of the traditional ceremony:

> As much as I loved a Seder with my sisters, what gnawed at me was the memory of the Seders I had at home, in my parents' house, Seders of men and women of several generations, with children running underfoot and spilling the wine. The Seder has always been a family celebration and, for me, a Seder just for women seems incomplete.

At the ideal Seder, Cantor concludes, "women would be as 'visible' as men, but neither men nor women would be the entire focus of the Seder."[115]

One ritual in which women are indisputably the entire focus is the traditional immersion in the *mikveh*, the ritual bath, related to the laws of family purity. Orthodox Jewish law requires married women to bathe thoroughly and then to immerse themselves in the *mikveh* prior to resuming sexual activity, following menstruation and seven "white" days. In some non-Orthodox communities, brides visit the *mikveh* before their weddings, even if they do not intend to maintain the family purity laws after marriage. Much to the surprise of older American Jews, many of whom regarded the *mikveh*—when they thought of it at all—as a quaint relic of outmoded attitudes and life-styles, interest in the *mikveh* has enjoyed a renaissance of sorts in certain circles. A key factor was Rachel Adler's positive discussion

---

[115]Aviva Cantor, "Jewish Women's Haggadah," in Koltun, ed., *The Jewish Woman*, pp. 94–102. See also "An Egalitarian Hagada," *Lilith*, no. 9, Spring/Summer 1982, p. 9.

in the first *Jewish Catalog*.[116] Feminists exploring Jewish women's spirituality and religious expression, together with well-educated younger generations of Orthodox women who take religious obligations seriously, and newly observant women who seek the structured environment and sexual limits of Orthodoxy, have revitalized *mikvehs* in many communities. Positive articles about *mikvehs* have appeared in several publications, including the *Reconstructionist* and *Hadassah Magazine*. Two students at the Reconstructionist Rabbinical College explain how *mikveh* ties in to their search for Jewish feminist spirituality:

> It appeals to the individual on the many levels of her spiritual existence and relationships. First, it addresses her relationship with her future husband—that intimate, binding relationship of two people who at times fuse in body and soul. Next, it addresses her relationship with other Jewish women, who have ancient and current ties to her through water. Finally, it addresses her relationship with all Jews, through Torah and its folkways.[117]

Their "Ceremony for Immersion" includes prayers and blessings in Hebrew and English, some drawn from traditional sources and some newly composed.

## Traditional Women and the Ba'alot Teshuvah

Ironically, the feminist striving for liberalization of the role of Jewish women has produced at least two species of backlash: right-wing emphasis on the intensification of woman's traditional role and increasing numbers of women who retreat from the sexual and social pressures of contemporary American life into highly structured Orthodoxy, within the *ba'al teshuvah* (religious renewal) movement.

During the past few years the *New York Times* has run attractive fullpage advertisements, paid for by the Lubavitch movement, showing a Jewish mother and daughter blessing the Sabbath candles. The texts of the advertisements speak of the importance of tradition in the lives of American Jewish women, and the importance of women in preserving Judaism. In their own way, these Lubavitch advertisements are a vivid testimonial to the new prominence and visibility of women in contemporary American Jewish life.

Davidman[118] and Kaufman[119] have documented the surprisingly feminist

---

[116]Rachel Adler, "Tumah and Taharah—Mikveh," in *The Jewish Catalog*, comp. and ed. Richard Siegel, Michael Strassfeld, and Sharon Strassfeld (Philadelphia, 1973), pp. 167–71.

[117]Barbara Rosman Penzer and Amy Zweiback-Levenson, "Spiritual Cleansing: A Mikveh Ritual for Brides," *Reconstructionist*, Sept. 1986, pp. 25–29.

[118]Lynn Davidman, "Strength of Tradition in a Chaotic World: Women Turn to Orthodox Judaism" (doctoral diss., Brandeis University, 1986).

[119]Debra Kaufman, "Coming Home to Jewish Orthodoxy: Reactionary or Radical

mentality that motivates some women to seek an Orthodox setting, in which they feel women are less harassed and more respected than in the outside world. Some of Davidman's Orthodox informants stated that Orthodox Judaism offers integrity for women in a way that contemporary society does not:

> ... [I]t also has to do with not being seen as a sexual object, which I think is a totally pro-woman attitude. You have to love me for what I am and not for what you can get off me, and that's the laws of *tum'ah* (ritual impurity) and *taharah* (ritual purity) in Judaism. . . . Take a look at what's going on out there, how women have been objectified. On the one hand you can say it's keeping women down on the farm by keeping their heads covered. On the other hand, you could say, hey, it's by maintaining a certain attitude towards women which is not to objectify them as a sexual object.

However, for some women seeking Orthodoxy, it is precisely the retreat from the pressures of feminism that is appealing. Women such as these often seek out Hassidic settings, where gender roles are most clearly defined—women are expected to be loving and pious wives and mothers. As one of Davidson's informants put it:

> ... [F]or many women, to relearn devotion, to replace narcissism with devotion, is really a very natural thing because it's more feminine to be devotional than to be narcissistic . . . just the way our bodies are built, a woman is, by nature, going to give of herself. . . . So when you teach a woman about devotion and marriage and selflessness and altruism, what you're really telling her is to be herself. . . . The biological function is consistent with the rest of her so that the way her body behaves is also the way the mind behaves and it's also the way the soul behaves.

In her study of modern Orthodox, Agudah-affiliated, and ultra-Orthodox women, Sarah Bunim[120] shows that many "have internalized the value system of the secular world." They are often highly educated and committed to careers, and they are also often agitated by what they perceive as inadequate religious roles for women in Orthodox Judaism—leading them to place even greater emphasis on the satisfactions of career achievement. Even among the most Orthodox *kollel* groups which Bunim studied, in which contact with secular values is kept to a minimum and women occupy a clearly subservient position as enablers of husbands who devote themselves to full-time study, feminism has had a curious impact: the status of the husband in the community is influenced by the money and prestige of his wife's job.

---

Women?" *Tikkun* 2, no. 3, July-Aug. 1987, pp. 60–63; idem, "Women Who Return to Orthodox Judaism: A Feminist Analysis," *Journal of Marriage and the Family,* Aug. 1985, pp. 541-55.

[120]Sarah Silver Bunim, "Religious and Secular Factors of Role Strain in Orthodox Jewish Mothers" (doctoral diss., Wurzweiler School of Social Work, Yeshiva University, 1986).

## "Get": The Unsolved Problem

A long-standing problem for Jewish women, one that has resisted solution, is in the area of Jewish marriage and divorce law. It is a problem that affects not just Orthodox and Conservative Jews, who follow Halakhah in this area, but any woman who wishes to marry or remarry in a Jewish religious framework.

According to traditional Jewish law, when a couple divorces, the man must place a *get*, a divorce contract, into the hands of his wife, indicating that she is no longer his wife. Without a *get*, the woman remains his wife in the eyes of Jewish law. If she then marries another man without receiving a *get*, she is legally an adulteress and children resulting from the new union are illegitimate, *mamzerim*. *Mamzerim* are not allowed to marry other Jews; they can only marry other *mamzerim*. Under certain circumstances, however, the husband can legally marry again even without a *get*.

Because women have far more to lose than men do if no *get* is obtained, some men have used this as a means to blackmail their wives during divorce proceedings. For example, they threaten not to give their wives a *get* unless they receive custody of the children, or unless their wives relinquish court-ordered financial settlements or alimony payments. Both feminists and concerned rabbis have worked for methods to prevent such extortion, either through use of a prenuptial agreement or through a religious annulment of the marriage. Several Orthodox lay leaders have banded together to form an organization to deal with the problem, appropriately named G.E.T., Getting Equitable Treatment. However, according to Honey Rackman, they have made little headway:

> Despite the attention *get* blackmail has been given in the Jewish media and the waste of young women spending their childbearing years in ugly and often vicious conflict with recalcitrant husbands, the Orthodox establishment has not responded. Ostrich-like, some Orthodox rabbis have even suggested that there is no problem. They maintain that they are dealing satisfactorily with the individual cases that come before them. With their best handwringing gesture, they gently shoo from their presence "feminist" troublemakers, with condescending assurances that they too are deeply troubled and suffer sleepless nights but cannot change the law.[121]

Rackman, for one, is convinced that the "patient is curable if only the qualified doctors would administer the medicine at their disposal."

It is not inconceivable that resistance to punishing men who will not comply with the *get* is related to general hostility to feminist goals, particularly in the Orthodox community. The rising rate of divorce among Jews is often attributed to the female independence, both emotional and occupa-

---

[121]Honey Rackman, "Getting a *Get*," *Moment*, May 1988, pp. 34–41, 58–59.

tional, fostered by feminism. Jewish women who divorce their husbands, like Jewish women who put on *tefillin* or study the Talmud, can be profoundly unsettling to a community long accustomed to the principle that women are ideally domestic, rather than public, beings.

In Israel, the *get* issue is of pressing concern to all women, since matters of marriage and divorce are controlled entirely by Orthodox rabbinic authorities. American Jewish feminists have been instrumental in supporting the Israel Women's Network—through the New Israel Fund—which has as one of its main goals the reform of the rabbinical courts.[122]

## CONCLUSION

In tandem with other factors making for change in American society, feminism has had a powerful impact on the American Jewish community. Increasing numbers of American Jewish women pursue career-oriented educational programs and the careers which follow. Partially as a result, they are marrying later and having fewer children than Jewish women 25 years ago. Moreover, a majority of today's American Jewish women, in contrast to the pattern of the past, continue to work even when they are the mothers of young and school-age children.

These demographic changes have affected the Jewish community in several important areas. First, they have created a large population of single adults, including never-married and divorced persons, who are far less likely to affiliate with the Jewish community in conventional ways. Second, they have produced a population of beginning families who are, as a group, older and more focused than beginning families 25 years ago. Third, they have fostered a dual-paycheck work ethic among Jewish parents, which makes both men and women disinclined to volunteer time for Jewish organizations. Fourth, they have resulted in a client population of Jewish children who are in need of child-care provision from birth onward, and a corresponding parental population demanding that the Jewish community provide Jewish-sponsored child care for children of varying ages.

Jewish religious life and Jewish culture have been profoundly transformed by Jewish feminism in all its guises. From birth onward, American Jewish girls today are more likely than ever before in Jewish history to be treated in a manner closely resembling the treatment of boys vis à vis their religious orientation and training. Increasing numbers of Jewish girls are welcomed into the Jewish world with joyous ceremonies, just as their brothers become official Jews with the ceremony of *Brit Milah*. American Jewish

---

[122]*New Israel Fund Annual Report*, 1988, p. 23.

schoolgirls receive some sort of formal Jewish education in almost the same numbers as their brothers. Bat Mitzvah has become an accepted rite in the American Jewish life cycle in all wings of Judaism, with the exception of the ultra-Orthodox.

Jewish women are counted for *minyanim* and receive *aliyot*, in all Reform and a majority of Conservative synagogues. Despite vehement attacks by some Orthodox rabbis, women's prayer groups around the country give Jewish women of every denomination the opportunity to participate in communal worship and Torah reading. College-age and adult Jewish women take advantage of greater access to higher Jewish education, with increasing numbers of women augmenting their knowledge of traditional Jewish texts. Reform, Reconstructionist, and Conservative female rabbis and cantors have been graduated and serve the Jewish community in pulpits and in other positions. Women hold tenured positions in Judaica in universities—including the Ivy League—and rabbinical seminaries. In addition, many women find meaning in traditional and innovative Jewish feminist liturgy and rituals. Through Jewish women's resource centers, networks, and publications of all types, Jewish feminists communicate with each other and increase communal understanding of Jewish feminist goals.

In the Jewish communal world, women assertively pursue both professional and volunteer leadership positions in local and national Jewish organizations. During the past 15 years, the number of women in such leadership positions has increased substantially, although neither the number of female executives nor the status and salary level of most of their positions comes close to matching that of male executives. Similarly, female representation on communal boards has improved in the past decade but does not come close to equaling that of men. Jewish women who express a desire for a more equal distribution of communal power have been advised by communal leaders that they must be prepared to fight aggressively for that power, including litigation, where necessary.

Despite the mainstreaming of feminist and Jewish feminist goals within the American Jewish community, the relationship between feminism and Judaism remains troubled. Some elements in rabbinical and communal leadership have a "knee-jerk" antifeminist response to any and all items on the Jewish feminist agenda. On the Jewish feminist side, there often exists a kind of tunnel vision which puts feminist agendas ahead of Jewish communal well-being and survival. In truth, there are certain areas in which the goals of feminism and the goals of Judaism are at odds with each other. In their "Orthodox response" to "Women's Liberation," Chana Poupko and Devora Wohlgelernter point up these differences:

> It is here that we come to the question of priorities. Of the 36 capital crimes of the Torah, 18 deal with crimes which undermine the family unit: homosexuality,

incest, etc. The other 18 are things which ensure the preservation of *Klal Yisrael*. . . . It seems clear that the priority is survival and for the sake of survival much must be sacrificed. . . . The concept of sacrifice is alien to the modern feminist movement. But, sacrifice is inherent in Jewish thought. The Midrash says that Yitzchak was blind after the *Akedah*. Perhaps what the Midrash is telling us is that when there is a priority involved, one never gets away as a whole person. The point of the *Akedah* is that every Jew is a sacrifice on the altar. The feminist notion of "self-fulfillment" is likewise foreign to Jewish thought and attempts at translation result in the derogatory expression, *sipuk atzmi*, which has a selfish connotation. . . . It seems that our Sages saw self-fulfillment in terms of the nation's preservation.[123]

Personal agendas, family agendas, and communal agendas—as we have seen in the preceding analysis—are often in conflict in the lives of contemporary American Jewish men and women. Personal fulfillment often conflicts directly or indirectly with optimum family life, and both personal and familial goals may diverge from communal goals. In resolving these conflicts, the American Jewish community is faced with an extraordinary challenge, one, Jewish feminists point out, that should not be perceived as a challenge facing women alone.

To strong proponents of feminism, the multifaceted flowering of American Jewish women overshadows any communal difficulties which may result. Jewish feminists argue that the personal needs of female individuals are as significant as the personal needs of male individuals. If those needs must be sacrificed for the sake of the family, the community, or *klal yisrael*, they contend, women should not bear the burden alone. Women will no longer consent to be the "sacrifice" that guarantees the well-being of a male-centered community.

Remembering that women comprise, after all, at least one-half of the Jewish people, it seems appropriate for Jewish survivalists of all denominations to reconsider the validity of feminist goals case by case and to search for constructive ways in which to reconcile Jewish feminism with the goals of Jewish survival. It is hard to imagine what communal good could be served by religious and communal leaders rigidly adhering to an automatic antifeminist stance. On the other hand, it seems appropriate for Jewish feminists, to the extent that they are serious about Jewish survival, to weigh carefully the repercussions of proposed changes and to consider their responsibility to the community as a whole. Indeed, it is one of the achievements of American Jewish feminism that women are now in a position to examine these issues—and to make choices.

---

[123]Chana K. Poupko and Devora L. Wohlgelernter, "Women's Liberation—An Orthodox Response," *Tradition,* Spring 1976, pp. 45–52.

# Recent Trends in American Judaism

by Jack Wertheimer

THE DECADE OF THE 1980s HAS witnessed a series of acrimonious confrontations between the leaders of various religious denominations within American Jewry. Some observers have voiced concern that American Jewry will soon be riven into contending camps that do not recognize each other's legitimacy as Jews. Others maintain that such a polarization has already come to pass; that a deep divide separates Orthodox from non-Orthodox Jews, with only a relatively small population of modern-Orthodox and right-wing Conservative Jews seeking to bridge the divide. And still others view the present confrontations as merely a passing stage in the continuing evolution of a distinctly American version of Judaism.[1]

This article seeks to go beyond the headline-making clashes between leaders of Jewish religious denominations in order to evaluate the state of contemporary Jewish religious life. It probes the following matters, among others: How do patterns of religious observance today compare with those of the recent past? What are the major concerns of the Jewish laity, and how have the rabbinic elites responded to these concerns? What new rituals and religious forms have captured the imagination of Jews in recent decades? What conclusions may be drawn about the condition of Judaism in the United States today?

The time period under discussion spans the two decades from the late 1960s to the late 1980s. This has been an era of perceptible change in patterns of behavior among American Jews, particularly in the religious sphere. Beginning in the mid-1960s, the agenda of American Jewish life shifted significantly in the wake of new social trends and reassessed priorities. In short, the changing character of Jewish life in America necessitated shifts within organized religious institutions, which in turn set off new chains of events. To set into bolder relief the far-reaching shifts that have occurred of late in the religious sphere, it would be well to begin with a brief consideration of Jewish religious life in the middle decades of the 20th century.

---

[1]For different assessments of American Jewish religious polarization, see the statements by Steven M. Cohen and Irving Greenberg in "The One in 2000 Controversy," *Moment*, Mar. 1987, pp. 11–22.

© 1989 Jack Wertheimer.

## MIDCENTURY GROWTH

The dominant characteristic of American Jewish life between 1940 and 1965 was numerical growth. Jews, like the larger American population, participated in a baby boom. As the Great Depression eased and veterans returned from World War II, Americans married in record numbers and began families. For Jews, this boom was propelled by the children and grandchildren of immigrants from Eastern Europe who had come to America in ever-swelling numbers between 1880 and the outbreak of World War I. Never before in the history of American Jewry had such a vast age cohort begun families in so short a span of time.

Simultaneously, large numbers of young Jewish families joined in the general American exodus to suburbia, an uncharted area devoid of Jewish institutions. This relocation represented not only a move from city to suburb, but also a departure from Jewish neighborhoods to settings populated mainly by Gentiles. Jews also began to move in substantial numbers to geographic regions of the United States that previously had only small Jewish communities, most notably southern California. These two developments—a burgeoning population and a major geographic shift—spurred the growth of religious institutions to provide prayer services and educational programs.[2]

The young families moving to suburbia in the 1940s and early 1950s often had only scant exposure to synagogue life prior to their move. Overwhelmingly second- and third-generation descendants of East European Jews, they had grown up either in homes where Judaism was taken for granted and Americanization had been given highest priority, or in socialist homes which rejected most religious practices. To be a Jew was primarily a matter of association with fellow Jews, not a conscious act of affiliation with a synagogue.[3]

This changed in the 1940s due to several factors: (1) When Jewish veterans returned from the war, they were eager to participate in the same kind of Americanized religious services that they had encountered in military chapels—services lead by an American-trained rabbi, who worked with a liturgy that incorporated both traditional and English readings. Hence, returning Jewish veterans were receptive to the program of evolving suburban synagogues.[4] (2) After moving to suburbia, transplanted Jewish urban-

---

[2]For a contemporary account of the Jewish move to suburbia, see Albert Gordon, *Jews in Suburbia* (Boston, 1959). On the geographic relocation of American Jews in the postwar era, see Marshall Sklare, *America's Jews* (New York, 1971), pp. 44–47.

[3]For an extended discussion of the Jewish associationalism that characterized second-generation Jews, see Deborah Dash Moore, *At Home in America: Second Generation New York Jews* (New York, 1981).

[4]The role of World War II in the Americanization of second-generation Jews and their Judaism has been insufficiently appreciated. Two essays written shortly after the war that

ites found themselves lonely for Jewish companionship. They looked to the synagogue to provide them with a network of Jewish friends and peers—a surrogate for the Jewish neighborhood. As one promotional leaflet stated: "The community needs a place for our children and we adults need some place to carry on our social lives. What better place can there be than our synagogues?"[5] (3) In the absence of a Jewish neighborhood where youngsters were socialized in Jewish customs and behaviors through a process of osmosis, it became necessary for parents to affiliate with a synagogue that would provide a formal Jewish education.[6] (4) Involvement in building a synagogue and sending children to a synagogue school were means for these Jews to participate in the larger revival of institutional religion that characterized midcentury America. By participating in seemingly parochial activities within their synagogues, these Jews were acting as quintessential midcentury Americans.[7]

The quarter century from 1940 to 1965 was a boom period in the establishment and construction of new Jewish religious institutions. The United Synagogue of America, Conservative Judaism's organization of synagogues, increased its affiliates from approximately 350 at the conclusion of World War II to 800 by 1965, with as many as 131 new congregations joining in a two-year period of the mid-1950s.[8] Similarly, the Reform movement's Union of American Hebrew Congregations boasted 664 congregations in 1966 compared to 334 in 1948. In the mid-1950s, 50 new congregations joined the UAHC within a two-year period.[9] Orthodox synagogues also experienced a period of growth as Young Israel branches and other modern Orthodox congregations sprang up in newly emerging urban and suburban areas.[10]

Not only were hundreds of new congregations established, but existing ones experienced unparalleled growth. It now became common for syna-

---

emphasize this point are Abraham Duker, "On Religious Trends in American Life," *YIVO Annual*, vol. 4, 1949, p. 63; and Moses Kligsberg, "American Jewish Soldiers on Jews and Judaism," *YIVO Annual*, vol. 5, 1950, pp. 256–65. The latter emphasizes anti-Semitism in the military as a factor promoting chapel attendance by servicemen and women.

[5]Gordon, *Jews in Suburbia*, p. 98.

[6]There is ample evidence from this period, in synagogue brochures as well as survey responses, that parents regarded the synagogue as primarily a vehicle for the education of youth. See, for example, Leonard Fein et al., *Reform Is a Verb* (New York, 1972), p. 90; and Marshall Sklare and Joseph Greenblum, *Jewish Identity on the Suburban Frontier: A Study of Group Survival in an Open Society* (Chicago, 1967), p. 190.

[7]See Sklare and Greenblum, *Jewish Identity*, chap. 5.

[8]For congregational growth in the Conservative movement, see the *Biennial Reports of the United Synagogue of America*—1952, p. 52; 1957, p. 97; 1959, p. 140; 1961, p. 3; 1963, pp. 184–85; 1965, p. 6.

[9]On the growth of the UAHC, see Marc Lee Raphael, *Profiles in American Judaism* (San Francisco, 1984), pp. 71, 198.

[10]On the spread of Orthodox synagogues, see Charles Liebman, "Orthodoxy in American Jewish Life," AJYB 1965, vol. 66, pp. 22–40, 59–60.

gogues to serve thousands of members. In 1937, the largest Reform temples numbered 500–800 families and only a half dozen had passed the 1,000-family mark. By 1963, 20 had passed the 1,400-family mark and a few exceeded 2,500 families.[11] Although Conservative, and especially Orthodox, synagogues rarely attracted such large membership bases, they too expanded dramatically.

The explosive growth of synagogues was matched by an equally dramatic expansion of synagogue schools. Enrollment figures demonstrate this clearly: in 1940, approximately 190,000 children attended Jewish schools; this figure rose to 231,028 in 1946; and then doubled to 488,432 by 1956; by the early 1960s, enrollments peaked at approximately 590,000. All in all, the number of young Jews attending Jewish schools tripled between the early 1940s and early 1960s. The vast majority of these children attended synagogue-based schools; only 8 percent were enrolled in intercongregational or noncongregational schools in 1962.[12]

There were important variations in the type of schooling adopted by the religious movements. Reform continued its earlier policy of emphasizing Sunday school, i.e., one-day-a-week education. In the peak years of the early 1960s, 60 percent of Sunday schools were under Reform auspices, 25 percent under Conservative auspices, and fewer than 10 percent under Orthodox auspices. By contrast, Conservative synagogues invested heavily in Hebrew-school education, i.e., schools that required attendance several times a week, usually on three separate days. In 1962, half the Hebrew schools were sponsored in Conservative synagogues, almost a quarter by Orthodox ones, and 13 percent by Reform temples. Within the Orthodox movement, the pattern was more complex. The figures cited above illustrate that Orthodox synagogues continued to sponsor Sunday schools as well as Hebrew schools. But in the postwar era, growing numbers of Orthodox Jews opted for education outside the synagogue in intensive all-day schools. The shift was especially dramatic outside of New York City where day schools grew from barely a handful in 1940 to 107 in 1959. Significantly, 85 percent of all day schools in America were under Orthodox auspices in 1962, even though close to one-third of their pupils were drawn from non-Orthodox homes.[13]

There were several important consequences of this rapid growth of synagogues and synagogue schools. First, there were insufficient numbers of personnel to staff them. It was estimated in 1962 that some 3,000 additional

---

[11]Jacob K. Shankman, "The Changing Role of the Rabbi," in *Retrospect and Prospect*, ed. Bertram W. Korn (New York, 1965), p. 246.
[12]Enrollment figures are taken from: Uriah Z. Engelman, "Educational and Cultural Activities," AJYB 1946–1947, vol. 48, p. 137; idem, "Jewish Education," AJYB 1963, vol. 64, pp. 152–53; and Walter Ackerman, "Jewish Education," in *Movements and Issues in American Judaism*, ed. Bernard Martin (Westport, Conn., 1978), p. 196.
[13]Engelman, AJYB 1963, pp. 152–53, 161–62.

rabbis and educators were needed to meet the growing institutional needs of American Jews.[14] The dearth of trained rabbis and educators limited the effectiveness of synagogue and educational programs at a time when Jews were joining institutions in record numbers. Second, the massive growth in the population of children reshaped the priorities of synagogues, with large percentages of synagogue budgets going to schooling. In Conservative synagogues, for example, education absorbed over a quarter of synagogue budgets, an allocation second only to the cost of salaries for personnel.[15] This represented a dramatic change from earlier models of synagogue life in which children played little role, and where most activity was focused on the needs of adult men. Now the synagogue was viewed as the primary vehicle for the socialization and education of young people in the ways of Judaism. Rabbis and teachers—and by extension, the synagogue—were assigned a role *in loco parentis*, as substitute Jewish role models.[16] Third, synagogues used their schools as a means to increase membership. Often, congregations did not even charge tuition, but rather financed their schools through membership dues—a strategy that, in the short run, compelled parents to join congregations if they wished to educate their children and have them celebrate a Bar or Bat Mitzvah, but that also resulted in parents dropping their membership once their youngest child had completed his or her Jewish education.[17]

## Conservatism

The expansive growth of religious institutions benefited all of the major Jewish religious movements, with Conservative Judaism being the greatest beneficiary. Not only did the number of Conservative congregations double in this period but Conservatism was the preferred religious self-identification of a plurality of American Jews.[18] This was not necessarily a matter of

---

[14] Freda Imrey, "Religion," AJYB 1963, vol. 64, p. 146.

[15] "Survey of Synagogue Finances," issued by the Department of Synagogue Administration, United Synagogue of America, Nov. 1963, p. 21.

[16] Many observers of Jewish life have remarked about the reliance of parents on the synagogue, rather than the home, to provide Jewish identity and knowledge to children. The frustration of rabbis over this state of affairs was summed up in Rabbi Arthur Hertzberg's cynical quip that the synagogue in America is "to a large degree, a parent-teacher association of the religious school." Quoted in Carolyn L. Wiener, "A Merger of Synagogues in San Francisco," *Jewish Journal of Sociology*, Dec. 1972, p. 189.

[17] On the relationship between synagogue schools and congregational membership, see Marshall Sklare, *Conservative Judaism: An American Religious Movement* (Glencoe, Ill., 1955), p. 77ff.

[18] *Jewish Identity: Facts for Planning*, Council of Jewish Federations, Dec. 1974, pp. 2–4. Local surveys also bore out these findings for many communities. See, for example, Sidney Goldstein and Calvin Goldscheider, *Jewish Americans: Three Generations in a Jewish Community* (Englewood Cliffs, N.J., 1968), pp. 176–77.

ideological commitment, as the most astute sociologist of the time noted already in the early 1950s, but rather a decision to opt for a moderate compromise between the extremes of Orthodoxy and Reform.[19] Jewish men serving in the military during World War II had been exposed to an essentially Conservative worship service, even though most Jewish chaplains were not Conservative rabbis, because such a service was deemed most appropriate to the spectrum of Jews in the military. When these veterans returned to found new synagogues in the suburbs, they generally opted for Conservative synagogues as a fair compromise.[20] As one synagogue organizer put it, "We figured that the Conservative [synagogue] was 'middle of the road,' and would not offend any group in the community. So we called it a Conservative congregation."[21]

While only a minority of synagogue members adhered to the religious commitments of the Conservative movement, significant numbers were attracted to specific programs offered by Conservative synagogues: principally, the more intensive schooling offered by Hebrew schools as compared to Sunday schools; but also the Conservative worship service that combined a high degree of fidelity to the traditional liturgy with innovations deemed appropriate to midcentury America; and a lavish panoply of social and recreational programs that Conservative synagogues sponsored more readily than their Reform or Orthodox counterparts.[22]

To meet the needs of Conservative youth, the Jewish Theological Seminary in conjunction with other arms of the Conservative movement founded the Ramah summer camps in 1948.[23] During the 1950s and 1960s, the Conservative leadership began to invest systematically in day schools, creating a network of 15 by 1961.[24] It was symptomatic of Conservative Judaism's self-confidence that it founded an international arm (the World Council of Synagogues) in November 1957, and in the 1960s developed a rabbinical seminary (the Seminario Rabinico Latinoamericano) to serve Latin American Jewry.[25]

Steps were also taken to clarify the movement's ideological stance. The

---

[19]See Sklare, *Conservative Judaism*, passim.

[20]At the conclusion of World War II, Philip Bernstein wrote that Jewish chaplains subordinated their ideologies to the needs of Jewish soldiers. "This led to more observance of tradition by the Reform, a liberalization of the Orthodox, and an expansion of Conservatism." See "Jewish Chaplains in World War II," AJYB 1945–1946, vol. 47, p. 174.

[21]Gordon, *Jews in Suburbia*, p. 97.

[22]Jack Wertheimer, "The Conservative Synagogue," in *The American Synagogue: A Sanctuary Transformed*, ed. Jack Wertheimer (New York, 1987), pp. 111–47.

[23]Shuly Rubin Schwartz, "Camp Ramah: The Early Years, 1947–52," *Conservative Judaism*, Fall 1987, pp. 12–42.

[24]Walter Ackerman, "The Day School in the Conservative Movement," *Conservative Judaism*, Winter 1961, p. 50ff.

[25]Marc Tanenbaum, "Religion," AJYB 1959, vol. 60, p. 64.

Rabbinical Assembly, the organization of Conservative rabbis, for the first time endorsed a *Sabbath and Festival Prayer Book* in 1946.[26] Two years later, relations between the Rabbinical Assembly and the Jewish Theological Seminary of America were revamped in a manner that gave wider latitude to the Conservative rabbinate's law committee. Within a short period, the law committee began to issue rulings on Halakhah (Jewish law) that departed significantly from Orthodox interpretations, most notably a ruling in the early 1950s concerning the permissibility of driving to a synagogue on the Sabbath.[27] Conservative leaders issued a series of volumes designed to disseminate information about their movement, most notably, Rabbi Mordechai Waxman's *Tradition and Change*, a compilation of ideological statements by prominent Conservative thinkers, Rabbi Moshe Davis's history of Conservative Judaism's origins, Evelyn Garfiel's guide to the prayer book, and various guides to the dietary laws and other observances, written by Rabbis Seymour Siegel and Samuel Dresner.[28] Gradually, rabbis and congregations managed to achieve a significant measure of uniformity in the practices of Conservative congregations, with mixed pews, mixed choirs, and Bat Mitzvah ceremonies for girls gaining wide, if not universal, currency.[29] All in all, the middle decades of the 20th century were a time of self-confidence for the Conservative movement.

## Reform

The same decades were a period of significant institutional growth for the Reform movement as well.[30] Throughout the postwar era, the Union of American Hebrew Congregations reported annual gains in new affiliates. Some of this growth resulted from deliberate efforts taken by the Reform movement to have a greater impact. Thus, in the late 1940s it launched an intensive campaign to "win the unaffiliated," a shift away from the policy of social exclusiveness that had characterized recruitment policies earlier in the 20th century.[31] The UAHC relocated from its former headquarters in

---

[26]The prayer book was edited by Rabbi Morris Silverman under the direction of a joint committee of the Rabbinical Assembly and the United Synagogue of America, headed by Rabbi Robert Gordis.

[27]Sidney Schwarz, "Law and Legitimacy: An Intellectual History of Conservative Judaism, 1902–1973" (unpublished doctoral diss., Temple University, 1982), pp. 221–22, 255–56.

[28]Jacob Neusner, "Religion," AJYB 1960, vol. 61, p. 57.

[29]Morris S. Goodblatt, "Synagogue Ritual Survey," *Proceedings of the Rabbinical Assembly*, 1942, pp. 105–09.

[30]On the institutional growth of the Reform movement, see Raphael, *Profiles in American Judaism*, pp. 71, 75, 198.

[31]Leon A. Jick, "The Reform Synagogue," in Wertheimer, ed., *The American Synagogue*, pp. 102–03.

Cincinnati to New York City, a move expressly designed to place the organization in the heartland of the American Jewish population.[32] Hebrew Union College expanded to reach new populations, merging with the Jewish Institute of Religion to create a New York school, establishing a Los Angeles branch in 1954, and opening a Jerusalem campus in 1963.

Under the leadership of Rabbi Maurice Eisendrath from 1943 to 1973, the Union of American Hebrew Congregations invested heavily in programs of social action. Eisendrath summed up his point of view in an interview when he received an award as clergyman of the year in 1959: Social action, he declared, "that's religion. The heart of religion concerns itself with man's relation to man." The Reform movement gave tangible expression to this concern in 1961, when it established a Religious Action Center, later renamed Social Action Center, in Washington, D.C. In the practical sphere, Reform rabbis assumed a leadership role in the movement to desegregate the South.[33]

Simultaneously, the Reform movement underwent important shifts in its approach to Jewish rituals. A survey conducted by the UAHC in the late 1940s found that virtually all responding congregations claimed to have moved toward "increased ritualism."[34] In a reversal of long-standing policy, congregations gradually permitted men to wear head coverings, if they so chose; and in a shift that had a broader impact, the Bar Mitzvah ceremony was reintroduced in virtually all temples. (It had earlier been rejected in favor of Confirmation services for older adolescents.) Congregations that had ushered in the New Year with trumpet blasts reverted to the traditional shofar, and cantors were hired to replace or supplement non-Jewish choirs. Studies of home observance indicated as well that members of Reform temples were more receptive to rituals such as candle lighting on Friday evenings and Hanukkah, as well as the celebration of the Passover Seder.[35]

This renewed interest in religious ritual engendered considerable soul-searching among the rabbinic elite of the Reform movement. In part, rabbis resented the pressures placed on them to reintroduce rituals that appealed to folk sentiments, e.g., the Bar Mitzvah ceremony, which now dominated Sabbath morning services. Equally important, the new turn to ritualism was regarded by many rabbis as a rejection of classical Reform ideology, an ideology that had attempted to purge Judaism of ceremonies that were seen as anachronistic. Typical of this view were remarks by Prof. Jacob Marcus

---

[32]On the UAHC's relocation to New York, see Maurice Eisendrath, "The Union of American Hebrew Congregations: Centennial Reflections," *American Jewish Historical Quarterly*, Dec. 1973, pp. 144–45.
[33]Raphael, *Profiles in American Judaism*, p. 73, and Neusner, AJYB 1960, pp. 55–56.
[34]Morris N. Kertzer, "Religion," AJYB 1952, vol. 53, p. 155.
[35]See Jick, "The Reform Synagogue," p. 104; Stephen Sharot, *Judaism: A Sociology* (New York, 1976) pp. 164–71; and Benjamin Efron and Alvan D. Rubin, "The Reality of Bar Mitzvah," *CCAR Journal*, Oct. 1960, pp. 31–33.

of the Hebrew Union College in a speech delivered in 1959: "There are today too many Reform Jews who have ceased to be liberals. Their Reform, crystallized into a new Orthodoxy, is no longer dynamic. Shocked by the Hitlerian catastrophe, many have turned their backs on the future to seek comfort in the nostalgia of a romanticized Jewish past which never existed. We cannot lead our people forward by stumbling backward."[36]

*Orthodoxy*

The crucial factor shaping Orthodoxy at midcentury was an infusion of new energy and leadership brought about by the arrival of refugees from Nazi Europe. The newcomers arrived from diverse Jewish environments, ranging from the rationalist yeshivah world of Lithuania to the Levantine Jewish society of the Balkans, from the Westernized, acculturated Orthodox *Gemeinden* of Germany to the insulated, self-segregating communities of Hungary. They came not out of a desire for self-advancement in America but simply because their communities had been decimated by the Nazi death machine. They were filled with nostalgia for the rich Jewish lives they had known in the Old World, and they were intent on recreating much of that life on American soil. Some built self-segregated enclaves in urban settings or rural environs, such as Boro Park and Williamsburg in Brooklyn and New Skvare in Rockland County, N.Y.; some insisted on wearing distinctive garb and communicating mainly in Yiddish; and most regarded American innovations in religious life with contempt. They saw themselves as the embodiment of a now destroyed European Judaism, the only Judaism, they insisted, with a claim to authenticity.[37] Gradually, the new immigrants assumed important roles within all sectors of Orthodox society, serving as rabbinic authorities, charismatic holy men, teachers, ritual functionaries, and organizers.

The arrival of a strong traditionalist element prompted a more combative Orthodox posture in this period. The new assertiveness was signaled at a meeting of Orthodox rabbis in 1945 devoted to the banning and public burning of Rabbi Mordecai Kaplan's *Sabbath Prayer Book*, a Reconstructionist *siddur*.[38] By the mid-1950s, there was a strong push for Orthodox self-segregation, much as it had existed in Europe. In a widely reported

---

[36]The outlook of classical Reform was enunciated in the Pittsburgh Platform of 1885 and revised in the Columbus Platform of 1937. Marcus's address is quoted by Alan Tarshish, "How 'Central' is the CCAR?" *CCAR Journal*, Jan. 1960, p. 32.

[37]On the impact of Orthodox refugees from Nazism on American Orthodoxy, see Shubert Spero, "Orthodox Judaism," in Martin, ed., *Movements and Issues*, pp. 86–87; and Charles Liebman, "Religion, Class, and Culture in American Jewish Life," *Jewish Journal of Sociology*, Dec. 1967, pp. 239–40. A full analysis of this group's immigration history and impact on American Jews and Judaism is urgently needed.

[38]Joshua Trachtenberg, "Religious Activities," AJYB 1945–1946, vol. 47, pp. 216–17.

edict issued in 1956, 11 *roshei yeshivah*, heads of rabbinic academies of advanced study, joined by the leader of the Hassidic Lubavitch movement, issued a ban on Orthodox participation in rabbinic organizations that included non-Orthodox rabbis. This ban was designed to place pressure on American-trained rabbis, particularly alumni of Yeshiva University and the Hebrew Theological College, to withdraw from umbrella organizations such as the Synagogue Council of America and local boards of rabbis.[39] The Rabbinical Council of America, the organization of modern Orthodox rabbis, was thrown into turmoil by the decision, with its president supporting the ban, but the majority of the rank and file rejecting it. (They could do so because the revered leader of the modern Orthodox rabbinate, Rabbi Joseph B. Soloveitchik, refused to sign the ban.) The issuance of the ban was symptomatic of the intention of the traditionalist leadership to pursue an exclusivist policy *vis à vis* the non-Orthodox community.[40]

The modern Orthodox community itself showed a more combative posture in these years. Rabbis affiliated with the Rabbinical Council of America engaged in a concerted effort to stem the massive tide of defection by Orthodox congregations into the Conservative camp. In legal challenges that were fought before state supreme courts, Orthodox leaders sought to prevent congregations that had previously relegated men and women to separate synagogue precincts from introducing mixed seating, a change that signified a congregation's defection from Orthodoxy to Conservatism. Yeshiva University also brought pressure on its rabbinic graduates not to serve in congregations that permitted mixed seating or the use of microphones on the Sabbath.[41] In the late 1950s, rabbis espousing the modern Orthodox position established a new journal, *Tradition*, both as a vehicle for expressing their own point of view as well as for combating non-Orthodox tendencies. Early issues of the journal were replete with hard-hitting critiques of Reconstructionist ideology, Conservative halakhic rulings on the marriage document and mixed seating, and the Reform movement's liturgical innovations.[42]

---

[39]On the ban, see Tanenbaum, AJYB 1959, p. 59, and "Religious Pluralism at Home: A Hundred Years of the NY Board of Rabbis," *Jewish Observer*, May 1981, pp. 44–47.

[40]Jacob Sloan, "Religion," AJYB 1957, vol. 58, p. 153.

[41]On the defection to Conservatism, see Wertheimer, "The Conservative Synagogue," pp. 124–25. On the issue of separate seating, see Louis Bernstein, "The Emergence of the English Speaking Orthodox Rabbinate" (doctoral diss., Yeshiva University, 1977), pp. 289–97; and Bernard Litvin, *The Sanctity of the Synagogue* (New York, 1959), pp. 49–77. See also Morris N. Kertzer, "Religion," AJYB 1955, vol. 56, p. 235, and Tanenbaum, AJYB 1959, pp. 60–62.

[42]See, for example, in *Tradition*: Eliezer Berkovits, "Reconstructionist Theology: A Critical Evaluation," Fall 1959, pp. 20–66; Norman Lamm, "Separate Pews in the Synagogue: A Social and Psychological Approach," Spring 1959, pp. 141–64; Emanuel Rackman, "Arrogance or Humility in Prayer," Fall 1958, pp. 13–26; and Walter Wurzburger, "The Oral Law and the Conservative Dilemma," Fall 1960, pp. 82–90.

Orthodox groups of all stripes invested heavily in this period in the establishment of day schools and yeshivahs. Leading the way was Torah U'Mesorah, which oversaw the growth of the day-school movement from approximately 30 before World War II to over 300 by the mid-1960s. Simultaneously, rabbinic figures recently arrived from Europe founded academies of higher study to support the continuing education of adult men, even after their ordination.[43] The latter institutions, *kollelim*, would produce the future leaders of right-wing Orthodoxy and provide teachers for the day-school movement.

Even with the emphasis on separate schooling, Orthodox Jews made important strides toward Americanization in these years. During the middle decades of the century, Orthodoxy ceased to be the province of relatively poor immigrant Jews, as its adherents participated in the upward mobility that brought affluence to large segments of American Jewry. Orthodox Jews now founded their own vacation resorts, as well as summer camps for youth. Perhaps even more important, they capitalized on changes in the marketing of American foodstuffs to convince manufacturers that it paid to carry kosher certification. Never before had so many non-Jewish food manufacturers carried kosher labeling in a direct effort to attract observant Jews concerned with dietary laws.[44]

Despite these important strides, however, Orthodoxy continued to be seen as a marginal grouping. In part this resulted from the selective blindness of contemporary observers, who were preoccupied with the widespread Jewish effort to integrate successfully into postwar America. From this perspective Orthodoxy was seen as a relic of past Jewish separatism. But there was also much objective evidence of Orthodox weakness. Hundreds of congregations that had been counted as Orthodox in the decades prior to World War II either folded or shifted their allegiance to Conservatism. Many who continued to identify as Orthodox were residual members of the movement; they did not observe Jewish religious laws with any thoroughness.[45] Even parents who sent their children to the expanding network of day schools did not practice consistently or meticulously.[46] As for their role in Jewish communal life, Orthodox Jews did not have a great impact on policy or philanthropy. Writing at midcentury, Marshall Sklare stated: "Orthodox adherents

---

[43]See Spero, "Orthodox Judaism," pp. 86–87.
[44]For an early article noting the revolution in the kosher food industry, see Morris Kertzer, "Religion," AJYB 1964, vol. 65, p. 81, which reports on a survey conducted in 1963 claiming that 2,000 products certified as kosher were manufactured by 400 companies, compared to half the number of both just a few years before.
[45]On the residual and nonobservant Orthodox, see Liebman, "Orthodoxy in American Jewish Life," pp. 30–36.
[46]Duker, "On Religious Trends in American Life," pp. 54–55.

have succeeded in achieving the goal of institutional perpetuation to only a limited extent; the history of their movement in this country can be written in terms of a case study of institutional decay."[47] Though this assessment proved incorrect in the long term, it accurately identified the more visible trend in Orthodox life at the time.

## Reconstructionism

The middle decades of the century also witnessed the emergence of a new Jewish religious movement—Reconstructionism. Since the 1920s, Rabbi Mordecai Kaplan and a coterie of his disciples had preached the ideology of Reconstructionism but had taken few steps to create a fourth religious movement. Kaplan steadfastly refused the entreaties of his followers to institutionalize his movement and focused instead on disseminating his views through a journal of opinion, *The Reconstructionist*, and a synagogue in New York, the Society for the Advancement of Judaism. Kaplan remained firmly within the Conservative camp, presenting his viewpoint to generations of rabbinical students at the Jewish Theological Seminary and arguing for change before his colleagues in the Rabbinical Assembly.[48]

In 1963 Kaplan retired from the Jewish Theological Seminary at age 82. This move freed him to support his followers' desire to expand Reconstructionism from an ideological movement to a distinct denomination within Judaism. Plans were made to establish a Reconstructionist Rabbinical College, which commenced operations in 1968.[49] Even before that, a federation of Reconstructionist congregations was founded to unify like-minded synagogues and to attempt to bring more groups into the fold.[50] By the late 1960s the movement was poised for growth but was still only a fringe phenomenon, overshadowed by Reform, Conservatism, and Orthodoxy, and numbering only a few thousand adherents.

The mushrooming of synagogues across the American landscape was not viewed by all observers as a sign of religious vitality. Will Herberg, for one,

---

[47]Sklare, *Conservative Judaism*, p. 43. A continuing high rate of defection from Orthodoxy was also predicted on the basis of surveys of younger Jews. The Riverton study, for example, found that most adolescents from Orthodox homes planned to identify as Conservative. See Marshall Sklare, Marc Vosk, and Mark Zborowski, "Forms and Expression of Jewish Identification," *Jewish Social Studies*, July 1955, p. 209.

[48]On Kaplan's allegiance to JTS and refusal to found a separate movement, see Schwarz, "Law and Legitimacy," pp. 191–96, 400–404; and Charles Liebman, "Reconstructionism in American Jewish Life," AJYB 1970, vol. 71, pp. 30–39.

[49]On the founding of the Reconstructionist Rabbinical College, see Liebman, "Reconstructionism," pp. 41–45.

[50]The Reconstructionist Foundation launched a Reconstructionist Fellowship of Congregations consisting of four affiliates in 1955. See Jacob Sloan, "Religion," AJYB 1956, vol. 57, p. 190.

questioned the depth of religiosity of those who were so eager to affiliate with synagogues. He characterized their involvement as "religiousness without religion, . . . a way of sociability or 'belonging' rather than a way of orienting life to God."[51] Among Jews there had been a notable rise in synagogue affiliation, but it was not matched by a rise in synagogue attendance. Survey research consistently found that Jews lagged far behind Catholics and Protestants in weekly attendance at a worship service.[52] Observers concerned with the quality of religious commitment, as measured by synagogue attendance and ritual observance, had reason to be skeptical about the depth of the religious revival.[53]

Beginning in the late 1960s, new currents began to sweep through American Jewish religious life. Arising from a range of circumstances, some specific to the Jewish condition, others generic to the American and even international mood at the end of the 20th century, these currents reshaped the agenda of both religious institutions and individual Jews. The landscape of Jewish religious life as described above was radically transformed. Among the factors helping to bring about this change were the following: the halt in the rate of growth of the American Jewish population; the soaring rate of intermarriage and concomitant preoccupation with strategies for Jewish survival; the impact of the State of Israel on the American Jewish consciousness, particularly after the Six Day War of 1967; structural shifts among American Jews, including the passing of the immigrant generation, geographical redistribution, and rising levels of higher education; the intensified social and political activism of the 60s; the resurgence of religious traditionalism and decline of secularism; and, finally, the women's movement.

These new developments affected all areas of American Jewish life. Their impact on the religious sphere is our particular concern.

## THE RELIGIOUS BEHAVIOR OF AMERICAN JEWS

An examination of the religious behavior of the masses of American Jews provides a convenient point of departure for a consideration of developments in American Judaism since the mid-1960s. The key sources of data

---

[51]Will Herberg, *Protestant, Catholic, Jew* (New York, 1955), p. 260; and idem, "The Triple Melting Pot," *Commentary*, Aug. 1955, pp. 101–08.

[52]According to a Gallup poll in 1964, 71 percent of Catholics, 37 percent of Protestants, and 17 percent of Jews claimed to have attended a religious service during the previous week. By 1970, the comparable figures were 60 percent, 38 percent, and 19 percent, respectively. See *The Yearbook of American and Canadian Churches*, 1972, p. 257.

[53]For an especially sober assessment, see Victor B. Geller, "How Jewish Is Jewish Suburbia," *Tradition*, Spring 1960, pp. 318–30.

on the religious behavior of American Jews are population studies. In the decade from 1977 to 1987, over 50 such studies were conducted under the auspices of local federations of Jewish philanthropies for the purpose of compiling profiles of the Jewish populations they serve. Virtually every large Jewish community has been surveyed, as have a considerable number of middle-size and small communities.[54] Included in these surveys are a

---

[54]The following population studies conducted under the auspices of local federations of Jewish philanthropies were utilized in the compilation of data for this section (relevant page numbers for data on religious issues follow). All data cited in this section are taken from these reports, unless noted otherwise. (I thank Jeffrey Scheckner, Administrator, North American Jewish Data Bank, for graciously making these studies available to me.) **Atlanta**: *Metropolitan Atlanta Jewish Population Study: Summary of Major Findings*, Atlanta Jewish Federation, 1983, pp. 8–9. **Baltimore**: Gary A. Tobin, Jewish Population Study of Greater Baltimore, Associated Jewish Charities and Welfare Fund, 1985, sect. 6 and *Summary Report*, pp. 21–32. **Boston**: Sherry Israel, *Boston's Jewish Community: The 1985 CJP Demographic Study*, Combined Jewish Philanthropies of Greater Boston, 1985, chap. 3. **Chicago**: Peter Friedman, *A Population Study of the Jewish Community of Metropolitan Chicago*, Jewish Federation of Metropolitan Chicago, 1982, pp. 42–45. Additional data that did not appear in the published report were generously provided to the author by Dr. Mark A. Zober, Senior Planning and Research Associate at the Jewish United Fund of Metropolitan Chicago. **Cleveland**: Ann Schorr, *From Generation to Generation*, and *Survey of Cleveland's Jewish Population*, Jewish Community Federation of Cleveland, 1981, pp. 42–49; **Dade County, Fla.**: Ira M. Sheskin, *Population Study of the Greater Miami Jewish Community*, Greater Miami Jewish Federation, 1982, pp. 157–211, 227–244. **Denver**: Bruce A. Phillips, *Denver Jewish Population Study* and *Supplement to the Denver Jewish Population Study*, Allied Jewish Federation of Denver, 1981, pp. iii-iv, 44–55; and pp. 14–25, respectively. **Hartford**: *Highlights from the Greater Hartford Jewish Population Study*, Greater Hartford Jewish Federation, 1981, p. 8. **Kansas City**: Gary A. Tobin, *A Demographic Study of the Jewish Community of Greater Kansas City: Executive Summary*, Jewish Federation of Greater Kansas City, 1985, pp. 3–19, 36–41. **Los Angeles**: Steven Huberman and Bruce A. Phillips, *Jewish Los Angeles: Synagogue Affiliation. Planning Report*, Jewish Federation Council of Greater Los Angeles, 1979, pp. 3–32, 37–51. Also Bruce A. Phillips, "Los Angeles Jewry: A Demographic Portrait," AJYB 1986, vol. 86, pp. 126–95. **MetroWest, N. J.**: Michael Rappeport and Gary A. Tobin, *A Population Study of the Jewish Community of MetroWest, New Jersey*, United Jewish Federation of MetroWest, N.J., 1985, pp. 61–96. **Milwaukee**: Bruce A. Phillips and Eve Weinberg, *The Milwaukee Jewish Population: Report of a Survey*, Milwaukee Jewish Federation, 1984, pp. iv, 1–17. Also *Summary Report*, pp. 1–5. **Minneapolis**: Lois Geer, *Population Study: The Jewish Community of Greater Minneapolis*, Minneapolis Federation for Jewish Service, 1981, chap. 5, pp. 1–19. Also *Executive Summary*, pp. 8–9. **Nashville**: Nancy Hendrix, *A Demographic Study of the Jewish Community of Nashville and Middle Tennessee*, Jewish Federation of Nashville and Middle Tennessee, 1982, p. 20. **New York**: Steven M. Cohen and Paul Ritterband, *The Jewish Population of Greater New York, A Profile*, Federation of Jewish Philanthropies of N.Y., 1981, pp. 22–34. Additional data were provided to me directly by Paul Ritterband. **Palm Beach County, Fla.**: Ira M. Sheskin, *Jewish Demographic Study*, Jewish Federation of Palm Beach County, 1987, pp. 101-40. **Philadelphia**: William Yancey and Ira Goldstein, *The Jewish Population of the Greater Philadelphia Area*, Federation of Jewish Agencies of Greater Philadelphia, 1983, pp. 109–162, 172–208. **Phoenix**: Bruce A. Phillips and William S. Aron, *The Greater Phoenix Jewish Population Study: Jewish Identity, Affiliation, and Observance*, Greater Phoenix Jewish Federation, 1983, pp. 3–10. **Pittsburgh**: Ann Schorr, *Survey of Greater Pittsburgh's Jewish*

series of questions pertaining to religious life: denominational affiliation, synagogue membership and attendance, selected measures of ritual observance, and intermarriage patterns. While these studies provide rich materials on contemporary trends, only a few such surveys exist from midcentury that can serve as a basis for comparative analysis. Still, when possible, comparisons will be made, taking account of, among other things, earlier surveys, as well as the National Jewish Population Study of 1970–71.[55]

*Denominational Preferences*

Recent population studies indicate that the preponderant majority of American Jews continue to identify with one of the denominations of American Judaism, albeit at varying rates and in declining numbers. (See table 1.) When asked how they identify their denominational preference, over two-thirds of Jews in all communities for which we have data indicated that they are either Reform, Conservative, or Orthodox. This kind of self-identification does not necessarily translate into synagogue membership or religious observance, but it indicates that the majority of American Jews accept some kind of religious label. However, compared to the National Jewish Population Study of 1970–71,[56] which found that only 14 percent of American Jews eschewed a denominational preference, it appears that in the 1980s a rising percentage of Jews do not identify with one of the religious movements. For the most part, it is only in smaller Jewish communities that approximately 85 percent of Jews accept a denominational label. By contrast, in the larger centers of Jewish population it is far more com-

---

*Population*, United Jewish Federation of Greater Pittsburgh, 1984, sect. 4. Also *Community Report*, pp. 6–15. **Richmond:** Ann Schorr, *Demographic Study of the Jewish Community of Richmond*, Jewish Federation of Richmond, 1984, pp. 9, 30–31, 42–48. **Rochester:** Gary A. Tobin and Sylvia B. Fishman, *The Jewish Population of Rochester, N.Y. (Monroe County)*, Jewish Community Federation of Rochester, N.Y., 1980, pp. i-iii, 19–33. **St. Louis:** Gary A. Tobin, *A Demographic and Attitudinal Study of the Jewish Community of St. Louis*, Jewish Federation of St. Louis, 1982, pp. iv-viii, 23–42. **Scranton:** *Demographic Census*, typescript report by Mrs. Seymour Bachman, Scranton-Lackawanna Jewish Federation, 1984. **Seattle:** James McCann with Debra Friedman, *A Study of the Jewish Community in the Greater Seattle Area*, Jewish Federation of Greater Seattle, 1979, pp. 8–11, 67–73. **Tampa:** Ray Wheeler, *A Social and Demographic Survey of the Jewish Community of Tampa, Florida*, Tampa Jewish Federation, 1980, pp. 60–66. **Washington, D.C.:** Gary A. Tobin, Janet Greenblatt, and Joseph Waksberg, *A Demographic Study of the Jewish Community of Greater Washington, 1983*, United Jewish Appeal Federation of Greater Washington, D.C., 1983, pp. 25, 39, 97–101, 139–50. **Worcester:** Gary A. Tobin and Sylvia Barack Fishman, *A Population Study of the Greater Worcester Jewish Community*, Worcester Jewish Federation, 1986, pp. 91–112.
[55]The results of the National Jewish Population Study were published in a series of pamphlets issued by the Council of Jewish Federations and Welfare Funds during the 1970s.
[56]See *Jewish Identity: Facts for Planning*, pp. 2–4.

TABLE 1. DENOMINATIONAL SELF-IDENTIFICATION (PERCENT)

| Community | Year of Study | Orthodox | Conservative | Reform | No Preference/Other |
|---|---|---|---|---|---|
| Atlanta | 1983 | 5 | 42 | 37 | 16 |
| Atlantic City | 1985 | 6 | 46 | 29 | 15 |
| Baltimore | 1985 | 20 | 35 | 29 | 16 |
| Boston | 1985 | 4 | 33 | 42 | 21 |
| Chicago | 1982 | 6 | 35 | 39 | 20[a] |
| Cleveland | 1981 | 9 | 39 | 47 | 5 |
| Denver[d] | 1981 | 7 | 28 | 35 | 30 |
| Hartford | 1981 | 6 | 38 | 40 | 16 |
| Kansas City | 1985 | 7 | 38 | 38 | 16 |
| Los Angeles | 1979 | 6 | 30 | 34 | 30 |
| MetroWest, NJ | 1986 | 6 | 38 | 34 | 20 |
| Miami (Dade County, FL) | 1982 | 11 | 35 | 24 | 30 |
| Milwaukee | 1983 | 7 | 27 | 52 | 14 |
| Minneapolis | 1981 | 5 | 53 | 32 | 10 |
| New York | 1981 | 13 | 35 | 29 | 23 |
| Palm Beach County, FL | 1987 | 2 | 43 | 3 | 25 |
| Philadelphia | 1984 | 5 | 41 | 25 | 22[b] |
| Pittsburgh | 1984 | 13 | 44 | 37 | 6 |
| Richmond | 1983 | 8 | 42 | 36 | 14 |
| Rochester | 1980 | 12 | 36 | 42 | 10 |
| St. Louis | 1982 | 8 | 26 | 52 | 14 |
| St. Paul | 1981 | 7 | 55 | 27 | 11 |
| Scranton | 1984 | 31 | 48 | 20 | |
| Seattle | 1979 | 16 | 30 | 46 | 8 |
| Tampa | 1980 | 2 | 43 | 41 | 14 |
| Washington, DC | 1983 | 4 | 35 | 41 | 18[c] |
| Worcester, MA | 1987 | 6 | 29 | 49 | 16 |

Source: Unless otherwise noted, tables are based on the studies listed in text footnote 54. Atlantic City and St. Paul data are from the Boston study, p. 154.
[a]Includes "Traditional."
[b]Includes 1.5% Reconstructionist; 7% "Traditional."
[c]Includes 3% Reconstructionist.
[d]Does not include converts.
Note: Figures rounded to nearest decimal.

mon for Jews to see themselves as "just Jewish" or without a religious preference.

The rejection of a denominational label by 23 percent of New York Jews, 28 percent of Los Angeles Jews, 30 percent of Miami Jews, 20 percent of Chicago Jews, and 22 percent of Philadelphia Jews is particularly noteworthy, given that these are the five largest Jewish communities in the United States and encompass close to 60 percent of the national Jewish population. (See table 2 for a ranking by size of the larger Jewish communities and their approximate populations when last surveyed.)

Table 1 illustrates the wide fluctuation in strength of the various denominations. Each of the major movements can claim great strength in particular communities. When we take the size of communities into account, it is

TABLE 2. LARGEST U.S. JEWISH COMMUNITIES

| Community | Jewish Pop. | Community | Jewish Pop. |
|---|---|---|---|
| New York, NY | 1,742,500 | Middlesex County, NJ | 39,350 |
| Los Angeles, CA | 500,870 | Oakland, CA | 35,000 |
| Chicago, IL | 248,000 | San Diego, CA | 35,000 |
| Miami (Dade County, FL)[a] | 241,000 | Monmouth County, NJ | 33,600 |
| Philadelphia, PA | 240,000 | Central New Jersey | 32,000 |
| Boston, MA | 170,000 | Denver, CO | 30,000 |
| Washington, DC | 157,335 | Houston, TX | 28,000 |
| MetroWest, NJ | 111,000 | Southern New Jersey | 28,000 |
| Baltimore, MD | 92,000 | Hartford, CT | 26,000, |
| San Francisco, CA | 80,000 | Milwaukee, WI | 23,900 |
| Cleveland, OH | 70,000 | Delaware Valley, PA | 23,000 |
| Detroit, MI | 70,000 | Minneapolis, MN | 23,000 |
| Bergen County, NJ | 69,300 | Kansas City, MO | 22,100 |
| Ft. Lauderdale, FL | 60,000 | Cincinnati, OH | 22,000 |
| Orange County, CA | 60,000 | Dallas, TX | 22,000 |
| South Broward, FL | 60,000 | New Haven, CT | 22,000 |
| Atlanta, GA | 50,000 | Seattle, WA | 19,500 |
| Phoenix, AZ | 50,000 | Northern New Jersey | 19,000 |
| Palm Beach County, FL | 45,000 | Buffalo, NY | 18,500 |
| Pittsburgh, PA | 45,000 | San Jose, CA | 18,000 |
| Rockland County, NY | 40,000 | Tucson, AZ | 18,000 |
| South County, FL | 40,000 | Rhode Island | 17,500 |
|  |  | Columbus, OH | 15,000 |

*Source:* Executive Summary, Kansas City study. See text footnote 54.
[a]AJYB 1988, p. 229.

possible to evaluate the relative strength of each denomination. (In most surveys, Reconstructionists were deemed numerically neglible and therefore were not listed separately. Even in Philadelphia, where the central institutions of the Reconstructionist movement are located, only 1.5 percent of respondents identified with Reconstructionism.)

A high level of identification with Orthodoxy is confined largely to New York. Even in New York, Orthodox allegiance is concentrated mainly in the boroughs of Brooklyn and the Bronx and is relatively weak in Manhattan. (Twenty-seven percent of heads of Jewish households in Brooklyn identified as Orthodox compared to 8 percent in Manhattan.)[57] The numerical strength of Orthodoxy in the largest Jewish community of the United States gives that movement a visibility that belies its actual size. In point of fact, some demographers contend that the percentage of Jews who identify as Orthodox has declined to under 10 percent in the late 1980s.[58]

Identification with Conservative Judaism continues at a high level in every Jewish community, but the dominance of the movement is now challenged by Reform in quite a number of localities. In some areas, such as Philadelphia and Minneapolis–St. Paul, Conservatism has maintained formidable strength. It also holds the allegiance of a high percentage of Jews in Sunbelt communities, both in areas where older Jews retire, such as southern Florida, and in burgeoning communities such as Atlanta. Nationally, the Conservative movement still commands the allegiance of a plurality of Jews, albeit a shrinking plurality.

The main beneficiary of Orthodox and Conservative losses seems to be the Reform movement (as well as the group of Jews with no preference). This is evident in Boston, for example, where, between 1965 and 1985, individuals who identified themselves as Orthodox declined from 14 percent to 4 percent, and as Conservative from 44 percent to 33 percent, while the percentage of those who identified as Reform rose from 27 percent to 42 percent, and the "no preference" group increased from 5 percent to 14 percent. Reform continues to exhibit great popularity in its traditional areas of strength—the Midwest and South—but is gaining many new adherents throughout the nation. Just as the middle decades of the 20th century witnessed dramatic numerical gains by the Conservative movement, the closing decades of the century appear as a period of particular growth for Reform Judaism. Indeed, some Reform leaders contend that their movement has already outstripped Conservatism. However, most demographers of American Jewry argue otherwise. On the basis of recent population studies, Barry Kosmin, director of the North American Jewish Data Bank, estimated in 1987 that American Jews were divided as follows: 2 percent

---

[57]Steven M. Cohen and Paul Ritterband, "The Social Characteristics of the New York Area Jewish Community, 1981," AJYB 1984, vol. 84, p. 153 and table 3.3.
[58]Barry Kosmin, "Facing Up to Intermarriage," *Jewish Chronicle* (London), July 24, 1987.

Reconstructionist, 9 percent Orthodox, 29 percent Reform, 34 percent Conservative, and 26 percent "other" or "just Jewish."[59]

To refine such figures and project likely trends for the near-term future, it is useful to examine patterns among generational and age groups. A dozen studies of Jewish communities provide data on the identification of various age groupings within each of the religious denominations. Among Jews who identify themselves as Orthodox, a consistent pattern emerges: higher percentages of Orthodox Jews are in the 18–34-year-old group than in middle-age groupings; but the highest percentages of Orthodox Jews in any age category are over age 65. This suggests both a source of future strength and future weakness for Orthodoxy. Unlike the other denominations, Orthodoxy is retaining the allegiance of its young and even showing a modest increase in attractiveness to younger Jews. By contrast, surveys conducted shortly after World War II repeatedly found that younger Jews from Orthodox homes intended to abandon an Orthodox identification. As a denomination with more adherents in the child-bearing years than in middle age, Orthodoxy can expect an infusion of new members through the birth of children to its younger population. But even as it maintains its attractiveness to its youth, Orthodoxy will have to contend with ongoing losses through the death of its older population, a group that is considerably more numerous than its youth population. In virtually every community for which data are available, with the notable exception of New York, between two and three times as many Orthodox Jews are over age 65 as are between ages 18 and 45. Thus, despite higher birthrates, Jews who identify as Orthodox are not likely to increase in the near future.

Adherents of Conservative Judaism form a different pattern. Self-identification with Conservatism is stronger among middle-age groups than among younger or older groups. In some communities, the largest segment of Conservative Jews is aged 35–44 and in others 45–64; but the percentage of Conservative Jews aged 18–35 is smaller than in either of the other two age categories. The apparent attrition among younger members constitutes the greatest demographic challenge facing the Conservative movement. At present it is unclear whether the movement has been unable to retain the allegiance of many of its youth, or whether children who grow up in Conservative families defer identifying with the movement until they have children of their own, in which case population studies conducted in the early 1990s should reveal a rise in the percentage of Conservative Jews in the younger age categories.[60] Which of these explanations holds true will

---

[59]Ibid.

[60]A strong case for the defection scenario has been made by Charles Liebman and Saul Shapiro in "A Survey of the Conservative Movement: Some of Its Religious Attitudes," unpublished paper, Sept. 1979, p. 22. Steven M. Cohen has argued that identification is tied to family status. See "The American Jewish Family Today," AJYB 1982, vol. 82, pp. 145–53.

determine whether the Conservative movement will age or retain a youthful character.

Of all the denominations, Reform maintains greatest stability across the age spectrum, with the exception of the oldest age cohorts. In virtually every community there are approximately as many Reform Jews in the younger age grouping (18–35) as in middle-age groupings. This would indicate the success of the movement either in retaining its youth or in recruiting younger Jews from the other denominations. From a numerical point of view, it is immaterial how Reform recruits its younger members, but it would still be interesting to know whether young people are attracted from within, or whether Reform is recruiting from outside its ranks.

*Synagogue Membership and Attendance*

Thus far, we have dealt with the relatively passive matter of denominational identification. Synagogue membership and attendance provide more active means of religious involvement. Once again there are significant variations between communities in the percentage of Jews who hold membership in a synagogue. (See table 3.) A recent study identified four variables that help determine rates of synagogue membership within communities.[61] (1) Marriage rates: Communities with a high proportion of married heads of household have a higher rate of synagogue membership; conversely, the larger the population of divorced or single adults, the lower the rate of affiliation. This conforms with a widely reported finding that American Jews generally join synagogues when they become parents and that divorce often leads to a lapse of synagogue membership. (2) Age structure: The higher the percentage of Jews in their 20s and 30s, the lower the rate of affiliation; since younger Jews are less likely to have children, they do not join synagogues in appreciable numbers. (3) Place of birth: Transients are less likely than Jews rooted in a community to invest in synagogue membership; where most Jews in a community are born locally, rates of synagogue membership are high. Thus it is not an accident that in cities in the North, synagogue membership is common, whereas in places like Phoenix it is relatively low. (4) Denominational identification: In communities where one of the religious movements is dominant, it becomes socially important to join a synagogue. In Minneapolis–St. Paul, for example, the high rate of affiliation is related to the great strength of local Conservative synagogues.

---

[61]Peter Friedman and Mark Zober, "Factors Influencing Synagogue Affiliation: A Multi-Community Analysis," North American Jewish Data Bank, Occasional Papers No. 3, May 1987, pp. 11–23.

TABLE 3. CURRENT SYNAGOGUE/TEMPLE MEMBERSHIP, BY COMMUNITY (PERCENT)

| Community | Year of Study | Members | Not Members |
|---|---|---|---|
| Atlanta | 1983 | Est. 27 | 73 |
| Atlantic City | 1985 | 51 | 49 |
| Baltimore | 1985 | 55 | 45 |
| Boston | 1985 | 41 | 59 |
| Chicago | 1982 | 44 | 50 |
| Cleveland | 1981 | 61 | 39 |
| Denver | 1981 | 39 | 61 |
| Kansas City | 1985 | 52 | 48 |
| Los Angeles | 1979 | 26 | 74 |
| MetroWest, NJ | 1986 | 53 | 47 |
| Miami | 1982 | 38 | 62 |
| Milwaukee | 1983 | 56 | 44 |
| Minneapolis | 1981 | 79 | 21 |
| Nashville | 1982 | 78 | 22 |
| New York | 1981 | 41 | 59 |
| Palm Beach County, FL | 1987 | 41 | 59 |
| Philadelphia | 1984 | 41 | 59 |
| Phoenix | 1983 | 33 | 67 |
| Pittsburgh | 1984 | 70 | 30 |
| Richmond | 1983 | 67 | 33 |
| Rochester | 1980 | 68 | 32 |
| St. Louis | 1982 | 66 | 34 |
| St. Paul | 1981 | 84 | 16 |
| Seattle | 1979 | 75 | 25 |
| Washington, DC | 1983 | 39 | 61 |
| Worcester, MA | 1987 | 60 | 40 |

Given the variation in membership figures from one community to the next, it is difficult to determine whether overall synagogue affiliation is rising or declining. One recent study found that synagogue membership varied from 66 percent in the North-Central states, to 48 percent in the Northeast, to 38 percent in the West. Nationwide, this amounted to a 53-percent rate of affiliation. Compared to the 48 percent of American Jews found to have been synagogue members in the 1971 NJPS, this would indicate a modest rise in synagogue affiliation. But judging from the low membership rates in the largest Jewish population centers, it appears doubtful that rates of synagogue affiliation have risen in the 1980s.[62] As for affiliation rates among adherents of the various denominations, a somewhat mixed pattern emerges from recent studies. (See table 4.) In some communities there is a clear spectrum in which Jews who identify as Orthodox have the highest rates of affiliation, self-identified Conservative Jews slightly lower rates, and self-declared Reform Jews dramatically lower rates. In other communities, Conservative Jews have the highest rates of synagogue membership, followed by the Orthodox and the Reform. The sharply lower affiliation rate of Jews who identify as Reform is one of many pieces of evidence that the Reform label is now utilized by many Jews who are not necessarily committed to the movement. Whereas at midcentury Jews with no strong religious allegiance often reflexively stated their affiliation as Conservative, today the reflex is to say Reform—particularly among the least committed.

TABLE 4. PERCENTAGE OF FAMILIES BELONGING TO SYNAGOGUE, BY DENOMINATIONAL PREFERENCE AND COMMUNITY

| Community | Orthodox | Conservative | Reform | Other |
|---|---|---|---|---|
| Baltimore | 71.0 | 58.0 | 54.0 | 27.0 |
| Boston | 67.0 | 60.0 | 35.0 | 9.0 |
| Chicago | 50.0 | 68.0 | 59.0 | 41.0 |
| Cleveland | 85.8 | 67.8 | 58.2 | 5.6 |
| Los Angeles | 42.0 | 45.0 | 24.0 | 8.0 |
| MetroWest, NJ | 71.0 | 75.0 | 51.0 | 16.0 |
| Miami (Dade County, FL) | 63.0 | 48.0 | 44.0 | 11.0 |
| Milwaukee | 63.4 | 64.8 | 82.8 | 23.5 |
| Philadelphia | 53.6 | 56.0 | 38.7 | 54.2[a] |
| Phoenix | 60.6 | 48.9 | 36.3 | 10.1 |
| Pittsburgh | 77.1 | 76.3 | 66.5 | 100.0[a] |

[a]Reconstructionist.

---

[62]On the results of a study conducted by Gary A. Tobin and Sylvia B. Fishman, see Ellen Bernstein, "Jewish Identity in the 80s," and Richard Bono, "Quandary: Establishment Struggles to Keep Jews in the Fold," both in the *Atlanta Jewish Times*, Mar. 25, 1988, p. 8, and Apr. 1, 1988, p. 7, respectively. It is worth noting that even with a synagogue-affiliation rate hovering near 50 percent, membership figures since World War II exceed those for earlier decades in this century. Thus, Stephen Sharot estimates synagogue affiliation in 1939 at between 25 and 33 percent. Admittedly, the Depression may have accounted for part of this low rate, but by 1939 the worst of the economic crisis had passed. See Sharot, *Judaism: A Sociology*, p. 146.

Since the early decades of the 20th century, surveys have demonstrated that Jews attend weekly religious services at far lower rates than their Christian neighbors. In the early 1980s, when approximately 44 percent of Americans claimed they attended services weekly, 24 percent of American Jews claimed to do so.[63] Surveys conducted under Jewish auspices in the 1980s suggest that this latter figure may well be inflated; in hardly any of the communities for which data are available do anywhere near 24 percent claim to attend synagogue "frequently"—a response that sometimes is interpreted to mean weekly attendance and sometimes attendance at least once a month. (See table 5.) Furthermore, in most communities, between one-third and one-half of all Jews attend religious services either never or only on the High Holy Days. While there is ample evidence that earlier in the century similar patterns obtained, it appears that in recent decades Jews are attending synagogue even less frequently. In Rochester, for example, 14

TABLE 5. FREQUENCY OF ATTENDANCE AT RELIGIOUS SERVICES, BY COMMUNITY (PERCENT)

| Community | Year of Study | Never | High Holidays Only | Occasionally | Frequently[a] |
|---|---|---|---|---|---|
| Atlantic City | 1985 | 15 | 31 | 39 | 15 |
| Baltimore | 1985 | 10 | 22 | 30 | 31 |
| Boston | 1985 | 28 | 36 | 28 | 8 |
| Chicago | 1981 | 2 | 29 | 51 | 18 |
| Kansas City | 1985 | 10 | 15 | 64 | 11 |
| MetroWest, NJ | 1985 | 12 | 18 | 45 | 21 |
| Miami | 1982 | 24 | 30 | 29 | 17 |
| New York | 1981 | 30 | 27 | 22 | 21 |
| Palm Beach County, FL | 1987 | 25 | 57 | 14 | 42 |
| Philadelphia | 1985 | 20 | 57[b] | 14[c] | 9[d] |
| Rochester | 1980 | 29 | 45 | 9 | 17 |
| St. Louis | 1982 | 18 | 30 | 30 | 20 |
| Seattle | 1979 | 20 | 30 | 30 | 20 |
| Washington, DC | 1983 | 16 | 14 | 61 | 9 |

[a]Defined differently in different studies.
[b]Few times per year.
[c]One-two times per month.
[d]Every week.

[63]*Yearbook of American and Canadian Churches*, 1984, pp. 283–84.

percent claimed to have attended services weekly in 1961, compared to 2 percent in 1980; attendance only on the High Holy Days rose from 19 percent to 45 percent. In Baltimore, the proportion who attended synagogue "a few times a year" rose from 37 percent to 52 percent between 1968 and 1985 (although levels for more frequent attendance also rose modestly in that period). In short, American Jews, never ardent synagogue-goers, appear to be avoiding religious services more than ever.

## Religious Observance

A third measure of religious behavior that has been utilized in recent community surveys is the observance of religious rituals and holidays. Since Judaism knows of several hundred rituals, social scientists surveying religious practices have been forced to limit their inquiries to a select number of observances which they see as symptomatic of broader patterns of behavior. However, matters are complicated by the range of attitudes within the denominations about which specific observances are still binding in the modern context. Thus, the observance of the dietary laws is optional in the Reform movement but mandatory in Orthodox and Conservative Judaism; refraining from using transportation on the Sabbath is viewed as mandatory by Orthodox rabbis, whereas Conservative rabbis have sanctioned such travel if it is necessary to attend synagogue services. Moreover, quantitative data shed little light on the quality of religious experience. Attendance at a Passover Seder, for example, may entail an intensive examination of the Exodus narrative and its religious implications or may simply provide the pretext for a family dinner. Still, for all their shortcomings, surveys of religious behavior provide important insights into religious life, particularly so since Judaism is a religion heavily oriented toward the performance of ritual actions.

Table 6 provides data on the ritual observances of Jews in 13 different communities that vary widely in size, geographic location, and social composition. Significantly, several universal patterns are evident. In every community, the most widely performed ritual is attendance at a Passover Seder, followed by the lighting of Hanukkah candles, the presence of a *mezuzah* on the front doorpost, and fasting on Yom Kippur. It is indeed noteworthy that over two-thirds of all Jews claim to observe these rituals. Moreover, it appears that in recent decades the observance of these four rituals has become more widespread than it was at midcentury.[64]

How do we explain the popularity of these four rituals and the relatively low rate of observance of other rituals? Marshall Sklare identified five

---

[64]See Sklare and Greenblum, *Jewish Identity on the Suburban Frontier*, p. 52, and Goldstein and Goldscheider, *Jewish Americans*, p. 201.

criteria that help explain why certain rituals are retained by American Jews, even as others are ignored. A ritual is most likely to be retained by Jews, he said, if it is capable of redefinition in modern terms; does not demand social isolation or the adoption of a unique life-style; accords with the religious culture of the larger community while providing a Jewish alternative when such is felt to be needed; is centered on the child; and is performed annually or infrequently.[65] The widespread observance of the Seder and Hanukkah accords well with all five criteria, while fasting on Yom Kippur fits in with the first and last. Affixing a *mezuzah* to a doorpost certainly conforms to the last criterion, but may also reflect the present eagerness of Jews to display their religious and ethnic identification in public.

Sklare's criteria also help to explain the relatively low levels of observance of the dietary laws and Sabbath prohibitions. In both cases, the rituals involved set Jews apart from their neighbors and require ongoing, rather than infrequent, attention. While observance of the dietary laws and the Sabbath had already suffered decline earlier in the century, there is some evidence of even further attrition in recent decades. In Baltimore in 1985, 23 percent of Jews surveyed claimed to light the Sabbath candles weekly, compared to 39 percent in 1968; in 1985, 24 percent of Baltimore Jews claimed they always purchased kosher meat, compared to 36 percent in 1965. In Boston, 31 percent of Jews in 1985 claimed they lit Sabbath candles regularly, compared to 62 percent in 1965; and 17 percent claimed to have a kosher home in 1985, compared to 27 percent who bought kosher meat and 15 percent who kept two sets of dishes in 1965.[66]

When patterns of observance are correlated with the denominational self-identification, it becomes evident that there is a significant degree of truth to the folk wisdom concerning differences between the various religious movements: Jews who identify as Orthodox observe rituals most frequently, Conservative identifiers less frequently, and Reform identifiers least frequently of all. (See table 7.) Still, a significant proportion of Jews who identify as Orthodox are not fully observant—e.g., almost one-third of Jews in New York who identify as Orthodox handle money on the Sabbath. Moreover, when it comes to such rituals as Seder participation, lighting Hanukkah candles, affixing a *mezuzah*, and fasting on Yom Kippur, rates of observance among Conservative Jews approximate the levels of the Orthodox; Reform Jews, by contrast, observe these rituals at far lower rates. Finally, it is worth noting that some rituals which the Reform movement

---

[65]Sklare, *America's Jews*, p. 114.

[66]It is still too soon to analyze the patterns of observance among fourth-generation Jews, as compared to their parents and grandparents. For a preliminary attempt that utilizes data from the New York survey, see Steven M. Cohen, *American Assimilation or Jewish Revival?* (Bloomington, Ind., 1988), pp. 54–56 and 129–30.

TABLE 6. PRACTICE OF SELECTED OBSERVANCES, BY COMMUNITY (PERCENT)

| Observances | N.Y. | Phila. | Balt.[a] | Wash. | Metrowest NJ[a] | KC[a] | St. Louis | Miami[a] | Phoenix[a] | Seattle[a] | Rochester[a] | Chicago[a] | Palm Beach County[a] |
|---|---|---|---|---|---|---|---|---|---|---|---|---|---|
| Attends Seder | 89 | 89 | 86 | NA | 78 | 76 | 71 | 70 | 81 | 84 | 80 | 88 | 75 |
| Lights Hanukkah candles | 76 | 78 | NA | NA | NA | NA | 80 | 57 | 78 | 78 | 78 | 78 | 67 |
| Has mezuzah | 70 | 71 | NA | NA | NA | NA | 76 | 77 | 57 | NA | NA | 64 | 69 |
| Fasts on Yom Kippur | 67 | 67 | 75 | 73 | 66 | NA | NA | 52 | NA | 63 | 63 | 64 | 52 |
| Lights Sabbath candles | 37 | 32 | 32 | 15[b] | 25 | 27 | 28 | 29 | NA | 38 | 33 | NA | 23 |
| Buys only kosher meat | 36 | NA | 24 | NA | 18 | NA | 19 | 24 | NA | NA | NA | NA | NA |
| Uses 2 sets of dishes | 30 | 16 | 23 | 10 | 16 | NA | 15 | 21 | 9 | 15[c] | 23[c] | 12.2 | 13[c] |

TABLE 6.—(Continued)

| Observances | N.Y. | Phila.[a] | Balt.[a] | Wash. | Metrowest NJ[a] | KC[a] | St. Louis | Miami[a] | Phoenix[a] | Seattle[a] | Rochester[a] | Chicago[a] | Palm Beach County[a] |
|---|---|---|---|---|---|---|---|---|---|---|---|---|---|
| Handles no money on Sabbath | 12 | NA | NA | NA | NA | NA | NA | NA | 4 | NA | NA | NA | NA |
| Refrains from transport on Sabbath | NA | 5 | 8 | 4 | 7 | NA | 5 | NA | 4 | NA | NA | 5 | NA |
| Has Christmas tree (sometimes or more frequently) | NA | NA | 16 | 25 | 13 | 21 | 14 | NA | NA | NA | 15 | NA | 9 |

NA Indicates data not available.
[a]Denotes always or frequently observed.
[b]Denotes always observed.
[c]"Keeps kosher home."

TABLE 7. PRACTICE OF SELECTED OBSERVANCES, BY DENOMINATIONAL PREFERENCE AND COMMUNITY (PERCENT)

| Observance | MetroWest NJ[a] O | C | R | New York[b] O | C | R | Boston[b] O | C | R | Philadelphia O | C | R | Baltimore[a] O | C | R | Miami[a] O | C | R | Chicago O | C | R |
|---|---|---|---|---|---|---|---|---|---|---|---|---|---|---|---|---|---|---|---|---|---|
| Attends Seder | 82 | 96 | 83 | 98 | 98 | 97 | 95 | 97 | 87 | 93 | 96 | 92 | 90 | 93 | 87 | 88 | 83 | 74 | 93 | 94 | 83 |
| Lights Hanukkah candles | NA | | | 97 | 95 | 88 | 93 | 95 | 90 | 90 | 87 | 77 | NA | | | 84 | 68 | 54 | 85 | 85 | 75 |
| Has mezuzah | NA | | | 95 | 93 | 78 | 97 | 89 | 77 | 85 | 87 | 65 | NA | | | 96 | 88 | 73 | 86 | 76 | 53 |
| Fasts on Yom Kippur | 77 | 86 | 61 | 96 | 90 | 77 | 89 | 85 | 77 | 98 | 85 | 59 | 90 | 87 | 67 | 88 | 68 | 38 | 85 | 76 | 56 |
| Lights Sabbath candles | 63 | 36 | 15 | 88 | 63 | 34 | 84 | 57 | 39 | 65 | 45 | 23 | 65 | 34 | 21 | 77 | 35 | 14 | NA | | |
| Buys only kosher meat | 82 | 36 | 4 | 91 | 56 | 16 | 72 | 32 | 7 | NA | | | 67 | 23 | 7 | 77 | 30 | 4 | NA | | |

TABLE 7.—(Continued)

Observance

Community and Denominations

| | MetroWest NJ[a] | | | New York[b] | | | Boston[b] | | | Philadelphia | | | Baltimore[a] | | | Miami[a] | | | Chicago | | |
|---|---|---|---|---|---|---|---|---|---|---|---|---|---|---|---|---|---|---|---|---|---|
| | O | C | R | O | C | R | O | C | R | O | C | R | O | C | R | O | C | R | O | C | R |
| Uses 2 sets of dishes | 72 | 26 | 4 | 90 | 48 | 9 | 83 | 26 | 4 | 52 | 26 | 1 | 67 | 21 | 4 | 75 | 27 | 3 | 64 | 14 | 1 |
| Handles no money on Sabbath | 68 | NA | | 68 | 8 | 2 | NA | | | NA | | | NA | | | 72 | 24 | 8[c] | NA | | |
| Has Christmas tree (sometimes or more frequently) | 13 | 3 | 16 | NA | | | 5 | 3 | 4 | NA | | | 1 | 5 | 13 | NA | | | NA | | |

O = Orthodox
C = Conservative
R = Reform
NA Indicates data not available.
[a]Denotes always or usually observed.
[b]Denotes synagogue members only.
[c]"Observes the Sabbath."

does not deem necessary, such as the purchase of kosher meat, continue to be practiced by small percentages of Jews who identify as Reform.

## Intermarriage

Intermarriage is generally defined as the marriage of a born Jew to a person who was not born Jewish. Some intermarriages result in conversionary marriages—i.e., one spouse converts to the religion of the other; others result in mixed marriages, where the two partners formally remain members of two separate religions. Strictly speaking, intermarriage does not provide a measure of religious behavior because one can be married to a non-Jew and continue to practice Judaism. Intermarriage is important in our context, however, for several reasons: it blurs religious boundaries between Jews and Christians; it serves as a potential source for new Jews if the non-Jewish spouse converts; it has a profound impact on the religious identity of children; and it raises serious questions of Jewish religious law and policy that bedevil the Jewish community today in an unprecedented manner. Our focus here will be on the quantitative aspects of intermarriage. In subsequent sections, attention will be given to the challenges raised by intermarriage for those who set policy within organized religious life.

Intermarriage has exploded on the American Jewish scene since the mid-1960s, rapidly rising in incidence to the point where as many as two out of five Jews who wed marry a partner who was not born Jewish. The NJPS was the first survey that drew attention to the changing dimensions of this phenomenon. When married Jews in the national sample were asked whether they were wed to someone who had not been born Jewish, roughly 2 to 3 percent who had married in the decades from 1900 to 1940 answered in the affirmative; the figure rose to 6.7 percent for those who had married in the 1940s and 1950s; jumped to 17.4 percent for those married between 1961 and 1965; and soared to 31.7 percent for those married between 1966 and 1970.[67] Recent population studies make it clear that intermarriage rates have remained high and dramatically exceed the rates of 20 years ago.

Table 8 lists the percentages of households in different localities that contain either a convert to Judaism or a non-Jewish spouse. In the localities listed, anywhere from 17 percent to 37 percent of Jewish households consist of intermarried families. If all these marriages resulted in the conversion of the non-Jewish partner, the matter of intermarriage would still raise important religious issues for American Jews, but they would revolve around the

---

[67]*Intermarriage: Facts for Planning*, Council of Jewish Federations, n.d., p. 10. For a critique of these figures, see Charles Silberman, *A Certain People: American Jews and Their Lives Today* (New York, 1985), pp. 289–92. While the figure for 1966–70 may have been inflated, intermarriage rates subsequently have reached that high level.

proper manner of integrating the converts into Jewish society. But in most communities, the percentage of households where no conversion has occurred—the mixed-marriage category—is far larger than the percentage of conversionary households. Thus the issue is not only how to deal with converts but also how to cope with the far larger population of Jews who choose to marry a non-Jew and still identify themselves as Jewish and raise their children as Jews.

TABLE 8. PERCENTAGE OF JEWISH HOUSEHOLDS WITH ONE CONVERTED OR NON-JEWISH SPOUSE, BY COMMUNITY

| Community | Convert | Non-Jew |
|---|---|---|
| Baltimore | 14.0 | 8.0 |
| Chicago | 4.0 | 13.0 |
| Denver | 6.6 | 30.1 |
| Metrowest, NJ | 23.0 | 14.0 |
| Milwaukee | 7.0 | 19.5 |
| Pittsburgh | 8.5 | 13.0 |

The dimensions of the problem are further highlighted by the age distribution of Jews involved in mixed marriages. Data are available from eight communities on the age composition of married couples who indicated that one spouse was an unconverted Gentile. (See table 9.) In comparing couples in three age categories—18–29, 30–39, 40–49—it becomes evident that marriage to a non-Jewish partner is more widespread the younger the couple. It may be that a certain percentage of these marriages will still become conversionary. Egon Mayer found that approximately one-quarter to one-third of intermarriages eventually lead to the conversion of the non-Jewish spouse, but Mayer's findings were based on research conducted in the late 1970s and early 1980s.[68] Since then, rates of intermarriage have continued to rise and both the Reform and Reconstructionist movements have formally stated that they now accept as Jewish a child who has only one Jewish parent. In all likelihood, these developments are affecting the incidence of conversion among the intermarried.

Only limited data are available on the incidence of intermarriage among adherents of the various denominations, but they help clarify why the Reform movement has been most active in formulating new responses in this area. In a survey conducted in 1985 at the biennial convention of the

---

[68]Egon Mayer, *Love and Tradition: Marriage Between Jews and Christians* (New York, 1985), p. 157.

TABLE 9. PERCENTAGE OF JEWISH HOUSEHOLDS WITH AN UNCONVERTED SPOUSE, BY AGE GROUP AND COMMUNITY

| Community | Age Group | | |
|---|---|---|---|
| | 18–29 | 30–39 | 40–49 |
| Chicago | 27.0 | 23.0 | 9.0 |
| Cleveland[a] | 23.5 | 19.1 | 14.3 |
| Denver | 66.0 | 40.0 | 13.3 |
| Los Angeles | 48.9 | 20.8 | 13.3 |
| Milwaukee | 23.5[c] | 27.1[c] | 7.7[c] |
| | 33.3[d] | 12.8[d] | 10.2[d] |
| Phoenix | 60.3 | 25.8 | 40.0 |
| Richmond | 43.6 | 29.4 | 20.7 |
| Pittsburgh | 26.5[b] | 23.0 | 17.1 |

[a]Denotes spouse other than Jewish or no religion.
[b]Under 30.
[c]Husband Jewish, wife not.
[d]Wife Jewish, husband not.

Union of American Hebrew Congregations, the congregational body of Reform Judaism, 31 percent of lay leaders of Reform temples reported having a child married to a non-Jewish spouse.[69] Table 10 provides information on the percentages of mixed-married couples among the children of those who identify with Orthodox, Conservative, and Reform Judaism. In the three communities for which data are available—Richmond, Philadelphia, and Cleveland—rates of intermarriage are highest among the offspring of those who identify as Reform, lower among those who identify as Conservative, and lowest among the Orthodox. At present, then, it appears that those who identify as Reform have the highest levels of mixed marriage among their children.

In terms of denominational identification, 40 percent of intermarried Jews in Los Angeles identify with the Reform movement, as do two-thirds of intermarried Jews in Milwaukee—in both cases versus 14 percent who identify with Conservative Judaism. Interestingly, 4 percent of intermarried Jews in Los Angeles identify as Orthodox. All of these data suggest that marriage to a non-Jewish partner is not regarded by many intermarrying Jews as a sign of defection from Judaism.

---

[69]Mark L. Winer, Sanford Seltzer, and Steven Schwager, *Leaders of Reform Judaism: A Study of Jewish Identity, Religious Practices and Beliefs, and Marriage Patterns* (New York, 1987), p. 66.

TABLE 10. INTERMARRIAGE STATUS OF GROWN CHILDREN, BY PARENTS' DENOMINATION (PERCENT)

| Children's Intermarriage Status | Orthodox | Parents' Denomination Conservative | Reform | Other |
|---|---|---|---|---|
| | | Richmond | | |
| Spouse born Jewish | 86.6 | 71.4 | 48.9 | 35.7 |
| Convert | 6.7 | 3.1 | 2.2 | 7.2 |
| Other religion/no religion | 6.7 | 25.5 | 48.9 | 57.1 |
| | | Philadelphia[a] | | |
| Both Jewish | 94.3 | 92.2 | 82.4 | |
| Convert | 2.5 | 1.6 | 4.0 | |
| Intermarriage | 3.2 | 6.2 | 13.5 | |
| | | Cleveland[b] | | |
| Both Jewish | 90.0 | 76.3 | 67.9 | |
| Convert | 0.0 | 5.4 | 7.4 | |
| Intermarried | 10.0 | 18.3 | 24.7 | |

[a]"Family of origin" instead of "Parents."
[b]Only adults over 50 included in "Parents."

Precisely because so many Jews who intermarry today continue to identify as Jews, the question of the status of their children has become a bone of contention in the Jewish community. In the present context, attention needs to be given to the religious outlook and behavior of children whose parents are mixed married. The most extensive analysis of this question appears in research conducted by Egon Mayer for the American Jewish Committee. Among his conclusions are the following:[70] children of conversionary marriages are more than three times as likely as children of mixed marriages to identify as Jews; 69 percent of children in conversionary

---

[70]Egon Mayer, *Children of Intermarriage: A Study in Patterns of Identification and Family Life* (New York, 1983), pp. 7, 11, 15–18. For a more recent discussion of the consequences of outmarriage, see U.O. Schmelz and Sergio DellaPergola, *Basic Trends in American Jewish Demography*, American Jewish Committee, 1988, pp. 20–24.

families definitely or probably want to be Jewish, compared to 26 percent of children of mixed marriages. According to Mayer, 81 percent of teenagers in mixed-married families never attend a synagogue, compared to 15 percent of teenagers in conversionary families; and only 14 percent of children of mixed marriages celebrate their Bar or Bat Mitzvah, compared to 73 percent of children of conversionary marriages. Mayer provides many additional measures confirming a widespread pattern—only a small minority of children of mixed marriages are socialized into Jewish religious life and identify their religion as Judaism. It remains to be seen whether children accepted as Jewish under the patrilineal definition will conform to the patterns of conversionary or mixed-married children.

## DENOMINATIONAL LIFE: REFORM JUDAISM

The most visible evidence of significant shifts in Jewish religious life may be observed in the new policies and procedures adopted by the various Jewish denominations. All of the movements have been challenged by their own constituents to respond to new social concerns, and in turn each movement has been forced to react to the new directions taken by other groups on the religious spectrum. As a result, all four major movements in American Judaism have adopted radically new programs that could not have been envisioned at midcentury.

Since the mid-1960s the official position of the Reform movement regarding a range of religious practices and ideological issues has been shaped by two seemingly contradictory impulses. On the one hand, Reform has sanctioned a number of radical departures from traditional practice: it was the first to ordain women as rabbis and cantors; it steadfastly refused to place sanctions on rabbis who officiated at mixed marriages; and most dramatically, it unilaterally redefined Jewish identity. On the other hand, the Reform movement has reintroduced or signaled its willingness to tolerate many religious practices that had been rejected in the past; in many temples men now don skullcaps and prayer shawls, kosher meals are prepared, and Hebrew usages have been reinstated. Reform, then, is changing in both directions—toward a more radical break with traditional practices and toward an unprecedented openness to traditional teachings.

This eclecticism has been made possible by a rethinking of the basic Reform position. Whereas Reform Judaism was formerly a movement that on principle said "no" to some aspects of the Jewish tradition, it is now a movement that is open to all Jewish possibilities, whether traditional or innovative. The guiding principle of Reform today is the autonomy of every individual to choose a Jewish religious expression that is personally meaningful. The result is a Judaism open to all options and therefore appealing to a broad range of Jews—including those who have long felt disenfranchised, such as Jews married to non-Jews and homosexuals. The dilemma this raises for the Reform movement is one of limits, of boundaries. If the autonomy of the individual prevails above all else, what beliefs and practices unite all Reform Jews? Is there, then, a model Reform Jew? And is there anything a Reform Jew can do that places him or her beyond the pale of acceptable behavior? Thus far, Reform Judaism has been unable to answer these questions.

## The Abandonment of Ideology

Not surprisingly, the issues that have prompted the most intense debate in the Reform movement have revolved around questions of definition and boundary. As noted above, the reintroduction of some rituals during the 1950s already engendered debate over the future direction of Reform, with some prominent rabbis expressing concern that the movement was losing its way and becoming less distinctive. The debate became considerably more vociferous as Reform Judaism instituted several radical new changes during the 1970s. Three issues especially sparked controversy: the introduction of a new prayer book to replace the venerated *Union Prayer Book* that had done service for 80 years; the decision of growing numbers of Reform rabbis to officiate at mixed marriages; and the desire of the movement to produce an updated platform to replace earlier ideological statements. In each case, Reform was torn between respect for the autonomous choice of the individual and the need to define a clear-cut position; and in each case, the former concern triumphed over the latter.

TOWARD A NEW REFORM LITURGY

The movement to compile a new prayer book for Reform Judaism to replace the *Union Prayer Book* (UPB)[71] began in earnest in the 1950s and gained momentum in 1966 when a symposium on liturgy was planned for the journal of the Reform rabbinate. Initially there was much resistance to change; it was argued that the venerable UPB, the Haggadah, and the Rabbi's Manual were "properties" of the Central Conference of American Rabbis (CCAR) and ought not be tampered with. If rabbis felt uncomfortable with parts of these works, the argument went, they could use them with greater selectivity. Others, however, contended that the UPB was no longer

---

[71]On the history of the UPB, see Lou H. Silberman, "The Union Prayer Book: A Study in Liturgical Development," in *Retrospect and Prospect*, ed. Bertram Korn (New York, 1965), pp. 46–80.

consonant with the mood of the movement and that an entirely new prayer book, compiled with the cooperation of rabbis, gifted writers, psychiatrists, philosophers, and educators, was needed. Proponents of a new prayer book complained that the UPB was written in archaic language and filled with obscure references, that its theology was dated, and its prayers remote from the actual concerns of Reform worshipers. As a tangible expression of dissatisfaction with the UPB, hundreds of Reform congregations began in the 1960s to compile informal "creative liturgies" that were distributed in photocopied form. Clearly, pressure was building among both rabbis and the laity for a new *siddur*.[72]

This ferment culminated in 1975 when the CCAR published the new prayer book, entitled *Gates of Prayer* (GOP), containing services for "weekdays, Sabbaths, Festivals, and prayers for synagogue and home." Among the innovations of this work were the following: a Hebrew, as well as an English, title; a partial attempt to deal with the male-oriented language of earlier liturgies; longer passages in Hebrew and from the traditional liturgy; a heavy emphasis on Israel and Zion; explicit references to the Holocaust; and—symptomatic of the new mood—the inclusion of ten distinct Friday-evening services (as well as a half-dozen Sabbath morning services), which have been described as ranging from "basically Conservative to Reconstructionist, to neo-Hassidic, UPB Reform, to polydox."[73]

Despite its near universal acceptance by Reform temples, *Gates of Prayer* continues to stir debate within the Reform movement.[74] A symposium held to mark the tenth anniversary of its appearance revealed a range of criticisms: some found it unwieldy because it was so heavy; others viewed it as essentially a rabbi's instrument; still others found it a poor pedagogic tool, since it lacked explanatory notes; and yet others resented its continued use of sexist language in reference to God. But the central issue of controversy continues to revolve around the issue of Reform definition.[75] One Reform rabbi indicated that the UPB "was torn from my hands by my trustees who

---

[72]On the creative liturgies of the 1960s, see Raphael, *Profiles in American Judaism*, pp. 66–67. For an extended discussion of the problems posed by the UPB, see the symposium in the *CCAR Journal*, Jan. and Oct. 1967, as well as Edward Graham, "Winds of Liturgical Reform," *Judaism*, Winter 1974, pp. 53–54.

[73]Eric Friedland, "Reform Liturgy in the Making," *Jewish Spectator*, Fall 1987, pp. 40–42. On "Polydoxy," see Alvin Reines, "Polydox Judaism: A Statement," *Journal of Reform Judaism*, Fall 1980, pp. 47–55. On the confusion regarding "theism," see David Polish, "An Outline for Theological Discourse in Reform," *Journal of Reform Judaism*, Winter 1982, pp. 2–3.

[74]On *Gates of Prayer*'s widespread acceptance, see CCAR *Yearbook*, 1979, p. 39, which claims that within four years of its appearance, it had been adopted by 75 percent of Reform temples.

[75]See the symposium on *"Gates of Prayer*: Ten Years Later," *Journal of Reform Judaism*, Fall 1985, pp. 13–61.

insisted that our congregation adopt the new [*Gates of Prayer*]. . . . I am not in sympathy with the new wave of Reform, the *kipa-talit-kashrut-milatevila* school which now seems to dominate the movement. I subscribe to the mission idea and the social justice emphasis in conventional Reform."[76] *Gates of Prayer* underscores the departure of Reform from its earlier position, but does not present a coherent vision of what Reform ideology constitutes today, other than an amalgam of contradictory tendencies within American Judaism.

THE CENTENARY PERSPECTIVE

The difficulty of defining a Reform outlook was further highlighted when the Central Conference of American Rabbis tried to draft a new ideological platform on the occasion of its centennial. This new platform was to take its place in a series of rabbinic pronouncements dating back to the Pittsburgh Platform of 1885 and the Columbus Platform of 1937. Yet when the committee empaneled to draft the platform met, it could not complete its work in time (1973), and instead the Centenary Perspective was issued in 1976.

In his preface to a special issue of the *CCAR Journal* introducing the Centenary Perspective, Rabbi Eugene Borowitz, chairman of the special committee that eventually drafted the statement, outlined some of the ideological differences that impeded progress. He described how, in the wake of the CCAR decision in 1973 urging rabbis to refrain from officiating at mixed marriages, "internal dissension among the rabbis had risen to such a point of intensity that there seemed the possibility of the Reform movement splitting. . . . Ideologically what troubled members of the [CCAR] was the place of freedom in Reform Judaism versus that of discipline." Borowitz went on to describe candidly how the Centenary Perspective was drafted in a deliberate attempt to avoid dissension and focus on commonalities. Three issues were deemed paramount: "What is the nature of a Reform Jew's religious obligations?" "What are our duties to the State of Israel and to the communities in which we live?" and "How do we balance our duties to our people and to humanity at large?" To these was added the issue of living with diversity within the Reform movement, "particularly since it seemed to have come to the point of tearing us apart."[77]

The Centenary Perspective responded to the last issue by turning diversity into a virtue: "Reform does more than tolerate diversity; it engenders it." Thus, it is not a common ideology that unites Reform Jews but rather

---

[76]Samuel M. Silver's letter in *Journal of Reform Judaism*, Spring 1986, p. 83.

[77]The Centenary Perspective, as well as analysis provided by members of the committee that drafted the statement, appears in *CCAR Journal*, Spring 1977, pp. 3–80.

a "spirit of Reform Jewish beliefs." These include: a belief in God, albeit a deity whose role is not clearly defined; an identification with the Jewish people, the bearers of Judaism; and a belief in Torah, which "results from meetings between God and the Jewish people." The chief manner in which these beliefs are acted upon is through the fulfillment of "obligations" that include "daily religious observance." Significantly, the Centennial Perspective qualifies what is meant by obligations: "Within each area of Jewish observance, Reform Jews are called upon to confront the claims of tradition, however differently perceived, and to exercise their individual autonomy, choosing and creating on the basis of commitment and knowledge." Once again, when confronted with the tension between freedom of choice and guidelines for belief and practice, Reform opted for the the former.

RABBINIC OFFICIATION AT MIXED MARRIAGES

The most bitter debate pitting movement discipline against the principle of individual autonomy erupted in 1973, when the Reform rabbinate debated a resolution that urged members of the CCAR to desist from officiating at mixed marriages. The proposed resolution not only reaffirmed Reform's long-standing view "that mixed marriage is contrary to the Jewish tradition and should be discouraged," but declared its "opposition to participation by its members in any ceremony which solemnizes a mixed marriage." The resolution went on to dictate a course of action to members of the CCAR who dissented from this view, urging them to: "1. refrain from officiating at a mixed marriage unless the couple" undertakes to study for conversion; 2. refrain from officiating at a mixed marriage for a member of another congregation served by a Conference member unless there has been prior consultation; 3. refrain from co-officiating or sharing with non-Jewish clergy in the solemnization of a mixed marriage; 4. refrain from officiating at a mixed marriage on Shabbat or Yom Tov." To give further weight to the resolution, the president of the CCAR published an essay in the official journal of the Reform rabbinate entitled "Enough," a plea to his members to desist from participating in "ecumenical marriages."[78]

---

[78]The entire debate appears in the CCAR *Yearbook*, 1973, pp. 59–97. For the original resolution, see pp. 63–64. See also David Polish, "Enough," *CCAR Journal*, Winter 1973, pp. 35–37. It is not entirely clear why the issue arose in 1973, but certainly one precipitating factor was the circulation within the CCAR in August 1969 of a list of colleagues who officiated at mixed marriages. This list for the first time confirmed that over 100 Reform rabbis participated in such ceremonies and made their names available to colleagues who wished to refer their congregants to them. As noted by Norman Mirsky, the circulation of this list "removed the matter from the realm of private to that of social dissent," and made it easier for rabbis who had desisted from officiating at such ceremonies to change their policies. See "Mixed Marriage and the Reform Rabbinate," *Midstream*, Jan. 1970, pp. 40–46.

In the ensuing debate, a range of passionately held views on the matter was expressed. Speaking for rabbis who officiated at mixed marriages, Irwin Fishbein pleaded with his colleagues to recognize that they did not have the power to prevent intermarriage by refusing to sanction such marriages; he urged them "not to slam a door that may be only slightly ajar" by refusing to officiate; and he called upon them to utilize their persuasive, rather than coercive, powers to encourage mixed-married couples to participate in Jewish life. Speaking for the CCAR members who supported the resolution, Joel Zion portrayed "mixed marriage without prior conversion [as] a serious threat to the survival of the Jewish people." He then raised the issue of drawing the line, describing his decision to enter the rabbinate in order "to lead my people, not to be lead by them; to set standards for Jewish survival, not to be set upon by those who seek a convenient answer to a religious problem. . . . We rabbis are the last bastion in the struggle for Jewish survival, and . . . the time has come for us to announce that our liberalism would go no further when survival is at stake."[79]

When the debate ended, the entire section of the resolution aimed at rabbis who officiated at mixed marriages was dropped. The resolution as adopted declared opposition to officiation at mixed marriages but also recognized that members of the CCAR "have held and continue to hold divergent interpretations of Jewish tradition." The principle of individual autonomy prevented the conference from passing a resolution that did anything more than urge what one rabbi called "voluntaristic responsiveness to the demands of Jewish law and the needs of the entire people."[80] Yet even this mild attempt at using a "collective voice to exert moral deterrence"[81] prompted over 100 dissident rabbis to form an "Association for a Progressive Reform Judaism" in September 1974, whose primary concern was upholding the right of every Reform rabbi to decide individually whether to officiate at a mixed marriage.[82] The failure to pass the original resolution and the splintering of the CCAR in response to the revised resolution further highlight the challenge posed by the Reform movement's

---

[79]CCAR *Yearbook*, 1973, pp. 96, 64–70.
[80]David Polish, "The Changing and the Constant in the Reform Rabbinate," *American Jewish Archives*, Nov. 1983, p. 327.
[81]Ibid.
[82]Judah Cahn, "The Struggle Within Reform Judaism," *CCAR Journal*, Summer 1975, p. 65. For more on the association, see Sylvin L. Wolf, "Reform Judaism as Process: A Study of the CCAR, 1960–75" (unpublished Ph.D. diss., St. Louis University, 1978), pp. 269–71. It appears that Reform rabbis opposed to their colleagues' officiation at mixed marriages continue to press their case. See Moshe Zemer, "An Halachic and Historical Critique of *Responsa on Jewish Marriage*," *Journal of Reform Judaism*, Spring 1988, pp. 31–47, which reports that 100 rabbis, including the heads of HUC-JIR, the UAHC, and the CCAR, issued a statement in Dec. 1985, declaring that there cannot be a Jewish marriage between a Jew and a non-Jew.

embrace of individual autonomy at the expense of movement discipline and coherence.

## Religious Practice—Change in Both Directions

Reform Judaism's commitment to individual autonomy has led to considerable revision in religious practice. Rituals that had long been deemed obsolete by the movement have been reinstated, while other traditional practices that Reform had never openly rejected in the past have now been abandoned. In its attitude toward tradition, the Reform movement has been open to change in both directions.

The openness to tradition is strikingly evident in a number of major publications issued by the CCAR since the early 1970s. Most of these works are part of a series of volumes whose titles contain the words "Gates of"; they provide liturgies and guidance for the High Holy Days, festivals, home observances, and even penitential prayers. In addition, there is a new Haggadah for Passover and a major new commentary on the Pentateuch. All of these volumes are handsomely produced and contain a goodly amount of Hebrew, as well as commentaries from a range of classical and contemporary Jewish sources. The "Gates of" series is unprecedented as a guide for the Reform laity.[83]

Perhaps the most important volume is a work entitled *Gates of Mitzvah: A Guide to the Jewish Life Cycle*. *Mitzvah*, the book declares, "is the key to authentic Jewish existence and to the sanctification of life. No English equivalent can adequately translate the term. Its root meaning is 'commandment' but *mitzvah* has come to have broader meanings." The book's introduction then goes on to clarify the radical departure implicit in a Reform emphasis on *mitzvah*. Formerly the movement had viewed ritual commandments, as opposed to ethical ones, as "optional or even superfluous." But this dichotomy is now rejected, for "the very act of doing a *mitzvah* may lead one to know the heart of the matter.... Ritual, as the vehicle for confronting God and Jewish history, can shape and stimulate one's ethical impulses." The volume then surveys a range of observances related to birth, childhood, education, marriage and the Jewish home, and death and mourning. One of the most striking passages deals with Jewish dietary laws: "The fact that *Kashrut* was an essential feature of Jewish life for so many centuries should motivate the Jewish family to study it and to consider whether or not it may enhance the sanctity of their home." Still,

---

[83]*Gates of Prayer* (1975); *Gates of Repentance* (1977); *Gates of the House* (1977); *Gates of Mitzvah* (1979); *The Five Scrolls* (with services, 1983); *Gates of the Seasons* (1983); *Gates of Song* (1987); *Songs and Hymns* (for *Gates of Prayer*, 1987); *Gates of Forgiveness-Selichot* (1987); *Gates of Understanding* (Commentary to *Gates of Prayer*, 1987).

the openness to tradition is continually qualified by a nondirective approach, summed up by the following disclaimer: "Even within the realm of *mitzvah* various levels of doing and understanding might exist." *Gates of Mitzvah* reaffirms the Reform movement's twin commitments to "Jewish continuity and to personal freedom of choice."[84]

A good deal of the pressure in the direction of greater traditionalism has emanated from rabbinical students at the various branches of Hebrew Union College. Much to the displeasure of some senior faculty members, rabbinical students in the 1970s began to don yarmulkes and introduce traditional rituals into their personal observance. Matters came to a head when some students began to lobby for the introduction of kosher food at Hebrew Union College to facilitate the observance of the dietary laws. For a brief period, the cafeteria at the Cincinnati branch dispensed food on two separate lines—one for kosher food and one for nonkosher food. (Subsequently, the alternatives became vegetarian food and nonkosher food.) Two branches of HUC signaled a desire to identify with a more traditional version of Judaism when they opted to refer to their chapels as synagogues.[85] It appears that rabbis ordained in recent years, as well as new faculty members appointed since the mid-1970s, are spearheading the turn to greater traditionalism.

The renewed interest in religious tradition also manifests itself in Reform temples, which over the past two to three decades have introduced the following: an increased number of readings in Hebrew (now spoken with an Israeli, Sephardic pronunciation); an *amidah* prayer, during which congregants are asked to stand; a cantor who serves as a *shaliah tzibur*, as the emissary of the congregation, something that non-Jewish choir members may not do; tolerance of male members who wear yarmulkes; and the near universal Bar and Bat Mitzvah.[86] Moreover, the liturgies employed reflect the emphasis on tradition found in the "Gates of" series.

Perhaps the most dramatic evidence of a move toward tradition in the Reform context was the Union of American Hebrew Congregations' decision in 1985 to support the establishment of Reform Jewish day schools. Earlier debates over this subject, beginning in 1969, had produced no such support. But despite vehement opposition and a relatively close vote, the 1985 motion carried. As of early 1986, there were ten day schools under

---

[84]Simeon Maslin, ed., *Gates of Mitzvah*, pp. 3–5, 40. It is noteworthy that the term "*mitzvah*" does not appear in the Centenary Perspective; the operative term there is "obligation."

[85]Norman Mirsky, "Nathan Glazer's *American Judaism* After 30 Years: A Reform Opinion," *American Jewish History*, Dec. 1987, pp. 237–38.

[86]Ibid., p. 241; Polish, "The Changing and the Constant," p. 330. On the dissatisfaction of some Reform rabbis with the Bar and Bat Mitzvah, due to the deleterious impact upon Sabbath-morning attendance, see Herman Snyder, "Is Bar-Bat Mitzvah Destroying Attendance at Synagogue Service?" *Journal of Reform Judaism*, Winter 1980, pp. 9–12.

Reform auspices in North America.[87] The creation of day schools by a movement that had long emphasized universal concerns and steadfastly supported public education represented a significant turn toward Jewish particularism.

These steps toward greater traditionalism within Reform have been counterbalanced by several radical departures from earlier Jewish practice. The first such departure came in response to the feminist movement. In the late 1960s, HUC began to enroll women in its rabbinic program, a decision that had already been sanctioned by the CCAR in 1922 but had never been acted upon until the women's movement spurred an interest in the matter. In 1972 Sally Priesand became the first woman to be ordained as a rabbi in North America. Since then, over 100 women have been ordained by HUC and other rabbinical seminaries in America.[88] HUC was first in investing women as cantors, beginning this in 1975. By the late 1980s the preponderant majority of students enrolled in the cantorial programs of the HUC were women.[89]

The openness of the Reform movement to women's participation is reflected in synagogue life as well. A survey of "Women in the Synagogue Today" conducted in 1975 found that virtually every Reform congregation included in the survey responded affirmatively when asked whether women participated in the following synagogue activities: being counted in a *minyan*, reading *haftarot*, opening the ark, having *aliyot* to the Torah, carrying a Torah on Simhat Torah, giving a sermon, chanting the service, and chanting *kiddush* and *havdalah*. Interestingly, a major variable determining the openness of Reform temples to women's participation was its age: "The classical Reform synagogues, which are older, allowed little nonrabbinical participation of any type. The rabbi . . . controlled the service. . . . However, the newer congregations, in moving back toward tradition, have reinstituted Sabbath morning services, including reading from the Torah, thus encouraging more participation by members in general. A by-product of these old-new forms is the availability of honors in the Torah service to women."[90]

A second area of radical departure for Reform was the decision to welcome homosexual congregations into the Union of American Hebrew Congregations. The issue first arose in the early 1970s, when Jewish homosexuals began to form synagogues in a number of localities across the nation. The head of the UAHC, Rabbi Alexander Schindler, turned for a

---

[87]Michael Zeldin, "Beyond the Day School Debate," *Reform Judaism*, Spring 1986, pp. 10–11.
[88]Raphael, *Profiles in American Judaism*, p. 69.
[89]Laurie S. Senz, "The New Cantors," *Reform Judaism*, Fall 1986, p. 18.
[90]Daniel Elazar and Rela Geffen Monson, "Women in the Synagogue Today," *Midstream*, Apr. 1981, pp. 25–26.

responsum to his colleague Solomon Freehof, the most respected adjudicator of Reform Jewish law. Freehof ruled that "homosexuality is deemed in Jewish law to be a sin. [But] . . . it would be in direct contravention to Jewish law to keep sinners out of the congregation. To isolate them into a separate congregation and thus increase their mutual availability is certainly wrong." Despite this ruling against the creation of separate congregations for homosexuals, a number of Reform rabbis encouraged the formation of homosexual congregations by offering their facilities for religious services.[91] In 1977 the UAHC resolved to support and welcome homosexual congregations as affiliates; in subsequent resolutions it urged the inclusion of homosexuals in all aspects of congregational life.[92]

Perhaps the most radical departures of the Reform movement in the realm of practice have come in response to the issue of mixed marriage. Reform's preoccupation with this matter stems largely from the high rate of intermarriage among its congregants. In addition, the movement has deliberately decided to recruit new members from mixed-married couples in the Jewish community. Reform leaders openly declare that as a result of these two trends, within the next few decades over half the families in some Reform temples will consist of intermarried couples and their children.[93]

To deal with the rising tide of mixed marriage, Reform temples have instituted programs to smooth the transition of non-Jews into the Reform community. Some congregations sponsor support groups for mixed-married couples; others permit such couples to become members, but limit the participation of the non-Jewish spouse;[94] and still others permit mixed-married couples to participate in the full range of ritual activities, including being called to the Torah together.[95] Moreover, a very large percentage of Reform rabbis—one survey put the figure at 50 percent—officiate at mixed marriages.[96] Still, such openness has not prevented the Reform movement

---

[91]See the symposium on "Judaism and Homosexuality" in *CCAR Journal*, Summer 1973, especially p. 33, on Freehof's decision, and pp. 33–41, on the founding of Beth Chayim Chadashim at the Leo Baeck Temple in Los Angeles.
[92]John Hirsch, "Don't Ghettoize Gays," *Reform Judaism*, Spring 1988, p. 15.
[93]See Mark L. Winer, "Jewish Demography and the Challenges to Reform Jewry," *Journal of Reform Judaism*, Winter 1984, p. 9.
[94]See Melanie W. Aron and David Jeremy Zucker, "The Structure, Function, and Organization of a Mixed Marriage Support System," *Journal of Reform Judaism*, Summer 1984, pp. 16–24.
[95]See Joseph A. Edelheit and Arthur Meth, "Accepting Non-Jews as Members of Synagogues," *Journal of Reform Judaism*, Summer 1980, pp. 87–92.
[96]Hershel Shanks, "Rabbis Who Perform Intermarriages," *Moment*, Jan./Feb. 1988, p. 14, reports on a survey taken by Rabbi Irwin Fishbein. See also the "Forum" section of the magazine's June 1988 issue for a discussion of the survey's reliability, as well as the letter of Rabbi David Ostrich which suggests that rabbinical students at HUC now overwhelmingly opt to officiate at mixed marriages, for "not to officiate would render the rabbi left out of the life of the congregation."

from emphasizing conversion to Judaism. When the rate of intermarriage began to rise in the 1960s, Reform established conversion programs that enrolled thousands of students.[97] By the early 1980s the movement announced an active outreach program aimed at all non-Jewish spouses married to Jews.

It was in the context of mixed marriage that the CCAR voted at its annual convention in 1983 to redefine Jewish identity. Rabbinic law defines a Jew as someone born to a Jewish mother or someone who has undergone conversion. In its 1983 ruling, the CCAR created new criteria to define Jewishness: that a child has at least one Jewish parent; and that the child's acceptance of Jewish identity be "established through appropriate and timely public and formal acts of identification with the Jewish faith and people."[98] Interestingly, Jewish identity is no longer automatic even if one is born to a Jewish mother, but now involves some unspecified test of creed as well. In the debate over the resolution, key supporters, such as Rabbi Alexander Schindler, argued that the resolution merely made explicit practices that had long existed on a *de facto* basis in the Reform movement; that it ameliorated the condition of Jewish fathers who wished to raise their children as Jewish; and that it continued the process of equalizing the status of males and females, since it avoided giving preferential treatment to either Jewish mothers or fathers. Opponents of the resolution maintained that the new definition would turn the Reform movement into a sect, with offspring who would not be acceptable as marriage partners for other Jews. Moreover, they feared that passage would lead to further attacks on the status of Reform in Israel.[99]

The decision on patrilineal descent and the other issues discussed here have evoked comparatively little debate within the Reform movement. Most Reform rabbis subscribe to these positions, and even more important, the Reform laity assents to them. Thus, when asked if a rabbi should officiate at a marriage only if both partners are Jewish, fewer than half the leaders of Reform temples agreed;[100] presumably, even fewer of the rank and file would agree. The decision on patrilineality has heightened tensions between the Reform movement and the other denominations, but it appears to reflect a consensus within the Reform movement itself.[101]

---

[97]*JTA Community News Reports*, July 25, 1969, reports on the School for Converts sponsored by the UAHC.
[98]For the complete text of the "Report of the Committee on Patrilineal Descent on the Status of Children of Mixed Marriages," see *American Reform Responsa: Collected Responsa of the CCAR, 1889-1983*, ed. Walter Jacob (New York, 1983), pp. 546-50.
[99]On the debate over patrilineal descent, see the CCAR *Yearbook*, 1983, pp. 144-60.
[100]Winer et al., *Leaders of Reform Judaism*, p. 55.
[101]This is not to suggest that all decisions are supported unanimously. For a particularly hard-hitting critique of recent Reform decisions, see Jakob Petuchowski, "Reform Judaism's

In the past two decades Reform has transformed itself from an insecure movement, uncertain of its agenda and viability, into a self-assured movement convinced that it "represents for most Jews the authentically American expression of Judaism."[102] Under a new generation of leaders who assumed executive office since the late 1960s, including Alexander Schindler of the UAHC, Joseph Glaser of the CCAR, and Alfred Gottschalk of HUC, Reform has charted a new course.[103] It has revamped its ideology and practice to broaden its appeal to sectors of the Jewish community that had often felt alienated from Jewish life—feminist women, mixed-married couples, homosexuals, as well as Jews in the other denominations who wish to exercise free choice in defining their Jewish commitments. Reform today is inclusive, reintroducing old practices while instituting new ones. Based on such an appealing program, the movement is confident that it will "harvest the demographic trends [within American Jewry] to its own benefit."[104] In their more expansive moods, some leaders express in public their belief that Reform will one day become *the* Judaism of all non-Orthodox Jews in America, encompassing liberal Jews ranging from classical Reformers to Reconstructionists to Conservative Jews.[105]

Demographic studies suggest that Reform's strategy has already begun to yield results. The movement is growing more rapidly than any other and at the expense of its competitors. It is too early to assess the long-term consequences of present trends within Reform, but no one can gainsay that it has reformed itself considerably in recent decades.

## DENOMINATIONAL LIFE: ORTHODOX JUDAISM

During the past quarter century, two major trends have marked the development of Orthodox Judaism in America. First, Orthodoxy has achieved an unprecedented degree of respectability in the eyes of both non-Orthodox Jews and non-Jews. Where once Orthodox Judaism had been written off as a movement of immigrants and poor Jews, it is now regarded

---

Diminishing Boundaries: The Grin That Remained," *Journal of Reform Judaism*, Fall 1986, pp. 15–24.

[102]Winer, "Jewish Demography," p. 14.

[103]On the emergence of the new leaders and the considerable controversy surrounding their appointments, see Eugene Borowitz, "Reform Judaism's Coming Power Struggle," *Sh'ma*, Mar. 19, 1971, pp. 75–78, and Mark Winer, "The Crisis in the Reform Movement," *Response*, Fall 1971, pp. 112–120.

[104]Winer, "Jewish Demography," p. 25.

[105]For evidence of this triumphalism, see Alexander Schindler, "Remarks by the President of the UAHC," CCAR *Yearbook*, 1982, p. 63. "Orthodoxy's mass strength was easily confined to the first generation of American Jews, and Conservative Judaism gives evidence of being essentially a second generation phenomenon. The future belongs to us."

as a denomination with staying power and appeal to Jews from across the religious spectrum. As sociologist Charles Liebman has noted, "This is the first generation in over 200 years—that is, since its formulation as the effort by traditional Judaism to confront modernity—in which Orthodoxy is not in decline."[106] Even though Orthodoxy is not growing numerically, its comparative stability, particularly as measured by the ability to inculcate a strong sense of allegiance among its young, has given the movement significant credibility and dynamism. Indeed, the movement's programs, particularly with regard to youth, are being increasingly imitated by the other denominations.

The second trend that characterizes Orthodoxy is the shift to the right in the thinking and behavior of Orthodox Jews. Orthodox Jews today observe ritual commandments more punctiliously than at midcentury; they regard rabbinic authorities who adjudicate Jewish law in a conservative manner with more favor than they do more liberal rabbis; and in their attitudes toward non-Orthodox Jews they tend to be more exclusivist than before. Both the emergence of a stronger Orthodoxy and the movement's shift to the right have reshaped relations between Orthodox and non-Orthodox Jews.

## Problems of Definition

Considerable difficulties inhere in any discussion of the Orthodox world. Like their counterparts in other religious movements, Orthodox Jews do not share a single articulated theology, let alone movement ideology. Where Orthodoxy differs, however, is in the degree of intolerance displayed by different sectors of the same movement toward each other. This is evident in the expressions of dismay that modern Orthodox Jews voice about "the black hats"—more right-wing Orthodox types[107] —moving into their neighborhoods.[108] Right-wing Orthodox rabbis often seek to delegitimate their more moderate Orthodox counterparts,[109] while the right-wing Orthodox

---

[106]Charles S. Liebman, "Orthodoxy Faces Modernity," *Orim*, Spring 1987, p. 13.

[107]The term "right-wing Orthodox," despite its problematic nature, is used in the present discussion because it is common parlance. The category roughly approximates the "sectarian Orthodox" identified by Liebman, the "traditionalist Orthodox" identified by Heilman and Cohen, and the "strictly-Orthodox" and "ultra-Orthodox" identified by Helmreich. See the discussion that follows.

[108]For an interesting account of such fears in one modern Orthodox community, see Edward S. Shapiro, "Orthodoxy in Pleasantdale," *Judaism*, Spring 1985, p. 170.

[109]See, for example, the views of Rabbi Moses Feinstein, who differentiated between *shomrei mitzvot*, observers of the commandments, and the community of "God-fearers," sectarians; and Ira Robinson, "Because of Our Many Sins: The Contemporary Jewish World as Reflected in the Responsa of Moses Feinstein," *Judaism*, Winter 1986, pp. 38–39.

press reserves its greatest scorn for the policies of moderate Orthodox groups.[110] Even on the Orthodox right, different Hassidic groups have battled with each other. The student of Orthodoxy is thus faced with the question of whether Orthodoxy can truly be viewed as a coherent and united movement.

Further, Orthodoxy is institutionally fragmented in a manner not paralleled within the other movements. Whereas Reform, Reconstructionist, and Conservative Judaism have within them a single organization of congregations, a single rabbinic organization, and a single institution for the training of rabbis, Orthodoxy has a multiplicity of organizations for each of these purposes.[111] Such institutional diffusion has apparently not hindered Orthodoxy but has created difficulties for the students of Orthodox life—particularly in determining who speaks for Orthodoxy. There are many conflicting voices.

The whole issue of authority is more complicated in Orthodoxy than in the other denominations. In some ways, Orthodox Jews are the most likely to accept the opinion of a rabbi as authoritative on matters pertaining to Jewish living. Indeed, some Orthodox Jews go so far as having their rabbis decide for them sensitive financial and professional matters, and even personal family questions, such as whom to marry and how many children to bring into the world. At the same time, Orthodox synagogues are less dependent on a rabbinic elite to guide their fortunes than are those of other denominations. Pulpit rabbis have less status in the Orthodox world than in any other segment of the Jewish community, and most Orthodox institutions rely heavily on lay rather than rabbinic leadership.

Sociologists have attempted to identify the major groupings within Orthodoxy by using various analytic schema. In a pioneering study published in the *American Jewish Year Book* 20 years ago, Charles Liebman differentiated between the "uncommitted Orthodox," the "modern Orthodox," and the "sectarian Orthodox."[112] The first were either East European immi-

---

[110]The most important English-language periodical of the Orthodox right is the *Jewish Observer*, which espouses the views of Agudath Israel. Its approach has been characterized by one modern Orthodox writer as one of "unrelieved negativism. Rather than articulating its own positive approach to issues, it is in most instances content merely to inveigh against positions adopted by others." David Singer, "Voices of Orthodoxy," *Commentary*, July 1974, p. 59.

[111]Orthodox rabbinic organizations include the Rabbinical Council of America, Agudath HaRabbonim, the Rabbinical Alliance of America, Agudath Ha'Admorim, and Hitachduth HaRabbonim HaHaredim. (See Raphael, *Profiles in American Judaism*, p. 155.) Among synagogue bodies there are the Union of Orthodox Jewish Congregations of America and the National Council of Young Israel. On the various rabbinical seminaries, aside from Yeshiva University's Rabbi Isaac Elchanan Theological Seminary, see William Helmreich, *The World of the Yeshiva: An Intimate Portrait of Orthodox Jewry* (New York, 1982).

[112]Liebman, "Orthodoxy in American Jewish Life," pp. 21–98.

grants who, out of inertia rather than religious choice, identified as Orthodox, or individuals who had no particular commitment to Jewish law but preferred to pray in an Orthodox synagogue. The modern Orthodox "seek to demonstrate the viability of the Halakhah for contemporary life . . . [and also] emphasize what they have in common with all other Jews rather than what separates them." The sectarians are disciples of either *roshei yeshivah* (heads of yeshivahs) or Hassidic rebbes, whose strategy it is to isolate their followers from non-Orthodox influences.

In contrast to Liebman's ideological scheme, sociologist William Helmreich utilizes behavioral measures to differentiate sectors of the Orthodox world.[113] Helmreich describes three separate groups—the "ultra-Orthodox," by which he means primarily Hassidic Jews; the "strictly Orthodox," referring to the products of Lithuanian-type yeshivahs transplanted in America; and the "modern Orthodox," by which he means Jews who look to Yeshiva University and its rabbinic alumni for leadership. Each group has its own norms of behavior, particularly with regard to secular education for children, the interaction between men and women, and even the garb they wear—e.g., the knitted *kippah*, the black velvet yarmulke, or the Hassidic *streimel*. Helmreich's contribution is to draw attention to the "yeshivah world" of the strictly Orthodox, a world that, as we will see, is transforming American Orthodoxy.

In a forthcoming study, sociologists Samuel Heilman and Steven M. Cohen speak of the "nominal Orthodox," the "centrist Orthodox," and the "traditionalist Orthodox."[114] The authors claim that Orthodox Jews, regardless of where they are situated on the religious spectrum, share with each other a high degree of similarity in what they regard as required ritual observances, belief in God and divine revelation, disagreement with potentially heretical ideas, feelings of bonding with other Orthodox Jews, and political conservatism on specific issues; in all of these areas, Orthodox Jews have more in common with each other than with non-Orthodox Jews. While the present essay will take note of the severe strains within the Orthodox movement, it does accept the premise that there are important religious beliefs and behaviors that unite Orthodox Jews and set them apart from non-Orthodox Jews.

## Orthodoxy's Newfound Confidence

All of the major groupings within the Orthodox camp have participated in an unprecedented revival during the past two decades. This revival may

---

[113]Helmreich, *World of the Yeshiva*, pp. 52–54.
[114]Samuel C. Heilman and Steven M. Cohen, *Cosmopolitans and Parochials: Modern Orthodox Jews in America*, forthcoming.

be measured in the following changes: Orthodox Jews have entered the public arena confident that a display of distinctive religious behavior will not hamper their economic and social mobility. Whereas at midcentury Orthodox Jews who wished to advance in non-Jewish environments believed it necessary to blend in, by the 1970s and 1980s male Orthodox students and professionals had taken to wearing yarmulkes on university campuses, in law offices, and on hospital wards, and in some cases, even in state and municipal legislatures. (Their female counterparts also may be identified by distinctive, though less obtrusive, items of dress, such as the modest garb of some Orthodox women and special hair coverings.) Orthodox Jews in recent decades have also demanded of their employers the right to leave their jobs early on Friday afternoons when the Sabbath begins early, as well as the right to absent themselves on religious holidays. In fact, a legal defense agency, the Commission on Law and Public Action (COLPA) was founded by Orthodox attorneys precisely to pressure employers to comply with the needs of Orthodox employees. It is now assumed by Orthodox Jews that observance of Jewish traditions ought not to limit one's professional opportunities.[115]

Orthodox Jews actively engage in the political process to further their own aims. In this regard, the most right-wing groups have been especially adept at taking advantage of political opportunities. It has now become routine in New York politics for local and even national politicians to pay court to Hassidic rabbis. What is less well known is the sophisticated lobbying effort that won for Hassidic groups the status of a "disadvantaged group," with entitlement to special federal funds.[116] It is symptomatic of Orthodoxy's political activism and self-assertion that in 1988 eight Orthodox groups banded together to form the Orthodox Jewish Political Coalition to lobby in Washington, D.C.[117]

Orthodox groups have taken advantage of new technologies to facilitate religious observance. The revolution in food manufacturing and the proliferation of food products have made it possible for Orthodox Jews to arrange for extensive kosher certification, a stamp of approval that many manufacturers regard as a means of increasing their market share among observant Jews, and even among non-Jews who deem such certification as evidence of a product's high quality. According to one report, there were 16,000 products with kosher certification in the late 1980s, compared with only 1,000 a decade earlier.[118] Advances in food technology have also made it

---

[115]See Natalie Gittelson, "American Jews Rediscover Orthodoxy," *New York Times Magazine*, Sept. 30, 1984, p. 41ff.
[116]*New York Times*, June 29, 1984, p. B5.
[117]*Jewish Journal* (New York), Mar. 11, 1988, p. 4.
[118]Joan Nathan, "Kosher Goes Mainstream," *New York Times*, Sept. 7, 1988, p. C1.

possible to produce new kinds of kosher products: frozen *hallah* dough, ersatz crab meat, *parve* ice cream and cheesecake, and high quality kosher wines. Technology has also been harnessed to create a new institution in American Jewish life—"the *eruv* community."[119] Beginning in the 1970s, dozens of Orthodox synagogues made use of the utility wiring around their geographic enclaves to create domains in which carrying items and pushing strollers are permissible on the Sabbath. There is no doubt that by making religious observance easier, the *"eruv* community" and the broad array of kosher products have rendered Orthodoxy that much more attractive.

Orthodox Jews have also employed new media technologies to disseminate Orthodoxy. One of the first Jewish groups to utilize cable television was the Lubavitch movement, which televises the speeches of its "rebbe," Rabbi Menachem M. Schneerson, from Lubavitch headquarters in Crown Heights, Brooklyn, throughout the world. The Lubavitch movement also publishes *Moshiach Times: The Magazine for Children,* in comic-book format.[120] More significantly, Orthodox publishing houses have produced a vast array of religious literature. Mesorah Publications, with its Artscroll series, is arguably the largest publisher of Jewish books in the world today.[121] Beginning with its first volume, *The Megillah: The Book of Esther*, and continuing with its *Complete Siddur* and High Holy Day prayer book, many of the books published by this private firm have sold over 100,000 copies. Significantly, this publishing house is identified with right-wing Orthodoxy. Its Bible commentaries and volumes on Jewish history give no credence to modern, critical scholarship.[122] Nonetheless, the Artscroll volumes, according to the firm's publisher, are purchased by readers spanning the spectrum from "Kollel families" to "Conservodox."[123]

Orthodox Jews have become so certain that their version of Judaism is the only correct one and the only avenue for Jewish survival that they have launched programs to help other Jews to "return" to Judaism, i.e., become Orthodox Jews. The pioneers in this endeavor have been Lubavitch Hassidim who, with much coverage in the general media, launched their "mitz-

---

[119]On the rise of this phenomenon, see Raphael, *Profiles in American Judaism*, p. 170. For a report on one such community, see the *Jewish Observer*, Sept. 1983, p. 37.

[120]See, for example, Joe Kubert's cartoon strip entitled "An Act of Resistance," *Moshiach Times*, Sept. 1985, pp. 12–13. On "Dial-A-Shiur" and Jewish cable television programs featuring study, see the advertisements in *Good Fortune: The Magazine About Jewish Personalities*, Jan.-Feb. and Mar. 1988.

[121]Barbara Sofer, "Bringing Artscroll to Israel," *Good Fortune: The Magazine About Jewish Personalities*, Apr. 1987, p. 13.

[122]On the scholarly perspective of Artscroll publications, see B. Barry Levy, "Artscroll: An Overview," in *Approaches to Modern Judaism* I (Chico, Calif., 1983), pp. 111–40.

[123]On the audience for Artscroll books, see Sofer, "Bringing Artscroll to Israel," pp. 13–14.

vah mobiles" in the early 1970s.[124] Stationing themselves in public areas and on university campuses in boldly marked trucks, they approached non-Orthodox Jews with the avowed purpose of convincing them to increase their levels of religious observance. As the Lubavitch movement and other Orthodox groups succeeded in wooing Jews from non-Orthodox backgrounds to their way of life, the organized Jewish community took note, particularly the non-Orthodox movements that sustained "defections." It is hard to gauge exactly how many non-Orthodox Jews have turned to Orthodoxy as so-called *ba'alei teshuvah* (literally, "those who have returned"). According to Herbert Danziger, an authority on the phenomenon, the number is significant, with the *ba'alei teshuvah* transforming Orthodoxy into a movement of choice rather than of birth.[125] It is too early to assess the long-term impact of *ba'alei teshuvah* on the Orthodox world. In the short term, however, the very phenomenon of nonobservant Jews turning to Orthodoxy has raised the movement's self-esteem and increased its prestige within the broader American Jewish community.

To a greater extent than any other denomination, Orthodoxy has been able to project itself as a movement attractive to young people. On an average Sabbath, many Orthodox synagogues are teeming with young parents and their children. At community parades and other public displays, Orthodox groups marshal vast numbers of youth. In general, Orthodox day schools, youth groups, and summer camps exude a sense of youthful vitality. The success of these programs is set into bold relief by the perception of many in other Jewish religious movements that their own youth are not sufficiently integrated into Jewish communal actitivities.

Orthodox Jews have assumed positions of power and influence in the organized Jewish community in an unprecedented manner. Within the past decade and a half, individual Orthodox Jews have risen to leading administrative posts in the Council of Jewish Federations, the American Jewish Committee, the American Jewish Congress, the Conference of Presidents of Major Jewish Organizations, the World Jewish Congress, and a range of local federations and other Jewish agencies. Their presence is symptomatic of a shift in priorities of these organizations to what are "survivalist" issues, rather than the traditional "integrationist" agendas. In turn, these officials have further spurred organizations to rethink their priorities. By insisting on assuming their rightful place within organized Jewish life, Orthodox Jews as individuals have also moved organizations to meet the minimal

---

[124]"Are You a Jew," *Time*, Sept. 2, 1974, pp. 56–57; "Jewish Tanks," *Newsweek*, July 15, 1974, p. 77.

[125]See M. Herbert Danziger, *Returning to Orthodox Judaism: The Contemporary Revival in America and Israel*, forthcoming.

religious needs of observant Jews: providing kosher food at Jewish communal events; not conducting business on the Sabbath or religious holidays; and providing the opportunity for public prayer.[126]

Orthodoxy has been the beneficiary of much media coverage and has learned to encourage and shape it in a positive direction. Unlike earlier coverage of some Hassidic groups in the general American press, which focused on their exoticism, more recent reporting has emphasized the warm communal spirit and decent values promoted by the Orthodox world. Jewish writers of a non-Orthodox outlook, often themselves searching for rootedness and meaning, have rhapsodized over the world of Orthodoxy. And the Orthodox, in turn, have cooperated in such ventures. It was a telling sign of the new perspective that a non-Orthodox Jewish woman on the staff of the *New Yorker* magazine was given entrée to the Lubavitch community of Crown Heights, to carry out research for a series of articles. Not only could her positive portrait not have been published in such a periodical earlier in the century, but it is doubtful that an Orthodox group would have been receptive to such an inquiry, let alone to a woman reporter, in a previous period.[127] Positive media coverage of this sort provides further evidence of Orthodoxy's new respectability, and in turn adds to the movement's self-confidence.

## Why the Revival?

How do we account for Orthodoxy's impressive rebound in recent decades? What factors prompted the emergence of programs for Orthodox revitalization? And why do they seem to succeed?

Perhaps the key to Orthodox success has been its educational institutions. As noted above, Orthodoxy began to invest heavily in all-day religious

---

[126]On the appropriation of traditional rituals within the federation world, see Jonathan Woocher, *Sacred Survival: The Civil Religion of American Jews* (Bloomington, Ind., 1986), p. 153. The battle to introduce religious observances into Jewish public life was not monopolized by Orthodox Jews; Conservative rabbis often played a pioneering, though unheralded, role. See Wolfe Kelman, "Defeatism, Triumphalism, or Gevurah?" *Proceedings of the Rabbinical Assembly*, 1980, p. 20.

[127]For examples of earlier reports emphasizing the exotic world of Hassidic communities, see Harvey Arden and Nathan Benn, "The Pious Ones," *National Geographic*, Aug. 1975, p. 276ff., which explores "the closed world of Brooklyn's Hassidic Jews—a bit of old Hungary transplanted to a tenement neighborhood in America's largest city." See also Ray Schultz, "The Call of the Ghetto," *New York Times*, Nov. 10, 1974. For a very different kind of reportage, see Lis Harris, *Holy Days: The World of a Hassidic Family* (New York, 1985), which originally appeared in three installments in the *New Yorker*.

For other examples of media attention to the Orthodox world, see Dorit Phyllis Gary, "The Chosen," *New York Magazine*, June 28, 1982, pp. 24–31; and Jan Hoffman, "Back to Shul: The Return of Wandering Jews," *Village Voice*, Apr. 21, 1987, p. 13ff.

schools at midcentury. In 1940 there were only 35 Jewish day schools in America, scattered in seven different communities, but principally located in the metropolitan New York area. Within the next five years the number doubled, and day schools could now be found in 31 communities. The postwar era witnessed an even more impressive surge, so that by 1975 there was a total of 425 Orthodox day schools, including 138 high schools, with a total enrollment of 82,200. It is estimated that by the 1980s approximately 80 percent of all Orthodox children were enrolled in day schools.[128]

Day schools serve the Orthodox community as the key instrument for formal education and socialization. With at least half of each day devoted to Jewish studies, day schools have the luxury of teaching students language skills necessary for Hebrew prayer and the study of Jewish texts in their original Hebrew or Aramaic, as well as ample time to impart information on the proper observance of rituals. Equally important, day schools provide an environment for building a strong attachment to the Orthodox group: they prescribe proper religious behavior and impart strong ideological indoctrination; and they create an all-encompassing social environment where lifelong friendships are made. According to one study of a leading Orthodox day school, even students from non-Orthodox homes developed a strong allegiance to Orthodoxy due to their ongoing exposure to the school's programs. Moreover, the majority of students were as religiously observant or even more observant than their parents.[129] At midcentury, the proliferation of day schools was creating a quiet revolution that few contemporaries noticed. By the 1970s and 1980s, Orthodoxy began to reap the benefits of its educational investments.[130]

Complementing the day-school movement is a series of other institutions designed to socialize the younger generation of Orthodox Jews. Orthodox synagogues of various stripes have introduced separate religious services for the young people as well as a range of social, educational, and recreational programs to provide an Orthodox environment while the youth are not in school. In addition, Orthodox groups have invested heavily in summer camps, which provide an all-embracing Orthodox experience during vaca-

---

[128]For data on the proliferation of day schools and the rise in enrollments, see Egon Mayer and Chaim Waxman, "Modern Jewish Orthodoxy in America: Toward the Year 2000," *Tradition*, Spring 1977, pp. 99–100. For more recent estimates, see Alvin I. Schiff, "The Centrist Torah Educator Faces Critical Ideological and Communal Challenges," *Tradition*, Winter 1981, pp. 278–79.

[129]Joseph Heimowitz, "A Study of the Graduates of the Yeshiva of Flatbush High School" (unpublished diss., Yeshiva University, 1979), pp. 102–03.

[130]Two surveys illustrating higher levels of education and observance among younger Orthodox Jews are: Egon Mayer, "Gaps Between Generations of Orthodox Jews in Boro Park, Brooklyn, N.Y.," *Jewish Social Studies*, Spring 1977, p. 99, and Heilman and Cohen, *Cosmopolitans and Parochials*, chap. 5.

tion months. Beyond that, it has become the norm for Orthodox teenagers to spend some time in Israel, again in an Orthodox ambience.

A second factor in the revitalization of Orthodoxy was the participation of Orthodox Jews in the postwar economic boom that brought unparalleled affluence to Americans in general. Like their counterparts in the other denominations, Orthodox Jews in increasing numbers acquired college and graduate degrees and entered the professions. These occupations freed Jews from the need to work on the Sabbath, thereby eliminating a conflict between economic necessity and religious observance that had bedeviled traditionally minded Jews in earlier periods. Thanks to their newfound affluence, Orthodox Jews could afford to send their offspring to day schools, from kindergarten through high school, and to pay for summer camps and trips to Israel for their children. In general, Orthodox Jews were now able to partake fully of American life even while adhering to traditional observances. The link between religious traditionalism and poverty and the backward ways of the Old World had been broken.[131]

An important consequence of this new affluence has been the ability of Orthodox Jews to insulate themselves more effectively from the rest of the Jewish community. With their host of synagogues, day schools, recreational programs, restaurants, summer camps, and the like, Orthodox Jews, in their largest centers of concentration, can live in separate communities that rarely interact with the larger Jewish populace. Even within the structures of existing communities, Orthodox Jews have obtained the right to separate programs geared to their own needs, or Jewish communal organizations tacitly set aside special resources for the sole use of Orthodox Jews.[132] Living in separate communities that insulate them from the larger Jewish community has helped to foster an élan among Orthodox Jews and a belief, particularly conveyed to the young, that the Orthodox community constitutes the saving remnant of American Judaism.

A series of developments in the broader American society has also given an important boost to Orthodoxy. Particularly during the 1960s and early 1970s, when experimentation and rebellion appeared to be the order of the day, those who were repelled by the new social mores found solace in the

---

[131]Charles Liebman noted this shift in the economic status of Orthodox Jews already in the mid-1960s ("Changing Social Characteristics of Orthodox, Conservative and Reform Jews," *Sociological Analysis*, Winter 1966, pp. 210–22). See also Bertram Leff's study of the occupational distribution of Young Israel members, cited in Gershon Kranzler, "The Changing Orthodox Jewish Community," *Tradition*, Fall 1976, p. 72, note 8; almost two-thirds of male members were professionals.

[132]In New York City, for example, Jewish Ys reserve special times for Orthodox Jews who require sex-segregated swimming. Other federation agencies sponsor special clinics and programs for Orthodox Jews, such as a program for developmentally handicapped Orthodox youth.

stability of Orthodoxy. More recently, the comparatively lower rates of divorce and substance abuse in the Orthodox grouping have encouraged many Jews to perceive Orthodox Judaism as a bulwark against social instability. At the same time, the openness of American culture has made it possible for Jews to identify with Orthodoxy without the need to defend their distinctive ways. As Charles Liebman has noted, "The very absence of rigid ideational and cultural structures which characterizes modernity, the undermining of overarching moral visions, and the celebration of plural beliefs and styles of life, invite culturally deviant movements."[133]

Finally, Orthodoxy has achieved increased stability in recent decades because it has policed its community more rigorously and has defined its boundaries ever more sharply. Where once a great range of behaviors was tolerated and the Orthodox movement contained a large population of nominal adherents, Orthodox Jews today are far less tolerant of deviance. Far more than any other movement in American Judaism, Orthodoxy—in its various permutations—has set limits and defined acceptable and nonacceptable behavior. This has a twofold psychological impact: first, it attracts individuals who want to be given explicit guidelines for proper behavior, rather than shoulder the burden of autonomy that is the lot of modern individuals; and second, it sharpens the group's boundaries, thereby providing adherents with a strong feeling of community and belonging.[134]

## *The Shift to the Right*

More rigorous self-policing is but one manifestation of Orthodoxy's shift to the right, a shift that is expressed in changed behavioral norms, political judgments, educational preferences, choice of leaders, and attitudes toward Western culture and non-Orthodox coreligionists. The move to the right has led the once distinctly modern Young Israel movement to move quite close to the strictly Orthodox Agudath Israel.[135] It has led to the veneration of yeshivah heads who seek to insulate their followers from Western modes of thought and torpedo efforts at cooperation between Orthodox and non-

---

[133] See Liebman, "Orthodoxy Faces Modernity," pp. 13–14.

[134] On the treatment of deviance within the Orthodox setting, see Egon Mayer, *From Suburb to Shtetl: The Jews of Boro Park* (New York, 1979), pp. 134–35; Helmreich, *World of the Yeshiva*, chap. 8; and Jeffrey Gurock, "The Orthodox Synagogue," in Wertheimer, ed., *The American Synagogue*, pp. 37–84.

[135] See, for example, Aaron Twerski's essay in the *Young Israel Viewpoint* denouncing the Denver conversion program (June 1985, p. 16). Note the broader observation of Gershon Kranzler that the Young Israel movement, which once supported religious Zionism, is now "solidly right-wing Agudah." ("The Changing Orthodox Synagogue," *Jewish Life*, Summer/Fall 1981, p. 50.)

Orthodox groups. And it has led to the demoralization of rabbis who formerly spoke for modern Orthodoxy.

Rabbi Walter Wurzburger has observed that "the mere fact that the term 'Modern Orthodoxy' is no longer in vogue and has been replaced by an expression ['Centrist Orthodoxy'] that deliberately avoids any reference to modernity speaks volumes."[136] Few Orthodox spokesmen any longer articulate the undergirding assumption of modern Orthodoxy, namely that a synthesis between traditional Judaism and modern Western culture is not only feasible but desirable.

The retreat from an ideology of synthesis is evident at what was formerly the fountainhead of modern Orthodoxy, Yeshiva University. The altered spirit was evident already by 1980, when the registrar of Yeshiva's Rabbi Isaac Elchanan Theological Seminary compared the present cohort of rabbinical students with their predecessors of the mid-1960s: "Things are entirely different . . . their whole outlook, sexual, religious, anti-college except in the narrowest, most utilitarian sense, is completely different from what it used to be. We have moved way to the right."[137] The shift is also apparent at Yeshiva College. In the mid-1980s the undergraduate student newspaper saw fit to publish a symposium on "Why Do [Yeshiva Men] Attend College?" As noted by the editor, this question should never have been raised at a college that had functioned for decades with the motto *Torah U'Mada* (Torah and Science), but "Yeshiva's motto does not offer a simple solution to this complex issue." In fact, one of the symposiasts, an American-trained talmudist, argued that "secular pursuits . . . for their own sake are dangerous on many grounds," particularly because they may not aid in "developing one's self Jewishly."[138] Thus, even within the walls of Yeshiva University, the insular views of the Orthodox right have made significant inroads.

The shift to the right is also evident in the declining authority of Yeshiva University's rabbinic alumni. *Tradition*, the journal established to represent the point of view of modern—now centrist—Orthodox rabbis, gives voice to a rabbinic establishment under siege from elements on the Orthodox right.[139] Virtually all contemporary *gedolim* (recognized rabbinic authori-

---

[136]Walter Wurzburger, "Centrist Orthodoxy—Ideology or Atmosphere," *Journal of Jewish Thought*, vol. 1, 1985, p. 67.

[137]The registrar is quoted by William Helmreich in a letter published in *Judaism*, Summer 1981, p. 380.

[138]Quoted in Jeffrey S. Gurock, *The Men and Women of Yeshiva: Higher Education, Orthodoxy, and American Judaism* (New York, 1988), pp. 254–55.

[139]Revealing evidence of a modern Orthodox rabbinate under siege is provided by the symposium on "The State of Orthodoxy" that appeared in *Tradition*, Spring 1982, pp. 3–83. The editor of the symposium, Walter Wurzburger, explicitly stated that "considerable segments of modern Orthodoxy are in retreat," and framed questions that underscored the

ties) identify with right-wing Orthodoxy and their views are rarely challenged.[140] Some insiders see this state of affairs as stemming from a failure to produce adjudicators of rabbinic law who have a modern Orthodox outlook.[141] Others feel that modern Orthodox leaders lack the charisma of the traditionalist *gedolim*, who are the products of the great European yeshivahs, and who appear uncompromised by any accommodation to modernity.[142] Yet others focus on ideology, noting the inability of modern Orthodox rabbis to confront the right and counter its message with a coherent program for modern Orthodox living.[143]

The weakness of the modern Orthodox rabbinate is tellingly revealed in its reliance on the Orthodox right for its official prayer book. The penultimate prayer book sponsored by the Rabbinical Council of America was translated and edited by David De Sola Pool, the spiritual leader of the Spanish Portuguese Synagogue in New York, and an exemplar of Americanized Orthodoxy. Its successor, the new authorized *siddur* of the RCA, is *The Complete Artscroll Siddur*, which in its original version explicitly traces its inspiration to rabbis associated with the rightist yeshivah world. For its edition of this *siddur* the RCA added only two modifications: a brief preface by Rabbi Saul Berman, in which he invokes "the Rov," Joseph B. Soleveitchik, the mentor of rabbis trained at Yeshiva University, and the insertion of the Prayer for the State of Israel, which the Artscroll editors had understandably omitted, given their non-Zionist ideology. There is no small irony in the fact that the RCA thus commissioned its opponents in the Orthodox world—traditionalists who do not accept the legitimacy of centrist Orthodox rabbis—to provide its official prayer book.[144]

The pulpit rabbis of centrist Orthodoxy face not only delegitimation but also a growing rate of attrition within their congregations. Younger members are increasingly attracted to small, informal synagogues (*shtieblach*) or

---

challenge he perceived: "How do you view the resurgence of right-wing Orthodoxy? Does it portend the eclipse of modern Orthodoxy? Do you regard modern Orthodoxy as a philosophy of compromise or an authentic version of Judaism?"

[140]David Singer, "Is Club Med Kosher? Reflections on Synthesis and Compartmentalization," *Tradition*, Fall 1985, p. 34.

[141]Bernard Rosensweig, "The Rabbinical Council of America: Retrospect and Prospect," *Tradition*, Summer 1986, pp. 8–10.

[142]On the charisma of noncompromisers, see Mayer and Waxman, "Modern Jewish Orthodoxy in America," pp. 109–10.

[143]See Joshua Berkowitz, "The Challenge to Modern Orthodoxy," *Judaism*, Winter 1984, pp. 101–06; and Shubert Spero, "A Movement in Search of Leaders," *Journal of Jewish Thought*, 1985, pp. 83–101.

[144]In the new RCA *siddur*, see especially p. xii for Berman's invocation of Soleveitchik and pp. 450–51 for the prayer for Israel. Other than these changes, the RCA *siddur* is identical to the *Complete Artscroll Siddur*; even the pagination has been retained by adding pp. 448a and 449b.

early services within established synagogues. In either event they separate themselves from the larger congregation. Writing in the mid-1970s, Rabbi Steven (Shlomo) Riskin, arguably the most charismatic figure in the modern Orthodox rabbinate, noted that inroads by Lubavitch and right-wing yeshivahs resulted in "the draw[ing] off from the modern Orthodox shul of many of the young yeshiva graduates, much to the chagrin of the local *Rav* [pulpit rabbi] who has tailored his sermons and rabbinic style to the tastes of the 'young people.'"[145]

Even within centrist Orthodox institutions, a palpable shift to the right is evident. One of the harbingers of change was the elimination of mixed social dancing at synagogue functions. Whereas in the mid-1950s it was commonplace for modern Orthodox synagogues, including Young Israel congregations, to hold square dances for their youth and social dancing at banquets, such activities are now banned by Orthodox synagogues.[146] Centrist Orthodox synagogues are also far more apt today to demand punctilious observance as a prerequisite for leadership within the congregation. There is also less tolerance today in Orthodox synagogues for members who are only nominally Orthodox. Not surprisingly, formerly modern Orthodox day schools are also moving to the right, as evidenced by curricular revisions that downgrade the study of Hebrew language and literature, as well as the erosion of coeducation. Whereas modern Orthodox day schools formerly separated the sexes around the age of puberty, they now are routinely separating boys and girls in the third and even lower grades. The new tenor is summed up in the somewhat self-mocking, somewhat bitter, joke about Orthodoxy's "Chumrah-of-the-Month Club," as growing numbers of Orthodox Jews accept the need for ever greater stringencies.[147]

## Why Is the Right Gaining Strength?

In light of the increased acculturation and upward mobility of Orthodox Jews, how is the move to the right to be explained? One would have expected that, as more Orthodox Jews attained a high level of secular education and entered the professions, they would move in the direction of "synthesis" rather than insularity. Why, then, has the Orthodox right made such deep inroads in the larger Orthodox community?

---

[145]Shlomo Riskin, "Where Orthodoxy Is At—And Where It Is Going," *Jewish Life*, Spring 1976, p. 27. See also Gershon Kranzler, "The Changing Orthodox Synagogue," *Jewish Life*, Fall 1981, pp. 43–51.

[146]Spero, "Orthodox Judaism," p. 89, describes the prevalence of mixed dancing. For a case study of one congregation, see Shapiro, "Orthodoxy in Pleasantdale," p. 169.

[147]The term appears in Silberman, *A Certain People*, p. 260. For a serious attempt to address the phenomenon, see Moshe Weinberger, "Keeping Up with the Katzes: The Chumra Syndrome—An Halachic Inquiry," *Jewish Action*, Rosh Hashana 1988, pp. 10–19.

A key factor, most certainly, is the day-school movement, which draws its personnel overwhelmingly from right-wing Orthodox circles. By contrast, few graduates of Yeshiva University's rabbinical program enter the relatively poorly paying field of Jewish education. As teachers of Jewish subjects in day schools, the products of the yeshivah world have imposed their worldview upon the schools and their youthful charges. They have made clear their distinct lack of enthusiasm for both secular education and the modern State of Israel, while arguing for the intense study of religious texts and punctilious halakhic observance.

A number of other factors have also facilitated Orthodoxy's move to the right. Within some sectors of the more acculturated Orthodox community, a kind of "discount theory of Judaism" prevails. This theory has been described by Lawrence Kaplan as follows: since " 'more is better'—for the children, that is ('they'll lose some of it later,' or so the theory goes)—it is the traditional Orthodox yeshivot which represent the 'more.' " Many highly acculturated Orthodox parents fear that their children will join the general slide into assimilation that characterizes so much of American Jewish life. They therefore expose their children in school to a Judaism that is far to the right of their own thinking in the hope that should their children move away from religious observance, they will end up at a position near modern Orthodoxy.[148]

Beyond these calculations, certain environmental factors have also favored the Orthodox right. One is the prosperity of Orthodox Jews, discussed above, which makes it possible for them to send their children to religious schools well into their college years. When Orthodox youth graduate from yeshivah high schools, their families can afford to send them to Israeli yeshivahs for further study—as a kind of finishing-school experience that is often located in an environment shaped by the attitudes of the Orthodox right. Then again, the waning decades of the 20th century have been a time of declining confidence in the viability of modern cultural norms. This mood has strengthened the hand of fundamentalists throughout the world, including traditionalists in the yeshivah world who reject the values of secular America. Finally, none of the communal circumstances that formerly put a brake on religious extremism in the European Jewish context any longer play a role in American Jewish life.[149] Orthodox halakhic authorities do not have to accommodate the broader needs of the Jewish community; on the contrary, they wish to segregate their followers from the non-Orthodox world.

---

[148]Lawrence Kaplan, letter, *Judaism*, Summer 1981, p. 382.
[149]See Charles Liebman, "Extremism as a Religious Norm," *Journal for the Scientific Study of Religion*, Mar. 1983, pp. 82–85.

## Responding to New Challenges

The consequences of Orthodoxy's shift to the right may be seen in the responses of centrist Orthodox rabbis to new challenges. One challenge was mounted from within by Orthodox women, members of centrist Orthodox synagogues who sought to reconcile their commitment to Orthodoxy with the new feminist consciousness of the 1970s and 1980s. Because they accepted the separation of men and women in their own synagogues, Orthodox women who wished to assume an active role in religious services founded a network of women's *tefillah* (prayer) groups in the 1970s. The new prayer circles took steps to avoid conflict with the larger Orthodox community: they scheduled services only once a month, so that members could continue to attend their own synagogues on three Sabbaths out of every four; they also omitted sections of the service that may only be recited by a quorum of men; and they eschewed using the term *minyan*, so as not to suggest that they were engaged in an activity reserved solely for men.[150]

With only a few exceptions, rabbis of centrist Orthodox synagogues responded negatively to these activities by their own female congregants.[151] As a consequence, the *tefillah* groups, for the most part, met in private homes. Moreover, when prayer groups did turn to rabbis for halakhic guidelines, they were rebuffed. As one of the leaders of the movement observed, this was one of the few times in Jewish history "that Jews turned to rabbis for halachic advice and were refused."[152]

Several years after the *tefillah* groups first appeared, the president of the Rabbinical Council of America brought the issue before a group of five talmudists at Yeshiva University, asking them for a legal responsum. The resulting one-page, undocumented statement prohibited women's prayer groups, ruling them a "total and apparent deviation from tradition." The statement added that "all these customs are coming from a movement for the emancipation of women, which in this area is only for licentiousness." The RCA, centrist Orthodoxy's rabbinic body, then approved the publication of the responsum, intending it as a "guideline" for Orthodox rabbis.[153]

There is no way to judge how such an issue would have been resolved in an earlier era in the history of American Orthodoxy. Women's prayer groups, after all, were responses to two new developments: the influence of the feminist movement of the late 1960s and 1970s on Orthodox women, and the coming of age of Orthodox women who had acquired a high level of literacy in Hebraica and Judaica in day schools. What is noteworthy,

---

[150]"Tsena-Rena," *Lilith*, no. 6, 1979, pp. 46–47.
[151]Ibid., and "Orthodox Women's Prayer Groups," *Lilith*, no. 14, Fall/Winter 1985, pp. 5–6.
[152]Rivkeh Haut, quoted in *Lilith*, no. 14, Fall/Winter 1985, p. 6.
[153]Ibid. See also the article by Hershel (Zvi) Schacter in *Beit Yitzhak*, vol. 17, 1985.

however, is the uncompromising stance adopted by centrist rabbis toward their own congregants. Rather than seeking a means to accommodate Orthodox feminists, or channel their energies productively, most rabbis in what was formerly the modern Orthodox rabbinate treated women's *tefillah* groups as deviant and undeserving of support, let alone a home in the Orthodox synagogue.

A similar hard-line stance has been taken toward challenges emanating from outside the Orthodox world. One symptom of this is the growing influence within the centrist Orthodox rabbinate of those who wish to follow the ruling issued in 1956 by yeshivah heads banning cooperation with non-Orthodox rabbis.[154] There is also a greater willingness on the part of Orthodox rabbis to express in public their disdain for the religious activities of Jews outside their camp. Already in the 1950s, Orthodox authorities had ruled that synagogues lacking a *mehitzah*, a barrier between men and women, were illegitimate,[155] and that marriages performed by Conservative and Reform rabbis were not religiously valid and therefore did not require a Jewish bill of divorce (*get*).[156] But in the 1980s, these decisions were openly proclaimed. Thus, the rightist Agudas Harabbonim began to place newspaper advertisements urging Jews to stay home on the High Holy Days rather than attend a non-Orthodox synagogue.[157] Moreover, in September 1988, the same organization announced a campaign to educate Jews that Reform Judaism "leads to mixed marriage" and Conservative Judaism is "even more harmful because it acts as a 'steppingstone' to Reform."[158]

This hardening of positions and shift to the right may be interpreted in two ways. It may be seen as a triumph of the elite religion of the yeshivah world over the folk religion that had previously been Americanized Orthodoxy.[159] The new elite Orthodoxy not only writes off non-Orthodox Jews who are unprepared to become *ba'alei teshuvah*,[160] but also insists that all

---

[154]Walter Wurzburger, "Orthodox Cooperation with Non-Orthodoxy," *Jewish Life*, Summer/Fall 1981, pp. 25–27, and press release, "Orthodoxy Should Follow a Policy of 'Creative Engagement' with Conservative and Reform Says President of RCA," May 20, 1987.

[155]For the unequivocal condemnation of non-*mehitzah* synagogues by Rabbi Joseph B. Soloveitchik, see the letters quoted in "A Call to 'Every Jew' and Some Responses," *Jewish Observer*, Jan. 1985, pp. 37–39.

[156]The ruling by Moses Feinstein, to the contrary, was intended as a leniency, so as to reduce the numbers of *mamzerim* whose parents had not properly divorced. See David Ellenson, "Representative Orthodox Responsa on Conversion and Intermarriage in the Contemporary Era," *Jewish Social Studies*, Summer/Fall 1985, pp. 215–18.

[157]Joseph Berger, "Split Widens on a Basic Issue: What Is a Jew?" *New York Times*, Feb. 28, 1986, p. 1.

[158]*Jewish Week* (New York), Sept. 20, 1988, p. 12.

[159]David Singer, "Thumbs and Eggs," *Moment*, Sept. 1978, p. 36.

[160]Note the observation of Norman Lamm, president of Yeshiva University: "Witness the readiness of our fellow Orthodox Jews to turn exclusivist, to the extent that psychologically,

compromises with modern culture are to be rejected as un-Jewish. The shift to the right may also be interpreted as a symptom of deep insecurity and retreat into insularity, of fear that the corrosiveness of modern American culture will eat away at the Orthodox population, just as it has sapped the non-Orthodox movements. Thus, even as it revels in the success of Orthodoxy, the *Young Israel Viewpoint* publishes an article entitled "Why Are Young Israel Children Going Astray?"[161] and the movement sponsors a symposium on "The Lifestyles of the Modern American Orthodox Jew— Halachic Hedonism?"[162]

## DENOMINATIONAL LIFE: CONSERVATIVE JUDAISM

Far more than the other denominations, Conservative Judaism has experienced severe turmoil, at times even demoralization, during the past quarter century. In part, this is the result of the letdown following the end of the Conservative movement's era of heady growth in the 1950s and 1960s. Equally important, Conservative Judaism has experienced turmoil because forces both within and outside the movement have confronted it with provocative new challenges. Conservatism had managed to paper over serious ideological differences within its ranks during the boom years, but by the late 1960s and early 1970s, internal dissent intensified and new alliances were being forged within the movement to press for change. With each step taken toward ideological and programmatic clarification, one faction or another of the Conservative coalition has felt betrayed.

In addition, Conservative Judaism's once enviable position at the center of the religious spectrum has turned to a liability as American Judaism has moved from an era of relative harmony to intense polarization. As the conflict between Reform on the left and Orthodoxy on the right has intensified, the Conservative movement, as the party of the center, has found itself caught in a cross fire between two increasingly antagonistic foes, and hard-pressed to justify its centrism. As Ismar Schorsch, chancellor of the Jewish Theological Seminary, has noted, the center "must produce an arsenal of arguments for use against both the left and right which, of necessity, often include ideas that are barely compatible."[163]

---

though certainly not halakhically, many of our people no longer regard non-Orthodox Jews as part of *Klal Yisrael*." See "Some Comments on Centrist Orthodoxy," *Tradition*, Fall 1986, p. 10.

[161]Reuven Fink, *Young Israel Viewpoint*, Sept. 1984, p. 24.

[162]Ibid., Sept./Oct. 1988, p. 20.

[163]Ismar Schorsch, "Zacharias Frankel and the European Origins of Conservative Judaism," *Judaism*, Summer 1981, p. 344.

## Strains in the Conservative Coalition

The Conservative movement has long been based on a divided coalition. Writing at midcentury, Marshall Sklare noted the gap between the masses of Conservative synagogue members and the rabbinic and lay elites of the movement.[164] Whereas the elites shared similar standards of religious practice and a common ideological commitment, the masses of synagogue members were unaware of Conservative ideology and often were only minimally observant. According to Sklare's analysis, "Conservativism represents a common pattern of acculturation—a kind of social adjustment—which has been arrived at by lay people. It is seen by them as a 'halfway house' between Reform and Orthodoxy."[165]

Even within the elite there was a considerable distance between the Seminary "schoolmen" and the rabbis in the field. As one of the rabbis bitterly put it: "Certain members of our faculty . . . have put us in shackles and in bonds . . . so that we cannot move. . . . [This] is humiliating to us. . . . [They] laugh at us as ignoramuses . . . [and imply] that we have been graduated as social workers and not as rabbis for humanity."[166] This statement draws attention to lack of empowerment and legitimacy accorded by the Seminary's faculty to its students during the first half of this century. But the gap within the Conservative elite also consisted of a tacit understanding concerning the division of labor within the movement. As Neil Gillman, a professor of theology at the Seminary observes:

> All of the groundbreaking Conservative responsa on synagogue practice [and] Sabbath observance . . . came out of the Rabbinical Assembly. . . . For its part, the Seminary Faculty remained within the walls of scholarship. It issued no responsa. If anything, it maintained a stance of almost explicit disdain toward all of this halakhic activity. . . . This relationship was actually a marriage of convenience. The Faculty could cling to its traditionalism, secure in the knowledge that the real problems were being handled elsewhere. The Rabbinical Assembly looked at its teachers as the hallmark of authenticity, holding the reins lest it go too far.[167]

The gap between the Seminary and the rabbinate was symbolized by the maintenance of separate seating in the Seminary's own synagogue until the 1980s, even as virtually every rabbi ordained by the institution served in a congregation that had instituted mixed seating of men and women.

By the late 1960s and early 1970s, the long-standing "discontinuities and

---

[164]Marshall Sklare, *Conservative Judaism: An American Religious Movement* (Glencoe, Ill., 1953), p. 229.
[165]Ibid., p. 229. See also Elliot N. Dorff, *Conservative Judaism: Our Ancestors to Our Descendants* (New York, 1977), especially pp. 110–57.
[166]Sklare, *Conservative Judaism*, p. 190.
[167]Neil Gillman, "Mordecai Kaplan and the Ideology of Conservative Judaism," *Proceedings of the Rabbinical Assembly* (hereafter "*RA*"), 1986, p. 64.

conflicts" within the Conservative movement, to use Sklare's formulation, had grown more aggravated. First, there was the gap between the rabbis and their congregants. This issue was directly confronted by Hershel Matt in the mid-1970s in a letter to his congregants explaining why, after 28 years in the rabbinate, he had decided to leave the pulpit: "The present reality is that affiliation with a congregation or even election to the Board or to committees does not require any commitment" to the primary purpose of a synagogue—"seeking to live in the holy dimension of Jewish life . . . trying to accept the obligation and joy of worshipping God, . . . trying to learn Torah from the rabbi."[168] A decade later, a younger colleague of Matt's, Shalom Lewis, published an essay describing the loneliness of the Conservative rabbi:

> The loneliness we suffer is not necessarily social but spiritual. We might bowl, swim, and *kibbitz* with the best of them, but we are still in another world entirely. We quote Heschel and no one understands. We perform *netilat yadayim* and our friends think we're rude when we are momentarily silent. . . . We walk home, alone, on Shabbos. I am blessed with a wonderful social community, but I have no spiritual community in which I have companions.[169]

Conservative rabbis have for decades bemoaned their inability to convince the masses of their congregants to live as observant Jews. In 1960, at a time of most rapid growth for the Conservative movement, Max Routtenberg noted the "mood and feeling among many of us that our achievements touch only the periphery of Jewish life and that our failures center around the issues that concern us most as rabbis and as Jews."[170] Almost two decades later, Stephen Lerner characterized the problem even more bluntly: "The major problem is that we have been or are becoming a clerical movement. We have no observant laity and even our lay leadership is becoming removed from the world of the traditional family."[171] In the intervening years, the journals and national conventions of the Conservative rabbinate repeatedly addressed this issue, and rabbis voiced their concern that the movement "had become less identifiable" and was in danger of "los[ing] its force and becom[ing] of less and less consequence on the American Jewish scene."[172] The mood in Conservatism was aptly captured by one rabbi who remarked to his colleagues that "self-flagellation appears to be the order of the day for the leadership of Conservative Jewry."[173]

---

[168]"On Leaving the Congregational Rabbinate," *Beineinu*, Nov. 1975, pp. 6–7.

[169]"The Rabbi Is a Lonely Person," *Conservative Judaism*, Winter 1983–84, pp. 40–41.

[170]Max Routtenberg, quoted by William Lebeau, "The RA Faces the Seventies," *Proceedings of the RA*, 1970, p. 99.

[171]"2001: Blueprint for the Rabbinate in the 21st Century," *Proceedings of the RA*, 1979, p. 122.

[172]William Greenfeld, quoted by Hillel Silverman in *Proceedings of the RA*, 1970, p. 111.

[173]See Jordan S. Ofseyer's contribution to the symposium discussion in *Conservative Judaism*, Fall 1972, p. 16.

The observations of leading sociologists further added to the pessimistic mood. Early in 1972, Marshall Sklare published an essay on "Recent Developments in Conservative Judaism" designed to update his study of 1953. As read by the editor of *Conservative Judaism*, Sklare "offered a thesis that the Conservative movement at the zenith of its influence, has sustained a loss of morale," attributable to "the emergence of Orthodoxy, the problem of Conservative observance, and the widespread alienation among Conservative young people."[174]

Charles Liebman and Saul Shapiro, in a survey conducted at the end of the 1970s and released at the 1979 biennial convention of the United Synagogue, came up with strong evidence to substantiate the thesis of the Conservative movement's decline.[175] Liebman and Shapiro found that almost as many young people reared in Conservative synagogues were opting for no synagogue affiliation as were joining Conservative congregations. Further, they contended that among the most observant younger Conservative families, particularly as defined by *kashrut* observance, there was a tendency to "defect" to Orthodoxy. Here was evidence of a double failing: a movement that had invested heavily in Jewish education in the synagogue setting seemingly did not imbue its youth with a strong allegiance to the Conservative synagogue; and rabbis who themselves had rejected Orthodoxy found their "best" young people—including their own children—rejecting Conservatism for Orthodoxy.

In truth, many of the best of Conservative youth were choosing a path other than Orthodoxy, one which would have a far more profound effect on the movement than denominational "defections." Beginning in the early 1970s, products of Conservative synagogues, youth movements, Ramah camps, and the Seminary were instrumental in the creation of a counterculture movement known as "*havurah* Judaism."[176] Although Conservative Jews did not completely monopolize the *havurah* movement, they played key roles as founders, theoreticians, and members. The first person to suggest the applicability of early rabbinic fellowships as a model for the

---

[174]Stephen C. Lerner, in his introduction to a symposium responding to Sklare's critique, which was entitled, significantly, "Morale and Commitment," *Conservative Judaism*, Fall 1972, p. 12. Sklare's essay forms the concluding chapter in the revised edition of his book (New York, 1972), pp. 253–82.

[175]Liebman and Shapiro, "Survey of the Conservative Movement"; and Saul Shapiro, "The Conservative Movement" (unpublished, dated Nov. 13, 1979). For critiques of the survey design and its assumptions, see Harold Schulweis, "Surveys, Statistics and Sectarian Salvation," *Conservative Judaism*, Winter 1980, pp. 65–69; and Rela Geffen Monson, "The Future of Conservative Judaism in the United States: A Rejoinder," *Conservative Judaism*, Winter 1983–84, especially, pp. 10–14.

[176]Stephen C. Lerner, "The Havurot," *Conservative Judaism*, Spring 1970, pp. 3–7; William Novak, "Notes on Summer Camps: Some Reflections on the Ramah Dream," *Response*, Winter 1971–72, p. 59. See also the symposium on Ramah in *Conservative Judaism*, Fall 1987, which points up the relationship between the camping movement and *havurah* Judaism.

present age was Jacob Neusner, who had been ordained at the Seminary.[177] The first and perhaps most influential of all *havurot* was founded in Somerville, Massachusetts, in 1968 by a group of Ramah and Seminary products under the leadership of Arthur Green, a rabbi ordained at the Seminary. The guiding force in the founding of the New York Havurah, as well as the journal *Response*, was Alan Mintz, who had earlier served as the national president of United Synagogue Youth. Finally, the books that served as primers of *havurah* Judaism, the *Jewish Catalogs*,[178] were compiled by products of Conservative youth programs.

Richard Siegel, one of the editors of *The Jewish Catalog*, provided the following analysis of the link between *havurah* Judaism and the Conservative movement, when he was invited to address the national convention of the Rabbinical Assembly:

> Ramah created a new Jewish lifestyle. . . . A group of discontents was created [due to experimentation at Ramah], a group of people who had a vision of something different from what went on in synagogues. . . . In essence, it was an internal development within the Conservative movement which had within it the seeds of internal contradiction, and its own destruction, in a way. The Conservative movement was unable to absorb . . . to meet the religious needs of a group of young people.[179]

For Siegel, then, it was the intense experience of participating in a Jewish religious community at Camp Ramah that prompted the emergence of the *havurah* movement as a substitute for what young people regarded as the formal and sterile atmosphere of the large Conservative synagogue. As Susannah Heschel put it to another group of Conservative rabbis: "The movement has succeeded too well in educating its children, because these children feel they have no proper place in Conservative life."[180]

In the short term, Heschel was correct in noting the alienation of some of these youth from Conservative synagogues. But there is substantial evidence to indicate that in the 1980s many of the formerly disaffected, including those who continue to worship within the *havurah* setting, increasingly participate in Conservative life: they send their children to Solomon Schechter schools and Ramah camps; they identify with the liturgy and ideology of Conservatism; and most importantly, they have moved from the

---

[177]Jacob Neusner, *Contemporary Judaic Fellowship in Theory and Practice* (New York, 1972).

[178]Richard Siegel, Michael Strassfeld, and Sharon Strassfeld, comps. and eds., *The Jewish Catalog* (Philadelphia, 1973); Sharon Strassfeld and Michael Strassfeld, comps. and eds., *The Second Jewish Catalog* (Philadelphia, 1976); idem, *The Third Jewish Catalog* (Philadelphia, 1980).

[179]"Futuristic Jewish Communities," *Proceedings of the RA*, 1974, p. 80.

[180]Susannah Heschel, "Changing Forms of Jewish Spirituality," *Proceedings of the RA*, 1980, p. 146.

periphery to the center of Conservatism's institutional life. It is this last development which accounts in large measure for the turbulence within Conservative Judaism in recent years. Put simply, leadership in the Conservative movement, its national institutions, synagogues, rabbinate, and various organizational arms, has passed into the hands of men and women who were reared in the pews of Conservative synagogues and socialized in its Ramah camps and USY programs. That transition has brought dislocation and turmoil to the Conservative movement for over a decade.

The biographies of recent Conservative leaders tell much of the story. When Gerson D. Cohen assumed the chancellorship of the Jewish Theological Seminary of America in 1972, he brought with him years of experience as an early participant in the Ramah experiment. His successor, Ismar Schorsch, shared such experiences and is himself the son of a Conservative rabbi. Equally important, the Conservative rabbinate has been recruiting ever growing percentages of its members from Conservative homes. During the first half of the 20th century, the preponderant majority of rabbinical students at JTS were drawn from Orthodox families and educational institutions. Since then, the percentage of such students has dwindled, so that hardly any current rabbinical students come from the Orthodox community. Instead, close to one-third are either from Reform backgrounds or unaffiliated families, or are converts to Judaism, while the other two-thirds are products of the Conservative movement.[181] The Seminary faculty, too, has been replenished with American-born Jews, who for the most part have been educated in Conservative institutions.

The new elite of the Conservative movement differs from its predecessors of earlier generations in two significant ways. Today's leaders regard the world of Orthodoxy as alien, and are far less emotionally tied to it. Accordingly, they feel fewer constraints in setting their own course. Second, and even more important, the new elite of the Conservative movement is far more prepared to put into practice the logical consequences of Conservative ideology. It is particularly significant that many of the new elite had experience in Ramah camps, because Ramah, as one observer noted, "is the battleground par excellence for Conservative Judaism, where theory and practice must and do meet. . . . [Only Camp Ramah] constantly turn[ed] to the central educational institution, the JTS, to ask what are the permissible limits of experimentation in Jewish prayer? What are the permissible limits of Shabbat observance? What precisely is the role of women in

---

[181]Aryeh Davidson and Jack Wertheimer, "The Next Generation of Conservative Rabbis," in *The Seminary at 100*, ed. Nina Beth Cardin and David W. Silverman (New York, 1987), p. 36. Other essays in the volume also point up the ability of the Conservative movement to recruit from within; see, for example, Burton I. Cohen, "From Camper to National Director: A Personal View of the Seminary and Ramah," pp. 125–34.

Conservative Jewish life?"[182] Precisely because it created a total Jewish environment, Ramah provided a setting in which to explore what it means to live as a Conservative Jew on a day-to-day basis. Products of Ramah, accordingly, have been prepared to put Conservative ideology into action once they have assumed roles of leadership within the movement.

As the Conservative elite has changed in character, the structure of alliances within the Conservative coalition has shifted dramatically. The "schoolmen" described by Marshall Sklare in the mid-1950s now include some women, but even more important, include home-grown products with strong ties to the Conservative movement and no allegiances to Orthodoxy. The same is true of the rabbinate and organizational leadership. Thus, coalitions for change cut across the movement, rather than remain solely in one sector, as had long been the case. The issue of women's ordination, which has agitated Conservative Judaism for a decade, has served as the symbol of change and the catalyst for further realignment within the movement.

## Womens' Ordination as Symbol and Catalyst

Although Conservative Judaism had long accepted the mixed seating of men and women in synagogues and, since the 1950s, had increasingly celebrated the coming of age of girls in Bat Mitzvah ceremonies, it was only in the early 1970s that more far-reaching questions concerning the status of women in religious life were addressed by the movement. A group of Conservative feminists, members of Ezrat Nashim,[183]—a Hebrew pun referring to the separate women's gallery in traditional synagogues, but also implying a pledge to provide "help for women"—pressed its agenda at the convention of the Rabbinical Assembly in March 1972, by holding a "counter-session" to which only women—wives of rabbis—were invited. The group demanded the following of the RA: that women be granted membership in synagogues; be counted in a *minyan*; be allowed to participate fully in religious observances; be recognized as witnesses before Jewish law; be allowed to initiate divorce; be permitted to study and function as rabbis and cantors; and be encouraged to assume positions of leadership in the Jewish community. These demands drew special attention because they were put forward by self-proclaimed "products of Conservative congregations, religious schools, the Ramah Camps, LTF, USY, and the Seminary."[184]

---

[182]Robert Chazan, "Tribute to Ramah on Its 25th Anniversary," *Beineinu*, May 1973, p. 31.
[183]Alan Silverstein, "The Evolution of Ezrat Nashim," *Conservative Judaism*, Fall 1975, pp. 44–45.
[184]Ibid.

Until a detailed history of Jewish feminism is written, it will not be possible to determine how many Conservative women actually supported these demands. What is clear, however, is that they evoked a sympathetic response within the Conservative rabbinate. This can be seen in the ever-increasing attention paid to the women's issues in both the journal and the convention proceedings of the Conservative rabbinate, beginning shortly after the aforementioned RA convention. In terms of action, in 1973 the Rabbinical Assembly's committee on Jewish law and standards adopted a *takkanah* (legislative enactment) permitting women to be counted as part of a *minyan*. The next year, the same committee considered whether women could serve as rabbis and as cantors, and whether they could function as witnesses and sign legal documents. Supporters of women's equality concluded that the minority opinions on these matters provided a sufficient basis for change in the status of women.[185]

When news about the decision on counting women in a *minyan* became public knowledge through articles in the general press, Conservative opponents of "egalitarianism"—the term that came to be applied to the equal treatment of women—began to organize. The decision had placed such rabbis on the defensive with their own congregants. How could individual rabbis committed to traditional role differences between men and women in the synagogue continue to justify their stance when a *takkanah* permitting the counting of women in the *minyan* had been passed by the legal body of the Conservative rabbinate? The action of the law committee, it was argued, undermined the authority of the individual rabbi. Furthermore, opponents contended, the committee had assumed an unprecedented role as an advocate of change. In short order, rabbis opposed to the decisions of the law committee organized a body initially known as the "Ad Hoc Committee for Tradition and Diversity in the Conservative Movement" and subsequently renamed "The Committee for Preservation of Tradition within the Rabbinical Assembly of America." Thus, even before the issue of women's ordination was formally raised, the battle lines were drawn within the Conservative rabbinate.[186]

Despite bitter divisions among its membership over questions of women's status, the Rabbinical Assembly assumed a leadership role in advocating a decision on women as Conservative rabbis. At its annual convention in 1977, the RA petitioned the chancellor of the Seminary to "establish an interdisciplinary commission to study all aspects of the role of women as

---

[185]Mayer Rabinowitz, "Toward a Halakhic Guide for the Conservative Jew," *Conservative Judaism*, Fall 1986, pp. 18, 22, 26, 29; see also Aaron H. Blumenthal, "The Status of Women in Jewish Law," *Conservative Judaism*, Spring 1977, pp. 24–40.
[186]Rabbi I. Usher Kirshblum headed these two committees; his correspondence with rabbinic colleagues, spanning the period from 1975 until 1983, is in the Archives of Conservative Judaism, at the Jewish Theological Seminary of America.

spiritual leaders in the Conservative Movement." Chancellor Cohen acceded to this petition and selected 14 individuals, evenly divided between rabbinic and lay leaders, to serve on the commission. The commission heard testimony around the country based on a variety of perspectives, including Halakhah, ethics, economics, sociology, psychology, and education. From the outset, however, it had committed itself to a guideline that "no recommendation would be made which, in the opinion of the members of the Commission, . . . would contravene or be incompatible with the requirements of Halakhah as the latter had been theretofore observed and developed by the Conservative Movement." Within two years, the commission concluded its work; it presented the RA with a majority opinion supported by 11 members, urging the JTS to admit women to the Rabbinical School, and a minority report issued by 3 members opposing such action.[187]

The majority, in its report, contended that since the role of the contemporary rabbi "is not one which is established in classical Jewish texts . . . [there is] no specifiable halakhic category which can be identified with the modern rabbinate." The halakhic objections to the ordination of women "center around disapproval of the performance by a woman of certain functions. Those functions, however, are not essentially rabbinic, nor are they universally disapproved, by the accepted rules governing the discussion of Halakhah in the Conservative Movement."

The minority report, in contrast, argued that the key halakhic issues had not been resolved to the satisfaction of many Conservative Jews, as well as Jews outside of the movement "who may be affected by practices in connection with testimony relating to marriage and divorce." The minority expressed concern that the ordination of women would drive opponents of egalitarianism out of the Conservative movement.

Once the commission reported its findings back to the Rabbinical Assembly, attention turned to the faculty of the Seminary. During the course of the commission's hearings, Chancellor Cohen had shifted his position from a desire to maintain the status quo to enthusiastic support of women's ordination. He took it upon himself to bring the matter before the faculty of the Seminary within one year, an undertaking that itself precipitated further controversy. It was not at all clear from Seminary rules of procedure that the faculty was empowered to decide on admissions policies. Some

---

[187]The "Final Report of the Commission for the Study of the Ordination of Women as Rabbis" was compiled by Gordon Tucker, executive director of the commission, and is printed in *The Ordination of Women as Rabbis: Studies and Responsa,* ed. Simon Greenberg (New York, 1988), pp. 5–30. See also the position papers of Seminary faculty members in the Greenberg volume. Several of the most forceful papers presented in opposition to women's ordination are not included in Greenberg's volume but appeared in a booklet entitled "On the Ordination of Women as Rabbis" (JTS, mimeo, early 1980s). See especially the papers of David Weiss Halivni, Gershon C. Bacon, and David A. Resnick.

argued that only talmudists on the faculty should have a right to decide; others objected to any faculty participating on the ground that admissions policies were a purely administrative matter; and still others claimed that halakhic questions had not been resolved satisfactorily, and therefore, no decision could be taken by the Seminary. In December 1979, the matter was brought before the faculty, but was tabled indefinitely so as to avoid a sharp split.[188]

Pressure for action on the ordination issue continued to mount, particularly within the Rabbinical Assembly. A number of women of Conservative background who had studied for the rabbinate at the Reform and Reconstructionist seminaries pressed for admission to the Rabbinical Assembly. The official organization of Conservative rabbis now was placed in the position of possibly admitting women who were as qualified as many male candidates ordained by non-Conservative institutions, even as the movement's own seminary refused to ordain women as rabbis. The issue came to a head in 1983, when Beverly Magidson, a rabbi ordained at the Hebrew Union College, successfully demonstrated her qualifications for admission to the Rabbinical Assembly. Like all candidates for admission not ordained by the JTS, Magidson needed the support of three-quarters of the rabbis present at the convention in order to gain admission; in fact she received the support of a majority. Some supporters of Magidson's admission opted to vote against her on the grounds that a woman ordained by the Seminary should be the first female admitted to the RA. Others felt that such a momentous decision should be reserved for a convention that drew a broader cross section of the membership (the convention met in Dallas, and attendance was lower than usual). But it was clear from the vote of 206 in favor to 72 opposed that it was only a matter of time before a woman rabbi would be admitted to the RA and that the Seminary could no longer defer a decision.[189]

In the fall of 1983, Chancellor Cohen once again brought the issue of women's ordination before the faculty. In the interval, several of the staunchest opponents of women's ordination had left the faculty, and Prof. Saul Lieberman, an intimidating figure even after his retirement from the faculty, had passed away. Clearly outnumbered, most other opponents of women's ordination, principally senior members of the rabbinics department, refused to attend the meeting. By a vote of 34 to 8, with one abstention, on October 24, 1983, the faculty voted to admit women to the rabbinical school. By the following fall, 19 women were enrolled in the Rabbinical School; one of them, Amy Eilberg, was ordained in May 1985,

---

[188]On the background to the faculty vote of 1979, see David Szonyi, "The Conservative Condition," *Moment*, May 1980, especially pp. 38–39.

[189]For the debate over Magidson's application, see *Proceedings of the RA*, 1983, pp. 218–51.

on the basis of her academic attainments during years of graduate studies.[190]

The protracted and bitterly divisive debate over women's ordination went beyond the issue of women's status in Judaism to the broader questions of movement definition. Predictably, given the centrism of the Conservative movement, advocates of opposing positions branded their opponents as either radical Reformers or Orthodox obstructionists. This was particularly evident during the debate over Magidson's application for admission to the RA. Opponents explicitly stated that if the RA voted affirmatively, "we are going to be publicly identified with the Reform movement";[191] supporters argued that by rejecting Magidson, "we will be subjecting ourselves to ridicule. . . . Our own communities and our congregants will lump us with Orthodox intransigents."[192]

Whereas earlier controversial decisions, such as the law committee's stance on the permissibility of driving to synagogue on the Sabbath, affected only individual Jews, the ordination of women as rabbis directly affected all segments of Conservative Jewry. Congregations eventually would have to decide whether to hire a woman as a rabbi; members of the Rabbinical Assembly would have to decide whether they could accept women as equals, particularly as witnesses in legal actions; and members of the Seminary faculty would have to decide whether they could participate in the training of women as rabbis. Once ordained as rabbis, women would assume a central role in the Conservative movement, a role that could not be ignored.

### Redefining the Movement

The crisis of Conservative morale during the late 1960s and the 1970s and the subsequent struggle over women's ordination prompted the leaders of Conservative Judaism to clarify the movement's program. The result was an outpouring of programmatic statements, halakhic works, and liturgical compositions. Even the decades-old plea of rabbis and lay people for an explicit statement of Conservative belief and practice was heeded. The result was the publication for the first time—over a century after the founding of the Jewish Theological Seminary—of a statement of Conservative principles issued jointly by all the major agencies of the movement. The Conservative movement was now clearly determined to stake out a clear position in the Jewish community and to maintain that position combatively.

---

[190]See Francine Klagsbrun, "At Last, A Conservative Woman Rabbi," *Congress Monthly*, May-June 1985, p. 11; and Abraham Karp, "A Century of Conservative Judaism," AJYB 1986, vol. 86, pp. 3–61.

[191]David Novak, in *Proceedings of the RA*, 1983, p. 223.

[192]Aaron Gold, in ibid., p. 237.

Beginning slowly in the early 1970s and then intensifying in the 1980s, a series of volumes appeared defining the Conservative position. First came a High Holy Day prayer book.[193] At the end of the decade there was Isaac Klein's *A Guide to Jewish Religious Practice*,[194] the first codification of Conservative halakhic rulings, albeit one written from the perspective of a highly traditional Conservative rabbi. In the 1980s came a Passover Haggadah,[195] a new *siddur*,[196] works on the Conservative approach to Jewish law, such as Joel Roth's *The Halakhic Process: A Systemic Analysis*,[197] and the collected responsa of the committee on Jewish law and standards.[198] Most notably, in 1988, a joint ideological committee, chaired by Robert Gordis, encompassing all organizational arms of the movement, issued *Emet Ve-Emunah*, a statement of beliefs and principles.[199]

Although the new publications do not speak with one voice or suggest anything resembling unanimity, several clear trends are evident. First and foremost, Conservative Judaism has reiterated its desire to occupy the center of the religious spectrum. Thus, the statement of principles speaks of "the indispensability of Halakhah" and the "norms taught by the Jewish tradition." By emphasizing a normative approach to Jewish religious behavior, the Conservative movement rejects the Reform and Reconstructionist positions. Simultaneously, the statement distances itself from Orthodoxy by taking note of "development in Halakhah," and affirms the right of Conservative religious authorities to act independently to interpret and adjust Jewish law.

It needs to be stressed that the Conservative position espoused in *Emet Ve-Emunah* is consciously centrist in that it seeks a path between extreme positions. As analyzed by Chancellor Ismar Schorsch, the statement of principles treats Halakhah as "a disciplinary way of life which is dynamic and evolving." It rejects Mordecai Kaplan's views on chosenness by reasserting "the meaningfulness of the concept of chosenness, and at the same time, claims that we are open to the wisdom of Gentiles." It "depicts Jewish prayer as something firm and fixed . . . and yet [the] liturgical form is open to development, to the refraction of contemporary tastes and anxieties."[200]

A second element of the reshaped Conservative Judaism of the 1980s is

---

[193]*Mahzor for Rosh Hashanah and Yom Kippur* (New York, 1972).
[194]New York, 1979.
[195]*The Feast of Freedom Passover Haggadah* (New York, 1982).
[196]*Siddur Sim Shalom: A Prayerbook for Shabbat, Festivals, and Weekdays* (New York, 1985).
[197]New York, 1986.
[198]*Proceedings of the Committee on Jewish Law and Standards of the Conservative Movement 1980–1985* (New York, 1988).
[199]*Emet Ve-Emunah: Statement of Principles of Conservative Judaism* (New York, 1988).
[200]Ismar Schorsch, "Reflections on *Emet Ve-Emunah*," an address circulated in typescript, unpaged.

an open embrace of pluralism in Jewish religious life. Within the movement itself an effort is made to embrace all Jews who identify themselves as Conservative. Even the newly published statement of principles need not be accepted "as a whole or in detail . . . [as] obligatory upon every Conservative Jew, lay or rabbinic." With regard to other Jewish groups, the statement of principles urges Jewish unity and seeks a common Jewish approach to conversion and religious divorces, vexing sources of friction between the various denominations.[201]

A third feature of the new Conservative position is strong support for gender equality. The statement of principles explicitly affirms the equality of the sexes. The new *Siddur Sim Shalom* takes cognizance in the Hebrew liturgy of the possibility that women will don *tallit* and *tefillin* and includes a blessing (*mi she-berakh*) for a female called to the Torah.[202] While stopping short of making equality of the sexes an absolute norm of Conservative Judaism, movement leaders have indicated clearly where their sympathies reside.

The emphasis on gender equality has led to widespread change. Surveys conducted during the 1970s suggested that growing numbers of Conservative congregations were electing women as officers and including them as equal participants in religious services by counting women in a *minyan*, calling them to the Torah, and permitting them to chant portions of the services. According to a 1988 survey conducted by Edya Arzt, "Better than half the congregations do count women in the *minyan* and do give them *aliyot* on all occasions. An additional 61 congregations give women *aliyot* on special occasions, such as an anniversary or a *Bat Mitzvah* or jointly with their husbands." Arzt found distinct patterns based on geographic location; opposition to women's participation was greatest in Brooklyn and Long Island, began to wane west of the Hudson, and was least evident on the West Coast, where the preponderant majority of congregations were egalitarian.[203]

Those opposed to egalitarianism and other recent changes in Conservatism have organized the Union for Traditional Conservative Judaism

---

[201] *Emet Ve-Emunah*, pp. 124, 40–41.
[202] *Siddur Sim Shalom*, pp. 2–3, 144.
[203] Edya Arzt, "Our Right to Rites," *Women's League Outlook*, Fall 1988, pp. 17–18. For some earlier surveys, see Zelda Dick, "Light from Our Poll on Women's Role," *Women's League Outlook*, Summer 1975, pp. 14–15; Daniel Elazar and Rela Geffen Monson, "Women in the Synagogue Today," *Midstream*, Apr. 1979, pp. 25–30; and Anne Lapidus Lerner and Stephen C. Lerner, "Report," *Rabbinical Assembly News*, Feb. 1984, pp. 1, 8. For two essays on the process by which individual congregations adopted egalitarianism, see Ruth R. Seldin, "Women in the Synagogue: A Congregant's View," *Conservative Judaism*, Winter 1979, pp. 80–88; and Esther Altshul Helfgott, "Beth Shalom's Encounter with the Woman Question," *Conservative Judaism*, Spring 1986, pp. 66–76.

(UTCJ) as a lobby within the movement. The UTCJ originally emerged in the fall of 1983 from the earlier pressure groups that had fought against changes in the status of women within religious law. Although it continues to speak out against egalitarianism, it has broadened its program to represent the interests of those within the Conservative coalition who oppose what they perceive as a move away from tradition. A recent article written by a lay member of the union, titled "Relief for Beleaguered Traditionalists," appeals to the disaffected: "Your rabbi is touting *Sim Shalom* as the greatest liturgical innovation since the Sh'ma. Your synagogue's ritual committee is again considering women's participation and seems to go along with whichever side seems the loudest. You've seen some food in the synagogue kitchen that makes you wonder whether you can eat there."[204] Although the union represents only a small proportion of Conservative Jews, whenever a decision is taken by the Conservative movement that does not conform with its views, it manages to get equal time in the Jewish press.[205]

The union's boldest challenge to the Conservative leadership has come through the establishment of a separate "Panel of Halakhic Inquiry," which, among other things, has restated the objection to women as rabbis and counting women in a *minyan*. A recent responsum dealing with the new Conservative prayer book argues that "it should not be used for the purpose of fulfilling one's prayer obligations," because it introduces "gratuitous changes," eliminates gender distinctions, "extirpates or modifies almost all positive references to . . . sacrificial ritual," and through its alternative readings, undermines the obligatory nature of Jewish prayer.[206]

Ironically, the rabbinic leaders of the Union for Traditional Conservative Judaism play much the same role today within the movement that the Reconstructionist wing played during the middle decades of the century. As analyzed by Gilbert Rosenthal, "The left wing believed itself the odd-man out. The Reconstructionist wing complained that our movement was too bound to tradition, too obsessed with nostalgia, too submissive to the rule of the Seminary faculty." Since the secession of Reconstructionism from the Conservative movement, "there is virtually no articulate left wing in our movement. Instead the odd-man out is the right-wing, which . . . has considered itself increasingly trampled upon and isolated. Today's critics decry our movement for being too obsessed with change, with radicalism,

---

[204]Douglas Aronin, *Hagahelet*, Spring 1987, p. 4.

[205]In a letter to the *Jewish Post and Opinion* (August 17, 1988, p. 15), Ronald Price, the UTCJ's executive director, claims that the union represents "500 rabbis (including some 150 Orthodox rabbis who identify with our philosophy) and over 5,000 lay families."

[206]See the responsum by Alan J. Yuter in *Tomeikh keHalakhah* I, ed. Wayne Allen (Mount Vernon, 1986), pp. 6–12.

with departures from Halakhic norms."[207] For their part, members of the UTCJ are convinced that Conservatism no longer has an articulate left wing because Reconstructionism has triumphed within the Conservative movement itself.

The leadership of Conservative Judaism has defined the shift differently. As enunciated by Kassel Abelson in his presidential address to the Rabbinical Assembly in 1987, Conservative Judaism is a "traditional *egalitarian* movement."[208] Traditionalism has been affirmed in the maintenance of Hebrew as the essential language of the liturgy; in the continuing assertion of the need for *Keva*, an established structure "for the times, content, and order of prayer"; for the reaffirmation that Judaism is a normative and binding legal system; and for the reiteration of the role of rabbis as arbiters of Jewish law. As a symbolic gesture of support for the traditional stance of Jewish law, the Rabbinical Assembly even went to the unusual length of affirming as a "standard" the belief that Jewish descent is only conveyed through the mother, thereby subjecting any rabbi who acts upon the patrilineal redefinition of Jewish identity to expulsion from the Rabbinical Assembly.[209] By affirming the need for conversion to Judaism as the only acceptable way for a non-Jew to enter the covenant and by rejecting the redefinition of Jewish identity introduced by Reform and Reconstructionist colleagues, the Conservative rabbinate sought to reiterate its fidelity to tradition on the most controversial and divisive issue on the Jewish religious agenda.

The repositioning of Conservative Judaism through the resolution of the issue of women's ordination served to relieve the paralysis besetting the Conservative movement. Conservative leaders began displaying a new feistiness in pressing the Conservative agenda on the American Jewish scene. Thus, Robert Gordis has challenged Reform to abandon patrilineality as a misguided departure from the unified approach of the Jewish people.[210] Similar challenges have been offered by movement leaders to the position of Orthodoxy *vis à vis* other issues. Ismar Schorsch has publicly declared his determination to become more denominational, to "bring a Conservative interpretation of Judaism to Europe as well as South America" and Israel, and to challenge opponents of the movement in the United States.[211] Conservative leaders have clearly resolved to assert in the public arena the

---

[207]Gilbert Rosenthal, "The Elements That Unite Us," *Proceedings of the RA*, 1984, p. 23.
[208]"Presidential Address," *Proceedings of the RA*, 1987, p. 45.
[209]For the debate over adopting the matrilineal principle as a "standard" within the RA, see *Proceedings of the RA*, 1986, pp. 313–22.
[210]Robert Gordis, "To Move Forward, Take One Step Back: A Plea to the Reform Movement," *Moment*, May 1986, pp. 58–61.
[211]Ismar Schorsch, "Centenary Thoughts: Conservatism Revisited," *Proceedings of the RA*, 1986, p. 79. See also the "Presidential Acceptance Speech" of Kassel Abelson, which points to Conservatism becoming a "more militant middle." Ibid., p. 76.

correctness of Conservative Judaism's recently modified, yet still centrist, position.

## DENOMINATIONAL LIFE: RECONSTRUCTIONISM

The most significant development in Reconstructionism during the past quarter century has been its reconstitution as a fourth religious movement, one which claims parity with the Orthodox, Conservative, and Reform branches of Judaism.[212] Ironically, however, the institutional growth of the movement has gone hand in hand with a reassessment of the teachings of its founder, Mordecai Kaplan. In fact, Reconstructionism has been reconstructed.

### Building a Fourth Movement

The emergence of Reconstructionism as a distinctive movement began when Mordecai Kaplan retired from his professorship at the Jewish Theological Seminary of America in 1963, at the age of 82. Reconstructionist institutions had existed before, but at Kaplan's behest they had not taken an independent course. Thus, when the Reconstructionist Rabbinical Fellowship was established in 1950, its founders declared they had "no intention of creating a new and competing denomination." Similarly, when the Reconstructionist Fellowship of Congregations was formed in 1955, it required all its constituents to hold dual membership in both the fellowship and in a congregational association of one of the three denominations. In the early 1960s, however, a number of Kaplan's disciples, including his son-in-law Rabbi Ira Eisenstein, convinced him of the need to establish an independent movement. Kaplan's retirement from the Seminary after 51 years freed him and his followers to pursue such a course.[213]

In the fall of 1968, the Reconstructionist Rabbinical College opened its doors in Philadelphia. The site had been chosen largely because of a special arrangement between the new college and the department of religion at Temple University in Philadelphia.[214] RRC, as it became known, was to

---

[212]The first sentence of the "Platform on Reconstructionism" announces that Reconstructionism is "one of the four major Jewish religious movements." *Newsletter* of the Federation of Reconstructionist Congregations and Havurot (hereafter *FRCH Newsletter*), Sept. 1986, page D.

[213]See Ira Eisenstein, *Reconstructing Judaism: An Autobiography* (New York, 1986), pp. 216-23.

[214]Temple University had recently come under public auspices and was eager to develop its seminary into a department of religion. The head of the department, Bernard Phillips, devised

train rabbis who combined a knowledge of the Jewish tradition with an understanding of other religious faiths. Accordingly, students were required to enroll simultaneously as Ph.D. students at Temple, while pursuing their rabbinical studies. The goal was "to produce a rabbi capable of confronting the secular world, acquainted with Christianity and other religions, and committed to the application of Judaism to the social problems of our day."[215]

Not surprisingly, the first years of the college were marked by considerable instability: a succession of deans and presidents oversaw operations; the requirement for students to earn a doctorate in religion was first modified and then dropped entirely; and faculty members came and went. But the basic conception of the curriculum remained intact. Guided by Kaplan's view of Judaism as "an evolving religious civilization," the curriculum each year introduces students to a different era of Jewish civilization—biblical, rabbinic, medieval, modern, and contemporary.

The 103 men and women ordained by RRC during its first two decades have provided the Reconstructionist movement with a cadre of rabbis imbued with a shared allegiance to Reconstructionist institutions and ideology. Most of these alumni do not occupy pulpits in Reconstructionist congregations. Rather, they hold positions in Reform and especially Conservative synagogues, where they serve as emissaries for Reconstructionism. These rabbis, far more than the relatively few congregations and *havurot* within the movement, provide Reconstructionism with a presence within the American Jewish community.[216]

## The Reconstruction of Reconstructionism

In the process of becoming a full-fledged denomination, Reconstructionism has moved boldly in several areas. One involved the thorny issue of mixed marriage. Whereas the Reform rabbinate drew widespread attention—and opprobrium—for its decision on patrilineal descent in 1983, the Reconstructionist movement had already passed a similar resolution at its annual convention 15 years earlier. In May 1968, Reconstructionism recognized as Jewish the "children of mixed marriage—when the mother is not

---

a master plan to bring seminarians of the Protestant and Catholic, as well as Jewish, faiths to Temple. See Bernard Phillips, "Where Religion Meets Scholarly Dialogue," *Reconstructionist*, Oct. 11, 1968, pp. 7–9.

[215]Reconstructionist Rabbinical College brochure, undated and unpaged.

[216]For a listing of alumni of the RRC and their present positions, see the school catalogue for 1988–90, pp. 60–63.

As of early 1988 there were 62 affiliates of the Federation of Reconstructionist Congregations and Havurot, many of them quite small. Some 2,000 families were estimated to belong to the Reconstructionist movement in the New York area. See *FRCH Newsletter*, Mar. 1988, p. 1.

Jewish—if the parents rear the child as a Jew (providing the boy with circumcision), matriculating the child in a religious school so that the child may fulfill requirements of bar or bat mitzvah or confirmation. No other formal conversion rites for the child will be required. . . ."[217] On a related matter, the Reconstructionist Rabbinical Association drafted "Guidelines on Intermarriage" in 1983 that outlined the proper role of rabbis at mixed marriages. Urging rabbis to reserve the use of the "traditional wedding ceremony (*kiddushin*) for the marriage of a Jew to a Jew," the guidelines affirmed the free choice of the rabbi "to attend and/or participate in a civil marriage ceremony between a Jew and a non-Jew" if the couple expressed a "determination to pursue, in the course of an on-going Jewish identification, ties with the Jewish community and the establishment of a Jewish home."[218]

A second area of far-reaching Reconstructionist innovation concerns the role of women in Jewish life. Kaplan's pioneering efforts in regard to women's participation in synagogue life are well known. His daughter Judith was the first girl to celebrate a Bat Mitzvah ceremony, this in 1922; in 1951, the Society for the Advancement of Judaism began to call women to the Torah and count them in a *minyan*. When the RRC was established, women were quickly admitted. Still, as noted by Rabbi Arthur Green, the current president of the RRC, it is only recently that gender equality has become a "bedrock principle" of Reconstructionism. This means that "in no move toward Jewish unity and interdenominational rapprochement will we compromise the following: the full participation of women on all levels of Jewish leadership, including the rabbinic; the welcome offered to women to participate and be counted as full equals in all areas of Jewish ritual life; the acceptance of women as partners with men in legal decision making, witnessing, and participation in a *bet din* (rabbinic court); or the right of a woman, in the absence of other good alternatives, to end a marriage with a Jewish divorce obtained in a non-degrading manner."[219] In recent years, Reconstructionists have sought to act on this principle not only with regard to ritual matters and policy decisions but also in the liturgical sphere. Thus, a new prayer book is being prepared that promises to eliminate the male-dominated imagery of the traditional liturgy.[220]

A third area for innovation has been in the conduct of congregational life.

---

[217] *Reconstructionist Newsletter*, Sept. 1968, p. 1.
[218] "RRA Guidelines on Intermarriage," *Reconstructionist*, Nov. 1983, pp. 18–23. A survey sponsored by the RRA found that 50 percent of the members wanted a strong statement against rabbinic officiation at mixed marriages, while 30 percent already did, or were prepared to, officiate at such marriages. See *Raayonot*, Spring/Summer 1982, p. 8.
[219] Arthur Green, "Reconstructionists and Jewish Unity," *Reconstructionist*, Sept. 1987, p. 12.
[220] See David Teutsch, "Seeking the Words of Prayer," *Reconstructionist*, Mar. 1988, pp. 10–11.

In recent years, Reconstructionists—especially rabbinic leaders—have rethought the relationship between rabbis and their congregants. The Reconstructionist rabbi "serves not as a judicial authority but rather as a learned teacher—someone who by virtue of his/her greater knowledge of Jewish civilization, can assist other Jews in studying the tradition and reaching their own decisions."[221] The ultimate arbiter, however, is the congregation, which is vested with the authority to make "all decisions, including decisions about ritual, . . . in a democratic fashion."[222] To insure democratization, Reconstructionists have developed clear-cut procedures for participatory decision making within smaller *havurot*, larger congregations, and the Federation of Reconstructionist Congregations and Havurot.[223]

As noted above, the institutional growth of Reconstructionism has been accompanied by a reevaluation of Kaplan's legacy. For example, in recent years, some prominent Reconstructionists have advocated a return to the belief in a supernatural God, a belief emphatically rejected by Kaplan. While the "Platform on Reconstructionism" draws a distinction between traditional Judaism's "conception of a supernatural God who possesses such attributes as goodness, justice, righteousness, and mercy," and the Reconstructionist affirmation of "a conception of God as the Power or Process that makes for salvation, or human fulfillment," it also affirms "that *belief in God* is more central to Jewish religion than a specific *conception* of God."[224] This cautious approach is necessary to accommodate the growing numbers of Reconstructionists who reject Kaplan's view of the matter. As one recent alumna and current faculty member at RRC has put it, "Claims about hope and goodness are quite implausible in anything *but* a supernatural context"; accordingly, she affirms her belief in a supernatural and personal God.[225] The emergence at the RRC of neo-Hassidism, with its emphasis on experiencing God through song and body movement in the

---

[221]Editor's Introduction, "Democracy and Lay-Rabbinic Relations in Reconstructionism," *Reconstructionist*, Sept. 1985, p. 8. See also Sidney H. Schwarz, "A Synagogue with Principles," *Reconstructionist*, June 1985, pp. 21–25.

[222]Rebecca T. Alpert and Jacob J. Staub, *Exploring Judaism: Reconstructionist Approach* (New York, 1985), p. 79.

[223]See the symposium on "Democracy and Lay-Rabbinic Relations in Reconstructionism," and especially the remarks of Richard A. Hirsh, "Clarifying Our Terms," in *Reconstructionist*, Sept. 1985, pp. 13–15. Hirsh is one of the few to object to this rejection of the traditional rabbinic model, noting that "while all Jews are *entitled* to an opinion, not all opinions are equally informed or equally valuable. I remain convinced that in lay-rabbinic interchange, a rabbi's perspective . . . is generally better informed (though not necessarily more correct) than that of a lay-person" (p. 15).

[224]*FRCH Newsletter*, Sept. 1986, p. E.

[225]Nancy Fuchs-Kreimer, "Reconstructionism Between the Generations," *Raayonot*, vol. 2, no. 2–3, pp. 44–45.

course of prayer, further threatens to undermine the traditional Reconstructionist conception of God. The newly elected president of the RRC and several faculty members are prominently identified with this trend.[226]

A similar challenge has been mounted to another long-standing principle of Reconstructionism: Kaplan's rejection of the chosen people concept. In a symposium on the future of Reonconstructionism conducted in 1982, several participants "indicated that the Kaplanian position on the chosen people might be *passé*."[227] Further evidence of rethinking on the matter is to be seen in the following statement issued by the Reconstructionist prayerbook commission in 1982: "There is a historical link between chosenness and the idea of holiness and covenant. Our sense of destiny has been necessary for Jewish survival. Thus, we should affirm what we consider ourselves to be chosen *for* rather than emphasize what we are chosen *from*. This principle can be implemented by emphasizing vocation."[228] These statements suggest that the concept of the chosen people, albeit somewhat redefined, is gradually being reinstated.

At least three factors are shaping Reconstructionism's changing ideological posture. First, there is the changing constituency of the movement. Writing at midcentury, Harold Schulweis, a leading disciple of Kaplan, characterized the original followers of Reconstructionism as the "twiceborn: Those who at one time experienced Orthodoxy and rejected it ... and who later feel the need to return but to a tradition nourished by a thoroughgoing intellectual modernity."[229] In the 1980s, in contrast, as an editorial in the *Reconstructionist* put it, "there are many members of FRCH affiliates who have joined because of the atmosphere and spirit of these groups. These people are unaware of the movement's philosophy in all its details."[230] Unlike the adherents cited by Schulweis, who were renegades from Orthodox homes, today's Reconstructionists are newcomers to Judaism. When Kaplan spoke of the right of tradition to cast a vote but not a veto, he appealed to a constituency that knew how tradition voted. Today, the task of Reconstructionism is to appeal to a generation that first must be exposed to Jewish tradition before it can even decide on its limits.

---

[226]The former president of the college, Ira Silverman, and a leading administrator of the movement, David Teutsch, also have advocated a reexamination of Kaplan's theology. See Sidney Schwarz, "The Reconstructionist Symposium," *Reconstructionist*, Mar. 1982, p. 21. See also Ari L. Goldman, "Reconstructionist Jews Turn to the Supernatural," *New York Times*, Feb. 19, 1989, p. A26.
[227]Ibid., p. 22.
[228]"Prayerbook-Committee Progress Report," *Reconstructionist*, Spring 1983, p. 21. See also the symposium on chosenness in the Sept. 1984 issue.
[229]"The Temper of Reconstructionism," in *Jewish Life in America*, ed. Theodore Friedman and Robert Gordis (New York, 1955), p. 74.
[230]*Reconstructionist*, Oct.-Nov. 1984, p. 7.

A second factor promoting ideological ferment is the presence on the RRC faculty of figures associated with countercultural tendencies in the religious and social spheres. Reconstructionism today prides itself on "being on the cutting edge of Jewish ritual and practice," and consciously reaches out to Jews who are eager to experiment.[231] Recent issues raised for discussion within the movement included the following: creation of "an ethical kashrut"—the prohibition of food produced through the oppression of workers, or in factories owned by the Mafia, or whose kosher certification is obtained unethically;[232] provision of "sanctuary for the stranger"—permitting members of a FRCH congregation to provide refuge for victims of political persecution who immigrate to the United States illegally;[233] and experimentation with female goddess imagery—as part of an effort to "dig up women's spiritual practices from the past and see what resonates," as proposed by a woman student at the RRC.[234]

Finally, the movement of Reconstructionism away from Kaplan is in part a result of the very decision to create a separate movement. As long as Kaplan played the role of gadfly to the Jewish community, the success of Reconstructionism was measured by the extent to which his views were adopted by the existing movements. Judged in those terms, Reconstructionism was enormously influential. As a separate movement, however, Reconstructionism has been under great pressure to define a distinctive approach to Jewish life in a community that has already accepted much of Kaplan's program. This pressure has done much to propel Reconstructionism toward new, and in some cases radical, positions that are far removed from the principles of Mordecai Kaplan. Thus, Reconstructionism, which began as the most sharply defined ideological group within American Judaism, today defines itself more by its process than by its united ideological commitments.

### DENOMINATIONAL RELATIONS

The foregoing analysis of shifts in the policies and practices of the various Jewish denominations provides the necessary context to assess why relations between the religious groups have deteriorated in recent years. All of

---

[231] Gary Rosenblatt, "Can a Reconstructionist Rabbi Go Too Far?" *Baltimore Jewish Times*, Mar. 27, 1987, pp. 66–68.
[232] Rebecca T. Alpert and Arthur Waskow, "Toward an Ethical Kashrut," *Reconstructionist*, Mar.-Apr. 1987, p. 13.
[233] Sissy Carpey, "Miklat Legerim: A Havurah for Sanctuary," *Reconstructionist*, May-June 1987, pp. 8–12.
[234] Rosenblatt, "Can a Reconstructionist Rabbi . . . ?" pp. 66–68.

the movements have responded to a series of new challenges faced by the American Jewish community: the rising level of intermarriage between Jews and non-Jews and the resulting question of how to integrate the children of such marriages into the Jewish community; the feminist revolution and the demands of Jewish women for equality in religious life; and declining levels of synagogue affiliation and involvement of third- and fourth- generation American Jews, which have forced Jewish institutions to compete for members. Each movement has responded differently to these issues and has embraced policies unilaterally, with little or no consultation with the other groupings in American Judaism. The resulting policies reflect profoundly different conceptions of Jewish identity, religious reform, and the future of American Judaism. The Reform and Reconstructionist position on patrilineality, for example, is incompatible with Conservative and Orthodox definitions of who is a Jew. The ordination of women as rabbis is viewed by the non-Orthodox as a logical extension of Jewish values and by the Orthodox as an unacceptable deviation from Jewish tradition. As Irving Greenberg, a modern Orthodox rabbi has suggested, both extremes on the religious spectrum act as if they have written each other off; they assume that those with opposing views will become increasingly irrelevant to the Jewish future.[235] Only those on the Conservative right and the Orthodox left seem concerned about this situation, perhaps because they have ties to all segments of the Jewish community.

One episode that symbolizes both the possibilities and the lost opportunities for greater religious unity is the so-called Denver experiment.[236] Beginning in 1978, Reform, Conservative, and Traditional[237] rabbis in that city formed a joint *bet din* to oversee conversions. (Orthodox rabbis refused to participate, and there was no Reconstructionist rabbi in Denver at the time.) The purpose of this program was to prevent a situation in which rabbis in Denver could not recognize each other's converts. While rabbis still retained the right to perform their own conversions, approximately 750 individuals underwent conversion in Denver through the joint court.

In order to function as a *bet din*, all participating rabbis compromised

---

[235]On Greenberg's views, see "Will There Be One Jewish People in the Year 2000?" *Perspectives*, National Jewish Center for Learning and Leadership, June 1985. See also Gary Rosenblatt, "Judaism's Civil War: How Deep Is the Rift?" *Baltimore Jewish Times*, Jan. 29, 1988, pp. 56–59.

[236]The most complete account of this experiment, which includes interviews with all of the participating rabbis, appears in "Conversion and Patrilineality," a special section of the *Intermountain Jewish News* (Denver), Dec. 2, 1983, pp.1–12.

[237]Traditional synagogues and rabbis are largely a Midwestern phenomenon; Traditional congregations permit men and women to sit together and utilize a microphone during religious services; their rabbis, mainly graduates of the Hebrew Theological Seminary in Skokie, Ill., identify with modern Orthodoxy.

some of their views. The Traditional rabbis "were prepared to say that even though . . . all of the students coming out of the general conversion process would not be authentic Orthodox Jews, . . . as long as they were beginning an effort to learn Judaism and aspire to be committed Jews, we were prepared to offer our signatures."[238] The Reform rabbis, in turn, agreed to teach about Jewish dietary laws, including the special Passover requirements in the home. In addition, the Reform rabbis acceded to the Traditional and Conservative rabbis' insistence that converts undergo ritual immersion in a *mikveh* and that males undergo a symbolic circumcision (*hatafat dam brit*). The lone Conservative rabbi in Denver, whose conception of conversion represented a centrist position, served as chairman of the group for most of its history, but the actual conversion ceremony was supervised by three Traditional rabbis.

After six years of relatively smooth functioning, the Denver *bet din* was dissolved in 1983. The precipitating factor was the resolution on patrilineality adopted that year by the Central Conference of American Rabbis. This decision to redefine Jewish identity, as well as the designation of Denver as a pilot community for a new Reform outreach effort—to seek out converts—convinced the Traditional and Conservative rabbis that they could no longer participate in the joint body. Although the Reform rabbis of Denver held varying views on the question of patrilineality, the decision of the Reform rabbinate on a national level placed the Traditional and Conservative rabbis in an untenable position. They could not cooperate in a conversion program with rabbis who held a very different conception of Jewish identity. Furthermore, they felt they could not supervise conversions that would occur with increasing frequency due to a Reform outreach effort that was inconsistent with their own understanding of how to relate to potential proselytes.

The possibility of future cooperation between the denominations in other Jewish communities was further undermined by the response of Orthodox groups to the Denver program. When the existence of the program became public knowledge (ironically, through the announcement of its demise), Orthodox groups raised a hue and cry over the folly of Traditional rabbis participating in a joint conversion effort. The *Jewish Observer* stated bluntly:

> While compromise for the sake of unity can often make good sense, when dealing with basic principles of faith, "compromise" is actually a sell-out. . . .It is time that all Orthodox rabbis recognize that Reform and Conservative Judaism are far, far removed from Torah, and that *Klal Yisroel* is betrayed—not served—when Orthodoxy enters in religious association with them.[239]

---

[238]"Conversion and Patrilineality," p. 2.

[239]Nisson Wolpin, "Compromise on the Great Divide: Questionable Conversions in Denver," *Jewish Observer*, Jan. 1984, pp. 32–34.

In the judgment of the *Jewish Observer*, "The Traditional rabbis of Denver have been party to an outrageous fraud."

Since the collapse of the Denver program, denominational relations have continued to deteriorate. Key flash points include: the veto exercised by Orthodox rabbis of the Rabbinical Council of America to prevent the Reconstructionist movement from joining the Synagogue Council of America;[240] the reconstitution of the JWB Chaplaincy Board in response to the application of a woman rabbi seeking to serve as a Jewish military chaplain;[241] and the placement of newspaper advertisements by rabbinic groups of the Orthodox right urging Jews to stay home on the Jewish High Holy Days rather than worship in non-Orthodox synagogues.[242] When the *New York Times* saw fit to publish a front-page article with the headline "Split Widens on a Basic Issue: What Is a Jew?" the divisions among rabbis began to attract more attention in the wider Jewish community.[243] One organization in particular, the National Jewish Center for Learning and Leadership, headed by Rabbi Irving Greenberg, sought to focus communal attention on the growing rift by inviting the leaders of all four Jewish religious movements to a conference that posed the provocative question—"Will There Be One Jewish People By the Year 2000?"[244]

In late 1988, rancor between the denominations reached new heights in response to Israeli political maneuverings. Both major Israeli political factions signaled to potential coalition partners representing various Orthodox constituencies their readinesss to guarantee passage of an amendment to Israel's Law of Return, stipulating that converts to Judaism be granted citizenship under that law only if they had been converted "according to Halakhah." From the perspective of non-Orthodox groups, this amendment could have only one purpose—the delegitimation of non-Orthodox rabbis. Since it is widely known that merely a handful of converts move to Israel annually, it was clear that this Orthodox demand had more symbolic than practical importance. The true issue was not so much "Who is a Jew?" but "Who is an authentic rabbi?"[245]

For several weeks in late 1988 the American Jewish community was in turmoil over this issue. The General Assembly of the Council of Jewish

---

[240]See *JTA News Bulletin*, Apr. 23, 1986, p. 4, and the editorial "The Synagogue Council of America," *Reconstructionist*, July-Aug. 1986, p. 6.

[241]When the CCAR placed a female candidate in the chaplaincy program, the commission was reconstituted as the Jewish Chaplains Council in 1986. See *JTA New Bulletin*, Aug. 29, 1985, p. 3, and AJYB 1986, vol. 86, p. 399, and AJYB 1987, vol. 87, p. 400, on the name change.

[242]*New York Times*, Feb. 28, 1986, p. A1.

[243]Ibid.

[244]Cohen and Greenberg, "The One in 2000 Controversy," pp. 11–22.

[245]Gary Rosenblatt, "Separating the Historical from the Hysterical," *Baltimore Jewish Times*, Dec. 9, 1988, p. 29ff., offers a helpful introduction to the controversy.

Federations devoted much of its agenda to the matter, particularly because community leaders feared that passage of an amendment to the Law of Return would do serious harm to fund-raising efforts and relations between American Jews and Israel.[246] The Jewish press carried an ongoing stream of reports and articles in response to this issue, including interviews with converts and debates among rabbis over the implications of the impending Israeli vote. Leaders of Jewish organizations threatened to urge their members to reconsider their funding allocations for Israeli charities and to withhold funding from Orthodox institutions in the United States. At the end of the year, Israeli political leaders forged a government that, in the short term at least, had no plans to amend the law—and so the immediate crisis passed.

The resentments unleashed by this controversy were unusually strong. Opponents of the amendment faulted Orthodox leaders in the United States, particularly the Lubavitcher Rebbe, for pressuring Israeli groups to pass the amendment. It was frequently argued that Orthodox Jews in America were taking their battle against the other Jewish denominations to Israel because they could not win such a battle in the United States. Moreover, non-Orthodox leaders claimed that their identity as Jews was under attack. As Shoshana Cardin, a former president of the CJF and chairwoman of that organization's committee on religious pluralism, put it: "What we're dealing with here is perceived disenfranchisement of millions of Jews. And in this case, perception is reality."[247]

Though some Orthodox organizations—principally, the Rabbinical Council of America—supported the campaign to remove the issue of "Who is a Jew?" from the Israeli political agenda, Orthodox groups joined together to blame Reform Judaism for creating a religious schism. In an "Open Letter to American Jews" signed by several Orthodox organizations, the halakhic definition of Jewish identity was described as "universally accepted among all Jews for thousands of years. Reform, however, has done away with Halacha; and the Conservative movement is forever tampering with it."[248] In a similar vein, Marc Angel, one of the most moderate members of the centrist Orthodox rabbinate, lashed out at those who criticized Orthodoxy for its stand:

---

[246]Arthur J. Magida, " 'Who Is a Jew' Dominates Assembly," *Jewish News* (Detroit), Nov. 25, 1988, p. 1.

[247]Cardin is quoted in the Magida article, noted above. See also " 'Who Is a Jew' Issue Threatens Funding," and "Leaders Protest 'Who Is,' " *Atlanta Jewish Times*, Dec. 2, 1988, pp. 12, 13, as well as " 'Who Is a Jew' Furor Erupts," in the same periodical, Nov. 8, 1988, p. 16A.

[248]The open letter appeared in the *New York Times*, Dec. 19, 1988, p. B9. On Orthodox divisions over the issue, see Alan Richter and Walter Ruby, "Rift Develops Among Orthodox over Law of Return," *Long Island Jewish World*, Dec. 2-8, 1988, p. 3.

Those leaders who speak so passionately for Jewish unity ought to have launched a major attack on the decision of Reform Judaism to consider "patrilineal Jews" as Jews. There has probably been nothing more divisive in modern Jewish history than this decision to unilaterally change the definition of Jewishness to include the child of a Jewish father.[249]

It is still too early to tell whether the bitterness generated by the "Who is a Jew?" debate will lead to further polarization or whether it will redouble efforts toward greater religious unity. The formation of an Israeli government intent on shelving the question will not in the long run make the divisions over Jewish identity disappear. For underlying the debate over "Who is a Jew?" are differences between Jewish religious factions over questions of religious authenticity, the nature of religious reform, and different conceptions of "What is Judaism?" Irving Greenberg has warned that by the end of the century there will be perhaps as many as half a million children, born to mothers converted by Reform rabbis or accepted as Jewish under the patrilineal definition, whose Jewishness will not be accepted by other Jews.[250] Moreover, within a generation, there will be rabbis of patrilineal descent who will not be recognized *as Jewish* by Orthodox and Conservative rabbis. Clearly, the inability of Jewish religious movements to act in concert in the recent past will have serious repercussions for American Judaism in the coming decades.

## NEW SETTINGS FOR RELIGIOUS REVIVAL

Although most Jewish religious activities in America continue to be channeled through the organized denominations, some important new programs for religious renewal have been launched independently—and sometimes in conscious rejection of—organized American Judaism. During the past 20 years, American Jews have experimented with new forms of religious communities, innovative liturgies that express contemporary concerns, and nontraditional settings for Jewish study. In time, some of these programs have been integrated into, or tacitly supported by, established religious institutions. But much of the impulse and energy for innovation has come from individual Jews seeking new ways to express their religious commitments.

---

[249]Marc D. Angel, "Leaders of U.S. Jewry Have Fear of Losing Power," *Jewish Week* (New York), Dec. 16, 1988, p. 26.
[250]See the exchange between Irving Greenberg and Steven M. Cohen in "The One in 2000 Controversy."

## The Havurah Movement

The most striking and influential attempt to foster religious renewal through the establishment of an alternative to established synagogues has been the *havurah* movement. In a new study of this phenomenon in American Judaism, Riv-Ellen Prell situates the movement in a particular historical context.[251] The *havurot*, she argues, were created by a particular generation—the grandchildren of immigrants from Eastern Europe, a generation that had come of age primarily in suburban America in the 1960s. Being swept up in the "youth culture" of the 1960s and 1970s, these young Jews sought a religious community that would alter "the relationship between the individual and society, between making and consuming, between membership and community, and between instrumentality and authenticity." The *havurah* model appealed to them because it provided the opportunity to form small intimate fellowships for study, prayer, and friendship that seemed impossible in the large, decorous, bureaucratized synagogues they knew from their youth. It allowed for individual participation and spontaneity, whereas established synagogues were dominated by professionals who "led" formal services.

The young Jews who joined *havurot* espoused the dominant political ideology of the time. They adopted the rhetoric of the New Left and supported the general critique of American society and especially of the Vietnam War. But what distinguished this group was its involvement with Jewish concerns. For even as they criticized established Jewish institutions, *havurah* organizers were engaged in the process of remaking Jewish life, rather than rejecting it wholesale. As Prell observes:

> This generation offered their own transformation of the key themes in American Judaism: authority, decorum, and organization. They neither transformed the voluntary structure of the American Jewish community, nor abandoned organizations, chiefly the prayer community, as the source of Jewish identity. Rather, they refashioned the nature of Jewish organizations in light of the aesthetics of the American counterculture. . . . Their counter-aesthetic and alternative decorum constituted a means by which they differentiated themselves from their parents and from American society.[252]

The first *havurah*, Havurat Shalom, was founded in Somerville, a suburb of Boston, in the fall of 1968, as an alternative rabbinical seminary. Within a short time, Havurat Shalom reoriented its program "to create a new and stimulating Jewish community." One year later the New York Havurah was formed, and within a few years, young Jews formed the Farbrangen in Washington and a similar *havurah* in Philadelphia. By the early 1970s,

---

[251] Riv-Ellen Prell, *Prayer and Community: The Havurah in American Judaism* (Detroit, 1989), pp. 69–72.
[252] Ibid., pp. 71–72.

*havurot* had proliferated on many college campuses. For the most part, these early *havurot* "were closed communities of young people... that were open to the rest of the Jewish community on Sabbaths and most holidays. ... The groups were run democratically, and generally included some program of communal study, in addition to regular communal meals and occasional weekend retreats."[253]

The *havurah* outlook of this period came to wider attention with the publication of *The Jewish Catalog* (1973) and *The Second Jewish Catalog* (1976), which along with a third such volume (1980) eventually sold over half a million copies. The first volume was oriented to a "do-it-yourself" approach aimed at "enabling the individual Jew to build his own Jewish life."[254] The volume paid attention to "the physical aspects of Jewish life, and provided a guide for the construcion of Jewish objects."[255] By contrast, the second catalog was more concerned with "proper ways to act rather than the simple how-to of doing Jewish things—more attention to the community, less to the self."[256] Surveying the Jewish life cycle, study, synagogue, prayer, and the arts, the second catalog offered a "mix of personal advice with halachic and other traditional sources, together with ideas, suggestions, illustrations, photographs, general information, and small-print commentary."[257] Both volumes featured an encounter with traditional Jewish sources and a concern with Halakhah, coupled with experimentation and eclecticism.

By the mid-1970s, this kind of approach came under attack from within. Some longtime members of the *havurah* movement grew impatient with what they saw as a casual approach to Jewish tradition, summed up by the semijocular remark of one insider: "We are a *havurah* so we examine Halakhah, then decide what we want to do."[258] Describing his early years in the *havurah* movement, Alan Mintz noted sardonically, "In those days my Judaism was a delicate flower of the Diaspora, a kind of aesthetic religion based on values and symbols which sacralized personal relations."[259] From a different perspective, William Novak challenged the *havurah* movement to stake out an alternative approach to Jewish tradition: "Is

---

[253]William Novak, "From Somerville to Savannah . . . and Los Angeles . . . and Dayton," *Moment*, Jan./Feb. 1981, p. 19.
[254]David Glanz review in *Congress Bi-Weekly*, June 21, 1974, p. 21.
[255]William Novak, "The Future of Havurah Judaism," *Moment*, Jan. 1977, p. 56.
[256]From *The Second Jewish Catalog*, quoted in Novak, "The Future . . . ," p. 56.
[257]Ibid.
[258]Quoted in Shira Weinberg Hecht, "Religious Practice and Organization in an Egalitarian Minyan Setting," a paper delivered at the annual meeting of the Society for the Scientific Study of Religion, Oct. 1988, p. 28, note 14. I thank the author for graciously sharing this paper and information on her research.
[259]Alan Mintz, in the symposium "Have You Sold Out?" *Response*, Spring 1976, p. 43.

it not time," he asked, "that those who find the Halakhah an inadequate surface begin to pave a more systematic alternative?"[260] In the 1980s, these issues began to pale as the *havurah* movement underwent important transformations. All the non- Orthodox versions of American Judaism expressed a new openness to the *havurah* form. Reconstructionism enrolled *havurot* as constituents in its Federation of Reconstructionist Congregations and Havurot; and Conservative and Reform congregations organized synagogue-based *havurot*. The latter were designed to offer synagogue members intimate fellowship, while simultaneously participating in the life of a larger congregation. In an influential essay, "Restructuring the Synagogue," Rabbi Harold Schulweis urged his colleagues "to offer the searching Jew a community which does not ignore his autonomy":

> We are challenged to decentralize the synagogue and deprofessionalize Jewish living so that the individual Jew is brought back into a circle of Jewish experience. ... I see one of the major functions of the synagogue as that of the *shadchan*—bringing together separate, lonely parties into *Havurot*. In our congregation, a *havurah* is comprised of a *minyan* of families who have agreed to meet together at least once a month to learn together, to celebrate together and hopefully to form some surrogate for the eroded extended family.[261]

Although definitive statistics are not available on the number of synagogue-based *havurot*, it is clear that the model proposed by Schulweis has been adopted by a significant number of congregations.[262] A survey conducted by a Reform commission headed by Rabbi Saul Rubin in the early 1980s found that at least 129 Reform temples sponsored *havurot*, with the largest numbers in the Northeast and on the West Coast. Most contained between 10 and 19 people, and revolved around educational activities, social programming, holiday observances, and Jewish family life.[263] Similar data are unavailable for Conservative synagogues, but the attention devoted to synagogue *havurot* at conventions of the Rabbinical Assembly suggests the proliferation of such fellowships.[264]

---

[260]Novak, "The Future ... ," p. 59. For a hard-hitting critique of *havurah* Judaism by an outsider, see Marshall Sklare, "The Greening of Judaism," *Commentary*, Dec. 1974, pp. 51–57. Sklare was particularly incensed over the rejection of Jewish norms in favor of the "youth culture," and the "superiority toward the conventional forms of American Jewish life" (p. 57).

[261]Harold Schulweis, "Restructuring the Synagogue," *Conservative Judaism*, Summer 1973, p. 19.

[262]Daniel Elazar and Rela Geffen Monson, "The Synagogue Havurah—An Experiment in Restoring Adult Fellowship to the Jewish Community," *Jewish Journal of Sociology*, June 1979, pp. 70–72.

[263]I am indebted to Rabbi Rubin for sharing some of his survey findings with me. As far as I know, they have not been published. On *havurot* on the West Coast, see Gerald B. Bubis and Harry Wasserman, *Synagogue Havurot: A Comparative Study* (Washington, D.C., 1983).

[264]See "Havurah Failures and Successes," *Proceedings of the RA*, 1979, pp. 55–75.

The introduction of fellowships into larger congregations has provided some adherents of *havurah* Judaism with the opportunity to reestablish their ties to the American synagogue. Whereas *havurot* once represented a break with establishment Judaism, they now serve as a bridge linking former members of the student movement with the larger Jewish community. This linkage was made especially evident by the formation of a national organization of *havurot* in 1979, which brings together both the independent and synagogue types.[265] The established community no longer views *havurot* as a threat, but has incorporated the fellowship ideal into some of its programs; in addition, it has recruited members of the *havurah* world to serve as rabbis, administrators, and educators within the larger Jewish community. In turn, members of *havurot* turn to the larger community in order to provide their children with Hebrew or day-school education, Jewish camping experiences, and social and recreational programs offered by Jewish community centers.[266]

A second dramatic change in *havurah* Judaism has been the shift from a community focused on study and social interaction to one primarily concerned with prayer services. Indeed, many a *havurah* has signaled the shift by renaming itself a *"minyan."* To some extent, this is a function of changes in the life situations of members. The undergraduate and graduate students who founded the *havurah* movement have taken on career, marriage, and family responsibilities that leave little time for intensive communal experiences. At the same time, the *minyan* may also represent a reaction to the loose, informal structure of earlier *havurot;* the goal of the *minyanim* is to enable members to fulfill a technical requirement of religious life—public prayer. The *havurah* and *minyan* are also distinguished by membership patterns. *Minyanim* are open to anyone who will participate regularly; as a result, "the typical *minyan* is larger than a *havurah*, and may reach a membership of eighty to a hundred."[267] But the growing population of attendees at *minyanim* has also led to dissatisfaction among those who feel that a large group works against spontaneity and brings in newcomers who lack the synagogue skills and *havurah* experience of veterans.[268]

A third important change in *havurah* Judaism has been the introduction of gender equality as a fundamental principle. As the women's movement

---

[265]Jeffrey Oboler, "The First National Havurah Conference," *Congress Monthly*, Dec. 1979, pp. 12–13.

[266]In Boston, however, Shira Weinberg Hecht found that many *havurah* members send their children to day schools, thereby obviating the need to join a synagogue.

[267]Lenore Eve Weissler, "Making Judaism Meaningful: Ambivalence and Tradition in a Havurah Community" (unpublished doctoral diss., University of Pennsylvania, 1982), cited in Hecht, "Religious Practice," p. 8.

[268]For some debate over this issue, see Steven M. Cohen, "Conflict in the Havurot: Veterans vs. Newcomers," *Response*, Summer 1979, pp. 3–4; and Michael Strassfeld, "Too Many for a Minyan," *Response*, Spring 1980, pp. 21–28.

developed in the 1970s, *havurot* incorporated egalitarianism as a basic ideal, albeit not without some strains. Since much of the liturgy of *havurot* was highly traditional, it took time for women to be integrated into nontraditional synagogue roles—as prayer leaders, Torah readers, etc. The movement as a whole also debated whether males of an Orthodox outlook, who insisted on praying in a *minyan* that separated the sexes, could be included in *havurah* Judaism.[269] The gradual evolution of egalitarian religious services within *havurah* Judaism not only transformed the prayer services of the movement but also served as a model for women in conventional synagogues. Moreover, with the intensification of their involvement in religious services, women in *havurot* began to experiment with new religious rituals and liturgies to express their separate concerns.

*Havurah* Judaism's relationship with the larger Jewish community is not without its ongoing challenges. Since its inception, the movement has been uncertain of its position *vis à vis* the established denominations. Does *havurah* Judaism represent a fifth religious movement? Is it postdenominational and, therefore, separate from all movements? A second challenge pertains to the relationship of *havurah* members to other generations of American Jews. Ironically, the young Jews who founded *havurot* to express the needs of their own generation have persuaded their elders of the value of their program, but have been far less successful with their juniors. Lamenting the absence of younger members, a *havurah* founder has observed: "No one beyond the generation that began the *havurah* joined or created new ones. Where are the college aged students today? They are becoming Orthodox Jews. We could only speak for ourselves."[270] As the former members of America's youth culture enter their 40s, they may find themselves without a successor generation within the *havurah* movement.

## New Women's Rituals and Liturgies

Jewish feminism has served as a second source of innovation outside of the mainstream of American Judaism.[271] Jewish feminists have created new ceremonies and liturgies, or reappropriated older forms to mark the particular life-cycle events of Jewish women. Though they communicate with each other in the pages of established journals, as well as new publications, such

---

[269]For a discussion of the principle of egalitarianism in *havurah* Judaism, see Novak, "From Somerville . . . ," pp. 58–59. For a case study of the struggle for egalitarianism within one *havurah*, see Prell, *Prayer and Community*, chap. 7, "Community, Visibility, and Gender in Prayer."

[270]Quoted in Prell, *Prayer and Community*, p. 317.

[271]Our discussion of denominational life noted the struggles for increased women's participation within established institutions, such as synagogues and seminaries. The present section is concerned with less formal and institutionalized expressions of Jewish feminism, many of which transcend ideology and denomination.

as *Lilith*, Jewish feminists appear to lack institutions to coordinate their activities. There are pockets of activists and small groups in many areas of the country, but little centralized activity. Moreover, Jewish feminists vary widely, from Orthodox women who will work only within the parameters set by Halakhah, to women who create nontraditional liturgies, to radical feminists who insist on breaking with the existing vocabulary of Judaism, claiming it is inherently distorted by patriarchal values and masculine religious categories. Due to the diffuse nature of Jewish feminism, it is difficult to assess just how many women are involved in its activities. But the proliferation of new liturgies and ceremonies attests to the creative engagement of those women who do participate in the movement.[272]

The initial focus of the Jewish women's movement within the religious sphere was to accord women a greater role in traditional ceremonial life. Hence, double-ring ceremonies were introduced at Jewish weddings so that brides could play a more active role; and the ceremony of *Brit Milah* was revised in order to accord mothers an opportunity to recite part of the liturgy at their sons' circumcisions. Once these hurdles were overcome, Jewish feminists shifted the focus of their attention to the celebration of women's life-cycle events.

Undoubtedly the most widely practiced of these were birth ceremonies for baby girls. These have ranged from the *Simhat Bat*, or *Shalom Bat*, which includes no new liturgy or formal ceremony, aside from remarks prepared by the newborn's parents, to the *Brit Banot*, which not only models itself after the liturgy of the *Brit Milah*, but in some instances seeks a substitute for the act of circumcision in analagous physical acts, such as immersing the baby girl in a ritual bath or washing her feet in water.[273] As noted by anthropologist Chava Weissler, such ceremonies strive to achieve several ends: (1) to create an elaborate celebration that rivals the *Brit Milah*; (2) to develop a liturgy initiating the child into the covenant that binds Israel to its God; (3) to define an approach to sex-role differentiation.[274]

---

[272]Much of the source material utilized in this section was gathered by Rabbi Debra Cantor, who, as a student at the Jewish Theological Seminary, compiled "A Compendium of New Jewish Women's Rituals" for a course I taught on contemporary American Judaism. The most important repository of materials on Jewish women's activities in the religious and other spheres is the Jewish Women's Resource Center (JWRC), housed at the headquarters of the National Council of Jewish Women in New York.

[273]Over 50 different birth ceremonies for girls are on file at the Jewish Women's Resource Center. See also: Susan Weidman Schneider, *Jewish and Female* (New York, 1984), pp. 121-30; and an issue of *Sh'ma* devoted to these rituals and liturgies (Dec. 23, 1983); Daniel I. and Myra Leifer, "On the Birth of a Daughter," in *The Jewish Woman: New Perspectives*, ed. Elizabeth Koltun (New York, 1976), pp. 91-100; Gary and Sheila Rubin, "Preserving Tradition by Expanding It," *Response*, Fall/Winter 1982, pp. 61-68; and "The Covenant of Washing," *Menorah: Sparks of Jewish Renewal*, Apr./May 1983, p. 22ff.

[274]Chava Weissler, "New Jewish Birth Rituals for Baby Girls," unpublished paper at the Jewish Women's Resource Center, p. 6.

A wide range of ceremonies was developed to celebrate other milestones in the lives of women. These include the redemption of the first-born daughter, *Pidyon Ha-bat*; weaning ceremonies; and special prayers that enable women to commemorate both pregnancy and miscarriage.[275] Further, an array of liturgies was created to mark the fertility cycle of women. The onset of menstruation is celebrated rather than perceived as a curse; it is designated as a "coming of age" to be proclaimed by daughter and mother in a public setting.[276] Jewish feminists have created other ceremonies to reappropriate the monthly ceremony of ritual immersion in the waters of the *mikveh*, as well as to mark the onset of menopause.[277] The value of such rituals for feminists is that they grant recognition to the unique experiences of women. For some feminists, however, the emphasis on women's biological functions represents a step backward. "Is the celebration of the recurrence of the menses feminism, or is it a ceremony honoring instrumentality?" asks Cynthia Ozick in a widely remarked essay. Feminism, she argues, must enable women to transcend biology; accordingly, Jewish feminism should seek to end the segregation of women.[278]

Feminist Judaism has found particular meaning for women in two Jewish holidays—Passover and Rosh Hodesh (Festival of the New Moon). Passover has become central to feminist celebrations for a number of reasons: it is the most widely celebrated of all Jewish holidays; it is thematically focused on liberation; it has traditionally been a time when women shoulder the burden of preparation; and the Exodus narrative itself draws attention to the roles of women—Yocheved and Miriam, Shifrah and Puah. Structurally, the twin Seder evenings provide an opportunity to experiment with new liturgies on the second evening, even for those who prefer the traditional ceremony on the first. Not surprisingly, there has been an outpouring of feminist Passover liturgies, generally focusing on women's liberation and their role in history.[279]

---

[275]Copies of such ceremonies are on file at the Jewish Women's Resource Center. For a survey, see Schneider, *Jewish and Female*, which contains a section on "Rituals for the Landmarks of Our Lives," pp. 117–48.

[276]For a ceremony marking the onset of menarche, see Penina V. Adelman, *Miriam's Well: Rituals for Jewish Women Around the Year* (New York, 1986), the section on "Sivan." See also *Siddur Nashim*, comp. Maggie Wenig and Naomi Janowitz (Providence, 1976), for a "Prayer on Menstruation."

[277]On the reappropriation of *mikveh*, see Evelyn Hutt v'Dodd's contribution in "The Ways We Are," *Lilith*, Winter 1976/77, pp. 7–9.

[278]Cynthia Ozick, "Bima: Torah as a Matrix for Feminism," *Lilith*, Winter/Spring 1985, pp. 48–49.

[279]For a survey of 13 feminist Haggadahs, see *JWRC Newsletter*, Winter/Spring 1981, pp. 1–2. See also Reena Friedman, "How Was This Passover Different from All Other Passovers?" *Lilith*, Spring/Summer 1977, pp. 33–36. For a new prayer to mark the pre-Passover cleaning, see Lynn Gottlieb, "Spring Cleaning Ritual on the Eve of Full Moon Nissan," in *On Being a Jewish Feminist: A Reader*, ed. Susannah Heschel (New York, 1983), pp. 278–80.

Some Jewish feminists have reappropriated the Festival of the New Moon, building upon its traditional association with women. Rabbinic texts had long enjoined women, as opposed to men, from engaging in their usual work routines on the New Moon Rosh Hodesh; some of those texts had in fact identified Rosh Hodesh as a reward to women, as a time when, in the world to come, "women will be renewed like the New Moons."[280] Rosh Hodesh is seen, thus, as a suitable occasion for exploring women's special spiritual needs. Since the early 1970s, when these celebrations gained popularity, Rosh Hodesh groups have met throughout the country, usually during the evenings when the new moon has appeared, to mark the occasion with the reading of mainly English liturgies (including their own versions of *"techinot,"* traditional women's supplications), movement in a circle, lighting candles, and eating a ritual feast.[281]

In all these activities, Jewish feminists have grappled with the tension between wishing to develop opportunities for women to express their own religious needs and a desire to integrate women into all facets of Jewish religious life. In discussions of liturgical revision, this issue is central: Is the goal of new liturgies to refer to God using pronouns that are feminine or using pronouns not associated with either gender? And if either approach is utilized, will Jews find a liturgy meaningful that differs radically from the hallowed prayers? The decades of the seventies and eighties have opened the way to experimentation with liturgy and ritual and to serious consideration of these issues.[282]

## Reaching Jews on the Periphery

The era of the 1970s and 1980s has also witnessed the emergence of a wide range of programs that appeal to Jews previously considered to be on the periphery of American Judaism. Some of these activities are "outreach" programs that reflect the internal agenda of the organized Jewish community—efforts to stem the tide of defections. Others are the spontaneous coming together of individuals seeking novel forms of religious community. Typical of the latter are humanistic synagogues, gay synagogues, rural

---

[280]For a good introduction to the historical, as well as the contemporary, observance of Rosh Hodesh by women, see Arlene Agus, "This Month Is for You: Observing Rosh Hodesh as a Woman's Holiday," in Koltun, ed., *The Jewish Woman*, pp. 84–93.

[281]Carol Glass, "A Festival of Joy," *JWRC Newsletter*, Winter/Spring 1981, reports on Rosh Hodesh groups. Numerous texts on the celebration of this ritual in different localities are on file at the Jewish Women's Resource Center.

[282]For a sampling of views in this debate, see the essays by Judith Plaskow, Rita M. Gross, and Arthur Green in Heschel, ed., *On Being a Jewish Feminist*, pp. 217–60; Naomi Janowitz and Maggie Wenig, "Selections from a Prayerbook Where God's Image Is Female," *Lilith*, vol. 1, no. 4, Fall/Winter 1977–78, pp. 27–29; Judith Plaskow, "Language, God and Liturgy: A Feminist Perspective," *Response*, Spring 1983, pp. 3–14.

communities, and informal networks for "Jewish renewal."

Jewish organizations spanning the spectrum from Jewish community centers and Ys to synagogues to special retreat centers have developed programs to attract unaffiliated Jews and teach them how to observe Jewish rituals. Many of the sponsoring organizations are nondenominational, such as Hadassah, but are eager to expose unaffiliated Jews to some type of religious observance—a traditional Sabbath, model Seder, or *sukkah* visit. Among the most innovative programs have been the retreats offered by the Brandeis-Bardin Institute on the West Coast and Project Connect, sponsored by the 92nd Street YM/YWHA in New York, both directed at unaffiliated families, including mixed-married couples. Synagogues of all denominations have been especially active in promoting outreach programs and separate religious services for single Jews, who tend to be unaffiliated. In New York and Washington, close to a thousand Jewish singles gather annually for their own High Holy Day services.[283]

In 1963, a Reform rabbi, Sherwin Wine, formed a "secular humanistic" Jewish congregation in Farmington Hills, Michigan, to provide a congregational setting for Jews who rejected belief in God but sought a communal structure to meet with fellow Jews. Wine's congregation now numbers 500 families and has been augmented by 25 additional congregations affiliated with the Society for Humanistic Judaism. These congregations hold Sabbath and holiday celebrations utilizing "non-theistic symbols (a *sukkah*, *lulav* and *etrog*, for instance), folk songs and celebrations, such as a Purim carnival—independent of services." Rites of passage are commemorated in ceremonies that do not include blessings or Torah readings, but do connect the life-cycle event to the larger tapestry of Jewish history. In general, congregational meetings consist of two parts: a period of time devoted to reading philosophical reflections, poetry, meditations, and songs; and a part devoted to a lecture or cultural program. Humanistic Judaism claims an international membership of 30,000 Jews.[284]

In 1972 homosexual men and women organized Beth Chayim Chadashim in Los Angeles, the first gay synagogue. Since then approximately 20 additional congregations have been established, with the largest, Congregation Beth Simchat Torah in New York, claiming 400 members and 1,000 worshippers at High Holy Day services. When interviewed, members of these congregations describe their early education in yeshivahs and Hebrew schools and their subsequent rejection of Judaism because of the conflict

---

[283]See, for example, Richard Bono, "Traditional Jewish Values Back in Vogue," *Atlanta Jewish Times*, Apr. 15, 1988, p. 1; and John L. Rosove, "A Synagogue Model for the Single Jew," *Journal of Reform Judaism*, Winter 1986, pp. 29–36.

[284]See Naomi Godfrey, "Taking the Theism Out of Judaism," *Jewish Week* (New York), Apr. 8, 1988, p. 28.

between their sexual orientation and traditional Jewish norms.[285] Gay synagogues provide these individuals with an opportunity to participate in Jewish worship with men and women who share their way of life. While much of the traditional liturgy is utilized at the services of gay synagogues, new prayers are added to "remove gender references to God, recognize the contributions of women as well as men . . . and to reflect the experiences of lesbian and gay Jews." A prayer included in the liturgy of Congregation Sha'ar Zahav in San Francisco expresses the hope: "Let the day come which is all Shabbat, when all people, all religions, all sexualities wil rejoice as one family, all children of Your creation."[286]

Throughout American Jewish history, some Jews have resided in small rural communities, separated by vast distances from the larger centers of Jewish life. Rural Judaism declined in the middle decades of the 20th century, as younger Jews sought higher education and settled in urban centers. In the late 1960s, this process was briefly reversed, as small numbers of Jews involved in the counterculture sought to escape from their suburban homes to rural America as part of a "back-to-the land" movement. In time, some confronted the isolation of their lives, in particular their loss of Jewish contacts. By the mid-1980s, the annual Conference on Judaism in Rural New England was convened to connect Jews in Vermont, New Hampshire, and Maine, who live far from a synagogue. A Klezmer band and a bimonthly journal—*KFARI: The Jewish Newsmagazine of Rural New England and Quebec*—help to provide a sense of community for these rural Jews. In Montpelier, Vermont, 80 families practice "New Age Judaism" in a nondenominational synagogue that functions without a rabbi.[287]

The "New Age Judaism" of rural Jews is part of a larger movement that has sought, since the 1960s, to merge Eastern religion, the self-actualization movement, and the counterculture outlook with Jewish religious traditions, particularly with Jewish mysticism. Led by a charismatic rabbi named Zalman Schachter-Shalomi, this loosely organized movement has gradually evolved an institutional network known as the P'nai Or Religious Fellowship, which currently numbers 11 American affiliates.[288] "Reb Zalman," as he is called by his disciples, has publicly spoken of his evolving Judaism,

---

[285]See Barry Alan Mehler, "Gay Jews," *Moment*, Mar. 1977, p. 22; Henry Rabinowitz, "Talmud Class in a Gay Synagogue," *Judaism*, Fall 1983, pp. 433–43; Janet R. Marder, "Getting to Know the Gay and Lesbian Shul," *Reconstructionist*, Oct.-Nov. 1985, pp. 20–25.

[286]Michael Rankin and Gary Koenigsberg, "Let the Day Come Which Is All Shabbat: The Liturgy of the 'Gay-Outreach' Synagogue," *Journal of Reform Judaism*, Spring 1986, p. 70.

[287]See Sam Allis, "In Vermont: When Woody Allen Meets L.L. Bean," *Time*, Sept. 26, 1988, pp. 10–11.

[288]See *P'nai Or*, undated brochure issued in 1989. Most affiliates call themselves P'nai or B'nai Or; one in Berkeley, Calif., is called the Aquarian Minyan. There are two affiliates in Europe.

one which began with intense study of Lubavitch Hassidism, later encompassed formal study of psychology, experimentation with LSD, and study with various masters of Asian religions.[289] He founded the P'nai Or Religious Fellowship to revitalize Judaism. As stated in its promotional brochure, "P'nai Or searches the inner meaning of Torah, Kabbalistic philosophy, Chasidic prayer, meditation, humanistic and transpersonal psychology, and *halakha* to gain a practical orientation to Jewish spiritual life. By understanding their intentions, the individual derives a new appreciation of Judaism as a path to inner balance and inter-connectedness with others, and with the world we live in."[290]

In light of its emphasis on self-expression, the Jewish renewal movement is particularly concerned with prayer. Schachter-Shalomi has developed what he refers to as a "Davvenology," an examination of Jewish prayer which "monitors each phase of the inner process and observes it in differing personality types." P'nai Or groups take great interest in dance, song, and movement, to invigorate their bodies and stimulate spiritual intensity.[291]

Designed as a self-consciously experimental movement, which "welcomes all Jews, including those who have been disenfranchised by the Jewish establishment,"[292] the Jewish renewal movement has begun to grapple with questions of definition and boundaries. A recent issue of *New Menorah: The P'nai Or Journal of Jewish Renewal* featured a debate over the "content" of Jewish renewal. As articulated by Arthur Waskow, one of the more politically active leaders of the movement, there is a vast difference between "Jewish restoration" and "Jewish renewal." The former continues to do what Jews have always done: "Keeping women in their separate place; keeping gay and lesbian Jews invisible; imagining God always and only as Lord and King; saying 'all my bones will praise You' while sitting locked into pews where no bone can move a quarter-inch; reciting the second paragraph of the Sh'ma while taking no responsibility to end the acid rain that is destroying earth." Jewish renewal, according to Waskow, requires the rejection of all these positions.[293] As the movement coalesces into what some regard as an emerging "fifth" Jewish religious movement, it will be forced to decide whether it is a movement of "content" as well as form.

There is considerable overlap in the populations of Jews who identify with several of the new and experimental movements. The *havurah* move-

---

[289]See "An Interview with Zalman Schachter-Shalomi," *New Traditions*, Fall 1985, pp. 9–25. His own account of some of his earlier experimentation is in "The Conscious Ascent of the Soul," in *The Ecstatic Adventurer*, ed. Ralph Metzner (New York, 1968), pp. 96–123.

[290]*Adventures in Jewish Renewal*, a publication of the P'nai Or Outreach Bureau (n.d., circa 1988), p. 2.

[291]See the pamphlets cited above.

[292]*Adventures in Jewish Renewal*, p. 2.

[293]*New Menorah*, Pessach 5749, pp. 6, 10. For more on Waskow's views, see his *These Holy Sparks: The Rebirth of the Jewish People* (San Francisco, 1983).

ment, feminist Judaism, Jewish renewal, and to some extent, gay Judaism, share an openness to innovation. They also share a common belief that they are disenfranchised from "establishment" institutions and synagogues. In fact, members of these movements are frequently invited to address rabbinic and synagogue conventions and publish articles in the journals of the religious movements. In limited but perceptible ways, their experimentation with new liturgies and ceremonies may even be having an effect on denominational Judaism. At the same time, their absence from the institutions of mainstream American Judaism deprives the "establishment" of important sources of enthusiasm and creativity. Conservative synagogues would take on a far more youthful and dynamic quality were they to regain the youth lost to *havurot*; and Reconstructionism would have greater momentum were the sympathies of its adherents not divided between it and the Jewish renewal movement.

CONCLUSION

In concluding this report on trends in American Judaism during the past two decades, it is appropriate to ask what they portend for the future of American Jewry. For the most part, the debate between sociologists of the American Jewish community revolves around the health of Jews as an ethnic group, and relatively little is said about the religious dimension of Jewish life. This is understandable, given the propensity of sociologists to focus on quantitative measures and on the survival of Jews as a viable and forceful group on the American scene. In light, however, of the uncertain future of ethnicity as an enduring bond within American society and the reemergence of religion as a powerful factor, the condition of American Judaism needs to be reevaluated. This question takes on particular importance for Jews, since Judaism has traditionally provided its adherents with patterns of behavior and reasons for identification that go beyond ethnicity, with a Jewish content that has motivated them to remain distinctive.[294]

The current debate between sociologists pits "transformationists" against "assimilationists," with the former arguing that American Jewry is undergoing dramatic changes that are transforming but not weakening Jewish life, whereas the latter perceive the changes within Jewish life as portents of decline and eventual assimilation into the fabric of American society.[295]

---

[294]For a contrary view stressing only the "structural" factors that account for Jewish identification, see Calvin Goldscheider and Alan Zuckerman, *The Transformation of the Jews* (Chicago, 1984).

[295]Two penetrating analyses of the debate between "assimilationists" and "transformationists" are presented in Cohen, *American Assimilation or Jewish Revival?* pp. 1–18, and Charles S. Liebman, *Deceptive Images: Toward a Redefinition of American Judaism* (New Brunswick, 1988), pp. 61–73.

Recent trends in American Judaism provide evidence to bolster both positions. Certainly American Judaism has been transformed within the past two decades: all of the religious movements have repositioned themselves on questions of ideology and, to a large extent, also practice. New movements of religious renewal have emerged which have particularly attracted young Jews. Indeed, there are more options for religious expression and more tolerance for religious pluralism than in any previous era in American Judaism. Moreover, there is a great curiosity today about religious expression, as distinct from the associational character of much of Jewish life in earlier decades of the century.

Simultaneously, demographic data suggest diminishing involvement in Judaism among the masses of American Jews. Surveys conducted during the eighties show a decline in the percentages of Jews who identify with any religious denomination. And compared to surveys conducted two decades ago, lower percentages of Jews attend synagogues with any regularity, keep kosher, or light Sabbath candles weekly. Most ominously, the rate of mixed marriage has skyrocketed in the past two decades, and is highest among the youngest Jews. Efforts to cope with this unprecedented challenge—which relates to the very transmission of Jewish identity—color all aspects of Jewish religious life.

All of these patterns suggest that in the religious sphere, a bipolar model is emerging, with a large population of Jews moving toward religious minimalism and a minority gravitating toward greater participation and deepened concern with religion. The latter include: newly committed Jews and converts to Judaism, whose conscious choice of religious involvement has infused all branches of American Judaism with new energy and passion; rabbinic and lay leaders of the official denominations, who continue to struggle with issues of continuity and change within their respective movements; and groups of Jews who are experimenting with traditional forms in order to reappropriate aspects of the Jewish past. These articulate and vocal Jews have virtually transformed American Judaism during the past two decades. At the same time, an even larger population of American Jews has drifted away from religious participation. Such Jews have not articulated the sources of their discontent but have "voted with their feet," by absenting themselves from synagogues and declining to observe religious rituals that require frequent and ongoing attention. To a great extent, their worrisome patterns of attrition have been obscured by the dynamism of the religiously involved. It remains to be seen, therefore, whether the transformation of American Judaism wrought by the committed minority during the past two decades will sustain its present energy and inspire greater numbers of Jews to commit themselves to a living Judaism.

# Review of the Year

UNITED STATES

# Civic and Political

## Intergroup Relations

THE YEAR 1987 BEGAN AND ended with concern about the impact of Israel-related events—the Pollard affair and the West Bank uprising. However, what was undoubtedly the most traumatic episode of the year resulted from a conjunction of Kurt Waldheim's presidency of Austria and his formal reception by Pope John Paul II, preceding the pope's visit to the United States. This episode contributed to a sense of despair over Catholic-Jewish relations as well as a growing fear among American Jews that the Nazi past was receding in the consciousness of America and the world.

### Waldheim, the Pope, and American Jews

The organized Jewish community, which had vigorously condemned the election of Kurt Waldheim to the Austrian presidency in 1986, was gratified when the U.S. government placed Waldheim on the "watch list" of persons barred from entering the country, the first head of state to be so designated. In April the Department of Justice and the State Department jointly announced that "a prima facie case of excludability exists with respect to Kurt Waldheim," based on the finding that he had "assisted or otherwise participated in the persecution of persons because of race, religion, national origin or political opinion." That was the language of the 1978 statute, which did not require proof that the proscribed person had personally committed war crimes, but only that he or she had played some role in such crimes.

In fact, a higher standard of proof could have been met. An official of the State Department told the *New York Times* on April 29 that "the more we dug, the stronger the case got." He said that the evidence of Waldheim's involvement in Nazi persecutions (as a German officer) was such that, if he had been a naturalized American citizen, the department would have sought his deportation. (By contrast, the British Foreign Office announced that there was not enough proof of Waldheim's wartime activity to bar him from visiting the United Kingdom.) Following the U.S. announcement, an Austrian newspaper poll found that more Austrians supported Waldheim, in the wake of the American action, than had elected him as president. More than 70 percent of the respondents did not want Waldheim to resign, and 57 percent thought he should file libel suits. Waldheim himself, in a televised speech to the Austrian nation, said he had "a clear conscience" about his wartime activity and promised to make public information that would clear him. Shortly thereafter, he gave his assent to the formation of a commission of historians that would investigate the charges against him.

In the May/June issue of *Present Tense,* Shlomo Avineri, noted professor of political science at the Hebrew University of Jerusalem, took sharp issue with the way in which the World Jewish Congress (WJC), which had taken the lead in exposing Waldheim's past, had handled the case. He complained that the group's allegations were often premature and amateurishly prepared, allowing the Waldheim defenders to counter too readily. Avineri also expressed the belief that the WJC should have consulted more closely with the State of Israel, and that it had pushed Israel into a confrontation with a friendly European country for which Israel was unprepared.

However, Avineri did not discount the larger importance of the Waldheim case, saying that it "revealed the fragility of the post-World War II consensus in both Austria and West Germany regarding the Nazi past. Like the furor over Bitburg, the Waldheim affair shows that attitudes and sentiments that were thought to have been finally buried needed only a hint of quasi respectability to reclaim some sort of legitimacy."

The Waldheim affair became the definitive benchmark against which to measure revisionist efforts to bury the uniqueness of the Holocaust, to depict it as merely part of the "normal" tragedy of wartime. Reference to the normal tragedy of wartime was a constant motif in Waldheim's defensive refrain. As a consequence, Jews in America and around the world were on the watch for efforts by various world governments to legitimize the Austrian leader. In midsummer, there was a rather unsurprising reception for Waldheim in Jordan, an official visit to Waldheim by Prime Minister Nikolai V. Ryzhkov of the USSR, and a private meeting with Chancellor Helmut Kohl of Germany, while he vacationed in Austria. But Western government leaders avoided official contact with the Austrian president.

Against this background, the announcement that Waldheim was to be received by Pope John Paul II in the Vatican in June, in an official state visit, was received by world Jewry as a highly disturbing signal of both legitimation of Waldheim and diminution of Holocaust consciousness. Although Jewish communities around the world joined in the protest, the consternation of the American Jewish community was particularly high because of the impending visit of the pope to this country in September.

AMERICAN-JEWISH REACTION

A special relationship existed between the Catholics and Jews of America. Both had been disadvantaged minorities in a Protestant-dominated land. In the first decades of this century they lived side by side in the large cities of the East. In immigrant neighborhoods, even if they did not become fast friends, they shared common problems and interests. Starting out in local political machines, both became influential in regional and national Democratic party politics. Although older Eastern European Jews still averted their eyes, or worse, when passing a Catholic church, a place they associated with past persecutions, and Father Coughlin's anti-Semitic movement during the 1930s, while finally opposed by the Church hierarchy, did not improve mutual images, a kind of ease developed between the Jewish and Catholic communities, based on common interests and experiences and a common sense of differentiation from the white Anglo-Saxon Protestant majority. Even after the Catholic and Jewish populations in America began undergoing social change, with many members of both groups moving out of the central cities, this "cultural-comfort" factor lingered. In addition, while good formal relations developed between the Jews and some liberal Protestant denominations, the Catholic Church still represented to many Jews the central and most authentic Christian church in the world.

For these and other reasons, the organized Jewish community felt it had a strong investment in a good relationship with the American Catholic Church. That feeling had blossomed, especially after the Second Vatican Council in 1965 called for a new institution of "the spiritual bond," "mutual respect," and "brotherly dialogues" between Catholics and Jews. In recent years the Catholic hierarchy had established special offices of liaison with American Jews throughout the country, which offices were expressly enjoined to avoid any hint of missionary interest but only to better relations based on mutual respect.

This background helps to explain why the news in June that the pope had granted an official audience to Kurt Waldheim stunned American Jews. On one level, the action was seen as a legitimation of Waldheim, even as an implied downgrading of wartime atrocities, including the Holocaust, as well as a failure to understand Jewish sensitivities on the subject. On another level, the pope's action raised the almost certain prospect of an unwanted confrontation with American Catholics, especially in light of the pontiff's planned visit to America in September. Wherever he was scheduled to appear, the local Catholic hierarchy had formally invited rabbis and Jewish leaders to participate fully in the general ceremonial affairs. In addition, a special meeting of the pope with American Jewish leaders had been arranged to take place in Miami.

The Vatican announcement on June 17 that an audience with Waldheim would take place a week later set off a wave of protest from American Jewish groups. The day after the announcement, "profound shock and dismay" was expressed jointly by the American Jewish Committee, the American Jewish Congress, the Anti-Defamation League, B'nai B'rith, the National Jewish Community Relations Council, and the Synagogue Council, a body comprising the rabbinical and lay leadership of all three major Jewish denominations. There were, as well, individual statements from these groups and others. The Synagogue Council said that "these developments cast a dark cloud on Jewish-Vatican relations and on the scheduled meeting of the Pope with leaders of the American Jewish community in Miami." The Vatican responded immediately that it was "surprised and profoundly grieved" that the planned meeting with Waldheim raised doubts about "the Holy Father's respect for the Jewish people." Theodore Ellenoff, president of the American Jewish Committee, anticipating one defense that was to come from Vatican circles, said that "it would be altogether a matter of personal conscience were the Pope to receive Dr. Waldheim as a private Catholic communicant seeking pastoral solace, [but for] the head of the Holy See to receive Kurt Waldheim as President of a state makes a mockery of truth and justice."

There was a moment of gratification as leaders of eight different Protestant denominations issued a joint statement saying that "the invitation disgraces the memory of the victims of the Nazi Holocaust." Archbishop John L. May of St. Louis, president of the National Conference of Catholic Bishops, also issued a statement expressing sympathy with Jewish concerns.

But American and world Jewish dismay was compounded by the substance itself of the meeting between the pope and Waldheim on June 25. The pope praised Waldheim for his activities in behalf of peace, making particular reference to his term as secretary-general of the United Nations, and made no mention of either the controversy surrounding his election or the Holocaust. A *New York Times* editorial the next day said that it had been waiting "to hear [the pope's] balancing remarks. There were none; only praise for Kurt Waldheim, peacemaker. The effect is to slight all the victims of Hitler's war."

The protests mounted. The American Jewish Congress and the Synagogue Council announced that they would boycott the scheduled September meeting with the pope in Miami. Other Jewish groups said that they were reconsidering their attendance at that meeting. By way of response, Agostino Cardinal Casaroli, Vatican secretary of state, met with American Catholic and Jewish leaders in July in New York to discuss the conflict. Another Vatican diplomat said that "the Holy Father is anxious that his meeting with the Jewish community in America go forward in a fruitful and friendly manner. It is very important."

JEWS MEET WITH POPE

Mutual efforts to repair the relationship led to an unusual two-day meeting in Rome—the first part, on August 31, between members of the Vatican's Commission on Religious Relations with the Jews and a nine-person delegation of the International Jewish Committee on Interreligious Consultations, composed primarily of American Jewish leaders; the second, on September 1, between the Jewish leaders and the pope. The conversation with the pope, lasting over an hour, was described by one participant, Rabbi Henry Siegman, executive director of the American Jewish Congress, as "a historic meeting which would have been inconceivable to previous generations."

The subject of the Waldheim visit was, of course, introduced by the Jewish delegation, but the agenda was much larger, including the Holocaust, anti-Semitism in general, and the Vatican's relations with Israel. A joint communiqué issued after the two meetings did not comment directly on the Waldheim affair but did announce the intended preparation of an official Catholic document "on the Shoah [Holocaust], the historical background of anti-Semitism and its contemporary manifestations." Further, the Vatican agreed to establish a mechanism enabling the Catholic Church and the Jewish community to keep in closer touch, to prevent such "surprises" as the Waldheim visit, and to provide access to the pope "whenever the need arises." One assessment of the meeting was expressed in this statement by the National Jewish Community Relations Council:

> In and of itself, the meeting with the Pope was historically significant and unusual; the very fact that it took place was reflective of the convergence of three critical factors: the regard the Pope has for the American Jewish community, the Vatican's sensitive relations with the American Catholic hierarchy, and the cordial relationship between the American Jewish community and the American Catholic church. . . . Those who participated in the Rome meetings were in agreement with one of their number who stated that the Vatican went as far—perhaps further—than we could expect them to go.

The Rome talks cleared the way for the scheduled meeting between Pope John Paul and American Jews in Miami on September 12. Although it was a well-publicized event, it was not as substantive as the Rome meeting, essentially recapitulating the points made in August.

Some Jewish groups did not respond favorably to the Rome and Miami meetings. Elan Steinberg of the World Jewish Congress claimed that very little was accomplished. Tensions remained, and some Jewish resistance was offered in the various American communities visited by the pope. In San Francisco, a local archdiocesan spokesman announced on television that the planned program for the pope's visit to that city had been cut back because of budgetary problems. He explained that a major reason was the curtailment of Jewish contributions to the planned program because of the controversy. A few Jewish communities felt it mandatory to present to the pope, through channels, statements of communal concern about the Waldheim visit.

Following the pope's visit there was a sense that the crisis in Catholic-Jewish relations had been blunted, that in fact new opportunities had been opened for deepening the relationship, especially in the United States. The Waldheim affair could not be expunged, certainly, but the promised Vatican document and educational program on the Holocaust and anti-Semitism might, in the long run, outweigh the negative effect of Waldheim's audience with the pope.

## Other Jewish-Catholic Issues

Considerable controversy had been generated at the end of 1986 over the projected visit to Israel of John Cardinal O'Connor, the archbishop of New York. He had been forbidden by the Vatican to visit formally with Israeli public officials in their Jerusalem offices, since such visits would appear to legitimate the status of Jerusalem as the Israeli capital, contrary to Vatican policy. This position exacerbated the Jewish community's bitterness at the failure of the Vatican to grant Israel formal recognition.

During his visit to Israel at the beginning of January, Cardinal O'Connor met with both President Chaim Herzog and Foreign Minister Shimon Peres in Jerusalem. However, he visited them pointedly in their residences, not their offices, and dressed in plain clerical garb, instead of the cardinal's crimson robes and decorations he wore elsewhere. Some question was raised by the press about his visit to Herzog's home, which served also as his office, but otherwise the problem of venue seemed to have been solved to the approximate satisfaction of both Israel and the Vatican.

Dissatisfaction, however, was expressed by 53 major American Jewish organizations, in a public statement on January 10, saying that they were "disquieted and distressed" by sympathetic remarks made by Cardinal O'Connor about Palestinian Arabs. O'Connor had said that he was shocked by conditions he found in a Gaza refugee camp and disturbed by the fact that Americans stereotyped Palestinian Arabs as terrorists. While speaking in a church in Jordan, he also called for self-determination for the Palestinian Arabs. However, later in January, in a meeting in New York, O'Connor and the leaders of eight major Jewish organizations largely resolved their differences. In a joint communiqué, they explained that the cardinal had clarified his remarks, which had been reported only partially by the media. When he called for Palestinian self-determination, for example, he also told his Jordanian audience that such self-determination had to take a form that would not endanger Israel's security.

Although this particular crisis was averted, the O'Connor episode further emphasized the two underlying critical issues in Catholic-Jewish relations, pinpointed by the statement of the 53 Jewish groups as: "First, the failure of the Vatican to establish de jure diplomatic relations with Israel. . . . Second, the failure of the Holy See to come to terms with the reality of a unified Jerusalem as the capital of Israel."

Certainly, these two issues had not come closer to resolution in the course of the Waldheim affair. In his statement to the Jews at the Miami meeting, the pope did say that "[a]fter the tragic extermination of the Shoah, the Jewish people began a new period in their history. They have a right to a homeland, as does any civil nation, according to international law." In Miami the pope also reiterated the belief that Israel should be accorded "the desired security and the due tranquility that is the prerogative of every nation." At the same time, he said that "the right to a homeland also applies to the Palestinian people, so many of whom remain homeless and refugees." And he came no closer to considering full-fledged and formal recognition of Israel.

Two other issues during the year troubled Catholic-Jewish waters. In May Pope John Paul beatified a Jewish-born Carmelite nun, Sister Teresia Benedicta, born Edith Stein, who had converted in 1922 and had been killed by the Nazis in 1942.

It was reportedly the first case of a Jewish-born Catholic having been beatified, the formal step leading to sainthood. There was scattered Jewish criticism of this act, led by the surviving family of Edith Stein. In part, the complaint was that it was in bad taste and out of keeping with the Second Vatican Council to honor a convert from Judaism, especially since she had been murdered by the Nazis because she was Jewish, not because she was Catholic. In short, she was a Jewish martyr, not a Catholic martyr. Others found awkward and somewhat offensive the pope's effort to fuse Edith Stein's identity, when he called her "a daughter of Israel who remained faithful as a Jew to the Jewish people, and, as a Catholic, to our crucified Lord Jesus Christ."

In November Joseph Cardinal Ratzinger, head of the Vatican Congregation for the Doctrine of the Faith, told a weekly Italian magazine that, with respect to Catholic dialogue with Jews, "the Pope has offered respect, but also a theological line. This always implies our union with the faith of Abraham, but also the reality of Jesus Christ, in which the faith of Abraham finds its fulfillment." This comment, which seemed to contravene efforts in recent years by representatives of the Church to affirm the independent and inviolable authenticity of Judaism, evoked vocal complaints from a number of American Jewish organizations. Subsequently, Cardinal Ratzinger "clarified" his remarks, and Dr. Eugene Fisher, executive secretary for Catholic-Jewish relations of the U.S. National Conference of Catholic Bishops, said that the cardinal's original words had been taken out of context.

Though the American Jewish community had reason to be unhappy with the Vatican in Rome, it was relatively satisfied with the conduct of the American Catholic Church. Speaking before an American Jewish Committee meeting in December, Dr. Fisher said, "While 1987 was a turbulent year in Catholic-Jewish relations, nevertheless, the delicate fabric of the new relationship that Catholics and Jews have been weaving in patient dialogue for the past 20 years in this country . . . remained intact." Not all Jews, certainly, but many, agreed with him.

## Jewish-Protestant Relations

Two major American Protestant denominations took historic steps in 1987 to change their theological stance toward the Jews.

In June, at its General Assembly, the Presbyterian Church (USA) adopted a document entitled "A Theological Understanding of the Relationship Between Christians and Jews." In essence this document asserted the authenticity of Judaism by affirming that "Jews are in a covenant relationship with God," and calling for a "reconsideration of the implications of this reality for evangelism." It also declared that Christians should put an end to "the teaching of contempt for Jews."

Jewish organizations hailed this aspect of the statement, but found the document's treatment of Israel somewhat less satisfying. The original formulation called Israel "the promised land for Jews." However, the Reverend Benjamin Weir, at times one of his church's workers among 50,000 Presbyterians in Arab countries, and a former hostage in Lebanon, said that he would find it "very difficult to live with" such language. The compromise document acknowledged God's promise of a homeland to the Jews, but said that "the State of Israel is a geopolitical entity and is not to be validated theologically."

At its convention in July, the United Church of Christ, which did not address the theological validity of Israel, adopted a declaration on Judaism which straightforwardly proclaimed for the first time in that Church's history that "Judaism has not been superseded by Christianity." The declaration, easily passed, also stated that "God has not rejected the Jewish people" and asked "God's forgiveness" for the violence to the Jews that resulted from the Christian Church's historical denial of "God's continuing covenantal relationship with the Jewish people."

CHRISTIAN FUNDAMENTALISTS

The Christian fundamentalist groups in America did not share the nonconversionary view expressed by both the United Church of Christ and the Presbyterians that Judaism had independent validity. To the contrary, the year's events provided food for American Jewry's continued ambivalence toward the fundamentalists.

On the positive side, a survey commissioned by the Anti-Defamation League, released in January, found that most evangelicals and fundamentalists did not "consciously use their deeply-held Christian faith and conviction as justification for anti-Semitic views of Jews." On an index of traditional anti-Semitic attitudes, fundamentalists registered at about the same level as the rest of the population on similar surveys in the past. Further, about nine out of ten fundamentalists said that Christians were not justified in holding negative attitudes toward Jews on grounds that the Jews killed Christ. Indeed, about a quarter of the fundamentalists felt that God viewed Jews "more favorably than other non-Christians [because] Jews are God's chosen people." That sentiment was the basis of the Christian fundamentalist bias in favor of Israel, along with the classic Christian missionary belief that Jesus would return only after the Jews were all gathered again in Israel, prefatory to their conversion to Christianity.

While fundamentalist groups favored the State of Israel, and their members did not seem to hold more traditional anti-Semitic attitudes than anyone else, their unchanging missionary stance was disturbing. In June the Reverend Bailey Smith told the Conference of Southern Baptist Evangelists that he loved the Jews, but that "unless they repent and get born again, they don't have a prayer." Smith had made substantially the same statement in 1980, and had subsequently apologized. But, said Rabbi A. James Rudin, director of interreligious affairs for the American Jewish Committee, "Smith's statement clearly reveals that he remains where he was seven years ago: a self-imposed prisoner in a theological swamp of narrow triumphalism and religious imperialism."

As the year ended, the fundamentalist cause suffered a setback when the Georgia Baptists, at their state convention, ousted their fundamentalist president and installed a more moderate leader. A moderate presidential candidate also won a landslide victory over a fundamentalist candidate at the North Carolina Baptist state convention. According to the *New York Times* of November 11, "Moderates hailed [the Georgia action] as the first major defeat of fundamentalist groups since they began gaining power over the nation's largest Protestant denomination [the Southern Baptists] eight years ago."

## Church-State Affairs

SCHOOL-RELATED ISSUES

Fundamentalists met with some significant defeats in the educational arena in 1987. In Mobile County, Alabama, a group of "Christian parents" had asked for the removal from elementary and secondary public schools of 44 textbooks in such fields as home economics, history, and social studies, on the ground that they promoted "secular humanism," which, the plaintiffs charged, was itself religion. It was unconstitutional, they said, and a violation of church-state separation to promote such a sectarian religion in the public schools.

In March federal district court judge W. Brevard Hand in Alabama agreed with the plaintiffs and ordered the textbooks removed from the state's public schools. It was Judge Hand who had previously upheld an Alabama statute permitting a moment of silent prayer in the public schools, a ruling that was overturned by the U.S. Supreme Court in June 1985. In the textbook case, Judge Hand ruled that "for purposes of the First Amendment, secular humanism is a religious belief system"; in the same decision, however, he found that the books he had excluded "discriminate against the very concept of religion, and theistic religions in particular." In August a federal appeals court reversed the decision, saying that Judge Hand had turned the First Amendment requirement that the government be neutral on religion "into an affirmative obligation to speak about religion."

In June a Louisiana statute forbidding the teaching of evolution in public schools unless equal time was given to "creation science," that is, the role of God in creating human beings and the world, was struck down by the Supreme Court, in a 7–2 decision, on the ground that it was an impermissible "establishment of religion." This decision was regarded as significant, not only because creationism was being pressed in many states but because it seemed to preclude the chance of successful appeals to the Supreme Court on the pending textbook cases. The American Jewish Congress, the American Jewish Committee, and the Anti-Defamation League had all filed friend-of-the-court briefs opposing the teaching of creationism in the schools.

Although President Ronald Reagan, in his January State of the Union address, called for a return to school prayer, fundamentalist groups failed to make progress on the public prayer front. A key case involving a "moment of silence" law was effectively lost by prayer proponents in the Supreme Court. In 1984 a U.S. court of appeals had invalidated a New Jersey law (*May v. Cooperman*) mandating a daily moment of silence in the classroom "for quiet and private contemplation and introspection." The appellate court ruled that the law unconstitutionally facilitated student prayer. In 1985 the Supreme Court struck down an Alabama "moment of silence" law (*Jaffree v. Wallace*), based on the finding that the "sole purpose" of the law was to foster prayer. There were about 25 states in which such laws existed, and all of them waited upon the Supreme Court hearing on the New Jersey appeal.

Conservatives had reason to think the New Jersey law might be upheld by the High Court, not only because the Reagan administration defended the statute but because it did not specifically mention prayer and cited a secular purpose for silent meditation. As it turned out, the court's decision, in December, to let the lower-court rulings stand, was purely on procedural grounds: since the state legislators who had filed the original suit were no longer in office when they filed the appeal, they had no standing. Thus, the substantive legal issues were left unaddressed. Despite the setbacks they had suffered, it was anticipated that fundamentalist groups would pursue their public-school objectives in other ways, including putting pressure on local school boards and on textbook publishers. While most Jewish groups hailed the judicial defeats which the Christian fundamentalists sustained during the year, Orthodox groups demurred at the Jewish organizational consensus on the subject of silent prayer in the public schools. Expressing the belief that private prayer was appropriate on all occasions, the Union of Orthodox Jewish Congregations had affirmed in 1980 that it did "not object to a period of silent meditation," and repeated that affirmation this year.

Even in nonfundamentalist quarters, questions began to be raised about the deeper implications of ignoring religion in the schools. The Association for Supervision and Curriculum Development, a nonpartisan professional organization of 80,000 school principals, teachers, and college professors engaged in curriculum matters, issued a report calling for an end to "the curricular silence on religion." The report complained that the textbooks had almost nothing to say "about the profound part religious belief has played in more recent U.S. history, from the Abolitionist movement to the civil rights movement." The study of world history suffered from the same deficiency, claimed the report, saying that "an elementary student can come away from a textbook account of the Crusades, for example, with the notion that these wars . . . were little more than exotic shopping expeditions."

The same complaint about the slighting of religion in the public schools was sounded in reports by two groups notably liberal on the church-state issue: People for the American Way and Americans United for Separation of Church and State. They made the distinction between teaching religion doctrinally and teaching about religion. The complaints indicated that such "silent treatment" for the role of religion in history and art was not only academically insupportable but added unnecessary fuel to the fundamentalist campaign to breach the principle of church-state separation.

The report of the curricular professionals noted parenthetically the existence in public schools of a "hidden curriculum" that might indeed foster certain unfortunate doctrinal and sectarian religious assumptions and practices. As examples, the report cited school events scheduled for "the most sacred hours of the Jewish week," and choral music which "typically conveys Christian belief and worship." In this connection, a federal court ruled in August that the North Babylon, New York, school board would have to change the date for its 1988 high-school graduation, scheduled for a Saturday, in order to accommodate the religious needs of an observant Jewish student.

OTHER CHURCH-STATE ISSUES

The perennial debate over government's role in either accommodating or limiting religion continued to produce mixed, often murky, results.

In February the U.S. Supreme Court ruled that states could not deny unemployment benefits to employees who were dismissed for refusing to work on their Sabbaths. The case was that of a woman who had been working in Florida for a store whose sales were heavy on Friday nights and Saturday. After becoming a convert to the Seventh Day Adventist Church, she refused to work any longer at those times—her Sabbath—and was dismissed. The state then refused to pay her unemployment benefits. The High Court stood on the "free exercise of religion" clause of the First Amendment, rejecting the state's argument that granting such benefits could violate the "establishment of religion" clause. While the case did not directly address the "religious accommodation" provisions in the civil rights law, the Anti-Defamation League said the decision "strengthens the obligation of employers to accommodate their employees' religious practices."

In March the U.S. Supreme Court upheld a ruling of the Oregon supreme court that had approved the suspension of a teacher for wearing Sikh religious clothing in her elementary- school classes. The Oregon court held that limiting the teacher's free exercise of religion was allowable in order to maintain religious neutrality in the schools, although it explicitly suggested that common decorations, such as a small cross or a Star of David, could not constitutionally be prohibited. In May, however, the U.S. Justice Department, which was not involved in the Oregon case, took a different position on the matter of religious garb. It accused the State of Pennsylvania and the Philadelphia school board of religious discrimination, for banning a teacher wearing an Islamic headpiece. The Justice Department indicated that while the Oregon case was based on the First Amendment, its Pennsylvania case rested on Title VII of the Civil Rights Act, which required employers to make reasonable accommodation for employees' religious observances and practices. The Justice Department also noted that the Pennsylvania case was not affected by the previous year's Supreme Court ruling upholding the right of the U.S. Air Force to ban the wearing of a yarmulke in military situations. Title VII, said the Justice Department, did not apply to the armed forces.

The issue of religious headgear in the armed forces was resolved this year, finally, through congressional action. An amendment to the Defense Authorization bill, passed in December, permitted members of the armed forces to wear "neat and conservative religious apparel which is part of the observance of the religious faith practiced by the members, while in uniform if it would not interfere with their military duties."

Various state and local jurisdictions took action during the year to accommodate Jewish religious needs. At the request of Agudath Israel, for example, the Los Angeles City Council passed a law to relax parking rules on religious as well as other major holidays. Agudath Israel had claimed that 40 to 50 Orthodox Jews received parking tickets after each Jewish holiday because religious observance prevented them from moving their cars. In a similar vein, and also initiated by Agudath Israel, the State of Ohio passed a law providing that autopsies would not be performed if they violated religious belief, except in cases of "compelling public necessity." California, New York, and New Jersey already had such laws. On another matter of concern to observant Jews, the U.S. Department of Housing and Urban Development rescinded a memorandum that would have required federally subsidized Jewish apartment complexes to offer nonkosher food in addition to their kosher meal programs.

In at least one instance, an accommodationist request was denied. A federal district court ruled in May that the Satmar Hassidic community of Kiryas Joel in suburban Rockland County, New York, could not demand that the publicly provided school buses for their United Talmud Academy be driven only by men.

Controversy continued over the placement of religious symbols on public property during Christmas and Hanukkah. In June a U.S. district court denied a suit by the American Civil Liberties Union to prevent both a crèche and a menorah from being displayed in and around the City-County Building in Pittsburgh. The ACLU was expected to appeal. In a contrasting case, a U.S. court of appeals held, in August, that the traditional Christmas-time crèche in Chicago's City Hall was unconstitutional. City Hall officials said they would not appeal. This court decision was particularly satisfying to the American Jewish Congress, which had filed suit against the crèche in 1985, because it reversed a previous U.S. district court ruling in which the judge said the crèche was appropriate because "America is a Christian nation."

## Nazis in the U.S.

The case of Karl Linnas was played out to its conclusion in 1987. Linnas had been sentenced to death *in absentia* by the Soviet Union in 1962 for his role as commandant of a concentration camp in Tartu, Estonia, where thousands of men, women, and children were executed during World War II. In 1981 he was stripped of his citizenship by a U.S. district court because of his war crimes and because he had entered this country illegally in 1951, concealing his wartime activity. He was ordered deported in 1983.

Appeals by Linnas to 14 different courts, including the Supreme Court, had all been turned down, and 17 different countries rejected his request for asylum. Earlier in April it was discovered that Attorney General Edwin Meese had arranged for Linnas to receive asylum in Panama. However, immediate representations by Jewish organizations caused Panama to reverse its position. On April 20, the Supreme Court rejected a request to stay the deportation order, and hours later Linnas was placed on a plane to the Soviet Union. Because Linnas was the first ex-Nazi to be forcibly deported by the United States to the USSR, questions were raised about the morality of sending someone to almost certain death. As it happened, on July 3, the official Soviet news agency, Tass, reported that Linnas had died in a Leningrad hospital of heart and kidney disease, even as he was awaiting action on an appeal for a pardon. Later that month, Feodor S. Fedorenko, a former Nazi who had been deported from the United States in 1984, was executed in the Soviet Union for war crimes.

Prior to Linnas's deportation, Attorney General Meese had come under attack for failing to carry out the deportation order with dispatch. According to Elan Steinberg, executive director of the World Jewish Congress, if the news of Meese's arrangement with Panama had not leaked out, Linnas would have been safely "vacationing" in Panama. Among those who supported Linnas was Patrick J. Buchanan, conservative columnist and former White House communications director, who argued that the case against Linnas was suspect, partly on the ground that some of the evidence had been fabricated by the Soviet Union, which was seeking to discredit Baltic nationalists.

Although the long delay in deporting Linnas was seen by some as a sign of the government's growing disinterest in prosecuting Nazi war criminals, the Office of Special Investigations (OSI) of the Department of Justice continued to pursue its investigations of alleged ex-Nazis. Neal M. Sher, director of the OSI, reported in November that since 1979, when that office began operations, it had prosecuted more than 50 immigrants who were found to have lied about their Nazi past. Of these, 26 had been stripped of their citizenship and 19 had been deported or had left the country voluntarily.

In November deportation proceedings were begun against 74-year-old Jakob Habich, from Chicago, who was charged with having lied to U.S. immigration officials about his involvement as a member of the Nazi SS at several death camps in Poland and Germany.

A troubling case to many Jews was that of 75-year-old Jacob Tannenbaum, a Polish Jew charged with complicity in Nazi war crimes because he had served as a kapo, or overseer, at a forced-labor camp in Gorlitz, in what became East Germany. He was accused of viciously beating fellow prisoners and with hiding his past when he entered the United States in 1949. In May the Justice Department moved to revoke Tannenbaum's citizenship as the first step toward possible deportation.

He was the fourth Jew ever to be charged by the U.S. government as a Nazi collaborator; only one of the previous three had been deported.

Wide coverage was given by the media during the year to the dramatic trials abroad of two well-known Nazi war criminals. The trial of John Demjanjuk, known as "Ivan the Terrible" because of the brutalities and killings he had committed as a camp guard at Treblinka, began in Israel in February and was still under way at year's end. Demjanjuk was a Ukrainian who had immigrated to the United States in 1952, settling in Cleveland, where he was employed as an automobile worker. He was extradited to Israel in 1986 after proceedings instituted by the OSI. (See AJYB 1988, vol. 88, pp. 154–55 and 405–06, as well as the article "Israel" elsewhere in this volume.)

The trial of Klaus Barbie began in France in May and ended in July. Known as "the butcher of Lyons," Barbie had been the wartime chief of the Gestapo in that French area during the German occupation. He was accused of having organized the roundup and deportation of several hundred Jews, including the 44 "children of Izieu," to Auschwitz, as well as the torture and deportation to death camps of non-Jewish members of the resistance movement. Barbie had been extradited to France from Bolivia in 1983, at the initiative of Serge Klarsfeld. Convicted by a Lyons court on July 4 and sentenced to life imprisonment, he was expected to appeal. (See the article "France" elsewhere in this volume.)

Neither case was without controversy in America. The Demjanjuk extradition continued to arouse criticism in the American Ukrainian community, based primarily on questions about the reliability of 40-year-old memories and evidence supplied by the Soviet Union. The Barbie case brought to light information about Barbie's rescue by U.S. intelligence agents after the war, who employed him and then—because he had been convicted of war crimes by the French government—arranged his escape to Bolivia.

## *Extremism and Racism*

The previous year's high level of concern about bigoted extremist groups tapered off in 1987. Some of the earlier furor resulted from the public exposure of violent and illegal extremist activity; 1987 was a year in which some of those exposed extremists were prosecuted and sentenced. In addition, the annual Anti-Defamation League study, "The Hate Movement in America," reported a general decline in the membership of those groups, to its lowest point in a decade. Ku Klux Klan membership was reported at about 5,000 in the nation, about half of what it had been in 1981. The neo-Nazi membership was reported at less than 500 nationally, a 10-to 20-percent decline since 1984, and other extremist groups, such as the Order and the Aryan Nations, had also dropped in numbers. In some cases this decline was seen as a direct result of vigorous prosecution of some law-breaking extremist leaders by law-enforcement agencies.

The leadership of the Order, for example, was severely decimated when two of its leaders were sentenced to 150-year prison terms in December. David Lane, 48, and Bruce Carroll Pierce, 33, had been convicted of the 1984 murder of a Denver radio talk-show host, Alan Berg, a Jew, who attacked white supremacists on his program. Lane was already serving a 40-year sentence on racketeering charges. Two other defendants, Richard Scutari and Jean Craig, were acquitted in the murder case, but were already serving 60 and 40 years, respectively, on racketeering charges. The man who planned Berg's killing, Robert T. Matthews, had been killed by federal agents in 1984, near Seattle.

By order of a federal court, in May, the national headquarters building of the United Klans, in Alabama, was turned over to the mother of Michael Donald, a black teenager who had been killed by members of that organization in 1981. (Two leaders of the United Klans, one of the nation's largest Ku Klux Klan organizations, had already been convicted of the crime, one sentenced to execution, the other to life imprisonment.) In February the youth's mother, Beulah Mae Donald, had won a $7-million damage suit against the United Klans, the first instance of a Klan organization being held financially liable for the actions of its members. Mrs. Donald was given the 7200-square-foot building and over six acres of wooded land in partial fulfillment of her suit, because few other assets could be found for United Klans. Her lawyer indicated that the court action was "pretty much a death blow" to that organization, which was already "in decline."

In January, in Forsyth County, Georgia, Klansmen demonstrated that despite declining numbers and legal setbacks, the Klan still had an appeal that extended beyond its formal membership. (See below, "Blacks, Jews, and Jesse Jackson.") However, in Greensboro, North Carolina, in June, and in Rumford, Maine, in September, Klansmen were heavily outnumbered by anti-Klan demonstrators when they held marches in those towns. Among the organizers of the anti-Klan protest in Maine was the Jewish Federation of Southern Maine, along with mainstream Christian, labor, and political groups.

In September Lyndon H. Larouche, Jr.—the right-wing purveyor of conspiracy theories—and seven of his leading supporters were brought to trial in a Boston federal district court on charges of criminal activity related to fund-raising for his 1984 presidential campaign. Five of his "front" organizations were also charged, including the National Caucus of Labor Committees and Independent Democrats for LaRouche. Many of LaRouche's supporters had run for political office in 1986, enjoying some initial success because they did not reveal their relationship to LaRouche, but in the end being defeated. LaRouche and his associates were charged with financing their political activities by illegally charging credit-card accounts and securing large loans with no intention of repaying them.

## Anti-Semitism

Although organized extremist groups were under attack and in a state of decline, the ADL's annual "Audit of Anti-Semitic Incidents" reported an increase of isolated incidents, after a five-year downward trend. The audit was based on reports gathered by ADL's 31 regional offices from individuals and law-enforcement agencies. (It was acknowledged that the figures might have been affected, up or down, by differences in reporting procedures.)

A large part of the overall increase reflected reports by the California offices of ADL that anti-Semitic incidents in that state had more than doubled over the previous year. New York and Illinois were up slightly; Florida and New Jersey were down slightly. Incidents of vandalism and desecration rose from 594 the previous year to 694. There were also 324 reports of threat or harassment against Jewish individuals or institutions, as compared with 312 the year before. Among its figures, the audit reported about a dozen "major crimes," including serious damage by arson to a synagogue in Massachusetts and one in California, as well as a Jewish home in Maryland; the pipe-bombing of a Jewish home in Georgia and one in Ohio; and unsuccessful arson attempts on Jewish institutions in New York, Pennsylvania, and Virginia. There were also two cemetery desecrations.

Of the 78 individuals arrested in connection with the reported incidents, four out of five were teenagers. According to a special ADL report on the phenomenon of the "skinheads," across the country several hundred shaven-headed teenagers were organized in gangs that used neo-Nazi insignia and talked about violence against Jews and blacks. One leaflet in Chicago said: "Skinheads of America, like the dynamic skinheads in Europe, are working-class Aryan youth. We oppose the capitalist and communist scum that are destroying our Aryan race....The parasitic Jewish race is at the heart of our problem."

In November, on the 39th anniversary of *Kristallnacht,* a gang of Chicago youth vandalized 11 Jewish and Korean-owned businesses and three synagogues. On the basis of substantial evidence, police arrested a member of the skinheads who was also a member of the SS Action Group, an organization with a national membership of 50.

Skinheads were arrested for criminal acts related to their gang activities in Ann Arbor, Michigan; Chicago, Cincinnati, Dallas, and Tampa Bay, Florida. They were involved in attacks on, or threats against, blacks in San Jose, California, and Orlando, Florida. The ADL cautioned that not all youths who shaved their heads or thought of themselves as skinheads were racists or neo-Nazis.

In the arena of less violent and more "conventional" anti-Semitism, the case of Ivan Boesky continued to reverberate. The stock-market arbitrager who was exposed at the end of 1986 and pleaded guilty to illegal "insider" activity was sentenced in federal court in New York in December to three years in jail. Because he had been highly publicized as a major contributor to Jewish institutions, much concern had been expressed in Jewish community circles that his activities would breed increased anti-Semitism. However, when the American public was asked, in a February survey by the Roper organization, what factors were to blame for the Boesky scandal, only 1 percent chose "a Jewish background." Indeed, just as many chose "a Catholic background." Most people blamed such general factors as "personal greed" or "insufficient governmental regulation." By the time of the April *New York Times*/CBS News survey, while they were generally disapproving, only one out of ten non-Jewish Americans said that the Boesky episode made them "angry." Twice that proportion of Jews gave that response.

In general, surveys during the year did not reveal any increase in the level of anti-Semitic attitudes. The April *New York Times*/CBS News poll reported that to the key question "Do the Jews have too much power?" about 21 percent answered in the affirmative, no significant departure from answers to the same question in recent decades. And when the earlier February Roper poll asked Americans to select from a list of different groups those that had "too much power," only about 7 percent picked the Jews, although multiple responses were accepted. Most people identified business corporations, labor unions, and news media. Even Arab interests, blacks, Orientals, and Catholics were more often identified as having "too much power" than were Jews. The only group lower than the Jews on the list was Hispanics. The response to this key question was about the same as it had been on other multiple-list surveys in recent years.

## Civil Rights

The Supreme Court took several significant actions during the year related to discrimination. In May the Court found unanimously that the post-Civil War Civil Rights Act of 1866, outlawing "racial" discrimination, also allowed private lawsuits against discrimination based on ancestry or ethnic identity. This ruling grew out of two cases, one involving an Arab-American and the other involving Jews. Majid Al-Khazraji had sued St. Francis College, in Loretto, Pennsylvania, charging that he was denied tenure on the faculty because of his Iraqi ancestry. Congregation Shaare Tefila in Silver Spring, Maryland, had sued to recover damages from eight men charged with defacing their synagogue with anti-Semitic slogans and swastikas in 1982. The suit had previously been denied by two lower courts which said that anti-Semitic acts did not come within the scope of federal law.

The High Court upheld both suits, which were brought under the 1866 law, on the ground that in 19th-century usage, Jews, Arabs, and other ethnic groups were commonly considered "races." The Court also referred to the demonstrated legislative intent of Congress to protect ancestral and ethnic groups from discrimination. Apart from the novelty of having Jews and Arabs on the same side of an issue, the ruling was widely hailed as a landmark in civil-rights protection.

In another action, the Supreme Court ruled in May that states could properly outlaw discrimination against women by Rotary Clubs. It was not clear, however, how specifically this ruling might apply to discrimination in general by private clubs. Also, in a matter of continuing interest to the Jewish community, in February the Supreme Court, by a 5–4 decision, ruled that judges could order employers to use strict racial quotas temporarily, in promotions as well as hiring, to counter severe past discrimination. The case involved the promotion of black state troopers in

Alabama. The subject of temporary court-ordered quotas in severe cases had long divided a number of Jewish organizations.

## Blacks, Jews, and Jesse Jackson

The year began with an episode that harked back to the racial unrest and upheavals of the sixties. On January 17, in Cumming, Georgia, only 30 or so miles from Atlanta but in all-white Forsyth County, hundreds of Ku Klux Klan members and supporters broke up a small civil-rights march, labeled a "walk for brotherhood," held to mark the birthday of Dr. Martin Luther King, Jr. The Klansmen hurled bottles, rocks, and verbal abuse at the small group of black and white marchers, forcing them back on their bus. Stunned by the intensity of racial hatred displayed in the incident, civil-rights leaders quickly organized a second, mass brotherhood march to take place in Forsyth County the following Saturday. The Atlanta chapters of the American Jewish Committee and the American Jewish Congress helped to organize the event, and Atlanta's largest Reform temple opened its doors to marchers who had no accommodations. Representatives of Jewish communities around the nation joined the march, which drew some 15,000–20,000 supporters from all parts of the country. Order was maintained by National Guard troops and local law-enforcement officers, but while local officials welcomed the marchers, a crowd of 1,000 to 2,000 Klan supporters jeered along the route.

Although this largest civil-rights demonstration since Martin Luther King, Jr., led the 1965 march in Selma, Alabama, was a heartening show of black-white solidarity, events during the year reflected the undeniable malaise that now afflicted the black-Jewish coalition. Nation of Islam leader Louis Farrakhan continued to arouse Jewish anger as he spoke around the country. In Syracuse, in November, he said that Jews should not "walk around like pompous peacocks." In December, New York Mayor Ed Koch criticized a black Catholic priest, Lawrence Lucas, who made a public statement accusing other Catholics of "murdering us in the streets," referring to the police, and then saying that still others "are killing us in the classroom. I do not have to tell you from what persuasion they come. You just have to look at the Board of Education, and it looks like the Knesset in Israel." Incidents periodically occurred to heighten tensions between blacks and Hassidim in Brooklyn.

The prime focus of the strained relationship was Jesse Jackson, who was preparing a major effort to gain the 1988 Democratic presidential nomination, with the overwhelming support of the black population. Still under criticism in the Jewish community for his "Hymietown" remark and his association with Louis Farrakhan during the 1984 election campaign, as well as for some of his attitudes toward Israel, Jackson made deliberate efforts during the year to mend fences. Speaking to delegates from the Union of American Hebrew Congregations in Washington, in April, Jackson said that "blacks and Jews demonstrate similar commitments to the values of social justice, civil rights and human dignity." He continued his public support for a more liberal Soviet emigration policy, and, in response to a Jewish request, wrote a letter to Syrian president Hafez al-Assad, asking for the extradition to West Germany of alleged Nazi war criminal Alois Brunner. He avoided public association with Louis Farrakhan, who, in turn, said that he would not publicly support Jackson's campaign.

In September, however, Jackson made certain remarks to a political action group of young Democrats in Los Angeles—in particular a comment about "Jewish support for South Africa"—that led some of the Jews present to stop the checks they had made out to his campaign. And an interview with Jackson on black-Jewish relations in the October issue of the magazine *Tikkun* was described by Rabbi Alexander M. Schindler, president of the Union of American Hebrew Congregations, as "bitterly disappointing." Rabbi Marc Tanenbaum, director of international relations for the American Jewish Committee, observed that the interview was "a regressive step in what many of us had taken to be a genuine effort on the part of Jesse Jackson to build bridges between himself and the Jewish community."

Although Jackson offended some readers of the *Tikkun* interview by refusing to condemn Pope John Paul's meeting with Kurt Waldheim, and by equating the South African situation with the Holocaust, the main area of contention between the Jewish community and Jesse Jackson was Israel and the Middle East. In the *Tikkun* interview, while calling for the security of Israel, Jackson again enunciated his even-handed support for a Palestinian homeland, at one point asserting that "affirmative action for Zionism had to do with uprooting people from lands."

In some views, Jesse Jackson's approach to the Middle East issued more from a general "third-world" and simplistic approach to international affairs than from any specific hostility to Israel. However, Jackson's continued close association with Arab political groups made pro-Israel supporters distinctly uneasy. In March, Jackson was the keynote speaker at a political conference of Arab Americans. Later, he met with some 20 Arab Americans in Washington, including James Zogby, president of the American Arab Institute, the most prominent American lobbyist for the Palestinian cause and the man Jackson had chosen to second his candidacy at the 1984 Democratic party convention.

In the April *New York Times*/CBS News poll, about half of the Jews, but only about a third of the non-Jews, said that they had an "unfavorable opinion" of Jackson. This despite the fact that Jews were disproportionately identified with the Democratic party and, even among Democrats, Jews voted disproportionately for black candidates, as in the case of the 1987 Chicago mayoralty election.

In the February Roper survey, the black public's attitudes toward the Middle East tended to mirror Jackson's. A quarter of the blacks, as against half the whites, said that they were more sympathetic to the Israeli cause than to the Arab cause. To put it another way: among those Americans who took a position on one side or the other, the ratio in favor of Israel was about six to one among whites, about two to one among blacks.

## Israel-Related Issues

According to conventional Jewish wisdom, two kinds of crises would be most likely to trigger an anti-Semitic backlash in the United States. One would be a devastating economic breakdown. Nothing of the kind was on the horizon in 1987. The other triggering crisis would be a radical break between Israel and the United States, raising in a heated context the question of American Jewish "dual loyalty." Such a crisis was not really on the horizon, either, but events were taking place that raised the issue more sharply than before in American Jewish minds.

A key concern was the case of Jonathan Pollard, former civilian intelligence analyst for the U.S. Navy, who pleaded guilty in June 1986 to spying on the United States for Israel. In March 1987 Pollard was sentenced to life imprisonment, and his wife, Anne, to five years in prison as an accessory.

The issue of American Jews' dual loyalties was occasionally hinted at, as in the case of one lead-off on an ABC-TV "Nightline" broadcast on the Pollard affair: "Is it a question of divided loyalties?" But there were no serious charges or debates on the subject of dual loyalty. However, an American Jewish fear of anti-Semitism resulting from charges of dual loyalty would not have been outlandish, given the fact that over the previous two decades of surveys, a quarter to a third of the American people had repeatedly said they thought Jews were more loyal to Israel than to America. But the Pollard case did not seem to affect that belief. In reply to the *New York Times*/CBS News survey in April, 28 percent of Americans expressed the belief that "most American Jews place the interests of Israel ahead of the interests of the United States." About the same proportion, 24 percent, agreed with the more typically worded proposition, in the February Roper poll, that most American Jews are more loyal to Israel than to the United States. That was, if anything, a lower proportion than had agreed with that proposition in recent years.

When asked by the *New York Times*/CBS poll whether Pollard had spied for Israel or for the Soviet Union, two-thirds of the non-Jews and one-third of the Jews said they did not know. The Jews who said they knew the answer to the question all answered correctly, but the non-Jews who said they knew named the Soviet Union almost as often as they mentioned Israel as the sponsor of Pollard's espionage. However, even after they were apprised of Israel's connection to the Pollard case, only a third of non-Jewish Americans thought the United States should take some action against Israel, and only about one out of ten recommended drastic action, such as sanctions or withdrawal of aid. About two-thirds of non-Jewish Americans thought the whole matter would "blow over fairly soon." Secretary of State George Shultz expressed the same opinion.

Although the Pollard case failed to evoke the feared anti-Semitic reaction, there was concern that other issues might. There was, for example, Israel's alleged role in the American sale of arms to Iran, including the diversion of some of those funds to the Nicaraguan *contras*. In the dramatic Senate investigation of these matters during the summer, Israel was frequently mentioned by witnesses, and Lt. Col.

Oliver North, the former National Security Council staff member who masterminded the affair, testified that the Israelis had cooperated in the fund diversion. The chairman of New York governor Mario Cuomo's Task Force on Bias-Related Violence warned that "moves within the Reagan administration to make Israel the scapegoat in the Iran arms scandal could result in a wave of anti-Semitism in the United States." However, when the Roper poll asked Americans to name those most responsible for the Iran affair, accepting multiple responses, only 5 percent of Americans mentioned Israel. Even Nicaragua was named more often. The Reagan administration received most of the blame.

Even though the Iran arms sale was apparently no more the issue that would ignite a wave of anti-Semitism in America than was the Pollard case, these jarring events brought American Jews closer to understanding the possible negative consequences of such events, not only for Israel but for themselves. (See "Jewish Communal Affairs," elsewhere in this volume.) A headline in the July 5th edition of the *New York Times* read: "American Jews Are Voicing Their Disquiet." And on November 22, a *New York Times* headline proclaimed: "U.S. Jews Are Anxious Over Mideast Violence." In this case the reference was to the Palestinian-Arab uprising that had erupted in the West Bank and Gaza. Daily front-page newspaper photos and nightly television coverage featured Israeli soldiers using guns and tear gas against Arab teenagers and children, armed mainly with rocks. As the year ended, American Jews were becoming increasingly disturbed, not only about the impact of that spectacle on their non-Jewish neighbors but also about the deeper implications of these events for Israel's future and for their own relationship with the State of Israel.

EARL RAAB

# The United States, Israel, and the Middle East

RELATIONS BETWEEN ISRAEL AND the United States remained at a high level in 1987, despite heightened tensions over Israel's part in the Iran-*contra* and Pollard affairs, as well as questions about Israel's role in the peace process. The evolution of U.S.-Israeli relations, involving greater strategic cooperation and the treatment of Israel as a true ally in the economic and military spheres, proceeded apace. The year was characterized by increasing concern—among the Arab states as well as the broader world community—over the expanding war in the Persian Gulf. It was only in the final days of the year, with the outbreak of large-scale rioting in Israel's occupied territories, that the Arab-Israeli conflict returned to the full glare of the international spotlight.

## United States-Israel Relations

### NATOIZATION

A major advance in U.S.-Israeli relations was the official designation in February by Secretary of Defense Caspar Weinberger and Secretary of State George Shultz of Israel as a major non-NATO ally. In May 1986 Israeli defense minister Yitzhak Rabin had broached the idea on a visit to Washington, and Rabin, Shultz, and Weinberger had discussed it in September 1986 on the occasion of another Rabin visit. In granting the new status, Secretary Weinberger advised Congress that Israel, like other major non-NATO allies, "represents a unique and strategic interest [that] . . . currently utilizes a wide range of U.S. systems and technology which it is in our long-term interests to improve and modernize." He went on to say that Israel "has the ability currently to contribute to U.S. conventional defense modernization through an established, sophisticated and innovative research and development base." This further acknowledgment of Israel's strategic value to the United States and the sophistication of its defense industry had practical as well as political benefits to Israel, including participation in cooperative research and development and joint military production. The new status did not guarantee Israel special benefits, but did provide opportunities for Israeli firms to compete fairly with formal U.S. allies in bidding on a wide range of Pentagon contracts. In December Secretary of Defense Frank Carlucci and Rabin signed a Memorandum of Understanding, to run through 1998, implementing the agreement.

VOICE OF AMERICA

Another cooperation project that reached fruition in 1987 was the plan for Israeli construction and maintenance of a radio transmitter in the Negev. The transmitter would be used to broadcast the Voice of America, Radio Free Europe, and Radio Liberty to the Communist bloc, Asia, and Africa. As a follow-up to the agreement signed in Israel in August 1986, providing that a station would be built, at a cost of $250 million, a more detailed 25-year agreement was signed on June 18, 1987. At the signing ceremony in Washington, President Ronald Reagan said, "Our special relationship will be given a new dimension. We could not be happier with this partnership with Israel because it will result in the broader dissemination of those values we have in common." It was noted by some analysts that the United States had sought a location for the transmitter since the early 1970s, but that other countries in the region had refused to provide sites. The agreement provided that the United States would lease the land from Israel for 25 years, from the time of the first transmission, which was expected to occur in five years. An Israeli firm would serve as the prime contractor for the project.

OTHER U.S.-ISRAELI COOPERATION

Other areas of cooperation between the two countries, begun in the earlier years of the Reagan administration, continued to develop. Regular meetings took place during the year between delegations of the two countries charged with enhancing strategic cooperation. The Free Trade Area agreement, signed in 1985, was being implemented, and in December Congress passed a bill in which aid to Israel remained at $3 billion, $1.2 billion in economic assistance and $1.8 billion in military assistance. Of the latter, Congress earmarked $150 million to be spent in the States and $300 million in Israel for advanced weapons systems.

Earlier in the year, in March, in testimony before the House Foreign Affairs subcommittee on Europe and the Middle East, Deputy Assistant Secretary of State for Near Eastern and South Asian Affairs Roscoe Suddarth broadly described the extensive cooperation between Israel and the United States in political, military, and economic matters. He reported that Israeli researchers had been awarded five Strategic Defense Initiative (SDI) contracts worth over $10 million; pledged the continuing U.S. commitment to help Israel maintain its "qualitative military advantages over any combination of opponents"; and said that Washington "takes pride" in the progress Israel and the United States had made in meeting "the external threat" to the region. Although strategic cooperation, the free-trade agreement, and financial aid all remained on track, two outstanding matters continued to trouble the relationship. One was the Iran-*contra* affair, which raised doubts about Israel's reliability and complicated relations with the Arabs and U.S. allies. The other, the Pollard case, called into question the very trust and credibility that formed the foundation of the special relationship.

## Iran-Contra Affair

The Iran-*contra* affair, which had begun late in 1986, dominated the headlines in 1987. (See AJYB 1988, pp. 165–70.) Investigations were held by both houses of Congress, by the Senate Intelligence Committee, by the special commission under former senator John Tower, and by the special prosecutor, Lawrence Walsh. At issue were charges that the administration had secretly traded arms to the Khomeini regime in Iran in exchange for American hostages; that monies from the sale of arms had been sent to the Nicaraguan *contras*; that President Reagan knew of this diversion; and that the United States had been led and/or misled by Israel from the affair's inception.

While the aspect of the affair that most sharply touched on political divisions in America was the diversion of funds to the *contras*, Middle East policy matters were involved as well. With regard to U.S.-Israeli relations, the critical issue was whether Israel would be blamed for the affair, with consequent harm to its standing in America and its future relations with U.S. officials. With regard to the Arab states and U.S. allies, the question was how the revelations would affect U.S. credibility in light of the overwhelming Arab concern about Khomeini, and in light of the gap between public U.S. opposition to terrorist Iran and the private policy of selling arms.

It was clear that Israel was heavily involved in various phases of the affair. Less clear, however, was whether Israel, because of its intelligence concerning Iran, was merely a useful conduit for American actions or whether Israel was more of an initiator. At the very least, Israel's involvement stemmed from a desire to demonstrate its usefulness to its American ally and benefactor. Assistance in freeing American hostages and in bringing Iran toward a more moderate posture vis à vis the West were goals clearly in the minds of Israeli policymakers.

Early in 1987, as the various investigations were going on, a multitude of stories surfaced in the media. One was a report that Lt. Col. Oliver North, a member of the National Security Council (NSC), which had carried out the arms deal, attributed the diversion of funds to the *contras* to a suggestion by David Kimche, former director-general of Israel's Foreign Ministry. Prime Minister Yitzhak Shamir responded immediately on Israeli radio that "it would be very easy to prove that such allegations are baseless." Shamir indicated that explanations would be made to U.S. congressmen investigating Israel's role in the arms deal. Kimche himself firmly denied a role in the *contra* funding, declaring that had he known profits from the sale of U.S. weapons to Iran were being directed to the *contras*, he never would have permitted Israel to participate in the operation.

While the Senate Intelligence Committee decided on January 5 not to make public its findings, leaks were abundant. The *New York Times* reported on January 10 that the study had raised new questions about Israel's role in persuading Reagan to violate his own policies of never paying ransom to terrorists for the release of hostages and of not supplying arms to Iran. The report allegedly referred to continual promises by Israel to the White House that in return for modest amounts of U.S. arms, all American hostages in Lebanon would be freed. And when these assurances were not fulfilled, and Washington came close to ending the sales, Israel succeeded in keeping the arms flowing. According to the *Times*, some State Department officials expressed irritation with Israeli denials that it had instigated the affair. Other officials in the State Department and the White House blamed North and NSC head Vice Adm. John M. Poindexter far more than Israel, portraying them as overeager to take risks to free the hostages, thereby avoiding the necessary critical scrutiny of promises made by Iranians and Israelis. One day earlier, January 9, the White House released the text of Reagan's January 17, 1986, intelligence finding formally authorizing arms sales to Iran. Also released was Colonel North's cover memo, recommending that the president sign the finding, in which he portrayed Israel as the initiator of the plan to supply the Iranian military. According to North's memo, Israeli counterterrorism adviser Amiram Nir had assured U.S. officials that with the shipment of 4,000 TOW anti-aircraft missiles to Iran, all U.S. hostages held in Lebanon would be released.

On January 11, senior Israeli officials reiterated their denial that Israel had led Washington into the arms deal. They indicated that Israel had acted at American request to help win the release of American hostages and had not known that profits from sales were being diverted to the *contras*. One Israeli official reflected concern about talking too much: "Obviously some American officials are trying to cover for themselves. We were prepared for this, and we do not believe that it is over. But we are the last ones who want to get into a mud-slinging contest with an administration that is basically friendly to us."

On January 12 it was reported that the administration had told Shamir the day before that it did not hold Israel responsible for the affair and was not seeking "to blame" Israel. The message, conveyed by U.S. ambassador to Israel Thomas Pickering, included the assurance that the various U.S. investigations were designed to get the facts and were "not an effort to make Israel a scapegoat for decisions made by Washington." The message followed days of press disclosures alleging special Israeli responsibility. Israeli sources welcomed the message as an indication that the special relationship between the two countries remained intact. Senior Israeli officials told the *Washington Post* that from the outset of the affair, Israel was determined to avoid comment when possible, or overt criticism of the administration, despite the growing feeling that Israel was being set up to take the blame—all to avoid a rupture in U.S.-Israeli relations.

On January 13, in testimony before a closed Knesset committee session, Peres said Nir told him that he had warned U.S. officials in January 1986 that chances for success of the arms-for-hostages scheme were "at best 25 percent."

The Senate Intelligence Committee report, released on January 29, concluded that the affair was a result of a "confluence of several factors," among them a reappraisal in the NSC of overall policy toward Iran; a desire to gain release of the hostages; and pressure from Israel to participate in its contacts with Iran. The report contended not only that Israel had played a key role as middleman in the sale, but that Israelis had a possible role in helping direct profits from those sales to the *contras*. On February 1, Israel again denied involvement in the diversion of funds or in transferring weapons to the *contras*; this charge was viewed by Israel as the most serious made, since it impinged on Israel's relations with Congress. Following release of the report, the intelligence subcommittee of the Knesset's Foreign Affairs and Defense Committee held two days of hearings with Nir and Kimche. The committee found that the testimony supported previous government statements that there was "no foundation whatsoever" to allegations that Israel delivered arms to the *contras*.

In February the issue shifted to the question of Israeli cooperation with various U.S. investigations. On February 5, Shamir indicated that Israeli officials involved in the sale would not be sent to Washington to testify directly, but would likely cooperate by providing written answers to questions. Four days later, Nir, Kimche, and arms dealers Al Schwimmer and Yaacov Nimrodi agreed to give written answers to questions from U.S. investigators. During the course of his visit to the States in mid-February, Shamir reached an agreement with Congress on the procedures for the congressional investigation of the Israeli role in the Iran-*contra* affair. Under the arrangement, the special investigative committees would jointly prepare a set of questions that would be submitted by the State Department to the Israeli government; no Israeli official would be subpoenaed or be asked to testify in public or private sessions. The Israelis would answer the questions in writing and would also submit to the committees a chronology of Israel's financial transactions and contacts relevant to the investigations.

Meanwhile, Shamir met Reagan at the White House on February 18 for discussions of what they described as cooperative approaches to a range of strategic and diplomatic issues. The White House meeting was seen as a clear effort to demonstrate that the Iran affair had not damaged relations between Israel and the United States.

On February 26, the Tower Commission, established in November 1986 and consisting of John Tower, former national security deputy Brent Scowcroft, and former secretary of state Edmund Muskie, issued its report. The report was unclear as to whether the operation was an Israeli or a U.S. initiative. It said, however, that "Israel had its own interests, some in direct conflict with those of the U.S.," and that lack of access to key Israeli players in the operation had prevented it from reaching conclusions about the full extent of Israel's role. As its bottom line, the commission said that "even if the government of Israel actively worked to begin the initiative and to keep it going, the U.S. government is responsible for its own decisions. . . . U.S. decision-makers made their own decision and must bear responsibility for the consequences."

Israeli officials reacted with some relief to the commission's findings. A spokesman for Shamir told the *New York Times* that "at first glance, it doesn't seem to stress especially the role of Israel. We are not being blamed."

On March 4, President Reagan gave a 13-minute nationally televised talk responding to the Tower Commission report, in which he acknowledged for the first time that the administration had swapped arms for hostages: "I undertook the original Iran initiative in order to develop relations with those who might assume leadership in a post-Khomeini government. It's clear from the board's report, however, that I let my personal concern for the hostages spill over into the geopolitical strategy of reaching out to Iran."

Despite Israel's offer to provide written answers to U.S. investigators, the issue of testimony by those involved did not go away. Independent counsel Lawrence E. Walsh continued to seek direct questioning, saying that he was "not a party to that agreement" made in February by Shamir with leaders of the House and Senate select committees. Walsh said that the written responses were a poor substitute in a criminal probe for face-to-face questioning.

Late in April, disagreement broke out over financial data Israel had collected on the sale of arms. Israel sought to have a veto on the public release of any of the materials it proposed turning over to the congressional committees and also asked for an assurance that the committees would not provide the material to Walsh. A prime concern of the Israelis was that their citizens not face prosecution by Walsh.

The conflict between Walsh and Israel continued. On May 21 he subpoenaed Kimche, who was in the States on a private visit, to testify before a grand jury; Israel protested, and on May 22 a federal judge, Aubrey E. Robinson, Jr., decided to allow Kimche to leave for Israel with the agreed promise to return should the courts uphold the subpoena. The government of Israel had described the subpoena as illegal, a "clear violation" of U.S.-Israeli agreements, and had ordered Kimche not to testify before the grand jury, fearing that he might be forced to divulge information affecting Israel's national security. Negotiations between Israel and Walsh continued into the summer without an agreement over whether his investigators would be allowed to question Israeli citizens directly. The issue was shifted to a federal judge.

CONGRESSIONAL HEARINGS

Meanwhile, the joint congressional committee held nationally televised hearings throughout the summer. The story dominated the headlines and television coverage, the witnesses becoming overnight stars. The hearings were notable for their lack of focus on Israel. In explanation, one Capitol Hill source was quoted as saying, "Whatever motivation or input the Israelis had, this was an American decision first, last and always." When the hearings ended early in August, Israeli officials expressed relief. One official was quoted as saying, "We really dodged a bullet—no make that a hail of fire." Thus Colonel North, in his testimony, offered praise for Israel rather than criticism, focusing on Israel's cooperation in the interception of the *Achille Lauro* hijackers (in 1985) and its general conduct in opposing terrorism. The hearings themselves revealed Poindexter and North as the key responsible figures, with no indication that the president had any role in the affair.

In November Prime Minister Shamir told the *New York Times* that he had no regrets about Israeli involvement in American covert arms sales to Iran. Israeli leaders had long maintained that they had been involved in order to help the United States free hostages and bring moderates to the fore in Iran. Shamir added, however, that in the future his government intended to adopt a totally neutral stance toward the participants in the Iran-Iraq war.

## Pollard Affair

The case of Jonathan Jay Pollard, an admitted spy for Israel, which had erupted on the scene late in 1985 and was followed by a guilty plea in June 1986, with sentencing postponed, did not go away in 1987. Several points of conflict between U.S. and Israeli officials continued to irritate relations for the first few months of the year. (See AJYB 1988, pp. 164–65; and AJYB 1987, pp. 161–63.)

### POLLARD SENTENCED

On January 6, the Justice Department submitted to Federal Judge Aubrey Robinson a memorandum recommending a stiff prison term for Pollard, asserting that he had compromised more than 1,000 classified documents, most of them marked top secret, and suggesting that the documents might have allowed Israel to identify American agents overseas. The memorandum attempted to show that greed rather than Israeli patriotism was his prime motivation. It said that Pollard was "consumed" by the "lure of money" and became "literally addicted to the high life-style funded by his espionage activities." The Justice Department memo disclosed that FBI agents traveled to Israel and retrieved 163 classified documents in December 1985. It also called on the judge not to consider whether Pollard had spied for a friendly or unfriendly country, only that he broke the law. The following day, the department submitted a second memorandum calling on Judge Robinson to send Anne Henderson-Pollard, wife of Jonathan, to prison for a "period of years" on the grounds that she was a "willing partner in crime" and that she had sought help from one of Pollard's Israeli "handlers" the first night Pollard was questioned.

Following a request by Pollard for information about other spy cases, the government, opposing this request, prepared another memorandum in which it claimed that "Pollard compromised a breadth and volume of classified information as great as in any reported espionage case and adversely affected U.S. interests vis-à-vis numerous countries, including potentially the Soviet Union." Pollard's attorney, Richard Hibey, strongly disagreed with the Justice Department's assertion of the damage his client had caused.

On February 26, Pollard submitted a presentencing statement to the court in which he said that he gave Israel military intelligence to help it maintain an up-to-date defense against hostile neighbors, chiefly Syria. "In my mind, assisting the

Israelis did not involve or require betraying the United States. I never thought for a second that Israel's gain would necessarily result in American loss," he stated. Asserting that deep Zionist convictions motivated his actions, he said he disagreed with the Navy's policy of giving Israel incomplete intelligence information: "I watched the threats to Israel's existence grow and gradually came to the conclusion that I had to do something." On March 4, Pollard was sentenced to life in prison and his wife to two concurrent five-year terms. Judge Robinson rejected the defense claim that the damage done to the United States was not serious; he cited a classified affidavit from Secretary of Defense Weinberger that outlined the precise nature of the harm done to U.S. intelligence sources and methods.

OTHER DEVELOPMENTS

In February the Justice Department notified three Israelis involved in the affair—Rafael (Rafi) Eitan, former chief of a small intelligence unit within the Israeli Defense Ministry; Yosef Yagur, a former science attaché in the Israeli consulate in New York; and Irit Erb, a former employee in the Israeli embassy in Washington—that it would seek to revoke their diplomatic immunity from prosecution. The department also informed Col. Aviem Sella, the Israeli Air Force officer who was Pollard's first "handler," that he might soon be indicted. This, in effect, would serve to bar him from ever traveling to the United States, where he would risk arrest.

Relations between the United States and Israel were further strained when the administration learned, early in March, that Colonel Sella had been assigned to command Israel's largest air base. On March 4, the State Department issued a statement criticizing Israel for the move: "The United States government believes that the promotion or reassignment to a position of major responsibility of any Israeli involved in violation of U.S. espionage laws is inconsistent with the spirit of cooperation in which we have wanted to proceed with the government of Israel in the Pollard affair." At the same time, the U.S. embassy in Israel lodged a protest with Israeli defense minister Rabin, noting that such a promotion, precisely at the time Pollard was being sentenced, hardly constituted making "accountable" those Israeli officials responsible for the "rogue" Pollard operation.

After initially refusing comment on any of these matters, on March 8 Prime Minister Shamir told a group of visiting American Jews that as far as Israel was concerned, the affair was over. On March 10, however, Abba Eban, in his capacity as head of the Knesset's Foreign Affairs and Defense Committee, announced that his intelligence subcommittee would be looking into the matter.

The following day, Secretary Shultz said that the Reagan administration was "deeply distressed" by Israeli espionage in the United States and had delivered "a strong message" to Israel on the need for further investigation. He said that new posts given to Sella and Eitan (who had been appointed head of Israel Chemicals, the largest state-owned company) were not warranted. Shultz's strong expression of concern contrasted sharply with State Department efforts the year before to play down the Pollard affair, a position that had angered the Justice Department. Meanwhile, Congressman David Obey (D., Wis.), chairman of the House appropriations subcommittee on foreign operations, said that he had summoned visiting U.S. ambassador to Israel Thomas Pickering to his office to tell him that "droves of members of Congress have expressed their anger" over Israel's decision to promote Sella and, earlier, Eitan.

On March 15, the government of Israel responded to this criticism. Defense Minister Rabin accused the Justice Department of reneging on its agreement with Israel by refusing to grant immunity to Sella. He claimed that the prosecutors reneged because they had already achieved their aim of forcing Pollard to confess— by using information from other Israelis who were questioned—and thus did not need Sella's help. Besides, he added, "there are certain people who would like to create tension" between Israel and the United States.

Criticism of Israel for the Sella promotion was not limited to American officials. Jewish leaders joined in. Morris Abram, chairman of the Conference of Presidents of Major American Jewish Organizations, called the promotion "a very deep wound" to the United States. Nathan Perlmutter, national director of the Anti-Defamation League of B'nai B'rith, said: "What began in stupidity quickly sank into irresponsibility. If this was a 'rogue operation,' it's a fair question to ask why Israel has promoted the rogues." Tensions eased a bit when Sella resigned, on March 29, from his post as commander of Tel Nof air base. Israeli officials, who had reportedly pressured Sella to resign, reacted with relief to his announcement and expressed the hope that it would lead to a lessening of tensions with Washington.

ISRAELI INVESTIGATIONS

Responding to pressures from Washington and within Israel itself, the government of Israel conducted two investigations into the Pollard operation. The inner cabinet of the Israeli government set up a two-member panel to "clarify" the affair. Yehoshua Rotenstreich, a retired attorney, and Zvi Tzur, former chief of staff of the Israel Defense Forces (IDF), comprised the panel, but they had no subpoena powers. In the Knesset, Eban's Foreign Affairs and Defense Committee carried out its own probe.

On May 25, the Rotenstreich panel and the Eban committee simultaneously disclosed their findings. Both cleared all of Israel's political leaders of any knowledge of or involvement in the affair. But the inquiries said that Israel's senior political leaders bore responsibility for failing to uncover and end the espionage operation. The Eban committee was particularly critical of Defense Minister Rabin and his predecessor, Moshe Arens, for their "lack of criticism, supervision and curiosity. They did not ask at any time, 'What is going on in this operation?' " The Rotenstreich commission placed responsibility on the full cabinet, which, on May 27, that body formally accepted. U.S. reaction was restrained. State Department spokeswoman Phyllis Oakley said that the U.S. government hoped the investigations would "contribute to insuring that espionage activities like Pollard's never occur again." A correspondent for the Israeli daily *Ha'aretz* summed up the state of affairs: "Everything now depends on the Americans. . . . [I]f the Americans will swallow these reports then it will be easy for the Israeli public to swallow them as well. If the Americans get angry, there will be demands here for the politicians to go home." Shamir told reporters that the cabinet's acceptance of the panel's report closed the matter: "In our view, this is the end. I hope we won't have to concern ourselves further with this affair." (For reaction in the United States to the Pollard affair, see "Intergroup Relations" and "Jewish Communal Affairs," elsewhere in this volume.)

## Lavi Project

A third area of some conflict between the two governments centered on the Israeli multibillion-dollar war plane, the Lavi. In 1986 the Pentagon had made the case against the Lavi, and the State Department had come around to that way of thinking by the end of the year.

Early in January 1987, Deputy Under Secretary of Defense for Planning and Resources Dov Zakheim visited Israel to convince Israeli leaders that the Lavi was neither a military necessity nor suited to Israel's financially strapped economy. At a press conference in Tel Aviv, Zakheim said that the Lavi would cost 45 percent more than the $15.2 million per plane that Israel had projected. Calling the Lavi an "unproven aircraft," he indicated that the United States would have "absolutely no interest" in purchasing the Lavi and might exercise its option to veto sales of the Lavi to other nations (55 percent of the aircraft's components were being manufactured by U.S. firms). Zakheim proposed to Israeli leaders alternatives involving coproduction of F-16s, which, it was said, would cost Israel less, would give Israel new planes sooner, and would compensate for some of the jobs lost by abandoning the Lavi. "What we're trying to do is to save some money . . . and offer Israel the possibility of in some way minimizing disruption to its defense budget and also to the military assistance program that we provide, which we think will be caused by the Lavi." Even while Israeli leaders indicated a willingness to consider the case, Israel Aircraft Industries pressed ahead with its test-flight program.

On February 22, the General Accounting Office (GAO) in Washington released a study which said that production costs for the Lavi would exceed $1 billion a year by 1990 and $1.4 billion by the year 2000. The report went on to say that even the lowest estimate of the funding required to produce 300 Lavi aircraft "will far exceed the spending cap set up by Israel ($550 million a year) and consume an increasingly larger share of Israel's defense resources." Debate raged within Israel for months, including within the military, and the cabinet continued to put off a decision. Reports circulated that Rabin and most senior Israeli military officers had reluctantly concluded that development and production of the Lavi could only be maintained by diverting large sums from other critical defense needs, a path they seemed unwilling to take. On the other hand, the government was under pressure because of the workers whose jobs would be threatened by the project's end and because national pride in the project was considerable.

On August 11, as the Israeli cabinet neared a decision on the fate of the Lavi, Washington, in its bluntest statement yet, urged Israel to scrap the program. State Department spokesman Charles Redman said: "Given the budgetary realities we and Israel face, we believe a decision by Israel to terminate the Lavi would be in the interest of both our countries." Officials indicated that the U.S. statement was intended, in part, to strengthen the hand of Israeli military officials and cabinet members who opposed the program on the basis of cost. In addition, Israeli officials acknowledged that Shultz had sent personal messages to Shamir, Peres, Rabin, Finance Minister Moshe Nissim, and Economics Minister Gad Yaacobi, urging the cancellation.

On August 30, the Israeli cabinet finally bit the bullet, voting 12-11, with one abstention, to end the project. In the final analysis, the IDF's fear that the project would draw away funding from other requirements was seen as the decisive factor. While the vote generally went along party lines, Labor for scrapping the project, Likud to continue it, the crucial vote to kill it came from Likud Finance Minister Moshe Nissim. Peres, who had long supported the Lavi, together with Nissim devised an alternative plan to cushion the blow by providing money for other weapons projects. How it would play out politically in Israel was unclear. Labor officials indicated that U.S. actions would be crucial; they said that if the United States helped Israel to coproduce the F16C (an updated F16) and permitted American aid to be spent on alternative Israeli-made weapons projects, Labor would reap the political benefits. If Washington did not come through, they said, Likud would use the issue successfully. Likud officials argued that the average Israeli, who took pride in the Lavi, would remember who killed it.

On September 10, the *Washington Post* reported that the administration had confirmed its commitment to ease the financial pain of the cancellation. In a letter to Nissim, Shultz indicated the administration's willingness to earmark $450 million to pay termination charges on contracts with U.S. and Israeli companies working on the plane. Also reported were U.S. commitments to try to increase from $300 million to $400 million a year Israel's unique authority to use part of its U.S. aid to buy Israeli-made products, and a continuation of the policy allowing Israel to require U.S. defense contractors to buy $150 million a year in Israeli products to "offset" the cost. As the year concluded, Israel was discussing with U.S. officials other ways to ease the economic blow of the Lavi cancellation. Included were Israeli proposals to participate in the manufacture of parts for the F-16; participation in the development of a new variant of the F-16 proposed by General Dynamics to lighten the plane and improve its performance; and a contract from the Defense Department to help pay the costs of research into an Israeli rocket, called the Arrow, which was designed to shoot down shorter-range missiles like the surface-to-surface missiles sold by the Soviet Union to Syria.

## The Peace Process

The impact of the continuing Iran-Iraq war and a related matter, the secret sale of U.S. arms to Iran, were issues that diverted attention from the Arab-Israeli arena and created additional obstacles to progress toward peace on a road already marked by innumerable obstacles.

The focus of the peace process in 1987 was the proposal for an international conference. The conference idea had a long history, going back to the 1970s; it was revived in February 1985, when Yasir Arafat and King Hussein reached an agreement which talked of an international conference with the participation of the Soviet Union. In speeches at the United Nations in 1985 and again in 1986, Shimon Peres indicated his willingness to attend an international conference if the Soviets restored relations with Israel and allowed Jewish emigration. Throughout 1987, differences between and among the main players effectively stalemated the idea. One obstacle was the widely publicized disagreement between Foreign Minister Peres and Prime Minister Shamir, who strongly opposed the conference idea. Another was the unclear U.S. position on the matter. Yet another was the disagreement between Peres on the one hand, and Arab and Soviet leaders on the other, concerning various aspects of the conference: its structure and powers and the nature of Palestinian representation to it.

As the year began, both President Hosni Mubarak of Egypt and Jordan's King Hussein were strongly urging U.S. officials to accept an international conference that would be attended by all regional parties and by both superpowers. Although the United States was formally opposed to a conference that would entail Soviet participation, late in 1986, when Shimon Peres, first as prime minister, then as foreign minister, began forcefully articulating his support under certain conditions, State Department officials agreed that the idea should be explored. This U.S. reassessment was seen as resulting only in part from the persistence of Peres. Washington's other concerns were the damage caused by the Iran arms affair (reinforced following a trip to the Middle East in January by Assistant Secretary of State for Near Eastern Affairs Richard Murphy) and the need to counter Moscow's skillful reemergence as a diplomatic player in the area.

SHULTZ-SHAMIR

Differences between Prime Minister Shamir and the United States over an international conference began to emerge early in the year. In mid-February, Shamir paid a visit to Washington during which a number of subjects were discussed, including that of the conference. On February 17, after a two-hour meeting with Shamir, Secretary Shultz told reporters that the administration did not "see exactly eye-to-eye" with Shamir, Shultz defending the conference idea, saying, "There may be something that carries that label that would be satisfactory." He added, however, that America's ultimate objective "is not an international conference. Our objective is direct negotiations." Shamir wholly rejected the conference idea as a "Soviet-inspired notion supported by radical Arab nations."

The next day President Reagan reiterated the Shultz position after meeting with Shamir, noting that the United States wanted direct talks and "any reasonable means, including an international conference, should be considered." Overall, however, Reagan played down the Shamir-Shultz clash of the day before, emphasizing Israel's status as a "major, non-NATO ally." Shamir said that this characterization of Israel added "a new dimension" to U.S.-Israeli relations, offering the possibilities of further American economic and military aid, as well as the psychological reinforcement of open U.S.-Israeli friendship.

One week later Peres was in Cairo, hoping to find common ground with Egyptian president Mubarak and his top policymakers with regard to the conference. A key issue was to find "an agreed Palestinian delegation" that could attend future negotiations. The talks brought no breakthrough on this matter, as the Egyptians insisted that the PLO should represent the Palestinians. On February 27, Peres and Egyptian foreign minister Esmat Abdel Meguid issued a joint communiqué calling for an international conference in 1987, leading to direct talks between Israel and the Arabs. Included in the communiqué was language referring to the "legitimate rights of the Palestinian people." Shamir reacted with anger toward Peres for conducting what he described as an independent foreign policy, and at a March 1 cabinet meeting a sharp clash ensued between the two. Peres did not force the issue to a cabinet vote, leading to speculation that he did not have enough support from his own Labor party to provoke a political crisis that might result in the collapse of the national unity government and the calling of elections.

INTERNATIONAL REACTION

Elsewhere, support for an international conference began to build. Soviet general secretary Mikhail Gorbachev wrote to the chairman of the European Community (EC) foreign ministers, Leo Tindemans, calling for an international conference, though he failed to spell out any particular conditions for participation. On February 23, the EC announced its unanimous support for Gorbachev's call. However, efforts by Washington to further this exploratory process were set back when both King Hussein and President Mubarak turned down invitations to visit Washington and confer with President Reagan. Both leaders indicated that the main reason for staying away was the continued shock and anger over U.S. arms sales to Iran. Between April 7 and April 9, Peres held a round of talks with two Soviet officials on the peace process at a meeting of the Socialist International in Rome. Attending the meeting as head of Israel's Labor party, Peres described his talks with the two Russians—Karen Brutents and Aleksandr Zotov, Middle East experts from the international department of the Soviet Communist party's Central Committee—as "serious and direct dialogue." Peres reiterated his position favoring participation by Moscow in a conference, once the USSR resumed diplomatic relations with Israel.

On April 9, Shamir reacted sharply, calling the conference an "insane and monstrous idea" that could bring "abundant disaster" to Israel. He continued, "[O]nly someone wishing the loss and destruction of his country, his freedom and his security would favor such a conference."

Meanwhile, in Washington on April 7, Jordanian president Zaid al-Rifai urged Shultz to end U.S. ambivalence and embrace Hussein's international conference. On leaving, Rifai indicated that the United States had accepted Jordan's plan in principle but disagreed on the details. Shultz, speaking to reporters after the meeting, seemed less positive than at the time of the Shamir visit. He indicated only that he was aware of the "importance" attached to a conference by Jordan and others, but stressed that any process had to lead to direct talks. Soon, however, there was a flurry of diplomatic activity, with reports circulating of a secret meeting in London on April 11 between Peres and Hussein. President Reagan sent a letter to Shamir urging him to consider the conference proposal. Shamir then sent Minister Without Portfolio Moshe Arens to Washington to tell Shultz that Likud leaders were firm in their opposition. According to reports, after Arens's visit, Shultz put off plans to travel to the Middle East in the near future to seek agreement on a conference between Israel and Jordan.

HUSSEIN-PERES

Reports of the Peres-Hussein meeting indicated that they had apparently agreed on the terms of a conference. The specific proposals, it was said, were for the UN to invite five permanent members to convene the parties, based on UN Security Council resolutions 242 and 338; for the conference to then quickly break up into three sets of "geographical bilateral committees" to conduct direct negotiations between Israel and Jordan, Israel and a joint Jordanian-Palestinian delegation, and between Israel and Syria. Finally, participation of the PLO would be conditional on that group's acceptance of 242 and 338 and renunciation of violence and terrorism. While Peres did not confirm that a meeting had taken place, he told an audience in northern Israel on April 28 that "this is a great opportunity. We must not miss out. It goes beyond all usual party strategy and if there is a need we will also go to the people."

Meanwhile, U.S. special envoy Wat Cluverius shuttled between Jerusalem and Amman, trying to resolve remaining points of disagreement concerning Soviet participation, who would represent the Palestinians, and whether the conference could reconvene to seek to break any deadlock in the bilateral talks.

Early in May, reports circulated that Peres had reached agreement with Hussein through U.S. mediation. There were indications that he believed Israel was closer to peace talks than ever before, because Hussein, recognizing a hardening of the PLO position, was no longer willing to wait for PLO change, and because of a new flexibility by Moscow. The *New York Times* reported on May 11 that Jordan had agreed to limit the Soviet role by not allowing the conference to have veto power over any accord reached by the bilateral committees. The *Times* went on to report that the final details of the understanding were said to have been ironed out with the help of Cluverius.

SHAMIR-PERES

Following those reports, the conflict within Israel itself intensified. In February the Israeli cabinet had achieved a functional compromise in the Labor-Likud dispute, enabling Shamir to continue to reject the idea of a conference publicly and Peres to press on legitimately with efforts to persuade various parties to agree to such a meeting. At a cabinet session on February 1, Shamir was reported to have enunciated the saving formula when he declared that while he opposed a conference, it was customary in the Israeli government to allow the foreign minister leeway to maneuver in the effort to achieve peace. The truce did not last long. When Peres went to Europe early in April to boost his plan, Shamir lashed out. The combination of increasing turmoil in the territories and the foreign minister's perception of the possibility of a breakthrough with Hussein emboldened Peres to bring matters to a head. On April 30 it was reported that Peres believed that he had achieved enough of a commitment from Hussein—a commitment to enter direct negotiations with Israel under the umbrella of an international conference—to justify asking the full Israeli cabinet to endorse the idea formally.

In an interview with the *New York Times* on May 8, Peres elaborated on his thinking. He said that the basic understanding between Israel, Jordan, the United States, and Egypt on an international conference was "an opportunity that we have not had since the creation of the State of Israel." He indicated that if the inner cabinet were to be deadlocked when he presented the issue, "then we will have to go to the people like in a real democracy. Let them decide whether to use this peace opportunity or lose it." He also said that he wished to see a more explicit declaration of support for the conference idea from the Reagan administration.

As noted, Washington had played a key role, through the Wat Cluverius shuttle, in the progress made to this point, but to avoid involvement in Israeli internal affairs had not given a vigorous endorsement. Thus, State Department spokeswoman Oakley said in reaction to Peres's remark about a breakthrough having been achieved: "We are convinced that peace can only be achieved through bilateral, direct negotiations. As we have said on several occasions, we are exploring with the parties in the region whether an international conference might contribute to that end." This statement was interpreted as reflecting American concern, despite basic agreement with Peres, that he was rushing matters by provoking a government crisis while important points of disagreement—the Soviet role, Palestinian representation—remained unresolved. On May 12, a sharp public exchange took place. Shamir accused Peres of being consumed by a "lust for power," adding that a conference was a "perverse and criminal idea," and that "every remnant and vestige of this plan must be wiped off the discussion table." Peres responded by accusing Shamir and

Likud of "demagogy," "hatred," and "character assassination." The following day, Israel's inner cabinet, consisting of five Likud and five Labor ministers, failed to endorse a Peres proposal to support the convening of an international conference. Subsequent efforts by Labor to dissolve the Knesset on this issue were frustrated when Shamir succeeding in putting together a bloc of 62 seats (one more than needed). The Prime Minister's Office now called on the foreign minister to inform all Israeli embassies that Peres no longer had a mandate to pursue the international conference, since Peres had refused to put the matter to a vote because it would have been rejected. Peres's supporters in the Foreign Ministry canceled the messages, instructing the embassies that since there had been no vote, there was no change in their instructions allowing them to articulate the foreign minister's interest in a conference. The ambivalence of the people of Israel themselves in the face of such conflict among their leaders was reflected in a poll made public in May: 52 percent favored participation in an international conference, but 59 percent said they would not support the idea if it meant collapse of the coalition government and early elections.

On May 19, the conference idea received another setback when a Soviet spokesman, Boris Pyadeshev, said in Moscow that a conference must be more than an "umbrella" for face-to-face negotiations between Israel and Jordan, and that the PLO should determine who would represent Palestinian interests at such a meeting. The spokesman said Soviet officials were prepared to be flexible on details, but clearly differences remained.

On May 21, Assistant Secretary of State for Near Eastern Affairs Richard Murphy told reporters that "significant progress" and "an encouraging convergence of views" had enhanced the prospects for a conference. He cited agreement that the conference would invite the parties to form "direct bilateral negotiations"; that it would not "impose solutions or veto agreements reached bilaterally"; that Palestinian representatives would participate in face-to-face negotiations "within a Jordanian-Palestinian delegation"; and that participants would be expected "to accept United Nations resolutions 242 and 338 and to renounce terrorism and violence." Murphy did not indicate which nations had agreed. With the Israeli government stalemated, with Washington promising to take no action without agreement of the full Israeli government, and with no evidence of major breakthroughs on the fundamental questions of representation at the conference and the role of the conveners, the perceived momentum of the conference idea slowed to a near halt. For months there was little activity on this front, until in August, Secretary of State Shultz sent his executive assistant, Charles Hill, to Israel to persuade Shamir to ease his opposition to a conference. He met with no success. On August 20, on a visit to Romania, Shamir met with Romanian president Nicolae Ceausescu in Bucharest for nine hours. No progress was made toward narrowing differences on the best way to proceed in Middle East peace negotiations.

On the occasion of the opening of the UN General Assembly session late in September, Peres met with Shultz and pressed his case. He reportedly described to

Shultz his perception of a more flexible Soviet attitude, reflected in talks with Foreign Minister Eduard Shevardnadze (also attending the UN session) on whether the PLO had to represent the Palestinians in any peace talks. He indicated that the language of the Soviets seemed much closer to that of the United States and Israel, suggesting possible acceptance of a Jordanian delegation with Palestinians "acceptable to the PLO." Shultz was reported to have told Peres that with the U.S.-Soviet arms-reduction agreement on track, the administration intended giving higher priority to the peace process; at the same time, he was reported to have said that while he supported the idea of an international conference, he would not pressure Shamir or other opponents to accept it.

SHULTZ VISIT TO MIDDLE EAST

Between October 16 and 18, Secretary Shultz, who had resisted pressures to visit the Middle East for two-and-a-half years, on the ground that he would not go until the parties showed signs of movement in their positions, made a trip to the region. The visit was attributed to two factors: concern that stagnation itself was dangerous and the challenge of a revived Soviet diplomacy—including meetings with Israelis and Arab representatives—in the region. It came at a time when attention was focused on the Persian Gulf, where a large U.S. fleet, supported by ships of other Western countries, was protecting Kuwaiti tankers from Iranian attack. Shultz met with Peres and Shamir in Israel, King Fahd in Saudi Arabia, Mubarak in Egypt, and then King Hussein in London.

Shultz's meetings, which saw no breakthrough, evoked a variety of reactions from the secretary of state. On the last day of his trip, Shultz called for "energy, unity and resolve" in restarting the Arab-Israeli peace process, warned that "no one helps the chances for peace by doing nothing," and said that "those who are reluctant to explore new ideas, or even revisit old ones, have an obligation to offer something different as an alternative to the status quo." Several hours later, in a news conference, when his remarks were interpreted by the Israeli press as criticism of Shamir, the secretary went out of his way to praise Shamir's desire for peace and announced that Shamir would pay an official visit to Washington in 1988.

On October 20, Shultz told reporters, "Realistically, I can't point to any particular thing that moves matters forward" in the Middle East peace process. On his flight from London to Helsinki (where he was stopping off before going to the Soviet Union), he left the impression in talking with reporters that he saw an international conference as an unworkable idea at the moment and felt that too much time had been spent discussing it. While Shultz had been supportive of the conference idea, he was not enthusiastic about the Soviet Union's vision of it. The conference envisioned by the Soviets, he said, was "exactly the kind of conference that the Israelis are shy of and I agree with the Israelis on this—a kind of conference that has a continuous role and a substantive role to play." Several days earlier, following the refusal by nine Palestinian leaders from the West Bank and Gaza, on instructions from the PLO, to meet with Shultz, he complained that it was "contradictory" for Palestinians to say they wanted to be represented but then refuse to participate in a dialogue. At the same time, Shultz appeared to criticize Shamir's opposition to a conference when he reiterated, "No one improves the chances for peace by doing nothing at all, by just sitting around."

On October 22, the *New York Times* cited an unnamed senior Israeli official to the effect that Shultz, at Peres's suggestion, had broached to Shamir a proposal under which Israel and Jordan would negotiate directly under joint U.S.-Soviet sponsorship. According to this official, Shultz insisted that there might be a way around an international conference, but not around Soviet involvement. The proposal called for Palestinian representatives to be part of a Jordanian delegation; Syria would be invited separately to hold direct talks with Israel. The new plan differed in its emphasis on direct talks and in the limitation of the number of Security Council permanent members present. This proposal, while moving away from the larger conference, seemed to represent something of a departure from the administration's stand on limiting Soviet involvement in the Middle East. The official indicated that while Shamir, wishing to make a "gesture" to the secretary, did not reject the plan outright, he had attached tough conditions for Soviet involvement—full diplomatic relations and unrestricted emigration for Soviet Jews. It was reported that Shultz would convey Shamir's terms to the Soviets on his visit to Moscow following his Middle East trip. On November 7, however, the *New York Times* quoted a very senior Jordanian official as saying that Jordan rejected this miniconference idea: "King Hussein wants a full international conference." Little thereafter was heard about this proposal.

## The PLO, Palestinians, and the Uprising

For the remainder of the year it was not the peace process but matters relating to the Palestinians and the PLO which dominated the news on the Arab-Israeli front.

Until December, the year had been characterized by both conflict and unity for the Palestinian movement. Early in January 1987, Arafat had publicly denounced the plan of King Hussein to channel $1.4 billion for development to the West Bank. The money, which was to go primarily for housing, was viewed as having a dual purpose: to prevent an exodus of Palestinians from the West Bank to Jordan and to enable Jordan to reassert its legal responsibility for the West Bank by providing an alternative source of aid to that of Israel. The plan had been opposed at the outset by radical Palestinians, who saw it as a step by Jordan to create its own Palestinian leadership and as a prelude to sharing power with Israel. Arafat joined in calling the plan a means "to improve the image of the Israeli occupation."

In April a meeting of the Palestine National Council (PNC) had taken place in Algiers, its main purpose to reconcile differences between PLO factions that had sharpened since the war in Lebanon. The PNC had last convened in 1984, in Jordan, but on that occasion anti-Arafat groups had boycotted the meeting. Reconciliation was the watchword of this session. Arafat, who was given a standing ovation by the 1,200 delegates and guests in the conference hall, was joined on the podium by George Habash, head of the Popular Front for the Liberation of Palestine (PFLP), and Naif Hawatmeh, head of the Democratic Front for the Liberation of Palestine (DFLP). Their appearance together appeared to be a blow to the Palestinian National Salvation Front, a radical coalition created by Syria in 1983 as a challenge to Arafat's leadership. In fact, three Syrian-based groups boycotted the meeting—Fatah Uprising, led by Col. Saeed Musa; Al-Saiqa; and PFLP General Command, led by Ahmed Jibril. The price for the display of unity was the adoption of a more hard-line stance on Arab-Israeli issues. To win the support of Habash and Hawatmeh, Arafat formally scrapped the PLO-Jordanian accord signed in 1985.

Whatever optimism resulted from this show of unity was counteracted by developments months later, at the Arab Summit Conference held in Amman in November. Reflecting the overwhelming fear of most Arab states of the spread of Iranian influence, the summit unanimously condemned Iran and supported Iraq, and cleared the way for Arab states to resume diplomatic relations with Egypt (broken off after Egypt signed a treaty with Israel). King Hussein put the return of Egypt to the Arab League on the agenda as the summit opened on November 8, in response to the desire of the Persian Gulf states to bring Egypt's military force back into the Arab fold as a counter to Iranian aggression.

For the first time since the founding of the Arab League, the Arab-Israeli conflict was not the main focus. The expected resolution was passed denouncing Israel and calling for an international conference under UN auspices, with the PLO playing a role on an equal footing with other parties. However, the English translation of the resolution omitted the standard reference to the PLO as the "sole legitimate representative of the Palestinian people." Arafat expressed outrage at this "scandal," and there was a general feeling that the status of the Palestinians had reached a low point.

Two weeks later an event took place that refocused attention on the Palestinian question. On November 25, a Palestinian guerrilla flew a hang glider from Lebanon into northern Israel and entered the Gibor army base, where he killed six Israeli soldiers and wounded seven others before being shot dead. The next day, much of the Arab world lauded the raider; a Palestinian writer praised the action's "very good effect on Palestinian morale."

It was in this atmosphere—where perceptions were about that the Arab world had placed the Palestinian problem on the back burner, generating increasing frustration among the residents of the territories, and where the example of the daring terrorist on the hang glider was fresh in Palestinian minds—that an incident took place in Gaza that caused a major Palestinian eruption. On December 6, an Israeli salesman was stabbed to death in Gaza. Two days later, December 8, an Israeli army truck collided with several vans in Gaza. Four Arabs were killed, 17 others were injured. A rumor spread that the collision was a premeditated Israeli action in reprisal for the stabbing death. The next day, December 9, large-scale riots broke out. (See article on 'Israel" elsewhere in this volume.)

On December 10, the violence continued in Gaza and spread to the West Bank. In Gaza, Palestinians gathered in throngs, burning tires, throwing stones at vehicles, and blocking roads. In Nablus, on the West Bank, Israeli soldiers fatally shot a 19-year-old man when a group of Palestinian youths surrounded a military patrol, pelting it with rocks and iron bars. The following day saw riots at the Balata refugee camp on the outskirts of Nablus. In Gaza, many men stayed away from their jobs in Israeli cities and towns and many students did not attend school. In a statement on December 11, the U.S. State Department said that it was "deeply saddened by the recent killings in the occupied territory."

By the end of the first week of rioting, the disturbances had spread to the entire Gaza strip. Israel increased its forces; rumors among the Palestinian population fueled the violence. On December 19, the rioting spread to Jerusalem, with crowds of rock-throwing youths attacking Israeli-owned banks and taking over the streets of the Arab district for hours. Police said it was the worst violence in Jerusalem in more than a decade. As the days passed, the riots, which had broken out spontaneously, appeared to be increasingly organized.

On December 20, the government of Israel, rebutting international criticism of its handling of the riots, declared that it was dealing with the situation "in a way that is more restrained than any other government in the world in similar circumstances." Israeli officials indicated that the army had not been prepared for the size and widespread nature of the protests and, as a result, soldiers found themselves in situations where "almost the only way to deal with it is to open fire." They indicated that more troops would be deployed and tactics would be altered, with an eye to reducing casualties. On December 21, Israeli Arabs in Nazareth rioted in sympathy with the Palestinians in the territories, and some 3,000 Israeli Arabs from the village of Umm al-Faham in the Galilee blocked the Wadi Ara road, a main artery connecting several Jewish villages. The same day, the U.S. State Department issued an advisory urging caution to travelers visiting the territories.

On December 22, the Security Council adopted a resolution strongly deploring Israel's handling of the disturbances in the territories. The United States abstained. Explaining this vote, Herbert Okun, the American representative, agreed that Israel's reaction to the riots was "unacceptably harsh," and indicated that the administration believed the riots were "spontaneous expressions of frustration and not externally sponsored." But, he said, the United States would not vote for the resolution because it contained "generalized criticism of Israeli policies and practices" and ignored the provocations faced by Israeli security forces. Meanwhile, the White House issued a statement saying both sides shared responsibility: "Demonstrations and riots on one side and harsh security measures and excessive use of live ammunition on the other hand cannot substitute for a genuine dialogue."

U.S. Jewish reaction to events in the territories became part of the story as well. One response was that of Morris Abram, speaking on behalf of the Conference of

Presidents of Major American Jewish Organizations, who said the violence had been "planned, instigated and incited by Palestinian terrorists led by the PLO and Moslem fundamentalist groups" and that "in the short range, order must be restored lest anarchy triumph." A different view was offered by Rabbi Alexander Schindler, president of the Union of American Hebrew Congregations. He said the violence "should shock Israel's government into realizing that a tense political situation cannot continue indefinitely without some kind of movement," adding that "Israel simply cannot sit in the territories and wait for peace to come."

On December 23, Israeli officials rejected the Reagan administration's assertion that Israeli troops had used excessive force in quelling Palestinian riots. In an unusual occurrence, the prime minister's and the foreign minister's offices offered similar responses. The prime minister's representative said that "to assign the same blame to those who caused the unrest and those who tried to prevent it can be interpreted wrongly." The Foreign Ministry said that U.S. criticism "came as a surprise" and would only encourage the PLO "to engage in further violence and undermine those truly committed to a real peace process." Later that day, the State Department again urged Israeli leaders to adopt nonlethal techniques to control the rioting. On December 24, more than 20 leaders of Jewish organizations met with State Department officials to complain about the administration's criticism of Israel.

The PLO's executive committee, meeting in emergency session in Tunis, considered establishing a government in exile and discussed the eventual composition of such a body. No action was taken, however.

Israeli leaders were perturbed by the news coverage of the disturbances, particularly that in the United States. Moshe Arens, former ambassador to Washington, spoke of an "information crisis" similar to the one he had faced in Washington during the 1982 war in Lebanon. A government spokesman castigated the foreign television coverage in particular for having the "chutzpah" to portray Israel as "a kind of South Africa."

Israeli leaders repeatedly and vehemently rejected U.S. criticism of their conduct. When Washington decried Israel's use of live ammunition in dealing with the protesters, Defense Minister Rabin said the Israel army had sought to use minimum force against the rioters, but he defended the use of live ammunition in situations in which the lives of soldiers were in jeopardy. When the United States complained about Israeli plans to deport a number of Palestinians, on the grounds that this would violate the Geneva Convention, Rabin said: "We are operating in accordance with our laws. We will continue the arrests, punishments, and deportations."

As the year ended, the long-term implications of the disturbances—for the peace process, for internal Israeli and Palestinian developments, for U.S.-Israeli relations, and for relations between Diaspora Jewry and Israel—were unclear. What did already seem evident was that a significant, possibly historic development was taking place, one that, unfortunately, through media coverage, was generating a negative image of Israel around the world.

## Terrorism

The gains made in 1986 in the fight against international terrorism, dramatically illustrated by the April 1986 U.S. raid on Libya, were severely undercut by revelations of the administration's secret arms deals with Iran. However, the administration demonstrated its continuing commitment to a strong policy in the case of Mohammed Ali Hamadei, a Lebanese accused of the 1985 hijacking of a TWA jet to Beirut and the murder of Robert Dean Stethem, a U.S. Navy diver, a passenger on that flight. In 1985, a U.S. grand jury had indicted Hamadei, who was presumably in Lebanon at the time, along with two others. On January 13, 1987, German officials arrested Hamadei on his arrival at the Frankfurt airport. The Reagan administration immediately requested that he be extradited to the United States, but the West German government said it would extradite Hamadei only if the U.S. government agreed not to seek the death penalty in the event of a conviction. On January 18, the Justice Department reluctantly agreed to the German condition, and U.S. officials expressed the hope that the extradition would happen soon.

However, Hamadei's Lebanese associates acted swiftly to prevent such a move. Within a few days of Hamadei's arrest, two West German businessmen, Rudolf Cordes of the Hoechst Chemical Company and Alfred Schmidt of the Siemens electrical concern, were kidnapped in Lebanon. On January 21, West German officials made clear that so long as these West Germans were being held hostage, there would be no quick extradition to the United States. It was noted by some analysts that in light of U.S. conduct in the Iran-*contra* affair, American officials were hardly in a position to demand the extradition.

For months the issue generated tension between U.S. and West German officials. Finally, on June 24, the Bonn government confirmed reports that it had decided not to extradite Hamadei but to try him itself for air piracy and murder. The government ruled out swapping Hamadei for Cordes and Schmidt, knowing that such a move would seriously harm U.S.-West German relations. Chancellery Minister Wolfgang Schmidt stressed that Hamadei would face the maximum sentence of life if convicted, and Washington expressed satisfaction at Bonn's strong stand.

On September 7, Alfred Schmidt was freed by his captors and driven to Damascus. His captors said they had received unspecified guarantees and assurances from West Germany, but German officials denied any deal and expressed gratitude to Syria for its positive role in the affair. No date had been set for Hamadei's trial by year's end; Cordes was still a captive in Lebanon.

Another kidnapping in Lebanon, occurring at the same time as that of the two Germans but apparently unrelated, provided another test of U.S. policy on terrorism. On January 24, gunmen posing as police abducted three American teachers and an Indian professor with an American passport from Beirut University College in West Beirut. President Reagan, reflecting a good deal of public sentiment, issued a statement saying, "There is a limit to what our government can do" to win the freedom of hostages. He indicated further that the latest victims had ignored official warnings and had remained in Beirut "at their own risk and their own responsibility."

Two days later the State Department barred U.S. citizens from traveling to Lebanon, citing the "chaotic" situation that posed "imminent peril" to all Americans there. It also gave the 1,500 Americans still in Lebanon 30 days to leave the country. On January 27 and 28, the Pentagon and the White House announced that the U.S. Navy was bolstering its presence in the Middle East, to aid the evacuation of Americans and to be ready to undertake military retaliation in the event that any American hostages were killed.

The kidnappers, identifying themselves as members of the Islamic Jihad for the Liberation of Palestine, demanded that Israel free 400 Palestinian prisoners by February 9 or they would kill the hostages. On February 1, Defense Minister Rabin rejected the demand, saying that Israel was not an "international reserve bank" for terrorist exchanges; Prime Minister Shamir said the next day that such a swap was "out of the question."

As a large U.S. fleet, including hundreds of aircraft and thousands of marines, gathered in the eastern Mediterranean, other groups holding hostages—Islamic Jihad and the Revolutionary Justice Organization—warned the administration not to mount a rescue operation or a reprisal raid. In response, the Pentagon attempted to ease the crisis atmosphere by downplaying any U.S. military plans and stressing that the navy buildup off Lebanon was "entirely precautionary." And on February 5, the administration admitted that it had given up plans to convene a conference of the seven leading industrial nations to deal with the Lebanese hostage crisis. It was reported that France, Great Britain, and West Germany had all argued that any appearance of collusion with Washington, particularly in the context of the U.S. military buildup in the region, would endanger the lives of the hostages.

On February 7, Lebanese Shi'ite leader Nabih Berri injected a new ingredient by offering to exchange an Israeli airman shot down in southern Lebanon in October 1986 for the 400 Palestinians, as well as to seek the release of the four teachers as part of the same deal. Pressure mounted. On February 8, the terrorists released a videotape of hostage Alan Steen pleading with the U. S. government to order Israel to free the 400 Arabs to prevent the hostages' execution. Shimon Peres responded immediately: "Israel cannot and will not operate according to ultimatums." But, he added, in what was seen as a softening of Israel's posture, "if anyone has any offers, he should please turn to Israel in an orderly fashion and he will be given an orderly answer."

On February 9, attention focused on the kidnappers and their midnight deadline. The Reagan administration once again ruled out concessions. Denouncing hostage takers as "animals," Secretary Shultz said that dealing with the hostage problem was particularly difficult because "we are sympathetic people and we all feel, as the President does, when an American overseas is kicked around, we're kicked around." He vowed that the United States would raise the cost to those who abducted Americans. Meanwhile, White House spokesman Marlin Fitzwater said that Washington "had not talked to the Israelis" about their demand, and that the U.S. position remained the same: "We will not ransom for hostages and we will not encourage others to do so. . . ."

Midnight passed and nothing happened. Shortly thereafter, the kidnappers said they would extend the deadline "until further notice." In a communiqué, the captors said the delay was prompted by the "repeated calls of the hostages themselves for a deferment of the deadline [and] mounting pleas by their families and national Lebanese bodies as well as the Indian government." The communiqué also referred to Peres's comments, which, it said, "contained certain positive points over the release" of the Palestinian prisoners. Later in February, General Antoine Lahad, commander of the South Lebanon Army Militia and an ally of Israel, said he was willing to trade 250 Shi'ite Amal prisoners for the four teachers if Amal would also release five members of the South Lebanese Army that it held. But again there were no developments.

Despite the ongoing Lebanese hostage situations and the fallout of the Iran-*contra* affair, there was in 1987 a general sense that progress had been made on the counterterrorism front. On the anniversary of the U.S. bombing raid on Libya, April 14, American officials cited figures showing a distinct drop in terrorist activity during the preceding year, which they attributed to the raid and also to increased security in Europe. On May 28, officials of the seven major democracies, as well as those of Belgium and Denmark, met in Paris to forge tighter links in the battle against international terrorism. U.S. attorney general Edwin Meese hailed the session as the first in a series of steps toward increased cooperation. Because of France's former reluctance to join international forums to fight terrorism, the fact that the meeting was organized by the French was seen as a significant victory for the Reagan administration.

One more indication of growing international seriousness on the subject was a UN vote on December 1 defeating a Syrian proposal for a UN conference to define the difference between terrorism and "legitimate" acts by national liberation movements. In an unusual consensus, the USSR and Third World countries joined the United States, Great Britain, and other Western countries in opposing the Syrian plan. This vote was seen as reflecting a new eagerness to deal with terrorism and an unwillingness to rationalize terrorist acts according to ideology.

## *PLO Office Closings*

The U.S. government took one more significant step in 1987 which reflected the complexity of its Middle East decision-making process: it closed the Washington office of the PLO. Factors leading up to this decision included the secretary of state's continuing determination to take a firm stand against terrorism; the initiative and stamina of a number of members of Congress; and the political input of American Jewish community leaders opposed to any PLO presence in the United States.

Movement to try to close both the PLO's Palestine Information Office in Washington and its UN Observer Mission in New York began in the fall of 1986. On October 17, 1986, ten senators sent a letter to President Reagan requesting the closing of the Washington office. In November 1986 a State Department spokesman indicated that there would be no action taken, claiming that the office did not contradict U.S. policy prohibiting contact with the PLO, nor did it conflict with U.S. opposition to terrorism.

In the spring of 1987, bills were introduced in both houses of Congress to close the Washington and New York offices. The bills, sponsored by Jack Kemp (R., N.Y.) in the House and Robert Dole (R., Kan.), Charles Grassley (R., Iowa), Frank Lautenberg (D., N.J.), Howard Metzenbaum (D., Ohio), and Rudy Boschwitz (Ind.-R., Minn.) in the Senate, said that the PLO was a "terrorist organization" and "a threat to the interests of the United States and its allies." The senators indicated that they had proposed the bill because the administration had not acted on their past requests to close the offices. Opposition to the bills outside the government focused on First Amendment issues—whether Congress had the right to bar American citizens or legal residents, those individuals running the PLO offices, from conducting advocacy activities at the direction of the PLO. Within the administration, concerns were voiced that the legislation would pose international legal problems, would make "martyrs" of the PLO representatives, and probably would be overturned by the World Court. Analysts also suggested that some in the administration opposed the bills because of a belief that the PLO eventually should be included in the peace process.

The prospect of the two pieces of legislation moving forward, together with the push for action from the organized Jewish community, generated a reassessment at the State Department. On July 31, Secretary Shultz wrote Grassley and Kemp rejecting their bills but leaving the door open for possible State Department action with regard to the less problematic issue, the Washington office. Finally, on September 15, State announced that it had informed the Palestine Information Office that it must close within 30 days. The State Department indicated that the action was being taken "to demonstrate U.S. concern over terrorism committed and supported by organizations and individuals affiliated with the PLO." As evidence in support of the move, officials cited the membership on the PLO Executive Committee of Abu Abbas, linked with the *Achille Lauro* hijacking; membership of groups "with a history of involvement with terrorism," such as the PFLP and the DFLP in the PLO; and contacts between "the mainline PLO" and the Abu Nidal group. At the same time, citing "special treaty obligations under the United Nations headquarters agreement," State Department officials disclosed that they would not seek to shut the PLO observer mission to the UN in New York City.

Lawyers for the information office challenged the State Department decision, but on December 2, a U.S. district court upheld the decision to close the Washington office. Judge Charles Richey ruled that the office constituted a "foreign mission" of the PLO, and that as a foreign political entity it had "no due process right under our Constitution." He added, however, that Palestine Information Office director

Hassan Rahman, a naturalized American citizen, remained "free as a citizen to espouse his political views." The court indicated that the State Department decision was a legitimate expression of "U.S. concern over terrorism committed and supported by individuals and organizations associated with the PLO."

Meanwhile, despite the hopes of the administration that the decision to close the Washington office would put the matter to rest, congressional legislation moved apace, and in mid-December, as part of the State Department authorization bill, Congress passed a measure requiring the closing of both offices within 90 days. Because it was part of the larger State Department bill, the measure received President Reagan's signature. However, the president expressed his displeasure, and Secretary Shultz warned that the effort to close the UN mission would be a "propaganda gain" for the PLO. As the year was coming to a close, the administration was struggling to find a way to avoid having to take the called-for action. It was reported that efforts would be made during the 90 days before the law went into effect to try to persuade lawmakers to abrogate the order.

KENNETH JACOBSON

# Communal

## Jewish Communal Affairs

THE MAJOR PREOCCUPATION of the American Jewish community in 1987 was, by far, the State of Israel. Issue after issue came up related to the Jewish state, each in its own way calling into question old assumptions about the American Jewish–Israeli relationship. The fate of Jews in another foreign country—the Soviet Union—was also a high communal priority, as it had been for two decades. And developments within the religious movements, as well as relations between them, continued to attract interest.

### Israel and American Jewry

In June of 1987 the American Jewish Committee released *Ties and Tensions*, a survey by Steven M. Cohen of American Jewish attitudes toward Israel and Israelis. It found that, by and large, American Jews continued to feel very close to Israel. Yet Cohen noted signs of distancing among the religiously less traditional and among the young. He suggested that certain Israeli policies over the preceding decade might have contributed to some disaffection among these groups. If this assessment was correct, events in 1987 could only have served to accelerate the trend. Though few American Jews went as far as Brown University professor Jacob Neusner, who declared, "It's time to say that America is a better place to be a Jew than Jerusalem" (*Washington Post*, March 8, 1987), many were viewing Israel more critically than they had before.

#### THE POLLARD AFFAIR

On March 4, Chief Judge Aubrey Robinson, Jr., of the U.S. district court for the District of Columbia, sentenced Jonathan Jay Pollard, an American Jew, to life imprisonment for espionage. Pollard had admitted to selling thousands of classified government documents to Israel while employed in naval counterintelligence. His wife, Anne Henderson Pollard, received a five-year sentence for being an accessory to the crime. The stiff jail terms reflected the recommendations of the Justice Department, which asserted that Jonathan Pollard's "breach of trust" caused "exceptional" danger to American national security. According to a memorandum filed by federal prosecutors, "the breadth and volume of the U.S. classified information sold by defendant to Israel was enormous, as great as in any reported case involving espionage on behalf of any foreign nation." Commented Secretary of Defense Caspar Weinberger, "It is difficult for me . . . to conceive of a greater harm to national security." (See "The United States, Israel, and the Middle East," elsewhere in this volume.)

For American Jews, who were used to thinking of Israel as a natural ally and close friend of the United States, these revelations came as a shock. The organized Jewish community was virtually unanimous in condemning the Pollards and praising their conviction. Expressing this consensus, Morris Abram, chairman of the Conference of Presidents of Major Jewish Organizations, asserted that "Pollard pleaded guilty in an American court to a serious crime. He received due process and a just punishment."

The Pollards had been arrested in November of 1985, with Jonathan Pollard accused of having delivered secret scientific, technical, and military information to the Israeli embassy in Washington every two weeks in exchange for payments totaling around $50,000. Four Israeli officials in the United States who were named as conspirators quickly returned to Israel. In June 1986, in order to avoid standing trial, and with the agreement of federal prosecutors, Pollard pleaded guilty.

At the time of Pollard's arrest, Israel, hoping to minimize the damage to American-Israeli relations, apologized, denied that the espionage had been authorized by its government, and promised full cooperation with American investigators. During 1986, however, the U.S. Justice Department came to believe that Israel was being less than forthcoming, and that, in fact, it was covering up the involvement of high-level officials. Indeed, Jonathan Pollard himself consistently said that his activities had Israeli government approval. The growing impression that the Israelis did not take this case as seriously as the Americans seemed confirmed when Aviem Sella and Rafael Eitan, two of the Israelis accused of conspiring with Pollard (Sella was about to be indicted by a federal grand jury), were appointed to prestigious new positions in Israel. And when Israel was called upon to return what had been stolen, it gave back just a small portion of the documents, and those were only copies of the originals.

American Jewish leaders warned that Israel's apparent nonchalance could antagonize Americans and make them less willing to support Israel. Interviewed by the *New York Times* (March 7), Rabbi Arthur Hertzberg, long active in Jewish communal affairs, expressed fear that this episode, coming amid allegations that Israel somehow instigated the Iran-*contra* fiasco, would add to the perception "that Israelis are so much at the center of the American agenda that they can do whatever they want." Furthermore, the uncovering of an American Jewish spy for Israel, by possibly resurrecting the old suspicion of Jewish dual loyalty, posed a potential threat to the status of all American Jews. Hyman Bookbinder, the American Jewish Committee's special representative in Washington, put the matter bluntly: "The fact that he's

Jewish could lead people to conclude erroneously that American Jews are less than 100 percent American citizens."

Jonathan Pollard's explanation of his acts reinforced this fear. Stung by allegations that he had spied for money, Pollard insisted that it was Zionist commitment that motivated him to spy on his own country to benefit the Jewish state. In letters from prison and in interviews, Pollard claimed that the information he provided Israel had to do with sophisticated new weaponry available to its enemies, information it was entitled to receive but which the United States was holding back. Since Israel's very existence was at stake, explained Pollard, he had reasoned that *"ein breira"*—he had no choice but to spy for Israel.

American Jewish leaders saw only one way to salvage American-Israeli ties and counter any perception of dual loyalty: convincing Israel to cooperate fully in uncovering the truth about the affair. "Israel is under a cloud," Abraham Foxman of the Anti-Defamation League (ADL) of B'nai B'rith told the *Washington Post* (March 12), "and it could have very serious consequences if the leadership doesn't come to grips with reality." American Jewish organizations vied with each other in sending delegations to Israel to convey this message. Indeed, the ADL and the Conference of Presidents of Major American Jewish Organizations got into a nasty tiff over which body had the right to speak for American Jewry to the Israelis on this issue.

Most Israelis, however, even those who considered the Pollard escapade a mistake, could not understand the sense of urgency that the Americans projected. Prime Minister Yitzhak Shamir at first rejected calls for a special investigation on the ground that the running of Pollard was a "rogue operation" that would never happen again. In March, when he reversed himself and ordered a probe—but one with no judicial powers—Shamir let it be known that this was done just to satisfy American Jews and the American government. Pressure from American Jews also had much to do with forcing Aviem Sella, Pollard's indicted Israeli contact, out of his new job as commander of an important air base and his reassignment as a military instructor.

Putting the best possible face on Israeli policy, American Jewish leaders hailed the decision to hold government and Knesset inquiries and Sella's resignation as indications that democracy was alive and well in Israel, and that the Jewish state intended to uncover the full story. But more bad news kept coming out of Israel. American correspondents stationed there reported overwhelming public sympathy for Pollard. While opinions varied over the wisdom of recruiting an American Jew as a spy, Israelis considered Pollard himself a Jewish hero who had sacrificed himself to save the Jewish state from destruction. A poll conducted by the Israeli newspaper *Yediot Aharonot* in mid-March found that 90 percent of Israelis thought Israel had a responsibility to help the Pollards. A group calling itself Citizens in Support of the Pollards raised tens of thousands of dollars in Israel to help pay the couple's legal fees.

Simmering differences between American and Israeli Jews over the Pollard affair burst into open conflict with the publication of an article in the *Jerusalem Post* (March 10) by Hebrew University political scientist Shlomo Avineri, a respected scholar long active in the Israeli Labor party. Avineri denounced the leaders of American Jewry as cowards, arguing that their excessively emotional response to the Pollard problem reflected their own sense of marginality and insecurity in America. If the United States was not a prejudiced country, why should the conviction of one Jewish spy alarm all the Jews? Why were American Jews so quick to distance themselves from Pollard and assert their own patriotism? Their disproportionate reaction proved, for Avineri, that American Jews felt just as vulnerable to anti-Semitism as all previous Diaspora communities, showing the truth of classical Zionist ideology: outside their own sovereign state, Jews will always be haunted by the specter of Jew-hatred. Contrary to the assumption of American Jewry, America was no exception.

American Jews were quick to respond. Abraham Foxman asserted angrily in an article in the *Jerusalem Post* (March 17): "If there is any collective neurosis among Jews over the Pollard affair, it exists in Israel, not the United States. It comes from the dissonance of declaring the Pollard scandal a 'rogue operation' and then rewarding the rogues. It's the sense of guilt over using, abusing, and then abandoning Pollard. It's you, not us, whose conscience is troubled by the moral cowardice of the Pollard affair."

Yet not all American Jews agreed with the views of the communal establishment. Prof. Alan M. Dershowitz of Harvard Law School was one of the first to call publicly for a reassessment of the case. In a *New York Times* op-ed piece (March 18), Dershowitz argued that Jonathan Pollard—who had, after all, confessed and cooperated with the government—should not have received a life sentence, especially since the espionage had been conducted for an ally, not an enemy, and the stolen documents had to do with Israel's regional security, not with global and strategic intelligence. Dershowitz added that "all countries spy on friends and foes alike. Certainly the United States spies on Israel . . . and Israel spies on us. The big news in the Pollard case is that the Israelis got caught." Like Avineri, he attributed American Jewish overreaction to fear of the dual-loyalty charge.

The influential columnist Charles Krauthammer seconded Dershowitz in the pages of the *Washington Post* (March 20). While allowing that American Jewish leaders acted properly in warning Israel of the potential danger of the Pollard affair for American-Israeli relations, he felt that "the rush of 65 Jewish leaders to Israel bears the sign of more than just an informational visit. There is about it an air of defensiveness bordering on panic." Krauthammer cited approvingly the words of Sen. Daniel Inouye (D., Hawaii): "To suggest that the act of one Jew should be borne by all Jews is an insult."

An April *New York Times*/CBS poll indicated that 40 percent of American Jews agreed with Dershowitz that Pollard's sentence was too harsh. Yet there was relatively little sympathy for him: 34 percent of American Jews were angry, and 27 percent embarrassed, at what he had done. As if to substantiate the Avineri thesis about American Jewish anxieties, fully 54 percent of American Jews surveyed feared a rise in anti-Semitism as a result of the affair. But the poll suggested that their concern was ill-founded: just 18 percent of non-Jews even knew that Pollard had spied for Israel, and, when informed of the fact, only 36 percent felt it would cause a rise in anti-Semitism. The percentage of non-Jews who believed that Jews had too much power in the United States registered at 21 percent, just about where it had been before Pollard.

PHILANTHROPY AND ZIONISM

Severe tensions emerged during 1987 between Israel and the American Jewish organizations that help defend and support it. The specific points of conflict—how to allocate American Jewish philanthropy in Israel, the composition and operation of the Jewish Agency, and elections to the World Zionist Congress—reflected a fundamental reassertion by American Jewry of its own values and priorities in relation to the Jewish state.

Over the years, local Jewish federations and individual contributors had become increasingly uneasy about their lack of control over distribution of the money they gave Israel through the United Jewish Appeal–Federation campaign. The money was distributed by the Jewish Agency, a body operating in Israel under the direction of an international governing board, whose activities include immigrant absorption, economic development, and education. Jewish leaders in the United States complained that the allocation process, controlled by Israeli political parties, was not only inefficient and possibly corrupt, but also unfair, since it divided the funds on a partisan basis and ignored worthy causes outside the political mainstream. Especially galling to many non-Orthodox activists was the dearth of funding for Reform and Conservative projects in Israel, which they attributed to an Orthodox stranglehold on allocations for religious institutions. Reflecting the growing mood of disaffection was the mounting popularity of the New Israel Fund, which granted money to Israeli causes not tied into the political system, and the well-publicized decision of the San Francisco Jewish Community Federation in December 1986 to earmark $100,000 directly to projects of its choice in Israel.

The United Jewish Appeal and the American Zionist movement viewed these developments with alarm, fearing that they could undermine the unified approach to providing aid to Israel. Stanley Horowitz, national president of the UJA, called the action of the San Francisco federation "a deviation from a process that has worked on a scale and with a degree of success few human enterprises can match." In January the American Zionist Federation, meeting in Philadelphia, denounced "any action by which public campaign funds of the community are disbursed outside the normal UJA–Federation allocations process, since it tends to divide the community and the unity of the combined campaign."

In March the powerful New York UJA–Federation—which raised fully one-fifth of all American contributions distributed by the Jewish Agency—released a report on how the Jewish Agency allocated funds to the Jewish religious movements in Israel. The result of a two-month investigation by a committee representing all the movements, the report found that, whereas at least 70 percent of donations in New York came from non-Orthodox sources, non-Orthodox movements in Israel received far less money than the Orthodox. The investigators stopped short of accusing the Jewish Agency of outright discrimination, attributing the situation instead to bureaucratic inertia and the relative indifference of donors about how their money was spent. On the basis of these findings, New York UJA–Federation called for a thorough overhaul and depoliticization of the Jewish Agency.

Under pressure from the Americans, the Jewish Agency took steps to deal with the criticism. Its board of governors recommended that chairman Arye Dulzin— whose reputation had been tarnished in a bank scandal—not serve beyond his current term, which would expire at the end of 1987. It also voted a $1.64-million allocation to the Reform movement in Israel, a step it hoped would end talk of a Reform boycott of the unified fund-raising system.

At the June meeting of the Jewish Agency Assembly in Jerusalem, American Jews pressed for a series of fundamental reforms drawn up by a "Committee of Twelve" prominent figures from the Zionist and philanthropic organizations. These suggestions included the removal of partisan considerations from the Agency, equal partnership between the Zionist movement and Diaspora philanthropists, accountability of officers to the board, and a clear distinction between the staff responsibilities of the Jewish Agency, on the one hand, and the World Zionist Organization, on the other. (The activities of the latter, composed of the national Zionist movements, overlapped in some areas with those of the Agency.)

The Americans got most of what they wanted, losing outright only on the issue of Jewish Agency–WZO staff duplication. The power and determination of the non-Orthodox religious movements achieved passage of two important resolutions: one reiterating a 1986 decision barring Agency funding for non-Zionist—i.e., ultra-Orthodox—religious schools, the other cutting off allocations to any Israeli body that refused to accept Ethiopian immigrants as Jews—a clear slap at the Orthodox rabbis and institutions that questioned the Jewishness of these immigrants.

The same American assertiveness came into play in connection with the World Zionist Congress, which meets once very five years, primarily to allocate its budget and choose half the members of the Jewish Agency's governing board. Since delegates to the 1982 congress had been appointed, it was now ten years since there had been an election to choose American representatives to what is the only semblance of a worldwide Jewish "parliament." On May 15 ballots were mailed out to the members of 16 American Zionist organizations; the voters would have until June 30 to select the 152 people who would constitute the American contingent within the 500-member congress. The election system was modeled on that used for the Israeli Knesset: the various movements presented lists of nominees, and each slate would be assigned delegates in proportion to its electoral strength.

Since most of the American Zionist organizations kept less-than-formal records of membership, a computing firm was hired to match each body's claim of membership against evidence of actual dues-paying members. It was agreed that any organization found to have overstated its membership by more than 7 percent would be penalized by losing delegates in proportion to the magnitude of the discrepancy. Even so, charges filled the air that one or another organization was inflating its membership lists, giving out unsolicited "guest memberships" to induce people to support a particular movement, or using the names and pictures of well-known personalities in its campaign literature without their permission.

These allegations were less important in the long run than the emergence of two relatively new Zionist movements in this election, both of which stressed the issue of religious pluralism. *Arza*, representing Reform Judaism, won 33 seats, the largest single contingent in the American delegation, and *Mercaz*, founded by the Conservative movement, won 20. It was clear that many American Jews who had in the past identified with mainstream Zionist movements like Hadassah and the Zionist Organization of America now felt so strongly about the need to combat the Orthodox monopoly in Israel that they opted for the explicitly denominational slates.

Several parties were stripped of delegates for having overstated their membership. The Religious Zionist Movement, made up of the Religious Zionists of America and allied organizations—the only group in the election that explicitly supported the religious status quo in Israel—was the biggest loser in this regard, sacrificing 13 of its 27 delegates. Rabbi Louis Bernstein, RZA board chairman, called the penalty "the greatest fraud since the Great Train Robbery" and warned that the election could mean "a reading of Orthodox Jews out of the American Zionist movement."

The American delegates proceeded to make their voices heard at the congress, which took place in Jerusalem in December. Allying themselves with other liberal Zionist movements and with the Israeli Labor party, they elected Labor's Simcha Dinitz as the new chairman of the Jewish Agency Executive and the WZO, and received important positions in the new administration in return. The importance of the religious pluralism issue to the non-Orthodox members of the American delegation was dramatically illustrated on the final night of the congress, when a proposal was passed favoring "complete equality of rights for all streams of Judaism," although when the Orthodox threatened to secede, the chairman asserted that the resolution did not bind the sovereign State of Israel.

When the congress adjourned in pandemonium, with delegates throwing flower pots at each other, one result was undeniable: American Jews would henceforth have considerably more influence in the Jewish Agency and the World Zionist Organization than in the past.

WHO IS A JEW?

The issue of religious pluralism bedeviled American Jewish–Israeli relations in other spheres besides the World Zionist Congress.

The great gap between the assumptions of Israeli Orthodoxy, on the one hand,

and the attitudes of the majority of American Jews, on the other, was illuminated in an interview with Israel's chief rabbis—something of a journalistic coup—published in the March issue of *Moment* magazine. Much of the article focused on the question of the Orthodox monopoly over Judaism in Israel, with the two rabbis, Avraham Shapiro (Ashkenazic) and Mordechai Eliahu (Sephardic), making it clear that Reform and Conservative Judaism had no legitimacy in their eyes. To be sure, both men insisted that non-Orthodox Jews were authentically Jewish, and urged them to settle in Israel. But Shapiro said that such "new" forms of Judaism constituted new religions, and that Reform was a "way-station to Christianity." Eliahu was even more hostile, comparing Reform rabbis to witch doctors and declaring that secular Jews were far preferable to non-Orthodox religious Jews, since the former, unlike the latter, recognized that Orthodoxy was the authentic version of Judaism.

American reaction came quickly. Rabbi Jack Stern, president of Reform's Central Conference of American Rabbis (CCAR), charged that the chief rabbis were "weakening the Jewish people" by rejecting pluralism. Another Reform leader, Rabbi Daniel Syme, claimed that the rabbis' "bigotry" reflected an underlying loss of confidence and a realization that "their base of support is crumbling." Rabbi Benjamin Kreitman, executive vice-president of the United Synagogue of America (Conservative), commented that Shapiro and Eliahu understood neither Jewish law nor talmudic philosophy. Even Rabbi Moshe Sherer, president of the Agudath Israel of America (Orthodox), who supported the chief rabbis' position, considered some of their remarks extreme and uncalled for.

This dispute was not taking place in a vacuum. The Shoshana Miller case that had inflamed passions during 1986 dragged on into 1987. In January Israel's interior minister Yitzhak Peretz, of the Orthodox Shas party, quit his cabinet post rather than obey the Israeli Supreme Court and register Miller, an American Reform convert to Judaism, as a Jew for the purposes of the Law of Return. At the same time, other Reform and Conservative converts in Israel began to take legal steps to have themselves denoted as Jews on their identity cards.

The Orthodox parties in the Knesset brought up their perennial demand for a change in the procedure for accepting foreign converts as Jews. One type of proposal, which had come up many times in the past, was for an amendment to the Law of Return that would require conversions to be "according to Halakhah" in order to gain acceptance. Another, seemingly more moderate, suggestion was to grant the Israeli chief rabbinate—controlled by the Orthodox—the authority to determine which foreign conversions were valid. In May, 23 national American Jewish organizations protested both ideas vehemently, and in July the Council of Jewish Federations and Welfare Funds, the umbrella organization for all local federations in the United States, sent a delegation to Israel to lobby against any change. The Knesset defeated the proposals, although one bill to give the rabbinate jurisdiction over conversions came within four votes of passage.

One by-product of the Knesset's action was a split within American Orthodoxy. The Religious Zionists of America, a modern Orthodox group affiliated with the

National Religious party in Israel, pointed out that nothing was gained by continually bringing up the "Who is a Jew?" issue when there was no chance of winning. On the contrary, said the organization's chairman, Rabbi Louis Bernstein, the battle had given an incentive to Reform and Conservative Jews to mount an aggressive anti-Orthodox campaign. However, the Agudath Israel of America and the Lubavitch movement remained firmly committed to a change in the law.

Another outcome of the controversy was a decision by the Council of Jewish Federations to circulate a six-point proposal suggesting a program to educate Israelis about the realities of American Jewish religious pluralism and to make American Jews more familiar with the Israeli political factors that influence the country's approach to religious matters.

In November, at the CJF's General Assembly in Miami, the organization's outgoing president, Shoshana Cardin, made this the primary topic of her address, warning that "deep divisiveness and widespread disaffection" would result from any change in the Israeli definition of Jewishness. A forum at the General Assembly that was devoted to the subject of religious pluralism attracted hundreds of delegates. Two of the featured speakers challenged Cardin's position from different perspectives: Rabbi Yedidyah Atlas, spokesman for the Israeli chief rabbis, insisted that only Orthodox conversion procedures, by providing a common denominator, could keep all Jews unified. Rabbi Haskel Lookstein, a modern Orthodox rabbi from New York City opposed to changing the Law of Return, nevertheless criticized the involvement of nondenominational American fund-raising agencies in Israel's internal politics.

CONTENTION OVER SOVIET JEWS

The question of what the Israelis called *"neshirah,"* the accelerating tendency of Soviet Jewish emigrants who had been given visas by Israel to "drop out" in Vienna and come to the United States as refugees, generated open conflict between Israel and American Jewry during the year.

With the Soviet government allowing more Jews out, and with good reason to believe that the numbers would go even higher, the over-80-percent drop-out rate was unacceptable to Israelis of all parties. For them, this was a matter of classical Zionist ideology: Israel was the only legitimate homeland for Jews. In addition, beleaguered Israel needed the demographic help and technical expertise that these refugees could provide.

The Israelis did not mince words. Moshe Arens, the cabinet minister in charge of Soviet Jewry issues, told a gathering of American Jews in March that "a strong Israel is synonymous with Jewish survival," and "if there were to be a large-scale emigration of Jews from the Soviet Union and the majority were not to go to Israel, it would be a tragedy of historic proportions for the Jewish people." He went so far as to accuse American Jews of securing refugee status for the Soviet Jews in order to "entice Jews from all over the world to come to the U.S." instead of to Israel.

Minister of Absorption Yaacov Tzur warned that the continued misuse of Israeli visas for travel to America could lead the Soviets to clamp down once again on emigration.

Prime Minister Shamir met with President Ronald Reagan and Secretary of State George Shultz in an effort to have them withdraw the "refugee" designation from Soviet Jews (and thus make it harder for them to enter the United States). He argued that the existence of a Jewish state ready and willing to welcome any Jew made it absurd to call Jews who had gotten out of the USSR refugees. But the American officials turned him down, largely because the American Jewish community was virtually united against him.

American Jewish leaders saw the situation very differently from the Israelis. To be sure, they wanted as many Soviet Jews as possible to go to Israel. But they felt that refugees should be able to choose freely where they wanted to live and not be coerced to settle in Israel, even if they had Israeli visas. Restriction of entry to the United States conjured up painful memories of an earlier period when desperate Jews were turned away from American shores.

One Israeli proposal for resolving the impasse was to convince the Soviet Union to allow flights from its territory to Israel, with a stopover in Eastern Europe, where tighter controls would eliminate the possibility of *neshirah*. American Jews objected, arguing that the lack of the drop-out option could dissuade many Soviet Jews from leaving altogether. The Americans favored a two-track system, with flights directly to the West and flights to Israel. However, even assuming that the Soviets would allow this, there were complications. Would the United States permit Soviet Jews who went straight to Israel to claim refugee status later, if they changed their minds and opted for America? The Israelis vehemently opposed such an arrangement. And what of those Soviet Jews in Israel who had close relatives in the United States? Should the principle of family reunification override Zionist sensibilities, enabling these Jews, at least, to retain the refugee designation? There were no easy answers.

By year's end, complicated negotiations involving Israel, the United States, the Soviet Union, and other parties resulted in an agreement in principle to route flights from the USSR through Romania to Israel, with the actual details still to be worked out. The underlying difference in outlook between Israelis and American Jews remained unresolved.

## *Defending Israeli Policies*

At least since 1967, the organized American Jewish community had made the support of Israeli foreign and defense policies in the court of American public opinion a central priority. In 1987 that became an increasingly difficult task.

IRAN-*CONTRA* AFFAIR

Fallout from the Iran-*contra* affair threatened Israel's reputation throughout the year. (See "The United States, Israel, and the Middle East," elsewhere in this volume.) Certain people involved in the scandal and a number of politicians insinuated that Israelis had not only acted as facilitators for the American sale of arms to Iran—which no one denied—but had masterminded the scheme to funnel proceeds of the sales to the Nicaraguan *contras*, in defiance of the American Congress. While the airing of such allegations raised fears in Jewish circles that Israel might be made a scapegoat for the bungled operation, in the end there was no clear evidence linking Israel to *contra* funding, and American Jewish organizations did not have to confront the issue publicly.

SOUTH AFRICA

American Jewry was not as fortunate in regard to Israel's ties with South Africa. For some time, Israel had been criticized for its heavy trade and military cooperation with the apartheid regime, the latter in contravention of a UN boycott on the supply of arms to South Africa. Although Israel justified these ties by citing similar South African relationships with other Western democracies, as well as continuing black African hostility toward the Jewish state, American Jews felt morally uneasy, especially since black Americans brought it up when Jews complained about anti-Semitism in their community.

The Israel–South Africa connection gained prominence when Congress required the administration to report by April 1987 on recipients of American aid who supplied military matériel to Pretoria; those nations deemed to have done so would have their aid cut off. Hoping to avert such a fate, Israel announced in March that it would not enter into any new military contracts with South Africa. It said nothing about the status of existing contracts.

Leaders of the congregational bodies of Reform and Conservative Judaism in America urged the Israelis to go further and cut all military links. Albert Vorspan, director of the Union of American Hebrew Congregations' Commission on Social Action, warned that American support for Israel was already declining because of the Jewish state's implication in the perpetuation of apartheid. "I think Israel has to look beyond tomorrow," he added, "because the present South African regime is not going to last beyond tomorrow." Benjamin Kreitman, executive vice-president of the United Synagogue of America, declared that "for Israel to be an armaments manufacturer and trader is mind-boggling. And certainly to send it to South Africa is a fearsome thing and gives the wrong signal."

Other American Jewish communal agencies took a more nuanced position. While arguing on pragmatic grounds for an end to Israeli military cooperation with the South Africans, Allan Kagedan, an American Jewish Committee policy analyst, noted that Israel was being singled out unfairly by pro-PLO elements eager to discredit its moral standing. Said the Committee's Washington representative, Hyman Bookbinder, "If we have to disagree with Israeli policy, we'll disagree. But we want to still put it in context, in perspective."

After Jewish pledges to support increased aid to black Africa induced black members of Congress to tone down the congressional apartheid report's language about Israel, Jews turned their attention to their own South African dilemma— whether Americans should divest holdings in South Africa as a way of striking at the apartheid system. On this issue, moral abhorrence at racism and the desire to maintain good relations with American blacks conflicted with the overwhelming opposition of the South African Jewish community to divestment.

Once again, the UAHC took a far-reaching stand, supporting not only divestment but also American trade sanctions against South Africa; indeed, the Reform movement's Central Conference of American Rabbis sold off the assets in its members' pension fund that had been invested in South Africa. To be sure, neither these organizations nor the New Jewish Agenda, which also backed divestment, believed that this approach would necessarily succeed in overturning apartheid. Rather, as Albert Vorspan put it, "We are at a moment of truth. Constructive engagement did not work, and now international pressures and economic pressures are being attempted. They have a chance of working."

The major nondenominational Jewish organizations again staked out a more moderate position. The Anti-Defamation League opposed divestment on the ground it could hurt most the very blacks in whose name it was advocated. The AJCommittee agreed with this assessment, although it did back limited economic sanctions against South Africa. It also urged American companies operating there to adhere to the so-called Sullivan Principles of equal employment practices and special training programs for nonwhites.

Interest in Israel's policy toward South Africa peaked again in June, when the Israeli government decided to follow the advice of a specially appointed committee and honor existing military contracts with Pretoria, a step that embarrassed liberal Jewish members of Congress eager to maintain a close working relationship with black colleagues. In July the UAHC issued a highly critical report on Israel–South Africa ties, which, it claimed, were far more extensive than South Africa's relations with other nations—an assertion that other Jewish organizations disputed.

ISRAEL AND THE PALESTINIANS

American Jewry became a battleground in 1987 for the conflicting approaches to the peace process of the two major components of Israel's "unity" government, Labor and Likud. Since most American Jews were used to backing the Israeli government whatever its point of view, the spectacle of a divided Israel, with each side seeking American Jewish support, led to considerable confusion.

On September 21 the American Jewish Congress announced its backing for an international peace conference on the Middle East, a decision that made the front page of the *New York Times*. The outcome of a visit by a 17-member task force to Israel during the summer, this statement set the organization squarely on the side of Foreign Minister Shimon Peres of the Labor party, and against Prime Minister Yitzhak Shamir of Likud, who opposed such a conference. Reactions to the AJCongress's statement varied. The Herut Zionists of America, affiliated with Shamir's party, blasted "this so-called Congress, who was elected by no one" for trying "to dictate Israeli foreign policy." Morris Abram was more circumspect, noting that it was ultimately up to the people of Israel to decide policy for themselves. Albert Chernin, executive director of the National Jewish Community Relations Advisory Council (NJCRAC), argued that the AJCongress ought to have conveyed its views privately to Israeli officials rather than broadcast them in the *Times*.

Congress president Theodore Mann explained that the task-force members had become convinced in Israel that the Jewish state simply could not go on ruling a large, hostile Arab minority and remain a democratic state. "I don't see AJCongress as being at war with the Israeli government," he said. "There is no official stance in Israel. The Israeli government has no position on an international conference." Both Mann and the group's executive director, Henry Siegman, claimed to be surprised at how little criticism their statement had evoked, and drew the conclusion that the other major Jewish organizations, though afraid to admit it publicly, really agreed with them. Emboldened by the the AJCongress move, Shimon Peres started to campaign openly for additional American Jewish support for an international peace conference. Addressing the Conference of Presidents of Major Jewish Organizations in New York on the night of October 1, he urged his audience to shed its traditional reluctance to intervene and to "decide for yourselves" on a peace strategy. If American Jewry felt justified in intervening on "Who is a Jew?" asked Peres, why the reticence about the peace process?

UAHC president Alexander Schindler was the only person in the room who announced support for the Peres plan. Abraham Foxman of the ADL warned that American Jewish intervention in the formation of Israel's foreign policy might "create discord within the American Jewish community and destroy the effectiveness of the united Jewish community on behalf of Israel." Bert Gold of the AJCommittee remarked, "I would be a little more cautious than Peres. American Jews have developed a nose about where and when it is proper to intervene. It is pretty much sacrosanct that the Israeli government has to make the decisions on basic security issues." Yet shortly thereafter, Gold's own organization endorsed the idea of an international conference, as did the UAHC, and both denied that they were interfering in Israel's affairs.

Prime Minister Shamir did not stand idly by as his rival sought the support of American Jewry. Immediately after Peres's appearance at the presidents' conference, Shamir called it a "dangerous precedent" for American Jews to dissent from Israel's foreign policy. When the prime minister visited the United States in November, he gave a series of speeches that drew large and enthusiastic crowds. Making light of the demographic argument for ceding territory, he said in New York,

"When the first pioneers came to Eretz Israel at the end of the last century, the Jewish population was but a handful. We were still a minority when the State was declared in 1948. . . . Throughout our long history, our strength lay in our faith in ourselves, in our strong conviction in the justice of our cause, and not in our numbers or our political power." Before returning to Israel, Shamir told the presidents' conference, "The sooner the international conference is removed from the agenda, the closer we'll be to peace."

The international conference was indeed removed from the agenda—by the outbreak of Palestinian violence in Gaza and the West Bank early in December. As Israeli efforts to quell the disturbances produced a rising toll of casualties and no prospect of calm, Israel's image in the United States suffered, especially in the media, and many American Jews agonized over the situation.

American Jewish groups that had sympathized with the Peres approach to peace now tended to criticize the Israeli response to the uprising and to urge talks over the status of the territories. Alexander Schindler of the UAHC urged Israel to "act to defuse the violence, to restore order and to actively seek and find appropriate partners for the process of negotiation." AJCongress's Henry Siegman said that, while Israel was justified in putting down the violence, "it is not at all clear that the deadly force used by the Israeli army was in every instance an appropriate response," and he reiterated his organization's view that only an international conference could bring peace. The American Committee for Israel Peace Center, an affiliate of an Israel-based organization, went further, calling on Israel to refrain "from acts of force that will aggravate the present situation and increase friction with the local population." Signing this statement were such well-known American Jews as author Leonard Fein, former cabinet member Philip M. Klutznick, and noted feminist Letty Cottin Pogrebin.

American Jewish organizations that had not previously endorsed an international peace conference put the onus for the bloodshed on the Arabs. Chairman of the presidents' conference Morris Abram charged that the uprising had been "planned, instigated and incited by Palestinian terrorists led by the PLO and Moslem fundamentalist groups," although he did call for talks between the Jewish state and "Palestinian representatives who are prepared to live in peace with Israel." As far as the ADL was concerned, "peace in the Middle East would be better served if those who are condemning the violence would also press the Arab states and the PLO to recognize Israel's existence." When the U.S. State Department criticized the Palestinian rioters and the Israeli steps against them in equal measure, mainstream Jewish leaders rushed to Israel's defense. B'nai B'rith president Seymour Reich suggested that the United States "learn to tell the difference between those who want to burn the house down and those who are seeking to protect it."

On December 27 more than 25 Jewish groups sent representatives to meet with State Department officials about the Palestinian uprising. After the session, Abram told reporters that its purpose had been to convince the administration that the Palestinians "are not college campus protestors. They come with Molotov cocktails and gasoline bombs." He did grant that Israel had an "image problem" and that "it would be better if Israel had better equipment for dealing with the riots."

Indeed, since the beginning of the uprising, the presidents' conference and other American Jewish organizations that publicly defended Israel's role had also been sending urgent private messages to Israeli leaders, urging them to moderate their military response and come to grips with the larger task of settling the Palestine problem. While these private communications played a role in the Israeli decision to minimize the use of live ammunition, the American Jewish leaders were not satisfied. Though few of them were willing to be quoted on the subject, as 1987 drew to an end, many told reporters, off the record, that the Likud policy of maintaining the status quo in the territories had reached a dead end. Alexander Schindler, who had never hidden his dovish sentiments, commented, "The explosion Shimon Peres has been talking about has finally happened. This situation cannot continue long."

## Soviet Jewry

Concern for the welfare of Jews in the Soviet Union had long been second only to the security of Israel on the public agenda of the American Jewish community. Still, there were divisions within the community over strategy. The National Conference on Soviet Jewry tended to take a comparatively moderate line toward the Soviet regime, while the Union of Councils for Soviet Jews and the Student Struggle for Soviet Jewry were more outspoken and confrontational. The major national Jewish organizations usually took positions somewhere between the two poles.

At the beginning of 1987, Soviet Jewry activists were pessimistic. Despite the emigration of Natan Sharansky and several other well-known Soviet Jews in 1986, the total number of Jews who had been allowed to leave during the year was a meager 914, the lowest in a long time. Furthermore, there was considerable fear that the growing rapprochement between the two superpowers could lead the United States to subordinate the issue of human rights in order to further its ties with the Soviets.

When Secretary of Commerce Malcolm Baldridge announced the lifting of a ban on exports of oil- and gas-drilling equipment to the Soviet Union, in January, the divisions in the organized Jewish community came to the fore. Both the AJCommittee and the AJCongress commented that a pledge of freer emigration should have been extracted in return for this concession. But the National Conference on Soviet Jewry declined to make it an issue. Instead, it urged that American companies doing business in the USSR exert their influence on behalf of human rights there.

Rumors began circulating in February of a fundamental change in Soviet policy. In March, Morris Abram and World Jewish Congress president Edgar Bronfman returned from a trip to Moscow and confirmed the news. Soviet officials told them that they would allow the emigration of 10,000–12,000 Jews and ease restrictions on Jewish life within the country. In addition, according to Abram, the Soviets promised that "substantially all refuseniks and their families will be free to go to

Israel within the year with the exception of cases in which national security claims may be legitimately made."

The prospect of a mass exodus of Soviet Jews had two immediate ramifications. For one, it increased tensions between Israelis and American Jews over the drop-out issue (see the discussion above). For the Americans, it also reopened the controversy over the Jackson-Vanik Amendment that barred most-favored-nation trading status for the Soviet Union: how high would the emigration rate have to go to merit revocation or waiver of the relevant provision—a step that would be of enormous help to the Soviet economy. While some American Jewish leaders suggested a carefully calibrated lifting of trade restrictions to match Soviet performance on emigration, the more militant groups, as well as a number of prominent former refuseniks, insisted that no concessions be made until the yearly emigration rate reached 50,000.

The rift within the Soviet Jewry movement was dramatically displayed in May at the Solidarity Sunday rally for Soviet Jewry in New York City. Natan Sharansky, a scheduled speaker, charged that Abram and Bronfman had been taken in by the Kremlin; once Jackson-Vanik was lifted, he predicted, the Soviets would clamp down once again on Jewish emigration. Former prisoner-of-conscience Yosef Mendelevich then grabbed the microphone, uninvited, and shouted to the crowd, "I know you have your leaders. You elected them. But don't send them anymore to Moscow. They don't know how to deal with the Russians." He called for an American trade embargo on the Soviet Union until freedom of emigration was a reality.

By June, Abram, and, to a lesser extent, Bronfman, expressed diappointment that the Soviet regime had not yet begun to carry out its earlier assurances. Abram charged that the Soviets "are trying to buy respectability at a bargain rate. They want to be praised for letting some of the high visibility cases out, for emptying the jails, except the big jail that is the Soviet Union." Bronfman commented, "I don't know what we can do except keep on talking, pushing and struggling," though he did feel that "things are a bit better than they were."

Things continued to get better. In September the last Jew still in prison for Jewish activity was released from Siberia, and reports from the Soviet Union indicated a decline in government interference with Jewish cultural and educational activity. Nevertheless, Morris Abram cautioned an AJCommittee audience that "the total emigration figures for this year will be only one-seventh of those under Brezhnev in 1979."

WASHINGTON MOBILIZATION

Soviet General Secretary Mikhail Gorbachev was scheduled to arrive in Washington on December 7 for meetings with President Reagan. In a rare display of unity, 50 national Jewish organizations and 300 local federations and community councils joined forces to organize a mobilization in the nation's capital on the day before the summit meeting that, its sponsors hoped, would focus attention on the USSR's human-rights and emigration policies. Only certain Orthodox elements refused to join in. A key to the success of this project was the choice of David Harris, the AJCommittee's Washington representative, as mobilization coordinator. Harris, who was not publicly identified with either the National Council or its critics, yet had been closely involved with the Soviet Jewry agenda, enjoyed the confidence of both camps.

As the day of the mobilization approached, its fragile unity was threatened when Morris Abram told a *New York Times* reporter: "The demonstration will be in support of American policy. . . .I have nothing but respect for the way they've been handling this." Glenn Richter, head of the Student Struggle for Soviet Jewry, reacted strongly: "It is incomprehensible to me that a man of intelligence and political acumen like Morris Abram is signaling this position of weakness to the Soviets and the Administration." Richter said that while his group would not do anything to disrupt the harmony required for the mobilization, it might "stage peaceful arrests" of its members on the following day "to get our point across."

The mobilization was strikingly successful and unmarred by ideological conflict. With local federations stimulating grass-roots participation and footing part of the bill, and Washington staffers of national organizations handling the logistics, over 200,000 demonstrators from all over the country turned up in Washington to see and hear former refuseniks, American Jewish leaders, prominent politicians, and popular entertainers. Stephen Solender, executive vice-president of the New York UJA–Federation, said, "It was beyond my expectations. I can't tell you how many calls I've been getting from people who participated and felt that this was one of the most extraordinary Jewish experiences in their lives."

After this high point, the actual Gorbachev-Reagan talks were a letdown, accomplishing virtually nothing to help Soviet Jews. Again the American Soviet Jewry movement had to wrestle with the question of whether to advocate linkage of closer American-Soviet economic ties to the human-rights issue. The Union of Councils for Soviet Jews decided to back the proposed Kemp-Roth bill barring private bank loans to the Soviet Union until it eased internal repression; the National Council for Soviet Jewry remained uncommitted on the measure, and the Student Struggle for Soviet Jewry went so far as to urge a boycott of American companies doing business with Moscow.

## The Religious Movements

Recrimination and invective among the various streams of religious Judaism in the United States abated noticeably in 1987. To an extent, the struggle over religious pluralism in Israel functioned as a lightning rod, diverting interdenominational animosities away from the American setting. But there was also a palpable cooling of rhetoric on the part of all the groups, a conscious stepping-back from confrontation.

PATTERNS OF COOPERATION

This mood was captured in a joint statement issued by the presidents of the Rabbinical Council of America (Orthodox), the Rabbinical Assembly (Conservative), and the Central Conference of American Rabbis (Reform). Released in early April, so that it might be read from pulpits on the Sabbath before Passover, this message asserted that, whatever the issues dividing Jews, "we have a common past, shared experiences. We have suffered together at the hands of tyrants from Pharaoh to Hitler, who made no distinction between Jews whether they were Orthodox, Conservative or Reform, whether religious or secular, whether Zionist, non-Zionist or anti-Zionist, whether committed or assimilated." And, the rabbis emphasized, "There is nothing that prevents us from dialogue and cooperation on matters of mutual concern."

The spirit of cooperation brought concrete progress in the nation's largest Jewish community on an intermovement issue of great importance—religious divorce. On May 13 the New York Board of Rabbis, its membership encompassing rabbis of all the movements, agreed on a program to deal with the problem of civilly divorced Jews who failed to obtain a *get* (religious divorce) and whose subsequent marriages were thus considered adulterous, and their children illegitimate, according to traditional Jewish law. The board called on rabbis to counsel congregants going through a divorce to arrange a *get* as well, suggested that synagogues enact sanctions against members who refuse to participate in *get* proceedings, and urged the use of prenuptial agreements in which both spouses promise that, in the event the marriage breaks up, they will go through a Jewish divorce. Board president Haskel Lookstein, an Orthodox rabbi, praised his non-Orthodox colleagues for subordinating their own theological preferences to the cause of Jewish unity. "Because our commitment to the Jewish people as a whole transcends whatever adjective may be prefixed to our interpretation of Judaism, we acted as one," he said.

Another straw in the wind augured well for the future of cooperation between the movements. Although Reform Judaism did not consider traditional Halakhah binding and stood for personal autonomy in matters of observance, its rabbis voted 91 to 61 to invite the other denominations to explore the creation of a joint *bet din* (rabbinical court) that might settle intermovement controversies over matters of personal status in Jewish law.

DENOMINATIONAL ISSUES

Each of the Jewish religious denominations went through its own internal strains during 1987.

For the Orthodox, differences between moderates and the so-called right wing continued to center on whether, and to what extent, there should be relations with non-Orthodox forms of Judaism, and with other religions. For extreme traditionalists, the other movements constituted illegitimate forms of Judaism that could not be legitimized. Rabbi Aaron Soloveitchik expressed this point of view at the annual convention, in May, of the Rabbinical Council of America, an organization associated with "modern" or "centrist" Orthodoxy. He attacked the pre-Passover unity statement: "What kind of common dialogue can there be between Jews of authentic faith and Conservative and Reform rabbis?" He carefully differentiated between non-Orthodox Jews and their form of religion: "I'm willing to risk my life to save the lives of Reform and Conservative leaders as individuals. But should the movements be entitled to recognition?"

Rabbi Haskel Lookstein, in contrast, cited the example of the New York Board of Rabbis' resolution on *get* to show that cooperative efforts with the other movements could be fruitful. He condemned Orthodox isolationism, urging joint action with the other movements on conversion and other religious matters. "We're not doing anything," he complained, "we can't just sit back."

A similar debate arose over the question of Orthodox participation in meetings with Pope John Paul II in Rome and Miami (see "Intergroup Relations," elsewhere in this volume). Gilbert Klaperman, an Orthodox rabbi, attended the Rome meeting in late August and was slated to be the Jewish spokesman when the pope came to Miami in September. But the Rabbinical Council of America, influenced by rabbis ideologically opposed to religious dialogue, vetoed his participation. Angry and bitter, Klaperman charged that his organization had been "maneuvered by some extremist people. . . . To have an Orthodox rabbi make the presentation would have raised the position of the Orthodox 100 percent. But they just couldn't do it."

In the Conservative movement, the issue of female cantors was resolved when the Jewish Theological Seminary announced that it would grant cantorial diplomas to women. Although a similar decision had previously been taken for rabbis, the traditional role of the cantor as representative of the congregation in prayer had created greater halakhic difficulties for those seeking equality of the sexes.

The decision came in for heavy criticism from the Union for Traditional Conservative Judaism, a group that had been established in 1983 in opposition to what it saw as a drift away from tradition within Conservatism. Rabbi Ronald Price, the union's executive director, charged that the step could not be reconciled with Jewish law. "Before we begin tampering with tradition," he added, "let us all look inward carefully and make sure that what we are asking of the tradition is a result of our commitment to living it."

It was not an issue of Jewish law, but one of power, that exercised Conservative leaders at the biennial convention of the United Synagogue of America in November. Franklin Kreutzer, the organization's president, publicly criticized his movement for failing to allocate sufficient authority to lay leadership. The rabbis were not doing enough, he said. "Being a rabbi doesn't make one a deity. We don't want rabbis to lower their halakhic standards, but rabbis need to come down from the bimah and deal with the real human problems that exist in the community. . . ." Focusing on two issues of particular concern to the laity, the delegates followed Kreutzer's lead and passed resolutions providing for binding arbitration in cases of disputes between rabbis and congregations, and calling for greater lay representation on joint lay-rabbinic commissions.

The Reform movement continued its ongoing internal debate over how to balance a modernist theology with the traditional teachings and practices of Judaism. Its leaders continued to advocate support for progressive social causes, such as help for AIDS victims, alleviating poverty, and banning nuclear weapons. Its Central Conference of American Rabbis even debated, but deferred action on, a proposal to ordain gay rabbis. At the same time, many in the movement called for a return to greater traditionalism. The 1983 resolution on patrilineal descent, recognizing as Jews—even without conversion—individuals with one Jewish parent, father or mother, so long as they identified publicly with the Jewish community, was still opposed by a significant minority of Reform rabbis. One of them, Eugene Lipman, newly elected president of the CCAR, said in January, "Where children of mixed marriages are concerned, I want them to be Jews for the whole world. Since the traditional community is never going to accept patrilineality, this means conversion, not just changing the definitions." Indeed, Lipman always had three Orthodox colleagues sign the certificates of his own converts, ensuring their universal acceptance as Jews.

Even among those satisfied with the patrilineal rule, there was widespread unhappiness over a lack of religious seriousness in the movement. Alexander Schindler put the matter bluntly: "As liberal Jews, we assert our autonomy and the right to choose. But all too often we choose nothing, or observe haphazardly. Because we make no demands on our congregants and constituents, except financial, we give substance to the perception by some that Reform Judaism is a religion of convenience." He advocated greater ritual observance as the way for Reform Jews to live lives of holiness.

A similar problem plagued the Reform educational system. With few committed Reform Jews as teachers, complained Rabbi Bernard Zlotowitz of the New York Federation of Reform Synagogues, "we have teachers who don't believe. We have Orthodox teachers in our schools who are opposed to what we teach." The Reform movement, he said, should strive to produce "people who can transmit love of the sacred word."

To some extent, these concerns reflected two disturbing findings of a survey of Reform lay leaders, issued in November. Even though patterns of ritual observance had risen—except for observance of *kashrut*—there had been a falloff in "associational" Jewishness: fewer Reform Jews lived in Jewish neighborhoods, had many Jewish friends, or were concerned with Jewish communal issues. An apparent gap between attitudes toward intermarriage and behavior also challenged the movement. Even though most of those surveyed said they opposed intermarriage, only 4 percent did not allow their children to date non-Jews.

The small Reconstructionist movement appeared to be redefining itself with the selection of Rabbi Arthur Green as president of its rabbinical college in Philadelphia. Green, a product of the 1960s Jewish counterculture and an eminent scholar of Jewish mysticism, seemed to many observers far removed from the scientifically oriented rationalism that had animated the movement's founder and chief ideologist, Mordecai Kaplan. At his inauguration in November, Green called for greater attention to ritual practice, Jewish study, and knowledge of the Hebrew language within Reconstructionism.

LAWRENCE GROSSMAN

# Jewish Population in the United States, 1988

THE JEWISH POPULATION OF the United States in 1988 was estimated to be 5,935,000. This figure represents hardly any change from that reported for 1987. The estimate is for the resident Jewish population of the country, including both that in private households and in institutional settings. Non-Jewish family members have been excluded from this total.

While the Jewish federations are the chief reporting bodies, their service areas vary in size and may represent several towns, one county, or an aggregate of several counties. In some cases we have subdivided federation areas to reflect the more natural geographic boundaries. Some estimates, from areas without federations, have been provided by local rabbis and other informed Jewish community leaders. In still other cases, the figures that have been updated are from past estimates provided by UJA field representatives.

The state and regional totals shown in Appendix tables 1 and 2 are derived by summing the individual estimates shown in table 3 and making three adjustments. First, communities of less than 100 are added. Second, duplicated counts within states are eliminated. Third, communities whose populations reside in two or more states (e.g., Kansas City and Washington, D.C.) are distributed accordingly.

The reader should be aware that population estimating is not an exact science and that collection procedures can result in annual fluctuations in community or state totals. It is also important to note that the results of a completed local demographic study often change the previously reported Jewish population figure, even where there has been no actual demographic change.

In determining Jewish population, communities count both affiliated and nonaffiliated residents. In most cases, counts are made by households, with that number multiplied by the average number of self-defined Jewish persons per household. Most communities also include those born and raised as Jews but who at present consider themselves of no religion. As stated above, non-Jews living in Jewish households, primarily the non-Jewish spouses and any non-Jewish children, are not included in the 1988 estimates presented in the appendix below.

Some areas, such as in the Sunbelt region, often include part-time residents in their totals. In the interest of accuracy and consistency, adjustments have been made for such overcounts. For 1988 we have more carefully scrutinized overcounts resulting from inclusion of non-Jews in Jewish population counts, double counting in areas with overlapping Jewish federation boundaries, and overestimation of average household size. This added circumspection has led to Jewish population decreases in areas where no actual decline has occurred. These areas include Kansas City and

Milwaukee as well as several suburban areas of Connecticut, Massachusetts, and New Jersey.

The community reporting the largest numerical gain since the last estimate was completed was the San Diego metropolitan area. In addition, the Ft. Lauderdale federation recently reevaluated its lists and thus determined significantly higher population figures. The increases in both communities exceeded 30,000 persons. Other Sunbelt communities reporting large increases are Orange County, California; and Brevard County, Tallahassee, and Orlando, Florida.

Significant increases have also been reported by Meriden, Connecticut; Bloomington, Indiana; Putnam County, New York; Charleston, South Carolina; Salt Lake City, Utah; Jersey City, New Jersey; Grand Junction, Colorado; Allentown, Pennsylvania; and Olympia, Washington.

While declines tend to be more gradual, some communities in the Northeast and Midwest whose economies are reliant on heavy industry or mining report Jewish population losses. The largest total decline, 5,000 persons, was reported in Cleveland, Ohio. Communities reporting declines include Wilkes-Barre and Pottsville, Pennsylvania; Youngstown and Zanesville, Ohio; Hibbing and Duluth, Minnesota; Holyoke, Massachusetts; Michigan City and Shelbyville, Indiana; Dubuque, Iowa; Quad Cities, Illinois-Iowa; Waukegan, Illinois; Gloversville, New York; and Battle Creek, Michigan, all reporting a reduction of more than 10 percent in their Jewish populations.

The footnotes detailing the areas included in particular communities have been expanded and grouped by state. Also: one asterisk indicates that the population includes the entire county; two asterisks indicate a two-county area; three asterisks indicate that the Jewish population figure has not been updated for several years.

BARRY A. KOSMIN
PAUL RITTERBAND
JEFFREY SCHECKNER

APPENDIX

TABLE 1. JEWISH POPULATION IN THE UNITED STATES, 1988

| State | Estimated Jewish Population | Total Population* | Estimated Jewish Percent of Total |
|---|---|---|---|
| Alabama | 9,400 | 4,052,000 | 0.2 |
| Alaska | 2,400 | 534,000 | 0.4 |
| Arizona | 69,300 | 3,319,000 | 2.1 |
| Arkansas | 2,100 | 2,372,000 | 0.1 |
| California | 905,500 | 26,981,000 | 3.4 |
| Colorado | 49,000 | 3,267,000 | 1.5 |
| Connecticut | 110,200 | 3,189,000 | 3.5 |
| Delaware | 9,500 | 633,000 | 1.5 |
| District of Columbia | 25,400 | 626,000 | 4.0 |
| Florida | 596,100 | 11,675,000 | 5.1 |
| Georgia | 63,300 | 6,104,000 | 1.0 |
| Hawaii | 8,000 | 1,062,000 | 0.8 |
| Idaho | 400 | 1,002,000 | 0.1 |
| Illinois | 257,900 | 11,552,000 | 2.2 |
| Indiana | 19,800 | 5,504,000 | 0.4 |
| Iowa | 6,600 | 2,851,000 | 0.2 |
| Kansas | 14,100 | 2,460,000 | 0.6 |
| Kentucky | 11,800 | 3,729,000 | 0.3 |
| Louisiana | 15,900 | 4,501,000 | 0.4 |
| Maine | 8,500 | 1,173,000 | 0.7 |
| Maryland | 209,600 | 4,463,000 | 4.7 |
| Massachusetts | 276,000 | 5,832,000 | 4.7 |
| Michigan | 84,000 | 9,145,000 | 0.9 |
| Minnesota | 30,800 | 4,214,000 | 0.7 |
| Mississippi | 2,200 | 2,625,000 | 0.1 |
| Missouri | 62,600 | 5,066,000 | 1.2 |
| Montana | 450 | 819,000 | 0.1 |
| Nebraska | 7,400 | 1,598,000 | 0.5 |
| Nevada | 19,500 | 963,000 | 2.0 |
| New Hampshire | 7,000 | 1,027,000 | 0.7 |
| New Jersey | 413,500 | 7,619,000 | 5.4 |
| New Mexico | 6,400 | 1,479,000 | 0.4 |
| New York | 1,844,000 | 17,772,000 | 10.4 |

| State | Estimated Jewish Population | Total Population* | Estimated Jewish Percent of Total |
|---|---|---|---|
| North Carolina | 14,500 | 6,333,000 | 0.2 |
| North Dakota | 800 | 679,000 | 0.1 |
| Ohio | 131,200 | 10,752,000 | 1.2 |
| Oklahoma | 5,300 | 3,305,000 | 0.2 |
| Oregon | 12,300 | 2,698,000 | 0.5 |
| Pennsylvania | 345,800 | 11,888,000 | 2.9 |
| Rhode Island | 16,100 | 975,000 | 1.7 |
| South Carolina | 8,700 | 3,377,000 | 0.3 |
| South Dakota | 400 | 708,000 | 0.1 |
| Tennessee | 19,700 | 4,803,000 | 0.4 |
| Texas | 97,500 | 16,685,000 | 0.6 |
| Utah | 3,300 | 1,665,000 | 0.2 |
| Vermont | 4,600 | 541,000 | 0.9 |
| Virginia | 65,000 | 5,787,000 | 1.1 |
| Washington | 22,500 | 4,462,000 | 0.5 |
| West Virginia | 3,000 | 1,918,000 | 0.2 |
| Wisconsin | 35,900 | 4,785,000 | 0.8 |
| Wyoming | 450 | 501,000 | 0.1 |
| U.S. TOTAL | **5,935,000 | 241,078,000 | 2.5 |

N.B. Details may not add to totals because of rounding.
*Resident population, July 1, 1986. (*Source:* U.S. Bureau of the Census, *Current Population Reports,* series P-22, No. 26.)
**Exclusive of Puerto Rico and the Virgin Islands, which previously reported Jewish populations of 1,500 and 350, respectively.

TABLE 2. DISTRIBUTION OF U.S. JEWISH POPULATION BY REGIONS, 1988

| Region | Total Population | Percent Distribution | Jewish Population | Percent Distribution |
|---|---|---|---|---|
| Northeast | 50,017,000 | 20.8 | 3,025,700 | 51.0 |
| New England | 12,737,000 | 5.3 | 422,400 | 7.1 |
| Middle Atlantic | 37,280,000 | 15.5 | 2,603,300 | 43.9 |
| North Central | 59,313,000 | 24.6 | 651,500 | 11.0 |
| East North Central | 41,737,000 | 17.3 | 528,800 | 8.9 |
| West North Central | 17,576,000 | 7.3 | 122,700 | 2.1 |
| South | 82,988,000 | 34.4 | 1,159,000 | 19.5 |
| South Atlantic | 40,916,000 | 17.0 | 995,100 | 16.8 |
| East South Central | 15,209,000 | 6.3 | 43,100 | 0.7 |
| West South Central | 26,864,000 | 11.1 | 120,800 | 2.0 |
| West | 48,760,000 | 20.2 | 1,099,500 | 18.5 |
| Mountain | 13,023,000 | 5.4 | 148,800 | 2.5 |
| Pacific | 35,737,000 | 14.8 | 950,700 | 16.0 |
| TOTALS | 241,078,000 | 100.0 | 5,935,000 | 100.0 |

N.B. Details may not add to totals because of rounding.

TABLE 3. COMMUNITIES WITH JEWISH POPULATIONS OF 100 OR MORE, 1988 (ESTIMATED)

| State and City | Jewish Population | State and City | Jewish Population | State and City | Jewish Population |
|---|---|---|---|---|---|
| ALABAMA | | **Little Rock | 1,350 | Monterey Peninsula | 1,500 |
| *Birmingham | 5,100 | Pine Bluff | 100 | *Napa | 450 |
| Decatur (incl. in Florence total) | | CALIFORNIA | | Oakland (incl. in Alameda County) | |
| *Dothan | 150 | Alameda County (listed under San Francisco Bay Area) | | Ontario (incl. in Pomona Valley) | |
| Florence | 150 | | | | |
| Huntsville | 750 | | | Orange County | 85,000 |
| **Mobile | 1,100 | Antelope Valley | 700 | Palmdale (incl. in Antelope Valley) | |
| **Montgomery | 1,300 | Bakersfield (incl. in Kern County) | | Palm Springs[N] | 9,500 |
| Selma | 100 | Berkeley (incl. in Contra Costa County total) | | Palo Alto (incl. in South Peninsula) | |
| Sheffield (incl. in Florence total) | | | | Pasadena (also incl. in L.A. Metro Area) | 2,000 |
| Tuscaloosa | 315 | *Chico | 500 | | |
| Tuscumbia (incl. in Florence total) | | Contra Costa County (listed under S.F. Bay Area) | | Petaluma (incl. in Sonoma County) | |
| ALASKA | | Corona (incl. in Riverside total) | | Pomona Valley[N] | 6,750 |
| **Anchorage | 2,000 | | | *Redding | 145 |
| ***Fairbanks | 210 | ***El Centro | 125 | Riverside | 1,620 |
| Juneau | 100 | ***Elsinore | 250 | Sacramento[N] | 10,000 |
| Ketchikan (incl. in Juneau total) | | *Eureka | 500 | Salinas | 500 |
| | | Fairfield | 800 | San Bernardino Area | 2,800 |
| ARIZONA | | Fontana (incl. in San Bernardino total) | | *San Diego | 70,000 |
| *Flagstaff | 250 | *Fresno | 2,000 | San Francisco Bay Area[N] | 196,000 |
| *Phoenix | 50,000 | Kern County | 1,400 | San Francisco | 45,500 |
| Prescott | 150 | Lancaster (incl. in Antelope Valley) | | North Peninsula | 22,000 |
| *Tucson | 18,500 | Long Beach (also incl. in L. A. Metro Area)[N] | 13,500 | South Peninsula | 19,500 |
| Yuma | 100 | Los Angeles Metro Area | 501,000 | San Jose | 32,000 |
| ARKANSAS | | | | Alameda County | 30,500 |
| Fayetteville | 120 | Merced | 170 | Contra Costa County | 21,000 |
| **Ft. Smith | 160 | *Modesto | 450 | Marin County | 17,000 |
| Hot Springs (incl. in Little Rock total) | | | | | |

[N]See Notes below. *Includes entire county. **Includes all of 2 counties. ***Figure not updated.

# JEWISH POPULATION IN THE UNITED STATES / 239

| State and City | Jewish Population | State and City | Jewish Population | State and City | Jewish Population |
|---|---|---|---|---|---|
| | | | | | |

Sonoma County ............... 8,500
*San Jose (listed under S. F. Bay Area)
*San Luis Obispo . 1,000
*Santa Barbara ... 3,800
*Santa Cruz ..... 1,200
Santa Maria ....... 200
Santa Monica (also incl. in L. A. Metro Area) ............... 8,000
Santa Rosa (incl. in Sonoma County)
Sonoma County (listed under S.F. Bay Area)
South Peninsula (listed under S.F. Bay Area)
*Stockton ........ 1,600
***Sun City ........ 800
Tulare & Kings County ................ 500
***Vallejo ......... 400
*Ventura County . 7,000

COLORADO
Aspen ............ 250
Boulder (incl. in Denver total)
Colorado Springs 1,500
Denver[N] ....... 45,000
*Ft. Collins ...... 1,000
Grand Junction .... 250
Greely (incl. in Ft. Collins total)
Loveland (incl. in Ft. Collins total)
Pueblo ........... 375
Vail ............. 100

CONNECTICUT
Bridgeport[N] .... 18,000
Bristol ........... 200
Cheshire (incl. in Meriden total)

Colchester ........ 575
Danbury[N] ...... 3,500
Danielson ......... 100
Darien (incl. in Stamford total)
Greenwich ...... 3,850
Hartford[N] ..... 28,000
Hebron (incl. in Colchester total)
Lebanon (incl. in Colchester total)
Lower Middlesex County[N] ...... 1,475
Manchester (incl. in Hartford)
Meriden[N] ....... 3,000
Middletown ..... 1,300
New Britain (incl. in Hartford)
New Haven[N] ... 28,000
New London[N] ... 4,000
New Milford ...... 400
Newtown (incl. in Danbury)
Norwalk[N] ...... 4,000
Norwich (also incl. in New London total) ............... 1,800
Putnam .......... 100
Rockville (incl. in Hartford)
Shelton (incl. in Valley Area)
Southington (incl. in Meriden total)
Stamford/New Canaan ............. 11,100
Storrs (incl. in Willimantic total)
Torrington ........ 560
Valley Area[N] ...... 550
Wallingford (also incl. in Meriden total) . 500
Waterbury[N] ..... 2,700

Westport (also incl. in Norwalk) ... 2,800
Willimantic Area .. 700
***Winsted ........ 110

DELAWARE
Dover[N] .......... 650
Wilmington (incl. rest of state) ... 9,500

DISTRICT OF COLUMBIA
Greater Washington[N] ............ 165,000

FLORIDA
Boca Raton-Delray Beach (listed under Southeast Fla.)
Brevard County . 3,000
*Crystal River ...... 100
Dade County (listed under Southeast Fla.)
**Daytona Beach . 2,000
Fort Lauderdale (listed under Southeast Fla.)
Fort Pierce ....... 500
Gainesville ...... 1,200
Hollywood (listed under Southeast Fla.)
**Jacksonville .... 7,200
Key West ......... 170
*Lakeland ......... 800
Lee County (incl. in Ft. Myers) .. 3,500
*Miami (incl. in Dade County)
Naples ........... 750
***Ocala .......... 100
Orlando[N] ...... 18,000
Palm Beach County (listed under Southeast Fla.)
**Pasco County .. 1,000
**Pensacola ........ 775
***Port Charlotte ... 150

| State and City | Jewish Population | State and City | Jewish Population | State and City | Jewish Population |
|---|---|---|---|---|---|
| **Sarasota | 9,000 | Kuaii | 110 | Ft. Wayne | 1,090 |
| *St. Petersburg (incl. Clearwater) | 9,500 | Maui | 250 | Gary (incl. in Northwest Ind. Calumet Region) | |
| Southeast Florida | 524,000 | **IDAHO** | | **Indianapolis | 10,000 |
| Dade County | 238,000 | **Boise | 220 | Lafayette[N] | 600 |
| Hollywood[N] | 60,000 | Lewiston | 100 | Marion | 100 |
| Ft. Lauderdale[N] | 116,000 | Moscow (incl. in Lewiston total) | | *Michigan City | 300 |
| Boca Raton-Delray Beach | 52,000 | | | Muncie | 160 |
| Palm Beach County (excl. Boca Raton-Delray Beach) | 55,000 | **ILLINOIS** | | Northwest Indiana-Calumet Region[N] | 3,000 |
| | | Aurora Area | 500 | South Bend[N] | 1,800 |
| | | Bloomington-Normal | 170 | *Terre Haute | 325 |
| Stuart-Port St. Lucie | 3,000 | Carbondale (also incl. in S. Ill. total) | 100 | | |
| Tallahassee | 1,500 | *Champaign-Urbana | 2,000 | **IOWA** | |
| *Tampa | 12,500 | Chicago Metro Area[N] | 248,000 | Ames (also incl. in Des Moines total) | 200 |
| Venice (incl. in Sarasota total) | | **Danville | 130 | Cedar Rapids | 430 |
| *Vero Beach | 300 | *Decatur | 210 | Council Bluffs (also incl. in Omaha, Neb. total) | 150 |
| Winter Haven (incl. in Lakeland total) | | East St. Louis (incl. in S. Ill.) | | Davenport (incl. in Quad Cities, Ill.) | |
| | | Elgin[N] | 600 | | |
| **GEORGIA** | | Freeport (incl. in Rockford total) | | *Des Moines | 2,900 |
| Albany | 400 | | | *Iowa City | 1,200 |
| Athens | 300 | Galesburg | 100 | **Sioux City | 645 |
| Atlanta Metro Area | 56,000 | *Joliet | 850 | *Waterloo | 235 |
| Augusta[N] | 1,400 | Kankakee | 200 | | |
| Brunswick | 100 | *Peoria | 1,000 | **KANSAS** | |
| **Columbus | 1,000 | Quad Cities[N] | 1,350 | Kansas City (incl. in Kansas City, Mo.) | |
| **Dalton | 225 | **Quincy | 125 | Lawrence | 175 |
| Fitzgerald-Cordele | 125 | Rock Island (incl. in Quad Cities) | | Manhattan | 100 |
| Macon | 900 | Rockford[N] | 1,000 | *Topeka | 500 |
| *Savannah | 2,500 | Southern Illinois[N] | 900 | Wichita[N] | 1,000 |
| **Valdosta | 110 | *Springfield | 1,000 | | |
| | | Waukegan | 500 | **KENTUCKY** | |
| **HAWAII** | | | | Covington/Newport (incl. in Cincinnati total) | |
| Hilo | 320 | **INDIANA** | | | |
| Honolulu (includes all of Oahu) | 7,300 | Bloomington | 1,000 | Lexington[N] | 2,000 |
| | | Elkart (incl. in South Bend total) | | *Louisville | 9,200 |
| | | ***Evansville | 1,200 | Paducah (incl. in S. Ill. total) | |

| State and City | Jewish Population | State and City | Jewish Population | State and City | Jewish Population |
|---|---|---|---|---|---|
| LOUISIANA | | MASSACHUSETTS | | Lynn-North Shore | |
| Alexandria | 350 | Amherst | 750 | Area[N] | 25,000 |
| Baton Rouge[N] | 1,200 | Andover[N] | 3,000 | *Martha's Vineyard | 260 |
| Lafayette (incl. in S. Central La.) | | Athol Area (also incl. in Worcester County total) | 300 | New Bedford[N] | 2,800 |
| | | | | Newburyport | 280 |
| Lake Charles | 300 | | | Newton (also incl. in Boston total) | 34,000 |
| Monroe | 525 | Attleboro | 200 | | |
| **New Orleans | 12,000 | Beverly (incl. in Lynn total) | | North Adams (incl. in N. Berkshire total) | |
| *Shreveport | 1,060 | | | | |
| South Central La.[N] | 250 | Boston Metro Region[N] | 228,000 | North Berkshire County | 750 |
| Tallulah (incl. in Vicksburg, Miss. total) | | Brockton[N] | 8,000 | Northampton | 700 |
| | | Brookline (also incl. in Boston total) | 26,000 | Peabody (incl. in Lynn total) | |
| MAINE | | Cape Cod (incl. all of Barnstable County) | 2,900 | Pittsfield (incl. all Berkshire County) | 3,100 |
| Augusta | 500 | | | | |
| Bangor | 1,250 | | | | |
| Biddeford-Saco (incl. in S. Maine) | | Clinton (incl. in Worcester County total) | | Plymouth | 500 |
| | | | | Provincetown (incl. in Cape Cod) | |
| Brunswick-Bath (incl. in S. Maine) | | Fall River | 1,780 | Salem (incl. in Lynn total) | |
| Lewiston-Auburn | 500 | Falmouth (incl. in Cape Cod) | | | |
| Portland | 3,900 | | | Southbridge (also incl. in Worcester County total) | 105 |
| Rockland | 110 | Fitchburg (also incl. in Worcester County total) | 300 | | |
| Southern Maine (incl. Portland)[N] | 5,500 | | | Springfield[N] | 11,000 |
| | | Framingham[N] | 10,800 | Taunton Area | 1,200 |
| Waterville | 300 | Gardner (incl. in Athol total) | | Webster (also incl. in Worcester County total) | 125 |
| MARYLAND | | Gloucester (also incl. in Lynn total) | 450 | | |
| *Annapolis | 2,000 | | | Worcester Area[N] | 10,100 |
| **Baltimore | 93,000 | Great Barrington (incl. in Pittsfield total) | | *Worcester County | 13,700 |
| Cumberland | 265 | | | | |
| ***Easton Park Area[N] | 100 | *Greenfield | 900 | MICHIGAN | |
| *Frederick | 600 | Haverhill | 1,500 | *Ann Arbor | 4,500 |
| *Hagerstown | 300 | Holyoke | 550 | Battle Creek | 180 |
| *Harford County | 1,000 | *Hyannis (incl. in Cape Cod) | | Bay City | 280 |
| Howard County | 7,200 | | | Benton Harbor | 500 |
| Montgomery and Prince Georges County | 104,500 | Lawrence (incl. in Andover total) | | **Detroit | 70,000 |
| | | | | *Flint | 2,000 |
| Salisbury | 400 | Leominster (also incl. in Worcester County total) | 750 | *Grand Rapids | 1,500 |
| Silver Spring (incl. in Montgomery County) | | | | **Jackson | 325 |
| | | | | *Kalamazoo | 1,000 |
| | | ***Lowell | 2,000 | *Lansing | 1,900 |

| State and City | Jewish Population | State and City | Jewish Population | State and City | Jewish Population |
|---|---|---|---|---|---|
| *Marquette County | 150 | NEVADA | | Englewood (incl. in Bergen County) Essex County[N] (also incl. in Northeastern N.J. total) | 76,200 |
| Midland | 200 | Carson City (incl. in Reno total) | | | |
| ***Mt. Clemens | 420 | *Las Vegas | 18,000 | | |
| Mt. Pleasant[N] | 120 | **Reno | 1,400 | | |
| Muskegon | 235 | NEW HAMPSHIRE | | North Essex | 15,600 |
| *Saginaw | 200 | Bethlehem | 100 | East Essex | 10,800 |
| MINNESOTA | | Claremont | 200 | South Essex | 20,300 |
| **Duluth | 560 | Concord | 450 | Livingston | 12,600 |
| *Minneapolis | 22,000 | Dover | 450 | West Orange-Orange | 16,900 |
| Rochester | 400 | Hanover-Lebanon | 360 | Flemington | 900 |
| **St. Paul | 7,700 | ***Keene | 105 | Freehold (incl. in Monmouth County) | |
| Winona (incl. in LaCrosse, Wis. total) | | **Laconia[N] | 270 | | |
| | | Littleton (incl. in Bethlehem total) | | Gloucester (incl. in Cherry Hill total) | |
| MISSISSIPPI | | | | | |
| Biloxi-Gulfport | 150 | Manchester[N] | 3,000 | Hoboken (incl. in Hudson County) | |
| Clarksdale | 100 | Nashua Area | 480 | | |
| **Cleveland | 120 | Portsmouth Area | 1,100 | Hudson County (also incl. in Northeastern N.J. total) | 15,750 |
| **Greenville | 480 | Salem (also incl. in Andover, Mass. total) | 150 | | |
| **Hattiesburg | 180 | | | Bayonne | 5,000 |
| **Jackson | 700 | | | Jersey City | 5,000 |
| **Vicksburg | 105 | NEW JERSEY | | Hoboken | 750 |
| MISSOURI | | Asbury Park (incl. in Monmouth County) | | North Hudson County[N] | 5,000 |
| Columbia | 350 | | | | |
| Hannibal (incl. in Quincy, Ill. total) | | *Atlantic City (incl. Atlantic County) | 15,800 | Jersey City (incl. in Hudson County) | |
| Joplin | 100 | | | | |
| Kansas City Metro Area | 20,000 | Bayonne (incl. in Hudson County) | | Lakewood (incl. in Ocean County) | |
| Springfield | 285 | Bergen County (also included in Northeastern N.J. total) | 85,000 | Livingston (incl. in Essex County) | |
| *St. Joseph | 280 | | | Middlesex County[N] (also incl. in Northeastern N.J. total) | 40,000 |
| **St. Louis | 53,500 | | | | |
| MONTANA | | ***Bridgeton | 325 | | |
| *Billings | 200 | Bridgewater (incl. in Somerset County) | | Millville | 135 |
| Butte | 110 | | | Monmouth County (also incl. in Northeastern N.J. total) | 33,600 |
| Helena (incl. in Butte total) | | Camden (incl. in Cherry Hill total) | | | |
| | | Cherry Hill[N] | 28,000 | Morris County (also incl. in Northeastern N.J. total) | 33,500 |
| NEBRASKA | | Edison (incl. in Middlesex County) | | | |
| Grand Island-Hastings (incl. in Lincoln total) | | | | | |
| Lincoln | 1,000 | Elizabeth (incl. in Union County) | | Morristown (incl. in Morris County) | |
| Omaha[N] | 6,500 | | | | |

| State and City | Jewish Population | State and City | Jewish Population | State and City | Jewish Population |
|---|---|---|---|---|---|
| Mt. Holly (incl. in Cherry Hill total) | | Warren County | 400 | Hudson | 470 |
| Newark (incl. in Essex County) | | Wayne (incl. in Passaic County) | | *Ithaca | 1,250 |
| | | | | ***Jamestown | 185 |
| New Brunswick (incl. in Middlesex County) | | Wildwood | 425 | Kingston[N] | 4,500 |
| | | Willingboro (incl. in Cherry Hill total) | | Lake George (incl. in Glens Falls total) | |
| North Hudson County (listed under Hudson County) | | | | Liberty (also incl. in Sullivan County total) | 2,100 |
| | | NEW MEXICO | | | |
| | | *Albuquerque | 4,500 | | |
| Northeastern N.J.[N] | 353,650 | Las Cruces | 525 | ***Massena | 140 |
| | | Los Alamos | 250 | Middletown (incl. in Orange County) | |
| Ocean County (also incl. in Northeastern N.J. total) | 9,500 | Santa Fe | 900 | Monroe (incl. in Orange County) | |
| | | NEW YORK | | | |
| Passaic County[N] (also incl. in Northeastern N.J. total) | 18,700 | *Albany | 12,000 | Monticello (also incl. in Sullivan County total) | 2,400 |
| | | Amenia (incl. in Dutchess County) | | | |
| Passaic-Clifton (also incl. in Passaic County total) | 8,000 | Amsterdam | 450 | New York Metro Area[N] | 1,671,000 |
| | | ***Auburn | 315 | Bronx | 85,000 |
| Paterson (incl. in Passaic County) | | Beacon (incl. in Dutchess County) | | Brooklyn | 418,900 |
| Perth Amboy (incl. in Middlesex County) | | *Binghamton (incl. all Broome County) | 3,000 | Manhattan | 274,300 |
| | | | | Queens | 321,200 |
| Phillipsburg (incl. in Easton, Pa. total) | | Brewster (incl. in Putnam County) | | Staten Island | 31,000 |
| | | | | Nassau County | 311,700 |
| Plainfield (incl. in Union County) | | *Buffalo | 18,500 | Suffolk County | 106,200 |
| Princeton | 2,600 | Canandaigua (incl. in Geneva total) | | Westchester County | 122,600 |
| Salem | 100 | Catskill | 200 | New Paltz (incl. in Kingston total) | |
| Somerset County[N] (also incl. in Northeastern N.J. total) | 4,900 | Corning (incl. in Elmira total) | | Newark (incl. in Geneva total) | |
| | | ***Cortland | 440 | Newburgh (incl. in Orange County) | |
| Somerville (incl. in Somerset County) | | Dunkirk | 120 | Niagara Falls | 395 |
| | | Ellenville | 1,600 | Olean | 120 |
| Sussex County (also incl. in Northeastern N.J. total) | 4,100 | Elmira[N] | 1,100 | **Oneonta | 250 |
| | | Fleischmanns | 115 | Orange County | 8,950 |
| Toms River (incl. in Ocean County) | | Fredonia (incl. in Dunkirk total) | | Oswego | 100 |
| | | Geneva | 300 | Pawling | 105 |
| Trenton[N] | 8,500 | Glens Falls[N] | 800 | Plattsburg | 275 |
| Union County[N] (also incl. in Northeastern N.J. total) | 30,000 | *Gloversville | 420 | Port Jervis (also incl. in Orange County total) | 560 |
| | | *Herkimer | 180 | | |
| Vineland[N] | 2,500 | Highland Falls (incl. in Orange County) | | Potsdam | 250 |

| State and City | Jewish Population | State and City | Jewish Population | State and City | Jewish Population |
|---|---|---|---|---|---|
| *Poughkeepsie.... | 6,500 | NORTH DAKOTA | | Youngstown total) | 400 |
| Putnam County.. | 1,000 | Fargo | 500 | Wooster | 125 |
| **Rochester | 23,000 | Grand Forks | 130 | Youngstown[N] | 4,000 |
| Rockland County | 60,000 | OHIO | | *Zanesville | 120 |
| Rome | 205 | **Akron | 6,000 | | |
| Saratoga Springs... | 500 | Athens | 100 | OKLAHOMA | |
| **Schenectady.... | 5,400 | Bowling Green (also incl. in Toledo total) | 120 | Norman (also incl. in Oklahoma City total) | 350 |
| ***Sharon Springs.. | 165 | | | **Oklahoma City. | 2,300 |
| South Fallsburg (also incl. in Sullivan County total).. | 1,100 | Butler County | 900 | *Tulsa | 2,750 |
| | | **Canton | 2,400 | | |
| Sullivan County. | 7,425 | Cincinnati[N] | 23,000 | OREGON | |
| Syracuse[N] | 9,000 | **Cleveland[N] | 65,000 | *Corvallis | 150 |
| Troy Area | 900 | *Columbus | 15,000 | Eugene | 2,300 |
| Utica[N] | 1,900 | **Dayton | 6,000 | **Medford | 500 |
| Walden (incl. in Orange County) | | East Liverpool | 200 | Portland | 9,000 |
| | | Elyria | 250 | **Salem | 250 |
| Watertown | 170 | Fremont (incl. in Sandusky total) | | | |
| Woodstock (incl. in Kingston total) | | Hamilton (incl. in Butler County total) | | PENNSYLVANIA | |
| | | | | Allentown | 6,000 |
| NORTH CAROLINA | | *Lima | 365 | *Altoona | 515 |
| Asheville[N] | 1,200 | Lorain | 600 | Ambridge[N] | 350 |
| **Chapel Hill-Durham | 2,750 | ***Mansfield | 600 | Beaver Falls (incl. in Upper Beaver County) | |
| Charlotte[N] | 4,000 | Marietta (incl. in Parkersburg, W.Va. total) | | Bethlehem | 810 |
| Elizabethtown (incl. in Wilmington total) | | ***Marion | 150 | **Bradford | 110 |
| *Fayetteville | 500 | Middletown (incl. in Butler County total) | | Brownsville (incl. in Uniontown total) | |
| Gastonia | 240 | | | Bucks County (lower portion)[N] | 14,500 |
| Goldsboro | 120 | New Philadelphia (incl. in Canton total) | | | |
| *Greensboro | 2,600 | | | *Butler | 300 |
| Greenville | 300 | **Newark | 105 | **Chambersburg.... | 470 |
| Hendersonville | 135 | Norwalk (incl. in Sandusky total) | | Chester (incl. in Phila. total) | |
| **Hickory | 100 | | | | |
| High Point (incl. in Greensboro total) | | Oberlin (incl. in Elyria total) | | Chester County (also incl. in Phila. total).... | 4,000 |
| Jacksonville (incl. in Wilmington total) | | Oxford (incl. in Butler County total) | | | |
| | | | | Coatesville (incl. in Chester County total) | |
| Raleigh | 1,375 | **Sandusky | 130 | | |
| Whiteville (incl. in Wilmington total) | | Springfield | 250 | Connellsville (incl. in Uniontown total) | |
| | | *Steubenville | 195 | | |
| Wilmington Area.. | 500 | Toledo[N] | 6,300 | Delaware Valley (see Bucks County) | |
| Winston-Salem.... | 440 | Warren (also incl. in | | | |

| State and City | Jewish Population | State and City | Jewish Population | State and City | Jewish Population |
|---|---|---|---|---|---|
| Donora (incl. in Pittsburgh total) | | Pittsburgh[N] | 45,000 | SOUTH CAROLINA | |
| Easton Area | 1,200 | Pottstown | 700 | *Charleston | 4,000 |
| *Erie | 800 | Pottsville | 250 | **Columbia | 2,000 |
| Farrell (incl. in Sharon total) | | *Reading | 2,800 | Florence Area | 210 |
| | | *Scranton | 3,200 | Georgetown (incl. in Myrtle Beach total) | |
| Greensburg (also incl. in Pittsburgh total) | 425 | Shamokin (incl. in Sunbury total) | | Greenville | 800 |
| **Harrisburg | 6,500 | Sharon (also incl. in Youngstown, Ohio total) | 260 | Kingstree (incl. in Sumter total) | |
| Hazleton Area | 410 | | | **Myrtle Beach | 425 |
| Homestead (incl. in Pittsburgh total) | | State College | 550 | ***Orangeburg County | 105 |
| Honesdale (incl. in Wayne County) | | Stroudsburg | 410 | | |
| | | Sunbury[N] | 160 | Rock Hill (incl. in Charlotte, N.C. total) | |
| Indiana | 135 | Tamaqua (incl. in Hazleton total) | | | |
| Jeanette (incl. in Greensburg total) | | Uniontown | 290 | *Spartanburg | 320 |
| | | Upper Beaver County | 200 | Sumter[N] | 175 |
| Johnstown | 395 | | | | |
| Kane (incl. in Bradford total) | | **Washington (also incl. in Pittsburgh total) | 250 | SOUTH DAKOTA | |
| | | | | Sioux Falls | 135 |
| Lancaster | 2,100 | Wayne County | 210 | | |
| *Lebanon | 400 | Waynesburg (incl. in Washington total) | | TENNESSEE | |
| Lewisburg (incl. in Sunbury total) | | | | Bristol (incl. in Johnson City total) | |
| | | West Chester (also incl. in Chester County) | 300 | Chattanooga | 2,000 |
| Lock Haven (incl. in Williamsport total) | | | | Jackson | 100 |
| McKeesport (incl. in Pittsburgh total) | | Wilkes-Barre[N] | 3,700 | Johnson City | 210 |
| | | **Williamsport | 415 | Kingsport (incl. in Johnson city total) | |
| Monessen (incl. in Pittsburgh total) | | York | 1,500 | | |
| Mt. Pleasant (incl. in Greensburg total) | | RHODE ISLAND | | Knoxville | 1,350 |
| | | Cranston (incl. in Providence total) | | Memphis | 10,000 |
| New Castle | 200 | | | Nashville | 5,490 |
| New Kensington | 380 | Kingston (incl. in Washington County total) | | Oak Ridge | 240 |
| Norristown (incl. in Philadelphia total) | | | | | |
| | | Newport-Middletown | 700 | TEXAS | |
| **Oil City | 145 | | | Amarillo[N] | 190 |
| Oxford-Kennett Square (incl. in Chester County) | | Providence Area | 14,200 | *Austin | 5,000 |
| | | Washington County | 1,200 | Bay City (incl. in Wharton total) | |
| Philadelphia Area[N] | 250,000 | | | Baytown | 300 |
| | | Westerly (incl. in Washington County total) | | Beaumont | 800 |
| Phoenixville (incl. in Chester County) | | | | *Brownsville | 325 |
| Pike County | 150 | | | College Station-Bryan | 400 |
| | | | | *Corpus Christi | 1,400 |

| State and City | Jewish Population | State and City | Jewish Population | State and City | Jewish Population |
|---|---|---|---|---|---|
| **Dallas | 24,500 | VIRGINIA | | Pullman (incl. in Moscow, Idaho total) | |
| El Paso | 4,800 | Alexandria (incl. Falls Church, Arlington, and Fairfax counties) | 35,100 | *Seattle<sup>N</sup> | 19,500 |
| *Ft. Worth | 4,100 | | | Spokane | 800 |
| Galveston | 800 | | | *Tacoma | 1,100 |
| Harlingen (incl. in Brownsville total) | | Arlington (incl. in Alexandria total) | | Tri Cities<sup>N</sup> | 240 |
| **Houston<sup>N</sup> | 42,000 | | | Vancouver (incl. in Portland, Oreg. total) | |
| Kilgore (incl. in Longview total) | | Blacksburg | 300 | | |
| | | Charlottesville | 950 | WEST VIRGINIA | |
| Laredo | 420 | | | Bluefield-Princeton | 250 |
| Longview | 200 | Chesapeake (incl. in Norfolk total) | | | |
| *Lubbock | 225 | | | *Charleston | 1,025 |
| Lufkin (incl. in Longview total) | | Danville | 100 | Clarksburg | 100 |
| | | Fredericksburg | 140 | Huntington<sup>N</sup> | 380 |
| Marshall (incl. in Longview total) | | Hampton (incl. in Newport News) | | Morgantown | 200 |
| *McAllen | 475 | Harrisonburg (incl. in Staunton total) | | **Parkersburg | 145 |
| Midland-Odessa | 150 | | | ***Weirton | 150 |
| Paris (incl. in Sherman-Denison total) | | ***Hopewell | 140 | **Wheeling | 500 |
| | | Lynchburg | 275 | | |
| Port Arthur | 260 | **Martinsville | 130 | WISCONSIN | |
| San Angelo | 100 | Newport News (incl. Hampton)<sup>N</sup> | 2,500 | Appleton | 250 |
| *San Antonio | 9,000 | | | Beloit | 120 |
| Sherman-Denison | 125 | Norfolk (incl. Virginia Beach) | 15,000 | Green Bay | 260 |
| | | | | *Kenosha | 200 |
| Tyler | 450 | Petersburg | 540 | LaCrosse | 150 |
| Waco<sup>N</sup> | 500 | Portsmouth-Suffolk (also incl. in Norfolk total) | 1,100 | *Madison | 4,500 |
| **Wharton | 130 | | | Manitowoc | 115 |
| Wichita Falls | 260 | Radford (incl. in Blacksburg total) | | Milwaukee<sup>N</sup> | 29,000 |
| UTAH | | | | Oshkosh | 150 |
| Ogden | 150 | Richmond<sup>N</sup> | 8,000 | *Racine | 375 |
| *Salt Lake City | 3,000 | Roanoke | 1,050 | Sheboygan | 190 |
| | | Staunton<sup>N</sup> | 375 | Superior (also incl. in Duluth, Minn. total) | 100 |
| VERMONT | | Williamsburg (incl. in Newport News total) | | | |
| Bennington | 100 | | | Waukesha (incl. in Milwaukee total) | |
| Brattleboro | 150 | Winchester<sup>N</sup> | 145 | | |
| **Burlington | 3,000 | WASHINGTON | | Wausau<sup>N</sup> | 240 |
| Montpelier-Barre | 500 | ***Bellingham | 120 | WYOMING | |
| Newport (incl. in St. Johnsbury total) | | Longview-Kelso (incl. in Portland, Oreg. total) | | Casper | 100 |
| | | | | Cheyenne | 230 |
| Rutland | 550 | | | Laramie (incl. in Cheyenne total) | |
| **St. Johnsbury | 100 | Olympia | 300 | | |

Notes

CALIFORNIA

Long Beach–includes in L.A. County, Long Beach, Signal Hill, Cerritos, Lakewood, Rosmoor, and Hawaiian Gardens. Also includes in Orange County, Los Alamitos, Cypress, Seal Beach, and Huntington Harbor.

Palm Springs–includes Palm Springs, Desert Hot Springs, Cathedral City, Palm Desert, and Rancho Mirage.

Pomona Valley–includes Alta Loma, Chino, Claremont, Cucamonga, La Verne, Montclair, Ontario, Pomona, San Dimas, and Upland. Portion also included in Los Angeles total.

Sacramento–includes Yolo, Placer, El Dorado, and Sacramento counties.

San Francisco Bay Area–North Peninsula includes northern San Mateo County. South Peninsula includes southern San Mateo County and towns of Palo Alto and Los Altos in Santa Clara County. San Jose includes remainder of Santa Clara County.

COLORADO

Denver–includes Adams, Arapahoe, Boulder, Denver, and Jefferson counties.

CONNECTICUT

Bridgeport–includes Monroe, Easton, Trumbull, Fairfield, Bridgeport, Shelton, Stratford, and part of Milford.

Danbury–includes Danbury, Bethel, New Fairfield, Brookfield, Sherman, Newtown, Redding, Ridgefield, and part of Wilton; also includes Brewster and Goldens Bridge in New York.

Hartford–includes most of Hartford County and Vernon, Rockville, Ellington, and Tolland in Tolland County.

Lower Middlesex County–includes Branford, Guilford, Madison, Clinton, Westbrook, Old Saybrook. Portion of this area also included in New London and New Haven totals.

Meriden–includes Meriden, Southington, Cheshire, and Wallingford. Portion also included in New Haven total.

New Haven–includes New Haven, East Haven, Guilford, Branford, Madison, North Haven, Hamden, West Haven, Milford, Orange, Woodbridge, Bethany, Derby, Ansonia and Cheshire.

New London–includes central and southern New London County. Also includes part of Lower Middlesex County and part of Windham County.

Norwalk–includes Norwalk, Weston, Westport, East Norwalk, part of Darien, part of New Canaan, and part of Wilton.

Valley Area–includes Ansonia, Derby, Shelton, Oxford, Seymour, and Beacon Falls. Portion also included in Bridgeport and New Haven totals.

Waterbury–includes Middlebury, Southbury, Naugatuck, Watertown, Waterbury, Oakville, and Woodbury.

DELAWARE
Dover–includes most of central and southern Delaware.

DISTRICT OF COLUMBIA
Greater Washington–includes Montgomery and Prince Georges counties in Maryland; Arlington County, Fairfax County, Falls Church, and Alexandria in Virginia.

FLORIDA
Ft. Lauderdale–includes Ft. Lauderdale, Pompano Beach, Deerfield Beach, Tamarac, Margate, and other towns in northern Broward County.
Hollywood–includes Hollywood, Hallandale, Dania, Davie, Pembroke, and other towns in southern Broward County.
Orlando–includes all of Orange and Seminole counties, and part of Lake County.

GEORGIA
Augusta–includes Burke, Columbia, and Richmond counties and part of Aiken County, South Carolina.

ILLINOIS
Chicago Metropolitan Area–includes all of Cook and DuPage counties and Southern Lake County. For a total of Jewish population of the Chicago metropolitan region, please include Northwest Indiana, Joliet, Aurora, Elgin, and Waukegan totals.
Elgin–includes northern Kane County, southern McHenry County, and western edge of Cook County.
Quad Cities–includes Rock Island, Moline (Ill.), Davenport, and Bettendorf (Iowa).
Rockford–includes Winnebago, Boone, and Stephenson counties.
Southern Illinois–includes lower portion of Illinois below Carlinville, adjacent western portion of Kentucky, and adjacent portion of southeastern Missouri.

INDIANA
Lafayette–includes Clinton, Montgomery, and Tippacanoe counties.
Northwest Indiana–includes Crown Point, East Chicago, Gary, Hammond, Munster, Valparaiso, Whiting, and the Greater Calumet region.
South Bend–includes St. Joseph and Elkhart counties and part of Berrien County, Mich.

KANSAS
Wichita–includes Sedgwick County and towns of Salina, Dodge City, Great Bend, Liberal, Russel, and Hays.

KENTUCKY
Lexington–includes Fayette, Bourbon, Scott, Clark, Woodford, Madison, Pulaski, and Jessamin counties.

LOUISIANA
Baton Rouge–includes E. Baton Rouge, Ascencion, Livingston, St. Landry, Iberville, Pt. Coupee, and W. Baton Rouge parishes.
South Central–includes Abbeville, Lafayette, New Iberia, Crowley, Opelousus, Houma, Morgan City, Thibadoux, and Franklin.

MAINE
Southern Maine–includes York, Cumberland, and Sagadahoc counties.

MARYLAND
Easton Park area–includes towns in Caroline, Kent, Queen Annes, and Talbot counties.

MASSACHUSETTS
Andover–includes Andover, N. Andover, Boxford, Lawrence, Methuen, Tewksbury, Dracut, and town of Salem, New Hampshire.
Boston Metropolitan Region–includes all towns south and west of Boston within approximately 35 miles, and all towns north of Boston within approximately 20 miles.
Brockton–includes Avon, Brockton, Easton, Bridgewater, Whitman, and West Bridgewater. Also included in Boston total.
Framingham–includes Maynard, Stow, Hudson, Marlborough, Framingham, Southborough, Ashland, Hopkinton, Holliston, Milford, Medway, Millis, Medfield, Billingham, and Franklin. Also included in Boston total.
Lynn–includes Lynn, Saugus, Nahant, Swampscott, Lynnfield, Peabody, Salem, Marblehead, Beverly, Danvers, Middleton, Wenham, Topsfield, Hamilton, Manchester, Ipswich, Essex, Gloucester, and Rockport. Also included in Boston total.
New Bedford–includes New Bedford, Dartmouth, Fairhaven, and Mattapoisett.
Springfield–includes Springfield, Longmeadow, E. Longmeadow, Hampden, Wilbraham, Agwam, and West Springfield.
Worcester–includes Worcester, Northborough, Westborough, Shrewsbury, Boylston, West Boylston, Holden, Paxton, Leicester, Auburn, Millbury, and Grafton. Also included in the Worcester County total.

MICHIGAN
Mt. Pleasant–includes towns in Isabella, Mecosta, Gladwin, and Gratiot counties.

NEBRASKA
Omaha–includes Douglas and Sarpy counties. Also includes Pottawatomie County, Iowa.

NEW HAMPSHIRE
Laconia–includes Laconia, Plymouth, Meredith, Conway, and Franklin.
Manchester–includes Manchester, Hookset, Merrimac, Amherst, Goffstown, Auburn, Derry, and Londonderry.

NEW JERSEY

Cherry Hill–includes Camden, Burlington, and Gloucester counties.

Essex County–East Essex includes Belleville, Bloomfield, East Orange, Irvington, Newark, and Nutley in Essex County, and Kearney in Hudson County. North Essex includes Caldwell, Cedar Grove, Essex Fells, Fairfield, Glen Ridge, Montclair, North Caldwell, Roseland, Verona, and West Caldwell. South Essex includes Maplewood, Millburn, Short Hills, and South Orange in Essex County, and Springfield in Union County.

Middlesex County–includes in Somerset County, Kendall Park, Somerset and Franklin; in Mercer County, Hightstown; and all of Middlesex County.

Northeastern N.J.–includes Bergen, Essex, Hudson, Middlesex, Morris, Passaic, Somerset, Union, Hunterdon, Sussex, Monmouth, and Ocean counties.

North Hudson County–includes Guttenberg, Hudson Heights, North Bergen, North Hudson, Secaucus, Union City, Weehawken, West New York, and Woodcliff.

Passaic County–includes all towns in Passaic County. Previous estimates for North Jersey have been distributed between Passaic, Bergen, and Morris counties.

Somerset County–includes most of Somerset County and a portion of Hunterdon County.

Trenton–includes most of Mercer County.

Union County–includes all of Union County except Springfield. Also includes a few towns in adjacent areas of Somerset and Middlesex counties.

Vineland–includes most of Cumberland County and towns in neighboring counties adjacent to Vineland.

NEW YORK

Elmira–includes Chemung, Tioga, and Schuyler counties. Also includes Tioga and Bradford counties in Pennsylvania.

Glens Falls–includes Warren and Washington counties, lower Essex County and upper Saratoga County.

Kingston–includes eastern half of Ulster County.

New York Metropolitan Area–includes the five boroughs of New York City, Westchester, Nassau, and Suffolk counties. For a total Jewish population of the New York metropolitan region, please include Fairfield County, Connecticut; Rockland, Putnam, and Orange counties, New York; and Northeastern New Jersey.

Syracuse–includes Onondaga County, Western Madison County, and most of Oswego County.

Utica–Southeastern third of Oneida County.

NORTH CAROLINA

Asheville–includes Buncombe, Haywood, and Madison counties.

Charlotte–includes Mecklenberg County. Also includes Lancaster and York counties in South Carolina.

OHIO
Cincinnati–includes Hamilton and Butler counties. Also includes Boone, Campbell, and Kenton counties in Kentucky.
Cleveland–for a total Jewish population of the Cleveland metropolitan region, please include Elyria, Lorain and Akron totals.
Toledo–includes Fulton, Lucas, and Wood counties. Also includes Monroe and Lenawee counties, Michigan.
Youngstown–includes Mahoning and Trumbull counties. Also includes Mercer County, Pennsylvania.

PENNSYLVANIA
Ambridge–includes lower Beaver County and adjacent areas of Allegheny County.
Bucks County (lower portion)–includes Bensalem Township, Bristol, Langhorne, Levittown, New Hope, Newtown, Penndel, Warrington, Yardley, Richboro, Feasterville, Middletown, Southampton, and Holland.
Philadelphia–includes Philadelphia City, Montgomery, Delaware County, Chester County, and central and upper Bucks County. For a total Jewish population of the Philadelphia metropolitan region, please include lower Bucks County, the Cherry Hill area of New Jersey, Salem and Mercer counties, New Jersey, and the Wilmington area of Delaware.
Pittsburgh–includes all of Allegheny County and adjacent portions of Washington, Westmoreland, and Beaver counties.
Sunbury–includes Shamokin, Lewisburg, Milton, Selinsgrove, and Sunbury.
Wilkes-Barre–includes all of Lucerne County except southern portion, which is included in Hazleton totals.

SOUTH CAROLINA
Sumter–includes towns in Sumter, Lee, Clarendon, and Williamsburg counties.

TEXAS
Amarillo–includes Canyon, Childress, Borger, Dumas, Memphis, Pampa, Vega, and Hereford in Texas, and Portales, New Mexico.
Houston–includes Harris, Montgomery, and Ft. Bend counties, and parts of Brazoria and Galveston counties.
Waco–includes McLellan, Coryell, Bell, Falls, Hamilton, and Hill counties.

VIRGINIA
Newport News–Includes Newport News, Hampton, Williamsburg, James City, York County, and Poquosson County.
Richmond–includes Richmond City, Henrico County, and Chesterfield County.
Staunton–includes towns in Augusta, Page, Shenendoah, Rockingham, Bath, and Highland counties.

Winchester–includes towns in Winchester, Frederick, Clark, and Warren counties Virginia; and Hardy and Jefferson counties, West Virginia.

WASHINGTON

Seattle–includes King County and adjacent portions of Snohomish and Kitsap counties.

Tri Cities–includes Pasco, Richland, Kennewick, and Yakima.

WEST VIRGINIA

Huntington–includes nearby towns in Ohio and Kentucky.

WISCONSIN

Milwaukee–includes Milwaukee County, eastern Waukesha County, and southern Ozaukee County.

Wasau–includes Stevens Point, Marshfield, Antigo, and Rhinelander.

# Review of the Year

OTHER COUNTRIES

# Canada

## National Affairs

CANADA ENJOYED A YEAR OF economic and political stability in 1987; however, the Progressive Conservative (PC) government of Prime Minister Brian Mulroney continued to sag in popularity, as evidenced by various public opinion polls. In an unprecedented situation, all three major parties (PCs, Liberals, and New Democrats) appeared to be competitive, with the mildly socialist New Democratic party holding the lead in a late summer poll for the first time ever. The PCs hoped that their accomplishments in office—chiefly, the Meech Lake constitutional accord, the free-trade agreement with the United States, and a significant reform of the income-tax system—would persuade the electorate to give them another term in the 1988 election. Since all three issues were controversial, however, particularly the free-trade agreement, the PCs' prospects were not encouraging.

For a while during the year national attention was focused on the September 10 legislative election in Ontario. Some 17 Jews ran in the election, including Larry Grossman, leader of the opposition PCs, as well as Liberals and New Democrats. The Liberals, led by Premier David Peterson, scored a decisive victory, forming a majority government for the first time in over four decades. Grossman himself went down to defeat and retired from politics. Five Jews won seats in the legislature, all Liberals: newcomers Ron Kanter and Chaviva Hosek joined veterans Monte Kwinter, Elinor Caplan, and Steve Offer. All were elected in Toronto-area constituencies. Three were named to cabinet posts: Kwinter as minister of industry, trade, and technology; Caplan as minister of health; and Hosek as minister of housing. Offer and Kanter were appointed as parliamentary assistants to other ministers. Further, Martin Barkin and Elaine Todres were appointed deputy ministers in the new government.

REFUGEES; CITIZENSHIP

Jewish issues were generally not central in national politics, although the continuing sagas of the anti-Semitic hatemongers James Keegstra and Ernst Zundel continued to attract headlines (see below). One national issue on which Jews were particularly outspoken was the question of refugee policy, especially in regard to illegal immigrants from such nontraditional places of origin as Sri Lanka. The government's inconsistent and often insensitive policies concerning the processing of claims for refugee status were criticized by, among others, Canadian Jewish Congress (CJC) president Dorothy Reitman, who recalled the unfair treatment accorded Jewish refugees from Nazism. MP David Berger joined in the criticism of the government's new, more stringent rules for determining refugee status, arguing that they amounted to a closing of the door to refugees. Minister of State for Immigration Gerry Weiner defended the policy, contending that its purpose was to curb illegitimate applicants and that "we are doing all we can to help real refugees."

In May the government introduced a controversial bill to deal with the issue, a major feature of which would allow applicants to be deported on the basis of a decision by a two-member screening panel. Joining other critics of the new law, Rabbi W. Gunther Plaut, who had earlier served on a commission that prepared a federal report on refugees, attacked the process as "badly flawed, probably not legal, and not humane." Other critics included professors Fred Zemans and Howard Adelman, the former a CJC committee chairman and the latter the head of York University's Refugee Documentation Center. CJC and B'nai B'rith worked with a number of other organizations in a coalition against the bill.

Ultimately Parliament passed two bills, the original one and another one providing severe deterrent and detention provisions. Jewish leaders opposed the bills to the end. Historian Irving Abella, coauthor of a notable book on Canadian refugee policy during the Nazi era, asked, "Isn't this bill an appeal to the innate racism of the Canadian people who responded so violently to the Sikhs and Tamils?" This and other contentions of unfairness and immorality were ignored.

The federal government raised concern among Jews with another piece of legislation, changes to the Citizenship Act. The proposals would make citizenship harder to obtain and easier to lose, with particular effect on dual citizens, such as Canadian Jews who had immigrated to Israel and who might now be unable to maintain dual citizenship. Among those groups vigorously opposing the suggested changes were the CJC, Parents of North American Israelis, and Jewish Immigrant Aid Services.

## Relations with Israel

Bilateral relations between Canada and Israel generally continued on a favorable basis, although the uprising of the Palestinian Arabs, which began in December, seemed a likely source of future difficulty. One indication of possible tension between the two countries was the refusal of the Canadian government to allow Gen. Amos Yaron to be accredited as the Israeli military attaché in Ottawa. Yaron, who was accredited in Washington, had been found negligent in connection with the 1982 Beirut massacre by the Israeli Kahan Commission investigating that episode. On the other hand, Canada was the only one of the 40 countries represented at the Francophone Summit meeting, held in Quebec City in September, to resist the temptation to support self-determination for the Palestinians or to endorse the idea of an international conference on the Middle East—both positions that received the support of the other 39 nations present.

The ambivalence of Canada's policy was underscored by the failure to invite Mayor Teddy Kollek of Jerusalem to an international conference of mayors of national capital cities, which Ottawa hosted in October. Kollek was not invited, presumably because of a reluctance of the organizers, including a federal government representative, to recognize Jerusalem as Israel's capital. Protests by members of the Ottawa Jewish Community Council, the Canada-Israel Committee (CIC), and others were to no avail. The fact that the mayor of Tripoli, Libya, was invited only highlighted the slight to Israel, because Canada generally did not include Libya in conferences that it sponsored.

Other official actions provoked disappointment in the community as well. The Liberal caucus in the House of Commons selected Marcel Prud'homme, an outspoken advocate of the PLO cause and one of the most pro-Arab MPs, as its chairman, arousing concern that the appointment might be the beginning of a shift away from traditional Liberal policy. On another front, Canada joined with 99 UN member nations in opposing the U.S. plan to close the PLO mission to the UN. Canada also abstained on a General Assembly resolution on UN activities on behalf of Palestinian rights that it had opposed in the past.

The Jewish community was also troubled about increasing expressions of anti-Israel and anti-Zionist attitudes in public discussions and in the media. At one of a number of symposia held to examine the question of media treatment of Israel, Ottawa columnist Ilya Gerol contended that many media people were ignorant about the Middle East and that Canadians generally were less sophisticated about world affairs than people of other nations. For these reasons, he said, it was necessary for the informed public to be particularly vigilant. One example of such vigilance was the protest launched by the CJC against a Vancouver radio station that ran a Voice of Palestine program that was intemperate in attacking Israel. The same station's newsletter also depicted an all-powerful Zionist lobby in Washington that insured American opposition to the Palestinian cause.

Supporters of Israel had some success this year in garnering backing in the Young Liberals and the Red Cross. In the former situation, a pro-PLO resolution that had been passed at a Quebec regional convention was defeated convincingly at the national convention. In the latter, the Canadian Red Cross Society expressed support for the Israeli Magen David Adom in that body's efforts to achieve international recognition of its emblem.

In an interesting historical note, recently released cabinet papers from the 1950s showed that the United States had urged Canada to sell arms to Israel in 1956, before the war with Egypt, because of fears that Israel was at a disadvantage against Soviet-backed Arab countries. At the time, the United States was not an arms supplier to Israel and wanted to avoid becoming too closely identified with Israel, in order to court the Arab states. The late Lester B. Pearson, then Canada's external affairs minister, supported the proposal. Although some arms were shipped, the idea of selling aircraft was dropped after war broke out.

The year brought several changes in diplomatic personnel. Israel Gur-Arieh succeeded Eliashiv Ben-Horin as Israel's ambassador in Ottawa. Benjamin Abileah and Chalom Schirman became the consuls-general in Toronto and Montreal, respectively.

## Anti-Semitism

The attention of Canadian Jewry continued to focus on three well-known anti-Semites: Ernst Zundel in Toronto, James Keegstra in Alberta, and Malcolm Ross in New Brunswick. (See AJYB, vol. 88, 1988, pp. 247–48.) In each case, most of the year's activity took place in the legal arena. Zundel and Keegstra were both appealing their earlier criminal convictions, while Ross waited to see if legal proceedings against him might be initiated.

Zundel's original conviction for "spreading false news"—publishing Holocaust-denial material—was overturned in January by the Ontario Court of Appeal, on procedural grounds. Citing errors related to jury selection, admissibility of evidence, and the charge to the jury, the court specifically rejected Zundel's contention that the law under which he was prosecuted for disseminating falsehoods about the Holocaust was unconstitutional. The unanimous decision left the prosecution with the choice of appealing to the Supreme Court of Canada, proceeding with a new trial, or dropping the charges. Attorney General Ian Scott of Ontario, who was urged by a number of Jewish organizations to take further action, decided to appeal to the Supreme Court. When that court declined to hear the appeal, Scott moved to hold a new trial, which was scheduled for January 1988.

Keegstra, who was convicted under the hate-propaganda provisions of the criminal code for using his high-school social-studies classroom as a forum for promoting anti-Semitism, took his case to the Alberta Court of Appeal. As with Zundel, he claimed both that the law under which he was convicted was unconstitutional and that there were errors in the trial. It was generally agreed that the appeal—which was still pending at year's end—constituted a major event in testing the limits of free speech under the relatively new Charter of Rights and Freedoms.

The Ross case was similar to that of Keegstra in that both were teachers who held anti-Semitic views. Ross had written several Holocaust-denial tracts and allegations of a Jewish conspiracy to dominate the world, but the provincial authorities in New Brunswick were indecisive about taking legal action. Julius Israeli, a concerned citizen, had been successfully publicizing the case for several years, but failed to persuade the authorities to act. He tried again when a new government took power in the province late in 1987, but was again rebuffed, the new minister of justice asserting that there was little chance of success in a prosecution. A major difference between the Ross and Keegstra cases was that Ross had not been accused of propagating his views in the classroom.

There were several anti-Semitic incidents in Canada during the year. In Hamilton, Ontario, a rash of vandalism was directed at synagogues and the Hamilton Hebrew Academy. The perpetrators were believed to be high-school-age members of a "skinhead" group. In Montreal, eight stores in a Jewish area were vandalized on the day before Yom Kippur, with swastikas painted in several places. Another tack was taken by anti-Semites in British Columbia, who circulated a flier in Toronto and Western Canada charging that non-Jews had to pay higher prices for food products because of *kashrut* certification, with the profits going to Israel and rabbis.

## Holocaust-Related Issues

In response to criticism about its past handling of alleged Nazi war criminals, in 1984 the government appointed Justice Jules Deschenes to investigate the situation and make recommendations. His long-awaited report was submitted in March and proved to be a source of controversy. Deschenes's key proposals were three amendments to the criminal code: to allow alleged Nazi war criminals in Canada to be prosecuted, to expedite extradition of suspects wanted in other countries, and to establish more effective laws for the lifting of Canadian citizenship obtained under false pretenses. However, Justice Minister Ray Hnatyshyn indicated that the government would accept only the first of the three recommendations. Both the CJC and B'nai B'rith's League for Human Rights welcomed the report and its findings and urged that the recommendations be implemented. During the period when Deschenes held hearings, representatives of Ukrainian bodies raised questions about allegations made against members of their community, expressing the fear that their group as a whole was being maligned. Indirectly, this raised tensions between the Ukrainian and Jewish communities.

Deschenes's voluminous study showed that immigration authorities had not been vigilant in past years in excluding possible Nazi war criminals from entry into Canada, partly because of a relaxation of government policy a few years after the end of World War II. For example, relevant forms did not include questions that might have elicited information regarding activities during the war.

With regard to specific allegations, Deschenes received about 1,700 names of possible war criminals in Canada, most submitted by Jews or Jewish organizations. After deleting duplications, persons who had died, persons who had left Canada, and those who could not be located, fewer than 200 remained. Allowing for the submission of additional names late in the process, Deschenes recommended investigation of about 250 people for possible action by the government. Of these, about 20 warranted immediate legal action.

Although the effect of the Deschenes Commission report was to reverse 40 years of Canadian ambiguity on the subject of war criminals, undoing the effects of four decades of neglect was expected to be a daunting task, both organizationally and politically. Jewish representatives argued that it was certainly worth the effort. Prof. Irwin Cotler, counsel for the CJC at the commission hearings, stated that every time a war criminal was brought to justice, "we strike a blow against the Holocaust denial movement, we repudiate all those who say that the Holocaust was a hoax or that this was simply a Jewish invention." After a few months of delay, late in June the government introduced a bill to provide for prosecution of war crimes. In addition, Hnatyshyn proposed changes to the immigration law that would bar suspected war criminals from Canada or allow them to be deported if found in the country. Quick passage of the bill was prevented by the objections of a few individual MPs, but the process was completed without amendments in September.

The first arrest of an alleged war criminal took place in December. Retired restaurateur Imre Finta was picked up as he attempted to leave the country and charged with forcible confinement, kidnapping, and manslaughter in connection with the deportation of about 8,000 Jews from Szeged, Hungary, in 1944. Earlier, Sabina Citron, founder of the Canadian Holocaust Remembrance Association, had won a libel judgment of $32,000 (Canad.) against Finta, who had accused her of lying when she alleged his participation in the deportation.

A supplementary aspect of the work of the Deschenes Commission had a sensational impact when it became public knowledge. Ottawa historian Alti Rodal carried out a major research project for the commission, including detailed information about immigration practices and the wartime activities of various groups. One of her most startling revelations was that two alleged Nazi war criminals were allowed to immigrate to Canada in 1983 with the aid of government officials who acted contrary to regulations. Another was that the United States had withheld vital information about potential immigrants to Canada after the war, thereby enabling some of them to escape detection by Canadian authorities. She also documented examples of Canadian officials who had decided to overlook SS tattoo marks on potential immigrants. Some of her findings reflected badly on the country's highest politicians, such as a description of efforts by Prime Minister Pierre Elliott Trudeau to oppose action against war criminals. This section was heavily censored in the public version of the document. Overall, the study represented a stinging indictment of government policy and practice over a protracted period.

Perhaps the public emphasis on war criminals made the case of Austrian president Kurt Waldheim more salient than it would otherwise have been. In any event, the increased sensitivity was reflected in Prime Minister Mulroney's decision that Waldheim would not be welcome in Canada because of his wartime activities. Not that the decision implied shunning the former UN secretary-general altogether. A minor flap was created by the disclosure that Canadian diplomats at the Vatican and in Jordan attended functions in honor of Waldheim when he visited those places. There was also widespread Jewish community criticism of Pope John Paul's reception of Waldheim at the Vatican in June.

## JEWISH COMMUNITY

*Demography*

The Jewish population of Canada remained at about 310,000. A recent study based on 1981 census data showed that Jews were the second largest ethnic group in metropolitan Toronto, after the Italians. The largest concentration of Jews was in the City of North York, where they constituted about 13 percent of the population. Overall, Jews represented about 4.6 percent of the Metro Toronto population.

Montreal's Jews faced specific demographic problems related in part to the political-economic environment of the province of Quebec. A matter of particular concern to the community was the low proportion of young adults. During the decade ending in 1981, about 9,000 Jews between the ages of 15 and 35 and 5,000 between the ages of 36 and 45 had left Montreal, out of a population of about 110,000. As a result, the relevant age cohorts were left badly depleted, with little likelihood that immigration would result in significant improvement. Although the community was unable to reverse the situation, it had introduced various programs aimed at stemming the tide of departures. These programs focused on employment and social needs.

The second problem resulted from the substantial Sephardic immigration that had entered Canada in the previous two decades. The estimated 20,000 Sephardic Jews in Canada, primarily in Montreal, were largely of North African—especially Moroccan—origin, and they had come either directly or after a period in Israel. Other Sephardim came from countries such as Tunisia, Egypt, Lebanon, and Iraq. While the influx compensated to a certain extent for the emigration losses, integrating the newcomers into the community had proved challenging. At first, the Sephardim, almost all of whom spoke French as their first or second language, concentrated on building up institutions to serve their own group. As they became more settled and confident, they began to make their presence felt in broader community settings. Substantial changes in the community's *modus operandi* were required in order to create an environment in which both Ashkenazim and Sephardim could work together effectively and comfortably. For example, major community bodies were making an effort to utilize French internally and externally and to offer services in French; Sephardic institutions became eligible for community funding; and steps were being taken to insure at least a modicum of Sephardic representation on community bodies.

Finally, the community faced a major challenge in dealing with a senior-citizen population that was probably, in proportional terms, second only to that of Miami among North American Jews. The increasing proportion of the elderly, compounded by abnormally small younger age cohorts, promised to place a great burden on community agencies for the foreseeable future.

The implications of structural changes in the community were another matter of concern. University of Toronto social work professor Benjamin Schlesinger found that single parents constituted about 12 percent of the Toronto community. He suggested that phenomena such as delayed parenthood, unmarried couples, dual-career families, and other developments necessitated a reexamination of conventional communal assumptions concerning the nature of Jewish families. He also expressed concern about the Jewish birthrate, currently about 1.5 children per family, well below the replacement rate.

Another dimension of Jewish family relationships was investigated by Prof. Stuart Schoenfeld of York University, who found that about one-fifth of Ontario's Jews married non-Jews. Intermarriage tended to be higher away from the large urban centers, and overall, Jews were still less likely to intermarry than others. Schoenfeld also reported that Reform and unaffiliated Jews and men were more likely to intermarry than more traditional Jews and women.

Somewhat contradictory intermarriage data were provided by Mitchell Jaffe of the JWB in New York, who estimated that the intermarriage rate for Canadian Jews was 8 percent. He also suggested that the average number of children per Jewish family was 1.9. Whatever the correct statistics, it was clear that Canadian Jews faced increasing problems of numbers and affiliation, as well as an age distribution that was skewed toward the higher ages when compared with the general population.

## Community Relations

The issue of public funding for Jewish schools continued to dominate the area of community relations. Increasing costs of providing educational services had induced Jewish schools in several provinces to turn to government for aid. Unlike their American counterparts, Canadian Jewish schools were not barred automatically from consideration for constitutional reasons, and the decision of whether to provide funding was essentially political.

Quebec was the most active province in the field, funding the Jewish schools on a per capita basis, in some cases at 85 percent of the amount available to public schools. In 1987 the annual subvention for primary and secondary schools exceeded $12 million (Canad.). Funding for private schools was available in several other provinces as well, though not always for Jewish schools. Ontario, which subvented the Catholic school system, declined to provide support to other private religious schools, many of which were Christian fundamentalist in orientation. The Jewish day-school system in Ontario, which educated some 8,000 students in 20 schools, was caught in the middle. Despite years of concerted effort, the community had been unsuccessful in the attempt to sway governments of both the PC and Liberal parties.

In the Supreme Court of Canada, groups representing Ontario's Jews faced stiff opposition in their appeal of an Ontario court's 1986 decision that upheld full funding of the Catholic schools but ruled out money for other religious schools. Particularly vigorous opposition to the Jewish position came from the Toronto public-school board, which feared that wider funding would weaken the public-school system. The Supreme Court upheld the lower-court decision, dashing Jewish hopes that the equality provisions of the constitution might be used to compel public funding for their schools.

In Montreal, the United Talmud Torahs, the largest day-school system on the continent, faced the loss of a school building it had been renting from the Protestant School Board of Greater Montreal (PSBGM) for 14 years. The board expressed its intention not to renew the lease but to reclaim the property for use as a school with a special curriculum, one that would include enough Hebrew studies on an optional basis to attract some Jewish families. As a public school, there would be no tuition fees, aside from modest amounts for optional programs. The UTT, with the backing of the broader Jewish community, vigorously resisted the PSBGM initiative for two reasons: (1) no alternative site for the UTT school was available, especially on such short notice, and (2) the competition for the same clientele undercut the UTT's general efforts to provide Jewish children with a full Jewish education. A high-level task force combining a number of Jewish community organizations was activated to try to persuade PSBGM director-general Joseph Rabinovitch to reconsider the alternative school idea. An undercurrent in the UTT-PSBGM dispute was the conflict between a number of Jewish parental supporters of the alternative school who wanted some Jewish education for their children, but rejected day schools, and Jewish educators apprehensive that the alternative-school model might siphon off current day-school parents faced with rapidly escalating tuition fees. In general, feelings were running high as the end of the year approached, with a denouement anticipated early in 1988.

Another troubling question of minority rights related to Sunday store closings, especially in Ontario, where Jews and others had been struggling for years to find means to circumvent the highly restrictive Retail Business Holidays Act. A late 1986 Supreme Court ruling upheld the law despite the court's acknowledgement that it infringed on religious freedom. In a significant development, the Ontario provincial government announced in December that it would henceforth allow municipalities to decide whether stores could remain open on Sundays. This move was viewed as most promising by the Jewish community. The City of North York promptly announced that it was considering easing restrictions on Sunday shopping in order to accommodate its large Jewish population.

## Communal Affairs

### ISRAEL AND ZIONISM

One of the highlights of the year was the election of delegates to the World Zionist Congress. Conducted by the CZF in the late spring, the hard-fought mail-ballot election, featuring nine organizational slates, was preceded by a spirited membership drive to determine who would be eligible to vote. One useful by-product of the process was an updated membership list, albeit amid charges that questionable mass-enrollment techniques had been used by some of the groups. Of the nearly 72,000 confirmed members, about one-third affiliated with the newly formed Orthodox United Torah Coalition. The Conservative Mercaz Canada was second, with about 14 percent of the members. Other groups that enrolled about 5 percent or more of the total included the Zionist Organization of Canada, Kadima (Reform), Canadian Sephardi Federation, Hadassah-WIZO, Na'amat Pioneer Women, Labor Zionist Alliance, and Herut Hatzohar of Canada.

Much of the intense interest in the membership drive was generated by the efforts of the Reform and Conservative religious groups to gain a foothold in Zionist politics and the Orthodox attempt to resist them. The formation of the United Torah Coalition was spurred by fears that any power gained by the Reform and Conservative Zionist groups could lead to diversion of funds from their traditional Orthodox destination, the Israeli *yeshivot.*

In the election itself, 3,871 ballots were cast for the United Torah Coalition (worth 5 of the 19 Canadian seats at the Congress); 3,134 for Kadima (4 seats); 2,274 for Labor Zionist (3 seats); 1,549 for ZOC (2 seats); and 1,297 for Mercaz (2 seats). Single seats went to a Hadassah-Sephardi coalition, a Herut-Tehiya combination, and Friends of Pioneering Israel. Compared to the previous election in 1983, the big winners were Kadima and Mercaz, while those that lost ground were Herut and the Labor Zionists.

An example of non-Orthodox assertiveness was the mission of North American Jewish leaders to Israel in August to try to dissuade members of the Knesset from voting for the "Who is a Jew?" amendment favored by the Orthodox. Donald Carr and Walter Hess of the United Israel Appeal, who represented Canadian Jews in the delegation, stressed to their Israeli interlocutors just how seriously Diaspora Jewry regarded the issue.

On the same question, a nasty conflict erupted in September when the CJC decided to align itself with other Diaspora organizations opposing any change in Israeli law related to the definition of a Jew. The move was immediately protested by the Orthodox rabbinate, which pointed out the CJC's inconsistency in claiming to be the representative body of Canadian Jewry while espousing a position that offended a major segment of the community. Nevertheless, the CJC Quebec regional executive narrowly defeated a motion to advocate rescinding the original decision. Efforts by Congress people to meet privately with key rabbis helped to defuse the situation to some extent, but the issue remained a divisive one.

#### OTHER COMMUNAL MATTERS

Whether it was desirable or even possible to maintain community unity in the realm of ideas was the topic of a one-day symposium, in September, on the topic "Must I Beg to Differ! Voices of Dissent and Non-Conformity Within the Montreal Jewish Community." The keynote lecture by Prof. Irving Abella of York University dealt with the history of dissent and pluralism in the Montreal community. Abella argued that the community had passed through various phases in its toleration of dissent. After a long period of relative conformity, from about 1948 to 1978, he contended, dissent was again acceptable and becoming more common, though not as intense as it had been during the 1930s, for example. Among the more hotly debated issues at the conference workshops were criticism of Israel, religious pluralism, and Jewish attitudes toward Quebec politics. Speakers in the debate included Milton Winston, Ariela Cotler, Peter Shizgal, and Jack Wolofsky.

A number of smaller organizations tried to establish themselves during the year. A spokesman for Chutzpah, a Toronto homosexual group, criticized the lack of facilities for helping Jews afflicted by AIDS. Francophone Jews in Montreal were instrumental in the establishment of the Union Mondiale des Juifs d'Expression Française, formed to promote the common interests of French-speaking Jews and the preservation of their heritage. Several Ottawa Jews formed the Jewish Association for Development, designed to provide a response to world poverty. In Montreal, a Jewish home for battered women was founded. Finally, the Winnipeg *Jewish Post* purchased the rival *Western Jewish News,* leaving the city with only one Jewish newspaper.

## Soviet and Ethiopian Jewry

Given the strong ties between Natan Sharansky and Canadian Jewry, his visit in September, preceded by his mother's visit in March, were the highlights of the year for those committed to the cause of Soviet Jews. Ida Milgrom met in Ottawa with members of Parliament, especially those who had been active in behalf of Soviet Jewry. Sharansky delivered the first Natan Sharansky Lecture in Human Rights at the Faculty of Law of McGill University in Montreal. He advocated a cautious stance toward the changes taking place in the Soviet Union, voicing skepticism about any real improvement in the protection of human rights and urging his listeners not to be lulled into complacency by the release of prominent dissidents. In Ottawa Sharansky met with Prime Minister Mulroney, External Affairs Minister Joe Clark, and opposition party leaders John Turner and Edward Broadbent. He received a standing ovation when he appeared in the gallery of the House of Commons and heard Prime Minister Mulroney pledge his government's continuing efforts to improve the state of human rights in the Soviet Union. Sharansky also addressed a cheering crowd in Toronto, where he finally received an honorary degree that York University had awarded him in 1982. At the ceremony, he recounted the history of the Soviet Jewry movement, stressing the contributions of Canadians.

In 1987 several of the Canadian families involved in the adoption of refusenik families were gratified to be able to receive their Russian "relatives" in freedom, among them Yuli Edelshtein, Alex Ioffe, and Lea and Alexander Mariasin. Other significant events during the year included a protest at a performance of the Red Army Choir in Toronto in February, a student meeting with the Soviet ambassador in April, a symposium in Ottawa in May, observance of the 35th anniversary of the execution of Soviet Jewish writers in August, a Simhat Torah protest in front of the Soviet consulate in Montreal in October, and the participation of hundreds of Canadians in the march to Washington, D.C., in December.

Ethiopian Jews were not forgotten either. Human-rights activist Irwin Cotler organized an international appeal for the remaining Jews in Ethiopia to be reunited with their families in Israel. Fifteen internationally prominent human-rights lawyers and jurists from four continents joined in the appeal, which was announced by Cotler at a rally in Jerusalem in July.

## Religion

Questions of religious practice were prominent in all three major movements. In a departure from conventional Reform behavior, Rabbi Dow Marmur of Toronto's Holy Blossom Temple urged his congregants to wear a *kippah* and *tallit* during services. He stated that "they are now badges of Jewish identity and characteristic features of Jewish worship." At Temple Emanu-El-Beth Shalom in Montreal, the policy on mixed marriages became an important factor in appointing a new rabbi. The congregation, which had tightened up somewhat its earlier liberal policy of allowing mixed marriages, rejected efforts by some members to relax restrictions. On the other hand, the temple insisted that its new rabbi be willing to perform mixed marriages, subject to specified conditions being met by the couple.

A dispute arose within the Toronto Orthodox community over the validity of the *eruv* (Sabbath boundary), although some observers suspected that the conflict only reflected broader religious differences between the right-wing and modern Orthodox.

The Union for Traditional Conservative Judaism, a breakaway Conservative faction, held its fourth annual conference in Toronto in September. The group opposed the decisions by the Jewish Theological Seminary of America to ordain female rabbis and cantors, which it regarded as a "clear breach" of Halakhah. Much of the conference was devoted to discussion of the women's issue.

The issue of pluralism continued to trouble rabbis and laity. Rabbi Marmur urged the creation of a joint rabbinical court (*bet din*) of all the religious movements in Toronto as a way of showing support for both pluralism and unity.

## Culture

Montreal's Yiddish Theater of the Saidye Bronfman Center celebrated its 30th anniversary. Originally known as the Yiddish Drama Group, it was responsible for the revival of a vibrant Yiddish theater in Montreal. Much of the credit belonged to Dora Wasserman, the driving force behind the group's success over the years. On the occasion of the anniversary, the musical *The Rothschilds* was produced.

Aviva Ravel's new play, *Vengeance,* dealing with the relationship of Poles and

Jews during the Holocaust, premiered in Montreal. At Montreal's annual World Film Festival, which had become a major cultural event, several of the entries were of Jewish interest. *Late Summer Blues,* an Israeli film that questioned conventional Israeli attitudes toward the military, was the first feature-length entry from that country. It was accompanied by another feature, *Tel Aviv-Berlin,* which dealt with the agony and torment of a German Jew living in Israel. It was the first Israeli nondocumentary film on the Holocaust. A short film, *Boker Tov Israel,* was also entered. Among the other films with Jewish themes that were screened in the festival were *Farewell Moscow,* an Italian film about Ida Nudel's struggle for her rights in the Soviet Union; *To Mend the World,* a Holocaust documentary based on survivors' accounts, by Toronto filmmaker Harry Rasky; *Weapons of the Spirit,* a French-American production about a French village that resisted the Nazis by saving Jews; *The Testament,* a French work based on a book by Elie Wiesel; *Wedding in Galilee,* a French-Belgian venture about Israeli-Arab relations; and a Canadian short, *The Rock 'n Roll Rabbi.*

The University of Toronto and Bar-Ilan University in Israel established a computer link giving researchers in Toronto access to Bar-Ilan's Global Jewish Database, which contained major classical texts. It was the first such connection in Canada. The University of Toronto added two courses in Yiddish and another on Jewish religious studies, aided by funding from the Toronto Jewish Congress Berman Fund. An annual prize for a Yiddish or Hebrew work was to be awarded by the Dr. Hirsch and Dvorah Rosenfeld Foundation for Yiddish Culture.

*Publications*

A number of important books were published during the year. The noted philosopher Emil Fackenheim's *What Is Judaism? An Interpretation for the Present Age* is a popular treatment of his theological concerns, with elements of autobiography added. Michael Marrus, author of works on various aspects of the Holocaust, confronts that phenomenon in its totality in *The Holocaust in History.* Rather than presenting another chronological treatment of the subject, Marrus investigates several key questions, such as the emergence of the Nazi extermination policy, the absence of a written record of Hitler's involvement in the Final Solution, collaborationist governments, and the role of outsiders.

In *The Myth of the Jew in France, 1967–1982,* Henry Weinberg examines the intensification of Jewish consciousness at a time when public life in France was often problematical for Jews. Weinberg contends that the late president Charles de Gaulle's criticism of the Jews in 1967, after the Six Day War, legitimated a wave of anti-Semitic activities.

Anti-Semitism in Canada was treated in two new works. Cyril Levitt and William Shaffir examine *The Riot at Christie Pits,* an outbreak in Toronto in 1933 in which Jews who used recreational facilities in a non-Jewish part of town were attacked by fascist thugs. Stanley Barrett's *Is God a Racist?* profiles extreme right-wing and anti-Semitic groups and their leaders.

*Justice Delayed: Nazi War Criminals in Canada* by David Matas is a timely examination of Canada's record of tolerating Nazi war criminals.

The often awkward relations between Jews and French-Canadians is the subject of *Jew or Juif? Jews, French-Canadians and Anglo-Canadians, 1759–1914* by Michael Brown. He contends that Jews have felt more comfortable in English Canada than in French Canada—despite considerable anti-Semitism among the English—and that an inability to integrate fully into either society led Jews to develop elaborate communal institutions.

Among other nonfiction works published during the year were the following: *The Jewish Thought of Emil Fackenheim* edited by Michael Morgan; *To Kill a Rabbi* by Rabbi Reuben Slonim; *Who Is a Jew: 30 Questions and Answers About This Controversial Issue* by Rabbi Immanuel Schochet; *The Best of Times, The Worst of Times* by Harry and Mildred Gutkin; *Derachim Vaderech B'Chinuch* by Rabbi Akiva Egozi; *Endurance: Chronicles of Jewish Resistance* by Amnon Ajzensztadt; *A Treasury of Sephardic Laws and Customs* by Rabbi Herbert Dobrinsky; *Shemot Exodus II,* by Rabbi Zvi Mond; *The Jew in Exile* by Rabbi Shmuel Yaakov Klein; and *The Main: Portrait of a Neighborhood* by Edward Hillel.

Ruth R. Wisse joined Irving Howe and Khone Shmeruk to edit *The Penguin Book of Modern Yiddish Verse.* Some 40 poets are examined in the work, 6 in detail. The poet Irving Layton published two books during the year—an autobiography, *Waiting for the Messiah,* and *Fortunate Exile,* a collection of poems on the theme of the Jews' encounter with history. *Lisa,* by Carol Matas, was a new work of fiction.

## Personalia

The Order of Canada was awarded to Boris Brott, Dr. Richard Goldbloom, Mitzi Dobrin, Jake Superstein, Ed Mirvish, George Cohon, Allan Gotlieb, Monty Hall, Dr. Harry Bain, and Harvey Webber. David Rome, Phyllis Godefroy-Waxman, and Alexander Brott received the Order of Quebec. Libby Greenfield, Robert Sachter, and Rita Finestone were appointed to the Canadian Multiculturalism Council, and Rabbi Reuven Bulka joined the Ontario Advisory Council on Multiculturalism and Citizenship. Chief Justice Alan B. Gold of Quebec Superior Court was named chancellor of Concordia University. Judith Loeb Cohen became the president of the National Ballet of Canada. Dr. Saul Cohen received the Saskatchewan Order of Merit. Jonathan Schneiderman was elected president of the youth wing of the Liberal party.

Yeshiva University awarded honorary degrees to the chief justice of the Supreme Court of Canada, Brian Dickson, and to Quebec's chief justice, Alan B. Gold. Quebec premier Robert Bourassa received an honorary degree from Tel Aviv University. Rabbi Reuven Bulka received the Joe Tannenbaum Literary Award for Jewish scholarship. Dr. Victor Goldbloom was awarded the René Cassin Medal.

Other awards included the Bronfman Medal to Harry Steiner; the Citation of Merit of the Royal Canadian Academy of Arts to Gershon Iskowitz; the Educator of the Year Award of the Educators Council of America to Rabbi Jay Braverman; J.J. Segal Foundation arts awards to Miriam Waddington, Pearl Weissenberg-Akselrod, Tova Shimon, and Pinchas Blitt; and the Rebecca Sieff Award to Irwin Cotler.

Major appointments within the Jewish community included: Ralph Snow, president of B'nai B'rith Canada; David Azrieli, president of the CZF; Mel Dobrin, president of Israel Bonds; Judge Irving Halperin, chairman of the National Budgeting Conference; Dr. Victor Goldbloom, president of ORT; Naomi Frankenburg, president of Hadassah-WIZO; Alfred Segall, president of the Canadian Magen David Adom for Israel; William Belzberg, North American campaign chairman for Israel Bonds; Murray Koffler, chairman of the board of the Weizmann Institute; Rabbi Michael Stroh, chairman of Arzenu—World Federation of Reform/Progressive Zionists; and Salomon Oziel, president of the Communauté Sepharade du Québec.

Among leading Jews who died in 1987 were the following: noted lawyer and senator Lazarus Phillips, in January, aged 91; community leader and philanthropist Lawrence Freiman, in January, aged 77; London community leader Bernard Wolf, in January, aged 96; Max Wolfe, founder of the Oshawa Group, in February, aged 94; Phil Cutler, judge and former labor lawyer, in February, aged 67; Rosa Singer, former Hadassah-WIZO president, in February, aged 94; teacher and Yiddishist Shaindele Elberg, in June, aged 74; Sephardic leader Léon Oziel, in June, aged 49; businessman Sam Rubin, in July, aged 78; Ethel Grossman, wife and mother of prominent Ontario politicians, in July, aged 74; Kingston community leader Sheldon Cohen, in July, aged 82; actor Lorne Greene, in September, aged 72; Louis Rosenberg, pioneer demographer and "one of the greatest Jewish civil servants Canada has ever known," in September, aged 94; Toronto congregational rabbi David Landy, in September, aged 72; Toronto congregational rabbi Louis Cashdan, in September, aged 81; Harry Steiner, Toronto community activist, in October, aged 75; Miriam Lieff, a founder of Emunah Women Canada, who had settled in Israel, in October, aged 82; long-time Toronto yeshivah teacher Rabbi Eliyahu Akiva Lipsker, in October, aged 70; linguistics professor Hans Stern, in October, aged 74; Dr. Ezra Lozinski, medical researcher and organizational activist, in November, aged 90; Philip Vineberg, prominent lawyer, teacher, and tax expert, in November, aged 73; David Kaye, Cornwall philanthropist, in December, aged 75; writer and former director of Montreal's Jewish Public Library Paul Trepman, in December, aged 71; and Herb Weinstein, social worker and director of the Hillel Foundation at McGill University, in December, aged 61.

HAROLD M. WALLER

# Latin America

## Argentina

*National Affairs*

MIDTERM ELECTIONS IN SEPTEMBER 1987, in which the opposition Peronists achieved significant victories in Congress and in provincial (state) and local elections, dealt a blow to the moderate center-left government of President Raúl Alfonsín. The victory of Alfonsín's Radical Civic Union (UCR) party in 1983—which brought to an end seven years of a harsh military regime—had created high expectations and hopes for the return of democracy and an amelioration of the country's economic distress. However, only the hopes of a political character had been fulfilled, and those only to a limited degree.

Alfonsín succeeded, especially at the start of his presidency, in creating an atmosphere of reconciliation with the Peronists and in keeping the military under his control as the legitimate president. Cultural life flourished, as seen in both the quantity and quality of intellectual debate, art exhibitions, popular concerts, film festivals, and the like. However, these achievements and the wide support Alfonsín enjoyed at the beginning of this period were counterbalanced by his failure to deal adequately with two serious and basic problems: meting out justice to those responsible for criminal acts during the 1976–1983 period of military rule, and the economic crisis.

The issue of justice had its roots in the last stages of the military regime, when its leaders decided to declare a general amnesty for those who stood to be accused of responsibility for the general repression, for the "disappearance" of leftist political opponents or perceived opponents, and for many other crimes committed during the so-called dirty-war years (1975–1982, including the last year of Isabel Peron's rule and most of the military regime). The government hoped that the amnesty law would preclude any further judicial action. When the democratic government came into office, however, the pressure of public opinion, national and international, combined with the new regime's own principles, created an atmosphere that required bringing the accused to trial. In the end, when only the members of the military *junta* were convicted and sentenced to long prison terms, many Argentineans were outraged.

Alfonsín faced a serious dilemma. On the one hand, any attempt to achieve absolute justice raised a threat of possible reaction by the military. (The attempted rightist coups of April 1987 and January 1988 were only the most serious expressions of the danger surrounding Alfonsín during most of his time in office.) On the other hand, the use of pragmatic solutions, such as the *"obediencia debida"* (due obedience) and *"punto final"* (full stop) laws, passed in 1986 and 1987, respectively, which in effect granted amnesty to the great majority of military personnel accused of violating human rights, aroused opposition not only from left-wing extremists but also from people who simply believed that democracy could not exist without the uncompromising application of unbiased justice. This lack of support from the left and the center diminished Alfonsín's ability to face down the military and deal firmly with the country's economic problems.

The main political opposition, the Partido Justicialista, the successor to the Peronista movement, generally supported the democratic regime, though not all party sectors did so enthusiastically or actively. Some Peronist leaders even maintained close contacts with military figures like Col. Aldo Rico, who was responsible for the failed coups d'état of April 1987 and January 1988. The General Confederation of Labor (CGT), led by the Peronist Saul Ubaldini, expressed its opposition to the government's economic policies through a continuing series of strikes, including countrywide general work stoppages, all of much longer duration and greater intensity than those experienced during the previous military and Peronist (1973–1976) regimes.

Despite the fact that the chaotic economic situation had been created in great measure by the policies of earlier governments, Alfonsín was held responsible. Fearful that payments on Argentina's $53-billion foreign debt could not be interrupted without creating a serious international crisis, Alfonsín followed International Monetary Fund advice and implemented strong restraining measures, such as drastic budgetary reductions and a freeze on wages and prices, with the ensuing decline of public services, increased unemployment, and so on. The situation of the majority became increasingly strained, and opposition to the government intensified. Alfonsín's position was further harmed by the demagogic demands of the opposition that the foreign debt be canceled unilaterally.

The government was shaken when the September 6, 1987, midterm elections resulted in a Peronist majority in the national Chamber of Deputies and Peronist victories in almost all the provincial governors' races. How this situation would influence both Alfonsín's ability to push through his policies and the future course of democracy in Argentina was not at all clear. One likelihood was that Alfonsín would complete his six-year term in 1989, having consolidated constitutional rule, and then deliver the office to the next legitimately elected civilian president—most probably Carlos Menem, a Peronist populist leader of Arab origin.

## JEWS AND THE GOVERNMENT

The opposition to the government had introduced a Jewish theme into the country's political debate, especially during the midterm 1987 election campaign. Rightwing members of the military and rightist elements within the Catholic Church and the Peronist trade unions charged that Alfonsín's government was in the hands of the so-called *Sinagoga Radical* (Radical synagogue), referring to the large number of Jews in high-level government positions.

Jews had in fact served in previous Argentinean governments in high positions, but never in such numbers as under Alfonsín. The fact that the number of Jews in the military administration (they occupied administrative, not military, positions, such as the directorship of the Internal Revenue Service) had been extremely low made the contrast all the more dramatic. Jewish visibility was heightened by the novel tendency among many Jewish officials to make public their Jewish identity or origin. Among Jews who occupied prominent positions in the government were Marcos Aguinis, secretary of culture and adviser to the president, and later the person responsible for organizing the First National Educational Congress; Cesar Jaroslavsky, president of the Radical Civic Union bloc in the Chamber of Deputies; Bernardo Grinspun, the first minister of the economy in Alfonsín's cabinet; Leopoldo Portnoi, president of the Central Bank; Jacobo Fiterman, public works commissioner in the Buenos Aires city administration (an influential, "visible" position). Fiterman had earlier been president of the Zionist Organization and head of the local United Jewish Appeal, called CUJA.

The warm acceptance of Jews by the Alfonsín regime was evident not only in the conspicuous presence of Jewish individuals within the government but in specific indications of support for Jewish issues. For example, the government issued a strong condemnation of the attack against the Jewish synagogue in Istanbul in September 1986. A warm reception was given to Edgar Bronfman, president of the World Jewish Congress, by President Alfonsín in December 1986, when Bronfman visited Argentina, Brazil, and Uruguay to express sympathy and support for their renewed democratic regimes. High government officials took part in Jewish community activities, as for instance, the presence of Federico Storani, president of the Foreign Relations Commission of the Chamber of Deputies, at the opening session of the Latin American Jewish Congress, in November 1987.

As part of the government's program of fostering cultural pluralism, different ethnic communities were given opportunities to present cultural programs in government-sponsored centers, especially the General San Martin Cultural Center in the city of Buenos Aires (an institution comparable to New York's Lincoln Center). The amount of attention given to Jews and Jewish cultural activity actually appeared to be disproportionate to the size of the Jewish population. Many observers regarded this as a reaction to the earlier disregard of a Jewish presence in the country.

The Israel Week organized in September 1986 at the San Martin Center, which attracted a large attendance, included addresses by the ambassador of Israel, a symposium on science, technology, and education in Israel, an exhibition which occupied most of the center's halls, and other activities. *Herencia* ("Heritage"), a Spanish version of Abba Eban's TV series on the history of the Jewish people, was presented nationally in prime time. (This event was in marked contrast to the difficulties encountered, under the military government, just in getting permission for the screening of a TV series on the Holocaust.) Other examples reflecting the positive change in attitude toward Jews under the democratic regime were the warm reception given to participants in the meeting of Latin American Friends of the Tel Aviv University held in Buenos Aires in August 1986, at which the subject of Jewish communities in the area was featured in the program; the offering by Universidad del Salvador (a Catholic institution) of a course in Yiddish, starting in 1987; and the awarding of a number of literary prizes to Jewish writers. In the Ministry of Culture's 1987 literary competition, second prize for essays and criticism was given to Isidoro Blastein, and third prize to Tamara Kamenszain (the daughter of a Jewish community leader); second prize in the Buenos Aires municipal literary competition was given to Marcos Ribak and third prize to Ricardo Feirstein, while first prize for essays was given to Geula Kosize and third prize for short stories to Eduardo Stilman, all of them Jews.

Jews were generally supportive of Alfonsín, but not all of one mind about how far to go in his support. On the one hand, Alfonsín represented democracy and a positive attitude toward the Jews. On the other hand, with the wounds inflicted on members of the Jewish community still fresh, many Jews demanded a firm stance from Alfonsín in prosecuting the officers responsible for the crimes of the "dirty war" period. (See "Communal Affairs," below.)

Support for the government by the DAIA (Delegación de Asociaciones Israelitas Argentinas), the representative political body of Argentine Jewry, was more outspoken and clear-cut than it had been in the previous 50 years. The greater involvement of the Jewish community in general issues and the feeling that the community had a stake in the existence of a democratic regime undoubtedly contributed to this attitude. In April 1987 the DAIA issued a call opposing antidemocratic attempts; it also signed a declaration, together with political parties and many other organizations, formally pledging to support the legal government. Still, many Jewish leaders, including the DAIA's own president, Dr. David Goldberg, criticized the government and those members of Congress who approved the *punto final* and *obediencia debida* laws mentioned above. In short, the "official" Jewish attitude was one of unconditional support for the legitimate democratic regime coupled with criticism of the failure to prosecute those responsible for violations of human rights during the "dirty war."

## Anti-Semitism

Although anti-Semitism was officially opposed, and its manifestations criticized by the president and other high officials, open attacks on Jews, mainly written and spoken, persisted. In theory—following the analysis of Harvard University sociologist Gino Germani, who lived and taught in Argentina for many years—there were two types of anti-Semitism in Argentina, the ideological and the traditional-popular; the former represented by extreme-right groups of upper-class origins and by certain sectors in the army and the Catholic Church; the latter by elements whose attitudes were rooted in more traditional prejudice. In practice it was hard to distinguish between the two types, especially because of the manipulation of popular anti-Semitism by the more ideological elements.

Certain Peronist groups, for example, manipulated popular prejudice for their own political purposes. During a mass political rally in November 1987, General Secretary Ubaldini of the CGT, the central trade-union federation, allowed thousands of demonstrators to shout *"Se va a acabar la sinagoga Radical"* ("An end to the Radical synagogue") and other anti-Semitic slogans, including personal insults of Jews in leading government positions. Preaching at a mass in October 1987, the priest Carlos Beltran condemned the Radical government, *"que se deja llevar por malos judios"* ("which let itself be led by bad Jews"). Public anti-Semitic outbursts occurred in periods of domestic tension, such as that prior to the September 1987 elections, or during the implementation of the government's new economic program, the Plan Austral, in June 1985, or in response to such international events as the Israeli attack on PLO headquarters in Tunis in September 1985, or the U.S. bombardment of Libya in April 1986.

While the government criticized individual anti-Semitic acts, its commitment to the democratic principle of freedom of expression, even when used by the enemies of democracy, prevented it from taking action. Anti-Semitic literature, for example, was offered freely in the central streets and on the newsstands of Argentinean cities.

In addition to anti-Semitic outbursts in connection with the September 6 elections, the shouting of *"Fuera los Judios"* ("Out with the Jews") and, again, *"Se va a acabar la sinagoga Radical"* at political rallies of the CGT and the Peronista party, 1987 saw intensified attacks on Jews in *Alerta Nacional, Masoneria, Cabildo,* and other anti-Semitic newspapers and periodicals. Similarly, the "Institute for Research on the Jewish Question" issued five books in a series called *Los judios son nuestros enemigos* ("The Jews are our enemies").

Jewish reaction to these events was different from what it had been under previous regimes (with the exception of a strike of Jewish businesses in 1962). Instead of relying solely on declarations or private, behind-the-scenes meetings with government officials, a mass rally was organized in Buenos Aires on November 26, 1987, attended by an estimated 40,000 persons, demonstrating "in repudiation of Nazi fascism and in support of the anti-discrimination law," namely, the then proposed law which would make expressions of anti-Semitism illegal.

## Former Nazis

The democratic government showed itself more willing to prosecute accused Nazi war criminals than had previous regimes, which had in effect protected them. However, the wheels of justice did not move quickly. The long drawn-out case of Walter Kutschmann, for example, ended abruptly with his death in 1986, before legal proceedings against him were completed. Kutschmann's extradition had been demanded by Germany as early as 1975, but the military coup of March 1976 effectively interrupted all legal proceedings. After years of pressure by Simon Wiesenthal and officials of B'nai B'rith's Anti-Defamation League, and with the help of a well-known Argentinean Jewish criminal lawyer, Elias Neuman, Kutschmann was arrested in 1985. Kutschmann, who had been living in Argentina since 1947, under the name of Pedro Olmos, had been a high-ranking SS officer responsible for mass executions of Jews in the Ukraine.

In November 1987 Josef Franz Leo Schwammberger, aged 75, was arrested in Huerta Grande, Córdoba, on an extradition request from West Germany, which had issued a warrant for his arrest in 1975. A former SS officer who had served as commandant of various labor and concentration camps, he was accused of shooting and torturing hundreds of Jews and stealing their valuables. The Simon Wiesenthal Center had named Schwammberger one of its most wanted Nazi fugitives. The legal proceedings were expected to continue into 1988.

Still other known Nazis who had found refuge in Argentina and whose capture and extradition were sought were Guido Zimmer, Karl Kirchmann, and Eich Heinrich.

## Argentina-Israel Relations

Argentinean Jews were gratified by the traditionally good relations that existed between the two countries, which meant that neither as individuals nor as a community were they placed in situations of conflict. With the country moving toward greater pluralism as a basic structural condition of democracy, the issue of "dual loyalty" was viewed as largely academic. Argentina was, however, a member of the developing countries group and as such had economic interests in Arab countries. The one area of tension in the relationship stemmed from Argentina's criticism of Israeli policies, first in regard to the Lebanon war and, at the end of the period reviewed, in regard to the occupied territories. The latter led to the indefinite postponement of a visit to Israel by President Alfonsín, which had been frequently mentioned as a real possibility.

Among the events which could be cited as demonstrating friendly relations between Argentina and Israel were the meeting between former Israeli president Ephraim Katzir and President Alfonsín, during the 1986 Latin American conference of the Friends of the Tel Aviv University; the signing of agreements on joint technological and scientific projects between the National Council for Scientific and

Technical Research (CONICET), the National Institute for Industrial Technology (INTI), and the Faculty of Physics and Sciences of the University of Buenos Aires, all from the Argentinean side, and the Weizmann Institute, from the Israeli side; the participation by Weizmann Institute experts in a seminar on aging in Buenos Aires; the visit of Peronista leader Antonio Cafiero to Israel in January 1987; and the visit to Israel of the deans of the University of Salvador and the National University of Rosario, Juan Alejandro Tobias and Juan Carlos Millet, respectively.

In April 1987, during the so-called Semana Santa rebellion, led by the rightist Colonel Rico who opposed the trials of senior military leaders on the ground that they had saved Argentina from chaos and/or communism, Foreign Minister Shimon Peres of Israel sent a message of support for the legal government of Argentina. Since the results of the confrontation were still not clear, the message was a breach of an unwritten Israeli diplomatic rule that required waiting until a crisis was resolved, in order not to endanger the position of the local Jewish community. The international backing expressed for the democratic regime, and the outspoken and clear-cut support of the Jewish community itself help to explain the Israeli foreign office's unusual move.

JEWISH COMMUNITY

*Demography*

Because the question about religion was dropped from the census after 1960, no reliable figures on Jewish population were available. The best estimate was that Jews numbered around 220,000, or 7 percent, in a population of some 30 million. Since the proportion of Jews was higher in the city of Buenos Aires as well as among the middle classes and in certain professions, Jews were more visible in Argentinean life than their small number would indicate.

In 1960, 80 percent of the Jewish population of Argentina was concentrated in the Buenos Aires metropolitan area (only 33 percent of the general population lived in the same area). The trend toward concentration seemed to be continuing, the other big communities being Córdoba, Rosario, La Plata, and Santa Fe. The trend toward decreasing population in smaller communities and in the few Jewish agricultural colonies also continued, with the exception of the "poles of development," such as the urban areas of Neuquen Province, though there too the figures were low.

Migration out of the country during the military regime included not only political refugees but also persons who had not been persecuted but left for economic or political reasons. The main destination for migration was Israel, but Europe, the United States, and other Latin American countries, such as Mexico and Venezuela, were also chosen. The return to democracy in Argentina influenced the remigration of many of those Jews who had left in the previous decade, as part of a general wave of returning Argentineans. However, when the initial enthusiasm linked with Alfonsín's election waned, and under the influence of continuing economic and political problems, this return stream slowed and emigration once again increased. For Jews, the paradoxical situation in which a democratic regime was less able to control anti-Semitism than a repressive one could be considered another "push" factor toward emigration.

## Basic Tensions

The return to democracy in 1983 opened up debate in the Jewish community on the role played by the community leadership during the period of the so-called dirty war. The families and friends of the estimated 1,500 Jewish *"desaparecidos"* (the disappeared ones), together with liberal sectors of the community, accused the Jewish leadership of those days of having collaborated with the previous regime by keeping silent. Among the most outspoken critics were Renee Epelbaum, one of the founders of the movement of Madres de la Plaza de Mayo, whose three children had disappeared; Herman Schiller, the editor of *Nueva Presencia,* since 1977 the first, and for a long period of time the only, newspaper to denounce human-rights violations; and Rabbi Marshall Meyer, who, since coming to Argentina in 1960 from the United States to introduce Conservative Judaism, had been a courageous leader in the cause of human rights. (Meyer returned to the United States in 1985, where he assumed a pulpit in New York City.) These three individuals initiated the Jewish Movement for Human Rights, in 1983—during the last year of the dictatorship—and in 1986–87 actively opposed the *punto final* and *obediencia debida* laws that effectively exonerated the military. During the years of the military regime, these leaders and many other individual Jews had been active within the general movement for human rights. The separate Jewish human-rights movement, which developed at the start of the Alfonsín period, played a central role in the community debates over Jewish leadership behavior during the dictatorship years. The movement was particularly influential among many young Jews and in left and liberal Jewish circles.

The debate in the Jewish community was a familiar one, centering on the conflict between ethical principle and pragmatic strategies of survival. The leaders of the Jewish Movement for Human Rights derided the "passive" behavior of the community leadership, and the leadership defended itself by arguing that using quiet influence with the junta had been more effective in saving lives and improving prisoners' conditions than lofty declarations and international pressure. On a personal level, some leaders also maintained that discreet measures were the only prudent ones, given the fact that they did not carry U.S. passports—a clear reference to Marshall Meyer's privileged position as an American citizen.

The role of the State of Israel and its representatives was greater than circumstances permitted making public. Jews were taken out of the country, and conditions of prisoners, once located, were improved, through the direct intervention and with the active help of Israeli representatives.

THE ECONOMIC SITUATION

The continuing economic crisis resulted in increasing economic polarization of the Jewish population. This in turn produced a situation in which those who had become richer and those whose economic situation had worsened—especially the latter—found it increasingly difficult to share the same social and institutional frameworks. In the case of membership in Jewish organizations and institutions, it was not just a matter of—for example—paying the dues, but of being able to afford appropriate clothes, tickets to the right social and cultural events, and so on. Among well-to-do Jews it had become common to purchase weekend cottages and apartments, frequently located on the extensive grounds of Jewish country clubs which offered all types of recreational facilities. Some of these clubs had started as relatively modest Jewish sport or social clubs that over the years became increasingly luxurious. The country-club installations were located within a radius of 10 to 35 miles of the center of Buenos Aires (where the clubs had their main social-cultural and sport centers), and those members who had houses at the country clubs used them as weekend retreats. Members who did not own houses were able to come just for the day, or to use the popular "dorms" (the English term was used) for an overnight, a weekend, or a brief summer vacation.

By contrast, wide segments of the Jewish population were not able to pay the tuition in Jewish schools (or to keep up with the style of life that sending children to these schools implied: presents for birthday parties, extracurricular activities, and the like). Parents were frequently not ready to accept—for psychological and cultural reasons—the scholarship aid generally available to those who needed it. This was not a new phenomenon, but economic conditions aggravated the trend. It should be noted that the majority of the Jewish community in Argentina was middle-class, not upper- or upper-middle class, as was the case in most Latin American countries.

The behavior of both the more and the less affluent posed dangers for the community's functioning. Growing assimilation among the former, as indicated, for example, by increased tendencies to bury the dead in private (not confessional) cemeteries and to join non-Jewish social circles and clubs, could result in loss of membership and income; so could the abandonment of Jewish institutions by the less affluent, for economic and social reasons—all this at a time when heavy demands were placed on institutional services by those in need. Reports based on professional social-work surveys showed that dealing with the poor was an important element in the work of the AMIA, the Buenos Aires *kehillah,* and many communal agencies. Despite a reluctance (as in the case of school fees) to turn to social services for help, numerous requests did come from people who had no income, or very low income; who needed a place to live or assistance with rent; who were unemployed, or had physical or mental health problems, or needed scholarships or services for the aged. In 1986 some 2,000 individuals were aided by various services of the AMIA, though the number of Jewish poor was estimated to be many more. In that year over

$600,000 was spent on these social services, a significant sum for the Jewish community's resources.

*Communal Affairs*

Several basic processes continued in the period surveyed, among them the trend toward greater professional management of community affairs. In the past, *askanim,* lay volunteers, were the leaders and doers, and the only professionals were teachers and rabbis. One major impetus for change was the expansion of Jewish institutional life that took place during the "dirty war" and junta years, as large numbers of Jews sought a haven from the turmoil around them, and as professionals who lost jobs in government and universities took positions in Jewish institutions. Other factors were a decrease in Zionist ideological factionalism and the example of Jewish communities elsewhere in the Diaspora, which put more emphasis on programs and service-delivery than on geographic origin or social standing or ideological ties among their members. Despite the growing influence of professionals, lay leaders maintained a prominent role; the normal kinds of conflicts occurred, and efforts were being made to forge a new type of relationship between professionals and volunteers.

The central organizations in Jewish life continued to be the local *kehillot,* or community bodies, such as the Buenos Aires AMIA (Asociación Mutual Israelita Argentina), which provided educational, cultural, social, and religious services; the representative national political body, the DAIA (Delegacíon de Asociaciones Israelitas Argentinas); and the OSA (Organizacíon Sionista Argentina), the Zionist roof organization. Communal activities centered around Jewish schools, the Jewish sport and social clubs, and the synagogues, which also provided cultural, social, and educational activities in addition to religious ones.

Elections in 1987 to the AMIA and the OSA gave some indication of the changes taking place in Jewish attitudes and communal life. The AMIA elections produced a surprise second-place victory for a brand new list, a coalition of representatives of certain sport and social clubs, lay leaders not identified with any Zionist political platform, and other groups, under the name Breira ("alternative"; not linked to the former U.S. Jewish organization of that name), whose platform called for changes in institutional life on a nonpartisan basis. A total of 9,518 voters (out of 25,000 members who had the right to vote) gave 49 percent of the votes to the Avoda-Labor Zionist list, 20 percent to Breira, and 16 percent to an Orthodox Aguda-Mizrahi list. In the previous election, in 1984, the total number of voters had been smaller, only 7,148. The increase was believed to be the result of the new democratic atmosphere prevailing in the country and the strong competition between the lists.

In the elections for the OSA, Breira fared poorly. The surprise this time was provided by Convergencia, a coalition of left-wing Zionists, intellectuals, and Voz Libre, an interesting group of leftists who had developed a sympathetic attitude toward Israel some years earlier, after becoming disenchanted with the policies of the Soviet Union. (In the thirties, forties, and early fifties, the leftist "progressive" sector had been much more active and influential in the Jewish community.) Convergencia publicized its slogans in the streets of Buenos Aires, "taking 'Zionism' into the open," as they put it.

The election results were as follows: Avoda (Labor Zionists)—3,538; Convergencia—2,166; MAS (linked to Breira)—1,092; Zionist Federation (Liberal Zionists) and Iona—999; Herut-Betar—521. The rest of the votes went to smaller lists.

While the 1987 elections did not mandate a clear direction of change, they did highlight the tension between those seeking changes which could be loosely defined as "modernization," and those who saw change in the structure of the community as a threat to Jewish life and to traditional Zionist attitudes. Those favoring modernization advocated nonpartisan community organization, rationalization of institutions, new techniques of community and institutional work, and so on. Modernizers, for example, considered the links of the "traditional" Zionists with Israeli ideologies or political parties an abnormal and negative phenomenon, whereas the traditional Zionists considered ideological differences a basic requirement for a democratic community and a sound Jewish education (in the youth movements, for instance). The traditionalists believed that pragmatic approaches, less emphasis on ideology, and a weakening of the Zionist parties would lead to greater assimilation, a less democratic community, and domination of communal life by the economically powerful. In actuality, while the main lines of debate were clear, the division between the two sectors was not so sharp, and there were many middle-of-the-road or "combined" positions. Historical loyalties to certain ideologies or institutions, class and other economic interests, and other factors all came into play.

## Education and Culture

Despite the serious economic crisis in the country, Jewish schools maintained high enrollments. According to the First Census of Jewish Schools in the Diaspora, carried out by the Israeli government, the Jewish Agency, and the World Zionist Organization in the early 1980s, the number of Jewish children in Argentina aged 3–17 was around 34,000; of this number 21,400 attended Jewish educational institutions, most of them all-day schools. This proportion, around 63 percent, was one of the highest among large communities in the Diaspora. In addition, hundreds of youngsters visited Israel through the Tapuz program (work in kibbutz, tours, seminars), and other educational tours and study programs.

Buenos Aires was home to several college-level Jewish educational institutions. Michlelet Shazar prepared Hebrew teachers for elementary and secondary schools. Sponsored by the AMIA and the WZO Education Department and academically supervised by the Tel Aviv University, the college had over 200 students. The Seminario Rabinico Latinoamericano of the Conservative movement trained rabbis, teachers, and youth leaders for Conservative congregations in Argentina and throughout Latin America.

ORT, which opened a new school in Buenos Aires, offered educational services to non-Jews as well as Jews. The organization had been successful not only in the area of higher technological education but also in the social and cultural spheres. The director of the Va'ad Hachinuch (the Jewish board of education), J. Barilko, was designated a member of the Honorary Commission of the First National Pedagogic Congress. Jewish educators participated in this congress and in other conferences involving institutions in the private education sector.

Only one Yiddish newspaper, *Di Presse,* continued to appear, several times a week. Several weekly Spanish newspapers, such as *Mundo Israelita, Nueva Sion, La Luz,* and *Nueva Presencia*—under a new publisher, not Herman Schiller—continued to publish.

An interesting phenomenon was the popularity of Israeli culture, especially folkdance groups—often sponsored by clubs or organizations—which performed at public and private functions. A well-attended dance festival took place once a year, as did a "Hassidic" festival (actually featuring many non-Hassidic Israeli and Jewish songs). Jewish Book Month, in September, continued to be an annual cultural event of great importance. Holocaust Memorial Day and Israel Independence Day were occasions for mass gatherings.

The Va'ad Hakehillot, in which the Buenos Aires AMIA was the main partner, continued to help small Jewish communities maintain their functioning. The Jews of La Plata celebrated the 80th anniversary of the creation of the local *kehillah,* while the community of Parana commemorated the 75th anniversary of its central organization.

The Seminario Rabinico Latinoamericano in Buenos Aires celebrated the 25th anniversary of its founding with a series of festive events. Through the Seminario's activity, the Conservative movement had succeeded in creating a new type of religious institution, one that offered an alternative to the basically non-Orthodox Jews of Argentina and other Latin American countries. Graduates of the Seminario headed Conservative congregations in Buenos Aires and several provincial cities.

The celebration of the 90th anniversary of the founding of the Bund party in Argentina (December 1987) had a nostalgic character. The Bund, a socialist-Yiddishist Jewish party, which had once had considerable influence in the development of the Jewish community, was now reduced to a small group of elderly members.

DAVID SCHERS
SHLOMO SLUTZKY

# Brazil

## National Affairs

THE SITUATION IN BRAZIL at the end of 1987 was one of profound crisis. Politically, the transition from dictatorship to democracy could be considered successful, since rule of law, freedom of the press, and civil rights prevailed. However, the country faced crushing social and economic problems that were not being solved and that raised doubts about the viability of the country's future as a stable democracy.

The process of *"abertura"* (opening), which opened the way for democracy at the beginning of the 1980s after 16 years of dictatorship, was mainly the result of the military regime's inability to deal with the economic crisis which its own adventurous plans of the 1970s—for Brazil to become a "big power"—had created. The military were also influenced by pressure from President Jimmy Carter's administration and the mass protests and demonstrations within Brazil which gained steadily in momentum. A key issue was *"diretas,"* direct election of the president, which the press and public opinion demanded, instead of the existing system of presidential selection by members of the National Congress and state legislatures. Although this demand was never met, Tancredo Neves, a popular candidate of the opposition Brazilian Democratic Movement party (PMDB), was elected. The present president, José Sarney, who once belonged to the rightist, promilitary Liberal Front party (PFL), had been added to the presidential slate as vice-presidential candidate in order to achieve a better political balance. Sarney assumed the presidency after Neves became ill and died before taking the oath of office; he set the country in a political direction more conservative than the one the late Neves was expected to follow.

The main achievement of the democratic government was the very fact that it survived. In addition, it successfully brought about the drafting of a socially progressive new constitution, through an open participatory process including presentations to the Constitutional Assembly and its committees by organized groups, among them the Jewish community. Adoption of the constitution had not been completed by the end of 1987, however, due to a dispute over the length of the presidential term of office, which could also affect how long Sarney himself remained in the position.

The Sarney government's "Plan Cruzado" (the name of the new monetary unit) was launched in February 1986. Based on strong control of inflation through price and wage freezes and budgetary restrictions, it produced positive short-term results that helped the PMDB perform well in the November 1986 elections to Congress and the state legislatures. However, many of the controls were abandoned after the election, and there was a return to double-digit monthly inflation. Another cause of the country's financial woes was the huge foreign debt incurred for large-scale development in the 1970s. When debt service depleted foreign reserves, early in 1986 the government decided to partially suspend further payments, which cut off access to new loans.

Social problems became ever more acute, with millions of children suffering from malnutrition and disease and millions of persons living in conditions of extreme poverty in rural areas or in the shantytowns, or *favelas,* of the cities, and urban violence on the increase. At the same time, because of the rapid economic development that had occurred over the previous 20 years, the already wide social gap between rich and poor grew even wider. While capable individuals in the lower and lower-middle classes often had a chance to better themselves, the underlying problems of economic and class structure and distribution of land and income mitigated against foreseeable improvement for the masses.

Because of Sarney's failure to take effective action, opposition to him grew stronger, even within his own party. The economic crisis and the lack of unity within the government and the ruling party in turn fostered a lack of faith in the democratic regime's ability to find solutions to Brazil's woes. Increasing emigration to Australia, Spain, Portugal, and elsewhere were clear and unprecedented indicators of the prevailing mood. Although a return to military rule was not likely, and support for democracy was strong, the result of any further deterioration in the situation was unpredictable.

## Brazil-Israel Relations

The attitude of Brazil toward Israel was complex and far from clear-cut. The central government continued to foster relations with the Arab countries and to observe a correct, cool attitude toward Israel. Its policies essentially followed the principle of "relative pragmatism." Israel's imports from Brazil, worth tens of millions of dollars a year, could not be compared with the billions of dollars of goods and services imported by Arab and Muslim countries, much of this in the form of weapons and the services of Brazilian companies in road building and other construction. Brazil imported 601,000 barrels of oil a day (21 percent from Saudi Arabia), and despite the drop in oil prices, because of its foreign debt, Brazil sought to maintain good relations with the Arab oil-producing countries, which were not only suppliers but also good customers. An additional element was the fact that millions of Brazilians were of Arab origin, some of them increasingly active in pro-Palestinian groups. The Parliamentary League of Arab-Brazilian Friendship and Cooperation, made up of 71 senators and representatives, 54 of them of Arab descent, functioned in effect as an Arab lobby demanding legal status for the PLO in Brazil (at the time, the PLO representative worked within the Arab League embassy). By contrast, there were only around 100,000 Jews in Brazil—and only one Jewish member of the National Congress.

Despite the central government's reserved policy, state governments, trade unions, and other public groups showed interest in increasing ties with Israel and acted accordingly. Some examples of this were: the celebration of Israel's Independence Day as an annual event in several cities; the sponsoring of an Israel Week in the city of Curitiba, capital of the important state of Paraná, on the occasion of the 39th anniversary of the State of Israel, in 1987, despite strong local Arab opposition; the naming of a Ben-Gurion Street in São Paulo, Brazil's biggest city, in November 1987; and an Israel Week held in the state of Goías in December 1987. Local politicians and officials, church, and trade-union leaders visited Israel, among them Bishop Ivo Lorscheiter of São Paulo, president of Brazil's Bishops' Conference, in April 1987, accompanied by Rabbi Henry Sobel, of São Paulo's leading Progressive congregation; and Joaquim dos Santos Andrade (Joaquinzao), the president of the CGT, the central trade-union federation, in November 1987, as a guest of the government and the Histadrut. The latter's attitude contrasted sharply with that of "Lula" (Luis Ignacio Lula da Silva), a member of the Constitutional Assembly and popular union leader, who stated publicly that he would not accept an invitation to visit Israel because of his identification with the PLO cause. In addition, groups of politicians, journalists, and other public figures visited Israel on tours organized by the Rio Jewish Federation. Local Jews encouraged these ties with Israel by initiating and supporting special events and visits by leading figures to Israel.

A high point in Brazil-Israel relations was the opening of new Israeli consular offices in São Paulo in August 1986. Shimon Peres's official visit to Brazil in December 1987 (the first by an Israeli foreign minister since Abba Eban's inauguration of the Israeli embassy in Brasilia, in 1973), during which he met with the highest officials, was viewed as a serious opening for improved relations. However, the eruption of violence in the occupied territories of Israel during the period that Peres was in Brazil created new tensions that neutralized the positive gains that had been made.

On the other side of the equation, in August 1986 an agreement was signed between the PLO and the Methodist University of Piracicaba—located in the interior of the state of São Paulo—for "cooperation and cultural exchange." Both parties declared themselves "dedicated to the democratic, anti-imperialist, anti-Zionist struggle." The Iranian embassy was forced by the Brazilian Foreign Ministry to stop publishing and distributing the "Protocols of the Elders of Zion," based on a 1967 Brazilian law banning that document. The PLO office, which functioned within the embassy of the Arab League, was active in distributing propaganda material and creating ties with Brazilian organizations. Farid Sawan, the PLO representative, was accused of distributing sabotage manuals to members of a union with which the PLO had close relations (Central Unica dos Trabalhadores, with which the above-mentioned Lula was associated) and to the Communist party of Brazil. A poster campaign in the streets of Brazil's major cities was mounted in behalf of Lamia Maraf Hassan, a Brazilian-Palestinian woman sentenced to life in Israel for the murder of an Israeli soldier. Still, while the PLO was visible, from a wider perspective it seemed that that organization's links with terrorism diminished the ability of its representatives to recruit any substantial public support in Brazil.

JEWISH COMMUNITY

*Demography*

The Jerusalem-based demographers U.O. Schmelz and S. DellaPergola estimated the Jewish population of Brazil in 1986 at 100,000 (out of a general population of over 138 million). Past overestimates of well over 100,000 were due mainly to lack of statistical sophistication; however, the present leaders of the community and of some international Jewish organizations were reluctant to accept the reduced figure suggested by the experts.

Recent estimates showed the majority of Brazilian Jews living in São Paulo (over 50,000) and Rio de Janeiro (over 30,000). Pôrto Alegre had fewer than 10,000 Jews; Curitiba, around 2,000; Belo Horizonte, 1,500; Belém, and Brasilia—the new capital—several hundred each. There were Jews in smaller cities as well. The São Paulo Jewish Federation had been active in the previous 10 years offering support to small communities in the state of São Paulo, such as Santos and Campinas.

The general demographic characteristics of Brazilian Jewry matched those of Jews in other Western countries: concentration in urban areas (although in Brazil this was not one main city, such as the capital, as in other countries, but two big cities and other less populated centers); aging of the population; low birthrate; increasing levels of education and income. As a result of these factors, and despite a small influx of Jewish immigrants from Egypt and Hungary in the 1950s, as well as from Israel and other South American countries, the Jewish population appeared to be stable in numbers, while raising its socioeconomic status. The one city with an increasing Jewish population was São Paulo, because of its dynamic economy, but the increase was based on internal migration from other parts of the country. There appeared to be an increase in the number of Brazilian Jews returning from Israel (though figures were not available). The number of Jews settling in Israel remained low, around 200 a year. (In 1985, 173 went on *aliyah* through the Zionist Organization; in 1986, 129; and in 1987, 134. Since others went to Israel as tourists and then decided to settle, the total immigration from Brazil could be estimated at around 200 persons a year.) Brazilian Jews were less sensitive to economic "push" factors than Argentinean Jewry; nevertheless, economic factors seemed to be decisive in most cases.

## Jewish Status and Identity

In Brazil, as in other developing countries, the lack of general economic development created conditions that enabled minority groups from Europe, the Middle East, and the Far East, including Jews, to advance rapidly, professionally and financially, and to enjoy greater access to higher education and other benefits than the citizenry as a whole.

For the majority of the Jewish community, the economic expansion and even the generally negative inflationary economic conditions prevailing during long periods of the previous 20 years had provided opportunities for economic advancement. Jews continued to move to better dwellings in better areas of the main cities, some of which offered private police protection, an important guarantor of well-being in the prevailing conditions of urban unrest and crime. As in other Latin American countries, many of those who had improved their economic status during the dictatorship tended to accept the regime, arguing that there was no other alternative to terrorism and leftist upheaval. Also, as in other countries and communities, these attitudes of many of the affluent, coupled with the organized Jewish community's failure to offer meaningful criticism of the government's human-rights violations, added to the alienation of liberal and leftist intellectuals and youth. Rabbi Henry Sobel, who was active in interfaith activities and also openly critical of human-rights violations, was a notable exception, as was Ronaldo Gomlevsky, president of the Jewish Federation of Rio de Janeiro. They, and a few others, served as a focus of identification for many of the estranged. (The criticism by some of Sobel's social activism, based on his enjoying the privilege of American citizenship, was similar to that voiced against Rabbi Marshall Meyer in Argentina.)

Liberal and leftist intellectuals and youth were further alienated by the complete identification (as they saw it) of the organized Jewish community with all the policies of the government of Israel, even in cases in which public opinion in Israel itself was sharply divided. This aloofness, in turn, served to accelerate the processes leading to assimilation. (A different reaction, active rather than passive, was that of a group critical of Israeli government policies that formed a local branch of the Israeli Peace Now movement.)

As elsewhere in the Diaspora, individual Jews faced problems of defining their Jewish identity and giving their links to the Jewish people concrete and positive expression. In Brazil these problems had a special character, owing to the powerful attraction of a tolerant, multiracial, culturally open society that displayed little anti-Semitism but that exerted both overt and subtle pressures for absolute loyalty to the country. These conditions, together with the opportunities for personal, professional, and economic advancement, made assimilation a pressing practical dilemma for many individuals and families and presented the community and its institutions with a major challenge.

Unlike Jewish politicians in Argentina, Brazilian Jewish politicians stressed their Jewishness in the hope of winning Jewish support and votes, even if the Jewish proportion of the electorate was not substantial. (This was part of a general social trend; members of spiritualist "macumba" groups, for example, also stressed their "religious" affiliation.) In politics, Jews had more influence than their numbers would indicate, because of their high status in the economic, social, and intellectual realms. In local elections, in areas in which Jews were concentrated, and because of the literacy qualification for voting, their votes weighed more heavily than their percentage in the population. Still, Jewish candidates for state and local office could not rely only on Jewish support. They ran on a variety of issues and had their own "clients," frequently—as was common in Brazilian "personalist-paternalist-patronage" politics—in poor areas, including *favelas,* where hundreds of thousands of poor people, mostly recent arrivals from rural areas, built their primitive huts and lived in extreme poverty.

## Communal Affairs

As in Argentina, the Jewish community was predominantly secular. In recent years, however, small ultra-Orthodox groups (mainly Chabad), on one side of the spectrum, and Reform and Conservative congregations, on the other side, continued to expand the alternatives available to those who did not find their place either in traditional Orthodoxy or in completely secular activities and frameworks.

Many Jews, including children, attended the big Jewish sport and social centers, such as Hebraica and Macabi. The Zionist youth movements had smaller numbers of members than in the past.

Jewish communal life continued to be organized along traditional Zionist party lines. In the 1987 elections for representatives to the World Zionist Congress, the Labor Zionists (Labor Alignment and Mapam) sent five delegates, and the other five places were distributed among other Zionist parties.

The Jewish federations in each state, united nationally under the Jewish Confederation of Brazil, were the roof organizations for all Jewish institutions in each state. Although the federation had started out as a political body, like the Argentinean DAIA, it aspired to a broader *"kehillah"* role, like that of the Argentinean AMIA. However, unlike Argentina, where the Hevra Kadisha (the burial society) was the central financial body in the community and basically supported the *kehillah's* activities, in Brazil the federations depended for their support on the Fundo Comunal, a joint fund-raising appeal for local needs. In some cases competition between the federation and Unificada (the Zionist Organization) created tensions, as when the Rio federation organized visits to Israel for local politicians, a function considered by Unificada to be in its domain. The federation in Rio, under the leadership of Ronaldo Gomlevsky, in fact had become the center of power within the local community.

The tension between the federations and Unificada was not unlike that in Argentina between "modernizers," who stressed local needs, and "ideologues," for whom Israel and traditional Zionist political issues were paramount. The state federations and Zionist organizations, especially those of São Paulo, Rio, and other main cities, tended to be more influential than the national roof bodies and were frequently competitive with each other. In this respect they followed the national Brazilian pattern, which stressed federalist-decentralized tendencies rather than the centralized pattern of other Latin American countries.

In São Paulo, the CIP (Congregação Israelita Paulista), led by Rabbi Henry Sobel, and in Rio de Janeiro the ARI (Associação Religiosa Israelita), led by Rabbi Roberto Graetz, were the largest non-Orthodox congregations. Both rabbis were active in interfaith activities and in behalf of civil rights. "Shalom" was a new Reform congregation developing in São Paulo. Although many small Orthodox synagogues were to be found in the main Jewish areas, attendance at religious services was generally low, except during the High Holy Days, when it increased dramatically. As in other Latin American communities, the Jews of Brazil expressed their Jewish identity mainly through cultural, social, and Zionist activities.

In the area of Jewish education, no major changes had taken place since the early 1980s. Out of an estimated 22,000 Jewish children aged 3 to 18, over 10,000 attended Jewish schools, almost all of them all-day institutions. The high proportion of enrollment in Jewish schools reflected the important place of private education in Brazil generally, especially for the middle and upper classes. Public, government-run schools which served the lower classes, had high rates of drop-outs and repeaters. Most of those Jewish children who did not attend Jewish schools attended other private schools. The Jewish schools, which maintained high standards of instruction, especially in the general subjects, were independent bodies. They received some communal support but were mainly financed by parents and interested groups of lay leaders who identified with the ideological character of a particular school— secular, traditional, or religious, more or less Zionist, and so on. The majority of schools were not Orthodox, but defined themselves as "traditional."

A board of Jewish education, the Va'ad Hachinuch, existed in cities with several schools (Rio and São Paulo), offering various services and distributing some financial help to the schools with funds received from the Chevra Kadisha or the Fundo Comunal. Some of the teachers were locally trained and received further training in Israel, mostly at the Machon Greenberg in Jerusalem. The role of Israeli teachers and advisers, who were sent through the World Zionist Organization education departments, was crucial in the area of Jewish studies. A central problem was the gap between the high level of attention paid to general studies—the ground on which competition took place with other Jewish and non-Jewish private schools—and the relatively low status of Jewish studies, especially in the higher grades. Still, the Jewish schools served as centers of Jewish social and cultural life for the Brazilian Jewish communities, and contributed to fostering—along with the family and other Jewish institutions—Jewish identity and links to the Jewish people and Israel.

## Jewish-Christian Relations

Although Brazilian Jewry was largely nonreligious, interfaith activities were understood by most Jews to enhance the prestige and position of the community within the general society, at the same time helping the Jewish people worldwide and the State of Israel. The pluralistic character of Brazilian society—the majority of its people Catholics but with a substantial minority of Protestant and spiritualist groups—combined with the progressive character of the Church leadership, provided a context conducive to successful collaboration and educational work between Jews and the Catholic Church. Bishop Lorscheiter's visit to Israel, mentioned above as an example of nongovernmental relationships with Israel, grew out of a process that had begun in 1981, when the National Commission for Jewish Catholic Dialogue was created. The process reached a high point with the first Pan-American Conference on Catholic-Jewish Relations, held in São Paulo in November 1985, which was attended by influential Catholic and Jewish representatives and theologians from all over Latin America. The sponsors of the meeting were the Brazilian Bishops' Conference (CNBB) and the American Jewish Committee, and the occasion, the 20th anniversary of "Nostra Aetate," the Vatican declaration on the Jewish people. Among the resolutions adopted was one stating that "Zionism is not racism," repudiating the infamous UN resolution of 1975.

The National Commission published a 187-page "Guide for Catholic-Jewish Dialogue in Brazil" and distributed it to all Catholic communities. The guide contained sections on the history of the Jewish people, anti-Semitism, the Holocaust, and how to deal with problems of prejudice. Among both Catholics and Jews some elements had reservations about the dialogue process—Orthodox Jews on the one hand, and Catholics who opposed the liberal, progressive attitudes of the CNBB in general, not only in regard to relations with the Jews. The Orthodox boycotted the 1985 conference because of the presence of Bishop Jean Lustiger of Paris, a converted Jew.

DAVID SCHERS
SHLOMO SLUTZKY

# Western Europe

## Great Britain

### National Affairs

THE DOMINANT POLITICAL EVENT of 1987 was the Conservative victory in the general election in June. Margaret Thatcher entered an unprecedented third term as prime minister with a total of 375 seats, giving her a slightly reduced majority over the previous term. Labor won 229 seats, a small increase; and the Liberal–Social Democratic Alliance, 22, a slight drop. While the results clearly confirmed the success of the "Thatcher revolution" among the enlarged middle class, they also revealed the ongoing divisions in British society, geographic and economic. The Conservatives scored heavily in London, southern England, and the Midlands, while Labor was strong in economically depressed areas in Wales, Scotland, and the north. In the election aftermath, the two parties constituting the Alliance, i.e., the Liberals and the Social Democrats, decided to go their separate ways, amid mutual recriminations, although an attempt was made by part of the Social Democrats to merge with the Liberals. On the Labor side, its third successive defeat gave impetus to a major reconsideration of traditional party policies.

The Tory victory reflected satisfaction with a generally improved economy. In March the chancellor of the exchequer was able to reduce income taxes without imposing any further taxes on gasoline, tobacco, or liquor. Unemployment, which had reached 3.25 million in February, declined by the end of the year to 2.8 million, less than 10 percent of the working population. During the whole year there were fewer than 1,000 separate strikes—for only the second time since 1940.

The number of Jews elected to Parliament fell to 23 (16 Conservative and 7 Labor) from 28 (17 Conservative, 11 Labor). In an analysis of the election and Jewish voting patterns, Prof. Ivor Crewe, head of Essex University's department of government, told the Board of Deputies of British Jews that the community had gradually moved to the political right since Jewish support for Labor peaked in the 1940s. Labor had become more hostile to Israel, he said, and now included some "virulently anti-Zionist tendencies," while the Tory party had moved the other way. The prospect was of a widening gap between the Jewish community and the Labor party, Crewe maintained, as the party was increasingly perceived as anti-Zionist and the Jewish community as non-Labor. Also, since the Jewish community was "largely middle class and prosperous," Crewe told the *Jewish Chronicle,* it was not surprising that it voted mostly Conservative.

A mini-opinion poll conducted after the June election in Finchley, North London, by Geoffrey Alderman of London University's Royal Holloway and Bedford College, suggested that three out of five Jews in that district had voted Conservative, one Labor and one Alliance. The results indicated a small shift away from the Alliance to the Conservatives.

## *Relations with Israel*

British criticism of Israel's handling of the occupied territories was the major irritant in a relationship otherwise characterized by amity and goodwill. In January Foreign Secretary Sir Geoffrey Howe warned that Israel could not indefinitely ignore the aspirations and frustrations of the two million Palestinians under its occupation without damaging the democratic values of Israeli society. In August new Foreign Office minister of state David Mellor, meeting with representatives of the Board of Deputies of British Jews, raised the question of conditions in the occupied territories resulting from the Israeli occupation. In December, on the eve of visiting Israel, Mellor stated that the government had registered serious concern at the upsurge in violent incidents, especially in Gaza, with the Israeli authorities. In an exclusive interview with the *Jewish Chronicle* in December, Prime Minister Thatcher appealed to Israel and the Arabs to show restraint in dealing with the disturbances and move forward to peace talks.

The government continued to advocate an international conference as the most practical way forward to negotiations between the parties directly concerned in the Arab-Israeli dispute. Foreign Secretary Howe saw the conference as a framework within which negotiations would take place, but without having the power to impose solutions. The government urged this position to Middle Eastern leaders who visited London during the year: King Hussein of Jordan; Osama el-Baz, adviser to President Hosni Mubarak, and Boutros Ghah, minister of state at the Egyptian Foreign Ministry; King Hassan of Morocco; and Israeli foreign minister and vice premier Shimon Peres, who met with Mrs. Thatcher in January, June, and November.

In December Israeli president Chaim Herzog was received by Queen Elizabeth and by Mrs. Thatcher, who described Israeli-British relations as better than they had ever been. Peace for Israel, she said, "can be obtained if we follow the lead set by men of courage—Arab and Israeli alike—who have shown a way ahead through peaceful negotiations in the framework of an international conference . . . ."

During his visit Herzog was made an honorary "bencher" of Lincoln's Inn, and an honorary fellow of University College, London, where he had studied. He had tea with the Lord Chancellor and met leading intellectuals, industrialists, and publishers. The high point of his visit was a dinner at London's Guildhall, organized by the Joint Israel Appeal (JIA) in association with the Board of Deputies, State of Israel Bonds, the Zionist Federation (ZF), and the National Zionist Council, to launch Israel's 40th-anniversary celebrations.

Britain rejected attempts by King Fahd of Saudi Arabia, in London in March, and by King Hussein in April, to persuade it to resume diplomatic relations with Syria, which it had broken off the previous fall. Syria, Mrs. Thatcher argued, had not proved that it had abandoned terrorism as state policy.

In April Saudi Arabia became the first foreign country to acquire the Alarm air-launched, antiradar missile for defending attacking aircraft, part of its £5-billion deal with British Aerospace. In August Israel expressed objection to the sale, on the ground that even if arms were sold to "nonconfrontation" states, there was no guarantee of their ultimate destination.

In the campaign preceding the general election, the Labor party promised "to actively seek stable peace which protects the security of Israel and recognizes the rights of the Palestinians to self-determination." Labor leader Neil Kinnock told the *Jewish Chronicle* that he would be prepared to meet PLO leaders if such a meeting helped to advance the peace process. At a pro-Palestinian caucus during the Labor party conference in September, opposition foreign secretary Gerald Kaufman, sharing a platform with the PLO's London spokesman, called on Israel to accept the PLO as the representative of the Palestinians.

Some signs of trade-union disaffection with Israel were evident during the year. At its June Blackpool conference, the National and Local Government Officers' Association (NALGO) voted to end its affiliations with the Trade Union Friends of Israel (TUFI) and Histadrut (the Israeli trade union movement). A group of pro-Israel NALGO members pledged to fight the decision. The conference also passed a motion appealing for a clear policy of opposition to all forms of Zionism and a campaign to support the struggle of the people of Palestine for liberation and freedom from oppression. Police were called to the conference when the director of Labor Friends of Israel (LFI) was physically intimidated by supporters of the National Black Members' Coordinating Committee. In October NALGO dismissed a branch administrator accused of being a hard-line Nazi. Elsewhere in the labor sector, the Trade Union Congress (TUC) passed a Fire Brigades Union motion condemning Israeli harassment of trade unions in the occupied territories, welcomed the European Community's call for a UN-sponsored Middle East peace conference, and described the PLO as the legitimate representative of the Palestinian people.

At a conference in March, the National Organization of Labor Students (NOLS) called for increased support for the Palestine Solidarity Campaign, speaking tours by people "involved in the liberation struggle," and twinning with West Bank universities. An effort by supporters of Israel in NOLS to pass an amendment declaring that Zionism expressed the legitimate right of the Jewish people to their homeland was defeated. However, Jewish students prevented the National Union of Students' conference in December from adopting NOLS's proposal for a pro-Palestinian policy.

## Nazi War Criminals

In March, in response to repeated calls from the Board of Deputies of British Jews for government investigation of suspected Nazi war criminals living in Britain, Home Secretary Douglas Hurd promised that inquiries would be initiated. This decision was influenced, as well, by meetings with American rabbis Marvin Hier and Abraham Cooper of the Simon Wiesenthal Center, which in 1986 had given the government a list of 17 suspected Nazi war criminals living in Britain. Members of the All-Party Parliamentary War-Crimes Group agreed with government policy not to release the names. "Our first priority is to see that no injustice is done to innocent individuals," said the group chairman, former home secretary Merlyn Rees. "It must be up to the Home Secretary to decide if there is sufficient evidence for further action to be taken." Further impetus for government action on war crimes was provided by revelations in the media about Antanas Gecas (formerly Gecevicius), aged 70, then living in Edinburgh, who was allegedly involved in atrocities when serving with the 12th Lithuanian Police Battalion in 1942–43. In addition, in October the antifascist monthly magazine *Searchlight* gave the home secretary dossiers on the alleged wartime activities of Latvian Paul Reinhards, living in Gravesend, Kent, and in December on Lithuanian Antas Derzinskas, a resident of Nottingham.

In October a rally at Manchester University Union launched a campaign by *Searchlight* and the Union of Jewish Students (UJS), backed by the National Union of Students (NUS), to change the law prohibiting prosecution of persons who were not British citizens at the time alleged crimes were committed. The campaign continued in November when 450 students from all over Britain came to London to lobby MPs on the subject. That month Hurd told a delegation from the All-Party Parliamentary War Crimes Group that he was considering an amendment to the Criminal Justice Bill, then before Parliament, to extend British jurisdiction retroactively to crimes by Nazis. He ruled out the possibility of extradition to the Soviet Union as a means of dealing with the problem. The Russians had requested such a procedure, since most of the alleged crimes had been committed in their territory. (Britain had no extradition treaties with either the USSR or Israel.) In November the American government offered to help the Home Office with investigations of accused Nazis.

JEWISH COMMUNITY

## Demography

The Jewish population of Great Britain was estimated at 330,000.

Figures for synagogue marriages continued to decline, from 1,144 in 1985 to 1,097 in 1986, the lowest total of the century, according to the Statistical and Demographic Research Unit (renamed the Community Research Unit in May) of the

Board of Deputies of British Jews. Of the 1986 total, 867 were performed under Orthodox auspices (compared with 891 in 1985); 160, Reform (169); and 70, Liberal (84 in 1985).

The number of burials and cremations under Jewish religious auspices in 1986, 4,838, was almost unchanged from 1985 (4,844). They comprised 3,906 Orthodox burials (3,905 in 1985); 580 Reform (551); and 352 Liberal (388 in 1985).

As before, roughly three-quarters of synagogue marriages were celebrated in London, indicating that city's centrality in Jewish life. Approximately 66 percent of all burials and cremations were recorded in London.

The London Beth Din was handling over 200 divorces annually, compared with 100 a few years earlier. Because of the rising divorce rate and increased demand for its services, the Jewish Marriage Council, a counseling agency for couples and families, appointed its first full-time director, thus freeing counselors from administrative duties.

## Community Relations

Chief Rabbi Sir Immanuel Jakobovits continued to press for practical Jewish involvement in helping to relieve Britain's inner-city problems. In March he appointed Alan Greenbat to devise a specifically Jewish project to help alleviate the situation. "We should produce an opportunity-offering project for disadvantaged young people with ability," Greenbat told the *Jewish Chronicle*. Two Board of Deputies committees were already engaged in related activities: its central Jewish lecture and information committee recommended that the board highlight any urban difficulties affecting the Jewish community; a committee under Sir Sigmund Sternberg was considering programs through which Anglo-Jewry could help in the wider community, such as adopting and helping regenerate a specific inner-city area. A four-month Jewish heritage festival was held in London's East End in the summer, helping to call attention to past cultural achievements of this disadvantaged inner-city area.

On a number of occasions throughout the year the chief rabbi publicly criticized the government's AIDS campaign, because it focused on means of avoiding sex-related problems instead of seeking to instill solid marital values.

On Holocaust Memorial Day, in April, the word "Perdition" was scrawled on the Holocaust memorial in London's Hyde Park, hours before a special service was to be conducted there by the chief rabbi. The reference was undoubtedly to Jim Allen's controversial play *Perdition,* whose opening several months earlier at the Royal Court Theater in London had been canceled in the wake of public protest. The play, based on the 1954 Kastner libel case in Israel, charged the Zionists with collaborating with the Nazis in wartime Budapest. Despite widespread debate over the play's historical accuracy, and a pending libel action brought against the play's publisher, Ithaca Press, by Nathan Dror, head of the Jewish Rescue Committee in Switzerland during the war, a book version of *Perdition* was published in July and a shortened version was read publicly in Edinburgh, amid demonstrations organized by the Board of Deputies and the Union of Jewish Students.

In June Lionel Kopelowitz, Board of Deputies president, conveyed to the Papal Nuncio in Britain the community's outrage at Kurt Waldheim's reception in Rome by Pope John Paul.

The Board of Deputies expressed concern, in May, that former members of the extreme-right National Front (NF) were running as Conservative party candidates in the elections. Robin Corbett, Labor MP, presented a motion in the House of Commons expressing regret over the party's "infiltration by extremists," but Norman Tebbit, Conservative party chairman, said that the party was "sufficiently strong to withstand any attempt at infiltration." Protests by the Board of Deputies and the Conservative Friends of Israel (CFI) caused Jean-Marie Le Pen, leader of France's National Front party, to cancel plans to address a caucus during the Conservatives' Blackpool conference in October. He had been invited by Jewish businessman Sir Alfred Sherman on behalf of Policy Search, a right-wing think tank.

NF Remembrance Day parades, to the Cenotaph in London and in the city of York, were banned after appeals by the Association of Jewish Ex-Servicemen and Women (AJEX) and the Board of Deputies.

## Communal Activities

The Board of Deputies' executive approved a reorganization plan that would cut the number of deputies from 667 to around 460, beginning in the 1988 session. The plan called for reducing the numbers of deputies representing both individual synagogues and the main synagogue organizations, such as the United Synagogue (US), and for eliminating Commonwealth community representation, except from Gibraltar. Conversely, the representation of youth and women was increased.

The board announced plans in November to raise an endowment fund of between £5 and £10 million for a community center in London to house its offices and the Jewish Museum and to provide facilities for cultural and educational activities. The board hoped to be able to purchase Woburn House, in London, from the United Synagogue, for this purpose.

In a move to achieve greater efficiency, in June the four largest Jewish welfare agencies—the Jewish Welfare Board (JWB), Jewish Blind Society (JBS), Norwood Childcare, and the Ravenswood Foundation—united to form the Federation of Jewish Family Services. Their combined annual budget of around £16 million accounted for over 70 percent of communal expenditure on welfare services. The agencies would retain their independence and identity but would increasingly draw on "a combined central resource, planning and development unit." They already worked closely together, had many common services and facilities, and shared offices in a building in Golders Green, North-West London. In September Ravenswood, which specialized in the care of the mentally handicapped, took over from JWB the administration of the Haven Foundation for mildly mentally handicapped adults in North London. JWB, which specialized in caring for the elderly and those recovering from mental illness, in June opened 17 sheltered apartments for the elderly at Westcliff, in conjunction with Southend and Westcliff B'nai B'rith. A £1.65-million sheltered housing development, consisting of 32 apartments, was dedicated in November in Finchley, North London. It was sponsored by JBS and the Jewish Association for the Physically Handicapped, which announced that the two organizations would merge resources starting in January 1988, with full integration planned by the end of 1990. The nonprofit South-West Region Jewish Housing Society, founded in 1984 and representing nine synagogues of all denominations, opened sheltered housing for 70 elderly in Kingston, Surrey, in June. In September the final stage of the AJEX House complex in Stamford Hill was completed, providing 50 sheltered apartments for aged Jewish war veterans. In the same month the Association of Jewish Refugees opened a day center in North-West London, and in November a new wing comprising 17 rooms was opened at Heinrich Stahl House for Jewish victims of Nazi oppression.

A Jewish National AIDS Coordinating Council was formed in November. Its purpose was to raise awareness of the disease and its implications and to support efforts to prevent its spread.

## Soviet Jewry

The government's continuing concern over Soviet treatment of Jews was high on the agenda when Prime Minister Thatcher and Foreign Secretary Howe met in December with General Secretary Mikhail Gorbachev and Foreign Minister Eduard Shevardnadze of the USSR, during their stopover in England en route to a summit meeting in Washington. The government used every possible opportunity during the year to press for a change in the Soviet policy toward Jews wishing to leave the Soviet Union.

In January Timothy Renton, minister of state in the Foreign Office, visited veteran refusenik Alexander Lerner in Moscow. All political parties welcomed Thatcher's statement, after she visited Moscow in April, where she met with refuseniks, that her goal was to achieve freer movement for those wishing to leave and greater religious freedom for those wishing to stay. In July the European Parliament member for Dorset East and Hampshire West, Bryan Cassidy, handed a letter to the naval attaché at the Soviet embassy calling on him to allow Prisoners of Zion to leave the USSR. In August Cassidy visited refuseniks in Russia on behalf of the Bournemouth Council for Soviet Jewry. Also in August, John Marshall, Conservative MP for Hendon South and Euro MP for London North, raised the case of 99-year-old refusenik Zalman Apterman with Howe and the Russian authorities.

The 35s, the women's campaign for Soviet Jewry, persuaded several trade unions to adopt refuseniks: NALGO adopted Victor and Batsheva Yelistratov of Moscow; the Inland Revenue Staff Federation campaigned for Vladimir and Masha Slepak; the Electrical Electronic Telecommunications and Plumbing Union adopted Mikhail Shipov; and the Transport and General Workers' Union (TGWU), the Kremen family. In July the British Medical Association conference passed a resolution expressing grave concern for Jewish doctors in Russia, who were persecuted after applying for exit visas.

The year saw visits to England from a number of former refuseniks: Galina Nabati, who addressed the JIA national assembly at London's Royalty Theater, in January; Dr. Vladimir Brodsky, a guest of the Medical Committee for Soviet Jewry, in March; Dima Ioffee, performer in the television documentary *No Exit,* who attended a June showing organized by the 35s and Conscience to draw attention to the second generation of refuseniks; Zakhar Zunshain, who addressed a rally in London's Hyde Park on Refusenik Sunday in July. In October Prime Minister Thatcher received Misha Taratuta in Blackpool. In November Viktor Brailovsky and his wife addressed several important bodies: a press conference organized by Scientists for the Release of Soviet Refuseniks; members of the All-Party Parliamentary Committee for the Release of Soviet Jewry; and the National Council for Soviet Jewry. The Soviet scientist received an honorary doctorate from the Open University.

At a demonstration in March, 2,500 people formed a human chain linking the Soviet and Israeli embassies, both in Kensington, West London. Demonstrations accompanied the performances of the Bolshoi Ballet Company in London and Manchester in July and August, and the Bolshoi Orchestra in Edinburgh. An intensive campaign by the Cherwell/Oxford Campaign for Soviet Jewry helped to win the release of refusenik Boris Nadgorny in November. In December British WIZO members delivered a petition with 4,000 signatures to the Soviet embassy, as part of a campaign to gain freedom for Evgeny Levin and his family.

## *Religion*

Chief Rabbi Jakobovits remained convinced that the only way to preserve the "oneness" of the Jewish people was for the Progressives to accept the definition of a Jew according to Halakhah, Jewish law. The problem of diversity, he said, had "assumed catastrophic proportions," and if not solved, could lead to irreparable schism. His statement was in response to a proposal made by Rabbi Sidney Brichto, director of the Union of Liberal and Progressive Synagogues (ULPS), that an Orthodox Beth Din formulate regulations enabling all denominations to achieve standard practice in conversion, divorce, and other matters of family law. Both ULPS and the Reform Synagogues of Great Britain (RSGB) indicated their willingness to discuss means to diminish differences between the various religious sections of Anglo-Jewry.

In February the United Synagogue (US) approved several significant constitutional changes. One would prevent officers from serving for over six consecutive years in one post; another redefined the membership rules to give women equal status with men. In May, for the first time, women were candidates in elections to newly created US management councils. In April the Congregation of Spanish and Portuguese Jews, in London, changed its constitution to give members' wives full membership rights, including voting power.

In February the US sold its oldest synagogue, the New Synagogue in Stamford Hill (North London), after membership fell to below 270 from a peak of 2,000 in the 1950s. The premises were to be used for educational purposes by the Bobover Hassidim. In December the East London Synagogue was sold for similar reasons. By contrast, a new synagogue was dedicated in Maidenhead in July, to house a congregation serving Berkshire and Buckinghamshire that had grown in five years from 80 to 400 families.

In September Rabbi Cyril Harris of St. John's Wood (North-West London) Synagogue accepted an invitation to become chief rabbi of South Africa.

The Orthodox Federation of Synagogues celebrated its centenary in October. The body comprised 15 constituent and 20 affiliated synagogues throughout London, with only four in the East End and the most active in Ilford and Edgware.

The Orthodox and Progressive movements both announced forthcoming publication of new prayer books. The former planned to issue a revised edition of Rev. Simeon Singer's Authorized Prayer Book of the United Hebrew Congregations of the British Commonwealth of Nations. Publication in the early 1990s would coincide with the 100th anniversary of the first edition and the 120th anniversary of the founding of the US. A new ULPS prayer book, edited by Rabbi John Rayner, was scheduled to replace *Service of the Heart,* which had been in existence for 20 years.

In November the government rejected a proposal by the government-appointed Farm Animals Welfare Council (FAWC) for compulsory stunning of animals before slaughter. The measure would have prohibited kosher slaughter (*shehitah*), which did not permit prestunning. In explaining the government's position, Agriculture Minister John MacGregor noted that *shehitah* was a fundamental obligation of Judaism that was not open to alteration.

Rabbi Jeremy Conway became the first director of the new Kashrut Division of the London Beth Din. In addition to promoting *kashrut* and existing *kashrut* facilities, he would work to broaden the range of kosher products on the market and increase kosher supervision of food producers.

*Education*

A new board of education replaced the old London Board of Jewish Religious Education, an autonomous body of nearly 300 members, financed by the Orthodox United Synagogue. The new board comprised 12 local community representatives elected by the US council, three US rabbis, the chief rabbi, the head of the London Beth Din, and three others. Its chairman was automatically one of the US's nine officers. In addition to overseeing the formal schooling offered in its part-time centers and three Jewish day schools, the board supervised US's youth programs and adult education. The US allocated over £1.8 million from its 1988 budget of £3.7

million for educational activities, 23 percent more than in 1987. The increase would be covered by a Rosh Hashanah education appeal. The first such appeal in 1986 had raised over £100,000.

A major recruitment and training program to improve the quality of senior personnel in Jewish education was announced in October. Sponsored jointly by the Jerusalem-based Jewish Agency's education department and the British Jewish Educational Development Trust (JEDT), the program was open to the whole spectrum of educational groups, from Progressive to ultra- Orthodox. The aim was to train people already in Jewish education as well as to recruit Jewish teachers currently employed in the non-Jewish sector, in order to fill between 40 and 60 senior posts in Jewish education that would become vacant in the next few years. The Institute of Jewish Education, established at Jews' College in 1984 to provide Orthodox teacher training and develop educational material for use in Jewish schools, appointed an Israeli, Haim Weinreb, as its first full-time director, in December. In July Jews' College broadened its joint B.Ed. course with the Polytechnic of North London to train secondary, as well as primary, teachers specialized in Jewish studies. Over 80 students registered for Jews' College courses in October, the highest enrollment in several years. More than 50 were enrolled in postgraduate and undergraduate programs; 30 studied for part-time cantorial qualifications.

The Center for Jewish Education, established by the RSGB at the Sternberg Center, Finchley, North London, in 1986, this year took over and incorporated the education departments of ULPS and the Leo Baeck College. The center was funded by the Advancement of Jewish Education Trust.

An independent educational trust was established in November, associated with the Board of Deputies, for the purpose of perpetuating the memory of the Holocaust. The group's first project was to be a traveling exhibition.

In February Cambridge University, whose Faculty of Oriental Studies had introduced a one-year postgraduate course in Hebrew studies, appointed its first lecturer in modern Hebrew. In July Lancaster University appointed Rabbi Dr. Louis Jacobs to a three-year visiting professorship in its religious studies department. On the other hand, the Bearsted Readership in Jewish Studies at Warwick University lapsed for lack of funds. University College, London, received gifts of two large private collections of Jewish books.

## Zionism and Aliyah

Elections to the World Zionist Congress, held in December, generated considerable conflict and confusion. The US affiliated with the Zionist Federation (ZF) in August, but withdrew the following month after the World Zionist Organization (WZO) in Jerusalem ruled that US members could not vote for Britain's delegates to the congress unless they had individually signed the Jerusalem Program. After months of wrangling, Pro-Zion, the Progressive movement's party, withdrew its insistence on elections "to bring democracy back to the Zionist movement," thus enabling British Zionist parties to reach an agreement on allocation of delegates without costly elections.

Poale Zion (PZ) chairman Ian Mikardo, MP, and Steve Erlick, editor of PZ's publication *Vanguard,* resigned in February over "persistent blocking of attempts to restructure the movement." "The majority of PZ branches," said Erlick, "are still inactive and moribund." In April Sidney Shipton resigned as director of the Jewish National Fund in Britain. In September the board of the Britain-Israel Public Affairs Committee (BIPAC) expressed unanimous support for its director, Jane Moonman, after charges of alleged irregularities against her had been disproved. Her husband, Eric Moonman, resigned from the board when faced with similar charges. The Joint Israel Appeal continued as BIPAC's major supporter, after assurances were given that the group had taken steps to rectify a lack of administrative control.

In March the ZF launched a campaign to have the 1975 UN resolution equating Zionism with racism amended or rescinded. A motion in the House of Commons to this effect was proposed by Reg Freeson, MP.

In October the British Aliya Movement joined the ZF as an observer for a provisional six months. About 750 Britains immigrated to Israel in 1987, compared with 776 in 1986, according to figures issued by the Aliyah Department of the WZO.

## Publications

Solicitor Ellis Birk became the new chairman of the *Jewish Chronicle,* succeeding David Kessler, who had been chairman since 1958. Recipients of the H. H. Wingate literary awards for 1987 were Israeli author Aharon Appelfeld for *The Age of Wonders* (fiction), and Italian-born Dan Vittorio Segre for *Memoirs of a Fortunate Jew* (nonfiction). The 1986 awards had been given to Conor Cruise O'Brien for *The Siege: The Saga of Israel and Zionism* (nonfiction) and David Pryce-Jones for *The Afternoon Sun* (fiction).

Noteworthy religious studies published this year were *Tradition and Transition,* essays presented to the chief rabbi to celebrate 20 years in office, edited by Jonathan Sacks; *A Jewish Book of Common Prayer* by Chaim Raphael; *The Ship Has a Captain: Judaism, Faith and Reason* by Julian G. Jacobs; *I Promise I Will Try Not to Kick My Sister (and Other Sermons)* by Progressive Rabbi Frank Hellner.

Dovid Katz published a *Grammar of the Yiddish Language,* and Tudor Parfitt produced *The Thirteenth Gate: Travels Among the Lost Tribes of Israel. Modern Hebrew Literature in English Translation,* edited by Leon Yudkin, was the first book published in Britain by the British committee of the International Center for University Teaching of Jewish Civilization, based in Jerusalem.

New historical works included *Fascism in Britain, a History, 1918–1985* by Richard Thurlow; *The Violent Society,* essays edited by Eric Moonman; *Turning Back the Pages: A Chronicle of Calcutta Jewry* by E.D. Ezra; and *A History of the Jews* by Paul Johnson. New works on local Jewish history included *Aspects of Scottish Jewry,* edited by Kenneth Collins; *Tales of Manchester Jewry* and *Manches-*

*ter in the Thirties* by Monty Dobkin; *Down in the East End,* an illustrated anthology, edited by Peter Marcan; *Story of the Grimsby Jewish Community* by Daphne and Leon Gerlis; and *Portsmouth Jewry, 1930s to 1980s* by Aubrey Weinberg.

Among new works on Palestine and Israel were *The Modern-day Conflict of Arab and Jew* by David Smith; *Arab and Jew: Wounded Spirits in a Promised Land* by David K. Shipler; *The Zealous Intruders: The Western Rediscovery of Palestine* and *The Mayor and the Citadel: Teddy Kollek and Jerusalem* by Naomi Shepherd; *The Railways of Palestine and Israel* by Paul Cotterell; *The Arab Jewish Conflict* by J.R. Gainsborough; and *The Making of Resolution 242* by Sidney D. Bailey.

Two new books on the Holocaust were *The Holocaust Denial: Antisemitism and the New Right* by Gill Seidel; and *The Italians and the Holocaust* by Susan Zuccotti.

Biographies published this year included *A Family Patchwork: Five Generations of an Anglo-Jewish Family* by Ruth Sebag-Montefiore; *Chaim Weizmann* by Norman Rose; *Victor Gollancz* by Ruth Dudley Edwards; *A Captive Lion,* a biography of Marina Tsvetayeva, by Elaine Feinstein, who also translated her *Selected Poems; Diaspora Blues,* Clive Sinclair's collection of essays and reflections; *Arnold Daghani* by Monica Bohm-Duchen; *Jack Kid Berg—The Whitechapel Windmill* by John Harding with Jack Berg; and *Don't Ask the Price* by Marcus Sieff.

New works of fiction published in 1987 included *Her Story* by Dan Jacobson; *Our Father* by Bernice Rubens; *Titch* and *The Companion* by Chaim Bermant; *The Fifth Generation* by Karen Gershon; *The Inventor* by Jacov Lind; *Summers of the Wild Rose* by Rosemary Harris; *Angel Cake* by Helen Harris; *A Sport of Nature* by Nadine Gordimer; *To the City* by Gillian Tyndall; and *Live in Peace,* the third part of Rosemary Friedman's trilogy.

Poetry of the year included *The Shoemaker's Wife and Other Poems* by Lotte Kramer; *Selected Poems* by Harry Fainlight, edited by his sister Ruth Fainlight; *Badlands,* a poetic record of Elaine Feinstein's 1984 sojourn in America's West; *Midsummer Morning Jog Log* by Michael Horovitz; *The Ship's Pasture* by Jon Silkin; *Leaseholder* by Daniel Weissbort; and *Masada Byzantium Celle* by Edward Lowbury.

## *Personalia*

Chief Rabbi Jakobovits received a number of honors this year. In March he was awarded an honorary fellowship by Queen Mary College, London University, for "distinguished public service." In October he was given the Lambeth Conference degree of doctor of divinity by the archbishop of Canterbury, Dr. Robert Runcie, for his contribution to the development of cooperation and understanding between the Jewish and Christian communities.

Four prominent Jews received knighthoods in 1987: the sculptor Anthony Caro; Arnold Elton, chairman of the Conservative Medical Society, which advised the government on the National Health Service; Dennis Landau, chief executive of the Cooperative Wholesale Society; and Mark Weinberg, founder of the Hambro Life

Insurance group. Sydney Brenner was made Companion of Honor for contributions to molecular biology. Yehudi Menuhin, the violinist, was awarded the Order of Merit, and Simone Ruth Prendergast was created a Dame for her political and public service.

Among British Jews who died in 1987 were Cecil Hyams, vice-chairman of AJEX, in January, aged 68; Rev. Joshua Sunshine, marriage authorization director in the office of the chief rabbi, in January, aged 62; Harry Leader, dance-band leader and composer, in February, in Brighton, aged 73; Julian Goldberg, Yiddish actor, in February, aged 77; Olga Katzin, the satirical writer "Sagittarius," in February, aged 90; Harold Rosenthal, music critic and author, in March, aged 69; Eric Sosnow, businessman and philanthropist, in March, aged 76; Myer Lew, *dayan* of the London Beth Din, in April, aged 79; Mordechai Dov Rogosnitsky, rabbi in Cardiff for over 40 years, in April, aged 78; Rae Taffler, women's rights activist, in April, aged 91; John Silkin, former Labor cabinet minister, in April, aged 64; Michael Sieff, former Marks and Spencer vice-chairman, in April, aged 76; Moshe Davis, executive director of the chief rabbi's office, 1973–1984, in May, aged 60; David Weitzman, Labor MP for Hackney North and Stoke Newington for 34 years, in May, aged 88; Louis Mintz, businessman and philanthropist, in May, aged 78; Yitzchak Golditch, Manchester Beth Din *dayan,* in May, aged 80; Harold Levy, Jewish educator, in June, aged 78, in London; Alfred S. Dresel, former chairman, Association of Jewish Refugees, in June, aged 96; Moses Friedlander, Hebrew scholar, in June, aged 85; Monty Levin, president, National Federation of Licensed Kosher Butchers and Poulterers for many years, in June, aged 86; Murray Mindlin, journalist, in June, aged 63; Alfie Bass, character actor, in July, aged 66; Lou Stoltzman, former JNF president, in July; Rabbi Dr. David Goldstein, Hebrew books curator at the British Library and translator, in July, aged 54; David Tack, national vice-president, AJEX, in July, aged 69; A.B. Levy, journalist, in August, aged 94; Sir James d'Avigdor-Goldsmid, soldier and politician, who achieved the rank of major general in the British forces, the highest obtained by any Jew, in September, aged 74; Lord Mancroft, businessman and government minister, 1954–1958, in September, aged 73; Arnaldo Dante Momigliano, historian and classicist, in August, in London, aged 79; George Mikes, author and humorist, in September, aged 75; Sonia Lipman, Anglo-Jewish historian, in London, in November, aged 61; Lt. Comdr. Julius Freedman, first Jewish officer in the regular Fleet Air Arm, in November, aged 70; Manny Cussins, Leeds businessman and philanthropist, in November, aged 81; Percy Cohen, Conservative party politician, in November, aged 95; Oliver Zangwill, professor of experimental psychology at Cambridge University, in November, aged 73; Richard Crown, B'nai B'rith national president, in December, at Gatwick, aged 69; Josef Fraenkel, Zionist historian, in December, in London, aged 84; Louis Littman, founder of the Littman Library of Jewish Civilization, in December, in London, aged 62.

MIRIAM & LIONEL KOCHAN

# France

OVERALL, 1987 WAS A MUCH quieter year than 1986, when France experienced a spate of terrorist attacks. Politically, the country was in between the 1986 legislative elections and the presidential election scheduled for 1988. While there was a wide consensus on matters of foreign policy—including the Middle East—between Socialist president François Mitterrand and the Right-centrist coalition government headed by Prime Minister Jacques Chirac, there were major debates on such domestic issues as the privatization of state-owned companies and other economic matters and the activities of the far-Right, xenophobic National Front of Jean-Marie Le Pen. Two issues that received widespread national attention this year held particular interest for Jews: the trial of Klaus Barbie and the threat posed by the National Front.

## National Affairs

### THE NATIONAL FRONT

In an atmosphere of deepening concern over unemployment (more than 10 percent of the work force by the end of 1986), and feeling strengthened by having more than 30 representatives in the National Assembly, the National Front (FN) took a more active stance in 1987. Its tactics during most of the year followed three main lines: the development of an anti-immigrant campaign; an attempt to trap the leaders of the traditional parties of the Right into an alliance against the Left (mainly the Socialists); and, more generally, a violent denunciation of politicians as a group, stressing an alleged separation between the people (*le pays réel*) and the institutions of government (*le pays légal*).

The front's organized anti-immigrant campaign, which had started by the end of 1986 and was based on the slogan "*être Français, ça se mérite*" ("One has to deserve to be French"), reached a peak in the spring of 1987. The FN attracted 10,000 people to a public meeting on April 2 in Paris and 20,000 demonstrators two days later in the streets of Marseilles, a city generally considered the FN's capital.

The extremist message of the campaign, which included appeals for non-European foreigners to be sent back to their countries, led a number of moderate Right leaders to differentiate publicly between the Right and the far Right. So, too, the two main parties of the Right—the Rally for the Republic (RPR, Rassemblement pour la République, led by Jacques Chirac), and the Union for French Democracy (UDF, Union pour la Démocratie Française, led by François Léotard and Giscard d'Estaing)—both declared that there would never be a national agreement between them and the FN. However, the situation was different on the local level. In July, for example, in Grasse, a small city in southern France, the UDF mayor was elected on a list that included six members of the National Front.

In September FN leader Le Pen provoked a major scandal when he declared on a popular radio program that the issue of Nazi gas chambers was one "discussed by historians" and was merely "a question of detail in the history of World War II." The statement, which made it clear that Le Pen was, to say the least, aware of the theories of historical revisionism, met with general disapproval in the press and among politicians and was the impetus for a demonstration organized by various antiracist movements. Although Le Pen was protected by parliamentary immunity from action by the public prosecutor, he was condemned in a civil action initiated by a coalition of antiracist groups and federations of former deportees and partisans. The court's decision stressed that Le Pen's language could be interpreted as a "consent to the horror" and a banalizing of the persecution of those who had been deported, particularly the Jews and the Gypsies, during World War II. As a protest of Le Pen's action, the National Assembly opened its autumn session on October 2 with a minute of silence in memory of the victims of Nazism. The session was boycotted by all the FN representatives, and Le Pen himself argued that he was a victim of the "pro-immigrant lobby," though without giving more details on the identity of that alleged body.

In the end, despite the deep emotions aroused, the impact of the incident remained unclear. The FN may well have benefited from the extensive media coverage it received, or at the least was not much harmed. A few months after the event, a poll showed that to a good number of French, Le Pen's reference to the gas chambers as "a detail" was nothing but a clumsy expression.

IMMIGRATION AND THE NATIONALITY CODE

In spite of the fact that immigration had been drastically limited since 1974, the issues of immigration and immigrant workers in France remained a major subject of debate, to a large extent focused on the "second-generation immigrants," i.e., the children of the foreign workers, mainly North Africans, who had settled in France in the 1960s and beginning of the 1970s.

Prior to the 1986 elections, the Right had proposed reforming the nationality code so as to (1) end the automatic granting of French citizenship to any child born on French soil; and (2) introduce in its place a "positive step": upon reaching their majority, children born in France of foreign parents would have to submit administrative petitions asking for French citizenship, but without any guarantee of a positive response. When the bill was drafted in the autumn of 1986, various sectors of the public claimed that it was discriminatory and would hamper the integration of children born and raised in France into French society. They also charged that the measure was a concession to the xenophobic views of the FN. The public debate aroused by the proposed bill led the government to withdraw the measure, at least temporarily.

In January 1987 Minister of Justice Albin Chalandon announced that the bill would be submitted for further consultation to a committee of 16 experts, among them Dominique Schnapper, a sociologist and the daughter of the late Raymond Aron. The committee proceeded to hold numerous hearings, portions of which were broadcast on TV. The testimony of Prof. Ady Steg, a well-known physician and president of the Alliance Israélite Universelle, made a particularly strong impression. The committee concluded that better tools were needed to aid the integration of second-generation immigrant youth, stressing the fact that since they had been born in France, they could be expected to remain and build their future in the country. Similar conclusions were reached in a report on racism prepared, at government request, by National Assembly member (RPR) Michel Hannoun.

Both reports evoked bitter reaction in the ranks of the National Front. In the Jewish community, which had not been on the front line on this issue, alarm was expressed over the growing spirit of intolerance shown by part of the French public. Jewish communal leaders stressed that while integration meant adopting the values of French society, it also meant being able to maintain one's own cultural characteristics.

TERRORISM

Considerable progress was made in the fight against terrorism—both domestic and of Middle Eastern origin. The legal apparatus was improved by the adoption of new laws (July) and the final ratification of the 1977 and 1979 international conventions of Strasbourg and Dublin against terrorism. Police and security forces were more successful than in 1986, and numerous arrests were made. At the same time, the fight against terror led to a serious diplomatic crisis with Iran.

On February 21 four of the five top leaders of the domestic radical group Action Directe—Jean-Marc Rouillan, Nathalie Ménigon, Joëlle Aubron, and Georges Cipriani—were arrested at an isolated farm in central France. On November 27 the fifth fugitive, Max Frérot, was arrested in Lyons. This put an end, at least for the year, to attacks initiated by the group. The police also arrested a number of activists in such independent terrorist movements as the Basque Iparretarak and the Alliance Révolutionnaire Caraïbe, a group active in the French territories in the Caribbean.

The problem of Middle Eastern terrorism was complicated by the continuing pressure exerted through the French hostages in Lebanon (one more, journalist Roger Auque, was kidnapped in January, and serious threats were made to the life of one of the "older" hostages in March), and by the potential consequences of antiterrorist measures on relations with Iran, the country believed to be behind most of the kidnappings.

On February 28 George Ibrahim Abdallah, a Lebanese terrorist convicted of complicity in the killings of an American and an Israeli diplomat in 1982, was sentenced by a French court to life imprisonment. Although the government had applied discreet pressure on the court to be more lenient, the court's decision coincided with the general climate of public opinion, which was against surrender to terrorist blackmail.

It was Abdallah whose release had been sought by those responsible for the wave of bombing attacks that hit France in the autumn of 1986. In March and April of 1987, 12 members of a network that had supplied logistical support to the architects of those attacks were arrested and indicted. In June another 57 persons—Islamic fundamentalists—were arrested, of whom 22 (9 Iranians and 10 Lebanese) were expelled from the country. The involvement of Iran in the 1986 terrorist attacks was confirmed when Wahid Gordji, who worked at the Iranian embassy in Paris in an unofficial capacity, disappeared when called to give evidence concerning the bombings. On July 2 Gordji reappeared at a press conference at the Iranian embassy; the same evening, President Mitterrand and the responsible ministers of government (Prime Minister Chirac, Minister of Foreign Affairs Jean-Bernard Raimond, Minister of Interior Charles Pasqua, and Minister of Police Robert Pandraud) held an emergency meeting at which they agreed to maintain a firm stand, insisting that Gordji be interrogated.

In the meantime, French police set up heavy guard around the Iranian embassy in Paris, in retaliation for which the French embassy in Teheran was virtually besieged. On July 14 the Iranians accused a French diplomat in Teheran of spying, and on the 17th, Paris announced the severing of diplomatic relations with Teheran. On July 24 a plane belonging to the French Air Afrique company was hijacked in Africa by a Lebanese Shi'ite; a French passenger was killed. After a French boat was attacked in the Persian Gulf by two Iranian motor launches, the French decided, on July 29, to send the aircraft carrier *Clémenceau* to the area "to ensure the protection of French interests."

The tension was relieved only in November. Iran showed its "goodwill" by helping to obtain the release of two of the French hostages in Lebanon and ordering Wahid Gordji to come forward. France, for its part, abstained from indicting Gordji, instead expelling him to Karachi, Pakistan, where he was exchanged for the French diplomat in Teheran. The sieges of both the Iranian embassy in Paris and the French embassy in Teheran were lifted and the diplomats on both sides allowed to return home. Yet another demonstration of goodwill was given in December when some 20 Iranians living in France, presumed to be opponents of the regime of the ayatollahs, were arrested and expelled to Gabon in Africa. Since some of them had earlier been granted the status of political refugees, this move aroused bitter protests both inside France and abroad. Some of the expelled were later allowed to return to France.

## Middle Eastern Policy

Despite the prime minister's alleged sympathy for Iraq (rumors in the summer that France might rebuild the atomic plant destroyed in June 1981 by Israeli planes were immediately denied) and the tension with Iran, France limited its involvement in the Persian Gulf war very carefully. It refused to join an American-sponsored international mine-sweeping team, though in July it did send specialized boats to the area.

As for the Arab-Israeli conflict, while the French supported the proposal for an international peace conference, they limited their activity in 1987 to quiet diplomatic contacts with the states involved. Among visitors to Paris were King Hussein of Jordan in January; the president of Lebanon, Amin Gemayel, in February; King Fahd of Saudi Arabia in April; followed by the prime minister of Israel, Yitzhak Shamir. President Mitterrand met with Algerian president Bendjedid Chadli in March, and with King Hassan of Morocco one month later; Jacques Chirac was in Egypt in September and in Israel in November; Minister of Foreign Affairs Raimond was in Damascus in October, seeking to renew ties with Syria. Relations with Israel continued to improve, with numerous visits made by Israeli and French ministers to each other's countries. High points of the year were the state visit of Prime Minister Shamir to Paris in April (27-30) and the reciprocal visit of Jacques Chirac to Israel six months later (November 1-3).

Events in the Israeli-occupied West Bank in December did not at first evoke much official reaction, perhaps because French attention was preoccupied with the situation in the Gulf. The French press, however, quickly denounced the methods being used by the Israelis in the territories, albeit more moderately—at first—than in previous instances, such as the 1982 war in Lebanon. On December 22 the government of France joined the other members of the UN Security council, except the United States, in condemning Israeli policy in the territories.

## *The Barbie Trial*

The trial of Klaus Barbie, which began on May 11, was certainly one of the major events of the year. Despite fears expressed when Barbie was extradited to France from Bolivia in 1983, the inevitable revelations about past events did not polarize the French public over the question of collaboration with the Nazis in World War II. Nor, despite the threats of Barbie's lawyer, Jacques Vergès—who a few months earlier had defended the terrorist George Ibrahim Abdallah—did the trial deteriorate into a debate over the Western democracies and their crimes, real or alleged, but remained focused on its subject—the crimes against humanity committed by the head of the Gestapo in the Lyons area.

Public opinion was virtually unanimous about the justification for the trial of Barbie, whose nickname, "the butcher of Lyons," seemed to speak for itself. The daily reporting, over several weeks, in newspapers and on the radio and TV, of the evidence given by the witnesses, highlighted the importance with which the trial was viewed. Adding to the air of solemnity was the fact that although the defendant had been a German officer, no attempt was made to conceal French collaboration with the Nazis and French responsibility for aspects of the Holocaust.

Four hundred journalists from all over the world attended the opening days of the trial, the first in French judicial history to be filmed (although the film would only be available to researchers in 20 years). Unfortunately, many of the journalists, mainly among the foreigners, seemed to miss the real significance of the trial and only to be awaiting revelations of scandal. When Barbie announced, on May 13, that he refused to attend his own trial, most of the visiting press left, leaving more room for the French press and for schoolchildren, who attended the trial in large numbers.

The trial reached its climax on May 15, when the prosecution presented the telex message signed by Barbie, containing an account of the deportation on April 16, 1944, of 44 Jewish children who had found shelter in a village close to Lyons, Izieu. None of those children survived, and Izieu became a symbol of the tragic fate of the Jews of France in World War II. The original of the critical document, whose authenticity had been questioned by lawyer Vergès, was shown to the court. On May 19 began the questioning of witnesses—parents of Barbie's victims (mothers of Izieu children), victims of Barbie who survived, and "general witnesses" such as author Elie Wiesel and historian Léon Poliakov. The very absence of Barbie on those days when Jews and non-Jews told their stories, naming Barbie as their tormentor, added a deeper emotional dimension to the testimony and was inevitably regarded as a sign of his cowardice.

The lawyers for the plaintiffs (there were no less than 39, representing more than 40 individuals or organizations, but who were able, on the whole, to coordinate their pleas) presented their case June 17–26. The public prosecutor, Pierre Truche, who had the floor on June 29 and 30, stressed Barbie's personal responsibility and the zeal with which he carried out his assignment in Lyons in 1943–44.

Barbie's defense was presented on July 1 and 2. On July 1 two lawyers from Third World countries, the Congo and Algeria, argued that crimes against humanity did not start and end with Nazi Germany, citing as examples of more recent perpetrators the United States in Vietnam, France in Algeria, and Israel. The Congolese defender also contended that Barbie could not be a racist since he had shaken hands with him. The day after this testimony, Vergès adopted a classic line of defense, minimizing Barbie's role and attempting to depict him solely as the executor of orders coming from above.

On July 3 Barbie was brought back to court. His last words before hearing the verdict were: "I have fought the Resistance, whom I respect, although with harshness. But it was war, and the war is over." The verdict came 40 minutes after midnight on July 4: the jury found Barbie guilty of the 17 crimes against humanity he was accused of and condemned him to life imprisonment.

Before, during, and after the Barbie trial the Jewish community, both nationally and locally, invested special efforts in public information and education. Before the trial, public lectures were offered on the Holocaust. During the trial, an exhibition in the city center of Lyons attracted more than 200,000 visitors, among them a large number of youth. After the trial, the community gave its support to the planned publication of the trial documentation. The community was also involved in the logistics of the trial—press conferences, hospitality for witnesses and lawyers, and the like.

## Anti-Semitism and Holocaust Denial

In February the Jewish weekly *Tribune Juive* revealed that a French version of the "Protocols of the Elders of Zion" was being distributed in a bookstore in the largely North African area of Ménilmontant in Paris. Prompt legal action resulted in seizure of the displayed copies and a ban on further distribution of the work. In itself, the incident could have been considered minor, for it was well known that certain Arab states and Islamic groups had been spreading anti-Semitic material in various countries for many years. However, viewed along with other manifestations of Arab hostility, it loomed much more significantly. It also pointed to a difficult dilemma for French Jews. On the one hand, they opposed the xenophobic campaigns of the National Front aimed at North African immigrants and their children. On the other hand, they feared that a subgroup in the population, one numbering more than three million and exposed to heavy doses of anti-Semitic propaganda, could become a threat to Jewish security.

Yet another matter of concern arose in May when, concurrent with the opening of the Barbie trial, the French Holocaust-denial movement published the first issue of a new quarterly, the *Annales d'Histoire Révisionniste* (Annals of Revisionist History). At the request of LICRA (the International League Against Racism and Anti-Semitism), a non-Jewish organization, the courts prohibited public distribution of the first issue of the journal, calling it, in the circumstances of the Barbie trial, a provocation to the victims of the Holocaust. A second issue was, nevertheless, published in the autumn, without interference.

JEWISH COMMUNITY

## Demography

According to most sources, the number of Jews in France was 550,000–600,000.

## Communal Affairs

Because of the seriousness with which it viewed the activities of the National Front, the French Jewish community was surprised and deeply dismayed when it learned, in February, that Jean-Marie Le Pen had met in the United States with a group of leaders of national Jewish organizations. French Jews feared that Le Pen would use his reception by that group to demonstrate his legitimacy. Even though it later turned out that the meeting was an unofficial, private gathering, leaders of

CRIF, the Representative Council of French Jewry, denounced the Americans for failing to consult with French Jewry about their intentions.

For most of the year—at least until December—there was less occasion than previously for Jewish communal activity in Israel's behalf. The community became aroused at the beginning of the year when three Lebanese Jews held hostage in Beirut were murdered. Although communal leaders tried to win public sympathy for the plight of Jews still living in Lebanon, this was a largely academic exercise, since the French were helpless to rescue even their own citizens who were hostages in Lebanon.

Toward the end of the year, CRIF expressed concern over the media's reporting of events in the West Bank and Gaza. One of its statements noted that "while the press had a duty to give an account of the events, nothing should prevent it from putting them in their context."

The struggle for freedom of emigration for Soviet Jews continued, with a private visit by Natan Sharansky in May helping to revitalize the effort. Non-Jews, too, shared the concern for Soviet Jews. During his official trip to Moscow in May, Prime Minister Chirac insisted on meeting with several refuseniks and drawing the attention of Soviet authorities to their plight. In September a group of Jewish community leaders visited the USSR, at the invitation of the Society for Friendship Between France and the Soviet Union, and were able to express publicly their support for the Jews of the USSR.

NEW CHIEF RABBI

On June 14, Joseph (Jo) Sitruk, chief rabbi of Marseilles, was elected chief rabbi of France, replacing René Samuel Sirat. Born in Tunis in 1944, Jo Sitruk spent his childhood in Nice; he received his rabbinic training at the Consistoire's Séminaire Israélite de France. In 1970 he was appointed assistant to the chief rabbi of Strasbourg, Max Warshawski. He became chief rabbi of Marseilles, the second largest Jewish community in France, in 1975. His personal charisma and talent as a speaker made him very popular in Marseilles, where he was able to open two Jewish schools and to increase greatly the number of Jewish children receiving a Jewish education.

In an interview with the daily *Le Monde* (December 29), Rabbi Sitruk discussed his view of his mission as chief rabbi. He named as his leading priority the development of a broad Jewish culture accessible to larger numbers of people—thus enlarging the notion of "education" which had been his predecessor's "priority of all priorities." The chief rabbi said he hoped to awaken in French Jews the "desire to discover or to know better the message of the Jewish people." To those who feared possible conflicts because of his strict Orthodoxy, he pointed to the communal unity he had been able to achieve in Marseilles.

## Jewish-Christian Relations

Although not specifically a French issue, the existence of a Carmelite convent at the site of the former extermination camp at Auschwitz-Birkenau in Poland remained a prime concern, with French Jews playing a leading role in international discussions of the matter. After the publication in 1986 of the "Zakhor" (Remember) declaration by Catholic and Jewish representatives, contacts between the parties continued. A follow-up meeting in Geneva on February 22 ended with an agreement in principle to have the convent moved outside the limits of the camp, this to be effected within 24 months.

A major participant in the negotiations on the convent was Albert Cardinal Decourtray, bishop of Lyons (as such, head of the French Roman Catholic hierarchy). At the end of June, when Pope John Paul II decided to receive Austrian president Kurt Waldheim at the Vatican, Cardinal Decourtray expressed his personal dismay at the pope's action. On the Jewish side, Jean-Paul Elkann, president of the Consistoire, the central Jewish religious body, and René Sirat, chief rabbi of France, strongly protested the meeting.

## Culture

Jewish tradition, history, and personalities continued to play a part in French cultural life. The Holocaust provided the setting for Louis Malle's *Au revoir les enfants*, a film that had immense popular success and was awarded an impressive number of Cesars (the French equivalent of American Oscars), besides the Gold Lion at the Venice festival. Another popular success was Gérard Oury's film *Lévy et Goliath*, a comedy about two Jewish brothers, one Orthodox and one assimilated, who join forces against a dangerous gang.

References to Jews and to Holocaust themes were also to be found in the theater. Some plays exploited the comic aspects of Jewish characters, such as the North African Jewish mother in *La femme sauvage* by Jean Yvane. The masterpiece of Soviet author Vassili Grossman, *Vie et Destin*, which takes place in the USSR during World War II, was adapted to theater under the title *Dernière lettre d'une mère juive soviétique à son fils* ("A Soviet Jewish Mother's Last Letter to Her Son") and was highly praised by both the public and the critics. Bernard Sobel's adaptation of Lessing's *Nathan le Sage* ("Nathan the Wise") was also a success.

This year saw the appearance of a new independent monthly, *Passages*, written by both Jews and non-Jews. By offering "a Jewish view of the news," the magazine aimed to create a bridge between the Jewish community and the rest of French society.

The subject of the 1987 Colloquium of Jewish Intellectuals was the Jewish perception of non-Jews, while the College of Jewish Studies of the Alliance Israélite Universelle presented a symposium on "Israel and the Nations." For the first time, the prize of the Foundation for French Judaism, whose panel of judges was headed by Emmanuel Levinas, was awarded to a non-Jewish author, Marthe Robert, "for her contribution to the understanding of the works of Kafka and Freud, particularly the understanding of their Jewish dimension."

With the inauguration of the Edmond Fleg School of the Mouvement Juif Libéral de France (Reform), the French Jewish community acquired its first Reform Jewish full-time school.

## Publications

The year brought a rich harvest of books on Jewish themes. Patrick Girard's *Pour le meilleur et pour le pire* ("For Better or Worse") is a popular history of the Jews in France. The history of the Jews in North Africa, an important segment of present-day French Jewry, is the subject of *Les Juifs d'Algérie, histoire et textes*, a compilation edited by Jean Laloum and Jean-Luc Allouche. The *Guide du Judaïsme français* ("French Jewish Guide") provides a short history of the community together with useful addresses and descriptions of 3,000 institutions, schools, restaurants, and other places of interest.

On the more personal level, a noteworthy autobiography by geneticist and Nobel Prize laureate (1965) François Jacob, *La statue intérieure* ("The Interior Statue"), evokes his experience as a Jew from a highly assimilated family.

Prof. André Neher's new work on Jewish mystics, *Faust et le Maharal de Prague, le mythe et le réel* ("Faust and the Maharal of Prague: Myth and Reality"), examines the similarities between the myth of the Golem and the myth of Faust. André Abécassis published the first two volumes of a "History of Jewish Thought" (in an original paperback edition). Maurice-Ruben Hayoun published a short biography of Maimonides (*Maïmonide*), and Adin Steinsaltz's *Essential Talmud* appeared in French translation.

Lucien Lazare produced the best documented history so far published, although a somewhat controversial one, of the Jewish Resistance in France during World War II (*La Résistance juive en France*). In it he stresses the difference between the non-Jewish French partisans, whose main duty was to fight, and the Jewish partisans, who had to fight but also to provide shelter, mainly for children. Stéphane Courtois and Adam Rayski's *Qui savait quoi? L'extermination des juifs 1941–1945* ("Who Knew What? The Extermination of the Jews 1941–1945") provides evidence of how much was already known in France about Nazi activities during the war. Pierre Vidal-Naquet's *Les assassins de la mémoire* ("The Memory Killers") analyzes the phenomenon of historical revisionism, specifically denial of the Holocaust, in France and elsewhere.

Three stars of the new generation of philosophers in France, all Jews, published controversial treatises this year. In *La Défaite de la pensée* ("The Failure of Thought"), Alain Finkielkraut denounces the indiscriminate inclusion of all cultural phenomena in the category of culture. In *Éloge des intellectuels* ("Praise of Intellectuals"), Bernard-Henri Lévy stresses the positive influence of intellectuals in France.

Finally, in *Descartes c'est la France* ("Descartes Is France"), André Glucksman attempts to rehabilitate the earlier philosopher's rationalism.

## Personalia

One of France's leading Jews, Nobel Peace Prize laureate René Cassin (1888–1976), was reinterred in the Pantheon, the resting place of France's heroes, in October, with full national honors. Cassin was an outstanding example of a French Jew who was involved in both the national affairs of his country and those of the Jewish community. A law professor and statesman, he represented France at the League of Nations from 1924 till 1938 and served as a legal adviser to De Gaulle's Free French Forces in London during the war. In 1946 he represented France on the committee that prepared the Universal Declaration of Human Rights and was president of the UN Commission on Human Rights in 1955. At the same time, he served as president of the Alliance Israélite Universelle, helping to rebuild postwar Jewish life and institutions in France. In 1967 Cassin bitterly criticized De Gaulle's decision to embargo French weapons to Israel. In conjunction with the Pantheon ceremonies, the Alliance organized a symposium in Cassin's memory on "Tradition and the Future of Human Rights."

Rabbi Paul Roitman, one of the organizers of Bnei Akiva in France and the creator of the Torah veTsion movement, which worked to integrate Algerian Jews into the French community structure, was made an officer of the Legion of Honor. Roger Ascot, chief editor of the Jewish monthly *L'Arche*; Lionel Stoleru, former minister and president of the France-Israel Chamber of Commerce; and Michel Topiol, head of the French section of the Jewish Agency and co-president of the UJA in France, were made knights of the Legion of Honor. Jacqueline Keller, the director of CRIF, became a knight in the National Order of Merit; Jean Kahn, vice-president of CRIF and president of the community of Strasbourg, and Chief Rabbi René Samuel Sirat were named officers in the order. Elie Wiesel received an honorary doctorate from the Sorbonne.

The Fédération Séfaradie de France elected a new president, Armand Amsellem, former president of the Jewish community in Toulouse. He replaced Albert Benattar, who had resigned. Liliane Klein-Lieber was elected president of Coopération Féminine, the women's organization of the FSJU, the United Jewish Philanthropic Fund.

Among prominent Jews who died this year were Yves Stourdze, a computer specialist (son of Marcel Stourdze, one of the witnesses at the Barbie trial and a leader of the Union Libéral Israélite de France, the Conservative religious movement), aged 38; Arnold Mandel, one of the most stimulating minds in the Jewish community, a talented poet, essayist, and novelist, a leader in the World War II Resistance, and contributor for 25 years (until 1986) of the article on France in the *American Jewish Year Book*, aged 74; Nicole Chouraqui, Algerian-born economist, member of the European Parliament since 1979 and a member of the Paris municipality, aged 49; Thérèse Spire, musicologist and librarian at the Sorbonne library and widow of poet André Spire, aged 88; Michel Borwicz, Polish-born historian and writer who settled in France in 1947, an officer in the Polish Resistance and an expert before the Polish Supreme Court in trials of Nazi war criminals, aged 76.

NELLY HANSSON

# The Netherlands

## National Affairs

THE YEAR 1987 WAS MARKED by relative political and economic stability. Despite controversy over several issues, there was no serious threat to the center-Right government headed by Premier Ruud (Rudolf) Lubbers, a coalition of Christian Democrats (CDA) and Liberals (VVD), which had been reinstated in July 1986.

In countrywide elections in March for the 12 provincial councils, both the CDA and VVD suffered small losses; however, by joining forces with fundamentalist Protestant parties they were able to retain their majority. In June the members of the provincial councils elected the 75 members of the Senate (the parliamentary First Chamber), giving the two coalition partners a narrow majority of 38 seats in that body.

Although the overall economy again showed growth, the government was forced to make drastic cuts in a budget that had grown dramatically throughout the 1970s and early 1980s. The government announced that by the year 1990, a total of 26,000 government employees would be dismissed, with most of the cuts to be made in education, public health, social welfare, and the Netherlands state railways. One proposed remedy was the privatization of certain government functions, such as the postal service. Implementation of the dismissals led to numerous demonstrations by affected groups, such as students and nurses, usually with little success. Unemployment, in the meantime, remained more or less stable, with estimates ranging from 500,000 to 680,000.

The Dutch police force had to cut its staff and scale down plans for constructing additional prisons or prison cells, despite the continuing increase in crime. Many of the frequent bank robberies (nearly one every day), thefts, burglaries, and shoplifting incidents were carried out in the larger cities, frequently by drug addicts, among them many young West Germans attracted to Holland by a relatively lenient drug policy.

Crimes with a political motive were committed by a group calling itself RARA (acronym of Revolutionary Anti-Racist Action), which set fire to enterprises that had branches in South Africa and damaged a number of Shell gasoline stations for the same reason, causing damage assessed at tens of millions of dollars. No members of this group had been caught by year's end. One of the main targets of the attacks, the Makro supermarket chain, was forced to withdraw from South Africa when it could no longer obtain insurance.

The number of individuals seeking political asylum in Holland increased to

13,500. In order to exercise better control over them, the government changed its approach from providing individual public assistance, allowing them to live where they wished, to placing them in newly created absorption centers, which provided free board and lodging and Dfl.300. ($150.) a month pocket money. The placement of some absorption centers in empty convents and boarding schools in villages created a certain amount of friction with local residents. Assistance was guaranteed for the duration of the refugees' stay, which could be as long as their request for political asylum had not been definitely rejected. Although nearly 85 percent of the requests for political asylum were in fact turned down, many immigrants succeeded in remaining in the country illegally by going into hiding.

## Holocaust-Related Issues

Still undecided was the controversy over the government pension of Flora Rost van Tonningen, the widow of Meinout Rost van Tonningen, a leading Nazi member of Parliament from 1937 to 1941 and later president of the German-controlled Netherlands State Bank, and herself an acknowledged neo-Nazi. (See AJYB 1988, vol. 88, pp. 284–85.) The Netherlands Council of State advised against withdrawal of her pension, but a special parliamentary commission, after studying the legal problem, thought withdrawal of the pension possible. Five members of the Second Chamber of Parliament, representing the three major parties, announced plans to submit a private members' bill to this effect, but had not yet done so by the end of the period under review. The adoption of such a bill would require a two-thirds majority in Parliament, which would not be easy to obtain.

It seemed unlikely that there would be further trials of war criminals in Holland, although about 40 names were still officially on the list of the government's special prosecutor for war crimes. Some of the accused were thought to have died and others were living in West Germany, Latin America, and elsewhere, having in the meantime obtained new citizenship, which protected them from extradition. What was probably the last Nazi trial in Holland was held in May, that of Marinus de Rijke, who as a camp guard at the German concentration camp Erica, in the town of Ommen, had allegedly committed serious atrocities, some resulting in the deaths of camp inmates. De Rijke, who escaped over the German border after liberation and took up residence in West Germany, was arrested during a visit to his relatives in Holland and brought to trial. Although he was acquitted because of conflicting evidence by a number of witnesses, the public prosecutor appealed the verdict. De Rijke, who returned to West Germany after his acquittal, could be tried again, but only *in absentia*.

Though the government made cuts in many categories of expenditure, including social benefits, it left untouched the level of payments allocated under the WUV, the law on payments to victims of World War II persecution. Two new developments relating to WUV took place during the year. One was a ruling by the

European Court of Justice in Strasbourg, binding on the Dutch government, entitling married women who were not breadwinners (i.e., housewives) to the same WUV benefits as men. The decision meant an additional outlay of $40 million annually for the government.

The second development was the report of the Van Dijke Commission, which had been established in January 1985 to examine continuation of WUV payments and propose means for simplifying the law's complex provisions. The commission aroused controversy with its recommendation that after the year 2010, when the last person born during the German or Japanese occupation turned 65 and became eligible for an old-age pension, no new application for WUV be accepted. (It did support continuation of existing payments, however.) The report also recommended a halt to new applications from so-called second-generation victims, though it approved payment for psychiatric treatment for the latter. The report was protested by several members of Parliament and by 20 different organizations, including the Jewish Social Welfare Foundation (JMW), whose representatives met with Minister of Social Welfare Elco Brinkman in September. No final decision was reached on the recommendations.

A subsidy from the Ministry of Social Welfare made possible production of an abridged version of Claude Lanzmann's film *Shoah* for showing to school classes, accompanied by a short guide for teachers. A symposium on "Teaching About the Holocaust in Elementary Schools" was held in May at the Commemoration Center at the site of the Nazi transit camp for Jews, Westerbork, with some 150 educators in attendance. The Ministry of Social Welfare announced that one million florins ($500,000) would be made available for producing teaching materials on the persecution of the Jews.

The "*Historikerstreit,*" the dispute among historians over interpretations of the Nazi past, which had been going on in West Germany for several years, had its echoes in Holland. Dr. Nanno K.C.A. in 't Veld, a staff member of the Netherlands State Institute for War Documentation for some 25 years, came out in support of Ernst Nolte, the German leader of the revisionist school of thought, which maintained that there was nothing novel or unique about the Holocaust.

The Dutch public was exposed to considerable media coverage of the Nazi war-crimes trial of John Demjanjuk in Jerusalem. One of the expert witnesses for the defense was Willem A. Wagenaar, professor of experimental psychology at the University of Leyden, who testified that after an interval of over 40 years, evidence given by prosecution witnesses was no longer reliable.

As in previous years, in connection with the May 4th observance of Memorial Day for the dead of World War II, a number of localities unveiled monuments to local Jews who had lost their lives during the Nazi period. One such monument was dedicated this year in Leeuwarden, and an education wing was opened in the Commemoration Center at Westerbork, the former Jewish transit camp. In Loosdrecht, near Hilversum, a modest monument was unveiled, erected at the private initiative of Miriam Waterman Pinkhof of Haifa, Israel, to the memory of the 23 children who lived on a Youth Aliyah farm in that village who perished at the hands of the Nazis. Mrs. Pinkhof and her late husband had been leaders at the farm.

## Relations with Israel

Although the Netherlands government continued to support the official position of the European Community—recognizing the legitimate rights of both Israel and the Palestinians—it refused to grant full diplomatic standing to the PLO in Holland, allowing it to maintain only an information office, in The Hague, and to have contact only with officials of the Foreign Ministry, not with the foreign minister himself. A private group, the Netherlands Palestine Committee, publicly advocated the Palestinian cause. In addition, there was an active Association of Palestinians in Holland, headed by PLO member Ibrahim el-Baz, and a related Association of Palestinian Women in Holland. The nucleus of the 500 or so Palestinians living in the country was a group of some 60 workers from Nablus who had been recruited as guest workers by a factory in Vlaardingen, west of Rotterdam, in 1963, and stayed on. Some of them later brought over their wives and children; others married Dutch women.

Many organized groups—Christian, left-wing, and certain left-wing Jewish groups—as well as the news media, expressed support for the Palestinian cause. The Christian groups included the Dutch branch of the Roman Catholic Pax Christi and the Dutch Reformed Church, which, in a 100-page memorandum on Christian policy on the occupied territories, expressed profound disappointment that "the same people which once gave justice to the world now commits much injustice in the occupied areas."

The Dutch branch of the Israeli Peace Now movement organized a public meeting with a Palestinian speaker and continued to publish its quarterly journal *Vrede Nu*. The Dutch news media—with some 12 resident correspondents in Israel, many of them working for more than one medium and most of them Jews—stepped up their already heavy coverage of the Palestinian problem when the Palestinian uprising broke out in December. The broadcasting companies in particular sent special correspondents to the occupied areas, many of whom had never visited Israel or the Middle East before but were accompanied by, or had established contacts with, Palestinians. Predictably, the coverage of events had an anti-Israel cast.

Despite growing public sentiment for the Palestinians, many Dutch people continued to support Israel, particularly those in Christian fundamentalist (more or less) circles. Active pro-Israel bodies were Christians for Israel, the Israel Committee Nederland, and the Evangelische Omroep Broadcasting Company.

A Dutch trade mission composed of 25 representatives of 13 small and medium enterprises in various technological fields visited Israel in February for an exchange of experiences. (Israel and the Netherlands had signed an agreement for technological cooperation in November 1986.) A Dutch agricultural commission visited Israel, the Gaza Strip, and the West Bank in May to explore arrangements for direct export of citrus from these areas to the European Community. During a visit to Israel in June, Foreign Minister Hans van den Broek discussed this matter with Israeli officials.

## Anti-Semitism

With one significant exception, anti-Semitic incidents were relatively few and minor—the shouting of anti-Semitic slogans by fans at soccer matches and occasional threats against Jews in connection with the situation of the Palestinians. The exception was the so-called Fassbinder affair, arising from the production of a controversial German play, Rainer Werner Fassbinder's *Garbage, the City and Death*. The play was to be produced in Dutch translation by students of the Amsterdam School of Drama, as the graduation project of a student in stage direction, 34-year-old Johan Doesburg.

The Fassbinder play had a history of controversy. Its scheduled performances in 1985 in Frankfurt—the scene of the play's action—were called off after vigorous protests by Frankfurt Jews, who labeled the work anti-Semitic or, at the very least, capable of inciting to anti-Semitism. In 1986 the Frankfurt supreme court ruled that the work contained "clearly derogatory and stereotype-like anti-Semitic tendencies."

The Amsterdam school first sought to have the play performed in a small theater in Amsterdam, but the theater's Jewish director, Leonard Frank, refused to make it available. A small theater in Rotterdam was then found, and what was advertised as the "European premiere" of the play was scheduled for November 18. Various Jewish organizations, as well as Liberal rabbi Avraham Soetendorp, tried to persuade both the drama school and the municipality of Rotterdam to cancel the public performances, but to no avail. The director and vice-principal of the school—Paul Sonke and Louk Zonneveld—Johan Doesburg himself, and the Rotterdam alderman for culture maintained that "cultural censorship" was contrary to the democratic principles for which so many of those who fought the Nazis had given their lives. Doesburg also said that one of his aims in presenting the play was to lift the long-standing taboo on public discussion of anti-Semitism.

On the night of the performance, 2,300 Jews, mostly members of youth organizations but also a number of prominent older people, demonstrated in front of the theater. In addition—and this had not been expected—as soon as the play started, some 80 people in the audience, including Rabbi Soetendorp, rushed onto the stage, refusing to move, thus preventing the performance from continuing. Lengthy negotiations produced a compromise: on Saturday evening, November 21, a performance was held for invited guests, half invited by the drama school and half by the Jewish organizations, followed by open discussion. Neither the performance nor the discussion changed the stand of either group. On November 23 the drama school announced that for the time being it would not perform the play, an important reason being the anonymous threats received by several of the actors—implying that these came from Jews.

The weekly *Haagse Post* devoted almost its entire issue of November 25 to publication of the text of the play (in Dutch), "so that the public can judge for itself," and the progressive VPRO Broadcasting Company broadcast the entire text on radio. Meanwhile, public comment in the media was predominantly critical of the Jews for preventing freedom of expression and cultural freedom and for resorting to "terrorism." Some Jews received threatening phone calls.

A strange related episode involved the actor Jules Croiset, who had been prominent among those protesting in front of the Rotterdam theater. On December 2 he was allegedly abducted by neo-Nazis in Bruges, Belgium, where he was appearing in a one-man show, but he managed to free himself the following day. This apparent manifestation of anti-Semitism aroused much concern, and a protest demonstration was held in Amsterdam, with the chairman of the Second Chamber of Parliament, Dick Dolman, as one of the main speakers. In the end, Croiset's abduction proved to be a hoax. Interrogated again by Belgian police on January 5, he admitted that he had made up the whole story, and that several of the threatening letters, including one to himself, had been written by him. Croiset, aged 50, emerged as a clearly troubled personality; among other things, he was the son of a Jewish father and a non-Jewish mother, an actress with Nazi sympathies, and he had become interested in his Jewish roots only a few years earlier.

## JEWISH COMMUNITY

### Demography

In the absence of any scientific census or survey, the number of Jews in the Netherlands was still estimated at about 25,000. Of these, 10,659 were considered official members of the Ashkenazi community (Nederlands Israelitisch Kerkgenootschap, NIK), distributed among 42 local communities throughout the country. Amsterdam, with nearly 8,000 members, The Hague, with 425 members, and Rotterdam, with 356 members, accounted for 82 percent of all NIK members. The Portuguese (Sephardi) community remained stable, with fewer than 1,000 members and one congregation, in Amsterdam; membership in the Liberal Jewish community was about 2,500, in six congregations. At least half of all persons of Jewish origin in Holland were not affiliated with the organized Jewish community.

### Communal Affairs

In June the Central Council of the NIK amended its regulations so as to require communities with fewer than 25 members to enter into a "cooperative association" with a nearby larger community, or be dissolved. The former's assets would go into a common fund, supervised by the NIK, to be used for the benefit of all small congregations. Some communities objected; though no longer able to provide the required services, they wanted to retain control of their assets for their own benefit. In Amsterdam, the 39-year-old ultra-Orthodox rabbi Shmuel J. Roth of Gateshead, England, who had been appointed a communal rabbi in July 1986 on a two-year contract, officially assumed his duties in January. Almost at once he became a source of irritation, even among the Orthodox, entering into conflicts with rabbinical colleagues and taking unpopular actions, such as dismissing the ritual slaughterer who had been in office for 40 years. As a result, his contract was terminated after eight months. When Roth contested his dismissal, arbitration was sought with the Beth Din of the United Synagogue in London, which at the end of the year confirmed the dismissal. An American, Aryeh L. Heintz, was appointed assistant rabbi of the Utrecht district—which comprised the whole of the Netherlands except the three main cities. Heintz was born in Houston, Texas, in 1958, received his rabbinical degree at the Chabad Yeshivah in Brooklyn, New York, and served as supervisor of the kosher dining facility at the State University of New York in Albany.

The Liberal Jewish Community (LJG) elected Frieda Brommet Menco as its head, to succeed Prof. Herman Musaph, who had occupied this position for two years. Mrs. Menco was for many years chairwoman of the women's group of the LJG and vice-chairwoman of its Amsterdam branch. Cantor Laszlo Pasztor, who had been cantor of the Amsterdam branch since 1983, left for West Berlin.

The Jewish women's society Deborah, established in 1979, continued to function actively. The group had some 200 members, many of whom were not otherwise connected with Jewish life. The Jewish women's journal *Kolenoe,* which had been in existence for five years and was largely produced by volunteers, ceased publication in January, for financial and other reasons.

The Netherlands Zionist Organization (NZB), with some 1,430 members in 16 local branches, concentrated its activity this year on the September elections to the 31st World Zionist Congress, in which the NZB was entitled to five seats. Only 570 members—less than half—used their right to vote, however. Of these, 246 voted for Arza (the Liberal Jewish Zionists), 130 for the Mizrahi, 104 for Poale Zion, 74 for the General Zionists, and 16 for Herut. Arza thus got two seats, and Mizrazhi, PZ, and the General Zionists one each.

The Tenth International Conference of Jewish Homosexuals was held in Amsterdam July 2–5, with some 260 participants. The host was the Dutch Society of Jewish Homosexuals, Shalhomo, which was established in 1979 and now had about 160 members. This was the first time the conference was held in Europe.

The long drawn-out lawsuit brought by a Jewish father, Robert Brucker, against the Jewish Maimonides Lyceum in Amsterdam for refusing to admit his 12-year-old son, Aram, as a pupil, because his mother was not Jewish according to Jewish law, continued to occupy public attention. In 1986 the Amsterdam lower district court had dismissed the father's suit, but on June 25, 1987, the Amsterdam higher district court ruled that the school had to admit the boy, on the ground that the boy's interest superseded that of the school. The court also ordered the school to pay a penalty of Dfl. 1,000 ($500.) for every day after the start of the new school year that the boy was not admitted. The school appealed to the Supreme Court, but as the decision of the latter would take several months, it applied for and was granted a postponement of the higher court's order until after a ruling by the Supreme Court. No decision had been reached by year's end. Meanwhile, the matter was widely covered in the general as well as the Jewish press, with much of the comment labeling the policy of the Maimonides Lyceum discriminatory, even racist, and attacking Orthodox Judaism for it. Although Rabbi David Lilienthal of the Amsterdam Liberal Jewish Congregation, to which the Brucker family belonged, testified in their behalf before the Amsterdam higher district court, all community leaders were concerned about the growing inter-Jewish polarization produced by the case. In a joint statement issued on October 2, the eve of the Day of Atonement, leaders of the Ashkenazi Congregation, the NIK, and the Liberal Jewish Congregation urged cooperation in the interest of all Jews in the country and in behalf of the State of Israel, Soviet Jewry, and oppressed Jews in other countries.

On March 16 the Committee for Solidarity with Soviet Jewry held its annual symbolic open-air seder, with some 80 participants. In light of reports about liberalization in the USSR—*glasnost*—the seder was held, not as previously, in front of the Soviet embassy in The Hague, but at Dam Square in Amsterdam.

## Culture

The main cultural event of the year was the opening of the Jewish Historical Museum on May 3 in its new premises, the converted complex of four former Ashkenazi synagogues dating respectively from 1671, 1686, 1700, and 1752—in Jonas Daniel Meijer Square in Amsterdam. The ancient synagogues, which were badly damaged during World War II and later sold to the city of Amsterdam by the Ashkenazi community, were renovated at a cost of $11 million, 80 percent of which was paid by the government and the Amsterdam municipality and the remaining 20 percent by private donations. The museum itself was under government auspices.

Some criticism was voiced when Austria donated a sum of $150,000 to the renovation, half of it from the Austrian government and half from Austrian industrialists. Austrian Chancellor Franz Vranitzky was invited to the official opening, which was also attended by Queen Beatrix, Premier Lubbers, Minister of Culture Elco Brinkman, and Amsterdam mayor Eduard van Thijn. The Orthodox rabbis boycotted the opening ceremony because the museum would remain open on the Sabbath and Jewish holidays, except the Day of Atonement. The festive opening was preceded by a performance in the new Music Theater across the square from the museum of the oratorio *Mechayeh Hametim* ("He who revives the dead"). Composed by Israeli composer Noam Sheriff and performed by the Israel Philharmonic

Orchestra and a Bavarian boys' choir, the work had been commissioned by a Dutch Jew, Bernhard Bronkhorst. The program was broadcast in its entirety by Dutch television.

## Jewish-Christian Relations

The Protestant gospel-preaching couple Lucas and Jenny Goeree were acquitted in June by the higher district court in Arnhem of charges of disseminating anti-Semitic material. The couple had been enjoined by the lower court in Zwolle in 1985 from distributing their publications, among them tracts charging that the Jews had brought the Holocaust upon themselves by rejecting Jesus as the messiah. The acquittal this year was based on the principles of free speech and freedom of religious expression. In January the Consultative Council of Jews and Christians (OJEC) asked the (Protestant) Council of Churches to distribute a statement to its member churches repudiating the concept of Jewish suffering as punishment for rejection of Jesus.

## Publications

Noteworthy books on Jewish subjects published this year included *Miep Gies Remembers Anne Frank* by Alison Lesly Gold; Jenny Wesly's *Joods* ("Jewish"), a photo-essay on Jewish life in the Netherlands in the 1980s; *Herlevend Bewaard* ("Preserved by Revival") by Henriette Boas, a collection of articles on Jewish aspects of Amsterdam, previously published in various periodicals. Monographs on small prewar Jewish communities continued to appear.

## Personalia

Willy Lindwer received two prizes at the Jewish Film Festival for his film *Menorah,* on the 350-year history of the Ashkenazi community of Amsterdam. Otto Treumann received the Yakir Bezalel Award in Jerusalem for his influence on graphic design worldwide and his contributions to the Bezalel Academy; Prof. Hans Bloemendal received the Award of Excellence of the American Research Institute Alcon.

Among prominent Jews who died in 1986 were Hartog Beem, an authority on the Dutch variant of Yiddish and on Jewish life in the prewar Dutch countryside, and author of some 400 books and articles, aged 94; Moses (Max) H. Gans, the author of, *inter alia,* the monumental *Memoir Book of Dutch Jewry, 1600–1940,* aged 70; Abraham Horodisch, a leading antiquarian and bibliophile, the founder in 1933 of the Erasmus Antiquariat in Amsterdam, aged 89; and Ben Elkerbout, TV documentary producer and founder of the Belbo Film Company, aged 46.

HENRIETTE BOAS

# Italy

## National Affairs

THE RARE POLITICAL AND SOCIAL stability enjoyed by Italy for three and a half years, under Socialist leader Bettino Craxi, came to an end in 1987. Mounting rivalry between the two main parties of the five-party governing coalition, the Christian Democrats and the Socialists, reached a climax early in the year. In March, after the Christian Democrats demanded the premiership, in accordance with an earlier agreement, Craxi resigned. When differences between the parties still proved irreconcilable, Parliament was dissolved and general elections were held in June, a year earlier than scheduled.

The elections saw a decline for the Communist party (from 29 percent in 1983 to 26 percent); a confirmation of Christian Democratic strength (33 percent in 1983, 34 percent in 1987); and a significant gain for the Socialist party, which had headed the government for four years (from 11 percent in 1983 to 14 percent). The small Republican party, a traditional friend of Israel, suffered a slight drop (from 5 percent in 1983 to 4 percent). The Radical party, which in previous years had distinguished itself in civil-rights campaigns, in the struggle against famine in the Third World, and in support for Soviet Jewry, remained stable (2.5 percent). The environmentalists' list (the Greens), which participated in the general elections for the first time, won 2.5 percent of the vote and 13 seats in the Chamber of Deputies.

The period after the elections saw a return to political instability: the coalition government formed in July, headed by Christian Democrat Giovanni Goria, was considered at best transitional by the main parties. The political spotlight focused during much of the year on five national referendums, three of them concerned with the use and development of nuclear energy, the remaining two calling for important changes in the criminal justice system. The referendums, held in November, were approved by a majority of the electorate. Under the Italian system, this meant that existing laws would be repealed and new legislation would have to be passed.

The social as well as the political stability that Italy had enjoyed since 1985 showed signs of distress. In the fall, local workers' organizations beyond the control of the central unions carried out a series of wildcat strikes, which completely paralyzed airports, railways, and public schools for brief periods.

Although Italy's economy continued to show growth, basic structural problems remained unsolved. The inflation rate, which dropped to 4.5 percent, the lowest since 1969, was twice as high as the European average. Manufacturing output increased and trade expanded; unemployment, however, reached 12 percent overall and 19 percent in southern Italy. The main sources of concern were still the enormous budget deficit, strong dependence on energy imports, and a low rate of productivity in public services. The deficit came to a record $92 billion—90 percent of Italy's GNP, compared with the average deficit elsewhere in Europe of 52 percent of GNP. Italy still depended on imports for 83 percent of its energy requirements, against a European average of 44 percent. Productivity in the public sector, already very low, dropped by 4 percent. Still, Italy continued to gain an important share of the international market, and its economy was the fastest growing in Europe.

## Relations with Israel

From May 1986, when Foreign Affairs Minister Giulio Andreotti visited Israel, to November 1987, Italy's relations with Israel saw no dramatic changes. However, with the outbreak of the Arab revolt in the territories in early December, relations deteriorated, and Italy explicitly condemned Israel's policy on several occasions. President Francesco Cossiga did, however, make a scheduled trip to Israel in December, the first visit by an Italian head of state to that country. Cossiga was accompanied by Foreign Affairs Minister Andreotti. The timing of the visit was criticized by circles sympathetic to the Arab revolt, even though it was described officially as a "private pilgrimage," and even though President Cossiga met first with a delegation of Palestinians from the territories and only later with President Chaim Herzog, Prime Minister Yitzhak Shamir, Foreign Minister Shimon Peres, and Speaker of the Knesset Shlomo Hillel. At Yad Vashem, the Holocaust memorial in Jerusalem, Cossiga took part in laying the cornerstone for a monument to Italian Jewish communities destroyed during the Nazi era. President Cossiga openly urged Israel to find a viable solution to the problem of the occupied territories and reaffirmed Italian support for the Palestinian right to self-determination.

Although Italy had previously been instrumental in bringing about special agricultural and tariff agreements between the European Community and Israel—to offset the growing presence of Spanish and Portuguese products on the European market—in the second half of 1987 Italy ceased its efforts in Israel's behalf. (See also "Culture," below.)

## Anti-Semitism

A portion of a survey on anti-Semitism in Italy that had been conducted in the summer of 1986 by the Intermatrix and Demoskopea research institutes, with the assistance of the Center of Contemporary Jewish Documentation of Milan (CDEC), was made public in March of this year. The survey was based on a questionnaire of 22 items that was administered to 2,000 people aged 15 to 65, living in 150 different localities scattered all over the country, belonging to all social classes and with different levels of education. Overall, the researchers evaluated the survey findings as "positive," saying they showed only a "normal" level of open anti-Semitism. They noted, however, a worrying tendency to racist attitudes toward

Arabs and blacks (Italy had about a million guest workers from Third World countries).

The responses showed a strong ignorance of Judaism and Jews, yet a low incidence of anti-Semitic stereotypes. Only 24 percent of those interviewed had ever personally known a Jew. The main sources of information about Jews were television, radio, and movies (56 percent), school (35 percent), the press (27 percent), and Catholic religious education (22 percent). Fifty-two percent had no idea how many Jews lived in Italy, 21 percent guessing between 50,000 and 100,000, and 27 percent between 100,000 and two million. Asked to give a definition of the Jews, 10 percent (mostly housewives) did not give an answer, while the balance, in equal proportions, said that they were a people, the heirs of a tradition, or members of a religion. Asked whether they liked or disliked Jews, 11 percent said they disliked Jews, 17 percent liked them, and 72 percent neither liked nor disliked them. The same proportion that admitted disliking Jews—11 percent—also said they would not become romantically involved with one. (By way of comparison, 21 percent rejected the idea of a love affair with an Arab, 24 percent with a black.) The rate of those admitting to dislike of Jews reached 14 percent among supporters of the leftist parties. On the subject of the Middle East conflict, 37 percent did not take a position, 23 percent considered the Arabs, in the main, responsible, and 10 percent thought that the responsibility fell on Israel.

While the survey was taken seriously and considered to be reliable, some observers felt it understated anti-Semitic attitudes in Italy. Anti-Semitic stereotypes, for example, continued to crop up in the Italian press. One instance of this occurred in June, when the well-known journalist Massimo Fini, writing in the weekly *L'Europeo* on the demonstration organized by Jews in St. Peter's Square to protest the pope's meeting with Kurt Waldheim (see below), strongly condemned the "Jewish incapacity to forgive and the desire for revenge, so deep-rooted in Jewish tradition." Fini added that it was time for the Jews to stop trying to impose their values on Western societies and blackmailing Europeans and Americans for their own goals. In November the economic weekly *Milano Finanza* published an article on the tycoon Carlo De Benedetti, written by Paolo Panerai, former chief editor of the leading Italian periodical on economics and finance, *Il Mondo*. (Born of a Jewish father and a Catholic mother, De Benedetti did not consider himself a Jew, but was often referred to as one in the press.) Focusing on De Benedetti's role in the October stock-market crash, Panerai pointed out that on this occasion, De Benedetti was among the few who had actually profited, by selling stocks and bonds in large amounts at the very last moment, when market values were still high. Noting that James Goldsmith and Edmund de Rothschild were the only other financiers who had not lost fortunes in October, he concluded that Jews were known to be shrewd and far-sighted, and that this was due to their big noses. (In Italian, "to have a nose" means, colloquially, "to be shrewd.") Other remarks by Panerai actually hinted at the responsibility of the "Jewish lobby" for the stock-market crash.

In the course of the year the popular Catholic weekly *Il Sabato* distinguished itself by frequent use of anti-Semitic statements. An October editorial charged that the American stock-market crash was caused by the maneuvering of the "Jewish lobby, overwhelmingly powerful in international finance." The same month, another editorial spoke of "Jewish misuse of the Western guilt complex for the Holocaust in order to achieve purely political goals." After the outbreak of the Arab revolt in December, similar remarks appeared in almost every article dealing with the situation in the territories and the Jewish-Arab conflict. The Jewish community strongly condemned each of these episodes through public statements.

## Religious Education in Public Schools

Under the concordat reached between the Italian government and the Catholic Church in 1984, which ended the status of Catholicism as the state religion, Catholic religious instruction in public schools was not eliminated but was made optional. As an extension of that principle, the Ministry of Education now allowed every religious group to organize religion classes in public schools for its adherents. The Jews, the Protestant Churches, and other non-Catholic groups objected that any sectarian teaching was a violation of the principle of equality and was thus inherently discriminatory. These groups had begun their fight for complete secularization of the public schools in 1985 and continued throughout 1987, but with no notable results. In October it was discovered that a public school in Rome had arranged Jewish religious teaching for its Jewish pupils, with the aid and support of some rabbis of the local community. When this provoked a wave of criticism and protest within the Roman and other Jewish communities, the classes were stopped.

JEWISH COMMUNITY

## Demography

An estimated 31,000 Jews were affiliated with one or other of the local Italian Jewish communities, with no significant change in number over the last year.

The results of recent research conducted in the three main communities (Rome, Milan, and Turin), carried out jointly by scientific researchers and Jewish communal bodies, were published in part by the monthly *Shalom,* the periodical of the Rome Jewish community. The findings showed demographic patterns among Italian Jews to be similar to those of the non-Jewish Italian population: significant aging, a significant decline in births, and a diminishing number of marriages. The average age in the three communities was about 42, with only about 15 percent of the Jewish population below the age of 15. The current marriage rate was 60 percent, and the individual rate of intermarriage about 30 percent. The steady rise in intermarriage among the longtime Jewish population was offset to some extent by the recent immigration of a few thousand traditional Jews from Iran, mostly settled in Milan, who tended to marry only Jews. Participation in the life of the community was low, with only about 30 percent voting in community elections. As to religious observance, some 12 percent observed the Sabbath and dietary laws and attended services regularly, while roughly the same percentage never attended synagogue; 70 percent claimed to fast on Yom Kippur; some 65 percent to eat only matzah during Passover.

The level of general education was high, with approximately 30 percent graduating from university. Some 64 percent had studied for at least a few years in a Jewish school, and 40 percent of those with children had enrolled them in Jewish schools. About 41 percent said they had some minimal knowledge of Hebrew.

## Communal Affairs

### NEW AGREEMENT WITH THE STATE

Until the end of 1987 the relationship of individual Jews with the organized Jewish community and the latter's relationship with the Italian state had been regulated by a law passed in 1929 and a royal decree enacted in 1930. In 1977, at a time when the Italian government was trying to renegotiate its "concordats," or legal agreements, with the Catholic and Protestant Churches, the government opened negotiations with the Unione delle Comunità Israelitiche Italiane (Union of the Italian Jewish Communities, UCII), the representative body of Italian Jews. The government and the UCII agreed to keep parts of the 1930 decree in the new accord, particularly the fourth article, which required Jews to affiliate with the organized Jewish community wherever they lived and to pay taxes for the support of communal institutions. In the late seventies, however, a case challenging this article was brought by an individual before the Corte Costituzionale (Italy's supreme court), and both parties decided to suspend negotiations pending the court's verdict. In 1984 the court ruled that the fourth article was unconstitutional.

The government and the UCII resumed negotiations, in the fall of 1986 reaching agreement on terms that were presented and discussed at the 12th congress of the UCII (December 1986). By that time the Craxi government had successfully concluded new *concordati* with the Catholic and Protestant Churches. On February 27, 1987, the UCII and the Italian government signed the new agreement, which then had to be approved by both the Jewish communities and the Italian Parliament. When, only a few hours after the signing, the government resigned, controversy erupted in the Jewish community, with critics accusing the leaders of UCII of surrendering to pressure and to Craxi's personal desire to be remembered as the leader who had reached new accords with all the religions. Some in the Rome community were extremely critical of the content of the agreements as well. Replying to the charges, Tullia Zevi, president of the UCII, said that the leadership had decided to sign the agreements before anyone knew that a serious political crisis was in the offing. Further, she pointed out, in the event of a prolonged government crisis, with the resulting absence of a partner to an agreement, the years of negotiation up to this point could all be lost. As to the content of the agreements, Zevi reminded her critics that the terms had been discussed by the 12th congress of the UCII just two months earlier, and approved.

The new agreement defined the Jewish communities as " . . . the traditional institutions of Italian Jewry . . . which . . . provide for religious practices, teaching and education, promote Jewish culture, guard the common interests of the Jews, and contribute to the welfare of their members, in accordance with Jewish law and tradition. . . ." Affiliation with the communities was already on a voluntary basis, following the above-mentioned ruling of the Corte Costituzionale of 1984. Jewish communities were no longer to be considered public bodies, and the Italian state would have no control of their activities. Contributions to the communities could, however, be deducted from taxes, up to a maximum of 10 percent of personal income. Jews would be entitled to observe fully the Sabbath and holidays, no matter where they were employed, and to request kosher food and religious assistance in public institutions (army, prisons, hospitals). Jews would have the right to take an oath, whenever required by Italian law, in accordance with Jewish law and with covered head.

The UCII changed its name to the Unione delle Comunità *Ebraiche* (instead of *Israelitiche*) Italiane (UCEI), which has a subtle difference in meaning in Italian, difficult to render in English. The UCEI itself was defined as the "body which represents Italian Jewry before the state. . . . It attends to and protects the religious interests of the Jews in Italy, promotes the preservation of Jewish traditions and treasures, coordinates the activities of the local communities, and maintains relations with Jewish communities abroad." Moreover, in the agreement the Italian republic committed itself to protecting the Jewish artistic and cultural heritage in Italy. Other matters pertaining to Jewish life, such as the status of rabbis, ritual slaughter, burials, and weddings, which were already regulated by Jewish law, remained substantially unchanged.

As a result of the new agreement with the government, revised by-laws governing the Union of Italian Jewish Communities had to be prepared, a task undertaken by an appointed commission. Only at the end of the year, in December, was a special congress convened in Rome, with delegates elected both by the communities and by individuals, in order to vote on the by-laws and the agreement. Several points in the documents aroused heated controversy. On the agreement, many delegates feared that if the Jewish communities became wholly voluntary, Jewish identification would decline and the viability of communal institutions would be endangered. The response to this argument was that compulsory affiliation with the communities had been ruled out by the Corte Costituzionale, and that the Italian constitution explicitly forbade any interference by the state in the life of religious communities. Another objection was raised by delegates of secular orientation to the almost exclusively religious definition of Italian Jewry implied in the agreement. Leaders of UCII and other delegates pointed out that the Italian constitution allowed special agreements only with religious, and not with national or ethnic, groups, and that the new agreement in fact recognized the unique historic, social, and cultural characteristics of the Italian Jewish community.

There was an impassioned confrontation between delegates of religious and secular orientation over articles of the new by-laws concerning qualifications for election to local community councils and the UCII. It was proposed that "... members of councils ... should show evidence of normal religious behavior" and that "... the rabbinical court [have] the authority to dismiss members whose behavior does not meet the necessary requirements." Secular delegates argued that these terms automatically ruled out secular Jews from community leadership and granted the rabbinical courts powers far exceeding the scope of their authority. A compromise was eventually reached between the parties, the revised article stating only that the public behavior of council members should not conflict with Jewish laws and values. As to the dismissal of council members, while the chief rabbi of the community could point out that the behavior of a member of a council failed to meet "necessary requirements," only the council itself had the authority to dismiss a member, whatever the reason. After three days of intense debate, the by-laws, with the above-mentioned changes, and the agreement, which remained untouched, were approved by the congress of UCII (from then on, UCEI). Italian political leaders expressed satisfaction with the new agreement, calling it a necessary step for the strengthening of democracy, tolerance, and equality in Italy; however, Parliament had taken no formal action on the matter by the end of 1987.

## Jewish-Catholic Relations

The visit of Pope John Paul II to the main synagogue of Rome in April 1986 had aroused expectations of further improvement in Jewish-Catholic relations in Italy. The hopes of many Italian Jews were dampened, however, by subsequent events. One was the elevation to sainthood in 1986 of Giuseppe Tomasi, a 17th-century ecclesiastic who was credited with many miracles, chief among them the conversion of Rabbi Mosè da Cave. Another event that aroused criticism was the beatification in May of Edith Stein, a German Jewish convert to Catholicism, a nun in the Carmelite order, who was gassed at Auschwitz. Many Jews were offended by the church's portrayal of her as a Christian martyr, when it seemed evident to them that she had been deported and killed as a Jew, not as a Catholic. Further, in June the authoritative journal *Renovatio,* published by the important bishopric of Genoa, affirmed that Jews were not included in the divine plan for salvation, since they had refused the truth and were cursed by Jesus.

The most provocative episode of all took place in June, when the pope received Austrian president Kurt Waldheim, who stood accused of participating in atrocities against partisans and Jews while serving in the German army during World War II. Just two months earlier Waldheim had been declared *persona non grata* by the

U.S. government because of his war record. To express their outrage, on June 25, Jews from all over the world organized a demonstration in St. Peter's Square in Rome, at the entrance to Vatican City. While the number of participants was not large—about a thousand—the event made a strong impression on the Italian media and public opinion. Responding to the chorus of protests over his meeting with Waldheim, the pope subsequently met with American Jewish delegations, in Italy and in the United States, to express his understanding of the Jewish position on matters relating to the Holocaust. Relations became strained again, however, in October, with the publication of an interview with Joseph Cardinal Ratzinger, secretary of Propaganda Fidae, the Vatican office for doctrine, in the popular Catholic weekly *Il Sabato,* in which he implied that in dialogue with Jews, Catholics should pursue the "theological line" that the true fulfillment of Judaism was represented by Christianity.

## Culture

The Italian National Jewish Library and Heritage Center, with the support and assistance of the Olivetti industrial group, continued the cataloging of Jewish community libraries and artistic treasures in Italy. The center also worked toward closer collaboration with Italian authorities. Current projects involving the center and Italian institutions included the restoration and opening to the public of the Jewish catacombs of the Villa Torlonia in Rome, the preservation and study of the Jewish catacombs of Venosa (Basilicata, southern Italy), and the restoration of the Sephardic synagogue of Pesaro, built in the 17th century. The Italian synagogue of Venice, built in 1575, underwent significant renovation.

Close collaboration between Italian and Israeli public institutions and scholars continued to flourish under the provisions of the cultural agreement signed in 1985. A catalogue of all Hebrew books published in the 16th century and housed in the public libraries of Emilia-Romagna was prepared by an Italian staff with the assistance of the Jewish National and University Library of Jerusalem. Important archaeological finds from several excavations in Israel were shown in Rome in April in an exhibition organized by the Israeli embassy in Italy and the Cultural Office of the Rome municipality. In connection with the "twinning" of the Israeli city of Acre with the Italian city of Pisa, an exhibition depicting the historical relations between some Italian towns and Acre during the period of the Crusades was presented in Rome in the summer. In July the municipality of Tel Aviv, the Dance Library of Israel, and the Italian Cultural Institute of Tel Aviv organized a conference in Pesaro on Guglielmo Ebreo, the 15th-century Jew who wrote the first modern treatise on the art of dance, *Trattato dell'arte del ballo* (ca. 1463).

A festival of Jewish culture took place in Milan in April and May, organized by Salone Pier Lombardo, a private theater. The program included theatrical presentations, conferences, and films. Among the participants were New York's Living Theater and the Israeli ballet company Kol Demamah.

Recent developments in anti-Semitism, its modern roots, and the rise of historical revisionism in Europe were analyzed at a conference on *"Ebraismo e Antiebraismo"* (Judaism and anti-Judaism), organized in Florence in March by the Gramsci Institute of Tuscany, a cultural center affiliated with the Communist party.

## Publications

This year saw the publication of the proceedings of two important international conferences held in Italy in recent years. One was the second international *"Italia Judaica"* conference, held in Genoa in 1984, on the history and culture of the Jews of Italy during the Renaissance and Baroque periods. *Italia Judaica,* an ongoing research project, was administered by a joint Italian-Israeli committee. The second conference, *"Ebrei a Venezia"* (Jews in Venice), held in Venice in 1983, had been organized by the Cini Foundation.

Among new works on the recent history of the Jews of Italy were Emanuela Trevisan Semi's *Allo specchio dei Falascià* ("In the Mirror of the Falashas"), a study of relations in the 1930s between the Fascist regime, Italian and Ethiopian Jews, and the Italian colonial adventure in Ethiopia. An in-depth study by the American scholar Susan Zuccotti, *The Italians and the Holocaust,* appeared in Italian translation at the beginning of the year.

Early in 1987, a few months after the publication of *I sommersi e i salvati* (*The Drowned and the Saved*), Primo Levi's reconsideration of his Holocaust experience, a related and already famous essay by Jean Améry on his ordeal in Auschwitz was published in Italian under the title *Intellettuale a Auschwitz* ("Intellectual in Auschwitz"). The Viennese-born Améry, son of assimilated Jews, went to Belgium in 1938, where he joined an anti-Nazi group. The essay first appeared in a book titled *Jenseits von Schuld und Sühne* ("Beyond Crime and Punishment"). Levi's and Améry's books both aroused wide attention and debate.

Other noteworthy new works about Italian Jews were *Perfidi giudei, fratelli maggiori* ("Wicked Jews, Elder Brothers"), the memoirs of Chief Rabbi of Rome Elio Toaff, and *Pagine ebraiche* ("Pages in Judaica"), a collection of articles and essays about Jewish history by Arnaldo Momigliano, a leading scholar of ancient history.

Israeli literature, previously unknown in Italy, achieved recognition this year. Three novellas by A. B. Yehoshua ("Facing the Forests," "Early in the Summer of 1970," and "The Continuing Silence of the Poet") were published in Italian in one volume titled *Il poeta continua a tacere* (from the title of the last work). An anthology of 11 short stories by as many Israeli contemporary writers, *La novella d'Israele* ("Tales of Israel"), was published as well.

## Primo Levi

The Italian public at large and the Jewish community in particular were shocked and saddened by the suicide, in April, of Primo Levi, a survivor of Auschwitz and one of Italy's best-known novelists. Born in Turin in 1919 into an assimilated, middle-class Jewish family, Levi graduated in chemistry from the University of Turin in 1941. In late 1943, after an armistice was concluded between Italy and the Allies, but with central and northern Italy still in German hands, he entered the Italian resistance and joined a military unit in the Piedmontese Alps. In December 1943, as the result of a betrayal, Levi was captured by the Fascists, soon confessed to being a Jew, and was sent first to the detention camp at Fossoli and later to Auschwitz. In the extermination camp, Levi worked as a chemist, a fact to which he attributed, at least partly, his survival. After the camp was liberated by the Russian Army, he wandered about Eastern Europe, returning to Italy in 1946, settling in Turin and resuming work as a chemist in a paint factory.

Levi wrote a book about his experiences in Auschwitz, which was first rejected by a famous publishing house, then issued in 1947 by a small firm under the title *Se questo è un uomo* (1947) (published in the United States under the title *If This Is a Man*, in 1959, and later reissued as *Survival in Auschwitz*). When the book was republished in 1957 by the same Italian publishing house that had first rejected it, becoming a best-seller and even a school textbook in Italy, Levi was encouraged to continue writing. His second work, *La tregua* (1963) (*The Truce*, 1965; U.S. edition, *The Reawakening*, 1965), was based on his wanderings and adventures in Eastern Europe after liberation. His next two works (not available in English) were *Storie naturali* (1966) ("Natural Stories"), a collection of moralistic and fantastic tales published over the years under the pseudonym of Damianos Malabaila—for which he was awarded the Bagutta, his first literary prize—and *Vizio di forma* (1971) ("Technical Error"), a book of stories. In 1975 Levi published *Il sistema periodico* (*The Periodic Table*, 1984), and the collection of poetry *L'osteria di Brema* ("The Tavern of Bremen"). *The Periodic Table*, which was widely praised, is a series of 21 autobiographical stories, each linked thematically to one of the chemical elements.

Even with his growing success as an author, Levi continued to work as a chemist, until retiring in 1977. In 1978 he published his first novel, *La chiave a stella* (*The Monkey's Wrench*, 1986), a long monologue by a workingman, a skilled rigger of derricks, discussing in vernacular Italian his adventures and his philosophy of life. This volume won the prestigious Strega Prize. In 1981 Levi edited an anthology of literary selections, ranging from the Bible to 20th-century writers, titled *La ricerca delle radici* ("Looking for Roots"). The same year he published another collection of stories, *Lilit e altri racconti* (*Moments of Reprieve*, 1986). *L'altrui mestiere*, published in 1985 (*Other People's Trades*, 1989), is an anthology of articles on various subjects, including the *Shulhan Arukh* and the culture of Eastern European Jews. His next work, turning away from autobiography, dealt with East European

Jewry and Ashkenazi culture, to which he had been introduced in Auschwitz and in his postwar odyssey. The novel *Se non ora, quando?* (1982) (*If Not Now, When?* 1985), which won the 1982 Viareggio and Campiello Prizes, is about a band of Jewish partisans seeking to make their way from Russia to Palestine at the end of World War II. In his last work, *I sommersi e i salvati* (1986) (*The Drowned and the Saved, 1988*), a book that can be considered his moral testament, the author reconsiders the Holocaust and his concentration-camp experiences. Primo Levi began to enjoy fame in Europe in the late 1960s and in the United States in the second half of the 1970s. His books reflect a wide culture, humanistic and scientific both, and his writing style has been lauded by both readers and critics for its clarity, lack of bitterness, and poetic elegance.

Levi considered himself an "integrated" Jew, whose main roots were in Italian rather than Jewish culture, which he confessed to not knowing enough about. He wrote that he became clearly aware of his Jewish identity as a result of the Fascist racial laws, the German persecution, and Auschwitz. His first contact with a deep Jewish life was in Auschwitz and his Eastern European wanderings after liberation. Primo Levi was decidedly secular: "The Holocaust confirmed my basic questions, rather than making me closer to religion," he said. In 1982 Levi signed a petition written by a group of Italian Jewish intellectuals, protesting the Israeli government's decision to invade southern Lebanon. The petition provoked controversy, and a wave of sharp criticism was directed at Levi in the Jewish community.

## Personalia

Bruno Zevi, a leading architect and architectural historian, was elected to the Lower Chamber of Parliament as a member of the Radical party. Zevi was born in Rome in 1918, studied at Harvard University, and returned to Italy after World War II, where, following Frank Lloyd Wright's theories and example, he championed an organic approach to architecture. He was appointed professor of modern architecture at La Sapienza University in Rome in 1948. Author of many books on architecture, he edited and published the monthly *L'Architettura* as well as writing on that subject for the popular weekly *L'Espresso*. Zevi was an active member of the Jewish community.

Arnaldo Momigliano, a world-famous scholar of ancient history, died in London in August, aged 79. Born into a traditional Piedmontese family in 1908, Momigliano studied at the universities of Turin and Rome, teaching in both from 1932 to 1938, when he left Italy because of the Fascist racial laws. He immigrated to England, where he taught at Oxford and Bristol Universities and London University College. From 1975 on he was professor of Roman history at the University of Chicago. Among his many noted publications were *Prime linee di storia della tradizione Maccabica* ("First Outlines of the History of the Maccabean Tradition," 1930); *The Conflict Between Paganism and Christianity in the Fourth Century* (ed., 1963); *Studies in Historiography* (1966); *Essays in Ancient and Modern Historiography*

(1977); *On Pagans, Jews, and Christians* (1987); and his series *Contributi alla storia degli studi classici* ("Contributions to the History of Classical Studies"). Among the numerous honors he received were the British Academy's Kenyon Medal, the Viareggio Prize, the Kaplun Prize of the Hebrew University of Jerusalem, and a knighthood from the British Crown.

SIMONETTA DELLA SETA

# Federal Republic of Germany

## National Affairs

FEDERAL ELECTIONS HELD ON January 25, 1987, after a calm and relatively uneventful campaign, produced no great surprises. The ruling Christian Democrats (CDU) dropped by about 3 percent to 37.5 percent of the vote; their coalition partner, the Free Democrats (FDP), increased by about 2 percent to 10 percent. On the opposition side, the Social Democrats (SPD) dropped one percentage point to 38 percent; and the Greens went up 3 percent to 8 percent. Some right-wing parties, such as the neo-Nazi National Democratic party (NPD), also increased their shares somewhat, but were far from getting any of their candidates elected.

Following the elections, Hans-Dietrich Genscher's FDP was prepared to form another coalition with Chancellor Helmut Kohl's CDU/CSU (Christian Social Union). Even before that, the party's leadership had decided to make concessions to the CDU/CSU, in particular, support for a crown's-witness statute offering reduced penalties to defendants in terrorist trials who were willing to testify against associates. Following the elections, the FDP also agreed to the imposition of criminal penalties for wearing masks at public demonstrations (by persons seeking to remain unidentifiable). Both concessions were decided on against strong opposition by the FDP's rank and file and under strong pressure from the CDU/CSU.

A major scandal that shook the country was the Barschel affair in Schleswig-Holstein. Premier Uwe Barschel was accused of conducting a "dirty tricks" electoral campaign against his political opponents. He was later found a suicide, albeit under mysterious circumstances, in a Geneva hotel. This and other scandals tarnished the image of the CDU/CSU party, and Chancellor Kohl was reelected party chairman with the lowest number of votes he had ever received. The party financing scandal (see AJYB 1988, vol. 88, p. 317), continued this year with court verdicts announced against top-ranking figures in business and government, including former Flick manager Eberhard von Brauchitsch, Hans Friderichs, and Count Lambsdorff, the former federal economics minister. The three were convicted of tax fraud and sentenced to payments of high penalties.

The Social Democrats (SPD) experienced two losses in 1987. First was the defeat of their candidate for chancellor, Johannes Rau, premier of North Rhine–Westphalia, in the federal elections. Second was the resignation of Willy Brandt, who had chaired the party for 23 years, in response to protests against some of his appointments. The new executive presented a more leftist image of the party, especially with Oskar Lafontaine, premier of the Saarland, as vice-chairman. This opening to the left involved greater sensitivity to ecological and women's issues and a willingness to deal with the alternative and Green-oriented movements.

The Green party continued to be divided by conflict between "Realists" and "Fundamentalists" in the party—the latter representing a hardline, more traditionally leftist position, the former advocating a closer working relationship with others, especially with the Social Democrats. One issue dividing the factions was the party's attitude to Israel. In the early 1980s, under the leadership of Jürgen Reents and the Fundamentalists, the party issued strong condemnation and criticism of Israel. In more recent years, however, the party expressed virtually unqualified support for Israel, as a result of efforts by Otto Schily and other members of the Realist wing in the party, which also made a number of moves toward closer relations with the Jewish leadership in the Federal Republic. In light of the continuing divisiveness, which had never been as bitter as this year, the party scheduled a crisis meeting in mid-December. The consensus was to seek cooperation and consolidation of the warring factions.

The economy, while slow overall, was relatively healthy, with record foreign-trade figures; however, the crisis in the steel industry worsened. There was serious unrest in the Ruhr and numerous strikes, especially by Thyssen steelworkers whose Duisburg-Rheinhausen steel plant was slated to be closed down, with a projected loss of 30,000 jobs. Negotiations between the DGB (German Federation of Unions) and the CDU government were largely unsuccessful. The government did, however, agree to subsidize the steel industry with DM 150,000, with the help of state and European Community (EC) funds.

CIVIL RIGHTS ISSUES

Overall, 1987 was not a good year for civil rights. While the state of Hamburg was the first in the Federal Republic to drop the *Berufsverbot* legislation barring leftists from civil-service jobs, the Bavarian government drafted legislation requiring mandatory AIDS tests for civil-service applicants, citizens from non-EC countries, and prisoners. Also in Bavaria, a court rejected the demand for a plebiscite on Wackersdorf, site of a highly contested nuclear plant, and there were regular reports that local citizens opposed to this project were being intimidated by police and local officials. A large demonstration at that site in September encountered massive police brutality, especially by a special crack unit brought in from West Berlin. The shooting of two policemen trying to break up a demonstration at a Frankfurt airport construction site in turn reinforced demands for greater limitations on the right to demonstrate.

Another major issue was the national census, with opponents concerned about confidentiality and the possibility that the data might be pooled with those in police computers. Despite the threat of severe penalties, an estimated 1 to 3 percent of the population boycotted the census, refusing to answer questions. In West Berlin, where both the opposition and police response were particularly strong, on May 1 police raids related to anticensus activities triggered riots. There was also some opposition in the Jewish community. While the Central Council of Jews in Germany had specifically endorsed inclusion of the question on religious affiliation, many other Jews opposed it, recalling that it was through the Nazi censuses that Jews had become easily identifiable targets. The boycott activities of the Jüdische Gruppe Berlin, a group that considered itself in critical opposition to the organized community, led to an official decision permitting Berlin Jews not to answer the question on religion. In addition, many of the court proceedings against Jewish boycotters were eventually dropped.

FOREIGN AFFAIRS; EAST GERMANY

In 1987 the Kohl government continued its overtures toward Eastern Europe and its efforts to ease Soviet–West German relations. In early July, President Richard von Weizsäcker and Foreign Minister Hans-Dietrich Genscher visited the USSR, the first in a series of planned mutual visits. In the course of the meetings, a number of agreements were ratified, including a memorandum concerning scientific-technical cooperation between the Federal Republic of Germany (FRG) and the Soviet Union. Although the Germans were received in a somewhat cool and businesslike manner, and the mission was considered to have been a difficult one, it was seen, in the end, as a great success for von Weizsäcker.

In December President Ronald Reagan and General Secretary Mikhail Gorbachev signed the INF (Intermediate-range Nuclear Forces) treaty that involved the destruction of all American and Soviet medium-range missiles. In West Germany, as elsewhere in Europe, there was considerable opposition to the proposed disarmament moves. While the more liberal forces in the coalition supported the initiative, it was surely with considerable reluctance that, at the beginning of May, Chancellor Kohl wrote to President Reagan to express support for the INF treaty. As A. Mechtersheimer, Green party defense expert, put it in a parliamentary debate on December 10, "The government boasts about a treaty that it was unable to stop."

In early September, East German leader Erich Honecker came to the Federal Republic on a five-day visit that had been planned originally in 1984 and been postponed several times due to disagreements between the two German governments. While Honecker's visit did not change the basics of East-West German relations—indeed, both sides reiterated their traditional positions—it did bring about a considerable improvement in the climate between the two countries. Other officials of the Federal Republic and the GDR exchanged visits as well during the year.

These improvements had no influence, however, on the frosty relations surrounding the status of West Berlin. On the occasion of Berlin's 750th anniversary, Honecker turned down an invitation from Lord Mayor Diepgen to come to West Berlin, and Diepgen in turn, some weeks later, decided not to visit the eastern part of the city. Visitors to West Berlin's anniversary celebrations included the heads of state of the three major Western allies—Queen Elizabeth II, President Reagan, and President François Mitterrand. President Reagan's presence caused major protests and riots, which were exacerbated by the repressive measures taken by local officials, including summarily closing off main arteries of the borough of Kreuzberg from the remainder of the city. In his public remarks, Reagan called on General Secretary Gorbachev to "tear down the Wall" and proposed holding the Olympic Games in both parts of the divided city.

## Relations with Israel

The most important event in German-Israeli relations this year was Israeli president Chaim Herzog's five-day visit to Bonn, beginning April 6. This visit, publicly endorsed by Prime Minister Yitzhak Shamir but opposed, on historical grounds, by many members of his own Likud party, reciprocated President von Weizsäcker's visit to Israel in 1985. Herzog was received with full military honors, and the German president described the visit as an exceptional event in the history of the two peoples. Herzog visited, among other places, Bergen-Belsen (which he had last seen only a few days after the camp's liberation in 1945), Berlin (with stops at the Jewish community headquarters and the memorial to resistance fighters at Plötzensee), and the Worms synagogue and cemetery, the oldest Jewish burial ground in Europe.

Herzog's visit was preceded by yet another internal controversy over proposed arms shipments by the FRG to Saudi Arabia. In the course of debate on the matter, Bavarian premier Franz-Josef Strauss criticized Israel and claimed that Germany had a special responsibility to "think about Israel and its problems." In his view, Saudi Arabia was a moderate Arab country, as such in a position to help integrate Israel into the Middle East, and therefore should be supported with arms shipments in order to help it realize a stabilizing role in the region. These statements aroused considerable criticism and protest in all parties, particularly in the opposition Social Democratic and Green parties.

The Israeli minister of agriculture made a visit to West Germany in February and two follow-up visits later in the year. Foreign Minister Shimon Peres came to Bonn at the end of June, reiterating his call for a Middle East peace conference, and Defense Minister Yitzhak Rabin arrived in September to discuss both military cooperation between the two countries and arms shipments to the Middle East. Chief German participants in the talks were Defense Minister Manfred Wörner, Franz-Josef Strauss, premier of Bavaria, and Foreign Minister Genscher. A highly publicized visit to Israel by a Green party delegation sought to counteract the negative effects of another Green party delegation three years earlier that had voiced extremely strong criticism of Israel.

## Neo-Nazism and Anti-Semitism

The continued growth of the extreme Right was clearly discernible in 1987. It could be seen in the annual report of the German secret service as well as in frequent newspaper accounts of trials of the new breed of young neo-Nazis who belonged to recently formed organizations that demanded a new order for Europe and opposed its present borders. Prominent among these groups was the Gemeinschaft Deutscher Osten/Deutsche Volksunion (DVU), founded in 1981, which was attempting to recover the eastern territories and considered itself a government in exile.

Two surveys of attitudes of German youth confirmed the existence of rightist trends. In one, which became the subject of a hearing in the Baden-Württemberg parliament, 13 percent of respondents thought that Nazism was a good idea, badly executed, and 32.9 percent thought that all talk about the murder of Jews should stop. Another study of German youth (aged 16–17) and neo-Nazism, conducted in Bielefeld (Wilhelm Heitmeyer, *Rechtsextremistische Orientierungen bei Jugendlichen*, Juventa Verlag), found that about 40 percent inclined to violence and power, favored inequality, and agreed with the concept of biological superiority; nevertheless, few appeared interested in joining radical groups. In addition, 44 percent wanted foreigners out of the Federal Republic, and 24 percent thought that, except for the action taken against Jews, Nazism was good.

Government policies toward neo-Nazism tended to be contradictory. The right-leaning, conservative federal interior minister, Friedrich Zimmermann, for example, decided not to ban the neo-Nazi Freiheitliche Arbeiterpartei (FAP). He and some of his colleagues expressed openly racist attitudes toward foreign workers and those seeking political asylum from Third World countries, while warmly welcoming Eastern European immigrants of "German descent." Similarly, despite protests by Jewish representatives, a high federal court acquitted a right-wing lawyer for making anti-Jewish statements. In his defense of an SS leader in the Warsaw ghetto, the lawyer, Jürgen Rieger, had claimed, among other things, that with even a minimum of solidarity among themselves, the Jews living in the ghetto could have avoided hunger and disease. He also asserted that the killings were carried out solely as measures to contain epidemics.

On the other hand, a number of neo-Nazi activists were convicted by lower courts, which sentenced them to substantial fines and jail terms. Moreover, when a DVU candidate won an election in Bremen, a statement denouncing this neofascist splinter group was published by labor unions, churches, and immigrant/foreigner groups. Similarly, when an anti-Semitic campaign was directed at a Jewish physician, Dr. Kiesel, in the Hessian town of Gedern, the magistrate of the city and the city council supported him and offered a reward for information about those responsible for the hate campaign. Many neo-Nazi meetings were sabotaged or demonstrated against by anti-Nazi coalitions, often composed of groups with Social-Democratic and Green leanings. In Schlüchern (Hesse), 1,500 people demonstrated outside a meeting attended by 40 neo-Nazis.

## JEWISH COMMUNITY

## Demography

As of January 1, 1988, the 65 local Jewish communities in the Federal Republic and West Berlin had a total of 27,612 members—14,017 males and 13,595 females. (Comparative figures for 1987 and 1986, respectively, were: 27,533—13,998 males and 13,535 females; 27,538—13,990 males and 13,548 females.) The age distribution of registered community members was as follows (the figure in parentheses is for the previous year): 0–15 years—3,668 (3,533); 16–30—4,513 (4,517); 31–40—4,327 (4,269); 41–60—7,067 (7,013); 61–70—3,934 (3,977); and over 70—4,103 (4,224). These figures confirm a trend observable since the early 1980s, namely, a slowing down of the severely overaged character of the population and noticeable increases in the category of young families (the 31–40 age bracket) and in the numbers of young children.

Estimates for Jews not registered with the organized community ranged from the 6,000–8,000 figure of the Central Jewish Welfare Agency (Zentralwohlfahrtsstelle der Juden) to the 25,000–30,000 cited by various other sources. Conversions to Judaism (43) were matched by membership cancellations (41). Total losses resulting from deaths (423) and emigration (237) essentially canceled out gains from births (11) and immigration (546). Most of the immigrants came from the USSR and a considerable number from Israel. Many of the Israelis settled in Frankfurt, while most of the Soviet Jews settled in West Berlin. The largest communities were West Berlin (6,132), Frankfurt (4,957), Munich (4,031), Hamburg (1,374), and Cologne (1,278). Together these six communities accounted for about two-thirds of the entire registered Jewish population in the Federal Republic. Many of the smaller communities had no, or only very few, younger Jewish members and were judged likely to disappear completely within the next few decades. All things considered, Jews in the Federal Republic still lacked critical mass. One indication of this was the frequent appeal for the involvement of the younger generation in community work; at the same time, the younger generation was too weak to consolidate and assume an identity of its own—at least inside the community structure. This was exemplified in the self-dissolution of the Federation of Jewish Youth at a January meeting. It was a small group that simply failed to attract new members.

## Communal Affairs

Elections to the board of the Central Council of Jews in Germany (Zentralrat der Juden in Deutschland), held in February, confirmed Werner Nachmann, a businessman from Karlsruhe, as chairman, by a large majority. Max Willner of Offenbach (Hesse), director for many years of the Central Jewish Welfare Agency, and Michael Fürst, a lawyer from Hannover, were elected vice-chairmen.

At meetings in Berlin in December, the council discussed the problem of mixed marriage, which it saw as a serious threat to the survival of the Jewish *Gemeinden* (local communities), one that was likely to produce Christian-Jewish rather than Jewish communities. It was pointed out that, especially in the small communities, young people faced considerable difficulty meeting suitable Jewish partners. Many more youth seminars and meetings were needed in order for younger people to meet each other, and it was suggested that young Jews should be encouraged to spend time at the Hochschule für Jüdische Studien (College for Jewish Studies) in Heidelberg.

Although the Jewish community in West Germany no longer felt isolated on the international Jewish scene, the council favored greater contact between the various Jewish communities in Europe in order to help keep the Jewish community in Germany "dynamic." Participants in the meetings warned against the revisionist theories of historian Ernst Nolte and others in the "historians' dispute" and urged the council to take a more active role in public debates of this type.

On the occasion of East German leader Erich Honecker's visit to the FRG, Werner Nachmann requested that scholars be granted access to the Central Archive of Jewish History in Germany now located in East Germany. Honecker promised that action would be taken on this request. In another matter, the Central Council was involved in negotiations that resulted in the creation of a final West German reparations fund of DM 5 million. Called *Hilfe für Opfer der NS Willkürherrschaft*, the monies were intended for those victims of Nazism who to date had not received any assistance.

In Darmstadt a foundation stone was laid for a new synagogue. The idea of rebuilding the synagogue originated in 1984 with non-Jewish citizens and was eventually taken up by the entire city council. In Freiburg a new synagogue was dedicated on November 5, close to the date of the pogrom in 1938 on which the old synagogue was destroyed.

The Central Jewish Welfare Agency of Jews in Germany (Zentralwohlfahrtstelle der Juden in Deutschland, ZWST), which was reestablished in 1951, celebrated its 70th anniversary in 1987. It was generally regarded as the most active, best-financed, and best-organized Jewish welfare and social-service organization in Europe. In terms of youth work, for example, in 1986 the ZWST conducted 13 summer camps with a total of 735 participants; the figure had been rising steadily over the years. The agency's youth department also conducted group Bar/Bat Mitzvah tours to Israel for 13–15-year-olds, twice a year. Two summer-camp sites and resorts, one in Wembach (Southern Black Forest) and the other in Sobernheim/Nahe, were available for younger children and the elderly. The ZWST assisted the major Jewish communities (except for Hamburg, but also including Stuttgart) in running nursery schools, which had a total enrollment of about 460 children. The three largest communities, in turn, also had Jewish day schools at the elementary level, with a total enrollment of almost 300 children. The ZWST awarded 779 student scholarships, up from 688 in 1984. Jewish nursing homes for the elderly in ten German cities served a total of 800 persons.

The ZWST saw as an important task demonstrating its solidarity with the Jewish communities of Eastern Europe. On various occasions it assisted the small remaining Jewish community in Poland with kosher food supplies and offered elderly Jews from Czechoslovakia medically supervised vacations in the Federal Republic.

THE JÜDISCHE GRUPPEN

Following the Israeli invasion of Lebanon in 1982, many younger Jewish intellectuals in West Germany voiced public opposition both to the invasion and the support given the Lebanon campaign by official Jewish representatives in the Federal Republic. As a result of threats and reprisals suffered by a number of these individuals—such as being barred from writing in Jewish publications—they joined together, first in small groups in several cities, eventually linking up nationwide and even including like-minded groups in Switzerland and Austria. Numerous meetings were held over the years, many at a retreat near Frankfurt, at the invitation of the Protestant Church; others in West Berlin, Zurich, and Vienna. Originally recruited from graduates of the 1968 student movement, the groups later began to draw younger people as well. While they continued to criticize Israeli policies and to explore ways to enter into dialogue with Palestinians, most of their activities related to the problems of living as Jews in Germany and to questions of neo-Nazism and racism in West German society. Some of Germany's most prominent younger Jewish professors, other intellectuals, and artists belonged to the groups, which had already produced a considerable number of publications, some receiving wide attention. In a few cities, notably Frankfurt, attempts were being made to bring the group closer to the organized Jewish community.

## Jewish-Christian Relations

The visit of Pope John Paul II to Germany on April 30, in part to officiate at the beatification of Edith Stein, a Jewish-born Carmelite nun who perished in the Holocaust, highlighted the ongoing controversy in the Catholic Church between conservative and reforming forces, those adhering to traditional anti-Jewish conceptions and those supporting change in Catholic-Jewish relations. Cologne prelate Dr. Jakob Schlafke, who had been promoting Stein's beatification for many years, argued in a television interview that she "died for the infidelity (*Unglauben*) of the Jewish people." He said, "She sacrificed herself so that Christ would be recognized by all." According to Schlafke, Edith Stein's last will included the following passage, which was an important factor in the drive for her beatification: "I ask the Lord that he may accept my life as atonement for the infidelity of the Jewish people and so that the Lord be accepted by his own [people] and his Kingdom come in eternity." Schlafke argued that while the Church had "deep respect for the faith of the Jews," it of course hoped that the time would come when the Jews recognized Christ. "We cannot take away," he said, "the fact that the Christian faith is the fulfillment of the Jewish faith."

The Central Council of Jews, whose delegates also had a brief ceremonial meeting with the pope, questioned Cardinal Höffner, head of the German Conference of Bishops, about the propriety of Schlafke's remarks. Höffner responded that Schlafke was expressing his own personal opinion and did not reflect the views of the cardinal, who, together with the Catholic Church in Germany, firmly supported the declaration "Nostra Aetate" of the Second Vatican Council. In cordial terms, Höffner also expressed his hope for a continuation of dialogue with the Jews.

Stein's American relatives reported that some Jews had tried to discourage them from coming to Germany to attend the beatification ceremonies. However, Susanne Batzdorff, a niece who resided in California, indicated that despite some misgivings, she considered the beatification an attempt by the Church to improve its relations with the Jews.

On the more positive side of Jewish-Christian relations, this year's Brotherhood Week featured the State of Israel as its theme, using as its motto *"Suchet der Stadt Bestes"* (Seek the Peace of the City—Jer. 29:7). The Coordinating Council of Associations for Christian-Jewish Cooperation awarded its Buber-Rosenzweig Medal to Neve Shalom, an interfaith Jewish-Arab settlement near Latrun, Israel. Gertrud Luckner, a non-Jewish former inmate of Ravensbruck concentration camp, received the Sir Sigmund Sternberg Award for her work in behalf of Christian-Jewish understanding and her help to Jews under Nazism. The award was presented by the International Council of Christians and Jews.

## The Börneplatz Controversy

In the course of excavations for the new administrative headquarters of Frankfurt's municipal gas company, the foundations of the Steinerne Haus, a palatial Jewish home built in 1717, and a *mikveh* (ritual bath) dating from 1462 were unearthed. The construction was taking place at the Börneplatz—named for Ludwig Börne, an important Jewish writer and contemporary of Heinrich Heine—which was also the site of the historic Jewish ghetto of Frankfurt. The discoveries raised questions about whether the original conception for the gas company's headquarters should stay unchanged and some of the remains simply be placed into a museum— as suggested by the city—or whether, as suggested by opposition groups, the plans should be thoroughly revised in order to preserve the remains *in situ*. After all, it was argued, this was the historic home of one of the most important Jewish communities in the Diaspora.

As discussions proceeded, more foundations were unearthed, mostly those of more ordinary living quarters of the Judengasse. The new excavations conveyed a sense of the cramped living conditions in the Jewish quarter before 1811, after which the Jews were allowed to leave the ghetto and live in other sections of town. (When the ghetto was razed in 1884, one of Frankfurt's most important synagogues was built on the site, together with the square. The Börneplatz synagogue, destroyed on November 9, 1938, was immortalized in one of Max Beckmann's most famous paintings, while the square was renamed Dominikanerplatz by the Nazis, a name kept until 1977.) A number of people in the Jewish community as well as some non-Jewish intellectuals had been urging for some years that the area be redesigned so as to preserve its historic significance.

In August a group of young opponents of the construction—Jewish and non-Jewish, representatives of the churches, of the SPD, and the Greens—began to occupy the construction site, blocking further work. A few days later they were carried off by police, and construction proceeded virtually without any changes, with the city agreeing merely to preserve the foundations of the *mikveh* and the Steinerne Haus.

Through all this, the Frankfurt Jewish community was divided. Before construction was even planned, its leaders had demanded that a memorial be built on the site. They had also, however, given permission for the construction to proceed. Once the foundations were excavated, the community tried to reopen the matter; however, when the city administration would not budge, except for the symbolic preservation of a few of the remains, Jewish representatives did not press their case. Without the engagement of the younger Jewish generation, the entire matter would never have become a hotly debated public issue.

## Cultural and Commemorative Events

Many of the events held in connection with the celebration of the 750th anniversary of the founding of Berlin focused on the important Jewish role in the city. The main anniversary exhibit included a large section on Jewish life, pointing to the presence of Jews in Berlin from its earliest years. The Fasanenstrasse Community Center featured an exhibit titled "Jewish Artists from Eastern Europe." A Jewish cultural festival (*Jüdische Kulturtage*) was held for the first time, in June, sponsored and organized by the Jewish community, with lectures, presentations on exiled Jewish writers, and a film retrospective. Other exhibits included one on artist Arthur Segal, originally from Berlin, and another on Jewish life in Berlin, in the Fasanenstrasse center. The villa of the noted Oppenheim banking family in Berlin featured an exhibit of paintings by Annemarie Oppenheim, a descendant of the family. The author of the novel *Alexanderplatz* was the subject of "Alfred Döblin as Example: City and Literature." Another exhibit was devoted to theater director and teacher Max Reinhardt. A public school was renamed the Moses Mendelssohn School.

This year was also the 45th anniversary of the Wannsee Conference, at which Nazi leaders planned "the Final Solution." Participating in a commemoration at the site were Lord Mayor Diepgen and the heads of all political parties. It was decided that the villa, currently a schoolchildren's resort, would be turned into a museum and study center. A museum was opened on the grounds of the former headquarters of the Gestapo and SS, with an exhibit called "Topography of Terror." The museum afforded access to the basement prison cells where victims of Nazism were held and tortured. Another noteworthy exhibit, entitled "T4, 1939–45," documented the Nazi euthanasia program. It was shown at Tiergartenstrasse 4, the building where the murders were planned. A commemorative exhibit opened at yet another infamous site, that of the Nazi party's former headquarters for mass events, the Reichsparteitaggelände, in Nuremberg.

Among many other commemorative events, too numerous to list in their entirety, both Munich and Düsseldorf featured exhibits of art works considered "degenerate" under Nazism (*Entartete Kunst*). Düsseldorf mounted a show honoring Alfred Flechtheim, a noted art collector and gallery owner in the 1920s. In Osnabrück, deliberations began concerning future use of the Nussbaum villa, built by the parents of Felix Nussbaum, the noted artist who lived in exile in Belgium and was killed in Auschwitz in 1944. The Cologne city archive opened an exhibit on the history of that city's Jews. Kassel and Frankfurt presented exhibits to mark the occasion of Franz Rosenzweig's 100th birthday.

Commemorative plaques and monuments were erected at the sites of numerous synagogues in small towns and villages. These were frequently accompanied by the publication of books, written by local teachers and amateur historians, on the history of the Jews in those locales. Such events included, this year, an exhibit on Jewish life in the town of Weiden (Upper Palatinate) and one in Viernheim, a small town near Mannheim. The latter, following the example of other towns, invited former Jewish inhabitants now living in the United States, Israel, and elsewhere, to visit as guests of the town. By contrast, the municipality of Dachau rejected a proposed Memorial and Youth Center, planned at the initiative of Aktion Sühnezeichen (Project Atonement). City officials said, "The CSU in Dachau will fight to the last drop of blood and with all determination against a youth meeting center. With the best of good will, it cannot be expected that we agree to a linkage between our city and the general guilt. Such centers would have to be built in Munich, Nuremberg or Berlin."

*Publications*

Noteworthy new books on general Jewish history included Ruth Beckermann, *Die Mazzesinsel. Juden in der Wiener Leopoldstadt von 1918–1938* ("Jews in the Viennese Leopoldstadt, 1918–1938"); Mario Offenberg, ed., *Adass Jisroel—die Jüdische Gemeinde in Berlin 1869–1942; Vernichtet und vergessen* ("Adass Yisroel, The Jewish Community in Berlin, 1869–1942, Annihilated and Forgotten"); Uwe Barschel, *Gabriel Riesser als Abgeordneter des Herzogtums Lauenburg in der Frankfurter Paulskirche 1848/49* ("Gabriel Riesser's Role as Deputy of the Duchy of Lauenburg to the Frankfurt Paulskirche"); Hans Otto Schembs, *Der Börneplatz in Frankfurt am Main—Ein Spiegelbild jüdischer Geschichte* ("The Frankfurt Börneplatz: A Mirror of Jewish History").

Among new works on the Holocaust were Elisabeth Endres, *Edith Stein. Christ-*

*liche Philosophin und jüdische Märtyrerin* ("Edith Stein: Christian Philosopher and Jewish Martyr"); Angelika Ebbinghaus et al., *Zwangsarbeit bei Daimler Benz* ("Forced Labor at the Daimler Benz Auto Works"); Angelika Ebbinghaus, *Opfer und Täterinnen. Frauenbiographien des Nationalsozialismus* ("Victims and Women Perpetrators: Biographies of Nazi Women"); Josef Tal, *Der Sohn des Rabbiners. Ein Weg von Berlin nach Jerusalem* ("The Rabbi's Son: A Road from Berlin to Jerusalem"); Ursula Büttner, ed., *Das Unrechtsregime*, 2 vols. (on Nazi ideology, defense of the Weimar Republic, Nazi system of rule, terror, resistance); Barbara Beuys, *Vergesst uns nicht. Menschen im Widerstand 1933–1945* ("Do Not Forget Us—People in Resistance 1933–1945"); Peter Steinbach, ed., *Widerstand. Ein Problem zwischen Theorie und Geschichte* ("Resistance: A Problem Between Science and History"), originally a lecture series at the University of Passau. A previously published work, *The International Biographical Dictionary of Central European Emigrés, 1933–1945*, edited by Werner Röder and Herbert A. Strauss, 3 vols., was awarded the Walter Meckauer Medal.

In the area of Jewish thought, new works included Aron Ronald Bodenheimer, *Wir und die anderen* ("We and the Others"); and Henryk M. Broder and H. Recher, eds., *Jüdisches Lesebuch 1933–1938* ("Jewish Reader"), texts from the *Jüdische Almanach* that appeared between 1933 and 1938 in Czechoslovakia. Among other new works of nonfiction were Peter Sichrovsky, *Schuldig geboren—Kinder aus Nazifamilien* ("Born Guilty—Children from Nazi Families"); Ralph Giordano, *Die zweite Schuld oder von der Last Deutscher zu sein* ("The Second Guilt, or, About the Burden of Being a German"); and Yohanan Meroz, *In schwieriger Mission—Als Botschafter Israels in Bonn* ("A Difficult Mission—Ambassador of Israel in Bonn").

A new magazine, published in Frankfurt, was *Babylon—Beiträge zur Jüdischen Gegenwart* ("Contributions on the Jewish Presence"), edited by Dan Diner, Susann Heenen-Wolff, Gertrud Koch, Cilly Kugelmann, and Martin Löw-Beer. *Dachauer Hefte II*, edited by Wolfgang Benz and Barbara Distel, includes an account of the trial of Norbert Wollheim v. I.G. Farben, 1952–53.

## Personalia

Ignatz Bubis, executive chairman of the Frankfurt community, member of the administrative council and the board of directors of the Central Council of Jews in Germany, president of the Keren Hayesod and of State of Israel Bonds, board member of a number of Jewish philanthropies, and a member of the Hesse State Rundfunkrat (media supervisory council), was elected to the executive of the Jewish Agency. At a reception hosted by him on his 60th birthday, he announced the establishment of a foundation for the advancement of Jewish education and scholarship, in honor of his parents.

Heinz Galinski, leader of the West Berlin community for 40 years, was made an honorary citizen of West Berlin, the city's highest distinction, on the occasion of his

75th birthday. In his honor, the *Gemeinde* established the Heinz Galinski Foundation.

Alisa Ilse Fuss, a retired teacher, was awarded the Ingeborg Drewitz Prize for her work with the International League of Human Rights and her campaigns against racism in the FRG.

Sen. Henry Ehrenberg, long active in German-Israeli relations, was honored with the Great Cross of the West German Order of Merit, on the occasion of his 70th birthday. Philosopher Hans Jonas was awarded the Peace Prize of the German Booksellers' Association. Rabbi Nathan Peter Levinson, long active in Jewish-Christian relations, retired this year from his post in Baden.

Fritz Stern, German-born professor (emeritus) of history at Columbia University, New York, delivered an address to the West German parliament on June 17, a national holiday marking the 1953 uprising in East Germany. (Stern's address was reprinted in the *New York Review of Books*, Dec. 3, 1987.)

Among prominent Jews who died in 1987 were Minna Aron, head of the Recklinghausen Jewish community since 1958, aged 73; Hans Rosenthal, a well-known TV entertainer who survived Nazism as a young orphan by hiding out in summer cottages outside Berlin, aged 62; Jacob Taubes, former professor at the Hebrew University, Harvard, Princeton, and Columbia, and since 1966 professor of Judaism and hermeneutics at the Free University of Berlin, aged 64; and Mary Gerold-Tucholsky, in Rottach Egern (Bavaria), aged 89.

Y. Michal Bodemann

# German Democratic Republic

## Holocaust-Related Issues

THE GDR GOVERNMENT'S current position regarding Germany's Nazi past was reflected in two major events in 1987. In June Rabbi Israel Miller of the Jewish Claims Conference visited Dresden and East Berlin, where he met with the East German head of state, Erich Honecker, to discuss restitution payments by the East German government to Jews who lived or owned property in what is now the German Democratic Republic. Negotiations regarding restitution payments proceeded throughout the year. In contrast to West Germany, the GDR, since its founding in 1949, had refused to make restitution payments to nonresident former Jewish citizens, or to Israel, on the grounds that as the antifascist Germany, it bore no responsibility for crimes committed under Hitler. That attitude had created tensions in the GDR's relations with international Jewish organizations.

Although it was barely noticed outside the GDR, the trial of former Nazi Henry Schmidt received wide publicity within the country. From April 1943 to February 1945, Schmidt served as head of the Dresden Gestapo and SS, in which capacity he organized the deportation of over 700 Dresden Jews. Schmidt disappeared during the bombing of Dresden in February 1945 and lived quietly and unnoticed in Leipzig until his former identity was discovered in April 1986. Many Jews participated in the trial as witnesses. Schmidt was sentenced to life imprisonment (there is no capital punishment in the GDR).

## Relations with Israel

Bitter complaints continued to be heard regarding coverage of the Middle East conflict in the East German press. There were still no official ties between the GDR and Israel, but contacts were expected to develop within the foreseeable future. First steps toward the eventual establishment of relations between the two states could be seen in the many visits of Israelis to the GDR. Ari Roth, publisher of the *Jerusalem Post*, and former minister of the interior and of religion Yosef Burg visited East Berlin in private capacities. Several Israelis were invited to take part in the Protestant Church conferences in East Berlin in June and in Buckow in September; in Buckow the Israelis constituted the largest foreign delegation. Israeli scholars also lectured at smaller events organized by the Jewish community and the Protestant Church. In 1987 the number of East German Jews—especially individuals below retirement age—who visited relatives in Israel was larger than previously, though not all Jews who applied were granted travel permits.

## Attitudes Toward Jews

Over the course of the year, popular manifestations of dissatisfaction with the government increased, largely in the form of unauthorized political demonstrations, requests to leave the country, and resignations from the Socialist Unity party. In this atmosphere of growing restlessness, diverse attitudes toward Jews were revealed.

On the one hand, several prominent Jews from within and without the GDR were invited to participate in the Protestant Church's major annual conference in East Berlin in June. The workshops on Christian-Jewish relations were the best attended at the conference, with 700 people registered and at times over 1,000 listeners in the auditorium. On the other hand, Jews both in and out of the Jewish community complained of increasing anti-Semitic harassment, especially from lower-level state and party functionaries and gangs of young men.

A significant anti-Semitic incident took place in East Berlin at the end of the year. A gang of young skinheads burst into a church-sponsored rock concert, shouted Nazi slogans, and began to beat up members of the audience. Jews and antifascists were distressed, first of all, by the violent and racist behavior of members of a generation that had no direct experience of Nazism. They were equally upset by the slow response of the East Berlin police to calls for aid and the light sentences—one to two years—handed the youthful offenders by the courts. As a result of massive protests, largely from within the Socialist Unity party, the sentences were later revised upwards.

## JEWISH COMMUNITY

### Demography

According to the League of Jewish Communities of the German Democratic Republic (GDR), approximately 400 Jews were registered with the GDR's eight organized Jewish communities: around 180 in East Berlin, 50 in Dresden, 40 in Leipzig, 30 in Erfurt, and very small groups in Schwerin, Magdeburg, Halle, and Karl-Marx-Stadt. In all the Jewish communities, after several years of decline, membership was stabilizing, although over half the members were above 65 years of age. An additional 2,000 to 3,000 GDR citizens of Jewish ancestry were not affiliated with any Jewish community. The Jewish community of East Berlin admitted 16 new members in 1987, this being the first gain in membership in several decades. Even with further additions of new members, the long-term outlook would still be affected by the low fertility rate and loss of population—especially of young people—resulting from increased emigration.

## Communal Affairs

The most dramatic event in the East German Jewish community in 1987 was the arrival of Rabbi Isaac Neuman of Champaign-Urbana, Illinois. After four years of negotiations involving the GDR government, the U.S. State Department, and the American Jewish Committee, arrangements were made for an American rabbi to serve in the GDR, where there had been no permanent rabbi since 1965. The East German government agreed to pay the rabbi a salary and to provide him with an apartment and a car. Rabbi Neuman's arrival created much excitement in East Berlin; over 1,000 people, including representatives of the governments and churches of both Berlins, attended his inauguration at the newly renovated and rededicated synagogue on the Rykestrasse. Although friction soon developed between the rabbi and the East Berlin community's board of directors, as a result of the contacts developed during the previous few years, relations between the East German Jewish community and the United States became closer and warmer. Over the course of the year, the community received visits from U.S. deputy foreign minister John Whitehead, Congressman William Lehmann of Florida and five other congressmen, and a delegation of 18 members of the American Jewish Committee. A member of the board of directors of the East Berlin Jewish community traveled to New York to make a film about her childhood in Washington Heights.

A new Jewish group was founded by approximately 150 East Berliners of Jewish or partly Jewish ancestry, most of them between the ages of 25 and 50. Most members of the group had grown up in the militantly atheistic Socialist Unity party—many of them children of party functionaries—and therefore had few ties to traditional Judaism or to the Jewish community. However, they had become interested in learning more about Judaism and getting involved in Jewish life. Working closely with the Jewish community's board of directors, the group sponsored a lecture and discussion series and organized a children's group; in addition, many members attended religious services and holiday celebrations. Despite this cooperative relationship, only about 15 percent of the new group's members had applied to join the Jewish community: for the many who still considered themselves atheists, the narrowly religious orientation and strict admissions procedures were deterrents. But the existence of the group meant that there was now an interested Jewish public around the Jewish community, this public consisting largely of writers, state and party functionaries, intellectuals, and artists, people whose ideas inevitably found their way into the political culture of the East German state.

Outside East Berlin, the seven Jewish communities, with 3 to 50 members each, remained largely wards of the Protestant Church. Besides communal celebrations of the most important holidays, their activity revolved around maintaining the local Jewish cemeteries, setting up commemorations of the 50th anniversary of *Kristallnacht* (now being called *Pogromnacht*) in November 1988, sponsoring an occasional lecture or concert around a Jewish theme, and representing the Jewish community at events organized by the churches, the Socialist Unity party, and the state. There were signs of new interest in Judaism among young East Germans and Jews, but, with the exception of Dresden, these small, isolated, and overaged communities maintained a marginal—and sometimes merely administrative—existence. Particularly important in breaking the isolation of the Jewish community in the GDR was the warming of ties between the Jewish communities of East and West Berlin. The leaders of the two Jewish communities exchanged visits, and the West Berlin community donated a photocopying machine to the East Berlin community. The West Berlin Jewish youth group attended Simhat Torah services in East Berlin, and the West Berlin Jewish dance group performed for the East Berlin Jewish community in December.

## Culture

Three major cultural events with Jewish themes took place in East Berlin during the year. The Deutsches Theater staged a new production of Lessing's *Nathan der Weise*, and the Deutsches Staatsoper performed Arnold Schönberg's *Moses and Aaron*, which had previously been banned in Berlin. Especially significant, for the first time since the founding of the East German state, in January a three-day festival of Yiddish culture, organized by Jalda Rebling and Jurgen Rennert, was held in East Berlin. Another event was the 100th anniversary of the birth of novelist and playwright Arnold Zweig, which was observed with lectures and ceremonies.

## Publications

Altogether, 31 new books on themes of Jewish interest were published in the GDR during the year. Among the most noteworthy were the following: *Bronstein's Kinder* ("Bronstein's Children"), a novel by East German Jewish author Jurek Becker about Germans and Jews working through the Nazi past, originally published in West Germany in 1986; *Erkundungen: 20 Erzähler aus Israel* ("Inquiries: 20 Israeli Writers"), edited by Jutta Jahnke, an anthology of short stories by three generations of writers in Israel, translated from Hebrew and Arabic; *Der Gelbe Fleck: Wurzeln und Wirkungen des Judenhasses in der Deutschen Geschichte* ("The Yellow Patch: The Roots and the Effects of Anti-Semitism in German History"), by Rosemarie Schuder and Rudolf Hirsch, the first comprehensive treatment of this theme in the historical literature of the GDR; Theodore Lessing's *Wortmeldungen eines Unerschrockenen: Publizistik aus 3 Jahrzehnten* ("Reports of an Intrepid Inquirer: Three Decades of Essays"); and Arnold Zweig's *Ein Bisschen Blut. Erzahlungen* ("A Little Bit of Blood: Short Stories"), a collection of his best short works.

ROBIN OSTOW

# Eastern Europe

## Soviet Union

### National Affairs

As COMMUNIST PARTY LEADER Mikhail Gorbachev pressed ahead with programs of political and economic reform in 1987, politicians, economists, and cultural figures engaged in open debate over these plans. The Soviet press, radio, and television, once dull and predictable, became livelier and more appealing. The media not only revealed more of the crimes and abuses that had occurred under Stalin, they also discussed hitherto taboo subjects, such as the shortcomings of "corrective labor" camps, environmental pollution, youth crime, AIDS, and abuses of their power by the police and the KGB.

The new policy of *glasnost'*, or openness, also allowed the formation of grassroots groups espousing a variety of ideas and causes. By the end of the year, the Communist party newspaper *Pravda* estimated that 30,000 nonofficial associations had been formed around the country, some of a political nature with names like "Federation of Socialist Clubs," "Club of Social Initiatives," and "Perestroika Club."

*Pravda* criticized some of the groups for "chauvinism, Zionism and anti-Semitism." One group that received a lot of media coverage was Pamiat' ("Memory"), originally formed to preserve Russian cultural monuments and traditions. Together with affiliated groups in several places around the country, Pamiat' spread ideas about a "Zionist-Masonic conspiracy" to rule the USSR. Criticizing the organization, the youth newspaper *Komsomolskaya Pravda,* among others, argued that it actually played into the hands of Zionists because it gave them "a reason to yell loudly about anti-Semitism in the USSR." The press reported receiving letters from readers who supported the theory of a "Zionist-Masonic conspiracy" or who blamed the "period of stagnation" under Leonid Brezhnev on Jews. One reporter referred to a statement made at a public lecture, "Nothing can be changed in our country without renouncing Marxism as a profoundly Zionist teaching," with the observation that "this really takes the cake." Admitting that it had not exposed anti-Semitic expressions in the past, the government newspaper *Izvestiia* argued that publicity might have aroused "uncalled-for feelings in some of our readers," tacitly admitting that popular anti-Semitism did exist. The party historical journal criticized a book on Zionism for taking a "subjective" approach and implied that the author's anti-Zionism had spilled over into anti-Semitism.

At a party Central Committee plenum in January, Gorbachev called for secret balloting and a choice of candidates in party and local Soviet elections. In June Gorbachev advocated a series of economic changes that included profit-and-loss accounting, linking a collective's income directly to its performance, decentralizing decision making, reforming the price system, and promoting individual initiative. Small-scale family farming was to be encouraged; farm managers were given greater say over what and how much they would grow and were permitted to sell up to 30 percent of their production above the quota at unregulated prices. These reforms did not meet with universal acclaim. Economists, historians, and other social scientists debated them in the media and in scholarly journals, while many middle-level party and state officials, fearful that the reforms would threaten their jobs or at least their routines, fought them with bureaucratic stratagems. Yegor Ligachev, a Politburo member often seen as second only to Gorbachev, publicly expressed his reservations about reforming the system too hastily and extensively.

A law was passed in June allowing citizens to initiate legal appeal against actions of public officials who violated their rights. Another expression of liberalization was the permission given to thousands of people to travel to the West, especially the United States, to visit relatives. By the fall, the U. S. embassy was issuing several thousand visitors' visas a month. A few exit visas were granted for visits to Israel. In addition, increasing numbers of émigrés now living in the United States were allowed to return to the Soviet Union for visits with relatives.

As a result of the campaign against alcoholism, consumption of legal vodka was down 43 percent from 1984. However, there were at least 390,000 arrests in 1987 for illegal home brewing, compared to fewer than 70,000 in 1985. One consequence of illegal alcohol manufacture was a sugar shortage in the country. Reduced alcohol consumption was said to be a possible reason for the rise in the Russian birthrate, although the national average was still short of that needed for population replacement. Infant mortality rates were still more than twice as high as in the United States.

*Relations with U.S.*

The Soviet Union continued to improve its relations with several countries, including the United States, from whom it resumed buying corn and wheat at prices subsidized by the American government.

At a summit meeting held in Washington in December, Secretary Gorbachev and U.S. president Ronald Reagan signed the first treaty reducing their nations' nuclear arsenals. They agreed to dismantle all Soviet and American medium- and shorter-range missiles and established the most extensive inspection of weapons ever negotiated between them, including placing technicians on each other's territories. As the two leaders seemed to establish better personal relations, it was decided not to let Reagan's "star wars" missile-defense system block negotiation of a new strategic missile pact. At the same time, economist Abel Aganbegyan reported that the USSR had received 300 proposals for joint economic ventures, 45 of them from the United States. By year's end, 13 such ventures were in operation, 1 with the United States.

Karl Linnas, an Estonian sentenced to death in the USSR for having killed people in a Nazi concentration camp, was deported from the United States to the Soviet Union in April. While awaiting action on an appeal for a pardon, Linnas, age 67, died in a Leningrad hospital.

## Relations with Israel

Cultural and diplomatic contacts between the USSR and Israel increased significantly during the year, reaching levels higher than at any time since 1967. The Soviet Gypsy Theater gave eight performances in Israel in March; the Bolshoi Ballet and Red Army Chorus scheduled Israeli appearances for 1989; and an Israeli film company agreed to make a film with a Soviet counterpart about a non-Jew from the Georgian Republic who travels to Israel.

When Syrian president Hafez al-Assad visited Moscow in April, Gorbachev remarked publicly that the absence of Soviet-Israeli relations "cannot be considered normal," and suggested that Israel was at fault. "We unambiguously recognize—to the same extent we do for all states—Israel's right to peace and a secure existence. At the same time, the Soviet Union continues to categorically oppose Tel Aviv's policy of force and annexation," Gorbachev said.

Israeli foreign minister Shimon Peres met with Yuri Dubinin, Soviet ambassador to the United States, in May, to discuss an international peace conference on the Middle East, and there were other Soviet-Israeli diplomatic contacts as well. The most dramatic event of the year was the arrival of eight Soviet officials in Israel in July, led by the deputy chief of the consular division of the Ministry of Foreign Affairs, Yevgeny Antipov, and including Alexei Chistyakov, deputy chief of the Foreign Ministry's Middle East Department. The delegation, whose stated task was to survey property belonging to the Russian Orthodox Church and renew the passports of Soviet citizens, had its original three-month visas extended, in October, for another three months. In an interview with *Izvestiia*, Antipov emphasized that "our trip has nothing to do with the problem of restoring relations." He noted that "Israeli officials have . . . taken an understanding view of the group's tasks and have given it all necessary assistance. . . . The Israelis' attitude toward us has been, on the whole, interested and well intentioned" (September 27, 1987). He noted, too, that Israel's climate was very hot, prices high, and soldiers ubiquitous.

The Soviet Union warned Israel several times not to continue development of the Jericho II medium-range missile, which was capable of reaching areas of the southern USSR. Foreign Minister Peres was reported to have refused a Soviet offer to establish interests sections in Tel Aviv and Moscow on the ground that while interests sections might be suitable to smaller powers such as Poland and Hungary, only full diplomatic relations would suffice for the USSR and Israel.

In October the USSR voted to exclude Israel from the UN General Assembly session, as it had in the past. Czechoslovakia, however, joined Poland, Hungary, and Bulgaria in not taking part in the vote. Romania and Yugoslavia voted for Israel's admission, leaving only the German Democratic Republic from the East European states voting with the USSR to exclude Israel.

## Human Rights

Early in the year it was announced that 140 prisoners convicted of subversive activities had been pardoned and that a comparable number of cases were being reviewed. Religious and political dissidents, as well as activists in behalf of several national movements, were among those released. In July 300 Crimean Tatars marched outside the Kremlin for over 24 hours. A commission headed by Anatoly Gromyko, chairman of the presidium of the Supreme Soviet, was appointed to look into their grievances.

In September, 17 campaigners for Jewish rights were arrested before they could launch a public demonstration against anti-Semitism. Permission to hold the demonstration was denied by Moscow city officials. There were other instances of harassment of human-rights activists, but a large group of them —eventually numbering some 400 and coming from Czechoslovakia, Sweden, and the United States, as well as the USSR—gathered for an independent human-rights seminar. In late December the Soviet government invited a delegation from the International Helsinki Federation for Human Rights to visit Moscow for a week of discussions with Soviet officials.

# JEWISH COMMUNITY

## Demography

No new data were available on the Jewish population, assumed to be about 1.8 million people. Mark Kupovetskii published a historical analysis of Moscow's Jewish population in *Sovetish haimland* (No. 7, 1987), in which he estimated that in the late 1970s there were 220,000–225,000 Jews in Moscow, where they constituted the second largest ethnic group. About 125,000 Jews were said to have migrated to Moscow, mostly from the Ukraine, in the years 1924–1933, after which migration to the capital was strictly regulated. Kupovetskii estimated that between one-third and one-half of the middle and younger generations of Moscow Jewry were married to non-Jews.

## Emigration and Emigration Activists

On January 1 a new law on emigration took effect, restricting family reunification to first-degree relatives, defined as parents, spouses, children, and siblings. The law also spelled out several procedures and regulations hitherto not publicized. Some viewed the statute as simply codifying existing practice, while others saw it as narrowing the possibilities of emigration. In practice, Jewish emigration increased dramatically, from 914 in 1986 to 8,011 in 1987. Only 2,108 of the emigrants went to Israel, the rest going to the United States and other Western countries.

Interior Minister Aleksandr Vlasov claimed that only 732 people were barred from leaving in the first 11 months of 1987, mostly for state security reasons. Gorbachev had mentioned the figure of 220 such persons just a week earlier, but most observers felt that both figures were far too low. In an interview with American television broadcaster Tom Brokaw, Gorbachev charged that the campaign for Jewish emigration was an attempt to organize a "brain drain," and that the USSR would "never accept a condition when people are being exhorted from outside to leave their country." He also asserted that the only reason people were not allowed to leave was security considerations. Indeed, on February 12, *Vechernaya Moskva* published a list supplied by OVIR (Office of Registration and Visas) of eight Jews who would not be allowed to leave on security grounds. Included were well-known refuseniks Alexander Lerner, Vladimir Slepak, and the Khasin family. In February public protests were mounted for several days in Moscow, demanding the release of Yosif Begun, a Hebrew teacher and *aliyah* activist who had been exiled, arrested after his return in 1978, and rearrested in 1983, sentenced to seven years in jail and five years in exile. On the fourth day of protest, plainclothesmen roughed up demonstrators and detained a few briefly. One week later Begun was released from Chistopol prison and was greeted by a crowd of about 100 people upon his arrival in Moscow.

In March, 75 wives of Prisoners of Conscience, members of separated families, and long-term refuseniks marked International Women's Day with hunger strikes and appeals in nine cities. Also in March, Michael Shirman, a 32-year-old leukemia patient, died in Israel, as his sister, who had been detained for over two years by Soviet authorities, arrived in Israel for a bone marrow transplant, too late to save him. Nine cancer patients in the USSR were denied permission to go to the West for treatment. Inna Meiman, a long-time refusenik, was allowed to leave without her husband, to undergo cancer treatment in the United States, but died soon after. Refusenik Yuri Shpeizman, a cancer victim, was allowed to leave but died in Vienna on his way to Israel.

Edgar Bronfman, president of the World Jewish Congress, and Morris Abram, chairman of the National Conference on Soviet Jewry and the Conference of Presidents of Major Jewish Organizations, met in March with Soviet officials Anatoly Dobrynin and Alexander Yakovlev. They were assured that there would be a major increase in Jewish emigration, direct flights to Israel via Bucharest, Romania, and improved opportunities for Soviet Jews to study Hebrew and religion. Abram reported that a kosher restaurant might be opened in Moscow and that Soviet rabbis would be trained, perhaps in the United States. If improvements were made, Abram told the Soviets, he would recommend repeal of the Stevenson amendment to the Foreign Trade Act, which limited credits to the USSR, and a waiver of the 1974 Jackson-Vanik Amendment, which barred the Soviet Union from getting most-favored-nation status. Bronfman and Abram were told that "substantially all" who had been refused permission to emigrate would be allowed to leave within the year, except for those who had access to state secrets. Some Soviet Jewish activists criticized Bronfman and Abram for advocating concessions on the basis of dubious assurances.

In an unprecedented gesture, U.S. Secretary of State George Shultz attended a Passover seder at the American embassy in Moscow, to which 50 refuseniks had been invited. Among them were Lerner, Slepak, Ida Nudel, Begun, Abe Stolar, Yevgeny Yakir, and Arkady Mai. Gorbachev commented to visiting American congressmen, "Not a single normal person was there, only people who complained."

In February Zionist activist Roald Zelichonok was released from prison after serving half his three-year term. In the spring, imprisoned Zionist activists Yosif Berenshtain, Yakov Levin, Mark Niepomniashchy, and Vladimir Lifshitz were released before completion of their respective sentences. Later, prisoners Leonid Volvovsky, Yuli Edelshtein, and Alexei Magarik were also released. This reduced the number of known "Prisoners of Zion" to near zero. (Edelshtein went to Israel in July.) In the fall, a few weeks before the summit with the United States, some well-known long-term refuseniks were given permission to emigrate. They included Yosif Begun, Viktor Brailovsky, Arkady Mai, Lev Sud, Lev Ovsishcher, and Simon Yantovsky. Ida Nudel, a refusenik for 16 years who had been exiled in Siberia from 1978 to 1982, was allowed to depart for Israel, as were 17-year refuseniks Alexander Lerner and Vladimir Slepak.

In the last days of 1986 and early 1987, several dozen families of Soviet émigrés to the United States returned to the USSR to resume permanent residence there.

## Culture

Among the grassroots organizations permitted by *glasnost'* were some aimed at promoting Jewish culture. In Moscow a retired military officer, Yuri Sokol, established a Jewish library of some 500 books in his apartment. He also applied to Moscow municipal authorities for a permit to open a museum featuring Soviet Jewish heroism in World War II. In Samarkand, Uzbekistan, a "Club for the History of the 'Eastern' Neighborhood," formerly the Jewish quarter, was formed under the leadership of Benyamin Benyaminov. In Baku, Azerbaijan, more than 70 Jews signed up for the first officially sanctioned Hebrew course, taught by Vladimir Farber, which was registered within the framework of grassroots organizations.

Jewish manuscripts in the Institute of Oriental Studies in Leningrad were described in an article in *Palestinskii Sbornik* (No. 28). There were 1,148 manuscripts in the collection, the oldest from the 9th century, most from the 16th through the 19th centuries. At the Fourth All-Union Conference of Young Orientalists, several scholars presented papers on Jewish subjects, including Hebrew language, other Jewish languages, and Krymchak (Crimean Jewish) family names. A hitherto unknown, unfinished story by Isaac Babel, "The Jewess," was published in Yiddish translation in *Sovetish haimland* (No. 9). Tass announced that a two-volume collection of Babel's works would be published the following year.

On the centenary of his birth, an exhibit of 90 paintings and 200 graphics by Marc Chagall opened at the Pushkin Fine Arts Museum in Moscow in September. (The Russian-born artist, who left his native land in the 1920s, died in France in 1985.) There were reports that a museum devoted to his works would open in his native city of Vitebsk. *Sovetish haimland* (No. 6) reproduced in color seven Chagall paintings, described as "relatively unknown," that were in Soviet collections.

Cultural performances of Jewish interest included a staging in Tbilisi, Georgia, of Arkady Stavitsky's play *40 Sholem Aleichem Street,* which dealt with Jewish emigration. A "mono-opera" based on Anne Frank's diary was staged by O. Iancu at the Kishinev Actors House. Fifty years after its debut, the film *Seekers of Happiness,* about the early settlers in Birobidzhan, was screened in the Minsk Literary House, in a Minsk theater, and on Belorussian television. *Commissar,* a film made in 1967 by Alexander Askoldov, a non-Jew, was finally released for showing to small audiences of foreigners and selected Soviet citizens at a Moscow film festival. The film portrayed Jewish suffering and bravery during the civil war, 1918–1921. A Russian version of the musical *Fiddler on the Roof* was performed in Odessa.

"Jewish Folk Music in Moldavia and Bukovina" was the subject of a lecture at the All-Union Geographical Society. Vladimir Bitkin of Kishinev accompanied his lecture with recordings of cantorial and folk music which he had made in those areas.

At the Sixth Moscow International Book Fair in September, three thousand publishers from 103 countries, including Israel, displayed their publications. The Association of Jewish Book Publishers in the United States was able to bring in books that had been banned at previous fairs. Even a Soviet newspaper (*Literaturnaya Gazeta,* September 16, 1987) admitted that the Jewish book displays were crowded, though it charged that "the exhibitors were interested in creating a propaganda stir, a sensational scandal . . . rather than in serious work."

It was announced that Birobidzhan would have its first institution of higher learning, a pedagogical institute. The plan called for an enrollment of 1,400 students and 150–180 faculty, including teachers of Yiddish language and literature. The school was scheduled to open in 1989–90. On a visit to Birobidzhan, *New York Times* reporter Philip Taubman was told that of 70,000 books and periodicals in the local library, 4,000 were in Yiddish. The mayor of the city of Birobidzhan, Mark

Kaufman, and the head of the Communist party organization, Boris Korsunsky, were Jews, as was the director of the largest industrial plant. Writing in *Sovetish haimland* (No. 7), Viktor Lenzon noted that the audience for the Moscow Drama Theater-Studio, a Jewish theater, had declined. As the novelty of Jewish theater dissipated, audiences were becoming more demanding, he claimed. In Lenzon's view, Yiddish theaters were underestimating their audiences and offering them too much light fare. In addition, the attempt to mix Russian and Yiddish had not been successful. "It's hard to imagine the Moscow Gypsy Theater visiting Japan, for example, and the Gypsies speaking Russian," he said. "Why, then, does the Yiddish theater at home act with such carelessness toward the Yiddish language?" Noting that the Yiddish theater is more a "theater about Jews" than a "Jewish theater," because the director and most of the actors lack sufficient knowledge of Jewish culture, Lenzon suggested that the theater make use of the more than 20 veterans of the former State Yiddish Theater still living in the USSR.

## Religion

According to the journal *Nauka i Religiia* (Science and Religion, No. 11), which published figures on the number of officially registered Jewish congregations, there had been a steady decline from 259 registered in 1961 to 109 in 1986.

The *mikvah* (ritual bath) at the Marina Roshcha Synagogue in Moscow, closed in 1986 by the authorities, was reopened this year. It was announced that kosher food, imported from Hungary, was being made available for lunches at the main Moscow synagogue on Arkhipova Street.

## Personalia

The Order of Lenin was awarded to Lev Borisovich Shapiro, first secretary of the (Birobidzhan) Jewish Autonomous Province party committee, on his 60th birthday.

Among prominent Jews who died during the year were Esther Karchmer, one of the first actresses in the State Yiddish Theater, in which she played over 50 roles, aged 88; sculptor Peisakh (Piotr Moiseevich) Krivorutskii, of Leningrad, whose subjects included many Jewish writers and actors, aged 66; Anatoly Efros, famed director of the Taganka Theater, aged 61; Arkady Raikin, the country's best-known humorist and satirist, aged 76; and Shaye Bronshtain, an artist who made scenery and costumes for the State Yiddish Theater, aged 78. Academician Yakov Borisovich Zeldovich, a physicist, a three-time winner of the Hero of Socialist Labor Award and the Lenin and USSR State Prizes, died at age 73. Rivke Rubin, Yiddish writer, critic, and translator, who had been on the editorial board of *Sovetish haimland* and later taught a course on Y. L. Peretz at the Gorky Literary Institute, died at age 81. Academician Mark Mitin, a philosopher, died at age 86.

ZVI GITELMAN

# Soviet Bloc Nations

## Czechoslovakia

THE REGIME IN CZECHOSLOVAKIA continued in 1987 to be one of the most conservative in the region. Seemingly traumatized by the unsuccessful attempt at economic and political reform in 1968, it did not rush to embrace the reforms being discussed in the USSR. In fact, it was political dissidents who took up the slogan of "Long live Gorbachev!" as their ironic rallying cry. In Jewish matters, too, the regime remained cautious, anti-Zionist, and highly critical of Israel.

A Communist party delegation, headed by Michal Stefanak, head of the Central Committee's International Department, visited Israel as guests of the Israeli Communist party. The Czechs met with a broad spectrum of Israelis. There was some speculation that this might lead to the kind of improvement in relations with Israel that had been observed with regard to Poland and Hungary.

### JEWISH COMMUNITY

The Jewish community was said to number some 5,000, though exact figures had not been available for many years.

In February a synagogue was consecrated in Karlovy Vary by Rabbi Daniel Mayer of Prague. It was housed in a building originally built for another purpose. The former main synagogue in this Bohemian spa and resort town had been blown up by the Nazis. Rabbi Mayer, educated at the Budapest Jewish Theological Seminary, was the only rabbi in Czechoslovakia, which had been without any rabbi for about 20 years.

## Hungary

In contrast to Czechoslovakia, Hungary had pursued a reformist economic course since 1968. The leadership took satisfaction in Soviet acknowledgment that Gorbachev's reforms were inspired in part by Hungarian precedents. However, Hungary was experiencing serious economic difficulties. Her foreign debt of $13 billion was the highest per capita among the socialist countries. The government announced plans to introduce a value-added tax and a significant income tax in 1988, with rates of the latter to reach as high as 60 percent. In March, 1,500 people marched in Budapest, demanding more political freedom and a reduction in Soviet influence in Hungary. Janos Kadar, party leader since 1956, was said to be less and less involved in administration and decision making. Major changes in leadership were expected.

During the course of the year several Israeli officials visited Hungary, mainly on commercial and cultural business. Jozsef Gyorke, deputy head of the party Central Committee's foreign department, led an official party delegation to Israel in April. Agreements were reached with Israel on cooperation in agriculture and irrigation. In September Hungary and Israel agreed to open interests sections in each other's capitals, each to be staffed by five diplomats. Deputy Foreign Minister Gabor Nagy said that the sections would facilitate contacts between the two countries. He reported that 20,000 Israelis were visiting Hungary annually and estimated that there were about 200,000–250,000 Israelis of Hungarian origin. The Israel Chamber Orchestra gave concerts in Budapest in September, and the Israel Philharmonic Orchestra toured the country the following month. Israel's Habimah Theater was invited to perform in Budapest, and the Hungarian National Theater was scheduled to appear in Israel, both in 1988.

JEWISH COMMUNITY

With no firm data available on the size of the Hungarian Jewish population, estimates ranged from 35,000 to 100,000.

In May the enlarged executive committee of the World Jewish Congress met in Budapest, the first time such a meeting was held in Eastern Europe. Hungarian president Pal Losonczi, Prime Minister Gyorgy Lazar, and Foreign Minister Peter Varkonyi met with WJC leaders. The latter attended the graduation exercises of the Rabbinical Seminary and also laid a wreath at a monument to Raoul Wallenberg that was unveiled in Budapest. The seminary, founded in the 19th century, was the only one of its kind in the socialist countries. It had in 1987 about a dozen students, half of them from Hungary and the rest from other socialist countries, including the USSR. The monument to Wallenberg, who was arrested by the Soviets in 1945 and whose fate remained unclear, was erected, without any public announcement, in a quiet residential section of Buda in April. Funds for the monument were provided by former U.S. ambassador Nicolas Salgo, a Jew of Hungarian origin. In January, Dr. Andras Losonci, president of the Central Board of Hungarian Jews, told New York City's mayor Edward Koch, who was visiting Hungary, that the Jewish community needed financial assistance. It was receiving $1 million annually from the Joint Distribution Committee, mainly for caring for the elderly, meals for the homebound, and elementary Jewish education, but the needs of the nursing homes and Jewish hospital were not being met.

In July the executive committee of the Memorial Foundation for Jewish Culture convened in Budapest, the first time this organization had met in Eastern Europe. On this occasion, three recently published Hungarian-language books on Judaism were introduced, and the Center for Judaic Studies, the only one of its kind in Eastern Europe, was inaugurated. Organizationally part of the Hungarian Academy of Sciences, the center was located in the Faculty of Arts and Sciences of the Eotvos Lorand University in Budapest.

An exhibit on the history of Hungarian Jewry was mounted in Goldmark Hall in Budapest. American actor Tony Curtis established the Emanuel Foundation, named for his Hungarian-born father, Emanuel Schwartz, to assist in the restoration of Budapest's Dohanyi Street Temple, the largest Jewish house of worship in Europe.

## Poland

Economic difficulties and political instability continued to plague Poland. Party leader Wojciech Jaruzelski enthusiastically embraced Soviet leader Mikhail Gorbachev's reforms, and many Poles hoped that liberalization in the USSR would spill over to Poland. In a remarkably frank article written by Jaruzelski, he described how the Polish Communist party was decimated by the Comintern in the late 1930s, and how the USSR divided Poland with Germany. These issues were hitherto almost unmentionable in the press, let alone in the Soviet and Polish party theoretical journals where his article appeared.

Poland's foreign debt rose to about $35 billion, more than it earned in hard currency in 1986 or 1987. Sharp increases in the prices of gasoline, food, and beverages brought protests from the Catholic Church and Lech Walesa, former leader of Solidarity. In February, U.S. President Ronald Reagan lifted economic sanctions against Poland on the ground that the human-rights situation had improved and political prisoners were being released. After four years without top-level diplomatic representation in either country, the United States and Poland agreed to exchange ambassadors. Vice-President George Bush visited Poland in September.

General Jaruzelski met with Pope John Paul II in Rome early in the year. The pope refused to establish diplomatic relations with Poland until disputes between the government and the local bishops were resolved. John Paul visited Poland in June and came out strongly for human rights, pointing to the Solidarity movement as an exemplar of those rights. Eight Jewish representatives from Polish-Jewish bodies were among those who met with the pope.

POLISH-JEWISH RELATIONS

Early in the year Catholic officials from Poland, France, and Belgium, meeting at the chateau of Baron Edmond de Rothschild in Geneva, agreed with European Jewish leaders that the Carmelite convent near the Auschwitz-Birkenau death camps should be closed, and that the ten nuns living in the convent would be relocated to an interreligious center a mile from the camps. The agreement had not yet been implemented by year's end.

Poland's government took several highly visible steps to improve relations with foreign Jewish communities and their leaders and with the State of Israel. Most observers suggested that the goal was to improve Poland's image among political and financial influentials who could help Poland out of her difficulties. In March a parliamentary delegation, headed by Politburo member Jozef Czyrek, met with Edgar Bronfman of the World Jewish Congress, Seymour Reich of B'nai B'rith International, and Morris Abram of the Council of Presidents of Major Jewish Organizations. In May the Jagellonian University in Krakow and the Jewish Historical Institute in Warsaw cosponsored a symposium on Polish-Jewish relations. In September an international conference, including Israeli scholars, was held in Bialystok on the subject "Five Hundred Years of Jewish Settlement in Podlasie."

At a four-day conference on the history and culture of Polish Jews, held in February at the Hebrew University in Jerusalem, Prof. Jozef Gierowski of the Jagellonian University in Krakow and director of its Research Center of Jewish History, stated that the Polish government would soon acknowledge "political error" in its 1968 anti-Semitic campaign. That campaign, which was triggered by then party leader Wladyslaw Gomulka's warning that Zionists had no place in Poland, had turned into a generally anti-Semitic onslaught led by some of Gomulka's political rivals. It resulted in a mass exodus of Jews, many of whom had been Communist party stalwarts. Gierowski said that he was authorized to make his statement by General Jaruzelski. Discussing this topic later, the influential Polish newspaper *Polityka* referred to the 1968 campaign in a front-page story as "infamous" and "an embarrassment" to Poland. On March 2, *Trybuna Ludu*, official organ of the Polish United Workers party, stated that most party and government officials had had nothing to do with the anti-Semitic campaign. "The Party as a whole and its leadership—though not always effective or timely—nonetheless tried to discourage an atmosphere of anti-Semitism." *Trybuna Ludu* admitted that 13,000 Jews left Poland in the period 1968–1971 and that the purge of Jews "caused harm to many people" and damaged Poland's intellectual life and image abroad.

At the same time, the Catholic newspaper *Tygodnik Powszechny* featured several articles debating the Polish role in the Holocaust. The well-known literary critic Jan Blonski and others discussed whether or not the Poles were guilty of any form of collaboration in the extermination of Poland's three million Jews. Not surprisingly, no definitive conclusions were reached. The major issue was whether Polish passivity was morally reprehensible or simply realistic, given the circumstances. Wladyslaw Sila-Nowicki, a lawyer who participated in the wartime resistance and who was once an adviser to Solidarity, wrote that Jewish passivity was "the first and basic impediment" to Poles helping the Jews more. An international conference on the extermination of Jews in the Belzec, Sobibor, and Treblinka camps was held in Lublin in August. Soviet and East European scholars participated. The U.S. Holocaust Memorial Council agreed to exchange documents with the Polish Main Commission for the Investigation of Nazi Crimes in Poland.

JEWISH COMMUNITY

The Jewish population of Poland was estimated at 5,000, of whom nearly 2,000 were registered with the religious community.

Ambassador Mordechai Paltzur, head of the Israeli interests section in Warsaw, participated in the commemoration of the Warsaw ghetto uprising of 1943, along with a delegation of Israeli youth. In Kielce, in August, a ceremony was held to commemorate the 1946 pogrom in that city. The ceremony also marked the restoration of the local Jewish cemetery, which was funded by the Nissenbaum Foundation and the Organization of Kielce Jews in the United States.

## *Romania*

The Romanian government was probably the least enthusiastic of any in the region about the reforms proposed in the USSR. Party leader Nicolae Ceausescu's "personality cult" reached heights unknown since the death of Stalin, the economic situation continued to deteriorate, and political repression showed no sign of letting up. At the beginning of the year, U.S. trade representative Clayton Yeutter announced that Romania would lose Generalized System of Preferences benefits, which waived import duties on selected goods from some developing countries. (Romania sold $50–60 million in goods annually to the United States.) In June the U.S. Senate approved an amendment to the trade bill that would suspend Romania's most-favored-nation status for six months after the bill's enactment. Only if the president recommended restoration and could point to assurances that Romania had improved its performance in the area of human rights and contacts could MFN status—first granted in 1975—be restored.

JEWISH COMMUNITY

The Jewish population of Romania was estimated at 21,500.

Jewish cultural and religious activity continued. Immigration to Israel went on at more or less the same levels as before, and Romania's relations with Israel remained cordial. There was considerable Israeli tourism to Romania and trade relations were considered satisfactory.

ZVI GITELMAN

# Israel

ISRAEL'S NATIONAL UNITY government limped through 1987, essentially marking time. Israel's leaders displayed unity only when forced to stave off a potential threat to their political lives from, ironically, the country's closest ally. When it came to the major challenge to Israel's long-term survival, the peace issue, the battering the two major coalition parties gave each other led some observers to suggest that Labor and Likud first had to show they could coexist themselves before setting themselves up as peacemakers on the international stage. In the national-security realm, new headline-making disclosures raised troubling questions about the iconization of security in Israel and the existence of a separate moral code for the security services. Finally, at the very end of 1987, a number of factors combined to set off the most intense and sustained outbreak of anti-Israel violence in the occupied territories since their capture by Israel 20 years earlier. While the exact nature of this uprising was as yet unclear, many saw it as signaling the start of a new era in Israel's history.

## Peace Initiatives

In 1987 public affairs in Israel were dominated by an unremitting clash between Prime Minister Yitzhak Shamir and Vice Premier and Foreign Minister Shimon Peres over the idea of an international peace conference to resolve the Arab-Israeli conflict. According to Peres, Jordan's insistence on such a conference as an "opening" or "accompaniment" to direct talks meant that this framework was a *sine qua non* for progress toward peace. Shamir, however, maintained that an international forum would inevitably exert pressure on Israel to withdraw from the occupied territories. Peres had built up international support for the idea during his two-year tenure as prime minister, and in September 1986, on the eve of the premiership rotation, had reached agreement with President Hosni Mubarak of Egypt on the general outlines for an international conference. The two had declared 1987 the "year of peace."

For the first four months of the year, Peres continued to promote the international conference idea intensively, making visits to London, Paris, and Brussels in January to drum up additional European support. Closer to home, another Peres visit to Cairo at the end of February for talks with President Mubarak and Foreign Minister Esmat Abdel Meguid produced a joint communiqué reaffirming the call for "the convening in 1987 of an international conference leading to direct negotiations between all the parties concerned based on UN Security Council Resolutions 242 and 338. The conference will offer an opportunity for direct negotiations that are to resolve the Arab-Israeli conflict in all its aspects and the legitimate rights of the Palestinian people." In a press conference on his return to Israel, Peres said that agreement had also been reached "on the principle that the [makeup of the] Palestinian delegation must be agreed to by all the sides, meaning also by Israel"—thus effectively enabling Israel to veto PLO participation.

Shamir, however, would not budge. He declared that the wording of the joint Israeli-Egyptian statement was "open to various interpretations" and during a ten-day visit to the United States in February took every opportunity to undermine the international conference idea. In an address to the Council for World Affairs in Los Angeles (February 20), Shamir said Soviet participation in such a conference would "increase subversion, intrigue and support of extremist elements" in the region. Instead, he proposed a "mini-international conference" in which Israel, Jordan, Egypt, and Palestinians from the territories would meet under U.S. auspices.

On April 9, Prime Minister Shamir brought the debate to a new pitch of intensity when he told a Liberal party meeting that only if Israel had "decided to commit suicide" could it ignore the arguments against an international conference. Labor, Shamir declared, "must follow the line I advocate" as long as it remained in the government. Peres, dismissing Shamir's attack as "election-campaign rhetoric," on April 12 briefed the cabinet on talks he had held earlier in the week on the international conference idea with two Soviet officials at a meeting of the Socialist International in Rome.

A sensational development underlay Peres's apparent equanimity. It later emerged that on Saturday, April 11, Peres had met with King Hussein in London. (Also present, according to *Yediot Aharonot*, which broke the story on May 10, was Defense Minister Yitzhak Rabin; the present account is based on an article in the *Ha'aretz* weekly magazine of May 22, 1987.) The seven-hour meeting capped two years of intensive efforts and produced a major breakthrough: a signed agreement on the procedural modalities for the holding of an international conference. The document was to be presented as an American plan, to make it more palatable both to the Likud and to "rejectionist" elements in the Arab world. Peres was certain he could ram the plan through the inner cabinet by inducing one or more Likud ministers to cross over in the vote (as he had previously done in connection with three other apparently intractable issues: Lebanon, the economy, and Taba). Wishing to take no chances, however, Peres worked to arrange a dramatic shuttle-diplomacy visit to the region by Secretary of State George Shultz of the United States.

Immediately upon his return from the meeting with Hussein on April 11, Peres huddled with U.S. ambassador to Israel Thomas Pickering. At Pickering's suggestion, Peres the next day dispatched his close adviser Yossi Beilin to Helsinki, to brief

Shultz, who was en route to Moscow. The cover story was that Beilin, the political director-general of the Foreign Ministry, was updating Shultz on Peres's recent contacts with Soviet officials. Impressed by what he heard from Beilin, Shultz decided to visit Israel on May 1 and to proceed from there to Egypt and Jordan. On April 13, Peres, at his initiative, met with Shamir for a private (and rare) 45-minute discussion. Peres read out the agreement with Hussein but refused to leave Shamir a copy, and, it later developed, made no mention of U.S. involvement. Shamir learned of the American angle only on April 22, in a meeting with Ambassador Pickering, who also informed the Israeli prime minister about Shultz's plan to launch a diplomatic mission in the region.

Shamir now proved that he, too, could rise to the occasion. First phoning Shultz and asking him to receive Minister Without Portfolio Moshe Arens on an urgent mission, Shamir then filled Arens in on the developments and sent him off to Washington. Now it was the Likud's turn to resort to a cover story to conceal the true purpose of Arens's trip, which, like all ministerial missions abroad, required cabinet approval. A call to Sen. Frank Lautenberg elicited an invitation to Arens to address an Israel Bonds meeting on Sunday (April 26), and a phone poll among the cabinet ministers elicited the necessary approval for Arens to address the meeting. Arens met with Shultz on April 24 and led him to understand that in the prime minister's opinion, his May 1 visit to Israel would not be desirable. Shultz, noting that he did not wish to intervene in internal Israeli politics, called off his mission.

Labor was outraged, but Shamir said blithely that the administration was well aware of the Likud's consistent opposition to an international conference. European pressure did not abate. In a visit to Paris at the end of May, Shamir heard President François Mitterrand of France say that he favored an international conference as the only viable route to advance the Middle East peace process. Similarly, the foreign minister of Belgium and current European Community (EC) president Leo Tindemans, who arrived in Israel via Jordan on May 9 for a 48-hour visit, stressed European backing for the international conference concept. In the meantime, a decision with potentially far-reaching implications taken by the Palestinian National Council, the PLO's "parliament," drew the usual dual response from Jerusalem. At the PNC meeting, held in late April in Algiers, PLO chairman Yasir Arafat abrogated the joint Jordanian-PLO strategy of 1985 for achieving a Middle East peace, and in return regained the support of the more radical Palestinian organizations. According to the Shamir camp, the PLO move was a boost for the hard-liners and put to rest the possibility of assembling an acceptable Palestinian delegation for an international conference; whereas the Peres camp saw the PLO decision as enabling Arab "moderates" to move ahead without being bound by the organization.

On May 5, King Hussein, while denying he had met with Peres, told the *Boston Globe* that Jordan would insist that the Palestinians accept Resolutions 242 and 338 and renounce terrorism as conditions for their participation in an international conference. In an unprecedented concession, he described as "unrealistic" the demand that Israel withdraw from all the territories it occupied in 1967, and added that the solution to the question of Jerusalem could not take the form of a return to a divided city.

Over the previous months, Peres's hesitation to bring the proposal for an international conference to the inner cabinet inevitably raised doubts about his credibility on this subject. In early May, however, the hour seemed propitious. Even if he failed to win over at least one Likud minister in the inner cabinet—a tie vote in the ten-member body, five each from the Likud and the Alignment, was tantamount to a defeat—he believed he could command a Knesset majority for early elections. Peres's confidence was further boosted by a message from Shultz to him and Shamir supporting an international conference.

The inner cabinet discussed the topic in two sessions, on May 11 and 13. The outcome was anticlimactic. According to a statement issued to the foreign press by the prime minister's media adviser immediately after the May 13 session, the Labor Alignment never submitted the proposal to a vote, but instead proposed calling a general election. The prime minister then announced that since the foreign minister's proposal had not been accepted by the inner cabinet, he "has no mandate to act in the international arena on the subject of an international conference." Although this interpretation was rejected by Peres in media interviews, the actual state of affairs was well summed up in a *Jerusalem Post* editorial on May 14:

> For good reason, no doubt, Mr. Peres wished to avoid a vote. That would have led to a draw and, therefore, by inner cabinet rules, rejection. For although the meeting, without a vote, did not—as Mr. Shamir claimed—formally mean a denial to Mr. Peres of a mandate to continue his conference-making diplomacy, it could only be interpreted as an indication that he simply did not have any such mandate, and that his usefulness as a peace-minded foreign minister had been destroyed and could not be restored as long as Mr. Shamir remained Israel's premier.

This analysis was borne out by developments during the remainder of the year. Peres had painted himself into a corner. His diminished standing at home due to his failure to ask for a vote in the inner cabinet and his inability to force an early poll (see also "Political Affairs" below) impaired his credibility in the international arena. In particular, it was clear to Washington that half a year after taking over as prime minister, Yitzhak Shamir was firmly in the driver's seat. This perception, combined with the Reagan administration's own domestic problems, its reluctance to be seen as intervening in Israeli internal affairs, and the consistently vacillating attitude it had shown toward the Middle East crisis in general, meant that concrete progress toward peace was all but ruled out in 1987.

Nevertheless, Peres continued to press ahead as though nothing had changed. On July 7 he met again with Egyptian president Mubarak, this time in Geneva, and the two reaffirmed that 1987 would be the "year of peace." Later that month, Shamir, replying to a message from Mubarak conveyed by Egyptian foreign minister Meguid during his visit to Israel (see also "Other Foreign Relations") suggested trilateral talks in Cairo involving Egypt, Jordan, and Israel, under U.S. auspices. Implicitly accepting Peres's contention that Jordan could not enter into direct talks without a broader framework, Shamir tried to narrow that framework considerably by arguing that the "international support and legitimacy" Amman insisted on would be provided by the presence of the United States and Israel. This conception was shrugged off by Mubarak.

In August Shamir demonstrated that he, too, was a player on the international stage. Briefing reporters during a visit to Romania, he said that he and President Nicolae Ceausescu—known for his good contacts in the Arab world and especially among the Palestinians—had agreed that "peace could be attained only through direct talks between the interested parties." However, Ceausescu did not budge one iota from his standard posture of insistence on an international conference with Soviet and PLO participation. In the final analysis, Shamir's three-day stay in Romania, although touted by his aides as the onset of a diplomatic offensive that would preempt Peres's globe-trotting, had as little impact as Peres's visit to Morocco a year earlier (see AJYB 1988, vol. 88, p.376).

Secretary of State Shultz finally turned up in Israel in October (16–19). After a series of separate talks with Shamir and Peres—a new form of shuttle diplomacy, in the unkind description of some observers—Shultz told a press conference in Jerusalem on October 18 that he "was not trying to talk anybody into or out of any particular thing," and that it might be productive to "rearrange" ideas previously put forward and "look for other ways" to advance toward peace. "An international conference as such," he said, "doesn't have any particular interest for the U.S.," and the sole purpose of international "umbrellas, auspices or a conference" was to bring about direct Arab-Israeli negotiations.

In an interview with the *Jerusalem Post* on the eve of the Shultz visit, Shamir was asked to sum up his first year in office as prime minister (since the rotation). "In the diplomatic field," he said, "Israel faces no special problems from the point of view of its international relations; there are no special pressures on us. It's true that there was no progress on the peace process, but there was no regression either." A somewhat different perspective was offered by Secretary of State Shultz in an address to the Weizmann Institute of Science in Rehovot during his visit to Israel. "We know," Shultz said,

> that no one—not the U.S., not Israel, not the Arabs—improves the chances for peace by doing nothing at all, by just sitting around. Those who are reluctant to explore new ideas, those who resist old ones, have an obligation to offer something different as an alternative to the status quo. . . . Surely there are risks in such a process. But equally surely there are risks to—and immense opportunities foregone by—Israel and its neighbors in not accepting those risks. No one helps the chances for peace by doing nothing.

## The Administered Areas

### DEMOGRAPHY

According to data released near the end of the year by the Central Bureau of Statistics, 21,500 Jews had moved to the territories in the three years since the installation of the national unity government. However, the trend was downward, from 9,200 new settlers in 1985, to 7,300 in 1986, and 5,000 in 1987. Moreover, a study by the West Bank Data Base Project, directed by Meron Benvenisti, found that 85 percent of the Jewish settlers resided in the Jerusalem and Tel Aviv metropolitan areas. Half of all the settlers resided in just five urban centers, of which the largest, Maaleh Adumim, just outside Jerusalem, had over 12,000 residents, nearly one-fifth of the approximately 60,000 Jews living in the territories at the end of 1987.

A forecast issued in May by the Central Bureau of Statistics showed that if present trends continued, the ratio of Jews to Arabs in Greater Israel (Israel plus the territories) in the year 2000 would be 57:43 at best, but could be a much narrower 54:46. Population parity would be reached a decade later. (Without the territories, the ratio would remain close to the current level inside Israel of 82 percent Jews and 18 percent Arabs.) In absolute figures, by the turn of the century there would be 4.2 to 4.3 million Jews in the country, including the territories, and 3.1 to 3.7 million Arabs (including 1.2 million Israeli Arabs). Already in 1987 more Arab babies were being born in Greater Israel than Jewish babies.

The existence of this demographic issue seemed to be seeping into the Israeli consciousness. On the one hand, its implications were a cause of the growing legitimacy "Kahanist" notions were enjoying in mainstream Israeli politics—as exemplified by the proposal of Deputy Defense Minister Michael Dekel (Herut) in July that the Arabs of the territories be "transferred" to Jordan with Western aid, and the suggestion made in October by Minister Without Portfolio Yosef Shapira (NRP) that the government pay $20,000 to any Arab willing to emigrate. On the other hand, according to a public-opinion poll published in *Ma'ariv* on May 12, the period between October 1986 and April 1987 saw an increase of 2 percent, to 51.8 percent, in the number of those willing to evacuate all or part of Judea-Samaria in return for a peace agreement with Jordan, and a leap of over 6 percent, to 35.2 percent, in the number of those willing to dismantle some or all of the settlements as part of a peace treaty.

### BACKGROUND TO THE UPRISING

On December 9, 1987, the situation that had existed in the territories occupied by Israel for over 20 years came to an end. Mass violence erupted on that date in a Gaza Strip refugee camp, touching off the heaviest and most sustained anti-Israel rioting since Israel captured the territories in June 1967.

One root cause of the December uprising was the leadership vacuum in the territories. Israeli leaders, particularly but not only in the Labor Alignment, constantly professed readiness to negotiate with Palestinian leaders in the territories, if such persons could only be found. In practice, however, the Israeli security forces seemed bent on stifling at birth any potential emergence of a local Palestinian leadership. Two of the favored methods of suppressing leadership stirrings in the areas were deportation and "administrative detention" (arrest without trial under the 1945 Defense [Emergency] Regulations promulgated by the British Mandatory authorities and not repealed by Israel). A striking example of how the latter method was applied in 1987 was the case of Faisal al-Husseini. Scion of a famous Palestinian family, Husseini was the founder of the East Jerusalem-based Arab Studies Society and was active in a group called the Israeli-Palestinian Committee Confronting the Iron Fist. On April 12, 1987, six weeks after the lifting of the last of a five-year series of "town arrest" orders which had confined him to Jerusalem, Husseini was arrested under a six-month administrative detention order, subsequently halved by the district court judge who reviewed the case. Husseini denied the charges against him—he was alleged to be a senior Fatah activist and political agitator—and stated that he advocated political dialogue between Israel and the PLO leading to the establishment of a Palestinian state alongside Israel. Immediately after being released from the three-month detention period he was served with a new six-month town-arrest order, was jailed for ten days at the end of August for interrogation concerning his "membership in a hostile terrorist organization" (and released when no evidence was produced to substantiate the accusation), and then on September 12, was rearrested under another six-month administrative detention order signed by Defense Minister Rabin.

Husseini's second and third arrests were apparently related to a somewhat bizarre episode involving himself and two other prominent Palestinians (and PLO supporters)—Sari Nusseibeh, an academic, and Salah Zuhaikah, the editor of an East Jerusalem paper—and a member of the Herut Central Committee, Moshe Amirav. Amirav, according to an article he published in *Ha'aretz* on September 22, had met with the three over a period of several months "to examine whether Palestinian radicals would agree to a political plan in the spirit of the Likud." A draft plan was worked out involving extensive self-rule ("autonomy") in the territories, though not a separate Palestinian state, and Amirav was scheduled to present it to PLO chairman Yasir Arafat in Geneva on September 6. In the meantime, Faisal al-Husseini was arrested on August 26 and held in custody for ten days, until September 4; on September 5 the Israel Air Force carried out a devastating raid at the Ein Hilweh refugee camp in Lebanon, killing some 50 of Arafat's supporters. Amirav then canceled his trip. On September 12, Husseini was rearrested; on September 21, after the story became public knowledge (at Amirav's doing), Dr. Nusseibeh was severely beaten by extremist Palestinian students at Bir Zeit University, where he taught philosophy, for daring to talk to Israelis. In Herut, moves were initiated to expel Amirav from the party.

Deportation was employed more sparingly than administrative detention (over 60

Palestinians were held under this form of arrest in 1987, including, on December 8, Radwan Abu Ayyash, the head of the Arab Journalists' Association in the territories). The expulsion to Jordan on January 26 of Mohammad Dahlan, 25, a student at Gaza's Islamic University, and on May 14 of two student leaders in the West Bank, Marwan Barghouti, 29, the head of the Bir Zeit student council, and Khalil Ashour, 39, a former head of the An-Najah University student council, was in keeping with the authorities' efforts to combat nationalist activity in the institutions of higher learning in the West Bank and Gaza, thus effectively blocking the emergence of local leadership.

An-Najah National University in Nablus was a key target in 1987. On January 3 the university was ordered closed for a week, and the shutdown was extended on the grounds that disturbances were being planned on the campus; at the same time, four students were placed under six-month administrative detention. On January 20 Defense Minister Rabin allowed An-Najah to reopen, but summoned West Bank university heads for a meeting at which he warned that Israel would not allow the universities to go on serving as a major center of incitement and unrest in the territories. On February 10 An-Najah was closed down for a month, and on March 27 for another two weeks. According to a statement issued by the university, the campus had been closed for a total of 90 days during the current semester. However, the longest unbroken closure in 1987 was of Bir Zeit University, which was ordered shut down for four consecutive months (from April 14, following a violent clash between students and Israeli troops in which a student was shot and killed, until August 13). Bethlehem University, relatively quiescent in recent years but the scene of considerable student unrest in 1987, was closed down for three months at the end of October. This followed a series of riots in and around Bethlehem after a 22-year-old student was shot and killed during a campus demonstration on October 29, held to commemorate the 1956 massacre at the Israeli Arab village of Kafr Kassem.

CONTINUING VIOLENCE

Violence was not lacking in the territories even before the events of December. Consistent with the pattern of recent years, such violence was directed both at the military and at civilians; some occurred on a relatively large scale, some took the form of terrorism perpetrated by individuals. One constant in the midst of the variations was that Israeli vehicles traveling in the territories were in perpetual danger of being struck by stones and rocks, often hurled by small children, and bearing potentially lethal effects. The mass demonstrations frequently coincided with an anniversary of significance to the Palestinians, such as Fatah's first operation against Israel (January 1, 1965) or the UN partition vote on Palestine (November 29, 1947). They might also be triggered by the visit of a high-ranking foreign personality to the area, by major events in the Arab world, such as a summit meeting, or by a desire to express solidarity with Palestinians caught in the internecine strife in Lebanon. (In 1987, as in previous years, all these fundamentally external causes were cited by the Israeli defense establishment to account for outbreaks of disturbances.) In contrast, individual terrorism was random, often impulsive, and usually deadly.

Some of the worst violence of the year prior to the December uprising occurred in April, in the wake of a hunger strike launched on March 25 by Arab security prisoners in Israel and the West Bank to protest alleged subhuman conditions and maltreatment. One trigger of the strike was the reopening of the so-called Ansar II prison camp in the Gaza Strip (named after the detention facility operated by the Israel Defense Forces—IDF—during the Lebanon War). Ansar II had been shut down at the end of 1986 following persistent reports that inmates had suffered physical abuse at the hands of their Israeli guards. It was reopened to cope with the arrest of about 150 persons aged 14 and up during a week of violent unrest in the Strip. As word of the strike, which at its height encompassed 3,000 prisoners, spread beyond the confines of the jails, serious rioting erupted throughout the West Bank. In the meantime, Jewish settlers were also increasingly restive because of the deteriorating security situation on roads in the territories. On March 4, after two buses on the Jerusalem–Kiryat Arba route were stoned, slightly injuring one passenger, settlers from Kiryat Arba and Hebron retaliated by driving through the nearby town of Halhoul after midnight, smashing windows of cars and houses.

It was in the midst of this charged atmosphere that the year's worst terrorist outrage was perpetrated. At about 7 P.M. on April 11—the same day, ironically, on which Foreign Minister Peres met secretly with King Hussein in London (see "Peace Initiatives")—a gasoline bomb struck the car in which Avraham and Ofra Moses and their three children, aged 5, 8, and 13, along with another boy, were traveling from their home in the Samaria settlement of Alfei Menasheh to Petah Tikvah. The car burst into flames. Avraham Moses managed to rescue the children, but his wife died in the flames. Five-year-old Tal died of his injuries on July 5, a few days after his father and the other children, all of whom sustained serious burns, were released from the hospital. Hours after the attack against the Moses family, hundreds of Jewish settlers went on the rampage in and around Kalkilya, torching fields and cars and smashing windows. During a visit to the site of the firebomb attack a few days later, Defense Minister Rabin told angry settlers that more Israeli troops were currently stationed in the territories than on the border with Lebanon. (On August 6 another couple from Alfei Menasheh suffered burns when a firebomb struck their car not far from the site of the attack on the Moses family. In December the security forces arrested a 25-year-old man from nearby Kalkilya in connection with both incidents; the orange grove from which he allegedly threw the incendiary bomb was uprooted by the IDF.)

In the meantime, the arrest of about one hundred Palestinian activists in the wake of the atrocity made no perceptible impact on the ongoing violence. On April 13 a Bir Zeit University student was killed when troops clashed with demonstrators near his home in the Gaza Strip town of Rafah. Three days later two Jewish women were injured when their car was stoned as they drove past the Deheishe refugee camp on the edge of Bethlehem. In response, the IDF threw up a fence 100 meters long and 6 meters high along the road in front of the camp. Another hundred persons were arrested in the Gaza Strip as unrest there continued, and in East Jerusalem about 20 youths were detained by police for exhorting shopkeepers to join a commercial strike.

Such measures were scoffed at by the Jewish settlers. Whether they had moved to the territories for religio-ideological reasons, or had been lured there by material inducements in the form of inexpensive, heavily subsidized housing and the promise of suburban "country living"—"five minutes from Kfar Sava," as the slogan went— they kept up intense pressure on the security forces to take a hard line against Palestinian "troublemakers." Following the stabbing of an Ethiopian immigrant in the Hebron *casbah* on May 1, and more violence on the roads, on May 6 Gush Emunim secretary-general Daniella Weiss led settlers on a rampage through Kalkilya, in an effort to intimidate the inhabitants.

The 20th anniversary of the Six Day War (June 5), which had brought the West Bank and Gaza under Israeli rule, saw a renewed flare-up of violent unrest throughout the territories, resulting in several Palestinian casualties in confrontations with Israeli troops. On June 6, after a Jewish woman was hit by a stone thrown at a bus near the Deheishe refugee camp, settlers retaliated in the year's most extreme "vigilante" action. That night, some 50 settlers from Kiryat Arba and Hebron, carrying firearms and clubs, blocked the Jerusalem-Hebron road outside the camp, smashed windshields of Arab cars, and dragged out the passengers and beat them. They then stormed into the camp, after clashing with Israeli soldiers, opening fire and throwing stones. O/C Central Command Maj. Gen. Avraham Mitzna called the attack an "abomination" and expressed his regret at the incident to the camp's inhabitants.

But the cyclical pattern of violence continued. On June 9 Deheishe residents again disrupted traffic by throwing stones at passing Israeli cars, injuring one woman. This provided the IDF with an opportunity to appease the Council of Settlements, which had dissociated itself from the June 6 rampage but had also professed outrage at General Mitzna's statements and "wimpish" attitude. Israeli forces carried out a search operation in Deheishe, and the wire fence separating the camp from the road was extended by about 250 meters and raised to a height of about 10 meters; one of the camp's access roads was sealed off with barbed wire.

SHIN BET ROLE

While the army tried to restrain the settlers and contain the growing popular unrest among the Palestinians, the General Security Service (Shin Bet) continued its intensive undercover antiterrorism efforts. On April 28 a Brazilian woman was sentenced to life imprisonment for having acted as an accomplice in the kidnapping and murder of an IDF soldier, David Manos, in 1984; a second woman received 12 years. (Both their husbands were jailed for life in October 1986 for the crime.)

In August a new form of anti-Israel activity, with overtones of fanatic religious fundamentalism, was revealed when the security forces announced the arrest of a joint Fatah-Islamic Jihad underground cell. The group had planned a suicide car-bomb attack in an Israeli city. On October 20 two West Bank residents, Ahmed Hanani, aged 31, and Muayid Abdel Samad, aged 25, both members of George Habash's Popular Front for the Liberation of Palestine, were sentenced to life imprisonment after being convicted by a Nablus military court of three murders and at least two attempted murders. Their most spectacular killing was of Nablus mayor Zafr al-Masri in March 1986, an action intended to undermine Israeli-Jordanian cooperation in the West Bank. They had also gunned down two Israelis in Nablus—Albert Buchris, from Afula, in June 1985; and a border policeman, Jamil Faris, in January 1986—and wounded two others, Uri Ovad in July 1985, and Haim TaMami in June 1986, in Jenin and Nablus, respectively.

Nor were Shin Bet efforts confined to the territories. On February 16 plainclothes police raided the office of the Alternative Information Center in downtown West Jerusalem, confiscated its files and archives, seized all the printing equipment on the premises, and arrested the entire staff, both Israelis and Palestinians. The AIC was ordered shut down for six months. During its three years of operation, the center, which functioned as a collective, issued a fortnightly bulletin, *News from Within*, which was legally registered at the Interior Ministry and whose contents were submitted for prior military censorship. Local and foreign journalists availed themselves of the AIC's generally reliable information on developments in the territories and on other issues related to the conflict. However, according to the "Closure and Seizure Order" signed by the inspector general of the Israel Police and issued under the 1948 Prevention of Terrorism Ordinance, the AIC "acted on behalf of the Popular Front for the Liberation of Palestine," printed "illegal publications of the organization and its affiliates," and distributed information which it received "from the organization's activists in the country and abroad." Despite the apparent gravity of the charge, all those arrested were released within 48 hours, with the exception of the center's director, Michael Warschawsky, who was kept imprisoned for two weeks and then remanded in custody until the completion of the legal proceedings against him. However, an appeal to the High Court of Justice secured his release as well, on NIS 75,000 bail.

The episode triggered protests in Israel and abroad by civil-rights activists and journalists, and raised anew the specter of the intrusion into the Israeli polity of practices employed by the authorities vis-à-vis the occupied territories. The Israel Association for Civil Rights petitioned the High Court of Justice against the closure of the AIC, and the Jerusalem branch of the Israeli Journalists' Association issued a statement assailing the shutdown of a licensed office. A petition deploring the AIC's closure, signed by some of Israel's leading intellectuals, appeared in *Ha'aretz*.

## TERRORISM INSIDE ISRAEL

Most of the actual terrorist outrages in 1987 occurred in the territories, and those attacks that took place inside the Green Line were also the handiwork of residents of the West Bank or Gaza. In Israel the most serious incidents in 1987 were: the stabbing murder of an IDF reserve soldier, Alexander Arad, aged 43, while hitchhiking at the Megiddo junction on September 24; the ax murder of another soldier a few days later—the body of Hanoch Steve Deneman, an immigrant from Holland and a convert to Judaism, was found in a field near Acre; the shooting death of a Jerusalem man, Yigal Shahaf, aged 25, in the Old City on October 10; bomb explosions on a Haifa-Jerusalem bus on February 1, wounding nine persons, and on an Ashkelon bus, on July 3, lightly wounding two passengers; and a bomb blast on a Haifa beach on June 27, seriously wounding a woman and injuring her small son.

## GAZA STRIP

It was in the Gaza Strip that the sheer weight of human misery seemed to engender a perpetual state of violent rage that finally issued in December's volcanic eruption. On August 2, in an unusually daring attack in the heart of Gaza City, the commander of the Military Police in the Gaza Strip, Capt. Ron Tal, aged 22, was shot to death at point-blank range in his car. On October 1, the IDF spokesman reported, three Palestinians were shot and killed by Israeli soldiers when they left their car and tried to flee after being ordered to stop at an IDF roadblock near the El-Bureij refugee camp. The army's version was widely disbelieved in Gaza when two of the victims were identified as well-known local figures, Mahmed Abdel Rahman Hassin, aged 33, a building contractor, and Mahmed Alian Ali al-Maganda, aged 40, a construction engineer (the third man carried no identification). Five days later, four Palestinian gunmen were killed in a shoot-out with Israeli security forces in Gaza City's Saja'iyeh neighborhood following a car chase; a Shin Bet agent, Victor Arjuan, from Beersheba, was also killed in the clash. Two of those killed turned out to be escaped security prisoners. The incidents sparked days of violent demonstrations throughout the Gaza Strip.

The visit to Israel of U.S. secretary of state George Shultz in mid-October (see also "Peace Initiatives") was the occasion for more unrest. With emotions running high in the territories, and heavy pressure exerted by local PLO activists, eight leading Palestinians from the West Bank and Gaza boycotted a planned meeting with Shultz. An Arab summit meeting held in Amman November 8–11 sparked a new wave of rioting. The sense of frustration and despair in the territories was heightened by King Hussein's humiliating treatment of Yasir Arafat at the meeting and by the almost total disregard of the Palestinian issue by the Arab leaders, who were concerned primarily with the Gulf War. In incidents on November 10 and 11 in which Jewish settlers opened fire, a 17-year-old Gaza girl was shot in the back and killed, and two other schoolgirls were wounded, one of them seriously. The coordinator of activities in the territories, Shmuel Goren, who took the rare step of visiting the seriously wounded girl in hospital, announcing that the Gaza Civil Administration would assist her family, told reporters that opening fire at schoolgirls "serves only the PLO."

THE UPRISING BEGINS

Goren spoke, of course, without benefit of foresight regarding the uprising that began a month later. Of the various events later cited as the "triggers" of the uprising—the fuses, as it were, that detonated the potent powder keg of human despair and political frustration—three bear special mention. A hang-glider attack at Kiryat Shemonah on November 25, in which a lone Palestinian raider killed six soldiers, gave Palestinians a big morale boost. (See "National Security," below.) Secondly, it was said, the Palestinians, disappointed in the results of the Arab summit meeting in November, took advantage of the Reagan-Gorbachev summit in Washington on December 8 to show that they were still a factor to be reckoned with in the international arena. Yet the proximate cause of the uprising, the authorities maintained, was nothing more out of the ordinary than a road accident. On the evening of December 8, four Gazans were killed and six injured when an Israeli truck was involved in a collision with two cars on the edge of the Gaza Strip. Two days earlier a Bat-Yam man, Shlomo Sakal, aged 45, had been stabbed to death in Gaza City, and a curfew imposed for two days as searches were carried out for the assailants. Apparently the ever-grinding rumor mill in Gaza had it that the truck driver was the murdered man's brother and that he deliberately caused the accident in an act of revenge. Whether this was folklore or fact, what was certain was that when the curfew was lifted on Wednesday, December 9, the lid blew off the Gaza Strip.

Symbolically, perhaps, it was a Gaza refugee-camp youth who was the first victim of the uprising. Hatham al-Sissi, a 17-year-old resident of the Jebalya camp, was shot and killed by Israeli troops that morning, and 17 other Gazans were wounded, four of them seriously, as waves of demonstrators hurled rocks, gasoline bombs, and other objects at Israeli troops, who were barely able to drive them back with live ammunition. Hundreds of enraged residents stormed the Shifa Hospital, seized the body of the youth who was killed, and held a mass funeral, which further enflamed passions. The few IDF troops regularly stationed in the Gaza Strip could not cope with either the scale or intensity of the disturbances.

On Thursday, December 10, the mass unrest spread to the West Bank. In Nablus another 17-year-old youth, Ibrahim al-Akliq, was shot dead and one person was wounded by Israeli marksmen using sniper rifles; two Israeli officers were hurt by flying glass. Serious rioting broke out in Nablus's Balata refugee camp, and a number of demonstrators were wounded by gunfire. Gasoline bombs were thrown at Israeli vehicles near Tulkarm and El-Bireh. In the Gaza Strip an 11-year-old boy, Wahid Abu Salem, from Khan Yunis, was killed and at least 15 persons were wounded. Commercial strikes were called and many residents of the territories employed in Israel did not report to work.

Security sources, still thinking in terms relevant to the past, attributed this "wave" of unrest primarily to the 20th anniversary of the founding of the Popular Front for the Liberation of Palestine. Similarly, no interconnection was perceived in the spread of the disturbances on a large scale from Gaza to the West Bank. As for the large number of casualties, although the IDF said troops were under strict orders to open fire only when they felt their lives were endangered, the fact was that such situations had grown increasingly frequent. For one thing, relatively small patrols found themselves under assault by crowds of an unprecedented size. For another, the Palestinians in the territories had apparently overcome the so-called fear barrier that had inhibited attacks on Israeli soldiers up to this point. Moreover, despite periodic pronouncements proclaiming the IDF's procurement and/or development of nonlethal riot-control equipment, the Israeli troops were as unequipped as they were untrained to cope with demonstrations of this magnitude.

On December 11 Defense Minister Yitzhak Rabin, after studying the situation, decided to go ahead with a ten-day visit to the United States. (He would later reject calls from his own party to cut short his stay, after completing the main business of the visit, because of the deteriorating situation in the territories.) It was Prime Minister Shamir who served as acting defense minister during the critical first period of the uprising. On the day the defense minister flew to the United States, border policemen in Balata shot and killed three individuals, aged 13, 19, and 57, and wounded seven others, in demonstrations that followed the Friday Muslim services. Many others were wounded in Gaza—about 15 according to the IDF, but 40 according to local sources, who said that many of the wounded refrained from applying to hospitals for fear they would be arrested. The Jebalya refugee camp remained completely sealed off. Tens of thousands of workers from Gaza employed in Israel stayed home, seriously affecting municipal sanitation services, construction projects, and numerous factories and businesses.

In its regular weekly meeting on Sunday, December 13, the cabinet heard the chief of staff, Lt. Gen. Dan Shomron, and the coordinator of activities in the territories, Shmuel Goren, offer an essentially upbeat assessment predicting that, as in the past, the demonstrations would cease as abruptly as they had begun. Shomron said the riots were in part the aftermath of the traditional yearly protests associated with the anniversary of the UN Partition Resolution. The cabinet resolved formally that no "civil revolt" was under way in the territories, that the media were to blame for inflating what was actually a passing wave of riots, and that the security forces had things under firm control. No need was seen for a change of policy in the territories. The cabinet communiqué further quoted Prime Minister and Acting Defense Minister Shamir as saying that the "terrorist organizations" had failed in their attempt to undermine the country's security and that the majority of the inhabitants in the territories "have no interest in disturbances and riots."

After two days without a death in the territories, a 25-year-old man from the Gaza

Strip town of Khan Yunis was shot and killed; according to the IDF spokesman, he had thrown gasoline bombs at soldiers. Military sources said the number of troops in the West Bank had been increased by 50 percent as compared with "normal" periods. While this beefing up of forces seemed to cause the scope and intensity of the unrest to taper off in the West Bank—although a commercial strike in Nablus and Ramallah persisted despite the security forces' efforts to force merchants to open for businesss—in Gaza there was no respite. Three more Palestinians, two aged 17 and the third aged 22, died in violent clashes with Israeli troops, and many others were wounded. A fourth man died in an Ashkelon hospital of wounds suffered earlier.

In the meantime, Israel found itself facing another front, the foreign media. Daily press reports and, more damaging, television footage showing Israeli soldiers in full battle gear firing on or clubbing civilians, often women and children, were taking a fearful image toll. Prime Minister Shamir on December 15 likened American TV coverage of the events in the territories to the "distorted" reporting during the Lebanon War. In a meeting with Chief of Staff Shomron, Shamir raised the possibility of closing the territories to reporters, a move he felt would have a salutary dampening effect on the unrest. Shomron dissuaded the prime minister from taking this course, as the IDF would be hard pressed to prevent journalists from entering the areas. Foreign Ministry Political Director-General Yossi Beilin said that not since the bombing of Beirut in August-September 1982 had Israel faced international media criticism on the present scale. On December 17 Beilin set up an emergency task force to handle the deluge of requests from Israel's legations abroad for concrete information and guidelines in order to refute the anti-Israel reporting. Quite often these requests were accompanied by the texts of condemnations of Israel by various individuals and organizations.

Of special concern to Jerusalem was Egypt's reaction. Ambassador Muhammad Bassiouny met on December 16 with Acting Foreign Minister Ezer Weizman (Peres was on a South American tour) to inquire what steps Israel was taking to prevent loss of life in the areas, particularly in Gaza. Israeli ambassador to Egypt Moshe Sasson reported that the atmosphere prevailing in Cairo and in the Egyptian press was the most hostile to Israel since the Beirut refugee-camps massacre in September 1982. On December 16 in the town of Rafah, which was split down the middle by the Israeli-Egyptian border, three local residents were shot when an Israeli patrol was attacked by an enflamed mob, one of whom stabbed an IDF soldier. The assailant later died of his wounds. A commercial strike continued throughout the Gaza Strip, curfews were imposed wholesale, and troops clashed with demonstrators in almost every refugee camp, using tear gas liberally—in some cases, according to Arab sources, in enclosed rooms, where the effects could be lethal.

Following a particularly turbulent Friday, December 18, on which two Gaza refugee-camp residents were shot dead and at least ten others were wounded when Israeli troops broke up mass demonstrations following the prayer services, and three West Bank refugee camps were placed under curfew, the disturbances spread to

Jerusalem. On December 19 East Jerusalem and the surrounding neighborhoods experienced what municipal officials said was the most serious rioting in the capital since 1967. The rioters, many of them elementary and high-school pupils, took to the streets in organized fashion, shouting religious and nationalist slogans, throwing stones, burning tires, and setting up barriers. Heavy damage was caused to the branches of three Israeli banks in East Jerusalem, and windshields of police cars were shattered. A total commercial and school strike was held in and around East Jerusalem. Many of the demonstrators shouted slogans against Industry and Trade Minister Ariel Sharon who, in a highly publicized and much criticized move, had taken up residence in the Muslim Quarter of the Old City of Jerusalem on December 15, at the height of the unrest. Some 300 police were needed to protect those who turned up for the housewarming party, among them Prime Minister Shamir, the guest of honor. (Another contributing factor to the situation in Jerusalem was the Energy Ministry's takeover on December 6 of 30 percent of the concession of the Jerusalem District Electricity Company, because it had incurred heavy debts to the Israel Electric Corporation, from which it was compelled to purchase nearly all its power. The JDEC supplied electricity to some of the post-1967 Jewish suburbs and settlements around Jerusalem and even to some IDF bases.)

In sharp contrast to the situation in the West Bank and Gaza, where troops trained for combat against enemy armies were at a loss when confronted with what was dubbed the "stone-age" warfare of civilians, in East Jerusalem, which had been officially annexed to Israel, the disturbances were handled by the Israel Police. The result was that in six consecutive hours of heavy rioting across a wide area, large quantities of tear gas were used but not a shot was fired. Three policemen were injured and 33 demonstrators arrested, 19 of them minors.

On December 20, the cabinet, at its regular weekly meeting, discussed the situation in the territories for four hours. A proposal by Acting Foreign Minister Weizman to send a special envoy to Cairo to forestall a crisis in relations between the two countries was rejected by Prime Minister Shamir. The latest assessment of the chief of staff was that the international reactions to the disturbances were motivating the population in the territories to persist with the riots. The cabinet communiqué released after the meeting, which consisted of Prime Minister Shamir's summation of the discussion, stated that the cabinet was "united in its support of the actions of the security forces . . . against terrorism and civil disorder, carried out with maximum effort to prevent the loss of life." Press reports concerning the number of casualties were described as "extremely exaggerated."

In the field, seven Palestinians in the West Bank and Gaza were wounded in clashes with troops on the tenth consecutive day of the disturbances. All 800 elementary and high schools in the West Bank were ordered closed for two days— subsequently extended to a week—by the head of the Judea-Samaria Civil Administration, Brig. Gen. Shaike Erez, to prevent organized incitement of the pupils. (Erez replaced Brig. Gen. Ephraim Sneh, who resigned in September after two years in the post, over policy differences with the coordinator of activities in the areas,

Shmuel Goren.) In East Jerusalem the commercial strike continued and about 30 more persons were arrested. In the Gaza Strip activists halted a bus carrying workers to Israel, ordered the passengers off, and burned the vehicle.

December 21 saw another ominous development: the spread of the unrest to the Israeli Arab population. The National Committee of Heads of Arab Local Authorities organized a one-day general strike of Israeli Arabs, under the slogan "Peace Day," to show solidarity with their Palestinian brethren in the territories. However, in contrast to other one-day strikes staged by the Israeli Arab population in 1987 (see "Other Domestic Matters"), Peace Day proved far from peaceful. In sporadic violence, 20 policemen were injured, one seriously, and 100 protesters were arrested (more arrests were made in the following days). Some 2,300 police and Border Police were deployed during the day. In yet another jolting "surprise" to the Israeli leadership, the unrest was not confined exclusively to "Arab sector" locales such as Nazareth and Umm al-Faham, where the influence of militants was pronounced, but encompassed also "mixed cities," including Jaffa, Lod, and Ramle. In addition, the Wadi Ara highway, a major east-west thoroughfare, was blocked for some hours when demonstrators set up barricades and stoned vehicles.

In an interview on Israel television two days later, Prime Minister Shamir asserted that by their actions Israel's Arabs were expressing "identification with the PLO." The riots had "lit a red light for many Israelis," the prime minister warned, and added, pointedly: "Our Arab citizens must . . . see the slope toward which they are sliding. Because they know what the end result was of such events [in the past]." Defense Minister Rabin also evoked the specter of 1948 when he took the opportunity of a statement to the Knesset on December 23 to address "a few words to the Israeli Arabs." For the most part, he noted, they had "passed the test of loyalty" to the state and were generally "unblemished." However, he went on: "In the distant past you experienced a tragedy, and it will be best for you and us if you do not revert to it or repeat it."

The events across the Green Line on December 21 produced a change of tone in the defense establishment. General Erez asserted that if the "rampage of the rabble" continued unabated, "we will have to employ harsh methods to restore order." As though to bear him out, 3 West Bank residents were killed and 16 wounded in clashes with Israeli forces; in the Gaza Strip one man died of wounds sustained 12 days earlier and about ten people were wounded. Two IDF soldiers suffered eye wounds when they were hit by stones in the Jebalya refugee camp. In both the West Bank and Gaza, a total and all-embracing general strike was held, described by security personnel as "unprecedented in scope" and tantamount to a "self-imposed curfew." Every area of life—commerce, education, services, public transportation, education—was affected. In the evening, Defense Minister Rabin, returning from the United States, told an airport press conference that "what is going on in the territories . . . is being perpetrated with a clear political aim behind which stand Iran, Iraq and Syria, and above all the PLO."

Two days later, in the Knesset statement already alluded to, Rabin offered a different explanation: "The violent public disorders in the past two weeks broke out against a backdrop of local events and were the fruit of spontaneous organizing. The PLO terrorist organizations and activists in the territories did everything they could, both inside and outside the territories, to heighten and intensify the events." Rabin also signaled that the military would take a tougher line. Larger forces would be deployed with the aim of quelling disturbances before they could get out of hand. Moreover, military commanders in the territories were under "no restrictions" in employing "the punishment of deportation and administrative detention" against "inciters" and "organizers," or in imposing curfew. According to the defense minister, between the outbreak of violence on December 9 and December 22, 21 residents of the territories had been killed and 158 wounded; 31 soldiers and border policemen and 19 Israeli civilians had been wounded.

Two of the deaths came on December 22. A 20-year-old Jenin resident died in Haifa's Rambam Hospital of wounds sustained earlier. In Gaza, a 19-year-old was shot and killed by troops who found themselves confronting a raging mob in the Jebalya refugee camp. Arab sources said IDF soldiers then entered homes in the camp, beat up the occupants, and used tear gas against them. In a new tactic, helicopters were used to drop tear-gas grenades on crowds of demonstrators. Mass arrests were made, under the guidance of the Shin Bet, in both Gaza and the West Bank.

On the international front, on December 22 the UN Security Council passed a resolution "[s]trongly deplor[ing] those policies and practices of Israel, the occupying power, which violate the human rights of the Palestinian people in the Occupied Territories, and in particular the opening of fire by the Israeli army, resulting in the killing and wounding of defenseless Palestinian civilians." The vote was 14–0, with the United States abstaining, following public rebukes of Israeli actions by President Ronald Reagan and administration spokesmen. As expected, the Israeli Foreign Ministry dismissed the resolution as "one-sided," complaining (on the same day that Rabin called the riots "spontaneous") that the resolution failed to mention "those hostile elements attempting to force their will upon the civilian population through violence and terrorism."

The first meeting of the inner cabinet since the uprising began took place only on December 23. According to press reports, the country's ranking policy-making body agreed that priority must be given to restoring order, even if this resulted in international condemnation. At the same time, in order to mitigate such condemnation, it was decided to enforce more stringently the order that troops could open fire only when their lives were endangered. The Israeli security forces, it was stressed, had to do all in their power to reestablish their authority and thus restore the IDF's damaged deterrent capability.

Within days of the inner cabinet meeting, over one thousand persons were arrested in the territories on charges of disturbing the peace and incitement. The Ansar II detention camp in Gaza was filled to capacity, and in the West Bank a new detention facility was set up at Dahariya, near Hebron, to handle the overflow from the other regional prisons. As the mass roundup of suspects continued, giving rise to rumors of large-scale expulsions or even a population "transfer," the level of protest and violence in the areas tapered off considerably. This was partially attributed to, besides the extensive arrests, unusually heavy December rains, pressure exerted on the activists by day-workers employed in Israel to resume their jobs, and the sealing off of various trouble spots, such as refugee camps. Nonetheless, sporadic violence continued, and commercial strikes, which the IDF tried unsuccessfully to break, were rampant. In the Jebalya camp, where a prolonged curfew was in force, residents complained about food shortages.

Dozens of lawyers were called up for emergency reserve duty, as prosecutors or defense counsel, to help handle the case load resulting from the unprecedented sweep of arrests. Lawyers from the territories decided to boycott the trials—which, like the detentions, were carried out under a combination of Jordanian law, the Defense (Emergency) Regulations promulgated by the British Mandate authorities in 1945, and decrees issued by the Israeli military since 1967. The local lawyers termed the proceedings "humiliating" and "farcical." The result was that many of the accused had no legal representation, and those who did find lawyers often met them for the first time in the courtroom. Twenty-three defendants were tried in Gaza military courts on December 27, and the number rose to 70 the next day. Jurists in Israel spoke of "assembly-line justice."

Most of the defendants were aged 17–30, though some were younger. Those convicted of taking part in demonstrations or throwing stones were given up to six months' imprisonment, along with extended probationary periods, and fined hundreds of shekels. There was no possibility of appeal. Persistent complaints about subhuman conditions and maltreatment of prisoners in the detention camps, particularly Ansar II, continued to be denied by the military.

The human-rights situation in the territories fueled dissent in Israel. Peace Now held a torchlight march through Jerusalem on December 26. In scenes reminiscent of the Lebanon War, the demonstrators were taunted, and in some cases assaulted, by supporters of the ultra-right Tehiya and Kach (Kahane) parties. The Yesh Gvul (There's a Limit/Border) movement, which originated in the Lebanon War, announced on December 24 that over 150 reserve soldiers, among them some officers, had signed a petition declaring that they would refuse to take part in "suppressing the uprising in the territories." In addition, a group of 16 high- school seniors wrote to Defense Minister Rabin declaring that they would refuse to serve in the territories after their induction into the army because they could not in good conscience carry out the "inhumane" orders entailed by the occupation. Two earlier groups totaling 50 12th-graders had already written similar letters to the defense minister.

Rabin, however, was digging in, and the defense establishment with him. Asked, in an interview in *Ha'aretz* on December 29, about American pressure on Israel not to carry out expulsions, Rabin replied: "The American stand is centered against administrative detentions and expulsions on the ground that they conflict with the Geneva Convention. But we act according to our own laws. We will continue with arrests, punishment and expulsions." Larger forces, the defense minister maintained, would have less resort to firearms. The previous day the chief of staff had told military correspondents that "far fewer" forces had been required to conquer the Gaza Strip in 1967 than were currently deployed there.

On December 30 a 17-year-old youth from the Jebalya refugee camp in Gaza died of wounds sustained some days earlier when he was shot in the head during a clash with troops. He was the 22nd resident of the territories to die since the uprising began three weeks earlier, and the last in 1987. His death sparked renewed mass demonstrations in Jebalya, but the army let the unrest run its course and did not confront the protesters. The year ended on a note of high tension as the security forces braced for expected trouble on January 1, Fatah Day—while suggesting that Fatah Day would also mark the climax of the unrest. In the meantime, sporadic disturbances continued throughout the territories, and dozens of persons were arrested each day, including, on December 29, a large number of convicted terrorists who had been released in the deal with Ahmed Jibril's organization in 1985. The trials in the military courts in both the West Bank and Gaza continued at an accelerated pace.

Two Israeli documents published on the last day of the year and an earlier statement by a leading Palestinian Arab encapsulate the views of some of the leading players on the unfolding events. A petition published in the press and signed by some 90 faculty members of Tel Aviv University gave voice to the despair many Israelis, particularly in the intellectual community, felt in the face of the official Israeli reaction to the uprising. Calling for a "reassessment of Israeli policy on the Palestinian issue in general and in the administered areas in particular," the signatories added:

> It is impossible to differentiate between the recent escalation in the expressions of violence between Arabs and Jews, and the protracted political deadlock. . . . It is unconscionable that IDF soldiers should find themselves in situations of opening fire against children and demonstrating civilians because of the government's refusal to address the real roots of the crisis. This state of affairs is morally oppressive and is corrupting every area of our life. . . . We call on the Israeli government to desist from its policy of threats and a hard hand in the territories and seek a political solution through dialogue and negotiation.

As though in answer to this and other appeals in the same vein, the IDF Spokesman's Office on the same day issued a policy statement, in English, directed to the foreign press and foreign legations, entitled "Maintenance of Public Safety in Judea, Samaria and Gaza Strip." After stating that the IDF "has taken various actions" against both individuals and institutions "for the purpose of maintaining public safety and returning life to normal" during this period, the information sheet stated: "These varied activities [of the IDF] have intensified in the wake of the disturbances of the last two [sic] weeks, but actually have been carried out routinely for several years." For the IDF, then, it was business as usual, only more so.

The third statement was that of deposed Gaza mayor Rashad ash-Shawwa, in an interview published in *Ha'aretz* on December 18, ten days after the uprising began:

> I call on the Jewish people and the lovers of peace among them: please, stop humiliating us and degrading us. Stop hurting another people which has done nothing wrong. We call on the Jewish people to return to their well-known revered values and stop treating our people as though they were not human beings. The people in the Gaza Strip feel they are being wronged and discriminated against, they feel they no longer have anything to lose. They work for you as garbagemen and dishwashers and they feel like slaves. . . . The disturbances are a spontaneous expression of the people's rage, beginning with the little pupil in elementary school and extending to the worker who returns every day from Israel and sees the good life there, but is forced to live in subhuman conditions here.

## National Security

### LEBANON

In 1987 Israel continued to face an array of adversaries in Lebanon, among them the Iranian-backed Hezballah (party of God), which occasionally teamed up with Palestinian groups trying to reestablish themselves in the country. The Israel Navy continued to play a key preemptive role in this regard, intercepting ships and small craft carrying PLO members to Lebanon.

On land, the year saw a considerable increase in the number of infiltration attempts into Israel (ten incidents, two more than in the previous two years combined), clashes in the security zone (54, nearly twice as many as in 1986), and the firing of Katyusha rockets into Israel (20 instances, as many as the two previous years combined). Because of the distance from which the rockets were launched, they generally landed harmlessly, although on April 16 three persons were slightly hurt when rockets struck a settlement in the Galilee panhandle.

It was in ground fighting, sometimes at close quarters, that the IDF's presence in Lebanon continued to take its toll. On April 10 two soldiers were killed in a Hezballah ambush in southern Lebanon, provoking massive Israeli artillery and tank fire. A few days later, outposts of the IDF and the Southern Lebanon Army (SLA), the 2,600-man Israeli-supported militia, came under massive Hezballah attack, with some 25 of the raiders killed. On April 19 another two Israeli soldiers were killed in hand-to-hand combat with terrorists who, for the first time since 1980, succeeded in getting across the security fence along the border, near Kibbutz Manara. On May 7 two terrorists were killed and three captured in a clash about 7 kilometers north of the border. Eighteen hours later the Israel Air Force (IAF) struck at "terrorist targets and departure bases for attacks on Israel" around the Ein Hilweh and Miyeh-Miyeh refugee camps near Sidon in southern Lebanon. It was the third such attack around Sidon within a week, and the 15th air raid on Lebanon since the beginning of the year. The declared aims of such attacks were to keep terrorists off balance and prevent the PLO from rebuilding its infrastructure in Lebanon. However, the Lebanese claimed that the air raids took a heavy toll in civilian casualties.

A controversial air strike was carried out on September 5 against Fatah strongholds, again around Sidon. In a major departure, this attack, reportedly the most devastating since 1982, came on a Saturday, and thus took Fatah personnel by surprise, resulting in about 50 persons killed and a like number wounded, including civilians. Some in Israel maintained that the attack was as much political as military, its intention being to torpedo an Israeli-Palestinian peace effort (see "Peace Initiatives"). Ten days after the big attack, an Israeli patrol was ambushed in the foothills of Mount Hermon in the security zone. The company commander, Ronen Weissman, from Moshav Maslul, was killed instantly; the platoon commander, Alexander Singer, an American who had settled in Israel two years earlier, was cut down when he tried to aid Weissman; and a third soldier, Oren Kamil, from Ramle, was felled as he tried to assist the two officers. Because of the difficult terrain, the remaining men had to fight on their own for some three hours before reinforcements could reach them (their medic and three others from the original 12-man unit were also wounded). But they held their ground until they were rescued.

Ten weeks later Lebanon was the origin of a particularly daring attack inside Israel, one with far-reaching consequences. On the night of November 25 a lone gunman from Ahmed Jibril's Popular Front for the Liberation of Palestine/General Command managed to fly a motorized hang glider from Syrian-controlled territory in Lebanon into Israel. Landing near Kiryat Shemonah, he killed an officer who happened to drive by in a military vehicle and then stormed a Nahal (paramilitary) camp, where he killed another five soldiers and wounded seven before being gunned down by one of the wounded men. The sentry at the camp gate fled in the face of the onrushing gunman without firing a shot. In the aftermath, the chief of staff reprimanded the brigadier general responsible for the sector where the camp was located, the colonel commanding the Nahal brigade was relieved of his duties and given another post, and the operations officer at the base, a captain, was ordered placed on trial before being dismissed from the army. It was later maintained that the incident at Kiryat Shemonah was one of the "triggers" of the uprising in the territories that erupted two weeks later.

Inside Lebanon itself, 1987 ended in what had become routine fashion, with three gunmen killed in two firefights with IDF patrols in the last two days of the year. All told, 15 Israeli soldiers were killed in clashes in or emanating from Lebanon (including the six killed in the hang-glider raid), double the number of the previous year, and over 20 were wounded. It was costing Israel about NIS 100,000 a day to maintain the SLA (which suffered about 50 men killed during the year) and the accompanying civil administration in southern Lebanon. About 1,150 Lebanese continued to cross the border each day to work in Israel.

THE NAFSU–SHIN BET CASE

Hardly had Israelis recovered from the revelations of the April 1984 Bus No. 300 hijacking (see AJYB 1988, vol. 88, pp. 368–73), when the country was rocked by another case involving the top-secret General Security Service (GSS, or Shin Bet in the Hebrew acronym). Although the 1987 scandal predated the earlier affair by some years, for the Israeli public it began with cryptic reports in the April 9 issue of a weekly news magazine, *Koteret Rashit*. The entire story emerged from the verdict subsequently handed down in the matter by the High Court of Justice.

On January 4, 1980, the Shin Bet arrested a man in his mid-20s named Izat Nafsu, from the Circassian village of Kafr Kama, on suspicion of treason. Nafsu was a career soldier in the IDF who held the rank of lieutenant when he left the army in October 1979. His final posting was in southern Lebanon, and it was in connection with his activities there that he was charged, and convicted—in a secret trial that concluded in June 1982—of treason, aggravated espionage, and aiding the enemy in wartime. Sentenced to 18 years' imprisonment and a dishonorable discharge, entailing loss of his military rank, Nafsu turned to the military appeals court, which in June 1986 upheld the original verdict. Nafsu then requested permission to appeal to the Supreme Court under a newly passed amendment to the Military Jurisdiction Law. His request was granted (Nafsu was the first person to take advantage of the new amendment), and in February 1987 the appeal was filed.

Nafsu maintained that his written confession was extracted under physical and mental duress. Since doubts had been expressed within both the military and the GSS about the conviction, the new GSS chief who took over after the departure of Avraham Bendor (Shalom), following the bus-hijacking affair, ordered a review of the case. Although Nafsu was all but cleared, the Shin Bet wanted to prevent the legal process from taking its course, contending that its secret interrogation methods would be revealed and its credibility in the courts damaged.

Supreme Court president Meir Shamgar headed the panel of three justices who heard Nafsu's case on May 24. They were informed by the chief military advocate that a plea-bargaining deal had been worked out involving the IDF, the GSS, and Nafsu. Under this arrangement, which was accepted by the court, the treason and espionage convictions were annulled, and Nafsu pleaded guilty to a far lesser charge of "exceeding his authority to the point of imperiling state security." The maximum penalty for this offense was five years' imprisonment, but the court, taking into account Nafsu's overall "positive military record" and the fact that he had already spent over seven years in prison on a conviction that "was devoid of any legal basis," sentenced Nafsu to two years' imprisonment and demotion from lieutenant to master-sergeant. Since he had already served far more than this term, he was ordered released immediately. (In August, the IDF said Nafsu would be paid NIS 70,000 in back pay, and Nafsu announced that he would also sue the state.) The court spoke also of the "gravity" with which it viewed the perjury committed by Shin Bet agents, which did "far-reaching harm to the credibility" of the GSS and its representatives in court. "[D]ecisive measures" were required "to eradicate this phenomenon, and we hereby draw the attorney general's attention to this," Justice Shamgar, who wrote the decision, added.

The ensuing developments were strongly reminiscent of the Bus No. 300 affair. The Supreme Court's ruling left Attorney General Harish no choice but to order a police investigation. However, in an effort to calm what was said to be an atmosphere of "rebellion" within the GSS, and help get Israel's intelligence community out of the headlines, on May 31 the cabinet decided to appoint a formal judicial commission of inquiry "into the procedures and methods of investigation of the General Security Service regarding Hostile Terrorist Activity and the giving of testimony in court concerning those investigations." On June 2 retired Supreme Court president Moshe Landau was appointed to chair the commission, with State Comptroller Yaakov Malz and former Mossad chief Maj. Gen. (res.) Yitzhak Hofi as members. This move neutralized the police probe (as had occurred in the Bus 300 case).

The Landau Commission's report, of which one section was made public on October 30 (the second part remained classified), cast a revealing light on one aspect of the changes wrought in Israeli society in the aftermath of the Six Day War. At the heart of the 98-page report (in the English version) was the official confirmation that perjury had been an "unchallenged norm" in the GSS "for 16 years," that is, since 1971. At that time, GSS interrogators (rather than representatives of the police) began to be called to testify in court regarding the legality of interrogation procedures used with accused terrorists. The problem for the GSS was that since, under Israeli law, a confession—usually the only evidence available in terrorist cases—was admissible only if "made voluntarily and of free will," any admission that pressure had been exerted on a suspect would almost certainly invalidate the confession. Moreover, in the Shin Bet perception, "telling the truth" would also entail the "exposure of interrogation methods," thus rendering them unusable "once they have been made known to the adversary." Faced, then, with this "severe dilemma," as the report termed it, the GSS interrogators took "the simplest and easiest way out . . . they simply lied, thus committing the criminal offense of perjury. . . ."

The commission placed the "principal responsibility" for the persistence of this "method" squarely on the shoulders of the three GSS chiefs who served between 1971 and 1987: Yosef Harmelim (1963–74), Avraham Ahituv (1974–80), and Avraham Shalom (1980–86). The commission also determined that none of the three prime ministers who held office in this period knew about the method. Equally important, for the sake of the Israeli legal system, the commission "was convinced that the senior echelon of the prosecution, both civil and military, not only knew nothing about the interrogators' routine giving of false testimony, but did not even imagine that such a custom existed."

Summing up, the commission declared that although the work of the GSS in "preserving Israel's security" was of "the utmost importance, . . . no activity in the field of security, however important and vital it may be, can place those acting above the law." However, the commission maintained, if the use of "pressure" were shown to be lawful, operatives could admit to its use in court, obviating the need for perjury. In the belief that the "effective interrogation of terrorist suspects is impossible without the use of means of pressure," the commission concluded that interrogation making use of such means was "permissible under the [law], as we interpreted it," such means to include "nonviolent psychological pressure . . . including acts of deception," and even "a moderate measure of physical pressure. . . ." In the second, secret, section of the report, the commission members delineated a "code of guidelines" to be followed by interrogators.

There remained the question of what action should be taken against present and former GSS personnel who had committed perjury. Consistent with its desire to set in motion a process of "rehabilitation and healing" within and toward the GSS, the commission, "after considerable soul-searching," recommended that no criminal proceedings be brought. Any other course was liable to cause "a far-reaching upheaval" within the GSS, "paralyze GSS investigations," and thus almost certainly lead to people dying "needlessly in terrorist activities that the GSS is capable of foiling."

The immediate result of the Landau Commission's report was the attorney general's cancellation of the police investigation. The cabinet, which officially endorsed the report on November 8, set up a committee to consider various matters relating to the GSS in the wake of the report. The Knesset on November 4 debated nine motions for the agenda stemming from the report. Several speakers, including two leading jurists, Amnon Rubinstein (Shinui) and David Libai (Alignment), added their voices to those of civil-rights activists who faulted the commission for sanctioning the use of force in GSS interrogations. The subject was referred to committee for further discussion. Condemnation of the report came from the person whose case had been its immediate cause, Izat Nafsu. Nafsu said he had expected justice to be meted out to those who had wronged him; he was very "bitter" that these people would not have to pay for their misdeeds.

On December 28 Prime Minister Shamir informed the Knesset's Defense and Foreign Affairs Committee that the relevant departments of the GSS had adopted the recommendations of the Landau Commission with regard to the interrogation of terrorist suspects and subsequent court testimony.

THE VANUNU CASE

The trial of Mordechai Vanunu, a former technician at the Dimona Nuclear Research Center (NRC), who was accused of passing top-secret information about the facility to the London *Sunday Times*, resumed on August 30, 1987. (The proceedings had officially opened in December 1986, with Vanunu pleading not guilty to charges of treason, aggravated espionage, and intent to harm state security. For the background, see AJYB 1988, vol. 88, pp. 373–75.) Earlier in the year

(January 29), the State Attorney's Office acknowledged that Vanunu had seriously impaired state security in an affidavit it filed in the Jerusalem district court in connection with Vanunu's request that he be allowed to meet with his girlfriend, an American named Judy Zimmet. (The request was rejected.)

In March, just days before the trial was scheduled to resume, Vanunu's family, who consistently gave him strong moral support, dismissed his lawyer, Amnon Zichroni, reportedly because of Zichroni's reluctance to conduct a "political trial" depicting Vanunu as a hero of the worldwide antinuclear cause. At a press conference in Jerusalem, Vanunu's two brothers, Meir and Asher, along with a number of well-known figures from the Israeli peace movement, assailed what they called the "lynch atmosphere" in the country against their brother, expressed concern for his state of mind—he had been held in solitary confinement since being brought back to Israel some five months earlier—and called for a public debate in Israel about the country's nuclear posture. Vanunu's family, allowed to visit him on April 7 after a lengthy ban on such visits was rescinded, reported that he seemed in good health.

The trial, however, was postponed for three months while Vanunu's new lawyer, Avigdor Feldman, a noted civil-rights activist, familiarized himself with the material. When the proceedings finally resumed on August 30 in the Jerusalem district court, before a panel of three judges, *in camera*, they did so under extraordinary security precautions. The windows of the courtroom and the back entrance to the building were covered, the windows of the police van in which Vanunu was brought to the court were whitewashed, and Vanunu himself was forced to wear a helmet to conceal his face. On the second day of the trial, the police turned on sirens and used force to restrain Vanunu when he shouted protests against having to wear the helmet.

On September 3 the Ministry of Justice released an abridged version of the indictment against Vanunu. According to this document, Vanunu was employed as a "technician and operator" at the NRC from November 2, 1976, to October 27, 1985. During this perod he "collected, prepared, copied and held in his possession secret information . . . with the intent to harm state security." Thus he had in his possession information about the NRC's "physical and organizational structure" and about "classified work methods and production processes" at the facility, as well as "code names for various secret developments at NRC."

The indictment charged that Vanunu had transferred the information to the *Sunday Times* knowing that it would be published and would thus "reach the enemy, or would most likely reach the enemy." By this means, Vanunu "intended to assist the enemy in his war against Israel." While the indictment described the material obtained by Vanunu as "secret information under the law," sources in the Justice Ministry noted that in Israeli law pertaining to security offenses, "information" was an all-embracing term encompassing also "incorrect information"—hence the state was admitting nothing concerning the "information" Vanunu gave the *Times*. This somewhat murky state of affairs grew even murkier when Defense Minister Rabin issued a "Certificate of Privilege" prohibiting any discussion in court of the accuracy or inaccuracy of the information published in the *Times*.

The first week of the trial, in which the prosecution rested its case, began with a "trial within a trial" in which Vanunu's lawyer argued that the manner in which his client had been brought to Israel invalidated both Vanunu's confessions and the court's jurisdiction to try him. The prosecution and the defense each called a psychiatrist to render an opinion on whether, in the light of these circumstances, Vanunu's confessions could be said to have been made of "his own free will." Vanunu himself took the stand for over three hours to testify on this question, although he was barred, by a Supreme Court order, from giving any details about how and from where he had been brought to Israel.

On September 2 one of the judges sitting in the case, Zvi Tal (who was also a judge in the Demjanjuk trial), suffered a heart attack and was hospitalized, causing a further delay in the trial. It was not until December that the defense began to present its case. On December 9 MK Abba Eban, chairman of the Defense and Foreign Affairs Committee, testified *in camera* for about 90 minutes, including a brief cross-examination by the prosecution. Eban, who was apparently called by the defense as an expert witness, quoted from a book on international treaties which he brought with him. On the same day that Eban appeared in court, Mordechai Vanunu was one of four persons awarded the $100,000 1987 international Right-Livelihood Prize for activity in behalf of peace and environmental causes. Meir Vanunu accepted his brother's share of the award at a Stockholm ceremony.

On December 22 the chief of Israeli military intelligence, Maj. Gen. Amnon Shahak, said in a lecture in Jerusalem that "the Vanunu affair, along with the reports about Israel's missile ability, accelerated Syria's buildup of its nonconventional warfare capability, in the area of chemical weapons." Upon the trial's resumption in 1988, the defense was expected to bring a gallery of international experts to testify on Vanunu's behalf.

## Israeli–U.S. Relations

Three major issues, all related to national security—of both countries—and all holdovers from previous years, dominated Israeli–U.S. relations in 1987. The Lavi, Pollard, and Iran-*contra* affairs dramatically highlighted Israel's ever-growing reliance on the United States and the extent of U.S. power to intervene in Israeli affairs. At the same time, Washington's inability to put together a coherent and comprehensive Middle East policy suggested that it was unable, or unwilling, to use its material influence to advance the peace process.

Secretary of State Shultz, indeed, was presented with what appeared to be a major opportunity to resurrect that process in the form of the April agreement between Jordan's King Hussein and Foreign Minister Shimon Peres. However, by the time Shultz finally got to the region, in October, he had missed the boat (see "Peace Initiatives," above). The deep-seated reluctance of the Reagan administration to get into a confrontational relationship with Jerusalem—except on matters of direct and immediate concern to U.S. national security—left Israel free to dismiss American criticism of its policies as "differences between friends" and, according to some observers, to behave on occasion as though it were the patron state and the United States its client.

A case in point was the U.S. attitude toward Israeli policy in the occupied territories. The sustained violence in the territories at year's end offered new occasions for American officials to chastise Israel. Thus, on December 12, Assistant Secretary of State Richard Murphy told reporters after a meeting with Foreign Minister Peres in New York that the United States "regrets deeply the violence" in the territories. Without "an active peace process," Murphy added, the administration saw a "danger that we will move backward if we are not moving forward." Some days later White House press secretary Marlin Fitzwater said President Reagan was "very concerned" about the situation and urged "direct negotiations" to "relieve tensions" in the region. On December 22 a U.S. abstention in the Security Council enabled the unanimous passage of a resolution condemning Israeli practices in the territories that "violate the human rights of the Palestinian people." Asked in an Israel TV interview about these and other American reactions, Prime Minister Shamir (who paid successful visits to the United States in February and November) expressed "regret" over such moves and said he would "always be grateful" for what the Reagan administration had done for Israel and the Jewish people. He then added: "But even with one's best friends differences sometimes crop up. . . . We will convince them, we will overcome these differences. But we must be aware that the cooperation and friendship between the U.S. and Israel are continuing [and] have reached new heights."

Shamir's analysis seemed perfectly sound. In June Israel and the United States signed an agreement for the construction of a powerful radio relay station in the Arava desert for use by the Voice of America and Radio Free Europe/Radio Liberty. Speaking at a White House ceremony, President Reagan asserted that the accord would "result in a broader dissemination of those values which we have in common." In November President Chaim Herzog paid the first-ever visit by an Israeli head of state to the United States, delivering five major speeches, including an address to a joint session of the Senate and the House of Representatives, and providing a natural opportunity for his host, President Reagan, to reaffirm the U.S. commitment to Israel's security.

One month later, at the height of the unrest in the territories, Defense Minister Rabin paid a ten-day visit to the States (December 11–21), during which he and Secretary of Defense Frank Carlucci signed a Memorandum of Understanding (MOU). The new accord, superseding a previous memorandum initialed four years earlier, granted Israel a status almost equal to that of NATO countries in dealings with the Pentagon—an outgrowth of the conferring on Israel of the formal status of a "major non-NATO ally" at the beginning of 1987. (Egypt was also accorded this status, the two countries thus joining Australia, Japan, and South Korea as major non-NATO allies of the United States.) In addition, Rabin was informed that the U.S. government would underwrite 80 percent of the preliminary development costs toward the production of an Israeli antitactical ballistic missile; that the U.S. military would test Israel's state-of-the-art "Popeye" air-to-ground missile, with a view toward its possible purchase; and that Washington would forego the usual surcharge on the Israeli-made components for the next 75 F-16 aircraft on order by Israel, thus reducing their final price by as much as $40 million. Much of this largesse was a result of Israel's cancellation of the Lavi project.

LAVI PROJECT

Nowhere, perhaps, was Israel's extensive dependence on the United States for its strategic needs, coupled with the conflicting belief that it could proceed independently of its patron, more evident than in the case of the Lavi project—Israel's effort to manufacture a jet fighter for the 1990s. In the past, Israel had ignored or shrugged off increasingly intensive signals from the Pentagon, chiefly in the person of Under Secretary of Defense for Planning and Resources Dov Zakheim, that the plane's cost, which was being borne by the United States, was getting out of hand. Following talks with Defense Minister Rabin and other ranking Israeli defense establishment personnel at the beginning of 1987, Zakheim held a press conference at the U.S. embassy in Tel Aviv. The rising cost of the Lavi, he argued, which he put at $1 billion per year, nearly twice the figure cited by Israeli experts, would compel Israel to forego other key defense projects, and Washington would not increase its current military aid to enable the project to continue. Moreover, he said, existing U.S. aircraft were equally good. (Three such planes, the first of 75 F-16s ordered by Israel, arrived in mid-February.)

In the meantime, Israel Aircraft Industries (IAI), the Lavi's manufacturer, continued to test the prototype of the aircraft, and senior IAI officials continued to scoff at Zakheim's data. On March 30 the second Lavi prototype made its maiden flight; by this time the first prototype had made 23 of a scheduled 1,800 test flights.

On May 20, following weeks of intensive meetings within the defense establishment to consider the Zakheim alternatives, Defense Minister Rabin placed the Lavi issue on the cabinet agenda. The Lavi lobby continued to argue that cancellation of the project would force thousands of highly skilled engineers to emigrate, and that Israel would have to pay $1 billion in penalties resulting from broken contracts. The major surprise for the ministers at the meeting was the adamant opposition to the Lavi voiced by the new chief of staff, Lt. Gen. Dan Shomron, and other senior officers. They argued that the Lavi, far from augmenting the IDF's strength, would instead detract from it by siphoning off the funds needed to acquire other essential sophisticated weaponry.

All told, the cabinet held seven discussions on the Lavi, spanning about a hundred days. From meeting to meeting, support for the project, which was virtually unanimous at the outset, dwindled, as ministers digested the facts and figures hurled at them by the country's economic hierarchy. In a report issued on June 30, State

Comptroller Malz presented a sorry history of mismanagement in which alternatives were not examined, costs spiraled without control, scrutiny was left in the hands of interested parties, and ministers raised their hands in favor of proceeding with a project that fed their national pride even as it ate away at the national purse.

Also on June 30, Defense Minister Rabin arrived in Washington for talks on the future of the Lavi, more specifically what the United States could offer Israel if it canceled the project. Rabin got his "sweeteners" to offset the bitter pill, including good terms for an Israeli purchase of 100 more F-16C fighters "off the shelf," and authorization to spend an extra $100 million of the military aid funds in Israel rather than in the United States. Rabin reported to the cabinet on July 7 about his talks, urging that the project be scrapped in order to take advantage of the Americans' goodwill. Rabin found a strong ally in Finance Minister Moshe Nissim, who noted that the $1.5 billion already spent on the plane's development was nearly twice the initial cost estimate of $800 million. Rabin himself was willing to go ahead with the project—but only if funding, to the tune of some $150–200 million a year for the next decade, could be found from outside the severely strained budget of the Defense Ministry and the IDF.

By now the future of the Lavi was a hot political issue, with the decisive vote scheduled for August 16. On August 11 the State Department said publicly what Shultz had been telling Israeli leaders privately. "Given the budgetary realities we and Israel face," the statement said, "we believe a decision to terminate the Lavi would be in the best interest of both our countries." To ensure that the Israeli leadership got the message, Shultz sent personal letters to Shamir, Peres, Rabin, Nissim, and Economy and Planning Minister Gad Yaakobi, reiterating the U.S. stance and assuring Israel that Washington would help with cheaper "alternatives" to the Lavi.

In the event, the final vote was deferred once more, this time for two weeks, to August 30, largely at the doing of Foreign Minister Peres. Peres was in a somewhat awkward position on the Lavi issue. As a founder of IAI and as an avowed believer in enhancing Israel's technological capability, Peres supported the project. On the other hand, Labor was generally disposed against the project, and, what was crucial, so was Defense Minister Rabin, whom Peres dared not cross if he wished to retain intraparty harmony. Seeking to resolve these contradictions, Peres obtained the assent of Rabin and of Nissim for a plan to discontinue the Lavi, but to allocate funds from the defense budget for "the continued development of advanced aviation technologies."

The conventional wisdom was that Prime Minister Shamir wanted the Lavi grounded—but wanted the work done by the Alignment. However, two days before the crucial August 30 cabinet meeting, Shamir, evidently willing to fly in the face of Washington, imposed "factional discipline" and compelled Justice and Tourism Minister Avraham Sharir to reverse his declared stand against the project. Since Labor's hawkish health minister, Shoshana Arbelli-Almoslino, made no secret of her support for the project, it appeared that a 12–12 vote was in the offing, which under cabinet rules would mean a go-ahead for the Lavi. At the decisive cabinet meeting, Peres requested a recess to enable the Labor ministers to consult privately. In a unanimous vote, "factional discipline" was imposed on a very unwilling Arbelli-Almoslino, who finally agreed to abstain—to the surprise and chagrin of Shamir and the Likud. The cabinet thus voted 12-11, with one abstention, in favor of Peres's plan. Following a pattern set in the two previous major decisions of the national unity government—the withdrawal from Lebanon and the economic stabilization plan—the vote went almost completely along party lines, with Labor victorious. In the case of the Lavi, Labor was joined by Nissim along with Zevulun Hammer (NRP) and Rabbi Yitzhak Peretz (Shas).

Immediately after the vote, Minister Without Portfolio Moshe Arens, an expert in aeronautical engineering who had served as vice-president of IAI for nearly ten years and was the Lavi's major proponent in the government, announced his intention to resign, asserting that he could "not share in the responsibility for the tragic decision." Although some Herut ministers, notably Ariel Sharon, David Levy, and former finance minister Yitzhak Modai, whipped up already furious IAI workers by intimating that they had new data at their disposal and would bring about a cabinet revote, and although thousands of IAI workers went on the rampage, blocking roads with burning tires, preventing access to Ben-Gurion Airport, and clashing with police in illegal demonstrations as they chanted anti-Peres slogans, it was clear that the Lavi was dead. Defense Minister Rabin ordered IAI to set in motion the procedures required to dismiss some 3,000 of the 5,000 IAI personnel involved in the Lavi project (out of a total work force of nearly 20,000).

The apocalyptic warnings uttered by ministers and defense establishment officials proved unwarranted. In November IAI announced that it was proceeding with the development of the Lavi's avionics systems, which were certain to be exportable. The Lavi's third prototype would also be built in a four-year project costing about $85 million—far less than the $125 million pumped into the Lavi during the 100 days in which the cabinet tried to make up its mind about the project. As for unemployment, some of the dismissed IAI workers were absorbed into other branches of the military industries and into private industry. The IDF announced tht it had over 500 vacancies for engineers and technicians, yet not a single laid-off IAI worker applied for these jobs—although many were threatening to emigrate to South Africa or other countries where lucrative employment was said to be available.

#### THE POLLARD AFFAIR

On March 4, 1987, U.S. district court judge Aubrey Robinson sentenced Jonathan Jay Pollard, a U.S. Navy civilian intelligence analyst who also happened to be Jewish, to life imprisonment on charges of spying for Israel. His wife, Anne Henderson Pollard, received a five-year prison term for her part in the affair. Thus ended the major stage in the drama that began on November 21, 1985, when Pollard was arrested by the FBI after being refused entry to the Israeli embassy in Washington. (For additional background, see AJYB 1988 and 1987.) Both Pollard and his wife pleaded guilty to the charges but appealed to the court to show compassion and leniency. Expressing remorse, they maintained that their motives had been not pecuniary—the Pollards were paid for their services—but ideological: their deep love for Israel.

In Israel there was shock. The Israeli leadership had maintained that the Pollard affair was the result of a "rogue" operation run by a former high-ranking Mossad official and a counterterrorism adviser named Rafi Eitan, within the framework of Lekem (Hebrew acronym for Scientific Liaison Bureau). Israel had officially apologized to the United States and said the unit had been disbanded. Israel had also promised to cooperate fully with Washington's investigation of the affair.

The day before Pollard's sentencing, an Israeli Air Force officer, Col. Aviem Sella, who was Pollard's recruiter and subsequent "handler," was indicted in the United States for his part in the affair. Three other Israelis, including Rafi Eitan, later had their immunity from prosecution lifted for being untruthful when they were questioned by American investigators in 1985. Yet amidst reports that the Pollard affair could seriously damage Israeli-U.S. relations, and in particular have detrimental effect on intelligence cooperation, came the astonishing news that Col. Sella had been appointed commander of the Tel Nof air base. Outraged, Washington informed Israel that it would boycott the Tel Nof base as long as Sella commanded it. (Rafi Eitan, too, far from being punished for his part in the affair, had been named managing director of Israel Chemicals, the country's largest government corporation, by Industry Minister Ariel Sharon.)

In the meantime, the Israeli political leadership set aside ostensible ideological differences and soon came out with the requisite denials. Defense Minister Rabin spoke on March 5 of this "very unique exception" to the "special relationship" between Israel and the United States, and one that had occurred "without the knowledge of the political authority." Foreign Minister Peres, asked by a reporter that day whether he felt Israel had a commitment to the Pollards, replied: "The government of Israel stated that this was done without its knowledge. This is what I can tell you." At the same time, Israeli-U.S. relations remained "very strong." On March 10 Prime Minister Shamir told Israel Radio: "The State of Israel has no connection with Pollard or his family. The State of Israel did not hire him and did not assign him espionage missions. Therefore the situation of the family may be a humanitarian problem or a moral problem, [but it is] not a problem with which the state, as such, need concern itself."

Shamir rejected calls for an official probe into the case as "hysterical and unreasonable." However, while the Israeli leadership could shrug off domestic discontent, the government was also under pressure from an outraged Washington and an equally outraged American Jewish community. (See "American Jewry" below, and the article "Jewish Communal Affairs" elsewhere in this volume.)

On March 11, a week after Pollard's sentencing, the inner cabinet decided, due to the "special significance" of the case—to set up a two-member "investigation commission." That move followed closely on the decision of MK Abba Eban, chairman of the Knesset's Defense and Foreign Affairs Committee, to have that body's subcommittee for intelligence and security services, which Eban also chaired, investigate the Pollard affair. After retired Supreme Court president Moshe Landau rejected a request to chair the commission, because it would not have the authority to subpoena witnesses who would testify under oath, the government appointed a well-known lawyer, Yehoshua Rotenstreich, the chairman of the Israel Press Council, to head the commission. The 76-year-old Rotenstreich was joined by Tsvi Tsur, a former chief of staff (1961–64) and the current chairman of the Zim Navigation Company.

On March 29 the relentless pressure exerted by Washington to bring about Col. Sella's replacement at Tel Nof, combined with the growing realization in Israel that the long-range national-security harm if Sella stayed on would outweigh his contribution to the building of the air force, resulted in an announcement of Sella's resignation. In a letter to the commander of the air force released to the press, Sella stated that his action was prompted by the "deterioration in Israel-U.S. relations" and his "concern for the future ties between the two countries and for relations with American Jewry."

Both reports, of the Rotenstreich-Tsur "investigation commission" and of the Eban subcommittee, were released on May 26 (five days before the appointment of the Landau Commission of Inquiry into Shin Bet procedures). Both reports reached basically the same conclusions, finding that the politicians had been unaware of the Pollard operation. But whereas Rotenstreich-Tsur bent over backward to absolve the specific ministers involved of responsibility or blame by applying the criterion that "the government as a whole should assume responsibility," the Eban committee tended to assign individual responsibility where this appeared warranted. But Eban, too, stopped well short of demanding that heads roll. Both reports also had secret annexes which were not made public and were not, it was stressed, transmitted to the Americans.

The Eban committee was composed of six MKs, three each from Labor and the Likud, who were unable, or unwilling, to agree on the interpretation of some of the events in question. As a result, their report contained differing versions of some of the key elements in the Israeli handling of the affair, which in large measure robbed the report of credibility. This did not prevent either Peres or Rabin from lashing out at Abba Eban, Labor's elder statesman, for lending a hand to a report that was far more critical of Labor than Likud politicians. Rabin even accused Eban of spitefully voting with the three Likud MKs in support of their version of events, and Eban was hauled over the coals on May 28 at a meeting of Labor's Central Committee called by Peres to express support for the party's leadership. The Eban report charged, for example, that Rabin, who served as defense minister for most of the period in which Pollard was run, "evinced no effort to maintain scrutiny . . . as he was duty-bound to do." Hence, "[t]he burden of ministerial responsibility devolving on him is beyond any doubt." Similarly, although Peres, Shamir, and Rabin "share responsibility" for the decisions made following Pollard's arrest, the parliamentary responsibility of Shimon Peres, who was prime minister at the time, was "preponderant."

Both reports noted, in virtually the same words, that Israeli credibility vis-à-vis the United States had been damaged by sloppy work done by the team set up to look into the affair after Pollard's arrest. Most tellingly, the Eban report assailed as "baseless" the description by Israeli officials of the Pollard affair as a "rogue" operation:

> It is an incontrovertible fact that the decision to handle Pollard as he was handled, as well as all the stages of implementation spanning a year and a half, were carried out by civil servants who received their appointments and drew their authority from the government, and more precisely, from Israel's defense establishment. All the actions of the operational personnel and the sums transferred to Pollard himself, derived from state resources without the approval or knowledge of the political echelon.
>
> That the political echelon did not know and did not grant approval cannot annul the responsibility of the Israel government in the situation that was created. . . .

Yet having gone this far, the Eban committee recoiled from making any "personal recommendations" and instead offered a conclusion strikingly similar to Rotenstreich-Tsur: "Despite the absence of any ministerial knowledge or approval for the operation, the government would do well to state unequivocally that Israel admits its responsibility and will continue to act to correct the damage, since some of its officials were involved in this operation."

The cabinet, clearly relieved, on May 27 voted to endorse the Rotenstreich-Tsur report—although the legal, and even the semantic, significance of the endorsement was unclear. (The cabinet was not called on to endorse or even acknowledge the existence of the Eban report, since it was a product of the legislative branch.) The indignation felt by many Israelis over the handling of the affair was expressed by the country's leading daily, *Ha'aretz*, in its May 28 editorial. Prime ministers and defense ministers who behaved as Peres, Shamir, Rabin, and Arens did in the Pollard affair, the paper wrote,

> can no longer be considered by the Israeli public as fit to handle the country's affairs . . . and their resignation is a primary precondition for the clearing of the turgid political atmosphere they created by their blundering. What is required now is their departure from the political stage and not the adoption of a meaningless Cabinet resolution or the [Labor party's] "backing" to those who do not deserve it.

In the final analysis, it was the existence of the national unity government that enabled Labor and the Likud to ride out scandals like the Pollard affair domestically. And as far as relations with Washington were concerned, U.S. secretary of the army John Marsh not only went ahead with a previously scheduled visit to Israel in mid-March but told Defense Minister Rabin that the Pollard affair was a "small" matter as compared with the "overall strength of our alliance." Rabin took the occasion to apologize for the affair, and told reporters that Israeli-U.S. strategic cooperation was continuing "without problems." As though to demonstrate this further, the chief of Israeli military intelligence, Maj. Gen. Amnon Shahak, held talks at the Pentagon at the end of March. White House spokesman Marlin Fitzwater, asked immediately after Pollard's sentencing whether the administration was contemplating a reduction in aid to Israel, replied: "Our relationship with Israel is long and strong, and is based on a myriad of strategic and mutual interests, and that will not change."

THE IRAN-*CONTRA* AFFAIR

As the investigation in the United States of the so-called Iran-*contra* affair gathered momentum, Israel's name, and more particularly the names of some of its prominent citizens in the national-security realm, continued to crop up. In this highly complex matter involving arms-for-hostages deals with Iran and the diversion of the profits to the antigovernment forces in Nicaragua known as the *contras*, in blatant violation of a ban imposed by Congress, Israel had already admitted shipping arms to Iran—solely at the request of the United States, it was emphasized—while totally denying any involvement in the transfer of funds to the *contras*. (For further background, see AJYB 1988, vol. 88, pp. 380–81.) In 1987 Israel continued to maintain this position, even in the face of contradictory evidence, such as that contained in the report of the Special Review Board appointed by President Ronald Reagan and headed by former senator John Tower. Thus, on February 27, one day after the panel released its report, the Defense Ministry in Tel Aviv dismissed as "totally groundless" a contention that Defense Minister Rabin in May 1986 "allegedly offered aid to the *contras* in the form of [military] instructors."

Whether Israel's singling out for denial only this one point in the Tower Commission report, out of a wealth of references to Israel in the document, most of them with far graver ramifications, implied admission of all the other "allegations," was unclear. What did become apparent was that, at best, Israel had become involved in an adventure over which it had no control but which, given its deepening military-strategic relations with Washington, it had no real option to refuse. The situation was aggravated by the fact that a large proportion of the Israeli denials referred to statements or reports issued by ranking American public figures. A few weeks before the publication of the Tower Commission report, the Defense Ministry had denied a claim, contained in a report of the Senate Intelligence Committee, that Defense Minister Rabin had told administration officials in September 1986 that Israel was willing to supply "a significant quantity of captured Soviet bloc arms" to the *contras*. The Senate report also indicated that Amiram Nir, the prime minister's adviser on counterterrorism, had known about the plan to fund the *contras*, and that Nir had passed on the information to his direct superior, Prime Minister Peres.

In the meantime, the subcommittee on intelligence and security services of the Knesset's Defense and Foreign Affairs Committee was also looking into "the cooperation between the U.S. and Israel relating to the delivery of arms to Iran," according to a communiqué issued by the subcommittee in February. The subcommittee (the same body that subsequently investigated the Pollard affair) gave credence to the government's account and was "convinced," its chairman, MK Abba Eban, told reporters, that Israel was not involved in transferring funds to the *contras*. At the bilateral level, Israel had reached an agreement with the State Department to submit two reports on the role it had played. The cooperation was on a strict "government-to-government" basis and exclusively in the form of written reports; no Israeli citizens would be allowed to testify in the United States. The first such report, focusing on financial issues, was drawn up by Maj. Gen. (res.) Rafael Vardi and forwarded in late April, after being approved by the Shamir-Peres-Rabin "triumvirate."

An unpleasant snag arose when Lawrence Walsh, the U.S. special prosecutor investigating the Iran-*contra* scandal, declared that he was not a party to the agreement with Israel and had two Israelis subpoenaed. The first was former Foreign Ministry director-general David Kimche, while he was visiting the United States; the second, a businessman and U.S. citizen, Al Schwimmer, was subpoenaed at his home in Israel, by an official from the U.S. embassy in Tel Aviv. Walsh reportedly wished to subpoena two other Israelis, Amiram Nir and another arms merchant, Yaacov Nimrodi. Israeli officials said they were displeased by this turn of events, which conflicted with the procedures set up by the two countries, and would fight it in the courts, but stated that the cooperation would continue as agreed. At the end of August the inner cabinet approved the second Israeli report and it was duly conveyed to Washington.

As fate would have it, Prime Minister Shamir paid a visit to the United States in November, a few days after the release of the two-part congressional report summing up the Iran-*contra* affair. The majority report, issued by the committee's Democratic members, found that Col. Oliver North, and not Amiram Nir, had conceived the idea of diverting money to the *contras*. (The minority, Republican, report deflected criticism from President Reagan and accepted North's sworn testimony that Nir had devised the plan in January 1986.) On the other hand, the majority report seemed to punch a major hole in Israel's consistently reiterated line that it knew nothing about the *contra* angle. Indeed, Israel was damned out of its own mouth: the report quoted the chronology submitted to the committee by Israel itself, according to which "North remarked to Israeli Ministry of Defense officials that he needed money and that he intended to divert profits from future transactions to Nicaragua."

However, the bottom line was that Washington and not Jerusalem bore responsibility for the affair. Moreover, it was stressed, the investigating committees had received "unprecedented cooperation from a sovereign nation, the State of Israel," which, while "not willing to allow its officials to be examined, [had] furnished the committees with extensive materials and information, including information affecting its national security." Prime Minister Shamir seemed to sum up this potentially very damaging episode in Israeli-U.S. relations when he was asked by the *New York Times* about the Israeli role in the arms-for-hostages deal: "It was," he said, "done by a common decision of our cabinet and we are convinced that our policy was a correct one. We did it together with the United States, and I do not see any reason to regret it."

## Other Foreign Relations

### EGYPT

The launching of the Taba arbitration process at the end of 1986 (see AJYB 1988, vol. 88, pp. 381–83) closed a major chapter in the history of the Arab-Israeli conflict. The fate of Taba, a tiny and nonstrategic strip of beach just south of Eilat, had been the last unresolved element in the implementation of the 1979 Israeli-Egyptian peace treaty. With the submission of the issue to a panel of international arbitrators—demonstrating that the two countries could settle their disputes by peaceful means—a new sense of solidarity and normalcy was discernible in relations between Cairo and Jerusalem in 1987.

Relations got off to a strong start with the second visit in six months to Egypt by Shimon Peres, this time (February 25–27) in his postrotation capacity of foreign minister. A joint communiqué issued at the conclusion of Peres's talks with President Hosni Mubarak and senior Egyptian officials noted that the meetings had "offered an opportunity for continuing the dialogue between the two countries concerning their mutual and firm commitment to intensify efforts in the search for a just and lasting peace in the Middle East, as well as their mutual desire to further improve bilateral relations."

Peres and Mubarak met once more during the year, on July 9, in Geneva, for a two-hour talk at which they reaffirmed their resolve to continue the search for a full regional peace. On July 20 Egyptian foreign minister Esmat Abdel Meguid paid the first visit to Israel in six years by a top Egyptian official. Besides holding talks with his host, Foreign Minister Peres, Meguid met also with Prime Minister Shamir and other Israeli leaders. The Egyptian diplomat urged Israel to assent to an international peace conference as an opening to direct talks and rejected two alternatives broached by Shamir, a "mini-international conference" or the renewal of the autonomy talks.

The year saw two anniversaries related to the Egyptian-Israeli peace. In June the Israeli Academic Center in Cairo marked its fifth anniversary. The center, under director Asher Ovadia, a professor of classics and art history from Tel Aviv University, provided guidance and assistance to Israeli academics doing research in Egypt and, in the other direction, welcomed Egyptian students seeking information about Israel.

Defense Minister Rabin took the occasion of the year's major anniversary—ten years since the visit of President Anwar Sadat to Jerusalem on November 19, 1977—to tour the ultimate result of that visit: the long but peaceful Egyptian-Israeli border, where few troops were stationed on either side. According to Rabin, the strategic effect of the peace with Egypt had been to tip the scales of the regional power balance to Israel's side. Unfortunately, just 11 days after Rabin's tour, an Israeli soldier was wounded when a grenade was thrown at an IDF patrol near Rafah—the first such incident in the 14 years since the Yom Kippur War. Both Israel and Egypt were quick to play down the incident as an aberration.

That maturity of approach was reflected as well when Israeli Foreign Ministry officials said they viewed positively the renewal of relations between Egypt and a number of Arab countries—Iraq especially—following the go-ahead for such a move given at an Arab summit conference in Amman in November. That Egypt was formally and publicly being readmitted to the Arab fold was perceived as implicit acceptance by the majority of the Arab nations of the Israeli-Egyptian peace treaty.

At year's end some quarters in Israel, notably Minister Without Portfolio Ezer Weizman, one of the architects of the Camp David accords that paved the way to the peace treaty, expressed apprehension about possible repercussions on the peace with Egypt of the IDF's measures in putting down the uprising in the territories. Cairo for its part utilized its diplomatic ties with Israel to fire off four protests within ten days as the violence surged, warning that Israel's "repressive methods" and its "violation of international commitments" were threatening "the peace march in the Middle East" and would have the effect of "deepen[ing] hatred and revenge." Yet the fact that Cairo did not recall its ambassador, as it had done in the wake of the Beirut refugee-camps massacre in 1982, held out hope that the peace between the two countries was now on a durable footing.

EUROPE

There were a number of firsts this year in Israel's relations with Western European countries, while the rapprochement with the Eastern European nations continued apace.

In April President Chaim Herzog became the first Israeli head of state to visit Germany, returning a visit paid to Israel in 1985 by President Richard von Weizsäcker. Herzog's host departed from diplomatic protocol by accompanying his Israeli guest throughout the visit (April 6–10). Shortly after his arrival in Bonn (following a brief visit to Switzerland, of which the highlight was a tour of Basel to commemorate the 90th anniversary of the First Zionist Congress), President Herzog flew to the site of the Bergen-Belsen death camp where he unveiled a memorial carved from Jerusalem stone.

During his visit, which received massive media coverage, Herzog also visited Worms and Mainz, where great Jewish communities once flourished, and met with the country's political leadership, including Chancellor Helmut Kohl and Foreign Minister Hans-Dietrich Genscher. At a luncheon in Herzog's honor, Kohl voiced his support for an international peace conference to resolve the Middle East crisis. President Herzog reiterated Israel's desire for peace and thanked the West Germans for their activity in behalf of Soviet Jewry.

In September Defense Minister Rabin paid a three-day visit to West Germany for talks with the military establishment. In the course of the visit Rabin viewed army maneuvers—the first Israeli defense minister ever to do so on German soil—and met with Chancellor Kohl and other senior officials. In a wreath-laying ceremony at the site of the Dachau concentration camp, Rabin declared: "We have learned the lessons of the Holocaust. One of them was to forge our own strength. It is in the name of that strength that I am here today. I shall be a voice for the murdered."

A different aspect of the Holocaust was marked later in the year, when President Herzog paid a visit to Denmark, the first to that country by an Israeli head of state. A highlight of the three-day stay (November 3–5) was Herzog's visit, accompanied by Queen Margrethe II, to the small fishing village of Gilleleje—the departure point for the daring rescue operation in October 1943 in which Jews were smuggled to neutral Sweden in small boats. Earlier in the year (February), Denmark's defense minister, Hans Engell, visited Israel together with his country's chief of staff and top aides.

Relations with Spain, established in 1986, were strengthened by another first—the first visit to that country by an Israeli foreign minister, Shimon Peres, in April. In November Israel and Spain signed a tourism agreement in a Jerusalem ceremony held during the visit of Spanish tourism minister Abel Ramon Caballero Alvarez.

In the other direction, French premier Jacques Chirac's three-day visit to Israel (November 1–3) was the first of its kind. Chirac paid a courtesy call on President Herzog and held working meetings with his host, Prime Minister Shamir, and with Foreign Minister Peres. His itinerary also included the dedication of a memorial to Jews in France who had been killed or deported by the Nazis. Chirac went on a "private" tour of the Old City of Jerusalem but refused to meet with Jerusalem mayor Teddy Kollek at the City Hall in West Jerusalem, since this might be construed as French acquiescence in Israel's annexation of East Jerusalem. At a press conference winding up the visit, Chirac, who had earlier met with a delegation of 11 leading Palestinians from the territories, expressed support for Palestinian self-determination but said he did not agree that the PLO was the "sole representative" of the Palestinians.

Earlier in the year French foreign minister Jean-Bernard Raimond, meeting with reporters to sum up a three-day visit to Israel (May 31–June 2), took a somewhat different line from Chirac, saying the PLO should be involved "in some way" once the peace process was launched. Raimond urged the convening of an international conference and said Israeli fears that the Soviet Union would impose its will at such a meeting were unfounded. These were also the views voiced by French president François Mitterrand in a three-day visit to France by Prime Minister Shamir at the end of April, and to more receptive ears, to Foreign Minister Peres, who demonstrated his Francophile leanings by visiting Paris three times in 1987. Defense

Minister Rabin was in France in June to attend the Paris Air Show. In December France, along with other Western European countries, expressed concern over the sustained violence in the occupied territories, noting that such outbreaks underscored the need for a peaceful solution.

From the other end of the Mediterranean, Foreign Minister Karolos Papoulias of Greece became the highest-ranking official from his country ever to visit Israel (November 30–December 2). Greece did not formally recognize Israel, though the two countries maintained "diplomatic representations" on each other's soil. Papoulias reiterated his country's traditional stand in favor of Israeli withdrawal from the occupied territories and Palestinian self-determination, while also stressing Israel's right to secure borders. Besides calling on President Herzog and holding talks with Prime Minister Shamir and Foreign Minister Peres, the Greek foreign minister met with a delegation of prominent Palestinians from the territories and with families of Israeli soldiers missing-in-action in Lebanon, pledging to use his good connections in the Arab world to try and discover their fate.

In 1987 Israel hosted a reigning monarch for the first time—the Grand Duke Jean of Luxembourg, accompanied by the Grand Duchess Josephine-Charlotte, who visited May 11–15. Speaking at a dinner in their honor, President Herzog recalled the efforts made in 1975 by Luxembourg's prime minister, Gaston Thorn, at that time president of the UN General Assembly, "to head off the vile attack on our people" in the form of the "infamous" Zionism-racism resolution. (Herzog was then Israel's ambassador to the UN.)

Relations with two more of Israel's traditional friends in Europe remained solid in 1987. Foreign Minister Peres visited Britain twice, in January and June, and heard Prime Minister Margaret Thatcher express her support for an international conference. Peres heard similar sentiments when he visited Italy in January. The Israeli foreign minister asked Defense Minister Giovanni Spadolini to convey a message from him to King Hussein, who visited Rome a few days later, and Spadolini reportedly brought Hussein's reply when he visited Israel later in the month, his third visit in two years. Spadolini, who was the guest of Defense Minister Rabin, also took the opportunity to meet with Palestinians from the territories. The meeting of another senior Italian visitor, Foreign Minister Giulio Andreotti, with Palestinians, took place in a very different atmosphere, as his visit was held in December, some ten days after the start of the uprising in the territories. Andreotti was in the entourage of Italian president Francesco Cossiga, who was making a Christmas pilgrimage to the Christian holy places.

THE VATICAN

Israel's relations with the custodian of many of those holy sites, the Vatican, were somewhat strained in 1987 as a result of two controversies. The first concerned John Cardinal O'Connor of New York, who arrived in Israel on January 1 from Jordan and initially refused to meet with Israeli leaders in their Jerusalem offices, in order to conform with the Vatican's nonrecognition of Israeli rule in the city. This was particularly problematic—from the cardinal's point of view—with regard to President Herzog, the head of state. The problem was solved when the meeting with Herzog was deemed to have taken place in the president's "residence" (in this case also his "office"), and Foreign Minister Peres also agreed to receive the prelate in his residence. However, Cardinal O'Connor did meet with Religious Affairs Minister Zevulun Hammer in his office and with Jerusalem mayor Teddy Kollek at City Hall. He also visited Yad Vashem and the Western Wall. Nevertheless, the entire matter left a lingering bad taste.

That bad taste turned sour in June following the Vatican's announcement that Pope John Paul II was to host Austrian president Kurt Waldheim, accused by Jewish and other groups of perpetrating or knowing about war cimes when he served as a German officer in World War II. The pope's decision was perceived as particularly insensitive as it followed hard on the heels of a visit to Poland where he prayed at the site of the Majdanek death camp for those murdered by the Nazis and their henchmen. On the day of the meeting (June 25), Prime Minister Shamir told reporters during a tour of Gaza that the pope's action was causing "anguish" and that implicitly, even if unintentionally, it "vindicated" the Nazis' crimes. Foreign Minister Peres said in an interview with French TV that the meeting would "put at risk" relations between the Jewish people and the Catholic Church. The pope eventually responded to a protest note sent to him by students and faculty from the Hebrew University of Jerusalem. A letter received by the institution's rector in August from the office of the Vatican Secretariat of State said the pope had "carefully noted" their message and expressed his "love and respect for the Jewish people and the victims of the Holocaust."

EASTERN EUROPE

The major event in the steady rapprochement between Israel and countries of Eastern Europe was undoubtedly the arrival in Israel of a Soviet consular delegation. The eight-member group, which flew in on July 12, was headed by Yevgeny Antipov, a senior official in the Soviet Foreign Ministry's consular directorate. The Soviet visitors said their main purpose in Israel was to prepare an inventory of Soviet property in the country, estimated to be worth $250 million.

On July 23, two weeks after the delegation's arrival, Israelis were taken aback at a Soviet warning that Moscow considered Israel's Jericho II medium-range missile a provocation and a threat to the USSR. The warning, broadcast over Moscow Radio's Hebrew-language service, followed a report in the *International Defense Review* that Israel had successfully tested the Jericho II ballistic missile, firing it 820 kilometers into the Mediterranean. The report added that the next generation of the Jericho II, with a range of 1,450 kilometers, would enable the missile to hit not only most of the Arab world but parts of the southern USSR as well. The Soviets called on Israel to back the initiative launched by Soviet leader Mikhail Gorbachev for the elimination of medium-range missiles in Asia. On July 26, Foreign Minister Peres issued an official statement noting that Israel "welcomes the willingness of the USSR to restrain the arms race in our region." However, Israel also "rejects the Soviet threats" against it, as it "holds no hostile intentions" toward the USSR. On the contrary, Israel advocated the creation of a "nuclear-free zone" in the region and an agreement "on the non-introduction of short- and medium-range missiles by either side."

Peres also took the opportunity to express Israel's agreement with Gorbachev's assessment (made in talks with Syrian president Hafez al-Assad in Moscow) "that the absence of diplomatic relations between the Soviet Union and Israel is an abnormal situation." Although the situation continued "abnormal," the renewed Israel-USSR dialogue persisted at a more intense level. In August Nimrod Novik, the foreign minister's political adviser, met in Bonn for a total of ten hours with Vladimir Terasov, a senior official in the Soviet Foreign Ministry's Middle East section, to discuss Middle East and bilateral issues, including the modalities of a possible international peace conference.

A month later, the head of the Soviet consular delegation in Israel, Yevgeny Antipov, met (after returning from a month-long visit to Moscow) with Foreign Ministry political director-general Yossi Beilin in what was the first unabashedly "political" contact with the visiting Russians. (The mission's three-month visas were later renewed for a further three months.) Finally, capping all these contacts, foreign ministers Shimon Peres and Eduard Shevardnadze held a two-hour meeting on September 23 at the Soviet Union's UN mission in New York during the UN General Assembly session. Peres told reporters the exchange of views had been "the most candid and the warmest" since Moscow broke relations in 1967. Shevardnadze, in distinct contrast to his furtive behavior when meeting with Peres in New York a year earlier, posed with Peres for photographers on the street after the meeting, saying that "contacts will continue—and Comrade Peres is of the same view."

While in New York, Peres also met with the foreign ministers of Poland and Hungary, two countries with which relations were thawing fairly quickly. In April Israel completed the renovation of the building that housed its diplomatic mission in Warsaw until 1967, and in May an Israeli interests section began functioning there, under the aegis of the Dutch embassy. A Polish interests section operated in parallel in Tel Aviv. An Israeli-Hungarian agreement to establish reciprocal interests sections was signed about a week before the meeting in New York and followed a trade agreement signed between the two countries in February. Peres also held a rare meeting with the Yugoslav foreign minister. In Israel, an agreement was signed with a visiting Yugoslav delegation to introduce direct charter flights between the two countries beginning in December. In August Prime Minister Shamir visited Romania, where his talks focused on the Middle East situation but encompassed also discussions with Prime Minister Constantine Descelescu on bilateral matters, including ways to bolster trade relations.

OTHER COUNTRIES

In June Prime Minister Shamir conducted a week-long swing through four African states, three of which—Liberia, Cameroon, and the Ivory Coast—had renewed diplomatic relations with Israel in recent years, while the fourth, Togo, announced its intention to follow suit a few days before Shamir's arrival. At a press conference on his return to Israel, Shamir said he had been "moved and impressed" by the reception he and the accompanying Israeli delegation had received in Africa. There was "no doubt," he said, that other African states would renew their relations with Israel "in the wake of the visit." Shamir said he had asked all the leaders he met with to intercede with the Ethiopian leadership in behalf of the remaining Jews in that country.

Where South Africa was concerned, Israel seemed to be prodded into action by fears of adverse repercussions in the U.S. Congress. On March 18 the inner cabinet decided (according to a statement in the Knesset the following day by Foreign Minister Peres) "to reiterate Israel's reservations, condemnation and refusal to compromise with a regime of discrimination," to "reduce" contacts with South Africa, and "not to sign any new contracts with South Africa in the sphere of defense"—probably the first public admission that such contracts already existed (and, by inference, would not be canceled). A government committee was to make proposals for "an approach toward South Africa in the spirit of the policy followed by the free world." Observers noted that Israel's action came shortly before the presentation to the U.S. Congress of a report drawn up by the administration on military ties maintained by various countries with South Africa, a report liable to bring in its wake congressional sanctions against offending countries.

Although the government committee, headed by Foreign Ministry political director-general Beilin, completed its report within the time allotted, the inner cabinet did not take it up until July 15 and then postponed "indefinitely" a final decision, as a number of ministers objected to the scope of the measures proposed. At the same time, Israeli tourism to South Africa was up by nearly 20 percent over the previous year, evidently boosted by the decline in the value of the rand. It was not until September 16 that the inner cabinet, once more spurred by fears of congressional action, passed a series of prohibitions regarding South Africa in the realms of the economy and tourism, cultural, scientific, and sports ties. Israel also declared that it would not act as an intermediary between South Africa and other countries seeking to break trade restrictions by redirecting goods through Israel.

Israel's ties with the Far East continued to show gradual improvement. On March 28 China's official Xinhua news agency reported that a meeting had been held the previous day at UN headquarters in New York between China's permanent representative to the world body, Li Luye, and Foreign Ministry director-general Avraham Tamir. Their discussion centered on recent developments in the Middle East, notably the possible convening of an international peace conference. While this was said not to have been the first high-level contact between the two countries, the fact that the Chinese had officially acknowledged it was termed unprecedented. The report of the meeting was seen as a signal that Beijing was interested in easing relations with Israel and ensuring that, as a permanent member of the Security Council, it was not passed over in a Middle East breakthrough. A breakthrough of another kind took place on September 30, when the foreign ministers of the two countries met for the first time at China's UN mission in New York. The one-hour meeting between Shimon Peres and Wu Xueqian was described as "businesslike." Peres told reporters after the meeting that agreement had been reached to maintain ongoing contact between the two countries through their UN envoys.

Whether the developments with China were in part the result of efforts by Australian Prime Minister Bob Hawke of Australia was not immediately known. Hawke, at any rate, had promised to push the Israeli cause with the Chinese when he visited Israel earlier in the year (January 26-29), the first-ever visit by an Australian prime minister to Israel. He also pledged to pursue his efforts in behalf of Soviet Jewry. A considerable portion of his talks with Prime Minister Shamir, Foreign Minister Peres, and other officials was given over to a review of the Middle East situation, with Hawke continuing to support Palestinian self-determination while also expressing a firm pro-Israeli posture.

Trade with Japan, a country that had long maintained a low profile toward Israel under pressure of the Arab boycott, was boosted in 1987. In October a delegation of leading Israeli industrialists held talks in Japan, and the following month Israel hosted a top Japanese trade delegation sponsored by a roof organization encompassing some 800 economic organizations.

Two presidential visits from Latin American countries reflected the strong ties Israel enjoyed in that part of the world. In May President Herzog hosted the world's only other Jewish president, Panama's Eric Arturo Delvalle. In the course of the five-day visit, the first by a Panamanian head of state, a tourism agreement was signed between the two countries. Less than a week after Delvalle's departure, Honduras president José Azcona Hoyo arrived for a six-day visit. Two days after the conclusion of that visit, Israel hosted the vice-president of El Salvador, Rodolfo A. Castillo Claramount. Other visitors to Israel from Latin America included the Argentinian and Mexican energy ministers. In June Israel concluded its first major coal deal in South America, signing a contract with Colombia for the purchase of over two million tons of coal by 1990. In December Foreign Minister Peres visited Brazil, accepting an invitation extended when he met with the Brazilian foreign minister at the UN in September.

## Political Affairs

The climax of the political year came at about 9 P.M. on May 19. It was then that the Knesset voted on motions of no confidence in the government submitted by four opposition parties on the Left. Over one hundred MKs were in the chamber. The motions dealt with the implications of the inner cabinet's inability to resolve the deadlock on the international conference issue, and with a recent cabinet decision stipulating that persons who did not serve in the IDF—i.e., Israeli Arabs—would pay higher university tuition fees.

The entire seven months since the premiership rotation took place had been building up to this moment. While Shimon Peres's efforts during his tenure as prime minister to gain support for an international conference had gone largely unchallenged, indeed were virtually ignored, by Yitzhak Shamir, who was then foreign minister, as soon as their roles were reversed Shamir fought the idea tooth and nail. The issue quickly became the dominant element in Israeli politics.

Since its two key decisions in 1985, on Lebanon and on economic stabilization, the national unity government had been marking time. The conventional wisdom was that the government would fall long before its appointed time of 50 months. But neither the pundits nor, perhaps, Peres himself, took sufficiently into account that Shamir was in a do-or-die situation. If he could not hold the government together a second time (as he had failed to do after Menachem Begin's retirement), his political career would be over.

Shamir got a boost when he overcame one major hurdle successfully—his party's convention, held at the end of March. In marked contrast to the Herut convention exactly one year earlier, which degenerated into violent chaos and broke off before completing its business, the 1987 gathering passed quietly. Shamir also scored points by managing to stay above the jockeying for position conducted by the three pretenders to the post-Shamir-era crown—David Levy, Ariel Sharon, and Moshe Arens. While the three of them battled it out for the top party functions, Shamir was unanimously acclaimed party leader, following a preconvention agreement.

Peres and other senior Labor figures had been hinting ominously that Labor would "go to the people" if the government did not conduct an active peace policy. To Likud charges that Peres's real goal was to bring about an early election because he could not reconcile himself to the number-two slot in the government, Labor countered with charges that the very idea of peace caused the Likud to break out in a rash. With the government speaking in two distinct—and irreconcilable—voices, it was not surprising that a public-opinion poll conducted by the Smith Research Center (and published in the *Jerusalem Post* in early May) showed a steep decline in Israelis' assessment of the government's performance. As compared with 63 percent of the 1,200 Israeli Jews polled in September 1986, on the eve of the rotation, who thought the government was "succeeding" or "mainly succeeding" in its tasks, by January 1987 this had fallen to 47 percent and to just 32 percent in April. At the same time, Shamir's "job rating" hit a new personal low of 36 percent, down from 55 percent in September 1986, while satisfaction with Peres also fell sharply, by 15 percent between September 1986 and April 1987, though it still stood at a respectable 62 percent.

It was against this political backdrop that Peres played his trump card—his secret London agreement with King Hussein (see "Peace Initiatives," above, for details). Although Shamir had demonstrated considerable tactical prowess, and outflanked

Peres by repulsing a Shultz visit to the region, Peres believed that the strategic momentum was still on his side. Specifically, Peres thought—or behaved as though he did—that at least one Likud minister in the inner cabinet would defect to Labor (as had happened in crucial votes in the past), and that even if this did not occur, Peres could command an absolute majority in the Knesset to force an early election. Thus, in an April 23 Israel TV interview, when asked what his reaction would be if there were no inner cabinet majority for his proposal on an international conference, Peres replied that there would then be "no justification for the government's existence." Immediately following the May 13 inner cabinet deadlock on his proposal, Peres told Israel Radio that a "parting of the ways" had been reached in the government and that "we must turn to the people" (a phrase he repeated seven times in a five-minute interview).

On May 19, then, the stage was set. Peres himself rushed back from an abbreviated U.S. visit that morning to take charge of Labor's strategy in the no-confidence challenges. If the government lost a no-confidence vote, it would be considered as having resigned. In that case, the overriding question was whether Labor could round up the 61 votes needed to dissolve the government and bring about an early poll. The problem was that a feasible alternative scenario also existed: that the Likud might succeed in finding enought MKs to form a narrow but workable majority without Labor. To that end, the Likud was engaged in some frantic vote-buying. The leader of Shas, the ultra-Orthodox Sephardi party, MK Rabbi Yitzhak Peretz, who had resigned as interior minister over the Shoshana Miller conversion case (see "Religious Issues," below), was lured back into the coalition by a Likud promise to amend within 60 days a 1927 religious ordinance in a manner enabling the Interior Ministry to refuse to register Reform or Conservative converts as Jews. In return, Peretz would vote against an early election. (In the wake of this deal, Peretz returned to the cabinet as a minister without portfolio, following a cabinet vote on May 24 and Knesset approval the following day.)

At the 11th hour, Labor, fearing it would suffer electorally because it would be perceived as splitting the nation, decided not to bring the government down, although observers estimated that it had the votes to do so. A number of Labor doves absented themselves when the roll call was taken, and some MKs crossed over to one side or the other in the vote. A particularly interesting case was that of Labor MK Abdel Wahab Darousha, who voted against the government, thus excluding himself from the coalition but remaining a Labor MK.

To ensure the government's survival until the November 1988 general election, the Likud engaged in some additional vote-buying. Minister without portfolio Yigael Hurvitz was promised two realistic places for his minuscule party on the Likud list in 1988, and MK Aharon Abuhatzeira, head of the defunct Tami ethnic party, was assured a high place on that same Likud list—both deals in return for pledges to oppose early elections should the issue resurface. At the same time, Labor suffered a blow when Shinui, its coalition ally, decided to leave the government, calling it a "two-headed monster." Shinui's cabinet representative, Communications

Minister Amnon Rubinstein, tendered his letter of resignation at the May 24 cabinet meeting which, ironically, reinstated Rabbi Peretz, and it took effect 48 hours later. Shinui's three MKs thus joined the opposition. (On June 7 the cabinet voted to appoint Labor's Gad Yaakobi minister of communications, in addition to his duties as minister of economy and planning; Knesset approval was given the following day.)

Another reason Rubinstein gave for leaving the government—its inability to agree on a replacement for the country's top diplomatic posting, ambassador to the United States, even though Meir Rosenne's term would conclude at the end of May—was resolved shortly after Rubinstein resigned. No longer needing the appointment as a possible political bargaining card, Shamir and Peres were able to agree on Moshe Arad, a career diplomat who had just completed service as ambassador to Mexico. Arad was approved by the cabinet as Israel's ambassador to Washington on June 7.

During the summer Labor made some half-hearted efforts to get Likud support for holding the next general election in the spring of 1988, half a year earlier than scheduled, noting that this was the final opportunity to advance the peace process before both Israel and the United States became involved in election campaigning. On August 6 Labor's ministerial forum voted to keep the party in the government while continuing to drum up domestic support for an international conference. At about the same time, the Likud proved it was a match for the Alignment in political impotence. Its attempt to pass legislation enabling the Interior Ministry to disqualify non-Orthodox conversions—as it had promised Shas—garnered so little support that it was not even brought up for preliminary discussion by the relevant Knesset committee.

Asked in a *Jerusalem Post* interview in October to sum up his first year in office and say where he had "left [his] mark on the government," Prime Minister Shamir replied: "I view my own main achievement as the navigation of the national unity government through all the storms of the past year. I see its continued existence as a supreme duty, as a symbol of national unity, and I am proud that I have succeeded in this and that the government serves and will continue to serve."

## *Economic Developments*

The economic year began dramatically with a new "package deal." On January 13 the shekel was devalued by 10 percent, standing at NIS 1.65 to the U.S. dollar and NIS 1.68 to a "currency basket" unit; subsidies of basic foods were cut by 5 to 20 percent; the Histadrut (Federation of Labor) agreed to forego a 2.7-percent cost-of-living increment; the industrialists pledged not to raise prices; and tax brackets were adjusted to increase net wages, with the top bracket, for salaries exceeding NIS 9,000 per month, reduced from 52.8 to 48 percent (this was almost all that remained of the "economic growth and stabilization program" trumpeted by the Treasury at the end of 1986). Also called for in the package deal was a reduction in the number of public-sector workers; and cuts of NIS 400 million to the state budget, with the major burden to be borne by health and education, between them accounting for 15 percent of the cuts. The package deal was formally signed on January 27.

On January 29 Finance Minister Moshe Nissim submitted to the Knesset the budget for the coming fiscal year (April 1, 1987–March 31, 1988), in the amount of NIS 39.3 billion. Due to the shortfall in tax collection in the wake of the income-tax reform, and the nonrenewal of the emergency aid from the United States, which had helped pull the country through the initial stages of the July 1985 economic stabilization program, a budget deficit of NIS 1.4 billion was envisaged. The budget was based on a forecast inflation rate of just 9 percent during the fiscal year. A major row, with clear political overtones, soon threatened to block passage of the budget. Labor was demanding cabinet approval of special aid, totaling over NIS 260 million, to help the United Kibbutz Movement defray its debts, while the Likud wanted any such aid "balanced" by aid to the settlements in the territories. The problem was resolved, apparently after a deal was struck between the two big parties, when the Knesset's Finance Committee approved a debt-rescheduling plan for the kibbutzim and, a few days later, included at least NIS 10 million for the settlements as part of an aid package for local authorities.

This paved the way for passage of the state budget by the Knesset plenum close to midnight on March 31, when it was due to come into effect. Although considerable dissatisfaction was expressed on all sides with various clauses in the budget, the debate itself, while lengthy, was stupefyingly dull. The budget passed totaled NIS 40.1 billion, of which some 20 percent was set aside for debt payments and nearly 25 percent for defense. The final amounts for both health and welfare were left pending, however, as the two ministers in question, Shoshana Arbeli-Almoslino and Yitzhak Navon, respectively (both Labor), balked at the cuts the Treasury was demanding.

A 20-year campaign ended when the Knesset passed a minimum-wage law in March. The minimum wage was set at 45 percent of the average countrywide salary as of April 1, 1987, with linkage to cost-of-living payments and other increments. However, the fact that premiums earned by workers, chiefly in low-paying jobs, would be considered part of their wages, effectively diluted the law's ability to close gaps in Israeli society.

Many of the country's 450,000 public-sector workers were found to need wage supplements to bring them up to the minimum-wage level, and on July 12 they staged a one-day general strike in support of the Histadrut's demands for higher salaries, pension benefits, and a five-day work week. On July 26 the cabinet approved in principle a shorter work week in terms of days, but with the proviso that there be "no reduction in the number of work-hours per week" and no falloff in productivity. Following additional industrial sanctions, an across-the-board salary hike of NIS 75 shekels per month was agreed on. However, a number of professional unions refused to sign the accord, pointing out that while the wage increase represented a substantial boost of up to 15 percent for unskilled or semiskilled workers, it was as low as 2 percent for professionals.

In at least one area the government showed an innovative approach, embarking on a program with potentially far-reaching implications and signaling a radical shift away from Israel's traditional socialist-oriented economic centralization. This was a thrust toward privatization, involving an effort to sell into private hands about 30 state-owned corporations, including El Al, Bezek Telecommunications, and Israel Chemicals. In August it was announced that a Wall Street firm, First Boston Corporation, was to act as the government's adviser in the privatization enterprise. Under the plan, revenues accruing from the sales would go toward defraying the country's domestic and external debts. Later in August the sale was announced of 51 percent of the shares of one such government corporation, Zion Cables Ltd., a subsidiary of Israel Chemicals, for $11 million.

Although Israel seemed to be divesting itself of some of its quasi-socialist trappings, the public furor and rancor generated by the Bank Leumi scandal suggested that rampant capitalism was not yet at hand. The story broke in bits and pieces in the wake of the Beisky Commission report (AJYB 1988, vol. 88, pp. 398–99), which condemned the directors of Israel's four largest banks, among them Ernest Japhet of Bank Leumi, and forced their resignations. Early in 1987 *Ha'aretz* revealed that Japhet was not only given $4.5 million in severance pay but was granted a monthly pension of $30,000, giving him a total package estimated to be worth in the neighborhood of $8 million. Compounding the issue was the fact that Bank Leumi was a public firm, founded and owned by the Jewish Agency through the Jewish Colonial Trust, and that its governor was the chairman of the Jewish Agency, Arye Dulzin. Japhet had long since betaken himself to New York, but on January 13 the entire board of directors of Bank Leumi resigned. However, the choice of Meir Heth as the new board chairman raised a storm because Heth, who headed the Tel Aviv Stock Exchange at the time of the bank shares' collapse, was also raked over the coals by the Beisky Commission. In April Bank Leumi went to court against its former seemingly omnipotent director, demanding that Japhet hand back the severance pay he received and another NIS 500,000 in pension and other payments. As for Dulzin, he was formally exonerated by the Diaspora fund-raisers on the Jewish Agency Board of Governors, but promised to resign at the end of the year. (See also "Israel and World Jewry," below.)

The consumer-price index stood at 16.1 percent in 1987, a decrease of 3.6 percent as compared with 1986, though still a good deal higher than the Treasury had envisaged. The Gross Domestic Product (GDP) rose by 5 percent and was accompanied by a decrease in unemployment of about 1 percent, to 6 percent. The GDP in the business sector performed even better, climbing by 7 percent, the highest in a single year since 1972. Industrial and agricultural production were up, and construction expanded by 9 percent, the first rise in that sector since 1979.

The widespread boom feeling was expressed in a rise of 6 percent in per capita private consumption, this on top of a 12-percent increase in 1986. An 11-percent rise in exports of goods and services was nearly double the 1986 increase, the total standing at $13.8 billion. Imports, however, continued to outpace exports, increasing by 19 percent, more than double the 1986 rise, and totaling $19.6 billion. The trade gap thus created of about $5.8 billion was up nearly 50 percent over 1986. A major part of the sharp increase in the trade deficit was accounted for by defense imports, which doubled in 1987, totaling $2.4 billion. Defense consumption overall was up by 31 percent in 1987, following a decline of 17 percent in 1986. Overall, the increase in imports over exports, combined with the decrease in direct government revenues, resulted in a deficit of just under $1 billion in the current account of the balance of payments.

Israel's foreign-currency reserves stood at $5.9 billion at the end of 1987, up by $1.2 billion over the previous year. However, this was exactly counterbalanced by the growth in Israel's foreign debt, which totaled $32.8 billion at the end of the year, as compared with $31.6 billion at the end of 1986—an increase of $1.2 billion of which $1 billion was due to the fall in the value of the dollar against other currencies. The country's total foreign assets at the end of 1987 were $13.6 billion (up from $12.4 billion a year earlier), meaning that net foreign liabilities stood at $19.2 billion, approximately the same as at the end of 1986.

## Extremism

In February the Knesset's House Committee, at the behest of Communications Minister Amnon Rubinstein, voted to deprive MK Meir Kahane, who espoused a theocratic Jewish state free of Arabs, "leftists," and "Hellenizing Jews," of the right to send out mail free via the Knesset. According to Rubinstein, Kahane had been abusing this privilege by sending hate mail to Israeli Arabs and Druze. The committee vote, which was open, was unanimous, but in a secret plenum poll, ten MKs voted against the proposal, which was nevertheless approved when it obtained the support of 34 MKs.

An issue of greater principle arose in June when Knesset Speaker Shlomo Hillel decided to divest Kahane of his parliamentary immunity and other privileges, over an incident dating back to the opening session of the 11th Knesset in August 1984. At that time Kahane added to his pledge of allegiance to the State and the Knesset a verse from Psalms, "So shall I keep thy law continually for ever and ever." In January 1987 the American-born Kahane, in an affidavit filed in a U.S. court against efforts by the State Department to lift his U.S. citizenship, declared that he had not taken an oath of allegiance to a foreign state and that his intention in citing Psalms was to show that his primary allegiance was to "the Law of God." Attorney General Yosef Harish then ruled that Kahane's original oath in the Knesset was invalid.

Speaker Hillel demanded that Kahane retake the oath in its proper form, but Kahane repeated the passage from Psalms. Hillel thereupon ruled that Kahane's status was that of an elected MK who was not yet a full-fledged member of the House.

Kahane had in the meantime petitioned the High Court of Justice against Hillel's demand to retake the pledge. However, the court threw out the petition on June 29, citing another verse in Psalms, to the effect that Kahane had not come before them "with clean hands": he had told the High Court that the biblical text was not meant to detract from his Knesset oath—the very opposite of what he stated in his U.S. affidavit. Kahane subsequently took the Knesset oath as prescribed.

Kahane won a significant court battle when the High Court of Justice in July ordered the Israel Broadcasting Authority to rescind its self-imposed boycott of Kahane's ideology. The court took a broad view of freedom of expression, declaring that only if the IBA were convinced that "public order" would be adversely affected could it impose a blanket ban, otherwise Kahane should be treated like any other MK.

In a case indirectly related to Kahane, the High Court of Justice in October ordered the parliamentary privileges of MK Muhammad Miarri (Progressive List for Peace) to be restored in full. The Knesset had partially lifted Miarri's parliamentary immunity in 1985 at the behest of the Likud, which wanted to "balance" similar measures taken against Kahane.

The results of a poll commissioned by the Van Leer Institute in Jerusalem and made public in October indicated that Kahanist notions were gaining ground among young Israelis. The poll, which encompassed 612 Jews aged 15–18, found that 42 percent of them favored reducing the rights of the country's Arab citizens. Israeli Arabs were named as one of the two groups (along with yeshivah students) "least worthy of respect." (IDF officers and combat troops were deemed "most worthy of respect.") Nearly 40 percent said they had little or no confidence in the media; political parties and Knesset members also ranked at the bottom of the list of trustworthy institutions.

Efforts continued to be made to gain clemency for the still imprisoned members of the Jewish terrorist underground by means of Knesset legislation. One such attempt, placed on the Knesset agenda by MK Avraham Verdiger (Morashah), was defeated in July, though it gained the vote of Prime Minister Shamir. In March President Herzog commuted to 24 years the life sentences meted out to three members of the underground convicted of murder. The three—Menahem Livni, Uzi Sharabaf, and Shaul Nir—would be able to get home leave and also have the commuted term reduced by another third for good behavior. This brought to 11 the number of convicted Jewish underground members whose sentences were reduced by the president.

## Religious Issues

Jerusalem continued to be the focus of ultra-Orthodox activism in 1987. The major issue was the opening of movie theaters in the capital on Friday evenings, in contravention of a local bylaw. The two movie theaters that began screening films on Sabbath eve—following a ruling by the Jerusalem municipality's legal adviser—circumvented the law by presenting a brief lecture before screening a film, thus creating a "cultural event" that satisfied the requirements of the law. On Friday evening August 7, ultra-Orthodox and secular demonstrators confronted each other in downtown Jerusalem outside one of the movie theaters, and on the Sabbath, 3,000 black-garbed demonstrators marched through downtown Jerusalem. Mounted police resorted to tear gas and clubs when the demonstrators stoned passing vehicles.

Escalation was swift. In the ultra-Orthodox Me'ah She'arim neighborhood, an 11-year-old boy was grabbed in the street and his earlocks shorn off. On August 24 about 15,000 ultra-Orthodox demonstrators gathered at the Western Wall to pray for an end to the Sabbath films. On the following Sabbath, 500 policemen were needed to prevent clashes betwen religious and secular demonstrators. Five movie theaters were by now open on Friday evenings.

On Friday, September 11, Prime Minister Shamir got into the act, consulting with Minister Without Portfolio Rabbi Yitzhak Peretz (Shas) and the two chief rabbis. Shamir told Israel TV that the "status quo" must be preserved and nothing done to impair Jerusalem's "special character." A week later a meeting attended by Shamir, Foreign Minister Peres, Religious Affairs Minister Zevulun Hammer, and Jerusalem mayor Teddy Kollek decided to create a committee to examine the entire issue.

On November 22 the situation took on a new aspect when Jerusalem district court judge Ayala Procaccia ruled that the relevant bylaw was null and void, and that only the Knesset was empowered to promulgate legislation curtailing freedoms in this manner. One immediate effect of this decision was to spur a cinema complex and two restaurants to open their doors on Friday evenings. Another was to push the religious parties and their allies in the Knesset to set to work drafting legislation in line with the court's ruling.

CONVERTS

Reverberations from the case of Shoshana (Susan) Miller were still being felt in 1987 (see AJYB 1988, vol. 88, pp. 400–01). Miller was the American-born Reform convert who successfully petitioned the High Court of Justice after the Interior Ministry refused to issue her a permanent identity card as a new immigrant to Israel. (She returned to the States soon thereafter.) Interior Minister Rabbi Yitzhak Peretz resigned over the issue on January 4 (the resignation took effect 48 hours later). Responsibility for the Interior Ministry thereby devolved upon the prime minister, who informally placed Deputy Minister Ronnie Milo in charge.

On January 25 the cabinet established a committee to examine the question of registering *olim* (new immigrants) who were converted abroad. The committee, chaired by Prime Minister Shamir, was to come up with unanimous recommendations within six months. Nearly nine months later (September 1), Shamir told an international gathering of Jewish lawyers that in its deliberations the committee had heard "a wide range of opinions" that "differ from each other in many respects." No recommendations, unanimous or otherwise, had been made by year's end.

In no other sphere, perhaps, was the growing recourse to the judiciary by both the executive and the legislative branches more blatant than in the realm of personal status, with both branches unable to resolve key questions. On February 1 the High Court of Justice acceded to the petition of the Israel Union for Progressive Judaism (the Reform movement) and issued a show-cause order against the Interior Ministry for refusing to abide by the Shoshana Miller precedent and register as Jews a Brazilian couple who underwent non-Orthodox conversion before immigrating to Israel. The Interior Ministry, however, now within the purview of the prime minister, seemed intent on abiding by a petition—signed by, among others, a number of rabbinical court judges (*dayanim*)—urging Interior to ignore the High Court ruling in the Miller case. Since the *dayanim* bore the status of judges, their signatures on such a petition were somewhat problematic. Yet only when Mapam MK Yair Tsaban took the issue to the High Court of Justice, leaving the *dayanim* open to a contempt-of-court charge, was a way found to avoid a showdown between the country's two court systems, the religious and the secular. (A similar clash was averted in the Nakash case; see "Other Domestic Matters," below.) The *dayanim* issued a "letter of clarification" declaring that the petition they had signed was an "opinion of halakhic principle" and was not intended to undercut "the rule of law."

In the meantime, the case of the Brazilian couple, as well as another case involving an American woman, dragged on amidst a series of deferments. At the end of June, Deputy Minister Milo declared that he could no longer bear responsibility for the Interior Ministry on behalf of Prime Minister Shamir, due to incessant friction with the ministry's director-general, Rabbi Arye Deri (Shas).

OTHER RELIGIOUS ISSUES

It was not only against converts that the ultra-Orthodox establishment was active. In March Leah Shakdiel, an Orthodox woman from the Negev development town of Yeroham, petitioned the High Court of Justice over the failure of the Ministry of Religious Affairs to approve her appointment to the local Religious Council. Although she had been lawfully nominated to the body, which had no halakhic authority but dealt with other aspects of local religious affairs, in practice the appointment had been held up for over a year, solely because of her sex. Shakdiel was the first woman in Israel ever nominated to serve on a Religious Council. In a similar case in December, the Tel Aviv municipal council voted 15–14 not to allow two women to serve on the 30-member panel that was to select the city's next

Ashkenazi chief rabbi. Both cases were pending before the High Court of Justice at year's end.

The annual battle against the introduction of summer (daylight saving) time was once more led by the cabinet's religious ministers, supported by the Likud. Nevertheless, on March 22, the cabinet voted 11–8 for five months of summer time (April 11–September 12). The starting date was then changed to April 14, after the Passover seder, so that the festive meal could begin earlier in the evening. In September Energy Minister Moshe Shahal announced that $6.2 million had been saved in energy outlays because of summer time.

In March the Mormons' Jerusalem Center for Near Eastern Studies, on Mount Scopus, which had been the target of intense Orthodox Jewish opposition in recent years, quietly opened its doors to its first group of students. The center, a branch of Brigham Young University in Utah, was still in the final stages of construction, but living quarters were available for 70 students previously housed at Kibbutz Ramat Rahel on the southern edge of Jerusalem.

## Israel and World Jewry

### THE DEMJANJUK TRIAL

Criminal trial 373/86, the State of Israel v. John Demjanjuk, opened on February 16 in a movie theater converted into a courtroom. The 67-year-old Demjanjuk, a retired auto worker from Cleveland, had been extradited from the United States, accused of being the notorious "Ivan the Terrible" ("*Ivan Grozny*") of the Treblinka death camp. About 850,000 Jews perished at Treblinka, and Demjanjuk, according to the indictment, "played an essential and active role in all stages of the annihilation of the Jews in the gas chambers," as well as beating and torturing Jews to death with his bare hands. Demjanjuk was charged on four counts under Israel's Nazi and Nazi Collaborators Punishment Law of 1950, carrying a maximum penalty of death. (For further background, see AJYB 1988, vol. 88, pp. 405–06.) Sitting in judgment on Demjanjuk were Supreme Court Justice Dov Levin and two district court judges, Zvi Tal and Dalia Dorner. The prosecution team was led by State Attorney Yona Blatman; the defense, which included an Israeli lawyer named Yoram Sheftel, by Demjanjuk's longtime American attorney, Mark O'Connor. The language of the trial was Hebrew, with simultaneous translation available into English and Ukrainian, Demjanjuk's native tongue. The newly fashioned courtroom could seat about 300 people, though about a quarter of those places were set aside for print journalists. Unlike regular trials in Israel, TV and still photography were permitted during the proceedings from a special area in the hall's upper gallery.

Demjanjuk, who was brought to Jerusalem every morning from his cell in Ramle, sat below and to the right of the judges, flanked by two policemen. No bulletproof glass cage was deemed necessary, such as was used to shield Adolf Eichmann when he was tried a quarter of a century earlier. But a more crucial difference existed between the Eichmann trial in 1961 and the Demjanjuk trial in 1987. In the former, the identity of the accused was not in question, and the focus of the trial was Eichmann's direct culpability and legal responsibility for implementing "the Final Solution." In the Demjanjuk trial the defense admitted everything concerning the Holocaust and the events at Treblinka but denied that the man in the dock was in fact "Ivan the Terrible." As a result, the bulk of the trial was taken up with the prosecution's efforts to establish, more than 40 years after the events, that John Demjanjuk and "Ivan" were one and the same. These efforts entailed the introduction of material evidence and expert opinion which to most ordinary citizens were abstruse. At times the proceedings slid into arguments over such seemingly trivial matters as pinholes in a photograph, or markings possibly made by a paper clip, which tended to eclipse and diminish the enormity of the actual crime.

The more technical discussion, however, occurred largely in the second phase of the proceedings. The trial's first month was given over to testimony by survivors of Treblinka whose harrowing accounts had an electrifying effect on the public. After a few days in which the hall was half empty, the survivors' testimony struck a responsive chord in the Israeli consciousness. Long lines formed for entry to the courtroom; electronic media coverage was expanded, with the entire proceedings broadcast live on two radio stations and on television; and schools arranged for classes to attend the trial. Large numbers of young people, including many soldiers in uniform, packed the hall.

Several of the survivors broke down in tears on the witness stand. In one incident that left a powerful impression, Demjanjuk offered his hand to witness Eliahu Rosenberg, who recoiled at the gesture and shouted at Demjanjuk in Polish, "*Grozny!*" and in Hebrew, "*Ratzhan!*" ("Murderer!"). At another point during Rosenberg's testimony, Demjanjuk shouted at him in Hebrew, "*Ata shakran!*" ("You are a liar!"). Like the other survivors who testified, Rosenberg described the inhuman brutality of "Ivan." Also like the others, he was challenged on minute details by the defense lawyers, who tried to pick holes in the survivors' testimony and thus demonstrate that after so many years their memories were imprecise and their testimony therefore unreliable. All the survivors identified John Demjanjuk as "Ivan the Terrible."

A leitmotif of the trial was the ongoing confrontation between the Israeli defense lawyer, Yoram Sheftel, and the president of the court, Justice Dov Levin. Sheftel's aggressive and abrasive courtroom manner rankled many and occasionally sparked clashes with Levin. On April 2 Supreme Court president Meir Shamgar rejected Sheftel's petition that the trial court disqualify itself, ruling that the judges had displayed "neither hostility nor bias" against the defense.

By this time the prosecution was calling to the stand official investigators from Israel and West Germany who had been involved in the Demjanjuk case and other Holocaust-related trials. In this stage much of the testimony was legalistic and technical, and attendance at the trial and general public interest fell off considerably.

In mid-May, proceedings in Jerusalem were suspended for five weeks while testimony was taken in West Germany from three former members of the Nazi apparatus. On June 25 the prosecution called its final witness, Dr. Antonio Cantu, an American expert on inks and paper. He was one of many who testified on the key item of material evidence in the trial, an ID card supplied by the USSR, which allegedly showed that Demjanjuk had been at the SS training camp at Trawnicki and later at Sobibor (though it did not mention Treblinka). Demjanjuk vehemently denied this, and the defense claimed the card was a KGB forgery. Cantu had subjected samples from the Trawnicki card to chemical and laser tests; he told the court that he found "no substance in [the card] that was introduced after 1942." On June 29 the court declared a recess until July 27, when the defense would begin presenting its case.

In the meantime the solemnity of the trial was marred by an element bordering on farce. On June 30 Demjanjuk informed the court that he was firing his lead counsel, Mark O'Connor. It was an open secret that O'Connor and Yoram Sheftel did not see eye to eye on the case—indeed, their bickering at times extended even to the courtroom. On July 15 the court granted a plainly confused Demjanjuk five days to make a final decision, during which he would consult with his son-in-law, who had flown in from the United States. On July 19 O'Connor formally resigned from the case, and the following day Demjanjuk confirmed the dismissal. In a letter to the court, O'Connor accused Sheftel of "negligence and misconduct."

John Demjanjuk took the stand a week later (July 27), as the defense began presenting its case. Demjanjuk pleaded with the court not to "put the rope around my neck" for something he had not done. He also declared that his "heart ache[d]" and that he felt "deep sympathy" toward the Jewish people "for what the Nazis did to you." Demjanjuk denied that he was "Ivan the Terrible" and said "I can't even kill a chicken. My wife has to do that." However, under cross-examination by the prosecution, Demjanjuk was unable to recall various dates concerning his activities during World War II. Nor could he account for his failure to mention in his U.S. hearings, under oath, the alibi he had produced in Israel, namely, that he had been a slave laborer at a prison camp for an 18-month period when he was alleged to have been at Trawnicki and then Treblinka. The prosecution also made much of a remark Demjanjuk had uttered during his pretrial interrogation in Israel. When asked whether he had ever been in the towns of Kossow and Mercizecz Podolski, he replied: "You are pushing me toward Treblinka." As the two little towns, hardly familiar to most people, lay between Sobibor and Treblinka, the inference, as drawn by the prosecution, was that Demjanjuk had served in one or both of the death camps.

After Demjanjuk, the defense called a series of expert witnesses of its own in an effort to refute the prosecution's witnesses regarding Demjanjuk's identity and the authenticity of the Trawnicki card, and to set the historical background to Demjanjuk's version of how he spent the war years. However, virtually all the defense witnesses were revealed to be less than expert under the intense and highly informed questioning of the prosecution's Michael Shaked.

One witness whom the prosecution found difficult to shake was Dr. Julius Grant, an 86-year-old British forensics expert with over 60 years' experience and an international reputation. Grant stated that in his opinion Demjanjuk's signature on the Trawnicki card was "unlikely to be authentic." He also had several other reservations, based on internal evidence, about the card. Nevertheless, the prosecution succeeded in getting Grant to qualify his testimony when it informed him that in the U.S. hearings Demjanjuk had said of the Trawnicki signature: "It is like I signed my name."

The trial testimony ended on December 29 (a seven-week delay had occurred when Judge Tal was hospitalized in September after suffering a heart attack), and the final summations by the prosecution and the defense were scheduled to begin in late January 1988. The courtroom had been largely empty for a few months. In the welter of technical evidence, the man and the events at the center of the proceedings had in some sense been lost sight of. With his four or five years of elementary schooling, it was unlikely that John Demjanjuk (whose original name was in fact Ivan), himself could follow the complicated testimony. That his placid, seemingly good-natured exterior masked one of the greatest mass murderers in human history was to many Israelis a certainty; to others it was still not 100 percent clear, even after 92 court sessions, 409 items of material evidence, 32 witnesses, the best efforts of eight prosecution and three defense lawyers, and nearly 9,000 pages of court protocol.

SOVIET AND ETHIOPIAN JEWS

For Ida Nudel, 17 years of being refused an exit visa by the Soviet authorities, including four years of exile in Siberia, ended when she landed at Ben-Gurion Airport on October 15. After being reunited with her sister, Elena Fridman, whom she had not seen since 1972, Ida Nudel stepped out of the plane to a tumultuous welcome. Besides a genuine movie star—the actress Jane Fonda, who had campaigned for Nudel's release and flew in especially for the occasion—the airport extravaganza featured Prime Minister Shamir and Foreign Minister Peres, who were seated on either side of Ida Nudel, as dozens of officials and press photographers buzzed about.

Through it all Ida Nudel evinced the inner dignity and fortitude which had helped her survive even greater ordeals in the USSR. She spoke by telephone to U.S. Secretary of State George Shultz from the airport and was able to express her appreciation in person when Shultz arrived in Israel the next day. Nudel urged all the Soviet Jewry activists to "continue the struggle" for the freedom of the remaining refuseniks, many of whom had given a party in her honor just before she left Moscow.

Among the other former Prisoners of Zion who were allowed to go to Israel in

1987 were Zachar Zunshine and his wife, Tatiana, in March; Simon Shnirman, who was jailed for refusing to serve in the Red Army but told reporters on his arrival in June that he wanted to serve in the IDF; Yuli Edelshtein, who astonished Israelis with his superb command of Hebrew when he arrived in July; Victor Brailovsky, a 15-year refusenik, who was reunited at the airport on September 24 with his brother, Mikhail, whom he had not seen in 10 years, and in Tel Aviv with his aged parents; Vladimir Slepak, a refusenik for 17 years, who in a speech at the Hebrew University a few days after his arrival in October said his first day in Israel was "like being reborn"; and, in November, Vladimir Lipshitz, a mathematician, who served 14 months of a 3-year prison term for promoting *aliyah* before being released.

A tragic case was that of Michael Shirman, who immigrated from the USSR in 1980 and died on March 5, aged 32, of leukemia. By the time his sister, Inessa Flerova, was allowed out of the Soviet Union in late 1986 to donate bone marrow for a transplant, Shirman was too ill for the surgery to be of help.

Despite the arrival of major names in the Jewish and human-rights struggle, a deep-seated malaise was affecting Soviet *aliyah*. In a public speech in March, Natan Sharansky spoke out against the bungling Israeli absorption bureaucracy and the country's failure to make new immigrants from Russia "feel at home here." This, he argued, was the primary reason the vast majority of Soviet Jews were opting for America instead of Israel. Statistically, 1987 was a relatively good year in this regard, with about 26 percent of the over 8,000 Jews allowed out of the USSR settling in Israel—ten times the 1986 figure. However, it was pointed out, this still constituted a "dropout" rate of 74 percent, in addition to which many of those permitted to leave were longtime refuseniks dedicated to Israel.

In his speech Sharansky also deplored the Israeli government's ongoing efforts to dissuade the U.S. government from granting Jews leaving the USSR refugee status, thereby virtually compelling them to immigrate to Israel. During his February visit to the United States, Prime Minister Shamir told reporters that it was an "insult to Israel" for Jews with Israeli visas to be admitted into the States as refugees. On this issue, at least, Shamir and Peres saw eye to eye. Chairing a cabinet meeting on February 22 as acting prime minister, Peres declared that the Jewish movement in the USSR was "first and foremost a Zionist and national movement and it must not be transformed into a mere movement of emigration." However, the government's plans hit a snag when Romania turned down Israel's request to help persuade the USSR to fly immigrating Jews to Bucharest, from where they would have to proceed directly to Israel without the possibility of "dropping out."

The Ethiopian Jews who arrived in Israel via "Operation Moses" continued to face a recalcitrant Orthodox rabbinical establishment. On March 11 the Institute for the Heritage of Ethiopian Jewry was finally inaugurated in Jerusalem. This was 6 months after a High Court injunction was handed down and 18 months after agreement was reached on its creation as part of an arrangement by which Ethiopian Jews could forego ritual immersion (thus symbolically "converting" to Judaism) before being allowed to marry. However, about a week later a spokesman for the

Ethiopians' Beta Yisrael organization termed the institute a sham and said that about 300 Ethiopian couples were being refused marriage permits unless they underwent a symbolic conversion ritual. The Beta Yisrael activists also held several demonstrations during the year to protest alleged government inaction in trying to extricate the thousands of Jews who remained in Ethiopia.

In December the Absorption Ministry reported that most of the Ethiopian immigrants resided in permanent housing in over 60 settlements throughout the country and that Ethiopian children had been "successfully integrated into formal educational frameworks." Other voices were less sanguine. In February Education Ministry officials warned of a "ghettoization" process in some neighborhoods where large numbers of Ethiopians lived, and in November, Ethiopians at the Pardes Hannah absorption center went on strike to protest substandard living conditions. In response, the Jewish Agency and the Absorption Ministry decided to spend $40 million to solve the housing problems of the approximately 1,000 Ethiopians still living in absorption centers.

## AMERICAN JEWRY

In March, an "open letter to an American Jewish friend," published in the *Jerusalem Post* by Prof. Shlomo Avineri, a leading member of the Israeli intellectual establishment, touched off a heated and at times rancorous debate about the very essence of the U.S. Jewish community and its relations with Israel. Avineri wrote that the reaction of the American Jewish leadership to the Pollard case recalled "trembling Israelites in the *shtetl*." This, he said, stemmed from a deep-rooted "anxiety" in the very soul of American Jewry that reflected a *galut* mentality— "ambivalence, alienation, homelessness." At bottom, Avineri proclaimed, American Jews were apprehensive "that despite all of [their] material success and intellectual achievements, [they] may not be seen by non-Jews as being truly American."

In reaction, Theodore Mann, the president of the American Jewish Congress, in an "open letter" of his own, wrote that if Israelis considered American Jews "vulnerable to the 'dual loyalty' charge," yet went ahead and recruited an American Jew as a spy, this smacked of "a disdain for American Jewry by Israeli leadership that is profoundly insulting." A statement released in March by Morris Abram, chairman of the Conference of Presidents of Major Jewish Organizations, sought, without reference to Avineri's article, to place the issue in a larger perspective. Pollard's spying was "a serious crime" and "inexcusable," Abram said, but the common interests of the two countries were "strong enough to weather this deplorable incident." Their "interdependence will and must be the overriding consideration binding the two countries in their common devotion to freedom, to justice and to human dignity." Abram's statement was issued in Jerusalem, where he was heading a 65-member mission for talks with the Israeli leadership.

A not unrelated controversy flared up in September when the American Jewish Congress (AJC) issued a position paper on the Middle East peace issue. Expressing support for the international conference concept espoused by Foreign Minister Shimon Peres, the AJC contrasted it with the "demographic and other dangers of continuing an unavoidably hostile occupation"—an unmistakable reference to Likud policies. In view of the "present stalemate" in Jerusalem on the peace process, the AJC maintained, it was "necessary and appropriate" for American Jews "to participate in the current historic debate." A few days later, on September 30, Peres, addressing the presidents' conference in New York, asserted that Diaspora Jewry not only had the right but also the duty to express itself "on the most essential issues" regarding Israel.

These developments drew an immediate condemnation from Prime Minister Shamir. In a letter dated October 1 to Morris Abram in his capacity as chairman of the presidents' conference, Shamir evoked the principle that "matters of security must be left to those who are called to shed their blood for the country." Shamir said there was a "shock of disbelief in Israel" at the "regrettable recent attempt to breach this understanding." About a week later, Abram, in a letter to both Shamir and Peres, dwelt on the traditional "restraint" exercised by the presidents' conference in offering advice to Israel regarding "matters of security." At the same time, he noted, "Israel and its governments have always been receptive to the expressions of diverse views by Jews abroad." That receptiveness was tested in practice when the American Jewish Congress published its position paper in the form of full-page ads in Israel's leading Hebrew-language papers.

### 31ST ZIONIST CONGRESS

One place where the clout of Diaspora Jewry was felt powerfully was within the Zionist movement, as evidenced in the events surrounding the 31st Zionist Congress, held in Jerusalem December 6–11. In October the leading Diaspora fund-raisers in the Jewish Agency continued the muscle-flexing they had shown in recent years by vetoing the Labor party's candidates for the positions of chairman and treasurer in the World Zionist Organization/Jewish Agency. Earlier in the year, the fund-raisers had indicated their desire for an overhaul of the veteran leadership by assuring the replacement of the current WZO/Agency chairman, Arye Dulzin, in the aftermath of the Bank Leumi scandal (see "Economic Developments," above). As part of this trend, Mendel Kaplan, from South Africa, was elected the first non-American chairman of the Jewish Agency board of governors.

The Zionist meeting was attended by nearly 600 delegates, about two-thirds of them from Israel and the United States, representing some 1.5 million members of Zionist organizations around the world. Such interest as there was in the congress among the Israeli public was centered on the election of the new chairman, in which the new Labor candidate, MK Simcha Dinitz, outpolled the Likud's Gideon Patt by 310–220. In the course of the deliberations, the congress passed (by a vote of 291–271) a resolution in favor of "complete equality for all streams within Judaism" and in rabbinical functions in Israel. The congress came to an undignified and unruly end around dawn on December 11, following an all-night session in which bleary-eyed delegates chose the new executive. When it came to the final issue on the agenda, the question of restructuring the executive, delegates from Herut, which objected to the proposed changes, first tried to prevent a vote and then, when the chairwoman, Hadassah president Ruth Popkin, declared the motion passed, stormed the speaker's platform, seized the microphone, and threw various objects at those who tried to restore order. "Shame on you," the chairwoman cried out in what were apparently the final words of the 31st Zionist Congress: "You have behaved like animals."

## Culture

THE ARTS

The arts in Israel got a boost in 1987 by being selected as the theme for the country's 39th Independence Day celebrations on May 4. Three of those honored to light the 12 torches (symbolizing the 12 tribes) in the traditional Mount Herzl Independence Eve ceremony represented major Israeli cultural institutions that celebrated anniversaries of their own during the Jewish calendar year: the Bezalel Academy of Art, the Habimah National Theater, and the Israel Philharmonic Orchestra (IPO), founded 80, 70, and 50 years earlier, respectively.

For Israelis, a major taste of Eastern European culture came in the form of Krakow's "Stary Teater" company, which presented its adaptation of Dostoevsky's *Crime and Punishment* at the annual Israel Festival/Jerusalem (May 18–June 14). Besides Poland, and of course Israel, artists representing music, dance, and theater from France, Italy, Ireland, Japan, Spain, Germany, and the United States performed in the festival. To mark the 20th anniversary of Jerusalem's reunification in the 1967 Six Day War, the festival opened with a breathtaking high-wire walk by France's Phillipe Petit across the 300 meters of the Hinnom Valley between West and East Jerusalem.

The capital was also the site of other major cultural events in 1987. In April about 1,000 publishers from 40 countries—including Poland, Hungary, Japan, and the Ivory Coast—exhibited over 100,000 books at the 13th Jerusalem International Book Fair. A highlight of the biennial event was the awarding of the Jerusalem Prize to South African writer J.M. Coetzee for giving expression in his work to "the freedom of the individual in society." As usual, tens of thousands of Israelis attended the fair, preserving its unique character as a popular event and not only a commercial enterprise.

On the stage, Motti Lerner's *Hevlei Mashiah* (Pangs of the Messiah's Coming), produced by the Cameri Theater, had as its theme the dilemmas faced—and created—by Jewish settlers in the West Bank. The Al-Hakawati Theater, based in East Jerusalem, produced *The Story of Kafr Shamma*, written by an American Jewish woman, Jackie Lubeck, which told (in Arabic translation) the story of a fictitious Palestinian village wiped off the map in the 1948 war. A play that stirred considerable controversy was Yehoshua Sobol's *Jerusalem Syndrome*, in which the action takes place during the Jewish revolt against the Romans in 70 CE, but with unmistakable allusions to ultranationalist trends in contemporary Israel. The situation in the territories was the subject of another play, adapted from David Grossman's book *The Yellow Wind*. Grossman had been commissioned by the weekly *Koteret Rashit* to document, with a novelist's eye, the situation in the West Bank 20 years after the Six Day War, and the resulting piece took up the magazine's entire Independence Day issue. Published in somewhat expanded form as a book, it became a best-seller.

In what was an extraordinary year for Hebrew fiction, new works were published by Israel's leading novelists: *Black Box* by Amos Oz; *Molcho* by A.B. Yehoshua; and *His Daughter* by Yoram Kaniuk. Yitzhak Ben-Ner's *Angels Are Coming*, set in 21st-century Israel, envisages a society ruled by draconian religious laws and rampant street violence. Haim Be'er's long-awaited second novel, *The Time of Trimming*, depicts macabre situations from his experiences in the military chaplaincy. Also set in an army camp is *Heart Murmur*, a major new work by one of Israel's prose masters, Yehoshua Kenaz. The novella-length title story of the new book by Daniella Carmi, *All the Time in the World for Picking Plums*, is a wrenching evocation of the life of a Gaza Strip refugee family. *A Trumpet in the Wind*, by the Iraqi-born writer Sammy Michael, tells of an Israeli Arab family in Haifa torn between two cultural worlds.

The world of traditional Jewish culture was evoked for Israelis in December, when the Israel Museum opened its renovated and expanded Judaica wing with an exhibit of the fabled collection of Joseph Stieglitz, a Tel Aviv dealer in Jewish ritual objects. Until its transfer to the museum, the collection, some of whose 280 items dated back to the 12th century, and which was miraculously saved from destruction during the Holocaust, was kept in the livingroom of the Stieglitzes' Tel Aviv home. Communities from the entire Jewish world, from Europe to India, many of them no longer extant, were represented in the collection.

In December the L.A. Mayer Museum of Islamic Art in Jerusalem exhibited an extraordinary collection of Islamic jewelry, including items from the 7th century and representing virtually every corner of the Islamic world. Israeli Arab schoolchildren came on organized visits to view the show. Earlier in the year the Israel Museum also had an impressive exhibition of Islamic jewelry, much of it uncovered in Israeli archaeological digs.

Two new museums opened in 1987. The Museum of Israeli Art in Ramat Gan devoted a show to the theme of the *Akedah* (the sacrifice of Isaac) in Israeli art. The Open Museum at Tefen, part of the high-tech Rose Garden Valley development created by industrialist Stef Wertheimer in Western Galilee, featured works by the late sculptor Yitzhak Danziger and a series of about 100 pieces in a variety of techniques by Uri Lifshitz. Entitled "Men and Machine," the works were to remain at the Tefen Industrial Park as decoration for factory walls.

## Archaeology

One of the high points in the ongoing excavations of the Old City of Jerusalem came in March, when, for the first time in nearly 2,000 years—since the destruction of the Second Temple—the whole 500-meter length of the Western Wall was uncovered. The event occurred when the dig, which was being carried out under the aegis of the Religious Affairs Ministry and the professional guidance of archaeologist Dan Bahat, reached the water tunnel that Herod sealed off as part of his struggle against the Hasmoneans. The entry to the site was just off the Western Wall plaza, but the area was not yet open to the general public.

In the south, a joint University of Maryland-Hebrew University archaeological team uncovered four churches at the Christian city of Rehovot, which was a way station on the Sinai-Palestine-Syria route 1,500 years ago. At another Negev dig, Tel Halif, where remains from the Bronze Age were discovered, archaeologists from a group of American universities, with the assistance of nearby Kibbutz Lahav and the Joe Alon Bedouin Study Center, were making use of space-age technology. NASA was providing data gleaned from satellites, and the U.S. Department of Agriculture supplied a unique sensory radar unit to assist underground mapping.

Israel's north also turned up some rich archaeological treasures in 1987. At Zippori (Sepphoris), the ancient capital of Galilee, not far from Nazareth, the third season of excavation by a Hebrew University-Duke University team revealed what one of the researchers called "the most beautiful Roman mosaic ever found" in Israel. Also, a 5,000-year-old port city, the oldest ever found in the country, was unearthed in the third season of a dig at Tel Rami, near Atlit, being conducted by a Haifa University team with assistance from European and American researchers.

Probably the year's most spectacular exhibition of archaeological treasures went on display at the Tel Aviv Museum in October. It featured about 250 items from the collection of Dr. Elie Borowski, who divided his time between Canada and Jerusalem. The entire collection was to form part of the Bible Lands Museum being built adjacent to the Israel Museum in Jerusalem. The sampling in the current exhibit included astonishing treasures spanning five millennia and encompassing virtually every land mentioned in the Bible, such as Phoenician ivories of the kind King Solomon used to decorate his palace.

## Other Domestic Matters

### POPULATION

Israel's population stood at 4,404,000 at the end of 1987, comprising 3.6 million Jews (82 percent), 615,000 Muslims (14 percent), 102,000 Christians (2.3 percent), and 75,000 Druze and members of other faiths (1.7 percent). The total population increased by 1.7 percent, as compared with 1986, and the Jewish population registered a 1.4-percent growth. Data released at the end of May to mark the 20th anniversary of Jerusalem's reunification showed that the city's population stood at 475,000 persons—340,000 Jews, 121,000 Muslims, and around 14,000 Christians. This constituted a population increase of approximately 80 percent since 1967, due primarily to natural growth. Overall, the proportion of the Jewish population in Jerusalem declined from 73.2 percent in 1967 to 71.6 percent in May 1987, while that of the Muslim population increased from 22 to 25 percent.

In comparative terms, immigration to Israel was well up in 1987—an increase of 36 percent over 1986. However, in absolute figures the situation was far less impressive: only 12,965 *olim* (new immigrants) arrived during the year, of whom nearly half (5,800) listed themselves in the category of "potential immigrants." Immigration was up from all continents, most notably from the USSR, which accounted for 16 percent of the year's total immigration. There was a decline of 10 percent in the number of *olim* from the United States (1,800, down from 2,000 in 1986). The Absorption Ministry tried this year to put an end to the perennial debate regarding the number of Israeli emigrants. A report commissioned by the ministry, based on an exhaustive study of both published and unpublished sources and statistical analyses, concluded that the maximum number of Israeli emigrants from 1948 until the end of 1985 stood at 346,000, of whom about half resided in North America.

ISRAELI ARABS

A major concern of Israeli Arabs, housing, was finally dealt with at cabinet level in 1987. The problem at issue was the rampant illegal construction of housing in Arab settlements due to a combination of factors: the refusal of the Interior Ministry to authorize master plans for Arab localities, the confiscation of Arab-owned land for Jewish development, and the Arab population's rapid growth rate (a nearly sixfold increase since 1948). A report drawn up by a committee under the chairmanship of Yaakov Markowitz, deputy director-general of the Interior Ministry, and approved by the cabinet on February 15, estimated the number of illegally built houses in the Arab sector at no fewer than 11,000. Of these it recommended leveling some 300 dwellings, with the final decision regarding thousands of others to await formal residential zoning plans. The cabinet decided that a special ministerial committee would deal with the issue, but little perceptible progress had been made by year's end.

Two other major issues on the agenda of Israel's Arabs were perceived discrimination in government budgetary allocations to Arab local councils, as compared with Jewish local councils, and serious shortages and disparities in education. Matters were not helped when the cabinet on May 17 decided (in a majority comprising Likud plus the religious parties) to impose a two-tier system of university tuition fees, with students who did not do army service—meaning, in practice, the country's Arab citizens—to pay $500 more per year than their Jewish counterparts. Following protest demonstrations, some of them violent, by both Jewish and Arab students, against "apartheid," the decision was rescinded.

This feeling of general neglect and second-class status was the background to a total general strike by Israel's Arab citizens on June 24. Organized by the National Committee of Heads of Arab Local Councils, the strike encompassed every sphere of activity in the approximately 50 Arab local councils and municipalities. However, "Equality Day," as it was called, passed quietly and generated few reverberations. By contrast, the sporadic violence that marked the "Peace Day" general strike by the Israeli Arabs on December 21, in solidarity with the uprising in the territories, led both Prime Minister Shamir and Defense Minister Rabin to warn these 18 percent of the country's citizens that, when all was said and done, they were in Israel at the sufferance of the Jewish majority.

### THE MEDIA STRIKE

Of all the strikes in Israel in 1987, one was particularly revealing about the nature of Israeli society, that of the electronic media. Called in support of wage demands by the journalists' union in the Israel Broadcasting Authority, the strike lasted seven weeks (October 7–November 27) and totally silenced Israel TV and Israel Radio, including news broadcasts. (Army Radio, barred by law from striking, partially filled the news gap.) The journalists, who evidently expected that the news-addicted public would exert pressure to end the walkout on their terms, soon found differently. Nor were the politicians, many of whom had little good to say about the news reporting on IBA, in any hurry to get radio and TV back on the air. Indeed, it was claimed that the blackout had helped preserve secrecy during talks held by U.S. Secretary of State George Shultz in Jerusalem. Road accidents declined by 25 percent during the strike, leading some to theorize that people were getting more sleep instead of staying up late to watch TV, or that without their daily fix of grim news, Israelis were under less stress. It was just such a stress-inducing item—the hang-glider attack at Kiryat Shemonah on November 25 in which six soldiers were killed—that finally allowed the journalists to back down gracefully and agree to return to work "for the national good," though their demands were unmet.

### NAKASH CASE

The case of William Nakash, whose extradition France sought on a murder charge dating from 1983, dragged on throughout the entire year. Nakash, a French Jew, had been convicted *in absentia* in France of killing an Arab in what the French police said was an underworld murder but which Nakash claimed was triggered by anti-Semitism. He fled to Israel where he was arrested during a robbery attempt. Nakash assumed some of the trappings of religiosity and gained the patronage of a lobby composed of the ultranationalist Right and the ultra-Orthodox rabbinical establishment. Their formal argument was that Nakash's life would be endangered in a French prison. (For additional background, see AJYB 1988, vol. 88, pp. 410–11.)

On March 10 the Supreme Court declared that the assumptions that had led Justice (and Tourism) Minister Avraham Sharir to decide against extraditing Nakash were "unfounded" and "generalized." Sharir was ordered to "reconsider" the case within 60 days. Six weeks later Attorney-General Yosef Harish was granted a further 60-day extension. On June 22, after a senior Justice Ministry official returned from a fact-finding mission to France and reported that the prisons in that country were safer than those in Israel (it had been suggested that Nakash be tried and serve his punishment in Israel), Sharir gave the go-ahead for the extradition. The Supreme Court, however, allowed a delay until July 2. In the meantime Nakash's lawyer flew to France, reportedly to try to persuade President François Mitterrand to intercede, and MK Haim Druckman (National Religious party) subsequently held talks in Paris with the French justice minister, but without practical result. Complicating the entire matter, and threatening to produce a head-on clash between the secular and religious court systems, was an order issued earlier by the Jerusalem rabbinical court barring Nakash from leaving the country after his wife, Rina, started divorce proceedings against him.

After the High Court of Justice reaffirmed its earlier decision, the rabbinical court gave Nakash an extra two weeks to decide whether he would grant his wife a divorce. In the meantime, the State Attorney's Office, in a step it had hoped to avoid, asked the rabbinical court to rescind its order barring Nakash from leaving the country. This was refused, the rabbinical court ruling that if Nakash left Israel without divorcing his wife she would become an *agunah* (a woman not allowed to remarry because her husband abandoned her), and this overrode the law. Picking up the gauntlet, the State Attorney's Office drew up a petition for submission to the High Court of Justice, contending that the rabbinical court had exceeded its authority. But the collision between the two courts was averted when Nakash informed the rabbinical court that he was willing in principle to grant the divorce, a move that prompted the court to declare that the order prohibiting Nakash from leaving Israel would expire on December 1. On December 2, after depositing a conditional writ of divorce with the rabbinical court and following a legal battle of two and a half years, Nakash was extradited to France.

## *Personalia*

Several key appointments were made in the Israel Defense Forces. On April 19 Maj. Gen. Dan Shomron was promoted to the rank of lieutenant general and took over as the IDF's 13th chief of staff, succeeding Lt. Gen. Moshe Levy, who retired from military service. Maj. Gen. Ehud Barak was appointed deputy chief of staff and was succeeded by Maj. Gen. Avraham Mitzna as O/C Central Command on May 7. The air force got a new commanding officer when Maj. Gen. Avihu Bin-Nun took over from Maj. Gen. Amos Lapidot (who retired from active service) on

September 22; Bin-Nun was replaced by Maj. Gen. Danny Yotam as head of the planning branch. In the civilian sphere, district court judge Yaacov Malz was elected by the Knesset's House Committee as Israel's fourth state comptroller on February 2, succeeding Yitzhak Tunik. In February, Mohammed Massarwa, deputy head of the Kafr Kari local council, was appointed Israel's consul general in Atlanta, the first Arab ever named to head an Israeli mission abroad.

Personalities who died during the year included Meir Ya'ari, a founder of Hashomer Hatzair, the first Zionist youth movement, and of the Kibbutz Ha'artzi movement, and a longtime leader of the Mapam party, on February 21, aged 90; Simha Flapan, the founder and first editor (for 25 years) of the English-language left-wing monthly *New Outlook*, on April 13, aged 77; Raphael Klatzkin, veteran actor in the Habimah National Theater and an Israel Prize winner for the performing arts, on May 27, aged 82; Shmuel Tamir, former justice minister and top trial lawyer, who established his reputation in the 1950s Kastner trial (concerning actions of the Hungarian Jewish leadership under the Nazi occupation), on June 29, aged 64; Moshe Ish-Kassit, proprietor of the traditional cafe haunt of Israel's bohemian-intellectual community in Tel Aviv, on July 14, aged 39; Shaike Ofir, versatile entertainer whose talents extended to stage, screen, TV, and stand-up comedy, on August 17, aged 58; Abba Kovner, an anti-Nazi fighter in the Vilna ghetto who became a major Israeli poet and a recipient of the Israel Prize, on September 25, aged 69; Nathan Axelrod, a pioneer of the local film industry in the prestate period, on October 6, aged 82; Pinhas Eylon, who for 36 consecutive years as mayor of Holon presided over its growth into Israel's fourth largest city, on October 30, aged 78; Eliahu Rimalt, former cabinet minister and a former head of the Liberal party and cochairman of the Likud, on November 5, aged 80; Michael Comay, veteran diplomat who served as ambassador to Canada, Britain, and the UN, on November 6, aged 79; and Prof. Yigal Shilo, director of the City of David excavations in Jerusalem, who was awarded the Jerusalem Prize for archaeology at a sick-bed ceremony just days before his death on November 14, aged 50.

RALPH MANDEL

# World Jewish Population, 1986

THE 1988 AMERICAN JEWISH YEAR BOOK (AJYB) contained new estimates of the Jewish population in the various countries of the world at the end of 1986, as well as background information and analysis. The statistical tables are reprinted here, without the accompanying text. Only two changes have been made in the figures for individual countries. The estimate for Australian Jewry has been raised by 3,000. The 1986 census of Australia, in which the question on religion was optional, enumerated 69,065 declared Jews. Since the census also indicated that about 25 percent of the country's whole population either did not specify their religion or stated explicitly that they had none, this large group must be assumed to contain persons who otherwise identify as Jews. Furthermore, although Australian Jewry is an aging population that also confronts demographic problems with regard to natural increase and assimilation, it has received migratory reinforcements during the last decade. Based on these factors, we arrive at a provisional estimate of 80,000—pending clarification of population trends since previous censuses. The second change regards India, where the population census held in 1981 counted 5,618 Jews. Allowing for both the known *aliyah* to Israel and natural increase, we have set the 1986 estimate at 5,200 (compared with 4,200 in 1985). The totals for Diaspora and World Jewry have been adjusted accordingly.

Our estimates for Soviet Jewry are updates of the figures from three population censuses (1959, 1970, and 1979). These were rather consistent among themselves, considering the probable evolution in the intervals. Our previously stated reservation about Soviet Jewish population figures bears repeating: While some underreporting is not impossible, it cannot be quantified and should not be exaggerated.[1]

The U.S. Jewish population in 1986 was estimated, in the AJYB article "Jewish Population in the United States," at 5,814,000, including "under 2 percent" non-Jewish household members. This was close to our own estimate for that year of 5,700,000. For 1987, the same article gave an estimate of 5,943,700, which was to be understood not as actual sudden growth but as a result of changes made in the counts of several local communities. A nationwide sample survey of U.S. Jewry, scheduled for 1990, is expected to provide benchmark information for a series of updated estimates.

---

[1]U.O. Schmelz and Sergio DellaPergola, "World Jewish Population," AJYB 1982, vol. 82, p. 285.

## Accuracy Rating

The three main elements which affect the accuracy of each estimate are the nature of the base data, the recency of the base data, and the method of updating. A simple code combining these elements is used to provide a general evaluation of the reliability of the Jewish population figures reported in the detailed tables below. The code indicates different quality levels of the reported estimates: (A) base figure derived from countrywide census or relatively reliable Jewish population surveys; updated on the basis of full or partial information on Jewish population movements in the intervening period; (B) base figure derived from less accurate but recent countrywide Jewish population investigation; partial information on population movements in the intervening period; (C) base figure derived from less recent sources, and/or unsatisfactory or partial coverage of Jewish population in country; updating according to demographic information illustrative of regional demographic trends; and (D) base figure essentially conjectural; no reliable updating procedure. In categories (A), (B), and (C), the years in which the base figures or important partial updates were obtained are also provided.

For a country whose Jewish population estimate of 1986 was not only updated but also revised in the light of improved information, the sign of "X" is appended to the accuracy rating.

The 1990 AJYB will present updated and, where necessary, revised Jewish population estimates for the countries of the world as of the end of 1988.

UZIEL O. SCHMELZ
SERGIO DELLAPERGOLA

TABLE 1. ESTIMATED JEWISH POPULATION, BY CONTINENTS AND MAJOR GEOGRAPHICAL REGIONS, 1984 AND 1986

| Region | Original 1984 | Revised Abs. Nos. | Revised Percent | 1986 Abs. Nos. | 1986 Percent | % Change 1984–1986 |
|---|---|---|---|---|---|---|
| Diaspora | 9,491,600 | 9,482,700 | 73.2 | 9,405,400 | 72.5 | −0.8 |
| Israel | 3,471,700 | 3,471,700 | 26.8 | 3,562,500 | 27.5 | +2.6 |
| World | 12,963,300 | 12,954,400 | 100.0 | 12,967,900 | 100.0 | +0.1 |
| America, Total | 6,469,000 | 6,461,100 | 49.9 | 6,454,700 | 49.8 | −0.1 |
| North[a] | 6,015,000 | 6,010,000 | 46.4 | 6,010,000 | 46.4 | 0.0 |
| Central | 47,300 | 46,300 | 0.4 | 45,500 | 0.3 | −1.7 |
| South | 406,700 | 404,800 | 3.1 | 399,200 | 3.1 | −1.4 |
| Europe, Total | 2,758,600 | 2,755,800 | 21.3 | 2,685,900 | 20.7 | −2.5 |
| West | 1,048,900 | 1,048,600 | 8.1 | 1,043,300 | 8.0 | −0.5 |
| East & Balkans[b] | 1,709,700 | 1,707,200 | 13.2 | 1,642,600 | 12.7 | −3.8 |
| Asia, Total | 3,509,300 | 3,509,300 | 27.1 | 3,598,000 | 27.8 | +2.5 |
| Israel | 3,471,700 | 3,471,700 | 26.8 | 3,562,500 | 27.5 | +2.6 |
| Rest[b] | 37,600 | 37,600 | 0.3 | 35,500 | 0.3 | −5.6 |
| Africa, Total | 147,400 | 149,100 | 1.1 | 145,200 | 1.1 | −2.6 |
| North | 16,700 | 16,700 | 0.1 | 15,200 | 0.1 | −9.0 |
| South | 119,100 | 119,100 | 0.9 | 116,200 | 0.9 | −2.4 |
| Rest[c] | 11,600 | 13,300 | 0.1 | 13,800 | 0.1 | +3.8 |
| Oceania | 79,000 | 79,100 | 0.6 | 84,100 | 0.6 | +6.3 |

[a]U.S.A. and Canada.
[b]The Asian territories of USSR and Turkey are included in "East Europe and Balkans."
[c]Including Ethiopia.

TABLE 2. ESTIMATED JEWISH POPULATION DISTRIBUTION IN THE AMERICAS, 1986

| Country | Total Population | Jewish Population | Jews per 1,000 Population | Accuracy Rating | |
|---|---|---|---|---|---|
| Canada | 25,612,000 | 310,000 | 12.1 | A | 1981 |
| United States | 241,596,000 | 5,700,000 | 23.6 | B | 1986 X |
| Total Northern America | | 6,010,000 | | | |
| Bahamas | 236,000 | 300 | 1.3 | C | 1973 X |
| Costa Rica | 2,666,000 | 2,000 | 0.8 | C | 1986 X |
| Cuba | 10,246,000 | 700 | 0.1 | D | |
| Dominican Republic | 6,416,000 | 100 | 0.0 | D | |
| Guatemala | 8,195,000 | 800 | 0.1 | A | 1983 |
| Jamaica | 2,372,000 | 300 | 0.1 | B | 1986 |
| Mexico | 79,563,000 | 35,000 | 0.4 | C | 1980 |
| Netherlands Antilles | 261,000 | 400 | 1.5 | D | X |
| Panama | 2,227,000 | 3,800 | 1.7 | C | 1986 |
| Puerto Rico | 3,502,000 | 1,500 | 0.4 | C | 1986 X |
| Virgin Islands | 107,000 | 300 | 2.8 | C | 1986 X |
| Other | | 300 | | D | |
| Total Central America | | 45,500 | | | |
| Argentina | 31,030,000 | 224,000 | 7.2 | C | 1960–86 |
| Bolivia | 6,547,000 | 600 | 0.1 | C | 1986 |
| Brazil | 138,493,000 | 100,000 | 0.7 | B | 1980 |
| Chile | 12,327,000 | 17,000 | 1.4 | C | 1986 |
| Colombia | 29,188,000 | 6,500 | 0.2 | C | 1986 |
| Ecuador | 9,647,000 | 1,000 | 0.1 | C | 1982 |
| Paraguay | 3,807,000 | 900 | 0.2 | C | 1984 |
| Peru | 20,207,000 | 4,000 | 0.2 | B | 1985 X |
| Suriname | 380,000 | 200 | 0.5 | B | 1986 |
| Uruguay | 2,983,000 | 25,000 | 8.4 | D | X |
| Venezuela | 17,791,000 | 20,000 | 1.1 | D | |
| Total Southern America | | 399,200 | | | |
| Total | | 6,454,700 | | | |

TABLE 3. ESTIMATED JEWISH POPULATION DISTRIBUTION IN EUROPE, 1986

| Country | Total Population | Jewish Population | Jews per 1,000 Population | Accuracy Rating |
|---|---|---|---|---|
| Austria | 7,565,000 | 6,400 | 0.8 | A 1986 |
| Belgium | 9,913,000 | 32,000 | 3.2 | D |
| Bulgaria | 8,959,000 | 3,200 | 0.4 | D |
| Czechoslovakia | 15,534,000 | 8,200 | 0.5 | D |
| Denmark | 5,121,000 | 6,600 | 1.3 | C 1984 |
| Finland | 4,918,000 | 1,200 | 0.2 | A 1986 |
| France | 55,392,000 | 530,000 | 9.6 | C 1972–78 |
| Germany, East | 16,624,000 | 500 | 0.0 | C 1986 X |
| Germany, West | 61,048,000 | 32,700 | 0.5 | B 1986 |
| Gibraltar | 29,000 | 600 | 20.7 | A 1981 |
| Great Britain | 56,763,000 | 326,000 | 5.7 | B 1986 |
| Greece | 9,966,000 | 5,000 | 0.5 | B 1986 |
| Hungary | 10,627,000 | 60,000 | 5.6 | D |
| Ireland | 3,537,000 | 2,000 | 0.6 | A 1986 |
| Italy | 57,221,000 | 31,800 | 0.6 | B 1986 |
| Luxembourg | 363,000 | 700 | 1.9 | C 1970 |
| Netherlands | 14,563,000 | 26,000 | 1.8 | C 1986 |
| Norway | 4,169,000 | 1,000 | 0.2 | A 1982 |
| Poland | 37,456,000 | 4,400 | 0.1 | D |
| Portugal | 10,291,000 | 300 | 0.0 | B 1986 X |
| Romania | 23,174,000 | 21,500 | 0.9 | B 1986 X |
| Spain | 38,668,000 | 12,000 | 0.3 | D |
| Sweden | 8,370,000 | 15,000 | 1.8 | C 1982 |
| Switzerland | 6,504,000 | 19,000 | 2.9 | A 1980 |
| Turkey[a] | 50,301,000 | 20,000 | 0.4 | C 1986 |
| USSR[a] | 280,144,000 | 1,515,000 | 5.4 | C 1979 |
| Yugoslavia | 23,271,000 | 4,800 | 0.2 | C 1986 |
| Total | | 2,685,900 | | |

[a]Including Asian regions.

TABLE 4. ESTIMATED JEWISH POPULATION DISTRIBUTION IN ASIA, 1986

| Country | Total Population | Jewish Population | Jews per 1,000 Population | Accuracy Rating |
|---|---|---|---|---|
| Hong Kong | 5,533,000 | 1,000 | 0.2 | C 1980 |
| India | 766,135,000 | 5,200 | 0.0 | A 1981 |
| Iran | 45,914,000 | 22,000 | 0.5 | D |
| Iraq | 16,450,000 | 200 | 0.0 | D |
| Israel[a] | 4,333,100[a] | 3,562,500 | 822.2 | A 1986 |
| Japan | 120,492,000 | 1,000 | 0.0 | C 1986 |
| Lebanon | 2,707,000 | 100 | 0.0 | D |
| Philippines | 56,004,000 | 100 | 0.0 | C 1982 |
| Singapore | 2,586,000 | 300 | 0.1 | C 1984 |
| Syria | 10,612,000 | 4,000 | 0.4 | D |
| Thailand | 52,094,000 | 300 | 0.0 | C 1980 |
| Yemen | 7,046,000 | 1,000 | 0.1 | D |
| Other |  | 300 |  | D |
| Total |  | 3,598,000 |  |  |

[a] End 1986.

TABLE 5. ESTIMATED JEWISH POPULATION DISTRIBUTION IN AFRICA, 1986

| Country | Total Population | Jewish Population | Jews per 1,000 Population | Accuracy Rating |
|---|---|---|---|---|
| Egypt | 49,609,000 | 200 | 0.0 | D |
| Ethiopia | 44,927,000 | 12,000 | 0.3 | D  X |
| Kenya | 21,163,000 | 100 | 0.0 | B 1986 |
| Morocco | 22,476,000 | 12,000 | 0.5 | D |
| South Africa | 33,221,000 | 115,000 | 3.5 | B 1980 |
| Tunisia | 7,234,000 | 3,000 | 0.4 | D |
| Zaire | 80,850,000 | 400 | 0.0 | D  X |
| Zambia | 6,896,000 | 300 | 0.0 | D |
| Zimbabwe | 8,406,000 | 1,200 | 0.1 | B 1986 |
| Other |  | 1,000 |  | D |
| Total |  | 145,200 |  |  |

TABLE 6. ESTIMATED JEWISH POPULATION DISTRIBUTION IN OCEANIA, 1986

| Country | Total Population | Jewish Population | Jews per 1,000 Population | Accuracy Rating |
|---|---|---|---|---|
| Australia | 15,974,000 | 80,000 | 5.0 | C 1986 |
| New Zealand | 3,248,000 | 4,000 | 1.2 | B 1981 |
| Other |  | 100 |  | D  X |
| Total |  | 84,100 |  |  |

TABLE 7. DISTRIBUTION OF THE WORLD'S JEWS, BY NUMBER AND PROPORTION (PER 1,000 POPULATION) IN VARIOUS COUNTRIES, 1986

| Number of Jews in Country | Total | Below 1 | 1–5 | 5–10 | 10–25 | 25 and over |
|---|---|---|---|---|---|---|
| | | | Number of Countries | | | |
| Total | 74[a] | 49 | 15 | 6 | 3 | 1 |
| Below 1,000 | 23 | 18 | 4 | — | 1 | — |
| 1,000–5,000 | 19 | 17 | 2 | — | — | — |
| 5,000–10,000 | 5 | 4 | 1 | — | — | — |
| 10,000–50,000 | 16 | 9 | 6 | 1 | — | — |
| 50,000–100,000 | 2 | — | 1 | 1 | — | — |
| 100,000–1,000,000 | 6 | 1 | 1 | 3 | 1 | — |
| 1,000,000 and over | 3 | — | — | 1 | 1 | 1 |
| | | Jewish Population Distribution (Absolute Numbers) | | | | |
| Total | 12,967,900 | 374,700 | 260,100 | 2,760,000 | 6,010,600 | 3,562,500 |
| Below 1,000 | 10,400 | 8,100 | 1,700 | — | 600 | — |
| 1,000–5,000 | 44,100 | 36,300 | 7,800 | — | — | — |
| 5,000–10,000 | 37,900 | 31,300 | 6,600 | — | — | — |
| 10,000–50,000 | 353,000 | 199,000 | 129,000 | 25,000 | — | — |
| 50,000–100,000 | 140,000 | — | — | 140,000 | — | — |
| 100,000–1,000,000 | 1,605,000 | 100,000 | 115,000 | 1,080,000 | 310,000 | — |
| 1,000,000 and over | 10,777,500 | — | — | 1,515,000 | 5,700,000 | 3,562,500 |
| | | Jewish Population Distribution (Percent of World's Jews) | | | | |
| Total | 100.0 | 2.9 | 2.0 | 21.3 | 46.3 | 27.5 |
| Below 1,000 | 0.1 | 0.1 | 0.0 | — | 0.0 | — |
| 1,000–5,000 | 0.4 | 0.3 | 0.1 | — | — | — |
| 5,000–10,000 | 0.2 | 0.2 | 0.0 | — | — | — |
| 10,000–50,000 | 2.7 | 1.5 | 1.0 | 0.2 | — | — |
| 50,000–100,000 | 1.1 | — | — | 1.1 | — | — |
| 100,000–1,000,000 | 12.4 | 0.8 | 0.9 | 8.3 | 2.4 | — |
| 1,000,000 and over | 83.1 | — | — | 11.7 | 43.9 | 27.5 |

[a]Excluding countries with fewer than 100 Jews.

TABLE 8. COUNTRIES WITH LARGEST JEWISH POPULATIONS (100,000 JEWS AND ABOVE), 1986

| Rank | Country | Jewish Population | In the Diaspora % | In the Diaspora Cumulative % | In the World % | In the World Cumulative % |
|---|---|---|---|---|---|---|
| 1 | United States | 5,700,000 | 60.6 | 60.6 | 43.9 | 43.9 |
| 2 | Israel | 3,562,500 | — | — | 27.5 | 71.4 |
| 3 | Soviet Union | 1,515,000 | 16.1 | 76.7 | 11.7 | 83.1 |
| 4 | France | 530,000 | 5.6 | 82.3 | 4.1 | 87.2 |
| 5 | Great Britain | 326,000 | 3.5 | 85.8 | 2.5 | 89.7 |
| 6 | Canada | 310,000 | 3.3 | 89.1 | 2.4 | 92.1 |
| 7 | Argentina | 224,000 | 2.4 | 91.5 | 1.7 | 93.8 |
| 8 | South Africa | 115,000 | 1.2 | 92.7 | 0.9 | 94.7 |
| 9 | Brazil | 100,000 | 1.1 | 93.8 | 0.8 | 95.5 |

Directories
Lists
Obituaries

# National Jewish Organizations[1]

## UNITED STATES

Organizations are listed according to functions as follows:
- Community Relations 445
- Cultural 449
- Overseas Aid 454
- Religious, Educational 456
- Social, Mutual Benefit 474
- Social Welfare 476
- Zionist and Pro-Israel 479

Note also cross-references under these headings:
- Professional Associations 489
- Women's Organizations 489
- Youth and Student Organizations 490

## COMMUNITY RELATIONS

AMERICAN COUNCIL FOR JUDAISM (1943). 298 Fifth Ave., NYC 10001. (212)947-8878. Bd. Chmn. Clarence L. Coleman, Jr.; Pres. Alan V. Stone. Seeks to advance the universal principles of a Judaism free of nationalism, and the national, civic, cultural, and social integration into American institutions of Americans of Jewish faith. *Issues of the American Council for Judaism; Special Interest Report.*

AMERICAN JEWISH ALTERNATIVES TO ZIONISM, INC. (1968). 501 Fifth Ave., Suite 2015, NYC 10017. (212)557-5410. Pres. Elmer Berger; V.-Pres. Mrs. Arthur Gutman. Applies Jewish values of justice and humanity to the Arab-Israel conflict in the Middle East; rejects nationality attachment of Jews, particularly American Jews, to the State of Israel as self-segregating, inconsistent with American constitutional concepts of individual citizenship and separation of church and state, and as being a principal obstacle to Middle East peace. *Report.*

AMERICAN JEWISH COMMITTEE (1906). Institute of Human Relations, 165 E. 56 St., NYC 10022. (212)751-4000. Pres. Sholom D. Comay; Exec. V.-Pres. Ira Silverman. Seeks to prevent infraction of civil and religious rights of Jews in any part of the world; to advance the cause of human rights for people of all races, creeds, and nationalities; to interpret the position of Israel to the American public; and to help

---

[1] The information in this directory is based on replies to questionnaires circulated by the editors.

American Jews maintain and enrich their Jewish identity and, at the same time, achieve full integration in American life. Includes Jacob and Hilda Blaustein Center for Human Relations, William E. Wiener Oral History Library, William Petschek National Jewish Family Center, Jacob Blaustein Institute for the Advancement of Human Rights, Institute on American Jewish-Israeli Relations. AMERICAN JEWISH YEAR BOOK (with Jewish Publication Society); *Commentary; Present Tense; AJC Journal; Capital Update.* Published in Israel: *Alon Yedi'ot,* a monthly bulletin of the Institute on American Jewish-Israeli Relations.

AMERICAN JEWISH CONGRESS (1918). Stephen Wise Congress House, 15 E. 84 St., NYC 10028. (212)879-4500. Pres. Robert K. Lifton; Exec. Dir. Henry Siegman. Works to foster the creative cultural survival of the Jewish people; to help Israel develop in peace, freedom, and security; to eliminate all forms of racial and religious bigotry; to advance civil rights, protect civil liberties, defend religious freedom, and safeguard the separation of church and state. *Congress Monthly; Judaism; Boycott Report; National Report.*

ANTI-DEFAMATION LEAGUE OF B'NAI B'RITH (1913). 823 United Nations Plaza, NYC 10017. (212)490-2525. Chmn. Burton S. Levinson; Dir. Abraham H. Foxman. Seeks to combat anti-Semitism and to secure justice and fair treatment for all citizens through law, education, and community relations. *ADL Bulletin; Face to Face; Fact Finding Report; International Reports; Law Notes; Rights; Law; Research and Evaluation Report; Discriminations Report; Litigation Docket; Dimensions; Middle East Notebook; Nuestro Encuentro.*

ASSOCIATION OF JEWISH CENTER WORKERS (1918). c/o JCC, 3505 Mayfield Rd., Cleveland Heights, OH 44118 (216)382-4000. Pres. Avrum I. Cohen; Treas. Alan S. Goldberg. Seeks to enhance the standards, techniques, practices, scope, and public understanding of Jewish Community Center and kindred agency work. *Kesher.*

ASSOCIATION OF JEWISH COMMUNITY RELATIONS WORKERS(1950). 443 Park Ave. S., 11th fl., NYC 10016. Pres. Jerome Levinrad. Aims to stimulate higher standards of professional practice in Jewish community relations; encourages research and training toward that end; conducts educational programs and seminars; aims to encourage cooperation between community relations workers and those working in other areas of Jewish communal service.

CENTER FOR JEWISH COMMUNITY STUDIES (1970). 1017 Gladfelter Hall, Temple University, Philadelphia, PA 19122. (215)787-1459. Jerusalem office: Jerusalem Center for Public Affairs. Pres. Daniel J. Elazar. Worldwide policy-studies institute devoted to the study of Jewish community organization, political thought, and public affairs, past and present, in Israel and throughout the world. Publishes original articles, essays, and monographs; maintains library, archives, and reprint series. *Jerusalem Letter/Viewpoints; Survey of Arab Affairs.*

COMMISSION ON SOCIAL ACTION OF REFORM JUDAISM (1953, under the auspices of the Union of American Hebrew Congregations). 838 Fifth Ave., NYC 10021. (212)249-0100. Chmn. Harris Gilbert; Dir. Albert Vorspan; Assoc. Dir. Rabbi David Saperstein. Develops materials to assist Reform synagogues in setting up social-action programs relating the principles of Judaism to contemporary social problems; assists congregations in studying the moral and religious implications in social issues such as civil rights, civil liberties, church-state relations; guides congregational social-action committees. *Briefings.*

CONFERENCE OF PRESIDENTS OF MAJOR AMERICAN JEWISH ORGANIZATIONS (1955). 515 Park Ave., NYC 10022. (212)-752-1616. Chmn. Seymour D. Reich; Exec. Dir. Malcolm Hoenlein. Coordinates the activities of 45 major American Jewish organizations as they relate to American-Israeli affairs and problems affecting Jews in other lands. *Annual report; Middle East Memo.*

CONSULTATIVE COUNCIL OF JEWISH ORGANIZATIONS-CCJO (1946). 420 Lexington Ave., Suite 1733, NYC 10170. (212)808-5437. Pres.'s Aldolphe Steg, Clemens Nathan, Joseph Nuss; Sec.-Gen. Warren Green. A nongovernmental organization in consultative status with the UN, UNESCO, ILO,UNICEF, and the Council of Europe; cooperates and consults with, advises and renders assistance to the Economic and Social Council of the UN on all problems relating to human rights and economic, social, cultural, educational, and related matters pertaining to Jews.

COORDINATING BOARD OF JEWISH ORGANIZATIONS (1947). 1640 Rhode Island Ave., NW, Washington, DC 20036. (202)-857–6545. Pres. Seymour D. Reich (B'nai B'rith), Leonard Kopelowitz (Board of Deputies of British Jews), David K. Mann (South African Jewish Board of Deputies); Exec. V.-Pres. Thomas Neumann (U.S.); Dir. Internatl. Council Warren Eisenberg. As an organization in consultative status with the Economic and Social Council of the UN, represents the three constituents (B'nai B'rith, the Board of Deputies of British Jews, and the South African Jewish Board of Deputies) in the appropriate UN bodies for the purpose of promoting human rights, with special attention to combating persecution or discrimination on grounds of race, religion, or origin.

COUNCIL OF JEWISH ORGANIZATIONS IN CIVIL SERVICE, INC. (1948). 45 E. 33 St., Rm. 604, NYC 10016. (212)689–2015. Pres. Louis Weiser. Supports merit system; encourages recruitment of Jewish youth to government service; member of Coalition to Free Soviet Jews, NY Jewish Community Relations Council, NY Metropolitan Coordinating Council on Jewish Poverty, Jewish Labor Committee, America-Israel Friendship League. *Council Digest.*

INTERNATIONAL CONFERENCE OF JEWISH COMMUNAL SERVICE (*see* World Conference of Jewish Communal Service)

JEWISH LABOR COMMITTEE (1934). Atran Center for Jewish Culture, 25 E. 21 St., NYC 10010. (212)477–0707. Pres. Herb Magidson; Exec. Dir. Martin Lapan. Serves as liaison between the Jewish community and the trade union movement; works with the AFL-CIO to combat anti-Semitism and engender support for the State of Israel and Soviet Jewry; strengthen support within the Jewish community for the social goals and programs of the labor movement; supports Yiddish cultural institutions. *Jewish Labor Review; Alumni Newsletter.*

———, NATIONAL TRADE UNION COUNCIL FOR HUMAN RIGHTS (1956). Atran Center for Jewish Culture, 25 E. 21 St., NYC 10010. (212)477–0707. Chmn. Sol Hoffman; Exec. Sec. Michael Perry. Works with trade unions on programs and issues affecting both labor and the Jewish community.

JEWISH PEACE FELLOWSHIP (1941). Box 271, Nyack, NY 10960. (914)358–4601. Pres. Rabbi Philip Bentley; Sec. Naomi Goodman. Unites those who believe that Jewish ideals and experience provide inspiration for a nonviolent philosophy and way of life; offers draft counseling, especially for conscientious objection based on Jewish "religious training and belief"; encourages Jewish community to become more knowledgeable, concerned, and active in regard to the war/peace problem. *Shalom/ Jewish Peace Letter.*

JEWISH WAR VETERANS OF THE UNITED STATES OF AMERICA (1896). 1811 R St., NW, Washington, DC 20009. (202)265–6280. Natl. Exec. Dir. Steven Shaw. Seeks to foster true allegiance to the United States; to combat bigotry and prevent defamation of Jews; to encourage the doctrine of universal liberty, equal rights, and full justice for all; to cooperate with and support existing educational institutions and establish new ones; to foster the education of ex-servicemen, ex-servicewomen, and members in the ideals and principles of Americanism. *Jewish Veteran.*

———, NATIONAL MEMORIAL, INC. (1958). 1811 R St., NW, Washington, DC 20009. (202)265–6280. Pres. Robert Zweiman; Museum Dir. Mark Dreyfuss. Operates a museum. and archives commemorating the activities and service of American Jews in the armed forces of the U.S. *Routes to Roots.*

NATIONAL CONFERENCE ON SOVIET JEWRY (formerly AMERICAN JEWISH CONFERENCE ON SOVIET JEWRY) (1964; reorg. 1971). 10 E. 40 St., Suite 907, NYC 10016. (212)679–6122. Chmn. Shoshana Cardin; Acting Natl. Dir. Myrna Shinbaum. Coordinating agency for major national Jewish organizations and local community groups in the U.S., acting on behalf of Soviet Jewry through public education and social action; stimulates all segments of the community to maintain an interest in the problems of Soviet Jews by publishing reports and special pamphlets, sponsoring special programs and projects, organizing public meetings and forums. *Newsbreak; annual report; action and program kits; Wrap-Up Leadership Report.*

———, SOVIET JEWRY RESEARCH BUREAU. Chmn. Charlotte Jacobson. Organized by NCSJ to monitor emigration trends. Primary task is the accumulation, evaluation, and processing of information regarding Soviet Jews, especially those who apply for emigration.

NATIONAL JEWISH COALITION (1979). 415 2nd St., NE, Suite 100, Washington, DC 20002. (202)547-7701. Hon. Chmn. Max M. Fisher; Natl. Chmn. Richard J. Fox. Promotes Jewish involvement in Republican politics; sensitizes Republican leaders to the concerns of the American Jewish community; promotes principles of free enterprise, a strong national defense, and an internationalist foreign policy. *NJC Bulletin; NJC for the Record.*

NATIONAL JEWISH COMMISSION ON LAW AND PUBLIC AFFAIRS (COLPA) (1965). 450 Seventh Ave., Suite 2203, NYC 10123. (212)563-0100. Pres. Allen L. Rothenberg; Exec. Dir. Dennis Rapps. Voluntary association of attorneys whose purpose is to represent the observant Jewish community on legal, legislative, and public affairs matters.

NATIONAL JEWISH COMMUNITY RELATIONS ADVISORY COUNCIL (1944). 443 Park Ave. S., 11th fl., NYC 10016. (212)684-6950. Chmn. Michael A. Pelavin; Sec. Barry Ungar; Exec. V.-Chmn. Albert D. Chernin. National coordinating body for the field of Jewish community relations, comprising 11 national and 114 local Jewish community relations agencies. Promotes understanding of Israel and the Middle East; freedom for Soviet Jews; equal status for Jews and other groups in American society. Through the NJCRAC's work, its constituent organizations seek agreement on policies, strategies, and programs for effective utilization of their resources for common ends. *Joint Program Plan for Jewish Community Relations.*

NEW JEWISH AGENDA (1980). 64 Fulton St., #1100, NYC 10038. (212)227-5885. Cochmn. Bria Chakofsky, Rabbi Marc Gruber; Codirs. Annette Jaffe, Clare Kinberg. Founded as "a progressive voice in the Jewish community and a Jewish voice among progressives." Works for nuclear disarmament, peace in Central America, Arab-Jewish reconciliation, feminism, and economic justice, and against anti-Semitism and racism. *Quarterly newsletter.*

SHALOM CENTER (1983). 7318 Germantown Ave., Philadelphia, PA 19119. (215)886-1510. Pres. Ira Silverman; Bd. Chmn. Viki List; Exec. Dir. Arthur Waskow. National resource and organizing center for Jewish perspectives on preventing nuclear holocaust and ending nuclear arms race. Trains community organizers, holds conferences, assists local Jewish committees and coalitions on nuclear weapons issues. Sponsors Sukkat Shalom. Provides school curricula, sermon materials, legislative reports, adult-education texts, and media for Jewish use. *Shalom Report.*

STUDENT STRUGGLE FOR SOVIET JEWRY, INC. (1964). 210 W. 91 St., NYC 10024. (212)799-8900. Natl. Dir. Jacob Birnbaum; Natl. Coord. Glenn Richter; Chmn. Avraham Weiss. Provides information and action guidance to adult and student organizations, communities, and schools throughout the U.S. and Canada; assists Soviet Jews by publicity campaigns; helps Soviet Jews in the U.S.; aids Rumanian Jews seeking emigration; maintains speakers bureau and research documents. *Soviet Jewry Action Newsletter.*

UNION OF COUNCILS FOR SOVIET JEWS (1970). 1819 H St., NW., Suite 410, Washington, DC 20006. (202)775-9770. Pres. Pamela Braun Cohen; Natl. Dir. Micah H. Naftalin. A confederation of 45 grass-roots organizations established in support of rescuing Soviet Jewry. Works on behalf of Soviet Jews through public education, representations to the administration and Congress, letter-writing assistance, news disseminaion, tourist briefing, speakers bureau, Adopt-A-Family, Adopt-A-Prisoner, Bar/Bat Mitzvah twinning, Tarbut, congressional vigil, congressional briefings, and publications programming; affiliations include Soviet Jewry Legal Advocacy Center and Medical Mobilization for Soviet Jewry. *UCSJ Quarterly Report; Refusenik Update; Congressional Handbook for Soviet Jewry.*

WORLD CONFERENCE OF JEWISH COMMUNAL SERVICE(1966). 15 E. 26 St., NYC 10010. (212)532-2526. Pres. Irving Kessler; Sec.-Gen. Solomon H. Green. Established by worldwide Jewish communal

## NATIONAL JEWISH ORGANIZATIONS / 449

workers to strengthen their understanding of each other's programs and to communicate with colleagues in order to enrich the quality of their work. Conducts quadrennial international conferences in Jerusalem and periodic regional meetings. *Proceedings of international conferences; newsletter.*

WORLD JEWISH CONGRESS (1936; org. in U.S. 1939). 501 Madison Ave., 17th fl., NYC 10022. (212) 755-5770. Pres. Edgar M. Bronfman; Chmn. N. Amer. Branch Leo Kolber (Montreal); Chmn. Amer. Sect. Rabbi Wolfe Kelman; Sec.-Gen. Israel Singer; Exec. Dir. Elan Steinberg. Seeks to intensify bonds of world Jewry with Israel as central force in Jewish life; to strengthen solidarity among Jews everywhere and secure their rights, status, and interests as individuals and communities; to encourage development of Jewish social, religious, and cultural life throughout the world and coordinate efforts by Jewish communities and organizations to cope with any Jewish problem; to work for human rights generally. Represents its affiliated organizations—most representative bodies of Jewish communities in more than 70 countries and 32 national organizations in Amer. section—at UN, OAS, UNESCO, Council of Europe, ILO, UNICEF, and other governmental, intergovernmental, and international authorities. Publications (including those by Institute of Jewish Affairs, London): *Christian Jewish Relations; Coloquio; News and Views; Boletín Informativo OJI; Batfutsot; Gesher; Patterns of Prejudice; Soviet Jewish Affairs.*

### CULTURAL

AMERICAN ACADEMY FOR JEWISH RESEARCH (1920). 3080 Broadway, NYC 10027. (212)678-8864. Pres. Isaac Barzilay; V.-Pres. David Weiss Halivni; Treas. Arthur Hyman. Encourages Jewish learning and research; holds annual or semiannual meeting; awards grants for the publication of scholarly works. *Proceedings of the American Academy for Jewish Research; Texts and Studies; Monograph Series.*

AMERICAN BIBLICAL ENCYCLOPEDIA SOCIETY (1930). 24 W. Maple Ave., Monsey, NY 10952. (914)352-4609. Exec. V.-Pres. Irving Fredman; Author-Ed. Rabbi M. M. Kasher. Fosters biblical-talmudical research; sponsors and publishes *Torah Shelemah* (Heb., 39 vols.), *Encyclopedia of Biblical Interpretation* (Eng., 9 vols.), *Divrei Menachem* (Heb., 4vols.), and related publications. *Noam.*

AMERICAN JEWISH HISTORICAL SOCIETY (1892). 2 Thornton Rd., Waltham, MA 02154. (617)891-8110. Pres. Phil David Fine; Dir. Bernard Wax. Collects, catalogues, publishes, and displays material on the history of the Jews in America; serves as an information center for inquiries on American Jewish history; maintains archives of original source material on American Jewish history; sponsors lectures and exhibitions; makes available historic Yiddish films and audiovisual material. *American Jewish History; Heritage.*

AMERICAN JEWISH PRESS ASSOCIATION (1943). c/o Atlanta Jewish Times, Suite 365, 1575 Northside Dr. NW, Atlanta, GA 30318. (404)355-6139. Pres. Vida Goldgar. Natl. Admin. Off.: 11312 Old Club Rd., Rockville, MD 20852-4537. (301)881-4537. Exec. Dir. L. Malcolm Rodman. Seeks the advancement of Jewish-journalism and the maintenance of a stong Jewish press in the U.S. and Canada; encourages the attainment of the highest editorial and business standards; sponsors workshops, services for members. *Membership bulletin newsletter; Roster of Members.*

AMERICAN SOCIETY FOR JEWISH MUSIC (1974). 155 Fifth Ave., NYC 10010. (212)-533-2601. Pres. Paul Kavon; V.-Pres. David Lefkowitz; Sec. Hadássah B. Markson. Seeks to raise standards of composition and performance in Jewish liturgical and secular music; encourages research in all areas of Jewish music; publishes scholarly journal; presents programs and sponsors performances of new and rarely heard works and encourages their recording; commissions new works of Jewish interest. *Musica Judaica.*

ASSOCIATION FOR THE SOCIAL SCIENTIFIC STUDY OF JEWRY (1971). City University of New York, 33 W. 42 St., NYC 10036. (212)642-2180. Pres. Rela Geffen Monson; V.-Pres. Steven M. Cohen; Sec.-Treas. Esther Fleishman. Arranges academic sessions and facilitates communication among social scientists studying Jewry through meetings, newsletter, and related materials. *Contemporary Jewry; ASSSJ Newsletter.*

ASSOCIATION OF JEWISH BOOK PUBLISHERS (1962). 838 Fifth Ave., NYC 10021. (212)249-0100. Pres. Charles D. Lieber. As a nonprofit group, provides a forum for discussion of mutual problems by publishers, authors, and other individuals and institutions concerned with books of Jewish interest. Provides national and international exhibit opportunities for Jewish books. *Combined Jewish Book Catalog.*

ASSOCIATION OF JEWISH GENEALOGICAL SOCIETIES 1485 Teaneck Rd., Teaneck, NJ 07666. (201)837-2700. Pres. Gary Mokotoff. Confederation of over 30 Jewish Genealogical Societies (JGS) in the U.S. and Canada. Encourages Jews to research their family history, promotes membership in the various JGS, acts as representative of organized Jewish genealogy, implements projects of interest to persons researching their Jewish family history. Annual conference where members learn and exchange ideas. Each local JGS publishes its own newsletter.

ASSOCIATION OF JEWISH LIBRARIES (1965). c/o National Foundation for Jewish Culture, 330 Seventh Ave., 21st fl., NYC 10001. (212)427-1000. Pres. Marcia W. Posner; V.-Pres. Elect Linda Lerman. Seeks to promote and improve services and professional standards in Jewish libraries; disseminates Jewish library information and guidance; promotes publication of literature in the field; encourages the establishment of Jewish libraries and collections of Judaica and the choice of Judaica librarianship as a profession; cocertifies Jewish libraries (with Jewish Book Council). *AJL Newsletter; Judaica Librarianship.*

B'NAI B'RITH KLUTZNICK MUSEUM (1956). 1640 Rhode Island Ave., NW, Washington, DC 20036. (202)857-6583. Chmn. Museum & Art Comm., Murray H. Shusterman; Dir. Gayle Weiss. A center of Jewish art and history in nation's capital, maintains temporary and permanent exhibition galleries, permanent collection of Jewish ceremonial and folk art, B'nai B'rith International reference archive, outdoor sculpture garden, and museum shop. Provides exhibitions, tours, educational programs, research assistance, and tourist information. *Semiannual newsletter; permanent collection catalogue; exhibition brochures.*

CENTER FOR HOLOCAUST STUDIES, DOCUMENTATION & RESEARCH (1974). 1610 Ave. J, Brooklyn, NY 11230. (718)338-6494. Dir. Yaffa Eliach. Collects and preserves documents and memorabilia, oral histories, and literary works on the Holocaust period for purposes of documentation and research; arranges lectures, exhibits, drama and music performances, and exhibitions of Holocaust art; conducts outreach programs to schools; maintains speakers bureau, oral history publication series, and audiovisual department. *Newsletter.*

CENTRAL YIDDISH CULTURE ORGANIZATION (CYCO), INC. (1943). 25 E. 21 St., 3rd fl., NYC 10010. (212)505-8305. Mgr. Jacob Schneidman. Promotes, publishes, and distributes Yiddish books; publishes catalogues.

CONFERENCE ON JEWISH SOCIAL STUDIES, INC. (formerly CONFERENCE ON JEWISH RELATIONS, INC.) (1939). 2112 Broadway, Rm. 206, NYC 10023. (212)724-5336. Hon. Pres. Salo W. Baron. Publishes scientific studies on Jews in the modern world, dealing with such aspects as anti-Semitism, demography, economic stratification, history, philosophy, and political developments. *Jewish Social Studies.*

CONGREGATION BINA (1981). 600 W. End Ave., Suite 1-C, NYC 10024. (212)873-4261. Pres. Elijah E. Jhirad; Exec. V.-Pres. Joseph Moses; Hon. Pres. Samuel M. Daniel. Serves the religious, cultural, charitable, and philanthropic needs of the Children of Israel who originated in India and now reside in the U.S. Works to foster and preserve the ancient traditions, customs, liturgy, music, and folklore of Indian Jewry and to maintain needed institutions. *Kol Bina.*

HEBREW ARTS SCHOOL (1952). 129 W. 67 St., NYC 10023. (212)362-8060. Chmn. Lewis Kruger; Pres. Alvin E. Friedman; Dir. Lydia Kontos. Offers instruction in music, dance, art, and theater to children and adults, combining Western culture with Jewish heritage. Presents in its Merkin Concert Hall and Ann Goodman Recital Hall frequent performances of Jewish and general music by leading artists and ensembles. *Newsletter,* bimonthly calendars.

NATIONAL JEWISH ORGANIZATIONS / 451

HEBREW CULTURE FOUNDATION (1955). 515 Park Ave., NYC 10022. (212)752-0600. Chmn. Milton R. Konvitz; Sec. Herman L. Sainer. Sponsors the introduction and strengthening of Hebrew language and literature courses in institutions of higher learning in the United States.

HISTADRUTH IVRITH OF AMERICA (1916; reorg. 1922). 1841 Broadway, NYC 10023. (212)581-5151. Presidium: Boris Shteinshleifer, Matthew Mosenkis, Rabbi Joseph P. Sternstein; Exec. V.-Pres. Aviva Barzel. Emphasizes the primacy of Hebrew in Jewish life, culture, and education; aims to disseminate knowledge of written and spoken Hebrew in the Diaspora, thus building a cultural bridge between the State of Israel and Jewish communities throughout the world. *Hadoar; Lamishpaha.*

HOLOCAUST CENTER OF THE UNITED JEWISH FEDERATION OF GREATER PITTSBURGH (1980). 242 McKee Pl., Pittsburgh, PA 15213. (412)682-7111. Chmn. Jack Gordon; Pres. UJF Leon L. Netzer. Develops programs and provides resources to further understanding of the Holocaust and its impact on civilization. Maintains a library, archive; provides speakers, educational materials; organizes community programs.

HOLOCAUST MEMORIAL RESOURCE & EDUCATION CENTER OF FLORIDA (1981). 851 N. Maitland Ave., Maitland, FL 32751. (407)628-0555. Pres. Dr. Earl Scarbeary; Exec. V.-Pres. Tess Wise. An interfaith educational center devoted to teaching the lessons of the Holocaust. Houses permanent multimedia educational exhibit; maintains library of books, videotapes, films, and other visuals to serve the entire educational establishment, offers lectures, teacher training, and other activities. *Newsletter.*

JEWISH ACADEMY OF ARTS AND SCIENCES, INC. (1926).888 Seventh Ave., Suite 403, NYC 10106. (212)757-1627. Act. Pres. Milton Handler; Hon. Pres. Abraham I. Katsh; Dir. Benjamin Saxe. An honor society of Jews who have attained distinction in the arts, sciences, professions, and communal endeavors. Encourages the advancement of knowledge; stimulates scholarship, with particular reference to Jewish life and thought; recognition by election to membership and/or fellowship; publishes papers delivered at annual convocations.

JEWISH MUSEUM (1904, under auspices of JewishTheological Seminary of America). 1109 Fifth Ave., NYC 10128.(212)860-1889. Dir. Joan H. Rosenbaum; Chmn. Bd. of Trustees Morris W. Offit. Repository of the largest collection of Judaica—paintings, prints, photographs, sculpture, coins, medals, antiquities, textiles, and other decorative arts—in the Western Hemisphere. Includes the National Jewish Archive of Broadcasting and the Tobe Pascher Workshop for the design and creation of ritual and ceremonial art objects. Tours of special exhibitions and permanent installations; lectures, film showings, and concerts; special programs for children. *Special exhibition catalogues.*

JEWISH PUBLICATION SOCIETY (1888). 1930 Chestnut St., Philadelphia, PA 19103. (215)564-5925. Pres. Edward E. Elson; Exec. V.-Pres. Richard Malina; Editor Sheila Segal. Publishes and disseminates books of Jewish interest for adults and children; titles include contemporary literature, classics, art, religion, biographies, poetry, and history. AMERICAN JEWISH YEAR BOOK (with American Jewish Committee).

JUDAH L. MAGNES MUSEUM—JEWISH MUSEUM OF THE WEST (1962). 2911 Russell St., Berkeley, CA 94705. (415)849-2710.Pres. Jacques Reutlinger; Exec. Dir. Seymour Fromer. Serves as museum and library, combining historical and literary materials illustrating Jewish life in the Bay Area, the Western states, and around the world; provides archives of world Jewish history and Jewish art; repository of historical documents intended for scholarly use; changing exhibits; facilities open to the general public. *Magnes News; special exhibition catalogues.*

JUDAICA CAPTIONED FILM CENTER, INC. (1983). PO Box 21439, Baltimore, MD 21208-0439. Voice (after 4 PM) (301)922-0905; TDD (301)655-6767. Pres. Lois Lilienfeld Weiner. Developing a comprehensive library of captioned and subtitled films and tapes on Jewish subjects; distributes them to organizations serving the hearing-impaired, including mainstream classes and senior adult groups, on a free-loan, handling/shipping-charge-only basis. *Quarterly newsletter.*

JWB JEWISH BOOK COUNCIL (1943). 15 E. 26 St., NYC 10010. (212)532-4949. Pres. Abraham J. Kremer; Dir. Paula Gribetz Gottlieb. Promotes knowledge of Jewish books through dissemination of booklists, program materials; sponsors Jewish Book Month; presents literary awards and library citations; cooperates with publishers of Jewish books. *Jewish Book Annual; Jewish Books in Review; Jewish Book World.*

JWB JEWISH MUSIC COUNCIL (1944). 15 E. 26 St., NYC 10010. (212)532-4949. Chmn. Leonard Kaplan; Coord. Paula Gribetz Gottlieb. Promotes Jewish music activities nationally; annually sponsors and promotes the Jewish Music season; encourages participation on a community basis. *Jewish Music Notes* and numerous music resource publications for national distribution.

JWB LECTURE BUREAU (1922). 15 E. 26 St., NYC 10010-1579. (212)532-4949. Dir. Sesil Lissberger; Chmn. Mark S. Mandell. Provides, and assists in the selection of, lecturers, performing artists, and exhibits for local Jewish communal organizations; advises on program design; makes booking arrangements. *The Jewish Arts; Learning for Jewish Living—A Listing of Lecturers; Available Lecturers from Israel; Lecturers on the Holocaust.*

LEAGUE FOR YIDDISH, INC. (1979). 200 W. 72 St., Suite 40, NYC 10023. (212)787-6675. Pres. Sadie Turak; Exec. Dir. Mordkhe Schaechter. Promotes the development and use of Yiddish as a living language. *Afn Shvel.*

LEO BAECK INSTITUTE, INC. (1955). 129 E. 73 St., NYC 10021. (212)744-6400. Pres. Yosef Haim Yerushalmi; Sec. Fred Grubel. A library, archive, and research center for the history of German-speaking Jewry. Offers lectures, exhibits, faculty seminars; publishes a series of monographs, yearbooks, and journals. *LBI Bulletin; LBI News; LBI Year Book.*

MARTYRS MEMORIAL & MUSEUM OF THE HOLOCAUST (1963; reorg. 1978). 6505 Wilshire Blvd., Los Angeles, CA 90048.(213)651-3175. Chmn. Jack I. Salzberg; Dir. Michael Nutkiewicz. Seeks to commemorate the events and victims of the Holocaust and to educate against future reoccurrences; maintains permanent and traveling exhibits, sponsors public lectures, offers school curricula and teacher training. West Coast representative of Israel's Yad Vashem; affiliated with the Jewish Federation Council of Greater Los Angeles.

MEMORIAL FOUNDATION FOR JEWISH CULTURE, INC. (1964). 15 E. 26 St., NYC 10010. (212)679-4074. Pres. Philip M. Klutznick; Exec. Dir. Jerry Hochbaum. Through the grants that it awards, encourages Jewish scholarship and Jewish education, supports communities that are struggling to maintain their Jewish identity, makes possible the training of Jewish men and women for professional careers in communal service in Jewishly deprived communities, and stimulates the documentation, commemoration, and teaching of the Holocaust.

NATIONAL FOUNDATION FOR JEWISH CULTURE (1960). 330 Seventh Ave., 21st fl., NYC 10001. (212)629-0500. Pres. George M. Zeltzer; Exec. V.-Pres. Abraham Atik. Provides consultation and support to Jewish community organizations, educational and cultural institutions, and individuals for Jewish cultural activities; awards fellowships and publication grants to individuals preparing for careers in Jewish scholarship;presents awards for creative efforts in Jewish cultural arts and for Jewish programming in small and intermediate communities; publishes guides to national Jewish cultural resources, traveling exhibitions, and plays; serves as clearinghouse of information on American Jewish culture; administers Joint Cultural Appeal on behalf of national cultural organizations; administers Council of Archives and Research Libraries in Jewish Studies, Council of American Jewish Museums, and Council of Jewish Theaters.

NATIONAL HEBREW CULTURE COUNCIL (1952). 14 E. 4th St, NYC 10003. (212)-674-8412. Cultivates the study of Hebrew as a modern language in American public high schools and colleges, providing guidance to community groups and public educational authorities; annually administers National Voluntary Examination in Hebrew Culture and Knowledge of Israel in the public high schools, and conducts summer seminar and tour of Israel for teachers and other educational personnel of the public school system, in cooperation with

Hebrew University and WZO. *Hebrew in Colleges and Universities.*

NATIONAL YIDDISH BOOK CENTER (1980). Old East Street School, PO Box 969, Amherst, MA 01004. (413)256-1241. Pres. Gail L. Perlman; Exec. Dir. Aaron Lansky. Collects used and out-of-print Yiddish books to distribute to individuals and libraries worldwide; provides resources to make Yiddish culture accessible to a new generation. *Yiddish Book News; Der Pakn-treger/The Book Peddler; Yiddish Bibliographic Notes.*

NEW YORK HOLOCAUST MEMORIAL COMMISSION (1982). 342 Madison Ave., Suite 717, NYC 10173. (212)687-5020. Cochmn.George Klein, Hon. Robert M. Morgenthau; Exec. Dir. David L. Blumenfeld; Museum Dir. David Altshuler. The commission is in the process of creating "A Living Memorial to the Holocaust-Museum of Jewish Heritage" in Battery Park City (lower Manhattan). The museum will contain permanent exhibitions on four themes—The World Before, The Holocaust, The Aftermath, and Renewal in America—as well as a state-of-the-art Learning Center and a varied program of changing exhibitions. *Newsletter.*

RESEARCH FOUNDATION FOR JEWISH IMMIGRATION, INC.(1971). 570 Seventh Ave., NYC 10018. (212)921-3871. Pres. Curt C. Silberman; Sec. and Coord. of Research Herbert A. Strauss; Archivist Dennis E. Rohrbaugh. Studies and records the history of the migration and acculturation of Jewish Nazi persecutees in various resettlement countries worldwide, with special emphasis on the American experience. *International Biographical Dictionary of Central European Emigrés, 1933-1945; Jewish Immigrants of the Nazi Period in the USA.*

ST. LOUIS CENTER FOR HOLOCAUST STUDIES (1977). 12 Millstone Campus Dr., St. Louis, MO 63146. (314)432-0020. Chmn.Fred Katz; Dir. Rabbi Robert Sternberg. Develops programs and provides resources and educational materials to further an understanding of the Holocaust and its impact on civilization. *Audio Visual and Curriculum Resources Guide.*

SEPHARDIC HOUSE (1978). 8 W. 70 St., NYC 10023. (212)873-0300. Exec. Dir. Janice Etzkowitz Ovadiah; Bd. Chmn. Rabbi Marc D. Angel. Conducts research and promotes Sephardic culture through courses, lectures, concerts, conferences, film programs, etc.; has an active publication program. *Sephardic House Newsletter.*

SKIRBALL MUSEUM, Los Angeles, CA (*see* Hebrew Union College-Jewish Institute of Religion)

SOCIETY FOR THE HISTORY OF CZECHOSLOVAK JEWS, INC. (1961). 87-08 Santiago St., Holliswood, NY 11423. (718)468-6844. Pres. and Ed. Lewis Weiner; Sec. Joseph Abeles. Studies the history of Czechoslovak Jews, collects material and disseminates information through the publication of books and pamphlets. *The Jews of Czechoslovakia* (3 vols); *Review; Review II.*

U.S. HOLOCAUST MEMORIAL COUNCIL (1980). 2000 L St., NW, Suite 588, Washington, DC 20036. (202)653-9220. Chmn. Harvey M. Meyerhoff. Established by Congress in 1980 to plan and build the U.S. Holocaust Memorial Museum in Washington, D.C., and to encourage and sponsor observances of an annual, national, civic commemoration of the Holocaust known as the Days of Remembrance. Also engages in Holocaust education and research programs. Consists of 55 members of all faiths and backgrounds appointed by the president, plus five U.S. senators and five members of the House of Representatives. *Newsletter* (monthly); *Directory of Holocaust Institutions* (annual).

YESHIVA UNIVERSITY MUSEUM (1973). 2520 Amsterdam Ave., NYC 10033. (212)-960-5390. Chmn. Bd. of Govs. Erica Jesselson; Dir. Sylvia A. Herskowitz. Collects, preserves, and interprets Jewish life and culture through changing exhibitions of ceremonial objects, rare books and documents, synagogue architecture, paintings, and decorative arts. Contemporary artists are featured. Special events and holiday workshops for adults and children. Guided tours are offered. *Seasonal calendar; special exhibition catalogues.*

YIDDISHER KULTUR FARBAND—YKUF (1937). 1133 Broadway, Rm. 1023, NYC 10010. (212)691-0708. Pres. and Editor. Itche Goldberg. Publishes a monthly magazine and books by contemporary and classical Jewish writers; conducts cultural forums; exhibits works by contemporary Jewish artists and materials of Jewish historical value; organizes reading circles. *Yiddishe Kultur.*

YIVO INSTITUTE FOR JEWISH RESEARCH, INC. (1925). 1048 Fifth Ave., NYC 10028. (212)535-6700. Chmn. Dr. Arnold Richards; Exec. Dir. Samuel Norich. Engages in social and humanistic research pertaining to East European Jewish life; maintains library and archives which provide a major international, national, and New York resource used by institutions, individual scholars, and laymen; trains graduate students in Yiddish, East European, and American Jewish studies; offers exhibits, conferences, public programs; publishes books. *Yedies fun Yivo—News of the Yivo; Yidishe Shprakh; Yivo Annual of Jewish Social Science; Yivo Bleter.*

———, MAX WEINREICH CENTER FOR ADVANCED JEWISH STUDIES (1968). 1048 Fifth Ave., NYC 10028. (212)535-6700. Dean Deborah Dash Moore. Provides advanced-level training in Yiddish language and literature, ethnography, folklore, linguistics, and history; offers guidance on dissertation or independent research. *The Field of Yiddish; Jewish Folklore & Ethnology Newsletter.*

## OVERSEAS AID

AMERICAN ASSOCIATION FOR ETHIOPIAN JEWS (1969). 2028 P St., NW, Washington, DC 20036. (202)223-6838. Pres. Nathan Shapiro; Dir. William Recant. Informs world Jewry about the plight of Ethiopian Jews; advocates rescue of Ethiopian Jewry as a major priority; provides relief in refugee areas and Ethiopia; and helps resettlement in Israel. *Release; Newsline.*

AMERICAN FRIENDS OF THE ALLIANCE ISRAÉLITE UNIVERSELLE, INC. (1946). 420 Lexington Ave., Suite 1733, NYC 10170. (212)808-5437. Pres. Henriette Beilis; Exec. Dir. Warren Green. Participates in educational and human rights activities of the AIU and supports the Alliance System of Jewish schools, teachers' colleges, and remedial programs in Israel, North Africa, the Middle East, Europe, and Canada. *Alliance Review.*

AMERICAN JEWISH JOINT DISTRIBUTION COMMITTEE, INC.—JDC (1914). 711 Third Ave., NYC 10017. (212)687-6200. Pres. Heinz Eppler; Exec. V.-Pres. Michael Schneider. Organizes and finances rescue, relief, and rehabilitation programs for imperiled and needy Jews overseas; conducts wide range of health, welfare, rehabilitation, education programs and aid to cultural and religious institutions; programs benefiting 600,000 Jews in over 30 countries overseas. Major areas of operation are Israel, North Africa, and Europe. *Annual report; JDC World.*

AMERICAN JEWISH PHILANTHROPIC FUND (1955). 386 Park Ave. S., NYC 10016. (212)OR9-0010. Pres. Charles J. Tanenbaum. Provides resettlement assistance to Jewish refugees primarily through programs administered by the International Rescue Committee at its offices in Western Europe and the U.S.

AMERICAN ORT FEDERATION, INC.—ORGANIZATION FOR REHABILITATION THROUGH TRAINING (1924). 817 Broadway, NYC 10003. (212)677-4400. Pres. David B. Hermelin; Exec. V.-Pres. Donald H. Klein. Provides vocational/technical education to over 158,000 students at ORT schools and training centers in 18 countries, with the largest program in Israel serving 92,000 students. Teaching staff numbers 5,200. Annual cost of program is about $119 million. *American ORT Federation Bulletin; ORT Yearbook.*

———, AMERICAN AND EUROPEAN FRIENDS OF ORT (1941). 817 Broadway, NYC 10003. (212)677-4400. Pres. Simon Jaglom; Hon. Chmn. Jacques Zwibak; Deputy Chmn. S. Alexander Strasun. Promotes the ORT idea among Americans of European extraction; supports the Litton ORT Auto-Mechanics School in Jerusalem and the ORT School of Engineering in Jerusalem. Promotes the work of the American ORT Federation.

———, AMERICAN LABOR ORT (1937). 817 Broadway, NYC 10003. (212)677-4400. Chmn. Sam Fine. Promotes ORT program of vocational training among Jews through activities of the ILGWU and the Amalgamated Clothing & Textile Workers Union. Promotes the work of the American ORT Federation.

———, BUSINESS AND PROFESSIONAL ORT (1937). 817 Broadway, NYC 10003. (212)-677-4400. Pres. Rose Seidel Kalich. Promotes work of American ORT Federation.

———, NATIONAL ORT LEAGUE (1914). 817 Broadway, NYC 10003. (212)677-4400. Pres. Judah Wattenberg; First V.-Pres. Tibor Waldman. Promotes ORT idea among Jewish fraternal *landsmanshaften* and individuals. Promotes the work of the American ORT Federation.

———, WOMEN'S AMERICAN ORT (1927). 315 Park Ave. S., NYC 10010. (212)505-7700. Pres. Reese Feldman; Exec. V.-Pres. Nathan Gould. Represents and advances the program and philosophy of ORT among the women of the American Jewish community through membership and educational activities; materially supports the vocational training operations of World ORT; contributes to the American Jewish community by encouraging participation in ORT campaigns and through general education to help raise the level of Jewish consciousness among American Jewish women; through its American Affairs program, cooperates in efforts to improve the quality of education and vocational training in the U.S. *Women's American ORT Reporter; Close-Ups.*

CONFERENCE ON JEWISH MATERIAL CLAIMS AGAINST GERMANY, INC. (1951). 15 E. 26 St., Rm. 1355, NYC 10010. (212)-696-4944. Pres. Israel Miller; Sec. and Exec. Dir. Saul Kagan. Monitors the implementation of restitution and indemnification programs of the German Federal Republic (FRG) arising from its agreements with FRG. Administers Hardship Fund, which distributes DM 400,000,000 appropriated by FRG for Jewish Nazi victims unable to file timely claims under original indemnification laws. Also assists needy non-Jews who risked their lives to help Jewish survivors.

HIAS, INC. (HEBREW IMMIGRANT AID SOCIETY) (1880; reorg. 1954). 200 Park Ave. S., NYC 10003. (212)674-6800. Pres. Ben Zion Leuchter; Exec. V.-Pres. Karl D. Zukerman. International Jewish migration agency with headquarters in the U.S. and offices, affiliates, and representatives in Europe, Latin America, Canada, Australia, New Zealand, and Israel. Assists Jewish migrants and refugees from Eastern Europe, the Middle East, North Africa, and Latin America. Via U.S. government-funded programs, assists in the resettlement of Indo-Chinese and other refugees. *HIAS Annual Report; HIAS Reporter; Quarterly Statistical Abstract.*

JEWISH RESTITUTION SUCCESSOR ORGANIZATION (1947). 15 E. 26 St., Rm. 1355, NYC 10010. (212)696-4944. Sec. and Exec. Dir. Saul Kagan. Acts to discover, claim, receive, and assist in the recovery of Jewish heirless or unclaimed property; to utilize such assets or to provide for their utilization for the relief, rehabilitation, and resettlement of surviving victims of Nazi persecution.

NORTH AMERICAN CONFERENCE ON ETHIOPIAN JEWRY (NACOEJ) (1982). 165 E. 56 St., NYC l0022. (212)752-6340.Pres. Jonathan Giesberg; Exec. Dir. Barbara Ribakove Gordon. Provides assistance to Ethiopian Jews in Ethiopia and in Israel; informs American and other Jewish communities about their situation; works to increase involvement of world Jewish communities in assisting, visiting, and learning about Ethiopian Jews. *Lifeline* (membership newsletter).

RE'UTH WOMEN'S SOCIAL SERVICE, INC. (1937). 240 W. 98 St., NYC 10025. (212)-666-7880. Pres. Ursula Merkin; V.-Pres. Ilse Rosenbaum. Maintains in Israel subsidized housing for self-reliant older people, old-age homes for more dependent elderly, Lichtenstadter Hospital for chronically ill, subsidized meals, Golden Age clubs. *Annual journal.*

THANKS TO SCANDINAVIA, INC. (1963). 745 Fifth Ave., Rm. 603, NYC 10151. (212)-486-8600. Natl. Chmn. Victor Borge; Pres. and Exec. Off. Richard Netter. Provides scholarships and fellowships at American universities and medical centers to students and doctors from Denmark, Finland, Norway, and Sweden in appreciation of the rescue of Jews from the Holocaust. Informs current and future generations of Americans and Scandinavians of these singular examples of humanity and bravery; funds books about this chapter of history. *Annual report; books, pamphlets.*

UNITED JEWISH APPEAL, INC. (1939). 99 Park Ave., NYC 10016. (212)818-9100. Natl. Chmn. Morton A. Kornreich; Chmn. Bd. of Trustees Martin F. Stein; Pres. Stanley B. Horowitz. The annual UJA/Federation Campaign is the primary instrument for the support of humanitarian programs and social services for Jews at home and abroad. In Israel, through the Jewish Agency, campaign funds help absorb, educate, and settle new immigrants, build villages and farms in rural areas, support innovative programs for troubled and disadvantaged youth, and promote the revitalization of distressed neighborhoods. UJA/Federation funds also provide for the well-being of Jews and Jewish communities in 33 other countries around the world through the American Jewish Joint Distribution Committee. Constituent departments of the UJA include the Rabbinic Cabinet, University Programs Department, Women's Division, Young Leadership Cabinet, the Young Women's Leadership Cabinet, and the Business and Professional Women's Council.

## RELIGIOUS AND EDUCATIONAL

AGUDATH ISRAEL OF AMERICA (1922). 84 William St., NYC 10038. (212)797-9000. Pres. Rabbi Moshe Sherer; Exec. Dir. Rabbi Boruch B. Borchardt. Mobilizes Orthodox Jews to cope with Jewish problems in the spirit of the Torah; sponsors a broad range of projects aimed at enhancing religious living, education, children's welfare, protection of Jewish religious rights, outreach to the assimilated, and social services. *Jewish Observer; Dos Yiddishe Vort; Coalition.*

———, AGUDAH WOMEN OF AMERICA– N'SHEI AGUDATH ISRAEL (1940). 84 William St., NYC 10038. (212)363-8940. Presidium Esther Bohensky, Aliza Grund. Organizes Jewish women for philanthropic work in the U.S. and Israel and for intensive Torah education. Seeks to train Torah-guided Jewish mothers.

———, CHILDREN'S DIVISION—PIRCHEI AGUDATH ISRAEL (1925). 84 William St., NYC 10038 (212)797-9000. Natl. Dir. Rabbi Joshua Silbermintz; Natl. Coord. Rabbi Mordechai Mehlman. Educates Orthodox Jewish children in Torah; encourages sense of communal responsibility. Branches sponsor weekly youth groups and Jewish welfare projects. National Mishnah contests, rallies, and conventions foster unity on a national level. *Darkeinu; Leaders Guides.*

———, GIRLS' DIVISION—BNOS AGUDATH ISRAEL (1921). 84 William St., NYC 10038. (212)797-9000. Natl. Dir. Devorah Pollack. Sponsors regular weekly programs on the local level and unites girls from throughout the Torah world with extensive regional and national activities. *Newsletters.*

———, YOUNG MEN'S DIVISION—ZEIREI AGUDATH ISRAEL (1921). 84 William St., NYC 10038. (212)797-9000. Pres. Avrohom Biderman; Dir. Rabbi Labish Becker. Educates youth to see Torah as source of guidance for all issues facing Jews as individuals and as a people. Inculcates a spirit of activism through projects in religious, Torah-educational, and community-welfare fields. *Zeirei Forum; Am Hatorah; Daf Chizuk; Ohr Hakollel.*

AGUDATH ISRAEL WORLD ORGANIZATION (1912). 84 William St., NYC 10038. (212)-797-9000. Cochmn. Rabbi Moshe Sherer, Rabbi Yehudah Meir Abramowitz. Represents the interests of Orthodox Jewry on the national and international scenes. Sponsors projects to strengthen Torah life worldwide.

AMERICAN ASSOCIATION OF RABBIS (1978). 350 Fifth Ave., Suite 3308, NYC 10001. (212)244–3350. Pres. Rabbi Jacob Friedman; Sec. Rabbi Robert Chernoff. An organization of rabbis serving in pulpits, in areas of education, and in social work. *Bimonthly newsletter; quarterly journal.*

ANNENBERG RESEARCH INSTITUTE (formerly DROPSIE COLLEGE FOR HEBREW AND COGNATE LEARNING) (1907; reorg. 1986). 250 N. Highland Ave., Merion, PA 19066. (215)667–1830. Dir. Bernard Lewis; Assoc. Dir. David M. Goldenberg. A center for advanced research in Judaic and Near Eastern studies at the postdoctoral level. *Jewish Quarterly Review.*

ASSOCIATION FOR JEWISH STUDIES (1969). Widener Library M., Harvard University, Cambridge, MA 02138. Pres. Ruth R. Wisse; Exec. Sec. Charles Berlin. Seeks to promote, maintain, and improve the teaching of Jewish studies in American colleges and universities by sponsoring meetings and conferences, publishing a newsletter and other scholarly materials, setting standards for programs in Jewish studies, aiding in the placement of teachers, coordinating research, and cooperating with other scholarly organizations. *AJS Review; newsletter.*

ASSOCIATION OF HILLEL/JEWISH CAMPUS PROFESSIONALS (1949). 6300 Forsyth Blvd., St. Louis, MO 63105. (314)726–6177. Pres. Rabbi James S. Diamond;

Exec. Off. Judith Schwartz. Seeks to promote professional relationships and exchanges of experience, develop personnel standards and qualifications, safeguard integrity of Hillel profession; represents and advocates before National Hillel Staff, National Hillel Commission, B'nai B'rith International, Council of Jewish Federations. *AHJCP Bulletin.*

ASSOCIATION OF ORTHODOX JEWISH SCIENTISTS (1948). 1373 Coney Island Ave., Brooklyn, NY 11230. (718)338-8592. Pres. Allen Bennett; Bd. Chmn. Sheldon Kornbluth. Seeks to contribute to the development of science within the framework of Orthodox Jewish tradition; to obtain and disseminate information relating to the interaction between the Jewish traditional way of life and scientific developments—on both an ideological and practical level; to assist in the solution of problems pertaining to Orthodox Jews engaged in scientific teaching or research. Two main conventions are held each year. *Intercom; Proceedings; Halacha Bulletin;* newsletter.

BALTIMORE HEBREW UNIVERSITY (1919). 5800 Park Heights Ave., Baltimore, MD 21215. (301)578-6900. Pres. Leivy Smolar; Bd. Chmn. Mark D. Coplin. Offers undergraduate and graduate programs in Jewish studies, biblical and Near Eastern archaeology, philosophy, literature, history, Hebrew language and literature; Joseph Meyerhoff Library.

———,BALTIMORE INSTITUTE FOR JEWISH COMMUNAL SERVICE. Joint certification program with University of Maryland, Towson State University, the Associated Jewish Charities and Welfare Fund, the UJA/Federation of Greater Washington, and Bnai Brith International sponsoring field work, seminars, and overseas study.

———,BERNARD MANEKIN SCHOOL OF UNDERGRADUATE STUDIES. Dean Judy Meltzer. BA program; the Isaac C. Rosenthal Center for Jewish Education; on-site courses throughout Maryland and in Jerusalem; interdisciplinary concentrations: contemporary Middle East, American Jewish culture, and the humanities.

———,PEGGY MEYERHOFF PEARLSTONE SCHOOL OF GRADUATE STUDIES. Dean Robert O. Freedman. PhD and MA programs; MA and MSW with University of Maryland School of Social Work and Community Planning in federation, community organization, center, and family services; MA and MEd in Jewish education and double MA in journalism with Towson State University; MA program in the study of Christian-Jewish relations with St. Mary's Seminary and University; MA program in community relations with University of Maryland Graduate School.

BETH MEDROSH ELYON (ACADEMY OF HIGHER LEARNING AND RESEARCH) (1943). 73 Main St., Monsey, NY 10952. (914)356-7065. Bd. Chmn. Emanuel Weldler; Treas. Arnold Jacobs; Sec. Yerachmiel Censor. Provides postgraduate courses and research work in higher Jewish studies; offers scholarships and fellowships. Annual journal.

B'NAI B'RITH HILLEL FOUNDATIONS, INC. (1923). 1640 Rhode Island Ave., NW, Washington, DC 20036. (202)857-6560. Chmn. B'nai B'rith Hillel Comm. Edwin Shapiro; Internatl. Dir. Richard M. Joel; Assoc. Internatl. Dir. Rabbi William D. Rudolph. Provides cultural, social, community-service, educational, and religious activities for Jewish college students of all denominational backgrounds on more than 400 campuses in the U.S., Canada, and overseas. Sponsors seminars in Israel, annual Washington Public Policy Conference, National Jewish Law Students Association, Student Secretariat; Arts and Culture Task Force, regional retreats and shabbatons; cosponsors Washington Soviet Jewry Lobby. *Jewish Life on Campus: A Directory of B'nai B'rith Hillel Foundations and Other Jewish Campus Activities; Igret; National Jewish Law Review; NJLS Newsletter.*

B'NAI B'RITH YOUTH ORGANIZATION (1924). 1640 Rhode Island Ave., NW, Washington, DC 20036. (202)857-6633. Chmn. Youth Comm. Edward Yalowitz; Internatl. Dir. Sidney Clearfield. Helps Jewish teenagers achieve self-fulfillment and make a maximum contribution to the Jewish community and their country's culture; helps members acquire a greater knowledge and appreciation of Jewish religion and culture. *BBYO Advisor; Monday Morning; Shofar; Hakol; Kesher.*

BRAMSON ORT TECHNICAL INSTITUTE (1977). 304 Park Ave. S., NYC 10010. (212)677-7420. Dir. Howard Friedman. A two-year Jewish technical college offering certificates and associate degrees in high technology and business fields, including computer programming and technology, electronics technology, business management, word processing, and ophthalmic technology. Houses the Center for Computers in Jewish Education.

BRANDEIS-BARDIN INSTITUTE (1941). 1101 Peppertree Lane, Brandeis, CA 93064. (818)348-7201. Pres. John Rauch. A pluralistic, nondenominational Jewish institution providing programs for people of all ages: Brandeis Camp Institute (BCI), a leadership program for college-age adults; Camp Alonim, a positive Jewish experience for children 8–16; House of the Book *shabbat* weekends for adults 25+, at which scholars-in-residence discuss historical, cultural, religious, and spiritual aspects of Judaism. *Brandeis-Bardin Institute Newsletter; BCI Alumni News.*

CANTORS ASSEMBLY (1947). 150 Fifth Ave., NYC 10011. (212)691-8020. Pres. Solomon Mendelson; Exec. V.-Pres. Samuel Rosenbaum. Seeks to unite all cantors who adhere to traditional Judaism and who serve as full-time cantors in bona fide congregations to conserve and promote the musical traditions of the Jews and to elevate the status of the cantorial profession. *Annual Proceedings; Journal of Synagogue Music.*

CENTRAL CONFERENCE OF AMERICAN RABBIS (1889). 192 Lexington Ave., NYC 10016. (212)684-4990. Pres. Rabbi Eugene J. Lipman; Exec. V.-Pres. Rabbi Joseph B. Glaser. Seeks to conserve and promote Judaism and to disseminate its teachings in a liberal spirit. *Journal of Reform Judaism; CCAR Yearbook.*

CLAL (see National Jewish Center for Learning and Leadership)

CLEVELAND COLLEGE OF JEWISH STUDIES (1964). 26500 Shaker Blvd., Beachwood, OH 44122. (216)464-4050. Pres. David S. Ariel; Bd. Chmn. Donna Yanowitz. Provides courses in all areas of Judaic and Hebrew studies to adults and college-age students; offers continuing education for Jewish educators and administrators; serves as a center for Jewish life and culture; expands the availability of courses in Judaic studies by exchanging faculty, students, and credits with neighboring academic institutions; grants bachelor's and master's degrees.

COALITION FOR THE ADVANCEMENT OF JEWISH EDUCATION (CAJE) (1976). 468 Park Ave. S., Rm. 904, NYC 10016. (212)-696-0740. Chmn. Betsy Katz; Dir. Eliot G. Spack. Brings together Jews from all ideologies who are involved in every facet of Jewish education, and are committed to transmitting Jewish knowledge, culture, and experience; serves as a channel of communication for its membership to share resources and methods, and as a forum for exchange of philosophical and theoretical approaches to Jewish education. Sponsors annual conference on Alternatives in Jewish Education. *Bikurim; Crisis Curricula; Mekasher; CAJE Jewish Education News.*

COUNCIL FOR JEWISH EDUCATION (1926). 426 W. 58 St., NYC 10019. (212)713-0290. Pres. Bernard Ducoff; Exec. Sec. Philip Gorodetzer. Fellowship of Jewish education professionals, comprising administrators and supervisors of national and local Jewish educational institutions and agencies, and teachers in Hebrew high schools and Jewish teachers colleges, of all ideological groupings; conducts annual national and regional conferences in all areas of Jewish education; represents the Jewish education profession before the Jewish community; cosponsors, with the Jewish Education Service of North America, a personnel committee and other projects; cooperates with Jewish Agency Department of Education and Culture in promoting Hebrew culture and studies; conducts lectureship at Hebrew University. *Jewish Education; Sheviley Hahinnukh.*

DROPSIE COLLEGE FOR HEBREW AND COGNATE LEARNING (see Annenberg Research Institute)

FEDERATION OF JEWISH MEN'S CLUBS, INC. (1929). 475 Riverside Dr., Suite 244, NYC 10115. (212)749-8100. Pres. Jerome Agrest; Exec. Dir. Rabbi Charles Simon. Promotes principles and objectives of Conservative Judaism by organizing, sponsoring, and developing men's clubs or brotherhoods; supports OMETZ Center for Conservative Judaism on campus; promotes Home Library of Conservative Judaism and the Art of Jewish Living series; sponsors Hebrew literacy adult education program; presents awards for service to American Jewry. *Torchlight.*

GRATZ COLLEGE (1895). 10th St. and Tabor Rd., Philadelphia, PA 19141. (215)329-3363. Bd. Chmn. Stephen Saks; Pres. Gary S. Schiff. Offers a wide variety of bachelor's, master's, teacher-training, continuing-education, and high-school-level programs in Judaic, Hebraic, and Middle Eastern studies. Grants BA and MA in Jewish studies, Bachelor and Master of Hebrew literature, MA in Jewish education, MA in Jewish music, certificates in Judaica librarianship, Jewish communal studies, Jewish chaplaincy, and other credentials. Joint bachelor's programs with Temple University and Beaver College and joint graduate program in Jewish communal service with U. of Pennsylvania. *Various newsletters, a yearbook, and scholarly publications.*

HEBREW COLLEGE (1921). 43 Hawes St., Brookline, MA 02146. (617)232-8710. Pres. Samuel Schafler; Bd. Chmn. Herbert L. Berman. Provides intensive programs of study in all areas of Jewish culture from high school through college and graduate-school levels, also at branch in Hartford; offers the degrees of MA in Jewish studies, Bachelor and Master of Jewish education, Bachelor of Hebrew letters, and teachers diploma; degrees fully accredited by New England Assoc. of Schools and Colleges. Operates Hebrew-speaking Camp Yavneh in Northwood, NH; offers extensive Ulpan program and courses for community. *Hebrew College Today.*

HEBREW THEOLOGICAL COLLEGE (1922). 7135 N. Carpenter Rd., Skokie, IL 60077. (312)267-9800. Pres. Rabbi Don Well; Bd. Chmn. Colman Ginsparg. An institution of higher Jewish learning which includes a division of advanced Hebrew studies, a school of liberal arts and sciences, a rabbinical ordination program, a graduate school in Judaic studies and pastoral counseling; the Fasman Yeshiva High School; a high school summer program combining Torah studies and computer science courses; anda Jewish studies program. *Or Shmuel Torah Journal;* quarterly newsletter.

HEBREW UNION COLLEGE-JEWISH INSTITUTE OF RELIGION (1875). 3101 Clifton Ave., Cincinnati, OH 45220. (513)221-1875. Pres. Alfred Gottschalk; Exec. Dean Eugene Mihaly; Exec. V.-Pres. Uri D. Herscher; Chmn. Bd. of Govs. Richard J. Scheuer. Academic centers: 3101 Clifton Ave., Cincinnati, OH 45220 (1875), Kenneth Ehrlich, Dean; 1 W. 4 St., NYC 10012 (1922), Norman J. Cohen, Dean; 3077 University Ave., Los Angeles, CA 90007 (1954), Uri D. Herscher, Chief Admin. Off.; 13 King David St., Jerusalem, Israel 94101 (1963), Michael Klein, Dean. Prepares students for Reform rabbinate, cantorate, religious-school teaching and administration, community service, academic careers; promotes Jewish studies; maintains libraries and a museum; offers master's and doctoral degrees; engages in archaeological excavations; publishes scholarly works through Hebrew Union College Press. *American Jewish Archives; Bibliographica Judaica; HUC-JIR Catalogue; Hebrew Union College Annual; Studies in Bibliography and Booklore; The Chronicle.*

———, AMERICAN JEWISH ARCHIVES (1947). 3101 Clifton Ave., Cincinnati, OH 45220. (513)221-1875. Dir. Jacob R. Marcus; Admin. Dir. Abraham Peck. Promotes the study and preservation of the Western Hemisphere Jewish experience through research, publications, collection of important source materials, and a vigorous public-outreach program. *American Jewish Archives; monographs, publications, and pamphlets.*

———, AMERICAN JEWISH PERIODICAL CENTER (1957). 3101 Clifton Ave., Cincinnati, OH 45220. (513)221-1875. Dir. Jacob R. Marcus; Codir. Herbert C. Zafren. Maintains microfilms of all American Jewish periodicals 1823-1925, selected periodicals since 1925. *Jewish Periodicals and Newspapers on Microfilm (1957); First Supplement (1960); Augmented Edition (1984).*

———, EDGAR F. MAGNIN SCHOOL OF GRADUATE STUDIES (1956). 3077 University Ave., Los Angeles, CA 90007. (213)-749-3424. Dir. Stanley Chyet. Supervises programs leading to PhD (Education), DHS, DHL, and MA degrees; participates in cooperative PhD programs with the University of Southern California.

———, JEROME H. LOUCHHEIM SCHOOL OF JUDAIC STUDIES (1969). 3077 University Ave. Los Angeles, CA 90007. (213)749-3424. Dir. David Ellenson. Offers programs leading to MA, BS, BA, and AA degrees; offers courses as part of the undergraduate program of the University of Southern California.

———, NELSON GLUECK SCHOOL OF BIBLICAL ARCHAEOLOGY (1963). 13 King David St., Jerusalem, Israel 94101. Dir. Avraham Biran. Offers graduate-level research programs in Bible and archaeology. Summer excavations are carried out by scholars and students. University credit may be earned by participants in excavations. Consortium of colleges, universities, and seminaries is affiliated with the school.

———, RHEA HIRSCH SCHOOL OF EDUCATION (1967). 3077 University Ave., Los Angeles, CA 90007. (213)749-3424. Dir. Sara S. Lee. Offers PhD and MA programs in Jewish and Hebrew education; conducts joint degree programs with University of Southern California; offers courses for Jewish teachers, librarians, and early educators on a nonmatriculating basis; conducts summer institutes for professional Jewish educators.

———, SCHOOL OF EDUCATION (1947). 1 W. 4 St., NYC 10012. (212)674-5300. V.-Pres. and Dean of Faculty Paul M. Steinberg; Dean Norman J. Cohen; Dir. Kerry M. Olitzky. Trains teachers and principals for Reform religious schools; offers MA degree with specialization in religious education; offers extension programs in various suburban centers.

———, SCHOOL OF GRADUATE STUDIES (1949). 3101 Clifton Ave., Cincinnati, OH 45220 (513)221-1875. Dean Samuel Greengus. Offers programs leading to MA and PhD degrees; offers program leading to DHL degree for rabbinic graduates of the college.

———, SCHOOL OF JEWISH COMMUNAL SERVICE (1968). 3077 University Ave., Los Angeles, CA 90007. (213)749-3424. Dir. Gerald B. Bubis. Offers certificate and master's degree to those employed in Jewish communal services, or preparing for such work; offers joint MA in Jewish education and communal service with Rhea Hirsch School; offers MA and MSW in conjunction with the University of Southern California School of Social Work, with the George Warren Brown School of Social Work of Washington University, and with the University of Pittsburgh School of Social Work; offers joint master's degrees in conjunction with USC in public administration or gerontology.

———, SCHOOL OF JEWISH STUDIES (1963). 13 King David St., Jerusalem, Israel, 94101. (02)20333. Dean Michael Klein; Assoc. Dean Rabbi Shaul R. Feinberg. Offers first year of graduate rabbinic, cantorial, and Jewish education studies (required) for American students; program leading to ordination for Israeli rabbinic students; undergraduate semester in Jerusalem and one-year work/study program on a kibbutz in cooperation with Union of American Hebrew Congregations; public outreach programs (lectures, courses, concerts, exhibits).

———, SCHOOL OF SACRED MUSIC (1947). 1 W. 4 St., NYC 10012. (212)674-5300. V.-Pres. and Dean Paul M. Steinberg. Trains cantors and music personnel for congregations; offers MSM degree. *Sacred Music Press.*

———, SKIRBALL MUSEUM (1913; 1972 in Calif.). 3077 University Ave., Los Angeles, CA 90007. (213)749-3424. Dir. Nancy Berman; Curator Barbara Gilbert. Collects, preserves, researches, and exhibits art and artifacts made by or for Jews, or otherwise associated with Jews and Judaism. Provides opportunity to faculty and students to do research in the field of Jewish art. *Catalogues of exhibits and collections.*

HERZLIAH-JEWISH TEACHERS SEMINARY (1967). Division of Touro College. 30 W. 44 St., NYC 10036. (212)575-1819. Pres. Bernard Lander; Dir. Jacob Katzman.

———, GRADUATE SCHOOL OF JEWISH STUDIES (1981). 30 W. 44th St., NYC 10036. (212)575-0190. Pres. Bernard Lander; Dean Michael Shmidman. Offers programs leading to MA in Jewish studies, including Hebrew language and literature, Jewish education, history, philosophy, and sociology. Admits men and women who have bachelor's degrees and backgrounds in Hebrew, Yiddish, and Jewish studies.

———, JEWISH PEOPLE'S UNIVERSITY OF THE AIR. (212)575-1819. Dir./Producer Dr. Jacob Katzman. The educational outreach arm of Touro College, it produces and disseminates Jewish educational and cultural programming for radio broadcast and on audio-cassettes.

## NATIONAL JEWISH ORGANIZATIONS / 461

INSTITUTE FOR COMPUTERS IN JEWISH LIFE (1978). 845 N. Michigan Ave., Suite 843, Chicago, IL 60611. (312)787-7856. Pres. Thomas Klutznick; Exec. V.-Pres. Irving J. Rosenbaum. Explores, develops, and disseminates applications of computer technology to appropriate areas of Jewish life, with special emphasis on Jewish education; provides access to the Bar-Ilan University Responsa Project; creates educational software for use in Jewish schools; provides consulting service and assistance for national Jewish organizations, seminaries, and synagogues. *Monitor.*

JEWISH CHAUTAUQUA SOCIETY, INC. (sponsored by NATIONAL FEDERATION OF TEMPLE BROTHERHOODS) (1893). 838 Fifth Ave., NYC 10021. (212)570-0707. Pres. Carl J. Burkons; Exec. Dir. Av Bondarin. Disseminates authoritative information on Jews and Judaism; assigns rabbis to lecture at colleges and secondary schools; endows courses in Judaism for college credit at universities; donates Jewish reference books to college libraries; sends rabbis to serve as counselor-teachers at Christian church summer camps and as chaplains at Boy Scout camps; sponsors institutes on Judaism for Christian clergy; produces motion pictures for public-service television and group showings. *Brotherhood.*

JEWISH EDUCATION IN MEDIA, INC. (1978). PO Box 180, Riverdale Sta., NYC 10471. (212)362-7633. Pres. Bernard Samers; Exec. Dir. Rabbi Mark S. Golub. Seeks to promote Jewish identity and commitment through the creation of innovative and entertaining media materials, including radio and television programming, film, and audio and video cassettes for synagogue and institutional use. Produces syndicated radio magazine, *L'Chayim.*

JEWISH EDUCATION SERVICE OF NORTH AMERICA, INC. (JESNA) (1981). 730 Broadway, NYC 10003. (212)529-2000. Pres. Bennett Yanowitz; Exec. V.-Pres. Jonathan Woocher. Coordinating, planning, and service agency for Jewish education in bureaus and federations; offers curricular advisement and maintains a National Educational Resource Center; runs regional pedagogic conferences; conducts evaluative surveys on Jewish education; engages in statistical and other educational research; provides community consultations; sponsors the National Board of License; administers Fellowships in Jewish Educational Leadership training program (FIJEL); provides placement of upper-level bureau and communal school personnel and educators. *Pedagogic Reporter; TRENDS; Information Research Bulletins; Jewish Education Directory; annual report; NISE Newsletter.*

JEWISH MINISTERS CANTORS ASSOCIATION OF AMERICA, INC. (1896). 3 W. 16 St., NYC 10011. (212)675-6601. Pres. Cantor Nathan H. Muchnick. Furthers and propagates traditional liturgy; places cantors in synagogues throughout the U.S. and Canada; develops the cantors of the future. *Kol Lakol.*

JEWISH RECONSTRUCTIONIST FOUNDATION (1940). Church Rd. and Greenwood Ave., Wyncote, PA 19095. (215)887-1988. Pres. Lillian S. Kaplan; Exec. Dir. Rabbi Mordechai Liebling. Dedicated to the advancement of Judaism as the evolving religious civilization of the Jewish people. Coordinates the Federation of Reconstructionist Congregations and Havurot, Reconstructionist Rabbinical Association, and Reconstructionist Rabbinical College.

———, FEDERATION OF RECONSTRUCTIONIST CONGREGATIONS AND HAVUROT (1954). Church Rd. and Greenwood Ave., Wyncote, PA 19095. (215)887-1988. Pres. Roger Price; Exec. Dir. Rabbi Mordechai Liebling. Services affiliated congregations and havurot educationally and administratively; fosters the establishment of new Reconstructionist congregations and fellowship groups. Runs the Reconstructionist Press and provides programmatic materials. Maintains regional offices in New York, Los Angeles, and South Bend, Ind. *The Reconstructionist;* newsletter.

———, RECONSTRUCTIONIST RABBINICAL ASSOCIATION (1974). Church Rd. and Greenwood Ave., Wyncote, PA 19095. (215)576-0800. Pres. Rabbi Joy Levitt; Admin. Michael M. Cohen. Professional organization for graduates of the Reconstructionist Rabbinical College and other rabbis who identify with Reconstructionist Judaism; cooperates with Federation of Reconstructionist Congregations and Havurot in furthering Reconstructionism in N. America. *Raayanot;* newsletter.

———, RECONSTRUCTIONIST RABBINICAL COLLEGE (see p. 465)

JEWISH TEACHERS ASSOCIATION—MORIM (1931). 45 E. 33 St., NYC 10016. (212)-684–0556. Pres. Phyllis L. Pullman; V.-Pres. Eli Nieman. Protects teachers from abuse of seniority rights; fights the encroachment of anti-Semitism in education; provides legal counsel to protect teachers from discrimination; offers scholarships to qualified students; encourages teachers to assume active roles in Jewish communal and religious affairs. *Morim Jewish Teachers Association Newsletter.*

JEWISH THEOLOGICAL SEMINARY OF AMERICA (1886; reorg. 1902). 3080 Broadway, NYC 10027–4649. (212)678-8000. Chancellor Ismar Schorsch; Bd. Chmn. Stephen M. Peck. Operates undergraduate and graduate programs in Judaic studies; professional schools for training Conservative rabbis and cantors; a pastoral psychiatry center; Melton Center for Jewish Education; the Jewish Museum; and such youth programs as the Ramah Camps, the OMETZ-Center for Conservative Judaism on Campus, and the Prozdor high-school division. Produces the "Eternal Light" radio and TV programs. *Academic Bulletin; Seminary Progress; The Second Century.*

———, ALBERT A. LIST COLLEGE OF JEWISH STUDIES (formerly SEMINARY COLLEGE OF JEWISH STUDIES-TEACHERS INSTITUTE) (1909). 3080 Broadway, NYC 10027. (212)678-8826. Dean Anne Lapidus Lerner. Offers complete undergraduate program in Judaica leading to BA degree; conducts joint programs with Columbia University and Barnard College enabling students to receive two BA degrees after four years.

———, CANTORS INSTITUTE AND SEMINARY COLLEGE OF JEWISH MUSIC (1952). 3080 Broadway, NYC 10027. (212)678-8038. Dean Rabbi Morton M. Leifman. Trains cantors, music teachers, and choral directors for congregations. Offers fulltime programs in sacred music leading to degrees of BSM, MSM, and DSM, and diploma of *Hazzan.*

———, DEPARTMENT OF RADIO AND TELEVISION (1944). 3080 Broadway, NYC 10027. (212)678-8020. Dir. Marjorie Wyler. Produces radio and TV programs expressing the Jewish tradition in its broadest sense: The "Eternal Light" weekly radio program on NBC network; one hour-long documentary on NBC-TV; TV program on ABC. Distributes cassettes of programs at minimum charge.

———, GRADUATE SCHOOL (formerly INSTITUTE FOR ADVANCED STUDY IN THE HUMANITIES) (1968). 3080 Broadway, NYC 10027. (212)678-8024. Dean Shaye J. D. Cohen. Graduate programs leading to MA, DHL, and PhD degrees in Jewish studies, Bible, Jewish education, history, literature, philosophy, rabbinics, and medieval studies; dual degree with Columbia University School of Social Work.

———, JERUSALEM CAMPUS, JTS (1962). PO Box 196, Jerusalem, Israel 91001. (02)-631121. Head of Campus Shamma Friedman. Offers year-in-Israel programs for college and postgraduate students seeking to combine Jewish studies with a community supportive of religious commitment and observance (Midreshet Yerushalayim). Academic and residential center for JTS rabbinical and cantorial students. Provides final year of training for rabbinical students of the Seminario Rabbinico of Argentina.

———, JEWISH MUSEUM (*see* p. 451)

———, LOUIS FINKELSTEIN INSTITUTE FOR RELIGIOUS AND SOCIAL STUDIES (1938). 3080 Broadway, NYC 10027. (212)678-8815. Dir. Gordon Tucker. A scholarly and scientific fellowship of clergy and other religious teachers who desire authoritative information regarding some of the basic issues now confronting spiritually minded individuals.

———, MELTON RESEARCH CENTER FOR JEWISH EDUCATION (1960). 3080 Broadway, NYC 10027. (212)678-8031. Dirs. Eduardo Rauch, Barry W. Holtz. Develops new curricula and materials for Jewish education; recruits and prepares educators through seminars and in-service programs; maintains consultant and supervisory relationships with a limited number of pilot schools; sponsors "renewal" retreats for teachers and principals. *Melton Journal.*

———, NATIONAL RAMAH COMMISSION (1951). 3080 Broadway, NYC 10027. (212)678-8881. Pres. Irving Robbin; Dir. Burton I. Cohen. Sponsors 7 summer camps conducted in Hebrew in the U.S. and Canada; offers opportunities for qualified Seminary students and others to serve as counselors, administrators, specialists, etc. Offers special programs in U.S. and Israel, including Bert B. Weinstein National Ramah Staff Training Institute, Ramah Israel Seminars, the Ulpan Ramah Plus Program, and Tichon Ramah Yerushalayim.

———, PROZDOR (1951). 3080 Broadway, NYC 10027. (212)678-8824. Principal Phyllis Hofman Waldmann. The highschool department of JTS, it provides a supplementary Jewish education for students who attend a secular (public or private) full-time high school. Classes in classical Jewish studies, with emphasis on Hebrew language, meet twice a week. *Prozdor Pages.*

———, RABBINICAL SCHOOL (1886). 3080 Broadway, NYC 10027. (212)678-8816. Dean Gordon Tucker. Offers a program of graduate and professional studies leading to the degree of Master of Arts and ordination; includes one year of study at the American Student Center in Jerusalem and pastoral psychiatry training.

———, SAUL LIEBERMAN INSTITUTE OF JEWISH RESEARCH (1985). PO Box 196, Jerusalem, Israel 92102. (02)631121. Dir. Shamma Friedman; Dir.-Gen. Shmuel Glick. Engaged in preparing for publication a series of scholarly editions of selected chapters of the Talmud. The following projects support and help disseminate the research: Talmud Text Database; Bibliography of Talmudic literature; Catalogue of Geniza Fragments; Teachers Training and Curriculum Development in Oral Law for Secondary Schools.

———, SCHOCKEN INSTITUTE FOR JEWISH RESEARCH (1961). 6 Balfour St., Jerusalem, Israel, 92102. (02)631288. Dir. Shamma Friedman; Dir.-Genl. Shmuel Glick. Comprises the Schocken collection of rare books and manuscripts and a research institute dedicated to the exploration of Hebrew religious poetry (piyyut). *Schocken Institute Yearbook (P'raqim).*

———, UNIVERSITY OF JUDAISM (1947). 15600 Mulholland Dr., Los Angeles, CA 90077. (213)879-4114. Pres. David L. Lieber; Sr. V.-Pres. Max Vorspan. West Coast affiliate of JTS. Serves as center of undergraduate and graduate study of Judaica; offers preprofessional and professional programs in Jewish education, nonprofit management, and allied fields, including a prerabbinic program and joint program enabling students to receive BA from UCLA and BHL from U. of J. after four years of undergraduate study. Offers degree programs in Jewish and Western studies as well as a broad range of adult education and Jewish activities. *Direction Magazine; Bulletin of General Information.*

MACHNE ISRAEL, INC. (1940). 770 Eastern Pkwy., Brooklyn, NY 11213. (718)493-9250. Pres. Menachem M. Schneerson (Lubavitcher Rebbe); Dir., Treas. M.A. Hodakov; Sec. Nissan Mindel. The Lubavitcher movement's organ dedicated to the social, spiritual, and material welfare of Jews throughout the world.

MERKOS L'INYONEI CHINUCH, INC. (THE CENTRAL ORGANIZATION FOR JEWISH EDUCATION) (1940). 770 Eastern Pkwy., Brooklyn, NY 11213. (718)493-9250. Pres. Menachem M. Schneerson (Lubavitcher Rebbe); Dir., Treas. M.A. Hodakov; Sec. Nissan Mindel. The educational arm of the Lubavitcher movement. Seeks to promote Jewish education among Jews, regardless of their background, in the spirit of Torah-true Judaism; to establish contact with alienated Jewish youth; to stimulate concern and active interest in Jewish education on all levels; and to promote religious observance as a daily experience among all Jews; maintains worldwide network of regional offices, schools, summer camps, and Chabad-Lubavitch Houses; publishes Jewish educational literature in numerous languages and monthly journal in five languages: *Conversaciones con la juventud; Conversations avec les jeunes; Schmuessen mit Kinder un Yugent; Sihot la-No-ar; Talks and Tales.*

MESIVTA YESHIVA RABBI CHAIM BERLIN RABBINICAL ACADEMY (1905). 1593 Coney Island Ave., Brooklyn, NY 11230. (718)377-0777. Pres. Sol Eiger; Exec. Dir. Y. Mayer Lasker. Maintains fully accredited elementary and high schools; collegiate and postgraduate school for advanced Jewish studies, both in America and Israel; Camp Morris, a summer study retreat; Prof. Nathan Isaacs Memorial Library; Gur Aryeh Publications.

NATIONAL COMMITTEE FOR FURTHERANCE OF JEWISH EDUCATION (1941). 824 Eastern Pkwy., Brooklyn, NY 11213.

(718)735–0200. Pres. J. James Plesser; Natl. Pres. Joseph Fisch; Exec. V.-Pres. Rabbi Jacob J. Hecht. Seeks to disseminate the ideals of Torah-true education among the youth of America; provides education and compassionate care for the poor, sick, and needy in U.S. and Israel; provides aid to Iranian Jewish youth through the Iranian Children's Fund; sponsors Camp Emunah and Camp Emunah Tiny Tots for girls; Camp Shalom for college youth; Operation Survival, War on Drugs; Hadar HaTorah, Machon Chana, and Ivy League Torah Study Program, seeking to win back college youth and others to Judaism; maintains schools and dormitory facilities, family and vocational counseling services. *Panorama; Passover Handbook; Seder Guide; Cultbusters; Intermarriage; Brimstone & Fire.*

NATIONAL COUNCIL OF YOUNG ISRAEL (1912). 3 W. 16 St., NYC 10011. (212)929–1525. Pres. Harold M. Jacobs; Exec. V.-Pres. Rabbi Ephraim H. Sturm. Maintains a program of spiritual, cultural, social, and communal activity aimed at the advancement and perpetuation of traditional, Torah-true Judaism; seeks to instill in American youth an understanding and appreciation of the ethical and spiritual values of Judaism. Sponsors kosher dining clubs and fraternity houses and an Israel program. *Viewpoint; Hashkafa series; Masorah newspaper.*

———, AMERICAN FRIENDS OF YOUNG ISRAEL SYNAGOGUES IN ISRAEL (1926). 3 W. 16 St., NYC 10011. (212)929–1525. Chmn. Jack Forgash; Cochmn. Michael Krengel; Dir. Israel Programs Isaac Hagler. Promotes Young Israel synagogues and youth work in synagogues in Israel.

———, ARMED FORCES BUREAU (1912). 3 W. 16 St., NYC10011. (212)929–1525. Advises and guides the inductees into the armed forces with regard to Sabbath observance, *kashrut*, and Orthodox behavior. *Guide for the Orthodox Serviceman.*

———, EMPLOYMENT BUREAU (1929). 3 W. 16 St., NYC 10011. (212)929–1525. Project Dir. Fed. Program Rabbi Ephraim H. Sturm; Project Dir. NYC Program Lisa S. Shmidman. Under federal contract in Cleveland and St. Louis and under contract to New York City, operates employment referral service for unemployed people, offering OJT (On-The-Job-Training). (No classroom training.) Counsels on jobsearch techniques. Low income limit. Serves all adults, including Sabbath observers. Reimbursement incentives available to employers.

———, INSTITUTE FOR JEWISH STUDIES (1947). 3 W. 16 St., NYC 10011. (212)929–1525. Pres. Harold M. Jacobs; Exec. V.-Pres. Rabbi Ephraim H. Sturm. Introduces students to Jewish learning and knowledge; helps form adult branch schools; aids Young Israel synagogues in their adult education programs. *Bulletin.*

———, YOUNG ISRAEL COLLEGIATES AND YOUNG ADULTS (1951; reorg. 1982). 3 W. 16 St., NYC 10011. (212)929–1525. Chmn. Kenneth Block; Dir. Richard Stareshefsky. Organizes and operates kosher dining clubs on college and university campuses; provides information and counseling on *kashrut* observance at college; gives college-age youth understanding and appreciation of Judaism and information on issues important to Jewish community; arranges seminars and meetings, weekends and trips; operates Achva summer mission to Israel for ages 18–21 and 22–27.

———, YOUNG ISRAEL YOUTH (reorg. 1968). 3 W. 16 St., NYC 10011. (212)929–1525. Dir. Richard Stareshefsky. Fosters a program of spiritual, cultural, social, and communal activities for the advancement and perpetuation of traditional Torah-true Judaism; strives to instill an understanding and appreciation of the high ethical and spiritual values and to demonstrate compatibility of ancient faith of Israel with good Americanism. Operates Achva Summer Mission study program in Israel. *Monthly newsletter.*

NATIONAL JEWISH CENTER FOR LEARNING AND LEADERSHIP—CLAL (1974). 421 Seventh Ave., NYC 10001. (212)714–9500. Chmn. Robert E. Loup; Pres. Irving Greenberg; Exec. V.-Pres. Paul Jeser. Devoted to leadership education and policy guidance for the American Jewish community. Conducts weekend retreats and community gatherings as well as conferences on various topics. *Perspectives.*

NATIONAL JEWISH HOSPITALITY COMMITTEE (1973). 201 S. 18 St., Rm. 1519, Philadelphia, PA 19103. (215)546–8293. Pres.-Rabbi Allen S. Maller; Exec. Dir. Steven S. Jacobs. Assists persons interested in Judaism—for conversion, intermarriage, or to respond to missionaries. *Special reports.*

NATIONAL JEWISH INFORMATION SERVICE FOR THE PROPAGATION OF JUDAISM, INC. (1960). 3761 Decade St., Las Vegas, NV 89121. (702)454–5872. Pres. Rabbi Moshe M. Maggal; V.-Pres. Lawrence J. Epstein; Sec. and P.R. Dir. Rachel D. Maggal. Seeks to convert non-Jews to Judaism and return Jews to Judaism; maintains College for Jewish Ambassadors for the training of Jewish missionaries, and the Correspondence Academy of Judaism for instruction on Judaism through the mail. *Voice of Judaism.*

NER ISRAEL RABBINICAL COLLEGE (1933). 400 Mt. Wilson Ln., Baltimore, MD 21208. (301)484–7200. Rabbi Yaakov S. Weinberg, Rosh Hayeshiva; V.-Pres. Rabbi Herman N. Neuberger. Trains rabbis and educators for Jewish communities in America and worldwide. Offers bachelor's, master's, and doctoral degrees in talmudic law, as well as teacher's diploma. College has four divisions: Mechina High School, Rabbinical College, Teachers Training Institute, Graduate School. Maintains an active community-service division. Operates special program for Iranian Jewish students. *Ner Israel Bulletin; Alumni Bulletin; Ohr Hanair Talmudic Journal; Iranian B'nei Torah Bulletin.*

OZAR HATORAH, INC. (1946). 1 E. 33 St., NYC 10016. (212)689–3508. Pres. Joseph Shalom; Sec. Sam Sutton. An international educational network which provides religious and secular education for Jewish youth worldwide.

P'EYLIM—AMERICAN YESHIVA STUDENT UNION (1951). 3 W. 16 St., NYC 10011. (212)989–2500. Pres. Jacob Y. Weisberg; Dir. Avraham Hirsch. Aids and sponsors pioneer work by American graduate teachers and rabbis in new villages and towns in Israel; does religious, organizational, and educational work and counseling among new immigrant youth; maintains summer camps for poor immigrant youth in Israel; belongs to worldwide P'eylim movement which has groups in Argentina, Brazil, Canada, England, Belgium, the Netherlands, Switzerland, France, and Israel; engages in relief and educational work among North African immigrants in France and Canada, assisting them to relocate and reestablish a strong Jewish community life. *P'eylim Reporter; News from P'eylim; N'shei P'eylim News.*

RABBINICAL ALLIANCE OF AMERICA (IGUD HARABONIM) (1944). 3 W. 16 St., 4th fl., NYC 10011. (212)242–6420. Pres. Rabbi Abraham B. Hecht; Menahel Beth Din (Rabbinical Court) Rabbi Herschel Kurzrock. Seeks to promulgate the cause of Torah-true Judaism through an organized rabbinate that is consistently Orthodox; seeks to elevate the position of Orthodox rabbis nationally, and to defend the welfare of Jews the world over. Also has Beth Din Rabbinical Court for Jewish divorces, litigation, marriage counseling and family problems. *Perspective; Nahalim; Torah Message of the Week; Registry.*

RABBINICAL ASSEMBLY (1900). 3080 Broadway, NYC 10027. (212)678–8060. Pres. Rabbi Albert L. Lewis; Exec. V.-Pres. Rabbi Wolfe Kelman. Seeks to promote Conservative Judaism, and to foster the spirit of fellowship and cooperation among rabbis and other Jewish scholars; cooperates with the Jewish Theological Seminary of America and the United Synagogue of America. *Conservative Judaism; Proceedings of the Rabbinical Assembly; Rabbinical Assembly Newsletter.*

RABBINICAL COLLEGE OF TELSHE, INC. (1941). 28400 Euclid Ave., Wickliffe, OH 44092. (216)943–5300. Pres. Rabbi Mordecai Gifter; V.-Pres. Rabbi Abba Zalka Gewirtz. College for higher Jewish learning specializing in talmudic studies and rabbinics; maintains a preparatory academy including a secular high school, postgraduate department, teacher-training school, and teachers seminary for women. *Pri Etz Chaim; Peer Mordechai; Alumni Bulletin.*

RABBINICAL COUNCIL OF AMERICA, INC. (1923; reorg. 1935). 275 Seventh Ave., NYC 10001. (212)807–7888. Pres. Rabbi Max N. Schreier; Exec. V.-Pres. Rabbi Binyamin Walfish. Promotes Orthodox Judaism in the community; supports institutions for study of Torah; stimulates creation of new traditional agencies. *Hadorom; Record; Sermon Manual; Tradition.*

RECONSTRUCTIONIST RABBINICAL COLLEGE (1968). Church Rd. and Greenwood Ave., Wyncote, PA 19095. (215)576–0800.

Bd. Chmn. Samuel Blumenthal; Genl. Chmn. Aaron Ziegelman; Pres. Arthur Green. Coeducational. Trains rabbis for all areas of Jewish communal life: synagogues, academic and educational positions, Hillel centers, federation agencies; confers title of rabbi and grants degrees of Master and Doctor of Hebrew letters. *RRC Report.*

RESEARCH INSTITUTE OF RELIGIOUS JEWRY, INC. (1941; reorg. 1964). 471 W. End Ave., NYC 10024. (212)874-7979. Chmn. Rabbi Oswald Besser; Sec. Marcus Levine. Engages in research and publishes studies concerning the situation of religious Jewry and its problems all over the world.

SHOLEM ALEICHEM FOLK INSTITUTE, INC. (1918). 3301 Bainbridge Ave., Bronx, NY 10467. (212)881-6555. Pres. Burt Levey; Sec. Noah Zingman. Aims to imbue children with Jewish values through teaching Yiddish language and literature, Hebrew and the Bible, Jewish history, the significance of Jewish holidays, folk and choral singing, and facts about Jewish life in America and Israel. *Kinder Journal* (Yiddish).

SOCIETY FOR HUMANISTIC JUDAISM (1969). 28611 W. Twelve Mile Rd., Farmington Hills, MI 48018. (313)478-7610. Pres. Lynne Master; Exec. Dir. Miriam Jerris. Serves as a voice for Jews who value their Jewish identity and who seek an alternative to conventional Judaism, who reject supernatural authority and affirm the right of individuals to be the masters of their own lives. Publishes educational and ceremonial materials; organizes congregations and groups. *Humanorah* (quarterly newsletter); *Humanistic Judaism* (quarterly journal).

SOCIETY OF FRIENDS OF THE TOURO SYNAGOGUE, NATIONAL HISTORICAL SITE, INC. (1948). 85 Touro St., Newport, RI 02840. (401)847-4794. Pres. Burton Fischler; Exec. Sec. Rabbi Chaim Shapiro. Assists in the maintenance of the Touro Synagogue as a national historical site; sponsors tours of synagogue. *History of Touro Synagogue.*

SPERTUS COLLEGE OF JUDAICA (1925). 618 S. Michigan Ave., Chicago, IL 60605. (312)922-9012. Pres. Howard A. Sulkin; Bd. Chmn. Stuart Taussig; V.-Pres. for Academic Affairs Byron L. Sherwin. Provides Chicago-area colleges and universities with specialized undergraduate and graduate programs in Judaica and serves as a department of Judaic studies to these colleges and universities; serves as Midwest Jewish information center, through its Asher Library, Maurice Spertus Museum of Judaica, Katzin Memorial Rare Book Room, and Chicago Jewish Archives. Grants degrees of MA in Jewish education, Jewish studies, and Jewish communal service; BA and Bachelor of Judaic studies. Has community outreach/extension studies program for adults.

SYNAGOGUE COUNCIL OF AMERICA (1926). 327 Lexington Ave., NYC 10016. (212)-686-8670. Pres. Rabbi Gilbert Klaperman; Exec. V.-Pres. Rabbi Henry D. Michelman. Serves as spokesman for, and coordinates policies of, national rabbinical and lay synagogal organizations of Conservative, Orthodox, and Reform branches of American Judaism.

TORAH SCHOOLS FOR ISRAEL—CHINUCH ATZMAI (1953). 167 Madison Ave., NYC 10016. (212)889-0606. Pres. Abraham Pam; Exec. Dir. Henach Cohen. Conducts information programs for the American Jewish community on activities of the independent Torah schools educational network in Israel; coordinates role of American members of international board of governors; funds special programs of Mercaz Hachinuch Ha-Atzmai B'Eretz Yisroel. *Israel Education Reporter.*

TORAH UMESORAH—NATIONAL SOCIETY FOR HEBREW DAY SCHOOLS (1944). 160 Broadway, NYC 10038. (212)227-1000. Pres. Sheldon Beren; Bd. Chmn. David Singer; Exec. V.-Pres. Joshua Fishman. Establishes Hebrew day schools in U.S. and Canada and provides the gamut of services, including placement and curriculum guidance; conducts teacher-training on campuses of major yeshivahs as well as seminars and workshops; publishes textbooks, workbooks, charts, and reading books. Runs Shabbatonim, extracurricular activities, and summer camp. National PTA groups; national and regional teacher conventions. *Olomeinu-Our World; Visions; Parshah Sheets.*

———, INSTITUTE FOR PROFESSIONAL ENRICHMENT (1973). 75 Varick St., Rm. 205, NYC 10013. (212) 941-9044. Dir. Bernard Dov Milians. Provides enriched training and upgraded credentials for administrative, guidance, and classroom personnel of Hebrew day schools and for Torah-community leaders; offers graduate and undergraduate programs, in affiliation with accredited universities which award full degrees: MA in early childhood and elementary education; MS in family counseling; MBA in management; MS in special education, reading; BS in education; BA in human relations, social sciences, education, gerontology. *Professional Enrichment News (PEN).*

——, NATIONAL ASSOCIATION OF HEBREW DAY SCHOOL ADMINISTRATORS (1960). 1114 Ave. J, Brooklyn, NY 11230. Pres. David H. Schwartz. Coordinates the work of the fiscal directors of Hebrew day schools throughout the country. *NAHDSA Review.*

——, NATIONAL ASSOCIATION OF HEBREW DAY SCHOOL PARENT-TEACHER ASSOCIATIONS (1948). 160 Broadway, NYC 10038. (212)227-1000. Exec. Sec. Mrs. Samuel Brand. Acts as a clearinghouse and service agency to PTAs of Hebrew day schools; organizes parent-education courses and sets up programs for individual PTAs. *Fundraising with a Flair; Monthly Sidrah Series Program; PTA with a Purpose for the Hebrew Day School.*

——, NATIONAL CONFERENCE OF YESHIVA PRINCIPALS (1956). 160 Broadway, NYC 10038. (212)227-1000. Pres. Rabbi Sholom Strajcher; Bd. Chmn. Rabbi Yitzchak Merkin; Exec. V.-Pres. Rabbi A. Moshe Possick. A professional organization of primary and secondary yeshivah day-school principals which seeks to make yeshivah day-school education more effective. *Newsletter; Directory of High Schools.*

——, NATIONAL YESHIVA TEACHERS BOARD OF LICENSE (1953). 160 Broadway, NYC 10038. (212)227-1000. Dir. Rabbi Yitzchok Merkin. Issues licenses to qualified instructors for all grades of the Hebrew day school and the general field of Torah education.

TOURO COLLEGE (1970). 30 W. 44 St., NYC 10036. (212)575-0190. Pres. Bernard Lander; Bd. Chmn. Max Karl. Chartered by NY State Board of Regents as a nonprofit four-year college with business, Judaic studies, health sciences, and liberal arts programs leading to BA, BS, and MA degrees; emphasizes relevance of Jewish heritage to general culture of Western civilization. Also offers JD degree and a biomedical program leading to the MD degree from Technion-Israel Institute of Technology, Haifa.

——, BARRY Z. LEVINE SCHOOL OF HEALTH SCIENCES AND CENTER FOR BIOMEDICAL EDUCATION. (1970) 300 Nassau Rd., Huntington, NY 11743. (516)421-2244. Dean Dr. Burton S. Sherman. Along with the Manhattan campus, offers 5 programs: Five-year program leading to MA from Touro and MD from Faculty of Medicine of Technion-Israel Institute of Technology, Haifa; BS/MA —physical therapy and occupational therapy programs; BS—physician assistant and health information management programs.

——, COLLEGE OF LIBERAL ARTS AND SCIENCES. 30 W. 44 St., NYC 10036. (212)575-0196. Exec. Dean Stanley Boylan. Offers comprehensive Jewish studies along with studies in the arts, sciences, humanities, and preprofessional studies in health sciences, law, accounting, business, computer science, and finance.

——, GRADUATE SCHOOL OF JEWISH STUDIES (1981) 30 W. 44 St., NYC 10036. (212)575-0190. Pres. Bernard Lander; Dean Michael A. Shmidman. Offers courses leading to an MA in Jewish studies, with concentrations in Jewish history or Jewish education. Students may complete part of their program in Israel, through MA courses offered by Touro faculty at Touro's Jerusalem center.

——, INSTITUTE OF JEWISH LAW. Based at Fuchsberg Law Center, serves as a center and clearinghouse for study and teaching of Jewish law. Coedits *Dinei Israel* (Jewish Law Journal) with Tel Aviv University Law School.

——, JACOB D. FUCHSBERG LAW CENTER (1980). Long Island Campus, 300 Nassau Rd., Huntington, NY 11743. (516)421-2244. Dean Howard A. Glickstein. Offers studies leading to JD degree.

——, JEWISH PEOPLE'S UNIVERSITY OF THE AIR. (1979) 30 W. 44th St., NYC 10036. (212)575-1819. Producer/Dir. Jacob Katzman. Produces and disseminates courses in Jewish subject matter for radio broadcasting and on audio-cassettes. Printed course outlines for all courses and discussion-leader's guides for some.

———, SCHOOL OF GENERAL STUDIES. 240 E. 123 St., NYC 10021. Dean Alfredo Matthew. Offers educational opportunities to minority groups and older people; courses in the arts, sciences, humanities, and special programs of career studies.

———, SHULAMITH SCHOOL. (1929). 1277 E. 14 St.,Brooklyn, NY 11230. (718)338-4000. Pres. Sy Knapel; Exec. Dir. Rabbi M. Zwick. Religious Hebrew elementary and high school.

UNION OF AMERICAN HEBREW CONGREGATIONS (1873). 838 Fifth Ave., NYC 10021. (212)249-0100. Pres. Rabbi Alexander M. Schindler; Bd. Chmn. Allan B. Goldman; V.-Pres.'s Albert Vorspan and Rabbi Daniel B. Syme. Serves as the central congregational body of Reform Judaism in the Western Hemisphere; serves its approximately 815 affiliated temples and membership with religious, educational, cultural, and administrative programs. *Keeping Posted; Reform Judaism.*

———, AMERICAN CONFERENCE OF CANTORS (1956). 1 Kalisa Way, Suite 104, Paramus, NJ 07652. (201)599-0910. Pres. Paul Silberscher; Exec. V.-Pres. Raymond Smolover. Members receive investiture and commissioning as cantors at ordination-investiture ceremonies at Hebrew Union College-Jewish Institute of Religion, Sacred School of Music. Through Joint Placement Commission, serves congregations seeking cantors and music directors. Dedicated to creative Judaism, preserving the best of the past, and encouraging new and vital approaches to religious ritual, music and ceremonies. *Koleinu.*

———, COMMISSION ON JEWISH EDUCATION (with CCAR and NATE) (1923). 838 Fifth Ave., NYC 10021. (212)249-0100. Dir. Rabbi Howard I. Bogot. Develops curricula and teachers' manuals; conducts pilot projects and offers educational guidance and consultation at all age levels to member congregations and affiliates and associate bodies. *Compass.*

———, COMMISSION ON SOCIAL ACTION OF REFORM JUDAISM (*see* p. 446)

———, COMMISSION ON SYNAGOGUE MANAGEMENT (with CCAR) (1962). 838 Fifth Ave., NYC 10021. (212)249-0100. Chmn. Dr. Paul Vanek; Dir. Joseph C. Bernstein. Assists congregations in management, finance, building maintenance, design, construction, and art aspects of synagogues; maintains the Synagogue Architectural Library.

———, NATIONAL ASSOCIATION OF TEMPLE ADMINISTRATORS (NATA) (1941). 1185 Sheridan Rd., Glencoe, IL 60022. (312)835-0724. Pres. Ilene H. Herst; Admin. Sec. Mark W. Weisstuch. Prepares and disseminates administrative information and procedures to member synagogues of UAHC; provides training of professional synagogue executives; formulates and establishes professional standards for the synagogue executive; provides placement services. *NATA Journal; Temple Management Manual.*

———, NATIONAL ASSOCIATION OF TEMPLE EDUCATORS (NATE) (1955). 707 Summerly Dr., Nashville, TN 37209-4218. (615)352-0322. Pres. Zena W. Sulkes; Exec. Sec. Richard M. Morin. Represents the temple educator within the general body of Reform Judaism; fosters the full-time profession of the temple educator; encourages the growth and development of Jewish religious education consistent with the aims of Reform Judaism; stimulates communal interest in and responsibility for Jewish religious education. *NATE News; Compass.*

———, NATIONAL FEDERATION OF TEMPLE BROTHERHOODS (1923). 838 Fifth Ave., NYC 10021. (212)570-0707. Pres. Richard D. Karfunkle; Exec. Dir. Lewis Eisenberg. Seeks to strengthen Judaism through family programming, by reaching out to college youth, and by promoting adult Jewish education. Through service programs, deals with current concerns of the changing Jewish family. Sponsors the Jewish Chatauqua Society, the brotherhoods' interfaith educational program. *Brotherhood.*

———, NATIONAL FEDERATION OF TEMPLE SISTERHOODS (1913). 838 Fifth Ave., NYC 10021. (212)249-0100. Pres. Dolores Wilkenfeld; Exec. Dir. Eleanor R. Schwartz. Serves more than 640 sisterhoods of Reform Judaism; promotes interreligious understanding and social justice;

awards scholarships and grants to rabbinic students; provides braille and large-type Judaic materials for Jewish blind; supports projects for Israel, Soviet Jewry, and the aging; is an affiliate of UAHC and is the women's agency of Reform Judaism; works in behalf of the Hebrew Union College-Jewish Institute of Religion; cooperates with World Union for Progressive Judaism. *Leaders Line; Notes for Now.*

———, NORTH AMERICAN FEDERATION OF TEMPLE YOUTH (NFTY; formerly NATIONAL FEDERATION OF TEMPLE YOUTH) (1939). 838 Fifth Ave., NYC 10021. (212)249-0100. Dir. Ramie Arian; Pres. David Barrett. Seeks to train Reform Jewish youth in the values of the synagogue and their application to daily life through service to the community and congregation; runs department of summer camps and national leadership training institute; arranges overseas academic tours, work-study programs, international student exchange programs, and college student programs in the U.S. and Israel, including accredited study programs in Israel. *Ani V'Atah; The Jewish Connection.*

UNION OF ORTHODOX JEWISH CONGREGATIONS OF AMERICA (1898). 45 W. 36 St., NYC 10018. (212)563-4000. Pres. Sidney Kwestel; Exec. V.-Pres. Rabbi Pinchas Stolper. Serves as the national central body of Orthodox synagogues; sponsors National Conference of Synagogue Youth, Our Way program for the Jewish deaf, Yachad program for developmentally disabled youth, Israel Center in Jerusalem, *aliyah* department, national OU *kashrut* supervision and certification service; provides educational, religious, and organizational guidance to synagogues and groups; represents the Orthodox Jewish community in relation to governmental and civic bodies and the general Jewish community. Publishes synagogue programming publications and books of Jewish interest. *Jewish Action magazine; OU Kosher Directory; OU Passover Directory; OU News Reporter; Synagogue Spotlight; Our Way magazine; Yachad magazine; Luach Limud Torah Diary Home Study Program.*

———, NATIONAL CONFERENCE OF SYNAGOGUE YOUTH (1954). 70 W. 36 St., NYC 10018. (212)244-2011. Pres. Alyson Maslansky; Dir. Rabbi Raphael Butler. Central body for youth groups of Orthodox congregations; provides educational guidance, Torah study groups, community service, programs consultation, Torah library, Torah fund scholarships, Ben Zakkai Honor Society, Friends of NCSY; conducts national and regional events including week-long seminars, Travel America with NCSY, Israel summer seminar for teens and collegiates, and Camp NCSY East. Divisions include Senior NCSY in 18 regions and 465 chapters, Junior NCSY for preteens, Our Way for the Jewish deaf, Yachad for the developmentally disabled, Mesorah for Jewish collegiates, and NCSY in Israel. *Keeping Posted with NCSY; Face the Nation—President's Newsletter; Oreich Yomeinu—Education Newsletter.*

———, WOMEN'S BRANCH (1923). 156 Fifth Ave., NYC 10010. (212)929-8857. Pres. Gitti Needleman; Admin. Sylvia Friedman. Seeks to spread the understanding and practice of Orthodox Judaism and to unite all Orthodox women and their synagogal organizations; services affiliates with educational and programming materials, leadership, and organizational guidance, and has an NGO representative at the UN. *Hachodesh; Hakol.*

UNION OF ORTHODOX RABBIS OF THE UNITED STATES AND CANADA (1900). 235 E. Broadway, NYC 10002. (212)964-6337. Dir. Rabbi Hersh M. Ginsberg. Seeks to foster and promote Torah-true Judaism in the U.S. and Canada; assists in the establishment and maintenance of *yeshivot* in the U.S.; maintains committee on marriage and divorce and aids individuals with marital difficulties; disseminates knowledge of traditional Jewish rites and practices and publishes regulations on synagogal structure; maintains rabbinical court for resolving individual and communal conflicts. *HaPardes.*

UNION OF SEPHARDIC CONGREGATIONS, INC. (1929). 8 W. 70 St., NYC 10023. (212)873-0300. Pres. Rev. Dr. S. Gaon; Bd. Chmn. Victor Tarry. Promotes the religious interests of Sephardic Jews; prepares and distributes Sephardic prayer books; provides religious leaders for Sephardic congregations.

UNITED LUBAVITCHER YESHIVOTH (1940). 841-853 Ocean Pkwy., Brooklyn, NY 11230. (718)859-7600. Pres. Eli N. Sklar; Chmn. Exec. Com. Rabbi S. Gourary. Supports and organizes Jewish day schools and rabbinical seminaries in the U.S. and abroad.

UNITED SYNAGOGUE OF AMERICA (1913). 155 Fifth Ave., NYC 10010. (212)533-7800. Pres. Franklin D. Kreutzer; Exec. V.-Pres. Benjamin Z. Kreitman; Sr. V.-Pres./Chief Exec. Off. Jerome M. Epstein. International organization of 850 Conservative congregations. Maintains 12 departments and 20 regional offices to assist its affiliates with religious, educational, youth, community, and administrative programming and guidance; aims to enhance the cause of Conservative Judaism, further religious observance, encourage establishment of Jewish religious schools, draw youth closer to Jewish tradition. Extensive Israel programs. *Program Suggestions; United Synagogue Review; Yearbook Directory and Buyers' Guide; Book Service Catalogue of Publications.*

———, COMMISSION ON JEWISH EDUCATION (1930). 155 Fifth Ave., NYC 10010. (212)260-8450. Cochmn. Harry S. Katz and Miriam Klein Shapiro; Dir. Rabbi Robert Abramson. Promotes higher educational standards in Conservative congregational schools and Solomon Schechter Day Schools and publishes material for the advancement of their educational programs. Provides guidance and resources for adult-education programs; publishes the *Jewish Tract* series; distributes El-Am edition of Talmud and black-and-white and color films of "Eternal Light" TV programs on Jewish subjects. *In Your Hands; Your Child; Kol Bana'yikh.*

———, COMMITTEE ON SOCIAL ACTION AND PUBLIC POLICY (1958). 155 Fifth Ave., NYC 10010. (212)533-7800. Cochmn. Rabbi Zachary Heller, Scott Kaplan; Dir. Tom Kagedan. Develops and implements positions and programs on issues of social action and public policy for the United Synagogue of America; represents these positions to other Jewish and civic organizations, the media, and government; and provides guidance, both informational and programmatic, to its affiliated congregations in these areas. *Today: Hayom.*

———, JEWISH EDUCATORS ASSEMBLY (1951). 15 E. 26 St., NYC 10010. (212)-532-4949. Pres. Rabbi Marim D. Charry; Exec. Dir. Benjamin Margolis. Advances the development of Jewish education on all levels in consonance with the philosophy of the Conservative movement. Promotes Jewish education as a basis for the creative continuity of the Jewish people. Serves as a forum for the exchange of ideas, programs, and educational media. *Bulletins; newsletters.*

———, KADIMA (formerly PRE-USY; reorg. 1968). 155 Fifth Ave., NYC 10010. (212)-533-7800. Exec. Dir. Daniel B. Ripps. Involves Jewish preteens in a meaningful religious, educational, and social environment; fosters a sense of identity and commitment to the Jewish community and the Conservative movement; conducts synagogue-based chapter programs and regional Kadima days and weekends. *Mitzvah of the Month;Kadima Kesher; Chagim; Advisors Aid; Games; quarterly Kadima magazine.*

———, NATIONAL ASSOCIATION OF SYNAGOGUE ADMINISTRATORS (1948). 155 Fifth Ave., NYC 10010. (212)533-7800. Pres. Harvey L. Brown. Aids congregations affiliated with the United Synagogue of America to further aims of Conservative Judaism through more effective administration (PALS Program); advances professional standards and promotes new methods in administration; cooperates in United Synagogue placement services and administrative surveys. *NASA Newsletter; NASA Journal.*

———, UNITED SYNAGOGUE YOUTH OF (1951). 155 Fifth Ave., NYC 10010. (212)-533-7800. Pres. Hillary Buff; Exec. Dir. Rabbi Paul Freedman. Seeks to strengthen identification with Conservative Judaism, based on the personality development, needs, and interests of the adolescent, in a Mitzvah framework. *Achshav; Tikun Olam; A.J. Heschel Honor Society Newsletter; SATO Newsletter; USY Alumni Assn. Newsletter; USY Program Bank.*

VAAD MISHMERETH STAM (1976). 4902 16 Ave., Brooklyn, NY 11204. (718)438-4963. Exec. Dir. Rabbi Yakov Basch. A nonprofit consumer-protection agency dedicated to preserving and protecting the halakhic integrity of Torah scrolls, phylacteries, and *mezuzot.* Makes presentations and conducts examination campaigns in schools and synagogues. *The Jewish Quill.*

NATIONAL JEWISH ORGANIZATIONS / 471

WEST COAST TALMUDICAL SEMINARY (Yeshiva Ohr Elchonon Chabad) (1953). 7215 Waring Ave., Los Angeles, CA 90046. (213)937-3763. Dean Rabbi Ezra Schochet. Provides facilities for intensive Torah education as well as Orthodox rabbinical training on the West Coast; conducts an accredited college preparatory high school combined with a full program of Torahtalmudic training and a graduate talmudical division on the college level. *Torah Quiz; Kobetz Migdal Ohr.*

WOMEN'S LEAGUE FOR CONSERVATIVE JUDAISM (1918). 48 E. 74 St., NYC 10021. (212)628-1600. Pres. Evelyn Auerbach; Exec. Dir. Bernice Balter. Constitutes parent body of Conservative (Masorti) women's groups in U.S., Canada, Puerto Rico, Mexico,and Israel; provides them with programs and resources in Jewish education, social action, Israel affairs, Canadian public affairs, leadership training, services to the disabled, community affairs, and publicity techniques; publishes books of Jewish interest; contributes to support of Jewish Theological Seminary of America and its residence halls. *Women's League Outlook; Ba'Olam.*

WORLD COUNCIL OF SYNAGOGUES (1957). 155 Fifth Ave., NYC 10010 (212)533-7693. Pres. Marshall Wolke; Exec. Dir. Bernard Barsky. International representative of Conservative organizations and congregations; promotes the growth and development of the Conservative movement in Israel and throughout the world; supports educational institutions overseas; holds biennial international conventions; represents the world Conservative movement on the Executive of the World Zionist Organization. *World Spectrum.*

WORLD UNION FOR PROGRESSIVE JUDAISM, LTD. (1926). 838 Fifth Ave., NYC 10021. (212)249-0100. Pres. Donald Day; Exec. Dir. Richard G. Hirsch; N. Amer. Dir. Martin Strelzer; Dir. Internatl. Relations & Development Rabbi Clifford Kulwin. International umbrella organization of Liberal Judaism; promotes and coordinates efforts of Liberal congregations throughout the world; starts new congregations, recruits rabbis and rabbinical students for all countries; organizes international conferences of Liberal Jews. *International Conference Reports; News and Views; Shalhevet* (Israel); *Teshuva* (Argentina); *Ammi.*

YAVNE HEBREW THEOLOGICAL SEMINARY (1924). PO Box 185, Brooklyn, NY 11218. (718)436-5610. Pres. Nathan Shapiro; Exec. Dir. Rabbi Solomon K. Shapiro. School for higher Jewish learning; maintains Machon Maharshal branch in Jerusalem for higher Jewish education and for an exchange student program. *Otzar Hashe'elot Vehateshuvot; Yavne Newsletter.*

YESHIVA UNIVERSITY (1886). 500 W. 185 St., NYC 10033. (212)960-5400. Pres. Norman Lamm; Chmn. Bd. of Trustees; Herbert Tenzer. The nation's oldest and largest independent university founded under Jewish auspices, with a broad range of undergraduate, graduate, and professional schools, a network of affiliates, publications, a widespread program of research and community outreach, and a museum. Curricula lead to bachelor's, master's, doctoral, and professional degrees. Undergraduate schools provide general studies curricula supplemented by courses in Jewish learning; graduate schools prepare for careers in medicine, law, social work, Jewish education, psychology, Semitic languages, literatures, and cultures, and other fields. It has six undergraduate schools, seven graduate and professional schools, and three affiliates, with its four main centers located in Manhattan and the Bronx. *Alumni Review/Inside YU.*

Undergraduate schools for men at Main Center: Yeshiva College (Dean Norman Rosenfeld) provides liberal arts and sciences curricula; grants BA and BS degrees. Isaac Breuer College of Hebraic Studies (Dean Rabbi Jacob M. Rabinowitz) awards Hebraic studies and Hebrew teacher's diploma, AA, BA, and BS. James Striar School of General Jewish Studies (Dir. Rabbi Benjamin Yudin) grants AA degree. Yeshiva Program/Mazer School of Talmudic Studies (Dean Rabbi Zevulun Charlop) offers advanced course of study in talmudic texts and commentaries.

Undergraduate school for women at Midtown Center, 245 Lexington Ave., NYC 10016: Stern College for Women (Dean Karen Bacon) offers liberal arts and sciences curricula supplemented by Jewish studies courses; awards BA, BS in education, AA, Jewish studies certificate, Hebrew teacher's diploma.

Sy Syms School of Business at Main Center (Dean Michael Schiff) offers undergraduate business study in conjunction with study at Yeshiva College or Stern College; grants BS in business. Sponsors one high school for boys (Manhattan) and one for girls (Queens). Universitywide services include the Irving and Hanni Rosenbaum Aliyah Incentive Fund; Jacob E. Safra Institute of Sephardic Studies; Ivan L. Tillem Program for Special Services for the Jewish Elderly; Holocaust Studies Program; Interdisciplinary Conference on Bereavement and Grief; Yeshiva University Gerontological Institute; Yeshiva University Museum; Yeshiva University Press.

———, ALBERT EINSTEIN COLLEGE OF MEDICINE (1955). 1300 Morris Pk. Ave., Bronx, NY 10461. (212)430–2000. Pres. Norman Lamm; Chmn. Bd. of Overseers Burton P. Resnick; Dean Dr. Dominick P. Purpura. Prepares physicians, conducts research in the health sciences, and provides patient care; awards MD degree; includes Sue Golding Graduate Division of Medical Sciences (Dir. Dr. Leslie Leinwand), which grants PhD degree. Einstein College's clinical facilities and affiliates encompass Jack D. Weiler Hospital of Albert Einstein College of Medicine, Bronx Municipal Hospital Center, Montefiore Hospital and Medical Center, and the Rose F. Kennedy Center for Research in Mental Retardation and Human Development. *Einstein; AECOM Today; Einstein Quarterly Journal of Biology and Medicine.*

———, ALUMNI OFFICE, 500 W. 185 Street, NYC 10033. 212)960–5373. Dir. E. Yechiel Simon. Seeks to foster a close allegiance of alumni to their alma mater by maintaining ties with all alumni and servicing the following associations: Yeshiva College Alumni (Pres. Henry Rothman); Stern College Alumnae (Pres. Rachel E. Oppenheim); Albert Einstein College of Medicine Alumni (Pres. Dr. Marvin Kirschner; Ferkauf Graduate School Alumni (Pres. Alvin I. Schiff); Wurzweiler School of Social Work Alumni (Pres. Eileen Stein Himber); Bernard Revel Graduate School—Harry Fischel School Alumni (Pres. Bernard Rosensweig); Rabbinic Alumni (Pres. Rabbi Steven Dworken); Benjamin N. Cardozo School of Law Alumni (Pres. Noel Ferris). Alumni Council (Chmn. Abraham S. Guterman) offers guidance to Pres. and Bd. of Trustees on university's academic development and service activities. *Alumni Review/Inside;*

*AECOM Alumni News; Jewish Social Work Forum.*

———, BELFER INSTITUTE FOR ADVANCED BIOMEDICAL STUDIES (1978). 1300 Morris Pk. Ave., Bronx, NY 10461. (212)430–2801. Dir. Dr. Ernst R. Jaffé. Integrates and coordinates the Medical College's postdoctoral research and training-grant programs in the basic and clinical biomedical sciences in the College of Medicine. Awards certificate as Research Fellow or Research Associate on completion of training.

———, BENJAMIN N. CARDOZO SCHOOL OF LAW (1976). 55 Fifth Ave., NYC 10003. (212)790–0310. Pres. Norman Lamm; Bd. Chmn. Jacob Burns; Dean Monroe E. Price. Provides innovative courses of study within a traditional legal framework; program includes judicial internships; grants Doctor of Law (JD) degree. Center for Professional Development assists students in obtaining employment. Leonard and Bea Diener Institute of Jewish Law explores American and Jewish jurisprudence. Bet Tzedek Legal Services Clinic provides services to low-income individuals; Samuel & Ronnie Heyman Center on Corporate Governance supports programs such as Tax Court Clinic. *Cardozo Law Review; Arts and Entertainment Law Journal; Women's Annotated Legal Bibliography; Assoc. of Student Internatl. Law Societies Internatl. Law Journal; Cardozo Law Forum.*

———, BERNARD REVEL GRADUATE SCHOOL (1937). 500 W. 185 St., NYC 10033. (212)960–5253. Dean Leo Landman. Offers graduate programs in Judaic studies and Semitic languages, literatures, and cultures; confers MS, MA, and PhD degrees.

———, BROOKDALE INSTITUTE FOR THE STUDY OF GERONTOLOGY (WURZWEILER SCHOOL OF SOCIAL WORK) (1978). 2495 Amsterdam Ave., NYC 10033. (212)960–0808. Dir. Celia B. Weisman. Aims to further advanced education in the field of gerontology and to introduce gerontology into the curriculum in the undergraduate and graduate schools.

———, DAVID J. AZRIELI GRADUATE INSTITUTE OF JEWISH EDUCATION AND ADMINISTRATION (1945). 245 Lexington Ave., NYC 10016. (212)340–7705. Dir.

Yitzchak Handel. Offers MS degree in Jewish elementary and secondary education; specialist's certificate and EdD programs in administration and supervision of Jewish education. Block Summer Education Program in administration and supervision of Jewish education. Prepares teachers and administrators in Jewish education for positions throughout the world.

———, FERKAUF GRADUATE SCHOOL OF PSYCHOLOGY (1957). 1300 Morris Pk. Ave., 5th fl., NYC 10461. (212)430–4201. Act. Dean Dr. Allan Goldstein. Offers MA in general psychology; PsyD in clinical and school psychology; and PhD in clinical, developmental-experimental (concentration in health) and school psychology. Center for Psychological and Psychoeducation Services offers counseling, diagnostic evaluation, and psychotherapy.

———, HARRY FISCHEL SCHOOL FOR HIGHER JEWISH STUDIES (1945). 500 W. 185 St., NYC 10033. Dean Leo Landman. Offers summer graduate programs in Judaic studies and Semitic languages, literatures, and cultures; confers MS, MA, and PhD degrees.

———, (affiliate) RABBI ISAAC ELCHANAN THEOLOGICAL SEMINARY (1896). 2540 Amsterdam Ave., NYC 10033. (212)960–5344. Chmn. Bd. of Trustees Judah Feinerman; Dean Rabbi Zevulun Charlop. Offers comprehensive program for preparing Orthodox rabbis; grants *semikhah* (ordination) and the degrees of Master of Religious Education, Master of Hebrew Literature, Doctor of Religious Education, and Doctor of Hebrew Literature. Includes Rabbi Joseph B. Soloveitchik Center of Rabbinic Studies, Marcos and Adina Katz Kollel (Institute for Advanced Research in Rabbinics, Dir. Rabbi Hershel Schachter), Kollel L'Horaah (Yadin Yadin; Dir. Rabbi J. David Bleich), Caroline and Joseph S. Gruss Kollel Elyon (Dir. Rabbi Aharon Kahn), Chaver Program (Dir. Rabbi J. David Bleich), Caroline and Joseph S. Gruss Institute in Jerusalem (Dir. Rabbi Aharon Lichtenstein). Brookdale Chaplaincy Internship Program trains prospective rabbis to work effectively with the elderly. Maybaum Sephardic Fellowship Program trains rabbis for service in Sephardic communities here and abroad. Morris and Nellie L. Kawaler Rabbinic Training Program emphasizes professional aspects of the rabbinate. Philip and Sarah Belz School of Jewish Music (Dir. Cantor Bernard Beer) provides professional training of cantors and other musical personnel; awards Associate Cantor's certificate and cantorial diploma. Max Stern Division of Communal Services (Assoc. Dir. Rabbi Kenneth Hain) provides personal and professional service to the rabbinate and related fields, as well as educational, consultative, organizational, and placement services to congregations, schools, and communal organizations throughout North America and abroad. Dr. Joseph and Rachel Ades Sephardic Community Outreach Program provides educational, religious, and cultural programs and personnel to Sephardic communities. Stone-Sapirstein Center for Jewish Education identifies and trains future educators through programs of learning, service, and internship; works with schools in the community and across the country; sponsors academic programs, lectures, and special projects throughout the university. National Commission on Torah Education and Educators Council of America formulate uniform educational standards, provide guidance to professional staffs, rabbis, and lay leaders with regard to curriculum, and promote Jewish education. Camp Morasha (Dir. Zvi Reich) offers Jewish studies program.

———, WOMEN'S ORGANIZATION (1928). 500 W. 185 St., Rm. BH 713, NYC 10033. (212)960–0855. Presidium: Inge Renner, Alice Turobiner, Judith Kirshenbaum; Dir. Liz Taffet. Supports Yeshiva University's national scholarship program for students training in education, community service, law, medicine, and other professions, and its development program. *YUWO News Briefs.*

———, WURZWEILER SCHOOL OF SOCIAL WORK (1957). 2495 Amsterdam Ave., NYC 10033. (212)960–0800. Chmn. Bd. of Governors Herbert H. Schiff; Dean Samuel M. Goldstein. Offers graduate programs in social casework, social group work, community social work; grants MSW and DSW degrees and postgraduate certificate in gerontology; two-year, full-time Concurrent Plan (Dir. of Admissions Naomi Lazarus) combines classroom study and supervised field instruction; the Extended Plan permits a period of up to five years to complete requirements for some master's degree candidates. Block Education Plan (Dir.

Frances A. Sosnoff) provides field instruction in Jewish communities in the U.S., Canada, Europe, and Israel. Clergy Plan provides training in counseling for clergy of all denominations. Plan for Employed Persons is specifically designed for people working in social agencies. *Jewish Social Work Forum.*

———, (affiliate) YESHIVA UNIVERSITY OF LOS ANGELES (1977). 9760 W. Pico Blvd., Los Angeles, CA 90035. (213)553-4478. Dean Rabbi Marvin Hier; Bd. Chmn. Samuel Belzberg; Dir. Academic Programs Rabbi Sholom Tendler. Grants BA degree in Jewish studies. Has university program and graduate studies department. Also provides Jewish studies program for beginners. Affiliates are Yeshiva University of Los Angeles High School and the Jewish Studies Institute.

———, SIMON WIESENTHAL CENTER (1978). 9760 W. Pico Blvd., Los Angeles, CA 90035. (213)553-9036. Dean Rabbi Marvin Hier; Assoc. Dean Rabbi Abraham Cooper; Dir. Gerald Margolis. Branch Offices: 320 N. Michigan Ave., Suite 1005, Chicago, IL 60601, (312)704-0027; 342 Madison Ave., Suite #320, NYC, 10017, (212)370-0320. Dedicated to preserving the memory of the Holocaust through education and awareness. Programs: museum; library; archives; "Testimony for the Truth" oral history; educational outreach; Scholars' Forum; International Social Action. *Simon Wiesenthal Center Annual; Response Magazine; Page One* (syndicated weekly radio news magazine presenting contemporary Jewish issues).

YESHIVATH TORAH VODAATH AND MESIVTA RABBINICAL SEMINARY (1918). 425 E. 9 St., Brooklyn, NY 11218. (718)-941-8000. Bd. Chmn. Chaim Leshkowiz. Offers Hebrew and secular education from elementary level through rabbinical ordination and postgraduate work; maintains a teachers institute and community-service bureau; maintains a dormitory and a nonprofit camp program for boys. *Chronicle; Mesivta Vanguard; Thought of the Week; Torah Vodaath News.*

———, ALUMNI ASSOCIATION (1941). 425 E. 9 St., Brooklyn, NY 11218. (718)941-8000. Pres. Marcus Saffer; Bd. Chmn. Seymour Pluchenik. Promotes social and cultural ties between the alumni and the schools through fund raising; offers vocational guidance to students; operates Camp Torah Vodaath; sponsors research fellowship program for boys. *Annual Journal; Hamesivta Torah periodical.*

## SOCIAL, MUTUAL BENEFIT

ALPHA EPSILON PI FRATERNITY (1913). 8815 Wesleyan Rd., Indianapolis, IN 46268-1185. (317)876-1913. Pres. Jonathan A. Tenzer; Exec. V.-Pres. Sidney N. Dunn. National Jewish fraternity active on many campuses; encourages Jewish students to remain loyal to their heritage and to assume leadership roles in the community; active in behalf of Soviet Jewry, the State of Israel, and other Jewish causes. *The Lion of Alpha Epsilon Pi* (quarterly newsletter/magazine).

AMERICAN FEDERATION OF JEWS FROM CENTRAL EUROPE, INC. (1938). 570 Seventh Ave., NYC 10018. (212)921-3871. Pres. K. Peter Lekisch; Bd. Chmn. Curt C. Silberman; Exec. Asst. Katherine Rosenthal. Seeks to safeguard the rights and interests of American Jews of Central European descent, especially in reference to restitution and indemnification; through its Research Foundation for Jewish Immigration sponsors research and publications on the history, immigration, and acculturation of Central European Jewry in the U.S.; sponsors social programs for needy Nazi victims in the U.S.; undertakes cultural activities, annual conferences, publications, and lecture programs; member, Council of Jews from Germany.

AMERICAN SEPHARDI FEDERATION (1973). 8 W. 40 St., Suite 1607, NYC 10018. (212)-730-1210. Pres. Leon Levy. Seeks to preserve the Sephardi heritage in the U.S., Israel, and throughout the world by fostering and supporting religious and cultural activities of Sephardi congregations, organizations, and communities, and uniting them in one overall organization; supports Jewish institutions of higher learning and those that train Sephardi lay and religious leaders; assists Sephardi charitable, cultural, religious, and educational institutions everywhere; publishes and/or disseminates books and other literature dealing with Sephardi culture and tradition in the U.S.; organizes youth and young-adult activities throughout the U.S.; supports efforts of the World Sephardi Federation to alleviate social disparities in Israel. *Sephardic Highlights.*

AMERICAN VETERANS OF ISRAEL (1949). c/o Samuel E. Alexander, 548 E. Walnut St., Long Beach, NY 11561. (516)431-8316. Pres. Murray Aronoff; Sec. Samuel E. Alexander. Maintains contact with American and Canadian volunteers who served in Aliyah Bet and/or Israel's War of Independence; promotes Israel's welfare; holds memorial services at grave of Col. David Marcus; is affiliated with World Mahal. *Newsletter.*

ASSOCIATION OF YUGOSLAV JEWS IN THE UNITED STATES, INC. (1941). 247 W. 99 St., NYC 10025. (212)865-2211. Pres. Mary Levine; Sec. Joseph Stock. Assists all Jews originally from Yugoslavia; raises funds for Israeli agencies and institutions. *Bulletin.*

BNAI ZION—THE AMERICAN FRATERNAL ZIONIST ORGANIZATION (1908). 136 E. 39 St., NYC 10016. (212)725-1211. Pres. Ernest Zelig; Exec. V.-Pres. Mel Parness. Fosters principles of Americanism, fraternalism, and Zionism; offers life insurance and other benefits to its members. Sponsors various projects in Israel: settlements, youth centers, medical clinics, Bnai Zion Home for Retarded Children (in Rosh Ha'ayin), the Haifa Medical Center, and the Herman Z. Quittman Center in Hakfar Hashwedi in Jerusalem. Has Young Leadership Division. *Bnai Zion Voice; Bnai Zion Foundation Newsletter; The Challenge; Haifa Happenings.*

BRITH ABRAHAM (1887). 136 E. 39 St., NYC 10016. (212)725-1211. Grand Master Robert Freeman. Protects Jewish rights and combats anti-Semitism; supports Soviet and Ethiopian emigration and the safety and dignity of Jews worldwide; furnishes regular financial assistance to Bnai Zion in Haifa, Haifa Medical Center, and other institutions to relieve the social burdens on the Israeli economy; aids and supports various programs and projects in the U.S.: Hebrew Excellence Program—Gold Medal presentation in high schools and colleges; Camp Loyaltown; Brith Abraham and Bnai Zion Foundations. *Voice.*

BRITH SHOLOM (1905). 3939 Conshohocken Ave., Philadelphia, PA 19131. (215)878-5696. Pres. Harold Sklar; Exec. Dir. Mervin L. Krimins. Fraternal organization devoted to community welfare, protection of rights of Jewish people, and activities which foster Jewish identity and provide support for Israel; sponsors Brith Sholom House for senior citizens in Philadelphia and Brith Sholom Beit Halochem in Haifa, a rehabilitation center for Israel's permanently war-wounded. *Brith Sholom Presents; monthly news bulletin.*

CENTRAL SEPHARDIC JEWISH COMMUNITY OF AMERICA (1941). 8 W. 70 St., NYC 10023. (212)787-2850. Pres. Emilie Levy; Treas. Victor Tarry. Pres. Women's Div. Irma Cardozo; Treas. Laura Capelluto. Promotes Sephardic culture by awarding scholarships to qualified needy students in New York and Israel; raises funds for hospital and religious institutions in U.S. and Israel. *Annual journal.*

FREE SONS OF ISRAEL (1849). 180 Varick St., 14th fl., NYC 10014. (212)924-6566. Grand Master Robert Grant; Grand Sec. Stanley Siflinger. Promotes fraternalism; supports State of Israel, UJA, Soviet Jewry, Israel Bonds, and other Jewish charities; fights anti-Semitism; awards scholarships. *National Reporter; Digest.*

JEWISH LABOR BUND (Directed by WORLD COORDINATING COMMITTEE OF THE BUND) (1897; reorg. 1947). 25 E. 21 St., NYC 10010. (212)475-0059. Exec. Sec. Joel Litewka. Coordinates activities of Bund organizations throughout the world and represents them in the Socialist International; spreads the ideas of socialism as formulated by the Jewish Labor Bund; publishes books and periodicals on world problems, Jewish life, socialist theory and policy, and on the history, activities, and ideology of the Jewish Labor Bund. *Unser Tsait* (U.S.); *Lebns-Fragn* (Israel); *Unser Gedank* (Australia); *Unser Shtimme* (France).

SEPHARDIC JEWISH BROTHERHOOD OF AMERICA, INC. (1915). 97-29 64th Rd., Rego Park, NY 11374. (718)459-1600. Pres. Bernard Ouziel; Sec. Michael Cohen. A benevolent fraternal organization seeking to further social, religiousl, and cultural goals of its members; offers funeral and burial benefits, scholarships, and aid to the needy. *Sephardic Brother.*

UNITED ORDER TRUE SISTERS, INC. (UOTS) (1846). 212 Fifth Ave., NYC 10010. (212)679-6790. Pres. Eileen B. Solomon; Exec. Admin. Dorothy B. Giuriceo. Philanthropic, community service, especially for indigent cancer victims; supports camps for children with cancer. *Echo.*

WORKMEN'S CIRCLE (1900). 45 E. 33 St., NYC 10016. (212)889-6800. Pres. Harold Ostroff; Exec. Dir. Jack Noskowitz. Provides fraternal benefits and activities, Jewish educational programs, secularist Yiddish schools for children, and community activities; supports institutions in Israel and promotes public-affairs activities in the U.S. on international and national issues. Underwrites "Folksbiene," worldwide Yiddish cultural, music, and theatrical festivals. Allied to *Jewish Forward* and WEVD. *Workmen's Circle Call; Kultur un Leben.*

## SOCIAL WELFARE

AMC CANCER RESEARCH CENTER (formerly JEWISH CONSUMPTIVES' RELIEF SOCIETY, 1904; incorporated as AMERICAN MEDICAL CENTER AT DENVER, 1954). 1600 Pierce St., Denver, CO 80214. (303)233-6501. Pres./Dir. Dr. Marvin A. Rich. Dedicated to advancing knowledge of cancer prevention, detection, diagnosis, and treatment through programs of laboratory, clinical, and community cancer control research. *Quarterly bulletin; annual report.*

AMERICAN JEWISH CORRECTIONAL CHAPLAINS ASSOCIATION, INC. (formerly NATIONAL COUNCIL OF JEWISH PRISON CHAPLAINS) (1937). 10 E. 73 St., NYC 10021-4194. (212)879-8415. (Cooperates with the New York Board of Rabbis and Jewish Family Service.) Pres. Rabbi Irving Koslowe; Exec. Off. Rabbi Moses A. Birnbaum. Supports spiritual, moral, and social services to Jewish men and women in corrections; provides a vehicle for Jewish chaplains in corrections to communicate mutual interests; stimulates support of correctional chaplaincy; provides spiritual and professional fellowship for Jewish correctional chaplains; promotes sound standards for correctional chaplaincy; schedules workshops and research to aid chaplains in counseling and with religious services for Jewish inmates. *Chaplains Manual.*

AMERICAN JEWISH SOCIETY FOR SERVICE, INC. (1949). 15 E. 26 St., Rm. 1304, NYC 10010. (212)683-6178. Pres. E. Kenneth Marks; Exec. Dir. Elly Saltzman. Conducts voluntary work-service camps each summer to enable high school juniors and seniors to perform humanitarian service.

ASSOCIATION OF JEWISH COMMUNITY ORGANIZATION PERSONNEL (1969). 1175 College Ave., Columbus, OH 43209. (614)-237-7686. Pres. Herman Markowitz; Exec. Dir. Ben M. Mandelkorn. An organization of professionals engaged in areas of fund raising, endowments, budgeting, social planning, financing, administration and coordination of services. Objectives are to develop and enhance professional practices in Jewish communal work; to maintain and improve standards, practices, scope and public understanding of the field of community organization, as practiced through local federations, national agencies, other organizations, settings, and private practitioners. *Prolog newsletter.*

ASSOCIATION OF JEWISH FAMILY AND CHILDREN'S AGENCIES (1972). 3084 State Hwy. 27, Suite 1—PO Box 248, Kendall Park, NJ 08824-0248. (201)821-0909. Pres. Bernard B. Nebenzahl; Exec. Dir. Bert J. Goldberg. The national service organization for Jewish family and children's agencies in Canada and the U.S. Reinforces member agencies in their efforts to sustain and enhance the quality of Jewish family and communal life. Operates the Elder Support Network for the National Jewish Community. *Bulletin* (bimonthly); *Directory; Job Openings Memo.*

ASSOCIATION OF JEWISH FAMILY AND CHILDREN'S AGENCY PROFESSIONALS (1965). c/o NYANA, 225 Park Ave. S., NYC 10003. (212)674-7400. Pres. Arnold Marks; Exec. Dir. Solomon H. Green. Brings together Jewish caseworkers and related professionals in Jewish family, children's, and health services. Seeks to improve personnel standards, further Jewish continuity and identity, and strengthen Jewish family life; provides forums for professional discussion at national conference of Jewish communal service and regional meetings; takes action on social-policy issues. *Newsletter.*

BARON DE HIRSCH FUND (1891). 130 E. 59 St., NYC 10022. (212)836-1798. Pres. Francis F. Rosenbaum, Jr.; Mng. Dir. Lauren Katzowitz. Aids Jewish immigrants and their children in the U.S. and Israel by giving grants to agencies active in educational and vocational fields; has limited program for study tours in U.S. by Israeli agriculturists.

B'NAI B'RITH INTERNATIONAL (1843). 1640 Rhode Island Ave., NW, Washington, DC 20036. (202)857-6600. Pres. Seymour D. Reich; Exec. V.-Pres. Thomas Neumann. International Jewish organization with affiliates in 43 countries. Offers programs designed to insure the preservation of Jewry and Judaism: Jewish education, community volunteer service to aid the needy, expansion of human rights, assistance to Israel, housing for the elderly, leadership training for youth and adults, rights of Soviet Jews and Jews of other countries to emigrate. *International Jewish Monthly; Shofar; Insider.*

———, ANTI-DEFAMATION LEAGUE OF (see p. 446)

———, CAREER AND COUNSELING SERVICES (1938). 1640 Rhode Island Ave. NW, Washington, DC 20036. (202)857-4992. Chmn. Burton M. Wanetik; Natl. Dir. Max F. Baer. Offers educational and career counseling to Jewish youth and adults on a group and individual basis through professionally staffed centers in New York, North Jersey, and Philadelphia.

———, HILLEL FOUNDATIONS, INC. (see p. 457)

———, KLUTZNICK MUSEUM (see p. 450)

———, YOUTH ORGANIZATION (see p. 457)

B'NAI B'RITH WOMEN (1897). 1640 Rhode Island Ave., NW, Washington, DC 20036. (202)857-6689. Pres. Hyla S. Lipsky; Exec. Dir. Elaine Binder. Promotes the principles of social advancement through education, action, and service. Offers programs that contribute to preservation of Jewish life and values; supports treatment of emotionally disturbed boys in BBW Children's Home, Group House in Israel; advocacy for women's rights. *Women's World.*

CITY OF HOPE NATIONAL MEDICAL CENTER AND BECKMAN RESEARCH INSTITUTE (1913). 1500 E. Duarte Rd., Duarte, CA 91010. (818)359-8111. Pres. and Chief Exec. Off. Dr. Sanford M. Shapero; Bd. Chmn. Abraham S. Bolsky. Offers care to those with cancer and major diseases, medical consultation service for second opinions, and pilot research programs in genetics, immunology, and the basic life process. *Pilot; President's Newsletter; City of Hope Quarterly.*

CONFERENCE OF JEWISH COMMUNAL SERVICE (1899). 3084 State Hwy. 27, Suite 1, Kendall Park, NJ 08824-1657. (201)821-1871. Pres. Daniel Thursz; Exec. Dir. Joel Ollander. Serves as forum for all professional philosophies in community service, for testing new experiences, proposing new ideas, and questioning or reaffirming old concepts; umbrella organization for eight major Jewish communal service groups. Concerned with advancement of professional personnel practices and standards. *Concurrents; Journal of Jewish Communal Service.*

COUNCIL OF JEWISH FEDERATIONS, INC. (1932). 730 Broadway, NYC 10003. (212)475-5000. Pres. Mandell Berman; Exec. V.-Pres. Carmi Schwartz. Provides national and regional services to more than 200 associated federations embracing 800 communities in the U.S. and Canada, aiding in fund raising, community organization, health and welfare planning, personnel recruitment, and public relations. *Directory of Jewish Federations, Welfare Funds and Community Councils; Directory of Jewish Health and Welfare Agencies* (biennial); *annual report.*

HOPE CENTER FOR THE DEVELOPMENTALLY DISABLED (1965). 3601 Martin L. King Blvd., Denver, CO 80205. (303)388-4801. Pres. Albert Cohen; Exec. Dir. George E. Brantley; Sec. Helen Fonda. Provides services to developmentally disabled of community: preschool training, day training and work activities center, speech and language pathology, occupational arts and crafts, recreational therapy, and social services.

INTERNATIONAL COUNCIL ON JEWISH SOCIAL AND WELFARE SERVICES (1961). c/o American Jewish Joint Distribution Committee, 711 Third Ave., NYC 10017. (NY liaison office with UN headquarters.) (212)687-6200. Chmn. Hon. L.H.L. Cohen; Exec. Sec. Leon Leiberg. Provides for exchange of views and information among member agencies on problems of Jewish social and welfare services, including medical care, old age, welfare, child care, rehabilitation, technical assistance, vocational training, agricultural and other resettlement, economic assistance, refugees, migration, integration and related problems, representation of views to governments and international organizations. Members: six national and international organizations.

JEWISH BRAILLE INSTITUTE OF AMERICA, INC. (1931). 110 E. 30 St., NYC 10016. (212)889-2525. Pres. Jane Evans; Exec. V.-Pres. Gerald M. Kass. Serves the religious, cultural, and educational needs of the Jewish blind, visually impaired, and reading-disabled by producing books of Judaica, including prayer books in Hebrew and English braille, large print, and on audio cassettes. Maintains free lending library of Hebrew, English, Yiddish, and other-language cassettes for the Jewish blind, visually impaired, and reading-disabled in 40 countries. *Jewish Braille Review; JBI Voice; Or Chadash.*

JEWISH CONCILIATION BOARD OF AMERICA, INC. (1930). 235 Park Ave. S., NYC 10003. (212)777-9034. Pres. Milton J. Schubin; Exec. Dir. Beatrice Lampert. Offers dispute-resolution services to families, individuals, and organizations. Socialwork, rabbinic, and legal expertise are available for family and divorce mediation and arbitration. Fee—sliding scale.

JEWISH FUND FOR JUSTICE (1984). 1725 K St., NW, Suite 301, Washington, DC 20006. (202)861-0601. Bd. Chmn. Si Kahn; Exec. Dir. Lois Roisman. A national grant-making institution supporting efforts to combat poverty in the U.S. Acts as a catalyst to increase Jewish communal and individual involvement in social-justice issues; participates in grant-making coalitions with other religious and ethnic groups. *Newsletter.*

JWB (1917). 15 E. 26 St., NYC 10010-1579. (212)532-4949. Pres. Donald R. Mintz; Exec. V.-Pres. Arthur Rotman. Leadership agency for North American network of Jewish community centers, YM-YWHAs, and camps, serving one million Jews. Provides Jewish educational and cultural programming through JWB Jewish Book and Music Councils, Lecture Bureau. U.S. government-accredited agency serving Jewish military families and hospitalized VA patients through JWB Jewish Chaplains Council. *JWB Circle; JWBriefing; Zarkor; JWB Personnel Reporter.*

———, JEWISH BOOK COUNCIL (*see* p. 452)

———, JEWISH CHAPLAINS COUNCIL (formerly COMMISSION ON JEWISH CHAPLAINCY) (1940). 15 E. 26 St., NYC 10010-1579. Chmn. Rabbi Aaron Landes; Dir. Rabbi David Lapp. Recruits, endorses, and serves Jewish military and Veterans Administration chaplains on behalf of the American Jewish community and the three major rabbinic bodies; trains and assists Jewish lay leaders where there are no chaplains, for service to Jewish military personnel, their families, and hospitalized veterans. *CHAPLINES newsletter.*

———, JEWISH MUSIC COUNCIL (*see* p. 452)

———, LECTURE BUREAU (*see* p. 452)

LEVI ARTHRITIS HOSPITAL (sponsored by B'nai B'rith) (1914). 300 Prospect Ave., Hot Springs, AR 71901. (501)624-1281. Pres. Harry Levitch; Chief Exec. Off. Patrick G. McCabe, Jr. Maintains a nonprofit, nonsectarian hospital for treatment of sufferers from arthritis; offers postoperative bone and joint surgery rehabilitation; stroke rehabilitation; and posttrauma rehabilitation. *Levi Voice.*

NATIONAL ASSOCIATION OF JEWISH FAMILY, CHILDREN'S AND HEALTH PROFESSIONALS (*see* Association of Jewish Family and Children's Agency Professionals)

NATIONAL ASSOCIATION OF JEWISH VOCATIONAL SERVICES (formerly JEWISH OCCUPATIONAL COUNCIL) (1940). 37 Union Square West, 5th fl., NYC 10003. (212)-243-0130. Pres. Harold E. Friedman; Exec. Dir. Harvey P. Goldman. Acts as coordinating body for all Jewish agencies in U.S., Canada, and Israel, having programs in educational-vocational guidance, job placement, vocational rehabilitation, skills-training, sheltered workshops, and occupational research. *Newsletter; NAJVS Reports.*

NATIONAL CONGRESS OF JEWISH DEAF (1956; inc. 1961). 4960 Sabal Palm Blvd., Bldg. 7, Apt. 207, Tamarac, FL 33319. TTY (305)977-7887. Pres. Dr. Martin Florsheim; Exec. Dir. Alexander Fleischman. Congress of Jewish congregations, service organizations, and associations located throughout the U.S. and Canada, advocating religious spirit and cultural ideals and fellowship for the Jewish deaf.

Affiliated with World Organization of Jewish Deaf. Publishes *Signs of Judaism,* a guide to American Sign Language. *NCJD Quarterly.*

NATIONAL COUNCIL OF JEWISH PRISON CHAPLAINS, INC. (*see* American Jewish Correctional Chaplains Association, Inc.)

NATIONAL COUNCIL OF JEWISH WOMEN (1893). 53 W. 23 St., NYC 10010. (212)-645-4048. Pres. Lenore Feldman; Exec. Dir. Dadie Perlov. Furthers human welfare through program of community service, education, advocacy for children and youth, aging, women's issues, constitutional rights, Jewish life and Israel. Promotes education for the disadvantaged in Israel through the NCJW Research Institute for Innovation in Education at Hebrew University, Jerusalem. Promotes welfare of children in U.S. through Center for the Child. *NCJW Journal; Washington Newsletter.*

NATIONAL INSTITUTE FOR JEWISH HOSPICE (1985). 6363 Wilshire Blvd., Suite 126, Los Angeles, CA 90048. (213) HOSPICE. Pres. Rabbi Maurice Lamm. Serves as a national Jewish hospice resource center. Through conferences, research, publications, video training courses, referral, and counseling services offers guidance, training, and information to patients, family members, clergy of all faiths, professional caregivers, and volunteers who work with seriously ill Jews.

NATIONAL JEWISH CENTER FOR IMMUNOLOGY AND RESPIRATORY MEDICINE (formerly NATIONAL JEWISH HOSPITAL/NATIONAL ASTHMA CENTER) (1899). 1400 Jackson St., Denver, CO 80206. (303)388-4461; 1-800-222-5864; Pres. Michael K. Schonbrun; Dir. Public Affairs Roy Raney. Leading medical center for study and treatment of respiratory diseases, allergies, and immune system disorders. Clinical emphasis on asthma, emphysema, tuberculosis, chronic bronchitis, and interstitial lung diseases; immune system disorders such as juvenile rheumatoid arthritis and immune deficiency disorders. *New Directions; Update; annual report; Lung Line Letter.*

NATIONAL JEWISH COMMITTEE ON SCOUTING (Boy Scouts of America) (1926). 1325 Walnut Hill La., Irving, TX 75015-2079. (214)580-2059. Chmn. Robert G. Kurzman; Dir. Fred Tichauer. Assists Jewish institutions in meeting their needs and concerns through use of the resources of scouting. Works through local Jewish committees on Scouting to establish Tiger Cub groups (1st grade), Cub Scout packs, Boy Scout troops, and coed Explorer posts in synagogues, Jewish community centers, day schools, and other Jewish organizations wishing to draw Jewish youth. Support materials and resources on request. *Hatzofe* (quarterly).

NATIONAL JEWISH GIRL SCOUT COMMITTEE (1972). Synagogue Council of America, 327 Lexington Ave., NYC 10016. (212)686-8670. Chmn. Rabbi Herbert W. Bomzer; Field Chmn. Adele Wasko. Under the auspices of the Synagogue Council of America, serves to further Jewish education by promoting Jewish award programs, encouraging religious services, promoting cultural exchanges with the Israel Boy & Girl Scouts Federation, and extending membership in the Jewish community by assisting councils in organizing Girl Scout troops and local Jewish Girl Scout committees. *Newsletter.*

NORTH AMERICAN ASSOCIATION OF JEWISH HOMES AND HOUSING FOR THE AGING (1960). 2525 Centerville Rd., Dallas, TX 75228. (214)327-4503. Pres.Dennis J. Magid; Exec. V.-Pres. Herbert Shore. Represents a community of not-for-profit charitable homes and housing for the Jewish aging; promotes excellence in performance and quality of service through fostering communication and education and encouraging advocacy for the aging. *Perspectives* (newsletter); *Directory.*

WORLD CONFEDERATION OF JEWISH COMMUNITY CENTERS (1947). 15 E. 26 St., NYC 10010. (212)532-4949. Pres. Ralph Goldman; Exec. Dir. Don Scher. Serves as a council of national and continental federations of Jewish community centers; fosters development of the JCC movement worldwide; provides a forum for exchange of information among centers. *Newsletter.*

## ZIONIST AND PRO-ISRAEL

ALYN—AMERICAN SOCIETY FOR HANDICAPPED CHILDREN IN ISRAEL (1934). 19 W. 44 St., NYC 10036. (212)869-8085. Chmn. Simone P. Blum; Exec. Dir. Nathan N. Schorr. Supports the work of ALYN Orthopaedic Hospital and Rehabilitation Center for Physically Handicapped Children, located in Jerusalem, which encompasses a 100-bed hospital and outpatient clinics, and houses the Helena Rubinstein Foundation Research Institute for research in neuromuscular diseases. *ALYN News.*

AMERICA-ISRAEL CULTURAL FOUNDATION, INC. (1939). 41 E. 42 St., NYC 10017. (212)557-1600. Bd. Chmn. Isaac Stern; Pres. Carl Glick. Raises funds to encourage the growth of culture in Israel through support of the arts; provides scholarships to gifted students and professionals in all the arts—music, dance, theater, the visual and plastic arts, film, and television. *Hadashot.*

AMERICA-ISRAEL FRIENDSHIP LEAGUE, INC. (1971). 134 E. 39 St., NYC 10016. (212)213-8630. Pres. Herbert Tenzer; Exec. V.-Pres. Ilana Artman. A nonsectarian, nonpartisan organization which seeks to broaden the base of support for Israel among Americans of all faiths and backgrounds. Activities include educational exchanges, tours of Israel for American leadership groups, symposia and public education activities, and the dissemination of printed information. *Newsletter.*

AMERICAN ASSOCIATES, BEN-GURION UNIVERSITY OF THE NEGEV (1973). 342 Madison Ave., Suite 1924, NYC 10173. (212)-687-7721. Pres. Isaac L. Auerbach; Bd. Chmn. Irwin H. Goldenberg; Chancellor Ambassador Yosef Tekoah. Serves as the university's publicity and fund-raising link to the U.S. The Associates are committed to publicizing university activities and curricula, securing student scholarships, transferring contributions, and encouraging American interest in the university. *AABGU Reporter; BGU Bulletin; Negev.*

AMERICAN COMMITTEE FOR SHAARE ZEDEK HOSPITAL IN JERUSALEM, INC. (1949). 49 W. 45 St., NYC 10036. (212)-354-8801. Pres. Charles Bendheim; Bd. Chmn. Ludwig Jesselson; Sr. Exec. V.-Pres. Morris Talansky. Raises funds for the various needs of the Shaare Zedek Medical Center, Jerusalem, such as equipment and medical supplies, nurse training, and research; supports exchange program between Shaare Zedek Medical Center and Albert Einstein College of Medicine, NY. *Heartbeat magazine.*

AMERICAN COMMITTEE FOR SHENKAR COLLEGE IN ISRAEL, INC. (1971). 855 Ave. of the Americas, NYC 10001. (212)-947-1597. Pres. David Pernick; Exec. Dir. Charlotte Fainblatt. Raises funds for capital improvement, research and development projects, laboratory equipment, scholarships, lectureships, fellowships, and library/archives of fashion and textile design at Shenkar College in Israel, Israel's only fashion and textile technology college. Accredited by the Council of Higher Education, the college is the chief source of personnel for Israel's fashion and apparel industry. *Shenkar Bulletin.*

AMERICAN COMMITTEE FOR THE WEIZMANN INSTITUTE OF SCIENCE (1944). 515 Park Ave., NYC 10022. (212)752-1300. Cochmn. Bram Goldsmith, Gershon Kekst; Exec. V.-Pres. Bernard N. Samers. Through 12 regional offices in the U.S. raises funds for the Weizmann Institute in Rehovot, Israel, and disseminates information about the scientific research under way there. *Rehovot; Interface; Research.*

AMERICAN FRIENDS OF HAIFA UNIVERSITY (1972). 41 E. 42 St., #828, NYC 10017. (212)818-9050. Pres. H. R. Shepherd; Exec. V.-Pres. Michael Weisser. Promotes, encourages, and aids higher and secondary education, research, and training in all branches of knowledge in Israel and elsewhere; aids in the maintenance and development of Haifa University; raises and allocates funds for the above purposes; provides scholarships; promotes exchanges of teachers and students. *Newsletter.*

AMERICAN FRIENDS OF RAMAT HANEGEV COLLEGE INC. (1983). 118 E. 25 St., NYC 10010. (212)460-8700. Pres. Meir Levin; Sec.-Treas. Jehuda J. Levin. Represents Ramat HaNegev College in fund raising and public relations in the U.S. Through various activities aids the college's efforts to improve the well-being of the Negev towns of Yeruham, Dimona, and Mitzpeh Ramon, and the development of the Negev south of Beersheva. *Newsletter.*

AMERICAN FRIENDS OF THE HAIFA MARITIME MUSEUM, INC. (1977). 236 Fifth Ave., NYC 10001. (212)696-8084. Chmn. and Treas. Bernard Weissman; Pres. Stephen K. Haber. Supports National Maritime Museum in Haifa. Promotes interest in maritime life among American Jews.

AMERICAN FRIENDS OF THE HEBREW UNIVERSITY (1925; inc. 1931). 11 E. 69 St., NYC 10021. (212)472-9800. Pres. Herbert D. Katz; Exec. V.-Pres. Robert A. Pearl-

## NATIONAL JEWISH ORGANIZATIONS / 481

man; Bd. Chmn. Harvey L. Silbert. Fosters the growth, development, and maintenance of the Hebrew University of Jerusalem; collects funds and conducts programs of information throughout the U.S., interpreting the work of the university and its significance; administers American student programs and arranges exchange professorships in the U.S. and Israel. *News from the Hebrew University of Jerusalem; Scopus magazine.*

AMERICAN FRIENDS OF THE ISRAEL MUSEUM (1972). 10 E. 40 St., Suite 1208, NYC 10016. (212)683-5190. Pres. Maureen Cogan; Exec. Dir. Michele Cohn Tocci. Raises funds for special projects of the Israel Museum in Jerusalem; solicits works of art for exhibition and educational purposes. *Newsletter.*

AMERICAN FRIENDS OF THE JERUSALEM MENTAL HEALTH CENTER—EZRATH NASHIM, INC. (1895). 10 E. 40 St., Suite 2701, NYC 10016. (212)725-8175. Pres. Burton G. Greenblatt; Exec. Dir. Mira Berman. Supports research, education, and patient care at the Jerusalem Mental Health Center, which includes a 250-bed hospital, comprehensive outpatient clinic, drug abuse clinic, geriatric center, and the Jacob Herzog Psychiatric Research Center; Israel's only nonprofit, voluntary psychiatric hospital; used as a teaching facility by Israel's major medical schools. *Friend to Friend; To Open the Gates of Healing.*

AMERICAN FRIENDS OF THE SHALOM HARTMAN INSTITUTE (1976). 1029 Teaneck Rd., Teaneck, NJ 07666. (201)837-0887. Pres. Robert P. Kogod; Dir. Rabbi Donniel Hartman; Admin. Dorothy Minchin. Supports the Shalom Hartman Institute, Jerusalem, an institute of higher education and research center, devoted to applying the teachings of classical Judaism to the issues of modern life. Founded in 1976 by David Hartman, the institute includes a Beit Midrash and centers for philosophy, theology, *halakhah,* political thought, and medical science, an experimental school, and programs for lay leadership. *A Word from Jerusalem.*

AMERICAN FRIENDS OF THE TEL AVIV MUSEUM (1974). 133 E. 58 St., Suite 704, NYC 10022. (212)319-0555. Pres. Roy V. Titus; Chmn. Milton J. Schubin; Exec. Dir. Ursula Kalish. Solicits contributions of works of art to enrich the Tel Aviv Museum collection; raises funds to support development, maintenance, and expansion of the museum and its educational and cultural programs. *Exhibition catalogues.*

AMERICAN FRIENDS OF THE TEL AVIV UNIVERSITY, INC. (1955). 360 Lexington Ave., NYC 10017. (212)687-5651. Board Chmn. Melvin S. Taub; Pres. Saul B. Cohen; Exec. V.-Pres. Jules Love. Promotes, encourages, aids, and advances higher education at Tel Aviv University and elsewhere. Among the many projects in the university's more than 50 research institutes are the Moshe Dayan Center for Middle & African Studies, the Jaffe Center for Strategic Studies; 25 institutes in different fields of medicine; and the Institute for Cereal Crops Improvement. *Tel Aviv University Report; Tel Aviv University Newsletter*

AMERICAN ISRAEL PUBLIC AFFAIRS COMMITTEE (AIPAC) (1954). 500 N. Capitol St., NW, Washington, DC 20001. (202)-638-2256. Pres. Ed Levy, Jr.; Exec. Dir. Thomas A. Dine. Registered to lobby on behalf of legislation affecting U.S.-Israel relations; represents Americans who believe support for a secure Israel is in U.S. interest. Works for a strong U.S.-Israel relationship. *Near East Report; AIPAC Papers on U.S.-Israel Relations.*

AMERICAN-ISRAELI LIGHTHOUSE, INC. (1928; reorg. 1955). 30 E. 60 St., NYC 10022. (212)838-5322. Pres. Mrs. Leonard F. Dank; Sec. Frances Lentz. Provides education and rehabilitation for the blind and physically handicapped in Israel to effect their social and vocational integration into the seeing community; built and maintains Rehabilitation Center for the Blind (Migdal Or) in Haifa. *Tower.*

AMERICAN JEWISH LEAGUE FOR ISRAEL (1957). 30 E. 60 St., NYC 10022. (212)-371-1583. Pres. Rabbi Reuben M. Katz; Bd. Chmn. Rabbi Aaron Decter. Seeks to unite all those who, notwithstanding differing philosophies of Jewish life, are committed to the historical ideals of Zionism; works, independently of class, party, or religious affiliation, for the welfare of Israel as a whole. Not identified with any political parties in Israel. Member, World Confederation of United Zionists. *Bulletin of the American Jewish League for Israel.*

AMERICAN PHYSICIANS FELLOWSHIP, INC. FOR MEDICINE IN ISRAEL (1950). 2001 Beacon St., Brookline, MA 02146. (617)-

232–5382. Pres. Dr. Edward H. Kass; Exec. Dir. Daniel C. Goldfarb. Helps Israel become a major world medical center; secures fellowships for selected Israeli physicians and arranges lectureships in Israel by prominent American physicians; runs medical seminars in Israel and U.S.; coordinates U.S. and Canadian medical and paramedical emergency volunteers to Israel; supports research and health care projects in Israel. *APF News.*

AMERICAN RED MAGEN DAVID FOR ISRAEL, INC. (1940). 888 Seventh Ave., Suite 403, NYC 10106. (212)757–1627. Pres. Dr. Robert L. Sadoff; Natl. Chmn. Louis Cantor; Exec. V.-Pres. Benjamin Saxe. An authorized tax-exempt organization; the sole support arm in the U.S. of Magen David Adom, Israel's Red Cross Service; raises funds for MDA's emergency medical services for Israel's military and civilian population, supplies ambulances, bloodmobiles, and mobile cardiac rescue units serving all hospitals and communities throughout Israel; supports MDA's 73 emergency medical clinics and helps provide training and equipment for volunteer emergency paramedical corps. *Lifeline.*

AMERICAN SOCIETY FOR TECHNION-ISRAEL INSTITUTE OF TECHNOLOGY (1940). 810 Seventh Ave., NYC 10019. (212)262–6200. Pres. Leonard L. Sherman; Exec. V.-Pres. Melvyn H. Bloom. Supports the work of the Technion-Israel Institute of Technology, Haifa, Israel's oldest university and premier technological institute, which educates 8,000 students in 20 engineering departments, in science and in medical school, and conducts research across a broad spectrum of science and technology. *Technion magazine; Technion-USA; UPDATE: News for ATS Insiders.*

AMERICAN SOCIETY FOR THE PROTECTION OF NATURE IN ISRAEL (1986). 475 Fifth Ave., 23rd fl., NYC 10017. (212)685–3380. Hon. Pres. Samuel W. Lewis; Pres. Daniel M. Singer; Exec. Dir. Tamar Podell. Seeks to increase the American public's awareness of, and support for, the critical conservation efforts conducted in Israel by the Society for the Protection of Nature in Israel (SPNI). Conducts educational programs and outdoor activities in the U.S. *Israel-Land and Nature* (published in Israel).

AMERICAN ZIONIST FEDERATION (1939; reorg. 1949 and 1970). 515 Park Ave., NYC 10022. (212)371–7750. Pres. Benjamin Cohen; Exec. Dir. Karen Rubinstein. Coordinates the work of the Zionist constituency in the areas of education, *aliyah,* youth and young leadership and public and communal affairs. Seeks to involve the Zionist and broader Jewish community in programs and events focused on Israel and Zionism (e.g., Zionist Shabbat, Scholars-in-Residence, Yom Yerushalayim) and through these programs to develop a greater appreciation for the Zionist idea among American Jewry. Composed of 16 national Zionist organizations, 10 Zionist youth movements, and affiliated organizations. Offices in Boston, Chicago, Los Angeles, New York. Groups in Baltimore, Detroit, Philadelphia, Pittsburgh, Rochester, Washington, DC. *Issue Analysis; Spectrum.*

AMERICAN ZIONIST YOUTH FOUNDATION, INC. (1963). 515 Park Ave., NYC 10022. (212)751–6070. Pres. Leon Levy; Exec. Dir. Ruth Kastner. Heightens Zionist awareness among Jewish youth through programs and services geared to high-school and college-age youngsters. Sponsors educational tours to Israel, study in leading institutions of science, scholarship, and the arts; sponsors field workers on campus and in summer camps; prepares and provides specialists who present and interpret the Israel experience for community centers and federations throughout the country. *Activist Newsletter; Guide to Education and Programming Material; Programs in Israel.*

AMERICANS FOR A SAFE ISRAEL (1971). 114 E. 28 St., NYC 10016. (212)696–2611. Chmn. Herbert Zweibon; Exec. Dir. Joseph Puder. Seeks to educate Americans in Congress, the media, and the public in general about Israel's role as a strategic asset for the West; through meetings with legislators and the media, in press releases and publications, promotes the notion of Jewish rights to Judea and Samaria. *Outpost.*

AMERICANS FOR PROGRESSIVE ISRAEL (1949). 150 Fifth Ave., Suite 911, NYC 10011. (212)255–8760. Pres. Mark Gold. A socialist Zionist movement that calls for a just and durable peace between Israel and its Arab neighbors; works for the liberation of all Jews; seeks the democratization of

Jewish communal and organizational life; promotes dignity of labor, social justice, and a deeper understanding of Jewish heritage. Affiliate of American Zionist Federation, World Union of Mapam, Hashomer Hatzair, and Kibbutz Artzi Fed. of Israel. *Israel Horizons; API Newsletter.*

AMIT WOMEN (formerly AMERICAN MIZRACHI WOMEN) (1925). 817 Broadway, NYC 10003. (212)477-4720. Pres. Daisy Berman; Exec. Dir. Marvin Leff. The State of Israel's official *reshet* (network) for religious secondary technological education; conducts social service, child care, Youth Aliyah villages, and vocational-educational programs in Israel in an environment of traditional Judaism; promotes cultural activities for the purpose of disseminating Zionist ideals and strengthening traditional Judaism in America. *AMIT Woman.*

AMPAL—AMERICAN ISRAEL CORPORATION (1942). 10 Rockefeller Plaza, NYC 10020. (212)586-3232. Pres. Michael Arnon. Finances and invests in Israeli economic enterprises; mobilizes finance and investment capital in the U.S. through sale of own debenture issues and utilization of bank credit lines. *Annual report; prospectuses.*

ARZA—ASSOCIATION OF REFORM ZIONISTS OF AMERICA (1977). 838 Fifth Ave., NYC 10021. (212)249-0100. Pres. Rabbi Charles Kroloff; Exec. Dir. Rabbi Eric Yoffie. Individual Zionist membership organization devoted to achieving Jewish pluralism in Israel and strengthening the Israeli Reform movement. Chapter activities in the U.S. concentrate on these issues, and on strengthening American public support for Israel. *ARZA Newsletter.*

BAR-ILAN UNIVERSITY IN ISRAEL (1955). 130 East 59 St., NYC 10022.. (212)832-0095. Chancellor Emanuel Rackman; Pres. Michael Albeck; Chmn. Global Bd. of Trustees Ludwig Jesselson; Pres. Amer. Bd. of Overseers Belda Lindenbaum. Supports Bar-Ilan University, a traditionally oriented liberal arts and sciences institution, where all students must take basic Jewish studies courses as a requirement of graduation; located in Ramat-Gan, Israel, and chartered by the Board of Regents of the State of NY. *Update; Bar-Ilan News.*

BETAR ZIONIST YOUTH ORGANIZATION (1935). 38 East 23 St., NYC 10010. (212)-353-8033. Central Shaliach Eli Cohen. Organizes youth groups across North America to teach Zionism, Jewish pride, and love of Israel; sponsors summer programs in Israel for Jewish youth ages 13–21; sponsors Tagar Zionist Student Activist Movement on college campuses. *Etgar.*

BOYS TOWN JERUSALEM FOUNDATION OF AMERICA INC. (1948). 91 Fifth Ave., Suite 601, NYC 10003. (212)242-1118. Pres. Michael J. Scharf; Exec. V.-Pres. Rabbi Ronald L. Gray; Chmn. Josh S. Weston. Raises funds for Boys Town Jerusalem, which was established in 1948 to offer a comprehensive academic, religious, and technical education to disadvantaged Israeli and immigrant boys from over 45 different countries, including Ethiopia and Iran. Enrollment: over 1,500 students in jr. high school, academic and technical high school, and a college of applied engineering. *BTJ Newsbriefs; Your Town Magazine.*

COUNCIL FOR A BEAUTIFUL ISRAEL ENVIRONMENTAL EDUCATION FOUNDATION (1973). 350 Fifth Ave., 19th fl., NYC 10118. (212)947-5709. Pres. Ruth Baum; Admin. Dir. Donna Lindemann. A support group for the Israeli body, whose activities include education, town planning, lobbying for legislation to protect and enhance the environment, preservation of historical sites, the improvement and beautification of industrial and commercial areas, and renovating bomb shelters into parks and playgrounds. *Quarterly newsletter.*

DROR—YOUNG KIBBUTZ MOVEMENT—HABONIM (1977). 27 W. 20 St., 9th fl., NYC 10011. (212)675-1168. Exec. Dir. Yoel Skolnick. Provides an opportunity for individuals who have spent time in Israel, on a kibbutz program, to continue their contact with the kibbutz movement through regional and national activities and seminars; sponsors two *garinim* to kibbutz each year and a teenage summer program. *New Horizons.*

———, CHAVURAT HAGALIL (1978). Exec. Dir. Shlomo Ravid. Aids those aged 27–35 in making *aliyah* to a kibbutz. Affiliated with TAKAM kibbutz association.

———, GARIN YARDEN, YOUNG KIBBUTZ MOVEMENT (1976). Exec. Dir. Shlomo Ravid. Aids those aged 20–30 interested in making *aliyah* to a kibbutz; affiliated with TAKAM kibbutz association.

EMUNAH WOMEN OF AMERICA (formerly HAPOEL HAMIZRACHI WOMEN'S ORGANIZATION) (1948). 7 Penn Plaza, NYC 10001 (212)564–9045. Pres. Gladys Baruch; Exec. Dir. Shirley Singer. Maintains and supports 200 educational and social-welfare institutions in Israel within a religious framework, including nurseries, daycare centers, vocational and teacher-training schools for the underprivileged, and a community college complex. Also involved in absorption of Ethiopian immigrants. *The Emunah Woman; Lest We Forget; Emunah Connection.*

FEDERATED COUNCIL OF ISRAEL INSTITUTIONS—FCII (1940). 4702 15th Ave., Brooklyn, NY 11219. (718)972–5530. Bd. Chmn. Z. Shapiro; Exec. V.-Pres. Rabbi Julius Novack. Central fund-raising organization for over 100 affiliated institutions; handles and executes estates, wills, and bequests for the traditional institutions in Israel; clearinghouse for information on budget, size, functions, etc., of traditional educational, welfare, and philanthropic institutions in Israel, working cooperatively with the Israeli government and the overseas department of the Council of Jewish Federations. *Annual financial reports and statistics on affiliates.*

FRIENDS OF LABOR ISRAEL (1986). 27 W. 20 St. (9), NYC 10011. (212)255–1796. Exec. Dir. Simmy Ziv-El; Asst. Dir. Ronny Brawer. The Israel Labor movement's newest support organization in the U.S. was established to bolster Labor representation in the World Zionist Congress and to promote a dialogue between labor leaders and American Jewry. *Folio.*

FRIENDS OF THE ISRAEL DEFENSE FORCES (1981). 15 E. 26 St., NYC 10010. (212)-684–0669. Bd. Chmn. Henry Plitt. Supports the *Agudah Lema'an Hahayal,* Israel's Assoc. for the Well-Being of Soldiers, founded in the early 1940s, which provides social, recreational, and educational programs for soldiers, special services for the sick and wounded, and much more. *Newsletter.*

FUND FOR HIGHER EDUCATION (1970). 1768 S. Wooster St., Los Angeles, CA 90035. (213)202–1879. Chmn. Exec. Comm. Max Candiotty. Raises funds and disseminates information in the interest of institutions of higher education in the U.S. & Israel. Over $18 million distributed to over 100 institutions of higher learning, including over $11 million in Israel and $6 million in the U.S. *In Response.*

GIVAT HAVIVA EDUCATIONAL FOUNDATION, INC. (1966). 150 Fifth Ave., Suite 911, NYC 10011. (212)255–2992. Chmn. Lucille R. Perlman. Supports programs in Israel to further Jewish-Arab rapprochement, narrow economic and educational gaps within Israeli society, and improve educational opportunities for various disadvantaged youth. Affiliated with the Givat Haviva Center of the Kibbutz Artzi Federation, the Menachem Bader Fund, and other projects. In the U.S., GHEF, Inc. sponsors educational seminars, public lectures and parlor meetings with Israeli speakers, as well as individual and group trips to Israel. *News from Givat Haviva; special reports.*

GOLDA MEIR ASSOCIATION (1984). 33 E. 67 St., NYC 10021. (212)570–1443. Pres. Alfred H. Moses; Exec. Dir. Avner Tavori. North American support group for the Israeli association, whose large-scale educational programs address the issues of democracy in Israel, Sephardi-Ashkenazi integration, religious pluralism, the peace process, and relations between Israeli Jews and Arabs. Its "Project Democracy" is the largest program dealing with the tide of extremism sweeping Israel's youth. *Newsletter.*

HABONIM-DROR NORTH AMERICA (1934). 27 W. 20 St., 9th fl., NYC 10011. (212)-255–1796. Sec.-Gen. Chuck Buxbaum; Exec. Off. Sarabeth Weiss. Fosters identification with pioneering in Israel; stimulates study of Jewish life, history, and culture; sponsors community-action projects, seven summer camps in North America, programs in Israel, and *garinei aliyah* to Kibbutz Ravid. *Batnua; Progressive Zionist Journal; Bimat Hamaapilim.*

HADASSAH, THE WOMEN'S ZIONIST ORGANIZATION OF AMERICA, INC. (1912). 50 W. 58 St., NYC 10019. (212)355–7900. Pres. Carmela E. Kalmanson; Exec. Dir. Aileen Novick. In America helps interpret Israel to the American people; provides basic Jewish education as a background for intelligent and creative Jewish living; sponsors Hashachar, largest Zionist youth movement in U.S., which has four divisions: Young Judaea, Intermediate Judaea, Senior Judaea, and Hamagshimim; operates six Zionist youth camps in this country; supports summer and all-year courses in Israel. Maintains in Israel Hadassah-Hebrew University Medical Center for healing, teaching, and research; Hadassah Community College; and Hadassah Vocational Guidance Institute. Is largest organizational contributor to Youth Aliyah and to Jewish National Fund for land purchase and reclamation. *Update; Headlines; Hadassah Magazine; Textures; The Catalist.*

———, HASHACHAR (formerly YOUNG JUDAEA and JUNIOR HADASSAH) (1909; reorg. 1967). 50 W. 58 St., NYC 10019. (212)355-7900. Pres. of Senior Judaea (high-school level) Gidon Isaacs; Coord. of Hamagshimim (college level) Eric Kleinman; Natl. Dir. Irv Widaen. Seeks to educate Jewish youth from the ages of 9–27 toward Jewish and Zionist values, active commitment to and participation in the American and Israeli Jewish communities; maintains summer camps and year programs in Israel. *Hamagshimim Journal; Kol Hat'nua; The Young Judaean.*

HASHOMER HATZAIR, SOCIALIST ZIONIST YOUTH MOVEMENT (1923). 150 Fifth Ave., Suite 911, NYC 10011. (212)929-4955. Sec. Morrie Hermon; Central Shaliach Chaim Broom. Seeks to educate Jewish youth to an understanding of Zionism as the national liberation movement of the Jewish people. Promotes *aliyah* to *kibbutzim.* Affiliated with AZYC and Kibbutz Artzi Federation. Espouses socialist ideals of peace, justice, democracy, and brotherhood. *Young Guard.*

HERUT ZIONISTS OF AMERICA, INC. (1925). 9 E. 38 St., Suite 1000, NYC 10016. (212)-696-0900. Pres. Hart N. Hasten; Exec. Dir. Glenn Mones. American branch of worldwide movement founded by Ze'ev Jabotinsky. Affiliated with Herut political party in Israel. Supports Israeli peace with security, free enterprise economy, and rights to settlement in the territories. Subsidiaries: Betar Zionist Youth; Tagar Zionist Student Activist Movement; Tel-Hai Fund, Inc. *The Herut Letter.*

JEWISH NATIONAL FUND OF AMERICA (1901). 42 E. 69 St., NYC 10021. (212)-879-9300. Pres. Joseph P. Sternstein; Exec. V.-Pres. Samuel I. Cohen. Exclusive fund-raising agency of the world Zionist movement for the afforestation, reclamation, and development of the land of Israel, including construction of roads, parks, and recreational areas, preparation of land for new communities and industrial facilities; helps emphasize the importance of Israel in schools and synagogues throughout the U.S. *JNF Almanac; Land and Life.*

KEREN OR, INC. (1956). 1133 Broadway, NYC 10010. (212)255-1180. Bd. Chmn. Dr. Edward L. Steinberg; Pres. Dr. Albert Hornblass; Exec. Dir. Paul H. Goldenberg. Funds the Keren Or Center for Multihandicapped Blind Children, in Jerusalem, providing long-term basic training, therapy, rehabilitative, and early childhood education to the optimum level of the individual; with major hospitals, involved in research into causes of multihandicapped blind birth; campaign under way for new multipurpose building on government land-grant in Ramot.

LABOR ZIONIST ALLIANCE (formerly FARBAND LABOR ZIONIST ORDER; now uniting membership and branches of POALE ZION—UNITED LABOR ZIONIST ORGANIZATION OF AMERICA and AMERICAN HABONIM ASSOCIATION) (1913). 275 Seventh Ave., NYC 10001. (212)989-0300. Pres. Menachem Z. Rosensaft; Exec. Dir. Sarrae G. Crane. Seeks to enhance Jewish life, culture, and education in U.S. and Canada; aids in building State of Israel as a cooperative commonwealth, and its Labor movement organized in the Histadrut; supports efforts toward a more democratic society throughout the world; furthers the democratization of the Jewish community in America and the welfare of Jews everywhere; works with labor and liberal forces in America. *Jewish Frontier; Yiddisher Kempfer.*

LEAGUE FOR LABOR ISRAEL (1938; reorg. 1961). 275 Seventh Ave., NYC 10001. (212)989-0300. Pres. Ezra Spicehandler; Exec. Dir. Rabbi Arthur Seltzer. Conducts Labor Zionist educational and cultural activities, for youth and adults, in the American Jewish community. Promotes educational travel to Israel.

MERCAZ (1979). 155 Fifth Ave., NYC 10010. (212)533-7800. Pres. Goldie Kweller; Exec. Dir. Hindy Kisch. The U.S. Zionist action organization for Conservative/Masorti Judaism, Mercaz works to attain religious rights for the Masorti movement in Israel. It fosters Zionist education and develops young leadership, sponsoring an annual mission to Israel. *Hatzioni Newsletter.*

NA'AMAT USA, THE WOMEN'S LABOR ZIONIST ORGANIZATION OF AMERICA, INC. (formerly PIONEER WOMEN/NA'AMAT) (1925; reorg. 1985). 200 Madison Ave., Suite 1808, NYC 10025. (212)725-8010. Pres. Gloria Elbling; Exec. Dir. Tehila Elpern. Part of a world movement of working women and volunteers, Na'amat USA helps provide social, educational, and legal services for women, teenagers, and children in Israel. It also advocates legislation for women's rights and child welfare in the U.S., furthers Jewish education, and supports Habonim-Dror, the Labor Zionist youth movement. *Na'amat Woman magazine.*

NATIONAL COMMITTEE FOR LABOR ISRAEL—HISTADRUT (1923). 33 E. 67 St., NYC 10021. (212)628-1000. Pres. Bruce C. Vladeck; Exec. V.-Pres. Eliezer Rafaeli; Chmn. Trade Union Council Morton Bahr. Promotes relations and understanding between American trade unions and the Israeli labor movement-Histadrut; offers educational programs on Israeli labor in the Jewish community and among the general public; raises funds for the educational, health, social and cultural projects of Histadrut for working people, Jews, and Arabs in Israel and for Histadrut's programs in the Third World. *Backdrop Histadrut; Amal Newsletter.*

NEW ISRAEL FUND (1979). 111 W. 40 St., Suite 2600, NYC 10018. (212)302-0066. Pres. Mary Ann Stein; Exec. Dir. Jonathan Jacoby. Supports the citizens'-action efforts of Israelis working to achieve social justice and to protect and strengthen the democratic process in Israel. Also seeks to enrich the quality of the relationships between Israelis and North American Jews through deepened mutual understanding. *A Guide to Arab-Jewish Peacemaking in Israel; quarterly bulletin; annual report.*

PEC ISRAEL ECONOMIC CORPORATION (formerly PALESTINE ECONOMIC CORPORATION) (1926). 511 Fifth Ave., NYC 10017. (212)687-2400. Pres. Joseph Ciechanover; Exec. V.-Pres. Frank J. Klein; Sec.-Asst. Treas. William Gold. Primarily engaged in the business of organizing, financing, and administering business enterprises located in or affiliated with enterprises in the State of Israel, through holdings of equity securities and loans. *Annual report.*

PEF ISRAEL ENDOWMENT FUNDS, INC. (1922). 41 E. 42 St., Suite 607, NYC 10017. (212)599-1260. Chmn. Sidney Musher; Sec. Harvey Brecher. Uses funds for Israeli educational and philanthropic institutions and for constructive relief, modern education, and scientific research in Israel. *Annual report.*

PIONEER WOMEN/NA'AMAT (*see* Na'amat USA)

POALE AGUDATH ISRAEL OF AMERICA, INC. (1948). 3190 Bedford Ave., Brooklyn, NY 11210. (718)377-4111. Pres. Rabbi Fabian Schonfeld; Exec. V.-Pres. Rabbi Moshe Malinowitz. Aims to educate American Jews to the values of Orthodoxy and *aliyah;* supports *kibbutzim,* trade schools, *yeshivot, moshavim, kollelim,* research centers, and children's homes in Israel. *PAI News; She'arim; Hamayan.*

———, WOMEN'S DIVISION OF (1948). Pres. Aliza Widawsky; Presidium: Sarah Ivanisky, Miriam Lubling, Bertl Rittenberg. Assists Poale Agudath Israel to build and support children's homes, kindergartens, and trade schools in Israel. *Yediot PAI.*

PROGRESSIVE ZIONIST CAUCUS (1982). 27 W. 20 St., NYC 10011. (212)675-1168. Shaliach Yoel Skolnick; Dir. Bruce Saposnick. A campus-based grass-roots organization committed to a progressive Zionist agenda. Students organize local and regional educational, cultural, and political activities, such as speakers, films, *Kabbalot Shabbat,* and Arab-Jewish dialogue groups. The PZC Kvutzat Aliyah is a support framework for individuals interested in *aliyah* to a city or town. *La'Inyan.*

RELIGIOUS ZIONISTS OF AMERICA 25 W. 26 St., NYC 10010. (212)689-1414.

———, BNEI AKIVA OF NORTH AMERICA (1934). 25 W. 26 St., NYC 10010. (212)-889-5260. Pres. Yitz Feigenbaum; V.-Pres. Admin. Jerry Yudkowsky. Seeks to interest youth in *aliyah* to Israel and social justice through pioneering *(haluztiut)* as an integral part of their religious observance; sponsors five summer camps, a leadership training camp for eleventh graders, a work-study program on a religious kibbutz for high school graduates, summer tours to Israel; establishes nuclei of college students for kibbutz or other settlement. *Akivon; Hamvaser; Pinkas Lamadrich; Daf Rayonot; Ma'Ohalai Torah; Zraim.*

———, MIZRACHI-HAPOEL HAMIZRACHI (1909; merged 1957). 25 W. 26 St., NYC 10010. (212)689-1414. Pres. Hermann Merkin; Exec. V.-Pres. Israel Friedman. Disseminates ideals of religious Zionism; conducts cultural work, educational program, public relations; raises funds for religious educational institutions in Israel, including *yeshivot hesder* and Bnei Akiva. *Newsletters; Kolenu.*

———, MIZRACHI PALESTINE FUND (1928). 25 W. 26 St., NYC 10010. Chmn. Joseph Wilon; Sec. Israel Friedman. Fundraising arm of Mizrachi movement.

———, NATIONAL COUNCIL FOR TORAH EDUCATION OF MIZRACHI-HAPOEL HAMIZRACHI (1939). 25 W. 26 St., NYC 10010. Pres. Rabbi Israel Schorr; Dir. Rabbi Meyer Golombek. Organizes and supervises *yeshivot* and Talmud Torahs; prepares and trains teachers; publishes textbooks and educational materials; organizes summer seminars for Hebrew educators in cooperation with Torah Department of Jewish Agency; conducts *ulpan*. *Hazarkor; Chemed.*

———, NOAM-MIZRACHI NEW LEADERSHIP COUNCIL (formerly NOAM-HAMISHMERET HATZEIRA) (1970). 25 W. 26 St., NYC 10010. (212)684-6091. Chmn. Rabbi Marc Schneier; V. Chmn. Sheon Karol; Dir. Jeffrey M. Weisberg. Develops new religious Zionist leadership in the U.S. and Canada; presents young religious people with various alternatives for settling in Israel through *garinei aliyah* (core groups); meets the religious,educational, and social needs of Jewish young adults and young couples. *Forum.*

SOCIETY OF ISRAEL PHILATELISTS (1948). 27436 Aberdeen, Southfield, MI 48076. (313)557-0887. Pres. Howard Chapman; Exec. Sec. Irvin Girer. Promotes interest in, and knowledge of, all phases of Israel philately through sponsorship of chapters and research groups, maintenance of a philatelic library, and support of public and private exhibitions. *Israel Philatelist; monographs; books.*

STATE OF ISRAEL BONDS (1951). 730 Broadway, NYC 10003. (212)677-9650. Internatl. Chmn. David B. Hermelin; Pres. Yehudah Halevy; Exec. V.-Pres. Morris Sipser. Seeks to provide large-scale investment funds for the economic development of the State of Israel through the sale of State of Israel bonds in the U.S., Canada, Western Europe, and Latin America.

THEODOR HERZL FOUNDATION (1954). 515 Park Ave., NYC 10022. (212)752-0600. Chmn. Kalman Sultanik; Sec. Isadore Hamlin. Cultural activities, lectures, conferences, courses in modern Hebrew and Jewish subjects, Israel, Zionism, and Jewish history. *Midstream.*

———, HERZL PRESS. Chmn. Kalman Sultanik. Serves as "the Zionist Press of record," publishing books that are important for the light they shed on Zionist philosophy, Israeli history, contemporary Israel and the Diaspora, and the relationship between them. Many of these volumes, because of their specialized nature, would not be attractive to commercial publishers, but are important as contributions to Zionist letters and history.

———, THEODOR HERZL INSTITUTE. Chmn. Jacques Torczyner; Dir. Sidney Rosenfeld. Program geared to review of contemporary problems on Jewish scene here and abroad, presentation of Jewish heritage values in light of Zionist experience of the ages, study of modern Israel, and Jewish social research with particular consideration of history and impact of Zionism. Lectures, forums, Encounter with Creativity; musicales, recitals, concerts; holiday celebrations; visual art programs, Nouveau Artist Introductions. *Annual Program Preview; Herzl Institute Bulletin.*

UNITED CHARITY INSTITUTIONS OF JERUSALEM, INC. (1903). 1141 Broadway, NYC 10001. (212)683-3221. Pres. Rabbi Zevulun Charlop; Sec. Sam Gabel. Raises funds for the maintenance of schools, kitchens, clinics, and dispensaries in Israel; free loan foundations in Israel.

UNITED ISRAEL APPEAL, INC. (1925). 515 Park Ave., NYC 10022. (212)688-0800. Chmn. Henry Taub; Exec. V.-Chmn. Herman Markowitz. As principal beneficiary of the United Jewish Appeal, serves as link between American Jewish community and Jewish Agency for Israel, its operating agent; assists in resettlement and absorption of refugees in Israel, and supervises flow of funds and expenditures for this purpose.

UNITED STATES COMMITTEE SPORTS FOR ISRAEL, INC. (1948). 275 S. 19 St., Suite 1203, Philadelphia, PA 19103. (215)546-4700. Pres. Robert E. Spivak; Exec. Dir. Barbara G. Lissy. Sponsors U.S. participation in, and fields and selects U.S. team for, World Maccabiah Games in Israel every four years; promotes education and sports programs in Israel; provides funds and technical and material assistance to Wingate Institute for Physical Education and Sport in Israel; sponsors coaching programs in Israel. *USCSFI Newsletter; commemorative Maccabiah Games journal.*

WOMEN'S LEAGUE FOR ISRAEL, INC. (1928). 515 Park Ave., NYC 10022. (212)838-1997. Pres. Muriel Lunden; Sr. V.-Pres. Linda Anopolsky; Exec. Dir. Bernice Backon. Promotes the welfare of young people in Israel; built and maintains homes in Jerusalem, Haifa, Tel Aviv; Natanya Vocational Training and Rehabilitation Center; the Orah Workshop for the Blind and Handicapped, and the National Library of Social Work. Also many facilities and programs on the campuses of the Hebrew University.*WLI Bulletin.*

WORLD CONFEDERATION OF UNITED ZIONISTS (1946; reorg. 1958). 30 E. 60 St., NYC 10022. (212)371-1452. Copres.'s Bernice S. Tannenbaum, Kalman Sultanik, Melech Topiol. Promotes Zionist education, sponsors nonparty youth movements in the Diaspora, and strives for an Israel-oriented creative Jewish survival in the Diaspora. *Zionist Information Views.*

WORLD ZIONIST ORGANIZATION—AMERICAN SECTION (1971). 515 Park Ave., NYC 10009. (212)752-0600. Chmn. Bernice S. Tannenbaum; Exec. V.-Chmn. Zelig Chinitz. As the American section of the overall Zionist body throughout the world, it operates primarily in the field of *aliyah* from the free countries, education in the Diaspora, youth and Hechalutz, organization and information, cultural institutions, publications; conducts a worldwide Hebrew cultural program including special seminars and pedagogic manuals; disperses information and assists in research projects concerning Israel; promotes, publishes, and distributes books, periodicals, and pamphlets concerning developments in Israel, Zionism, and Jewish history. *Israel Scene; Five Fifteen.*

——, DEPARTMENT OF EDUCATION AND CULTURE (1948). 515 Park Ave., NYC 10022. (212)752-0600. Exec. Counselor Arthur Levine; Exec. Dir. Mordecai Peled. Seeks to foster a wider and deeper knowledge of the Hebrew language and literature and a better understanding and fuller appreciation of the role of Israel in the destiny of Jewry and Judaism, to introduce the study of Israel as an integral part of the Jewish school curriculum, and to initiate and sponsor educational projects designed to implement these objectives.

——, NORTH AMERICAN ALIYAH MOVEMENT (1968). 515 Park Ave., NYC 10022. (212)752-0600. Pres. Tamar B. Harris; Exec. Dir. Robert Berl. Promotes and facilitates *aliyah* and *klitah* from the U.S. and Canada to Israel; serves as a social framework for North American immigrants to Israel. *Aliyon; NAAM Newsletter; Coming Home.*

——, ZIONIST ARCHIVES AND LIBRARY OF THE (1939). 515 Park Ave., NYC 10022. (212)753-2167. Dir. and Librarian Esther Togman. A depository for books, pamphlets, newspapers, periodicals, ephemera, and archival material; a primary center in the U.S. for research and authentic information on Israel, Zionism, the Middle East, and Jewish life in the Diaspora.

ZIONIST ORGANIZATION OF AMERICA (1897). ZOA House, 4 E. 34 St., NYC 10016. (212)481-1500. Pres. Milton S. Shapiro; Exec. V.-Pres. Paul Flacks. Seeks to safeguard the integrity and independence of Israel, assist in its economic development, and foster the unity of the Jewish people and the centrality of Israel in Jewish life in the spirit of General Zionism. In Israel, owns and maintains both the ZOA House in Tel Aviv, a cultural center, and the Kfar Silver Agricultural and Technical High School in Ashkelon, with a full-time student enrollment of 700 students. Kfar Silver, under the supervision of the Israel Ministry of Education, focuses on academic studies, vocational training, and programs for foreign students. *American Zionist Magazine; Zionist Information Service Weekly News Bulletin (ZINS); Public Affairs Action Guidelines; Public Affairs Action Report for ZOA Leaders.*

## PROFESSIONAL ASSOCIATIONS*

AMERICAN ASSOCIATION OF RABBIS (Religious, Educational)

AMERICAN CONFERENCE OF CANTORS, UNION OF AMERICAN HEBREW CONGREGATIONS (Religious, Educational)

AMERICAN JEWISH CORRECTIONAL CHAPLAINS ASSOCIATION, INC. (Social Welfare)

AMERICAN JEWISH PRESS. ASSOCIATION (Cultural)

AMERICAN JEWISH PUBLIC RELATIONS SOCIETY (1957). 234 Fifth Ave., NYC 10001. (212)697–5895. Pres. Robert L. Kern; Treas. Hyman Brickman. Advances professional status of workers in the public-relations field in Jewish communal service; upholds a professional code of ethics and standards; serves as a clearinghouse for employment opportunities; exchanges professional information and ideas; presents awards for excellence in professional attainments, including the "Maggid Award" for outstanding literary or artistic achievement which enhances Jewish life. *AJPRS Newsletter; AJPRS Directory.*

ASSOCIATION OF HILLEL/JEWISH CAMPUS PROFESSIONALS (Religious, Educational)

ASSOCIATION OF JEWISH CENTER WORKERS (Community Relations)

ASSOCIATION OF JEWISH COMMUNITY ORGANIZATION PERSONNEL (Social Welfare)

ASSOCIATION OF JEWISH COMMUNITY RELATIONS WORKERS (Community Relations)

CANTORS ASSEMBLY (Religious, Educational)

CENTRAL CONFERENCE OF AMERICAN RABBIS (Religious, Educational)

CONFERENCE OF JEWISH COMMUNAL SERVICE (Social Welfare)

COUNCIL OF JEWISH ORGANIZATIONS IN CIVIL SERVICE (Community Relations)

JEWISH CHAPLAINS COUNCIL, JWB (Social Welfare)

JEWISH EDUCATORS ASSEMBLY, UNITED SYNAGOGUE OF AMERICA (Religious, Educational)

JEWISH MINISTERS CANTORS ASSOCIATION OF AMERICA, INC. (Religious, Educational)

JEWISH TEACHERS ASSOCIATION—MORIM (Religious, Educational)

NATIONAL ASSOCIATION OF HEBREW DAY SCHOOL ADMINISTRATORS, TORAH UMESORAH (Religious, Educational)

NATIONAL ASSOCIATION OF SYNAGOGUE ADMINISTRATORS, UNITED SYNAGOGUE OF AMERICA (Religious, Educational)

NATIONAL ASSOCIATION OF TEMPLE ADMINISTRATORS, UNION OF AMERICAN HEBREW CONGREGATIONS (Religious, Educational)

NATIONAL ASSOCIATION OF TEMPLE EDUCATORS, UNION OF AMERICAN HEBREW CONGREGATIONS (Religious, Educational)

NATIONAL CONFERENCE OF YESHIVA PRINCIPALS, TORAH UMESORAH (Religious, Educational)

RABBINICAL ASSEMBLY (Religious, Educational)

RABBINICAL COUNCIL OF AMERICA (Religious, Educational)

RECONSTRUCTIONIST RABBINICAL ASSOCIATION, JEWISH RECONSTRUCTIONIST FOUNDATION (Religious, Educational)

UNION OF ORTHODOX RABBIS OF THE U.S. AND CANADA (Religious, Educational)

WORLD CONFERENCE OF JEWISH COMMUNAL SERVICE (Community Relations)

## WOMEN'S ORGANIZATIONS*

AMIT WOMEN (Zionist and Pro-Israel)

B'NAI B'RITH WOMEN (Social Welfare)

BRANDEIS UNIVERSITY NATIONAL WOMEN'S COMMITTEE (1948). 415 South St., PO Box 9110, Waltham, MA 02254–9110. (617)736–4160. Natl. Pres. Barbara Miller; Exec. Dir. Harriet J. Winer. Responsible for support and maintenance of Brandeis University libraries; sponsors

---

*For fuller listing see under categories in parentheses.

490 / AMERICAN JEWISH YEAR BOOK, 1989

University on Wheels and, through its chapters, study-group programs based on faculty-prepared syllabi, volunteer work in educational services, and a program of New Books for Old sales; constitutes largest "Friends of a Library" group in U.S. *Imprint.*

HADASSAH, THE WOMEN'S ZIONIST ORGANIZATION OF AMERICA (Zionist and Pro-Israel)

NA'AMAT USA, THE WOMEN'S LABOR ZIONIST ORGANIZATION OF AMERICA (Zionist and Pro-Israel)

NATIONAL COUNCIL OF JEWISH WOMEN (Social Welfare)

NATIONAL FEDERATION OF TEMPLE SISTERHOODS, UNION OF AMERICAN HEBREW CONGREGATIONS (Religious, Educational)

UOTS (Social, Mutual Benefit) (*See* United Order True Sisters)

WOMEN'S AMERICAN ORT, AMERICAN ORT FEDERATION (Overseas Aid)

WOMEN'S BRANCH OF THE UNION OF ORTHODOX JEWISH CONGREGATIONS OF AMERICA (Religious, Educational)

WOMEN'S DIVISION OF POALE AGUDATH ISRAEL OF AMERICA (Zionist and Pro-Israel)

WOMEN'S DIVISION OF THE UNITED JEWISH APPEAL (Overseas Aid)

WOMEN'S LEAGUE FOR CONSERVATIVE JUDAISM (Religious, Educational)

WOMEN'S LEAGUE FOR ISRAEL, INC. (Zionist and Pro-Israel)

WOMEN'S ORGANIZATION, YESHIVA UNIVERSITY (Religious, Educational)

## YOUTH AND STUDENT ORGANIZATIONS*

AMERICAN ZIONIST YOUTH FOUNDATION (Zionist and Pro-Israel)

B'NAI B'RITH HILLEL FOUNDATIONS (Religious, Educational)

B'NAI B'RITH YOUTH ORGANIZATION (Religious, Educational)

BNEI AKIVA OF NORTH AMERICA, RELIGIOUS ZIONISTS OF AMERICA (Zionist and Pro-Israel)

BNOS AGUDATH ISRAEL, AGUDATH ISRAEL OF AMERICA, GIRLS' DIVISION (Religious, Educational)

DROR—YOUNG KIBBUTZ MOVEMENT—HABONIM (Zionist and Pro-Israel)

HABONIM-DROR NORTH AMERICA (Zionist and Pro-Israel)

HASHACHAR, HADASSAH (Zionist and Pro-Israel)

HASHOMER HATZAIR, SOCIALIST ZIONIST YOUTH MOVEMENT (Zionist and Pro-Israel)

KADIMA, UNITED SYNAGOGUE OF AMERICA (Religious, Educational)

NATIONAL CONFERENCE OF SYNAGOGUE YOUTH, UNION OF ORTHODOX JEWISH CONGREGATIONS OF AMERICA (Religious, Educational)

NOAM-MIZRACHI NEW LEADERSHIP COUNCIL, RELIGIOUS ZIONISTS OF AMERICA (Zionist and Pro-Israel)

NORTH AMERICAN FEDERATION OF TEMPLE YOUTH, UNION OF AMERICAN HEBREW CONGREGATIONS (Religious, Educational)

NORTH AMERICAN JEWISH STUDENTS APPEAL (1971). 165 Pidgeon Hill Rd., Huntington Station, NY 11746. (516)385-8771. Pres. Cindy Rubin; Chmn. Gerald A. Flanzbaum; Exec. Dir. Brenda Gevertz. Serves as central fund-raising mechanism for five national, independent Jewish student organizations; insures accountability of public Jewish communal funds used by these agencies; assists Jewish students undertaking projects of concern to Jewish communities; advises and assists Jewish organizations in determining student project feasibility and impact; fosters development of Jewish student leadership in the Jewish community. Beneficiaries include local and regional Jewish student projects; current constituents include Student Struggle for Soviet Jewry, *Response,* Yugntruf Youth for Yiddish, and the newest constituent, Progressive Zionist Caucus.

---

*For fuller listing see under categories in parentheses.

NATIONAL JEWISH ORGANIZATIONS / 491

NORTH AMERICAN JEWISH STUDENTS' NETWORK (1969). 501 Madison Ave., 17th fl., NYC 10022. (212)755-5770. Pres. Moshe Ronen; Natl. Chmn. Ayall Schanzer; Exec. Dir. Alan Oirich. Coordinates information and programs among all Jewish student organizations in North America; promotes development of student-controlled Jewish student organizations; maintains contacts and coordinates programs with Jewish students throughout the world through the World Union of Jewish Students; runs the Jewish Student Speakers Bureau; sponsors regional, national, and North American conferences. *Network Spectrum; Jewish Students of America.*

STUDENT STRUGGLE FOR SOVIET JEWRY (Community Relations)

YUGNTRUF YOUTH FOR YIDDISH (1964). 3328 Bainbridge Ave., Bronx, NY 10467. (212)654-8540. Chmn. Itzek Gottesman; Editor Paul Glasser. A worldwide, nonpolitical organization for high school and college students with a knowledge of, or interest in, Yiddish. Spreads the love and use of the Yiddish language; organizes artistic and social activities, including annual conference for young adults; sponsors Yiddish-speaking preschool for non-Orthodox children; disseminates new Yiddish teaching materials. *Yugntruf.*

ZEIREI AGUDATH ISRAEL, AGUDATH ISRAEL OF AMERICA, YOUNG MEN'S DIVISION (Religious, Educational)

CANADA

B'NAI BRITH CANADA (1875). 15 Hove St., Suite 200, Downsview, ONT M3H 4Y8. (416)633-6224. Pres. Dr. Brian Feldman; Exec. V.-Pres. Frank Dimant. Canadian Jewry's senior organization; makes representations to all levels of government on matters of Jewish concern; promotes humanitarian causes and educational programs, community volunteer projects, adult Jewish education, and leadership development; dedicated to human rights; sponsors youth programs of B'nai Brith Youth Org. and Hillel. *Covenant; Communiqué; Hillel Voice.*

———, INSTITUTE FOR INTERNATIONAL AND GOVERNMENTAL AFFAIRS (1987). Identifies and protests the abuse of human rights throughout the world. Monitors the condition of Jewish communities worldwide and advocates on their behalf when they experience serious violations of their human rights. *Comment.*

———, LEAGUE FOR HUMAN RIGHTS (1970). 15 Hove St., Downsview, Ont. L453E7. (416)633-6227. Natl. Chmn. Harry Bick; Natl. Dir. Alan Shafman. Dedicated to monitoring human rights, combating racism and racial discrimination, and preventing bigotry and anti-Semitism, through education and community relations. Sponsors Holocaust Education Programs, the R. Lou Ronson Research Institute on Anti-Semitism; distributor of Anti-Defamation League materials in Canada. *Review of Anti-Semitism.*

CANADA-ISRAEL SECURITIES, LTD., STATE OF ISRAEL BONDS (1953). 1255 University St., #200, Montreal, PQ H3B 3B2. (514)-878-1871. Pres. Melvyn A. Dobrin; Exec. V.-Pres. Julius Briskin. Sells Israel bonds and notes.

CANADIAN ASSOCIATION FOR LABOR ISRAEL (HISTADRUT) (1944). 7005 Kildare Rd., Suite 14, Cote St. Luc, PQ H4W 1C1. (514)484-9430. Pres. Harry J. F. Bloomfield; Exec. Dir. Yaacov Erez. Conducts fund-raising and educational activities on behalf of Histadrut, Kupat Holim, and Amal schools in Israel.

CANADIAN FOUNDATION FOR JEWISH CULTURE (1965). 4600 Bathurst St., Willowdale, ONT M2R 3V2. (416)635-2883. Pres. Mira Koschitzky; Exec. Sec. Edmond Y. Lipsitz. Promotes Jewish studies at university level and encourages original research and scholarship in Jewish subjects; awards annual scholarships and grants-in-aid to scholars in Canada.

CANADIAN FRIENDS OF THE ALLIANCE ISRAÉLITE UNIVERSELLE (1958). PO Box 578, Victoria Station, Montreal, PQ H3Z 2Y6. (514)481-3552. Pres. Joseph Nuss. Supports the educational work of the Alliance.

CANADIAN FRIENDS OF THE HEBREW UNIVERSITY (1944). 208-1 Yorkdale Rd., Toronto, ONT M6A 3A1. (416)789-2633. Pres. Edward J. Winant; Exec. V.-Pres. Shimon Arbel. Represents and publicizes the Hebrew University in Canada; serves as fund-raising arm for the university in

Canada; processes Canadians for study at the university. *Scopus; Ha-Universita.*

CANADIAN JEWISH CONGRESS (1919; reorg. 1934). 1590 Dr. Penfield Ave., Montreal, PQ H3G 1C5. (514)931–7531. Pres. Dorothy Reitman; Exec. V.-Pres. Alan Rose. The official voice of Canadian Jewish communities at home and abroad; acts on all matters affecting the status, rights, concerns and welfare of Canadian Jewry; internationally active on behalf of Soviet Jewry, Jews in Arab lands, Holocaust remembrance and restitution; largest Jewish archives in Canada. *National Small Communities Newsletter; Intercom; Ottawa Digest; National Soviet Jewry Newsletter; National Archives Newsletter; Community Relations Newsletter;* regional newsletters.

CANADIAN ORT ORGANIZATION (Organization of Rehabilitation Through Training) (1942). 5165 Sherbrooke St. W., Suite 208, Montreal, PQ H4A 1T6. (514)481–2787. Pres. Dr. Victor C. Goldbloom; Exec. Dir. Mac Silver. Carries on fundraising projects in support of the worldwide vocational-training-school network of ORT. *ORT Reporter.*

———, WOMEN'S CANADIAN ORT (1948). 3101 Bathurst St., Suite 604, Toronto, ONT M6A 2A6. (416)787–0339. Pres. Harriet Morton; Exec. Dir. Diane Uslaner. *Focus.*

CANADIAN SEPHARDI FEDERATION (1973). c/o Or Haemet School, 210 Wilson Ave., Toronto, ONT M5M 3B1. (416)483–8968. Pres. Maurice Benzacar; Sec. Laeticia Benabou. Preserves and promotes Sephardic identity, particularly among youth; works for the unity of the Jewish people; emphasizes relations between Sephardi communities all over the world; seeks better situation for Sephardim in Israel; supports Israel by all means. Participates in *La Voix Sépharade, Le Monde Sépharade,* and *Sephardi World.*

CANADIAN YOUNG JUDAEA (1917). 788 Marlee Ave., Suite 205, Toronto, ONT M6B 3K1. (416)787–5350. Exec. Dir. Alon Szpindel; Natl. Shaliach Avi Gur. Strives to attract Jewish youth to Zionism, with goal of *aliyah;* educates youth about Jewish history and Zionism; prepares them to provide leadership in Young Judaea camps in Canada and Israel and to be concerned Jews. *Judaean; The Young Judaean.*

CANADIAN ZIONIST FEDERATION (1967). 5250 Decarie Blvd., Suite 550, Montreal, PQ H3X 2H9. (514)486–9526. Pres. David J. Azrieli; Exec. Dir. Rabbi Meyer Krentzman. Umbrella organization of all Zionist and Israel-related groups in Canada; carries on major activities in all areas of Jewish life through its departments of education and culture, *aliyah,* youth and students, public affairs, and fund raising for the purpose of strengthening the State of Israel and the Canadian Jewish community. *Canadian Zionist.*

———, BUREAU OF EDUCATION AND CULTURE (1972). Pres. David J. Azrieli; Exec. Dir. Rabbi Meyer Krentzman. Provides counseling by pedagogic experts, in-service teacher-training courses and seminars in Canada and Israel; national pedagogic council and research center; distributes educational material and teaching aids; conducts annual Bible contest and Hebrew-language courses for adults. *Al Mitzpe Hachinuch.*

FRIENDS OF PIONEERING ISRAEL (1950s). 1111 Finch Ave. W., Suite 154, Downsview, ONT M35 2E5 (416)736–0977. Pres. Norman Auslander. Conducts educational activities supporting the kibbutz movement in Israel; supports a progressive Israel.

HADASSAH—WIZO ORGANIZATION OF CANADA (1917). 1310 Greene Ave., Suite 900, Montreal, PQ H3Z 2B8. (514)937–9431. Natl. Pres. Naomi Frankenburg; Exec. V.-Pres. Lily Frank. Extends material and moral support to the people of Israel requiring such assistance; strengthens and fosters Jewish ideals; encourages Hebrew culture in Canada and promotes Canadian ideals of democracy. *Orah Magazine.*

JEWISH IMMIGRANT AID SERVICES OF CANADA (JIAS) (1919). 5151 Cote Ste. Catherine Rd., Montreal, PQ H3W 1M6. (514)-342–9351. Pres. Sheldon Sper; Exec. Dir. Herb Abrams. Serves as a national agency for immigration and immigrant welfare. *JIAS Bulletin.*

JEWISH NATIONAL FUND OF CANADA (KEREN KAYEMETH LE'ISRAEL, INC.) (1901). 1980 Sherbrooke St. W., Suite 500, Montreal, PQ H3H 1E8. (514)934–0313. Pres. Neri J. Bloomfield; Exec. V.-Pres. Michael Goldstein. Fund-raising organization affiliated with the World Zionist Organization; involved in afforestation, soil reclamation, and development of the land of Israel, including the construction of roads and preparation of sites for new settlements; provides educational materials and programs to Jewish schools across Canada.

LABOR ZIONIST MOVEMENT OF CANADA (1939). 7005 Kildare Rd., Suite 10, Cote St. Luc, PQ H3W 1C1. (514)484-1789. Chmn. Natl. Coord. Com. Harry Simon; Admin. V.-Pres. Abraham Shurem. Disseminates information and publications on Israel and Jewish life; arranges special events, lectures, and seminars; coordinates communal and political activities of its constituent bodies (Na'amat of Canada, Labor Zionist Alliance, Poale Zion party, Habonim-Dror Youth, Israel Histadrut, affiliated Jewish elementary and high schools in Montreal and Toronto). *Bulletin; Brief Facts; Newsletter.*

MIZRACHI-HAPOEL HAMIZRACHI ORGANIZATION OF CANADA (1941). 159 Almore Ave., Downsview, ONT M3H 2H9. (416)-630-7575. Pres. Kurt Rothschild; Exec. Dir. Rabbi Menachem Gopin. Promotes religious Zionism, aimed at making Israel a state based on Torah; maintains Bnei Akiva, a summer camp, adult education program, and touring department; supports Mizrachi-Hapoel Hamizrachi and other religious Zionist institutions in Israel which strengthen traditional Judaism.

*Mizrachi Newsletter; Or Hamizrach Torah Quarterly.*

NATIONAL COUNCIL OF JEWISH WOMEN OF CANADA (1897). 1110 Finch Ave. W., #518, Downsview, ONT M3J 2T2. (416)-665-8251. Pres. Penny Yellen; Exec. Dir. Eleanor Appleby. Dedicated to furthering human welfare in Jewish and non-Jewish communities, locally, nationally, and internationally; provides essential services, and stimulates and educates the individual and the community through an integrated program of education, service, and social action. *New Edition.*

NATIONAL JOINT COMMUNITY RELATIONS COMMITTEE OF CANADIAN JEWISH CONGRESS (1936). 4600 Bathurst St., Willowdale, ONT M2R 3V2 (416)635-2883. Chmn. Joseph J. Wilder; Exec. Dir. Manuel Prutschi. Seeks to safeguard the status, rights, and welfare of Jews in Canada; to combat anti-Semitism and promote understanding and goodwill among all ethnic and religious groups. *Community Relations Report.*

ZIONIST ORGANIZATION OF CANADA (1892; reorg. 1919). 788 Marlee Ave., Toronto, ONT M6B 3K1. (416)781-3571. Pres. Max Goody; Exec. V.-Pres. George Liban. Furthers general Zionist aims by operating six youth camps in Canada and one in Israel; maintains Zionist book club; arranges programs, lectures; sponsors Young Judaea, Youth Centre Project in Jerusalem Forest, Israel.

# Jewish Federations, Welfare Funds, Community Councils

## UNITED STATES

### ALABAMA

**BIRMINGHAM**

BIRMINGHAM JEWISH FEDERATION (1936; reorg. 1971); PO Box 130219 (35213); (205)-879-0416. Pres. Suzanne Bearman; Exec. Dir. Richard Friedman.

**MOBILE**

MOBILE JEWISH WELFARE FUND, INC. (inc. 1966); One Office Park, Suite 219 (36609); (205)343-7197. Pres. Irving Silver; Admin. Barbara V. Paper.

**MONTGOMERY**

JEWISH FEDERATION OF MONTGOMERY, INC. (1930); PO Box 20058 (36120); (205)-277-5820. Pres. Jeff Kohn; Admin. Beverly Lipton.

### ARIZONA

**PHOENIX**

JEWISH FEDERATION OF GREATER PHOENIX (incl. surrounding communities) (1940); 32 West Coolidge, Suite 200 (85013); (602)-274-1800. Pres. Irv Sattler; Exec. Dir. Harold Morgan.

**TUCSON**

JEWISH FEDERATION OF SOUTHERN ARIZONA (1942); 635 N. Craycroft (85711); (602)327-7957. Pres. Carol Karsch; Exec. V. Pres. Charles Plotkin.

### ARKANSAS

**LITTLE ROCK**

JEWISH FEDERATION OF ARKANSAS (1911); 4942 West Markham, Suite 5 (72205); (501)-663-3571. Pres. Jane B. Mendel; Exec. Dir. Errol Imber.

### CALIFORNIA

**FRESNO**

JEWISH FEDERATION OF FRESNO (org. 1911; inc. 1978); 5094 N. West Ave. (93711); (209)-432-2162. Pres. Lee Horwitz; Exec. Dir. Carol Reba.

**LONG BEACH**

JEWISH FEDERATION OF GREATER LONG BEACH AND WEST ORANGE COUNTY (1937; inc. 1946); (sponsors UNITED JEWISH WELFARE FUND); 3801 E. Willow St. (90815); (213)426-7601. Pres. Gordon Lentzner; Exec. Dir. Sandi Goldstein.

**LOS ANGELES**

JEWISH FEDERATION COUNCIL OF GREATER LOS ANGELES (1912; reorg. 1959); (sponsors UNITED JEWISH FUND); 6505 Wilshire Blvd. (90048); (213)852-1234. Pres. George Caplan; Exec. V. Pres. Wayne Feinstein.

**OAKLAND**

JEWISH FEDERATION OF THE GREATER EAST BAY (Alameda and Contra Costa coun-

---

This directory is based on information supplied by the Council of Jewish Federations.

## JEWISH FEDERATIONS, FUNDS, COUNCILS / 495

ties) (1918); 401 Grand Ave. (94610); (415)-839-2900. Pres. Amy R. Sternberg; Exec. V. Pres. Ami Nahshon.

### ORANGE COUNTY
JEWISH FEDERATION OF ORANGE COUNTY (1964; inc. 1965); (sponsors UNITED JEWISH WELFARE FUND); 1385 Warner Ave., Suite. A, Tustin (92680–6442); (714)259–0655. Pres. Jeff Schulein; Exec. Dir. Merv Lemmerman.

### PALM SPRINGS
JEWISH FEDERATION OF PALM SPRINGS-DESERT AREA (1971); 611 S. Palm Canyon Dr., Suite 215 (92264); (619)325–7281. Pres. Sondra Landau; Exec. Dir. Nat Bent.

### SACRAMENTO
JEWISH FEDERATION OF SACRAMENTO (1948); PO Box 254589 (95865); (916)486–0906. Pres. Barbara Ansel; Exec. Dir. Arnold Feder.

### SAN DIEGO
UNITED JEWISH FEDERATION OF SAN DIEGO COUNTY (1936); 4797 Mercury St. (92111); (619)571–3444. Pres. Shearn Platt; Exec. V. Pres. Stephen M. Abramson.

### SAN FRANCISCO
JEWISH COMMUNITY FEDERATION OF SAN FRANCISCO, THE PENINSULA, MARIN, AND SONOMA COUNTIES (1910; reorg. 1955); 121 Steuart St. (94105); (415)777–0411. Pres. Annette Dobbs; Exec. Dir. Rabbi Brian Lurie.

### SAN JOSE
JEWISH FEDERATION OF GREATER SAN JOSE (incl. Santa Clara County except Palo Alto and Los Altos) (1930; reorg. 1950); 14855 Oka Rd., Los Gatos (95030); (408)-358-3033. Pres. Eli Reinhard; Exec. Dir. Michael Papo.

### SANTA BARBARA
SANTA BARBARA JEWISH FEDERATION (org. 1974); PO Box 90110, Santa Barbara (93190); (805)966–7860. Pres. Steven A. Amerikaner; Exec. Dir. Ina F. Frank.

### COLORADO
DENVER
ALLIED JEWISH FEDERATION OF DENVER (1936); (sponsors ALLIED JEWISH CAMPAIGN); 300 S. Dahlia St. (80222); (303)321–3399. Pres. Joseph F. Pells; Exec. Dir. Sheldon Steinhauser.

### CONNECTICUT
BRIDGEPORT
JEWISH FEDERATION OF GREATER BRIDGEPORT, INC. (1936; reorg. 1981); (sponsors UNITED JEWISH CAMPAIGN); 4200 Park Ave. (06604); (203)372–6504. Pres. Irving Kern; Exec. Dir. Gerald A. Kleinman.

### DANBURY
JEWISH FEDERATION OF GREATER DANBURY (1945); 54 Main St., Suite E (06810); (203)792–6353. Pres. S. Benedict Levin; Exec. Dir. Sharon Garelick.

### EASTERN CONNECTICUT
JEWISH FEDERATION OF EASTERN CONNECTICUT, INC. (1950; inc. 1970); 28 Channing St., New London (06320); (203)442–8062. Pres. Reuben Levin; Exec. Dir. Jerome E. Fischer.

### GREENWICH
GREENWICH JEWISH FEDERATION (1956); 22 W. Putnam Ave., Suite 18 (06830); (203)-622-1434. Pres. Nancy Zisson; Exec. Dir. Rabbi Melvin Libman.

### HARTFORD
GREATER HARTFORD JEWISH FEDERATION (1945); 333 Bloomfield Ave., W. Hartford (06117); (203)232–4483. Pres. Richard Suisman; Exec. Dir. Don Cooper.

### NEW HAVEN
NEW HAVEN JEWISH FEDERATION (1928); 419 Whalley Ave. (06511); (203)562–2137. Pres. Mary Lou Winnick; Exec. Dir. Susan Shimelman.

### NORWALK (See Westport)

### STAMFORD
UNITED JEWISH FEDERATION (inc. 1973); 1035 Newfield Ave., PO Box 3038 (06905); (203)322–6935. Pres. Ben Zinbarg; Exec. Dir. Debra Stein.

### WATERBURY
JEWISH FEDERATION OF WATERBURY, INC. (1938); 359 Cooke St. (06710); (203)756–7234. Pres. Gary Broder; Exec. Dir. Eli J. Skora.

### WESTPORT, WESTON, WILTON, NORWALK
UNITED JEWISH APPEAL/FEDERATION OF WESTPORT-WESTON-WILTON-NORWALK (inc. 1980); 49 Richmondville Ave. (06880);

(203)266-8197. Pres. Michael Stashower; Exec. Dir. Robert Kessler.

## DELAWARE

### WILMINGTON

JEWISH FEDERATION OF DELAWARE, INC. (1934); 101 Garden of Eden Rd. (19803); (302)478-6200. Pres. Stephen E. Herrmann; Exec. V. Pres. Robert N. Kerbel.

## DISTRICT OF COLUMBIA

### WASHINGTON

UNITED JEWISH APPEAL-FEDERATION OF GREATER WASHINGTON, INC. (1935); 6101 Montrose Rd., Rockville, MD 20852. (301)-230-7200. Pres. Joseph B. Gildenhorn; Exec. V. Pres. Ted B. Farber.

## FLORIDA

### DAYTONA BEACH

JEWISH FEDERATION OF VOLUSIA & FLAGLER COUNTIES, INC.; 533 Seabreeze Blvd., Suite 300 (32018-3996); (904)255-6260. Pres. Dr. Michael D. Kohen; Exec. Dir. Iris E. Gardener.

### FT. LAUDERDALE

JEWISH FEDERATION OF GREATER FT. LAUDERDALE (1968); 8358 W. Oakland Pk. Blvd. (33351); (305)748-8400. Pres. Harold L. Oshry; Exec. Dir. Kenneth B. Bierman.

### JACKSONVILLE

JACKSONVILLE JEWISH FEDERATION, INC. (1935); 8505 San Jose Blvd. (32217); (904)-448-5000. Pres. Elliot Zisser; Exec. V. Pres. Isaac Lakritz.

### LEE COUNTY

JEWISH FEDERATION OF LEE COUNTY (1974); 3628 Evans Ave., Ft. Myers (33901); (813)275-3554. Pres. Dr. Ingeborg Mauksch; Exec. Dir. Helene Kramer.

### MIAMI

GREATER MIAMI JEWISH FEDERATION, INC. (1938); 4200 Biscayne Blvd. (33137); (305)576-4000. Pres. Donald E. Lefton; Exec. V. Pres. Myron J. Brodie.

### ORLANDO

JEWISH FEDERATION OF GREATER ORLANDO (1949); 851 N. Maitland Ave., PO Box 1508, Maitland (32751); (305)645-5933. Pres. Betty Monroe; Exec. Dir. Jordan Harburger.

### PALM BEACH COUNTY

JEWISH FEDERATION OF PALM BEACH COUNTY, INC. (1938); 501 S. Flagler Dr., Suite 305, W. Palm Beach (33401); (305)832-2120. Pres. Alec Engelstein; Exec. Dir. Jeffrey L. Klein.

### PINELLAS COUNTY

JEWISH FEDERATION OF PINELLAS COUNTY, INC. (incl. Clearwater and St. Petersburg) (1950; reincorp. 1974); 301 S. Jupiter Ave., Clearwater (34615); (813) 446-1033. Pres. Sylvan Orloff; Exec. Dir. Robert F. Tropp.

### SARASOTA

SARASOTA-MANATEE JEWISH FEDERATION (1959); 580 S. McIntosh Rd. (34232); (813)-371-4546. Pres. Max Bussel; Exec. Dir. Jack Weintraub.

### SOUTH BROWARD

JEWISH FEDERATION OF SOUTH BROWARD, INC. (1943); 2719 Hollywood Blvd., Hollywood (33020); (305)921-8810. Pres. Ron Rothchild; Exec. Dir. Sumner G. Kaye.

### SOUTH COUNTY

SOUTH PALM BEACH COUNTY JEWISH FEDERATION (inc. 1979); 336 NW Spanish River Blvd., Boca Raton (33431); (407) 368-2737. Pres. Marvin Zale; Exec. Dir. Rabbi Bruce S. Warshal.

### TAMPA

TAMPA JEWISH FEDERATION (1941); 2808 Horatio (33609); (813)875-1618. Pres. Walter H. Kessler; Exec. V. Pres. Gary S. Alter.

## GEORGIA

### ATLANTA

ATLANTA JEWISH FEDERATION, INC. (1905; reorg. 1967); 1753 Peachtree Rd. NE (30309); (404)873-1661. Pres. William E. Schatten; Exec. Dir. David I. Sarnat.

### AUGUSTA

AUGUSTA JEWISH FEDERATION (1937); PO Box 3251, Sibley Rd. (30904); (404)736-1818. Pres. David Alalof; Exec. Dir. Louis Goldman.

### COLUMBUS

JEWISH WELFARE FEDERATION OF COLUMBUS, INC. (1941); PO Box 6313 (31907); (404)568-6668. Pres. Warren Pomerance; Sec. Irene Rainbow.

## SAVANNAH

SAVANNAH JEWISH FEDERATION (1943); (sponsors UJA-FEDERATION CAMPAIGN); PO Box 23527 (31403); (912)355-8111. Pres. Sheldon Tanenbaum; Exec. Dir. Stan Ramati.

## HAWAII

### HONOLULU

JEWISH FEDERATION OF HAWAII (1956); 677 Ala Moana, Suite 803 (96813); (808)531-4634. Pres. Richard I. Kersten.

## ILLINOIS

### CHAMPAIGN-URBANA

CHAMPAIGN-URBANA JEWISH FEDERATION (1929); 503 E. John St., Champaign (61820); (217)367-9872. Pres. Helen Levin; Exec. Dir. Janie Yairi.

### CHICAGO

JEWISH FEDERATION OF METROPOLITAN CHICAGO (1900); One S. Franklin St. (60606); (312)346-6700. Pres. Maynard I. Wishner; Exec. V. Pres. Steven B. Nasatir.

JEWISH UNITED FUND OF METROPOLITAN CHICAGO (1968); One S. Franklin St. (60606); (312)346-6700. Pres. Richard L. Wexler; Exec. V. Pres. Steven B. Nasatir.

### DECATUR

DECATUR JEWISH FEDERATION (member, Central Illinois Jewish Federation) (1942); c/o Temple B'nai Abraham, 1326 W. Eldorado (62522); (217)429-5740. Pres. Cheri Kalvort; Treas. Marvin Tick.

### ELGIN

ELGIN AREA JEWISH WELFARE CHEST (1938); 330 Division St. (60120); (312)741-5656. Pres. Charles Zimmerman; Treas. Stuart Hanfling.

### PEORIA

JEWISH FEDERATION OF PEORIA (1933; inc. 1947); 3100 N. Knoxville, Suite 19 (61603); (309)686-0611. Pres. Dr. Thomas Halperin; Exec. Dir. Barry Nove.

### QUAD CITIES

JEWISH FEDERATION OF THE QUAD CITIES (incl. Rock Island, Moline, Davenport, Bettendorf) (1938; comb. 1973); 224 18 St., Suite 303, Rock Island (61201); (309)793-1300. Pres. Martin Rich; Exec. Dir. Ida Kramer.

### ROCKFORD

ROCKFORD JEWISH COMMUNITY COUNCIL (1937); 1500 Parkview Ave. (61107); (815)-399-5497. Pres. Jay Kamin; Exec. Dir. Tony Toback.

### SOUTHERN ILLINOIS

JEWISH FEDERATION SERVING SOUTHERN ILLINOIS, SOUTHEASTERN MISSOURI AND WESTERN KENTUCKY (1941); 6464 W. Main, Suite 7A, Belleville (62223); (618)398-6100. Pres. Carol Korein; Exec. Dir. Rabbi Zalman Stein.

### SPRINGFIELD

SPRINGFIELD JEWISH FEDERATION (1941); 730 E. Vine St. (62703); (217)528-3446. Pres. Howard Feldman; Exec. Dir. Lenore Loeb.

## INDIANA

### EVANSVILLE

EVANSVILLE JEWISH COMMUNITY COUNCIL, INC. (1936; inc. 1964); PO Box 5026 (47715); (812)477-7050. Pres. Jon Goldman; Exec. Sec. Maxine P. Fink.

### FORT WAYNE

FORT WAYNE JEWISH FEDERATION (1921); 227 E. Washington Blvd. (46802); (219)422-8566. Pres. Lawrence Adelman; Exec. Dir. Vivian Lansky.

### INDIANAPOLIS

JEWISH FEDERATION OF GREATER INDIANAPOLIS, INC., INC. (1905); 615 N. Alabama St., Suite 412 (46204-1430); (317)637-2473. Pres. Jerry Litwack; Exec. V. Pres. Harry Nadler.

### LAFAYETTE

FEDERATION JEWISH CHARITIES (1924); PO Box 708 (47902); (317)742-9081. Pres. Arnold Cohen; Finan. Sec. Louis Pearlman, Jr.

### MICHIGAN CITY

MICHIGAN CITY UNITED JEWISH WELFARE FUND; 2800 S. Franklin St. (46360); (219)-874-4477. Chmn. & Treas. Harold Leinwand.

### NORTHWEST INDIANA

THE JEWISH FEDERATION, INC. (1946); 2939 Jewett St., Highland (46322); (219)972-2251. Pres. Alan Hurst; Exec. Dir. Martin Erann.

## SOUTH BEND

JEWISH FEDERATION OF ST. JOSEPH VALLEY (1946); 105 Jefferson Centre, Suite 804 (46601); (219)233–1164. Pres. Dr. Martin I. Jacobs; Exec. V. Pres. Kim Marsh.

## IOWA

### DES MOINES

JEWISH FEDERATION OF GREATER DES MOINES (1914); 910 Polk Blvd. (50312); (515)277–6321. Pres. Martin Brody; Exec. Dir. Elaine Steinger.

### SIOUX CITY

JEWISH FEDERATION (1921); 525 14 St. (51105); (712)258–0618. Pres. Sandra Baron; Exec. Dir. Doris Rosenthal.

## KANSAS

### KANSAS CITY
(See Missouri)

### WICHITA

MID-KANSAS JEWISH FEDERATION, INC. (1935); 400 N. Woodlawn, Suite 8 (67208); (316)686–4741. Pres. Dr. Hilary Zarnow; Exec. Dir. Beverly Jacobson.

## KENTUCKY

### LEXINGTON

CENTRAL KENTUCKY JEWISH FEDERATION (1976); 333 Waller, Suite 5 (40504); (606)-252-7622. Pres. Gail Cohen; Admin. Linda Ravvin.

### LOUISVILLE

JEWISH COMMUNITY FEDERATION OF LOUISVILLE, INC. (1934); (sponsors UNITED JEWISH CAMPAIGN); 3630 Dutchmans Lane (40205); (502)451–8840. Pres. Ronald W. Abrams; Exec. Dir. Dr. Alan S. Engel.

## LOUISIANA

### ALEXANDRIA

THE JEWISH WELFARE FEDERATION AND COMMUNITY COUNCIL OF CENTRAL LOUISIANA (1938); 1227 Southhampton (71303); (318)445–4785. Pres. Alvin Mykoff; Sec.-Treas. Roeve Weill.

### BATON ROUGE

JEWISH FEDERATION OF GREATER BATON ROUGE (1971); 11744 Haymarket Ave., Suite B; PO Box 80827 (70898); (504) 291–5895. Pres. Dr. Steven Cavalier; Exec. Dir. Yigal Bander.

### NEW ORLEANS

JEWISH FEDERATION OF GREATER NEW ORLEANS (1913; reorg. 1977); 1539 Jackson Ave. (70130); (504)525–0673. Pres. Dr. Marshall Gottsegen; Exec. Dir. Jane Buchsbaum.

### SHREVEPORT

SHREVEPORT JEWISH FEDERATION (1941; inc. 1967); 2032 Line Ave. (71104); (318)-221–4129. Pres. Neal Nierman; Exec. Dir. Monty Pomm.

## MAINE

### LEWISTON-AUBURN

LEWISTON-AUBURN JEWISH FEDERATION (1947); (sponsors UNITED JEWISH APPEAL); 74 Bradman St., Auburn (04210); (207)786–4201. Pres. Joel Goodman.

### PORTLAND

JEWISH FEDERATION COMMUNITY COUNCIL OF SOUTHERN MAINE (1942); (sponsors UNITED JEWISH APPEAL); 57 Ashmont St. (04103); (207)773–7254. Pres. Larry Plotkin.

## MARYLAND

### BALTIMORE

ASSOCIATED JEWISH CHARITIES & WELFARE FUND, INC. (1920; reorg. 1969); 101 W. Mt. Royal Ave. (21201); (301) 727–4828. Chmn. Samuel K. Himmelrich, Sr.; Pres. Darrell D. Friedman.

## MASSACHUSETTS

### BERKSHIRE COUNTY

JEWISH FEDERATION OF THE BERKSHIRES (1940); 235East St., Pittsfield (01201); (413)-442-4360. Pres. Alexandra Warshaw; Exec. Dir. Rhoda Kaminstein.

### BOSTON

COMBINED JEWISH PHILANTHROPIES OF GREATER BOSTON, INC. (1895; inc. 1961); One Lincoln Plaza (02111); (617)330–9500. Pres. Joel B. Sherman; Exec. V. Pres. Barry Shrage.

### FRAMINGHAM

GREATER FRAMINGHAM JEWISH FEDERATION (1968; inc. 1969); 76 Salem End Rd., Framingham Centre (01701); (508) 879–3301. Pres. Carl Chudnofsky; Exec. Dir. Lawrence Lowenthal.

### LEOMINSTER

LEOMINSTER JEWISH COMMUNITY COUNCIL, INC. (1939); 165 Grove Ave. (01453);

(617)534–6121. Pres. Milton Kline; Sec.-Treas. Howard J. Rome.

## MERRIMACK VALLEY

MERRIMACK VALLEY UNITED JEWISH COMMUNITIES (Serves Lowell, Lawrence, Andover, Haverhill, and Newburyport) (1988); 805 Turnpike St., N. Andover (01845); (508)688–0466. Pres. Larry Ansin; Exec. Dir. Leonard Gravitz.

## NEW BEDFORD

JEWISH FEDERATION OF GREATER NEW BEDFORD, INC. (1938; inc. 1954); 467 Hawthorn St., N. Dartmouth (02747); (508)997–7471. Pres. Barry Russell; Exec. Dir. Jerry Neimand.

## NORTH SHORE

JEWISH FEDERATION OF THE NORTH SHORE, INC. (1938); 4 Community Rd., Marblehead (01945); (617)598–1810. Pres. Dr. Bertil F. Wolf; Exec. Dir. Bruce Yudewitz.

## SPRINGFIELD

JEWISH FEDERATION OF GREATER SPRINGFIELD, INC. (1925); (sponsors SJF/UJA CAMPAIGN); 1160 Dickinson St. (01108); (413)737–4313. Pres. Betsy Gaberman; Exec. Dir. Joel Weiss.

## WORCESTER

WORCESTER JEWISH FEDERATION, INC. (1947; inc. 1957); (sponsors JEWISH WELFARE FUND); 633 Salisbury St. (01609); (508)756–1543. Pres. Gilbert Slovin; Exec. Dir. Joseph Huber.

# MICHIGAN

## ANN ARBOR

JEWISH COMMUNITY ASSOCIATION/UNITED JEWISH APPEAL; 2939 Birch Hollow Dr. (48108). (313)971–7183. Pres. Dr. David Schteingart; Exec. Dir. Rabbi Earl A. Jordan.

## DETROIT

JEWISH WELFARE FEDERATION OF DETROIT (1899); Fred M. Butzel Memorial Bldg., 163 Madison (48226); (313)965–3939. Pres. Dr. Conrad L. Giles; Exec. V. Pres. Martin Kraar.

## FLINT

FLINT JEWISH FEDERATION (1936); 619 Wallenberg St. (48502); (313)767–5922; Pres. Gary Hurand; Exec. Dir. David Nussbaum.

## GRAND RAPIDS

JEWISH COMMUNITY FUND OF GRAND RAPIDS (1930); 2609 Berwyck SE (49506); (616)956–9365. Pres. Joseph N. Schwartz; Admin. Dir. Judy Joseph.

# MINNESOTA

## DULUTH-SUPERIOR

JEWISH FEDERATION & COMMUNITY COUNCIL (1937); 1602 E. 2 St., Duluth (55812); (218)724–8857. Pres. Aaron Glazman; Sec. Admin. Gloria Vitullo.

## MINNEAPOLIS

MINNEAPOLIS FEDERATION FOR JEWISH SERVICE (1929; inc. 1930); 7600 Wayzata Blvd. (55426); (612)593–2600. Pres. Herbert Goldenberg; Exec. Dir. Max L. Kleinman.

## ST. PAUL

UNITED JEWISH FUND AND COUNCIL (1935); 790 S. Cleveland, Suite 201 (55116); (612)690–1707. Pres. Rhoda Mains; Exec. Dir. Sam Asher.

# MISSISSIPPI

## JACKSON

JACKSON JEWISH WELFARE FUND, INC. (1945); 5315 Old Canton Rd. (39211–4625); (601)956–6215. Pres. Ruth Friedman; V. Pres. Erik Hearon.

# MISSOURI

## KANSAS CITY

JEWISH FEDERATION OF GREATER KANSAS CITY (1933); 5801 W. 115th St., Overland Park, Kansas (66211–1824); (913)469–1340. Pres. Ann R. Jacobson; Exec. Dir. A. Robert Gast.

## ST. JOSEPH

UNITED JEWISH FUND OF ST. JOSEPH (1915); 509 Woodcrest Dr. (64506); (816)-279–7154. Pres. Dorathea Polsky; Exec. Sec. Martha Rothstein.

## ST. LOUIS

JEWISH FEDERATION OF ST. LOUIS (incl. St. Louis County) (1901); 12 Millstone Campus Dr. (63146); (314)432–0020. Pres. Thomas R. Green; Exec. V. Pres. William Kahn.

# NEBRASKA

## LINCOLN

LINCOLN JEWISH WELFARE FEDERATION, INC. (1931; inc. 1961); PO Box 80014

(68501); (402)423-5695. Pres. Charles H. Coren; Exec. Dir. Robert Pitlor.

## OMAHA

JEWISH FEDERATION OF OMAHA (1903); 333 S. 132 St. (68154-2198); (402)334-8200. Pres. Saranne Gitnick; Exec. Dir. Howard Bloom.

## NEVADA

### LAS VEGAS

JEWISH FEDERATION OF LAS VEGAS (1973); 1030 E. Twain Ave. (89109); (702)732-0556. Pres. Arnold Rosencrantz; Exec. Dir. Norman Kaufman.

## NEW HAMPSHIRE

### MANCHESTER

JEWISH FEDERATION OF GREATER MANCHESTER (1974); 698 Beech St. (03104); (603)627-7679. Pres. Gary Wallin; Exec. Dir. Earnest Siegel.

## NEW JERSEY

### ATLANTIC COUNTY

FEDERATION OF JEWISH AGENCIES OF ATLANTIC COUNTY (1924); 5321 Atlantic Ave., Ventnor City (08406); (609)822-7122. Pres. James Cooper; Exec. Dir. Bernard Cohen.

### BERGEN COUNTY

UNITED JEWISH COMMUNITY OF BERGEN COUNTY (inc. 1978); 111 Kinderkamack Rd., PO Box 4176, N. Hackensack Station, River Edge (07661); (201)488-6800. Pres. Paula Cantor; Exec. V. Pres. Dr. James Young.

### CENTRAL NEW JERSEY

JEWISH FEDERATION OF CENTRAL NEW JERSEY (1940; merged 1973); (sponsors UNITED JEWISH CAMPAIGN); Green Lane, Union (07083); (201)351-5060. Pres. Jim Shrager; Exec. V. Pres. Burton Lazarow.

### CLIFTON-PASSAIC

JEWISH FEDERATION OF GREATER CLIFTON-PASSAIC (1933); (sponsors UNITED JEWISH CAMPAIGN); 199 Scoles Ave., Clifton (07012). (201)777-7031. Pres. Jon Gurkoff; Exec. Dir. Yosef Muskin.

### CUMBERLAND COUNTY

JEWISH FEDERATION OF CUMBERLAND COUNTY (inc. 1971); (incorp. JEWISH COMMUNITY COUNCIL and ALLIED JEWISH APPEAL); 629 Wood St., Suite 204, Vineland (08360); (609)696-4445. Pres. Gerald Batt; Exec. Dir. Daniel Lepow.

### ENGLEWOOD

(Merged with Bergen County)

### JERSEY CITY

UNITED JEWISH APPEAL (1939); 71 Bentley Ave. (07304); (201)332-6644. Gen. Chmn. Mel Blum; Exec. Sec. Madeline Mazer.

### MERCER COUNTY

JEWISH FEDERATION OF MERCER AND BUCKS COUNTIES NJ/PA (formerly Delaware Valley); (1929; reorg. 1982); 999 Lower Ferry Rd., Trenton (08628); (609)883-5000. Pres. Jon Parker; Exec. Dir. Haim Morag. (Also see listing under Pennsylvania.)

### METROWEST

UNITED JEWISH FEDERATION OF METROWEST (1923); (sponsors UNITED JEWISH APPEAL); 60 Glenwood Ave., E. Orange (07017); (201)673-6800; (212)943-0570. Pres. Sam Oolie; Exec. V. Pres. Howard E. Charish.

### MIDDLESEX COUNTY

JEWISH FEDERATION OF GREATER MIDDLESEX COUNTY (formerly Northern Middlesex County and Raritan Valley) (org. 1948; reorg. 1985); 100 Metroplex Dr., Suite 101, Edison (08817); (201)985-1234. Pres. Larry Zicklin; Exec. V.-Pres. Michael Shapiro.

### MONMOUTH COUNTY

JEWISH FEDERATION OF GREATER MONMOUTH COUNTY (formerly Shore Area) (1971); 100 Grant Ave., PO Box 210, Deal (07723-0210); (201)531-6200-1. Pres. Sharon Portman; Exec. Dir. Marvin Relkin.

### MORRIS-SUSSEX COUNTY

(Merged with MetroWest)

### NORTH JERSEY

JEWISH FEDERATION OF NORTH JERSEY (formerly Jewish Community Council) (1933); (sponsors UNITED JEWISH APPEAL DRIVE); One Pike Dr., Wayne (07470); (201)595-0555. Pres. Joanne Sprechman; Exec. Dir. Barry Rosenberg.

### NORTHERN MIDDLESEX COUNTY

(See Middlesex County)

### OCEAN COUNTY

OCEAN COUNTY JEWISH FEDERATION (1977); 301 Madison Ave., Lakewood (08701); (201)363-0530. Pres. Robert Singer; Exec. Dir. Michael Ruvel.

**RARITAN VALLEY**
(See Middlesex County)

**SOMERSET COUNTY**
JEWISH FEDERATION OF SOMERSET, HUNTERDON, & WARREN COUNTIES (1960); 120 Finderne Ave., Bridgewater (08807); (201)-725-6994. Pres. Ted Gast.

**SOUTHERN NEW JERSEY**
JEWISH FEDERATION OF SOUTHERN NEW JERSEY (incl. Camden, Burlington, and Gloucester Counties) (1922); (sponsors ALLIED JEWISH APPEAL); 2393 W. Marlton Pike, Cherry Hill (08002); (609)665-6100. Pres. Robert Paul; Exec. V. Pres. Stuart Alperin.

## NEW MEXICO

**ALBUQUERQUE**
JEWISH FEDERATION OF GREATER ALBUQUERQUE (1938); 12800 Lomas NE, Suite F (87112); (505)292-1061. Pres. Shirlee R. Londer; Exec. Dir. Elisa M. Simon.

## NEW YORK

**ALBANY**
(Merged with Schenectady; see Northeastern New York)

**BROOME COUNTY**
JEWISH FEDERATION OF BROOME COUNTY (1937; inc. 1958); 500 Clubhouse Rd., Binghamton (13903); (607)724-2332. Pres. Howard Rittberg; Act. Exec. Dir. Victoria Rouff.

**BUFFALO**
JEWISH FEDERATION OF GREATER BUFFALO, INC. (1903); (sponsors UNITED JEWISH FUND CAMPAIGN); 787 Delaware Ave. (14209); (716)886-7750. Pres. Stuart G. Lerman; Exec. Dir. Harry Kosansky.

**ELMIRA**
ELMIRA JEWISH WELFARE FUND, INC. (1942); Grandview Rd. Ext., PO Box 3087 (14905); (607)734-8122. Pres. Arnold Rosenberg; Exec. Dir. Cy Leveen.

**KINGSTON**
JEWISH FEDERATION OF GREATER KINGSTON, INC. (inc. 1951); 159 Green St. (12401); (914)338-8131. Pres. Dr. Howard Rothstein.

**NEW YORK**
UJA-FEDERATION OF JEWISH PHILANTHROPIES OF NEW YORK, INC. (incl. Greater NY; Westchester, Nassau, and Suffolk Counties) (Fed. org. 1917; UJA 1939; merged 1986); 130 E. 59 St. (10022); (212)980-1000. Pres. Peggy Tishman; Bd. Chmn. Joseph Gurwin; Exec. V. Pres.'s Ernest W. Michel, Stephen D. Solender.

**NIAGARA FALLS**
JEWISH FEDERATION OF NIAGARA FALLS, NY, INC. (1935); Temple Beth Israel, Rm. #5, College & Madison Ave. (14305); (716)-284-4575. Pres. Howard Kushner; Exec. Dir. Linda Boxer.

**NORTHEASTERN NEW YORK**
UNITED JEWISH FEDERATION OF NORTHEASTERN NEW YORK (formerly Albany and Schenectady) (1986); Latham Circle Mall, 800 New Loudon Rd., Latham (12110); (518)783-7800. Pres. Ernest Kahn; Exec. Dir. Norman J. Schimelman.

**ORANGE COUNTY**
JEWISH FEDERATION OF GREATER ORANGE COUNTY (1977); 360 Powell Ave., Newburgh (12550); (914)562-7860. Pres. Harold Levine; Exec. Dir. Nancy Goldman.

**POUGHKEEPSIE**
DUTCHESS COUNTY JEWISH WELFARE FUND; 110 S. Grand Ave. (12603). (914)471-4594. Pres. Roslyn Tinkelman; Exec. Dir. Ira Minot.

**ROCHESTER**
JEWISH COMMUNITY FEDERATION OF ROCHESTER, NY, INC. (1939); 441 East Ave. (14607); (716)461-0490. Pres. Paul Goldberg; Exec. Dir. Avrom Fox.

**ROCKLAND COUNTY**
UNITED JEWISH COMMUNITY OF ROCKLAND COUNTY (1985); 240 W. Nyack Rd., W. Nyack (10994-1700). (914)627-3700. Pres. Barbara Grau; Exec. Dir. Michael A. Bierman.

**SCHENECTADY**
(Merged with Albany; see Northeastern New York)

**SYRACUSE**
SYRACUSE JEWISH FEDERATION, INC. (1918); 101 Smith St.; PO Box 510, DeWitt (13214-0510); (315)445-0161. Pres. Helen Marcum; Exec. V. Pres. Barry Silverberg.

**TROY**
TROY JEWISH COMMUNITY COUNCIL, INC. (1936) (incorp. into Northeastern NY); 2430

21 St. (12180); (518)274-0700. Pres. Steven Gimberg.

## UTICA

JEWISH FEDERATION OF UTICA, NY, INC. (1933; inc. 1950); (sponsors UNITED JEWISH APPEAL OF UTICA); 2310 Oneida St. (13501); (315)733-2343. Pres. Richard Dinerstein; Exec. Dir. Meyer L. Bodoff.

## NORTH CAROLINA

### ASHEVILLE

WESTERN NORTH CAROLINA JEWISH FEDERATION (1935); 236 Charlotte St. (28801); (704)253-0701. Pres. Robert J. Deutsch; Exec. Dir. Ellen Sandweiss-Hodges.

### CHARLOTTE

CHARLOTTE JEWISH FEDERATION (1938); PO Box 13369 (28211); (704)366-5007. Pres. Mrs. Bobbi Bernstein; Exec. Dir. Michael Minkin.

### DURHAM-CHAPEL HILL

DURHAM-CHAPEL HILL JEWISH FEDERATION & COMMUNITY COUNCIL (1979); 1310 LeClair St., Chapel Hill (27514); (919)967-1945. Pres. Barry Nakell.

### GREENSBORO

GREENSBORO JEWISH FEDERATION (1940); 713A N. Greene St. (27401); (919)272-3189. Pres. Bernard Gutterman; Exec. Dir. Marilyn Chandler.

## OHIO

### AKRON

AKRON JEWISH COMMUNITY FEDERATION (1935); 750 White Pond Dr. (44320); (216)-867-7850. Pres. Joseph Kanfer; Exec. Dir. Stanley H. Bard.

### CANTON

CANTON JEWISH COMMUNITY FEDERATION (1935; reorg. 1955); 2631 Harvard Ave., NW (44709); (216)452-6444. Pres. Neil Genshaft; Exec. Dir. Jay Rubin.

### CINCINNATI

JEWISH FEDERATION OF CINCINNATI (1896; reorg. 1967); 1811 Losantiville, Suite 320 (45237); (513) 351-3800. Pres. David Lazarus; Exec. V. Pres. Aubrey Herman.

### CLEVELAND

JEWISH COMMUNITY FEDERATION OF CLEVELAND (1903); 1750 Euclid Ave. (44115); (216)566-9200. Pres. Max R. Friedman; Exec. Dir. Stephen H. Hoffman.

### COLUMBUS

COLUMBUS JEWISH FEDERATION (1926); 1175 College Ave. (43209); (614)237-7686. Pres. B. Lee Skilken; Exec. Dir. Alan Gill.

### DAYTON

JEWISH FEDERATION OF GREATER DAYTON (1910); 4501 Denlinger Rd. (45426); (513)854-4150. Pres. Bernard Rabinowitz; Exec. V. Pres. Peter H. Wells.

### STEUBENVILLE

JEWISH COMMUNITY COUNCIL (1938); 300 Lovers Lane (43952); (614)282-9031. Pres. Morris Denmark; Exec. Sec. Jennie Bernstein.

### TOLEDO

JEWISH FEDERATION OF GREATER TOLEDO (1907; reorg. 1960); 6505 Sylvania Ave., PO Box 587, Sylvania (43560); (419)885-4461. Pres. Marla Levine; Exec. Dir. Steven J. Edelstein.

### YOUNGSTOWN

YOUNGSTOWN AREA JEWISH FEDERATION (1935); PO Box 449, 505 Gypsy Lane (44501); (216)746-3251. Pres. Esther L. Marks; Exec. V. Pres. Sam Kooperman.

## OKLAHOMA

### OKLAHOMA CITY

JEWISH FEDERATION OF GREATER OKLAHOMA CITY (1941); 2800 Quail Plaza Dr. (73120). (405)752-7307. Pres. Charles Fagin; Exec. Dir. Garth Potts.

### TULSA

JEWISH FEDERATION OF TULSA (1938); (sponsors UNITED JEWISH CAMPAIGN); 2021 E. 71 St. (74136); (918)495-1100. Pres. Edward I. Cohen; Exec. Dir. David Bernstein.

## OREGON

### PORTLAND

JEWISH FEDERATION OF PORTLAND (incl. state of Oregon and adjacent Washington communities) (1920; reorg. 1956); 6651 SW Capitol Highway (97219); (503)245-6219. Pres. Dr. Leonard Goldberg; Exec. Dir. Charles Schiffman.

JEWISH FEDERATIONS, FUNDS, COUNCILS / 503

## PENNSYLVANIA

**ALLENTOWN**
JEWISH FEDERATION OF ALLENTOWN; 702 N. 22 St. (18104); (215)821-5500. Pres. Milton Sheftel; Exec. Dir. Ivan C. Schonfeld.

**ALTOONA**
FEDERATION OF JEWISH PHILANTHROPIES (1920; reorg. 1940); 1308 17 St. (16601); (814)944-4072. Pres. Morley Cohn.

**BUCKS COUNTY**
JEWISH FEDERATION OF MERCER AND BUCKS COUNTIES NJ/PA (formerly Delaware Valley); (1929; reorg. 1982); 999 Lower Ferry Rd., Trenton, NJ (08628); (609)883-5000. Pres. Jon Parker; Exec. Dir. Haim Morag. (Also see listing under New Jersey.)

**ERIE**
JEWISH COMMUNITY COUNCIL OF ERIE (1946); 701 G. Daniel Baldwin Bldg., 1001 State St. (16501); (814)455-4474. Pres. Leonard Lechtner.

**HARRISBURG**
UNITED JEWISH FEDERATION OF GREATER HARRISBURG (1941); 100 Vaughn St. (17110); (717)236-9555. Pres. Morton Spector; Exec. Dir. Elliot Gershenson.

**JOHNSTOWN**
UNITED JEWISH FEDERATION OF JOHNSTOWN (1938); 601 Wayne St. (15905); (814)-539-9891. Pres. Isadore Suchman.

**PHILADELPHIA**
FEDERATION OF JEWISH AGENCIES OF GREATER PHILADELPHIA (1901; reorg. 1956); 226 S. 16 St. (19102); (215)893-5600. Pres. Miriam A. Schneirov; Exec. V. Pres. Robert P. Forman.

**PITTSBURGH**
UNITED JEWISH FEDERATION OF GREATER PITTSBURGH (1912; reorg. 1955); 234 McKee Pl. (15213); (412)681-8000. Pres. Edward Perlow; Exec. V. Pres. Howard M. Rieger.

**READING**
JEWISH FEDERATION OF READING, PA., INC. (1935; reorg. and inc. 1972); (sponsors UNITED JEWISH CAMPAIGN); 1700 City Line St. (19604); (215)921-2766. Pres. Victor H. Hammel; Exec. Dir. Daniel Tannenbaum.

**SCRANTON**
SCRANTON-LACKAWANNA JEWISH FEDERATION (incl. Lackawanna County) (1945); 601 Jefferson Ave. (18510); (717)961-2300. Pres. Joseph Dubin; Exec. Dir. Seymour Brotman.

**WILKES-BARRE**
JEWISH FEDERATION OF GREATER WILKES-BARRE (1935); (sponsors UNITED JEWISH CAMPAIGN); 60 S. River St. (18702); (717)-822-4146. Pres. Connie Roth; Exec. Dir. Irving Ginsberg.

## RHODE ISLAND

**PROVIDENCE**
JEWISH FEDERATION OF RHODE ISLAND (1945); 130 Sessions St. (02906); (401)421-4111. Pres. Norman Tilles; Exec. V. Pres. Elliot Cohan.

## SOUTH CAROLINA

**CHARLESTON**
CHARLESTON JEWISH FEDERATION (1949); 1645 Raoul Wallenberg Blvd., PO Box 31298 (29407); (803)571-6565. Pres. Ellis I. Kahn; Exec. Dir. Michael Wise.

**COLUMBIA**
COLUMBIA JEWISH FEDERATION (1960); 4540 Trenholm Rd., PO Box 6968 (29260); (803)787-0580. Pres. Samuel Tenenbaum; Exec. Dir. Alexander Grossberg.

## SOUTH DAKOTA

**SIOUX FALLS**
JEWISH WELFARE FUND (1938); National Reserve Bldg., 513 S. Main Ave. (57102); (605)336-2880. Pres. Laurence Bierman; Exec. Sec. Louis R. Hurwitz.

## TENNESSEE

**CHATTANOOGA**
CHATTANOOGA JEWISH FEDERATION (1931); 5326 Lynnland Terrace, PO Box 8947 (37411); (615)894-1317. Pres. Charles B. Lebovitz; Exec. Dir. Louis B. Solomon.

**KNOXVILLE**
KNOXVILLE JEWISH FEDERATION (1939); 6800 Deane Hill Dr., PO Box 10882 (37939-0882); (615)693-5837. Pres. Arnold Schwarzbart; Exec. Dir. Conrad J. Koller.

## MEMPHIS
MEMPHIS JEWISH FEDERATION (incl. Shelby County) (1935); 6560 Poplar Ave., PO Box 38268 (38138); (901)767-7100. Pres. Edward R. Young.

## NASHVILLE
JEWISH FEDERATION OF NASHVILLE & MIDDLE TENNESSEE (1936); 801 Perry Warner Blvd. (37205); (615)356-3242. Pres. Nedda Pollack; Exec. Dir. Dr. Jay M. Pilzer.

# TEXAS

## AUSTIN
JEWISH COMMUNITY COUNCIL OF AUSTIN (1939; reorg. 1956); 11713 Jollyville Rd. (78759); (512)331-1144. Pres. David Kruger; Exec. Dir. Marilyn Stahl.

## DALLAS
JEWISH FEDERATION OF GREATER DALLAS (1911); 7800 Northhaven Rd., Suite A (75230); (214)369-3313. Pres. Howard Schultz; Exec. Dir. Morris A. Stein.

## EL PASO
JEWISH FEDERATION OF EL PASO, INC. (incl. surrounding communities) (1937); 405 Wallenberg Dr., PO Box 12097 (79913-0097); (915)584-4437. Pres. Joan Johnson; Exec. Dir. David Brown.

## FORT WORTH
JEWISH FEDERATION OF FORT WORTH AND TARRANT COUNTY (1936); 6801 Dan Danciger Rd. (76133); (817)292-3081. Pres. Sandra Freed.

## GALVESTON
GALVESTON COUNTY JEWISH WELFARE ASSOCIATION (1936); PO Box 146 (77553); (409)763-5241. Pres. Dr. Mark Sanders; Treas. Charna Graber.

## HOUSTON
JEWISH FEDERATION OF GREATER HOUSTON (1936); 5603 S. Braeswood Blvd. (77096-3999); (713)729-7000. Pres. Sandra Weiner; Exec. Dir. Hans Mayer.

## SAN ANTONIO
JEWISH FEDERATION OF SAN ANTONIO (incl. Bexar County) (1922); 8434 Ahern Dr. (78216); (512)341-8234. Pres. Joe Westheimer, Jr.; Exec. Dir. Robert Posner.

## WACO
JEWISH FEDERATION OF WACO AND CENTRAL TEXAS (1949); PO Box 8031 (76714-8031); (817)776-3740. Pres. Simone Bauer; Exec. Sec. Martha Bauer.

# UTAH

## SALT LAKE CITY
UNITED JEWISH COUNCIL AND SALT LAKE JEWISH WELFARE FUND (1936); 2416 E. 1700 South (84108); (801)581-0098. Pres. Richard McGillis; Acting Exec. Dir. Eve Bier.

# VIRGINIA

## NEWPORT NEWS—HAMPTON—WILLIAMSBURG
UNITED JEWISH COMMUNITY OF THE VIRGINIA PENINSULA, INC. (1942); 2700 Spring Rd., Newport News (23606); (804)930-1422. Pres. Dr. Steven Seltzer; Exec. Dir. Norman Olshansky.

## RICHMOND
JEWISH COMMUNITY FEDERATION OF RICHMOND (1935); 5403 Monument Ave., PO Box 17128 (23226); (804)288-0045. Pres. Dr. Walter N. Rabhan; Exec. Dir. Robert S. Hyman.

## TIDEWATER
UNITED JEWISH FEDERATION OF TIDEWATER (incl. Norfolk, Portsmouth, and Virginia Beach) (1937); 7300 Newport Ave., PO Box 9776, Norfolk (23505); (804)489-8040. Pres. Bootsie Goldmeier; Exec. V. Pres. Gary N. Rubin.

# WASHINGTON

## SEATTLE
JEWISH FEDERATION OF GREATER SEATTLE (incl. King County, Everett, and Bremerton) (1926); 2031 Third Ave. (98121); (206)622-8211. Pres. Francine Loeb; Exec. Dir. Michael Novick.

# WEST VIRGINIA

## CHARLESTON
FEDERATED JEWISH CHARITIES OF CHARLESTON, INC. (1937); PO Box 1613 (25326); (304)346-7500. Pres. Carl Lehman; Exec. Sec. William H. Thalheimer.

# WISCONSIN

## KENOSHA
KENOSHA JEWISH WELFARE FUND (1938); 6537 Seventh Ave. (53140); (414)658-8635. Pres. Nathaniel S. Lepp; Sec.-Treas. S. M. Lapp.

## JEWISH FEDERATIONS, FUNDS, COUNCILS

### MADISON
MADISON JEWISH COMMUNITY COUNCIL, INC. (1940); 310 N. Midvale Blvd., Suite 325 (53705); (608)231-3426. Pres. Lawrence Shapiro; Exec. Dir. Steven H. Morrison.

### MILWAUKEE
MILWAUKEE JEWISH FEDERATION, INC. (1902); 1360 N. Prospect Ave. (53202); (414)-271-8338. Pres. R. Todd Lappin; Exec. V. Pres. Robert Aronson.

### RACINE
RACINE JEWISH WELFARE COUNCIL (1946); 944 S. Main St. (53403); (414)633-7093. Chmn. Arthur Schaefer.

## CANADA

### ALBERTA

#### CALGARY
CALGARY JEWISH COMMUNITY COUNCIL (1962); 1607 90th Ave. SW (T2V 4V7); (403)-253-8600. Pres. Hal Joffe; Exec. Dir. Drew J. Staffenberg.

#### EDMONTON
JEWISH FEDERATION OF EDMONTON (1954; reorg. 1982); 7200 156 St. (T5R 1X3); (403)487-5120. Pres. Sheldon Maerov; Act. Exec. Dir. Maxine Fischbein.

### BRITISH COLUMBIA

#### VANCOUVER
JEWISH FEDERATION OF GREATER VANCOUVER (1932); 950 W. 41 Ave. (V5Z 2N7); (604)266-8371. Pres. Daniel U. Pekarsky; Exec. Dir. Steve Drysdale.

### MANITOBA

#### WINNIPEG
WINNIPEG JEWISH COMMUNITY COUNCIL (1938; reorg. 1973); (incl. COMBINED JEWISH APPEAL OF WINNIPEG); 370 Hargrave St. (R3B 2K1); (204)943-0406. Pres. Evelyn Katz; Exec. Dir. Robert Freedman.

### ONTARIO

#### HAMILTON
JEWISH FEDERATION OF HAMILTON WENTWORTH & AREA (1932; merged 1971); (incl. UNITED JEWISH WELFARE FUND); PO Box 7258, 1030 Lower Lion Club Rd., Ancaster (L9G 3N6); (416)648-0605. Pres. Phillip Leon; Exec. Dir. Sid Brail.

#### LONDON
LONDON JEWISH COMMUNITY COUNCIL (1932); 536 Huron St. (N5Y 4J5); (519)673-3310. Pres. Gloria Gilbert; Exec. Dir. Gerald Enchin.

#### OTTAWA
JEWISH COMMUNITY COUNCIL OF OTTAWA (1934); 151 Chapel St. (K1N 7Y2); (613)-232-7306. Pres. Stephen Victor; Exec. Dir. Gerry Koffman.

#### TORONTO
TORONTO JEWISH CONGRESS (1917); 4600 Bathurst St.; Willowdale (M2R 3V2); (416)-635-2883. Pres. Herb Rosenfeld; Exec. Dir. Steven Ain.

#### WINDSOR
JEWISH COMMUNITY COUNCIL (1938); 1641 Ouellette Ave. (N8X 1K9); (519)973-1772. Pres. Alan R. Orman; Exec. Dir. Joseph Eisenberg.

### QUEBEC

#### MONTREAL
ALLIED JEWISH COMMUNITY SERVICES (1965); 5151 Cote St. Catherine Rd. (H3W 1M6); (514)735-3541. Pres. Peter Wolkove; Exec. Dir. John Fishel.

# Jewish Periodicals[1]

## UNITED STATES

### ARIZONA

ARIZONA POST (1946). 635 N. Craycroft, #202, Tucson, 85711. (602)325-5864. Sandra R. Heiman. Fortnightly. Jewish Federation of Southern Arizona.

GREATER PHOENIX JEWISH NEWS (1947). PO Box 26590, Phoenix, 85068. (602)870-9470. Flo Eckstein. Weekly.

### CALIFORNIA

B'NAI B'RITH MESSENGER (1897). PO Box 57991, 2510 W. 7 St., Los Angeles, 90057. (213)380-5000. Shelly Rubin, Rabbi Yale Butler. Weekly.

HERITAGE-SOUTHWEST JEWISH PRESS (1914). 2130 S. Vermont Ave., Los Angeles, 90007. (213) 737-2122. Dan Brin. Weekly. (Also SAN DIEGO JEWISH PRESS-HERITAGE, San Diego [weekly]; CENTRAL CALIFORNIA JEWISH HERITAGE, Sacramento and Fresno area [monthly]; ORANGE COUNTY JEWISH HERITAGE, Orange County area [weekly]).

JEWISH JOURNAL (1986). 3660 Wilshire Blvd., Suite 204, Los Angeles, 90010. (213)738-7778. Gene Lichtenstein. Weekly.

JEWISH NEWS (formerly ISRAEL TODAY) (1973). 4211 Laurel Canyon Blvd., Studio City, 91604; PO Box 1909-245, Studio City, 91604-3791. (818)786-4000. Phil Blazer. Monthly.

JEWISH SPECTATOR (1935). PO Box 2016, Santa Monica, 90406. (213)393-9063. Trude Weiss-Rosmarin. Quarterly.

JEWISH STAR (1956). 109 Minna St., Suite 323, San Francisco, 94105. (415)421-4874. Nevon Stuckey. Bimonthly.

NORTHERN CALIFORNIA JEWISH BULLETIN (1946). 88 First St., Suite 300, San Francisco, 94105. (415)957-9340. Marc Klein. Weekly. San Francisco Jewish Community Publications Inc.

SAN DIEGO JEWISH TIMES (1979). 2592 Fletcher Pkwy., El Cajon, 92020. (619)-463-5515. Carol Rosenberg. Biweekly.

TIKKUN (1986). 5100 Leona St., Oakland, 94619. (415)482-0805. Nan Fink. Bimonthly. Institute for Labor & Mental Health.

WESTERN STATES JEWISH HISTORY (1968). 2429 23rd St., Santa Monica, 90405. (213)-450-2946. Norton B. Stern. Quarterly. Western States Jewish History Association.

### COLORADO

INTERMOUNTAIN JEWISH NEWS (1913). 1275 Sherman St., Suite 214, Denver, 80203. (303)861-2234. Miriam H. Goldberg. Weekly.

### CONNECTICUT

CONNECTICUT JEWISH LEDGER (1929). PO Box 1688, Hartford, 06101. (203)233-2148. Berthold Gaster. Weekly.

### DISTRICT OF COLUMBIA

B'NAI B'RITH INTERNATIONAL JEWISH MONTHLY (1886 under the name MENORAH). 1640 Rhode Island Ave., NW,

---

[1]The information in this directory is based on replies to questionnaires circulated by the editors. For organization bulletins, see the directory of Jewish organizations.

Washington, 20036. (202)857-6645. Marc Silver. Ten times a year. B'nai B'rith.

JEWISH VETERAN (1896). 1811 R St., NW, Washington, 20009. (202)265-6280. Pearl Laufer. Bimonthly. Jewish War Veterans of the U.S.A.

MOMENT (1975). 3000 Connecticut Ave., NW, Suite 300, Washington, 20008. (202)-387-8888. Hershel Shanks. Monthly (ten issues a year). Jewish Educational Ventures, Inc.

NEAR EAST REPORT (1957). 500 N. Capitol St., NW, Washington, 20001. (202)638-1225. Eric Rozenman. Weekly. Near East Research, Inc.

UCSJ QUARTERLY REPORT. 1819 H Street, NW, Suite 230, Washington, 20006. (202)-775-9770. Jennifer Kane. Quarterly. Union of Councils for Soviet Jews.

WASHINGTON JEWISH WEEK (1965). 1910 K St., NW, #601, Washington, 20006. (202)872-1100. Lisa S. Lenkiewicz. Weekly.

### FLORIDA

JEWISH FLORIDIAN GROUP (1927). 120 NE 6 St., Miami, 33101. (305)373-4605. Leo Mindlin. Weekly.

JEWISH JOURNAL (1977). PO Box 189006, Ft. Plantation, 33318. (305)581-2244. Steven Sands. Weekly. Worrell South Florida Newspaper Network.

JEWISH WORLD (1982). 2405 Mercer Ave., W. Palm Beach, 33401. (305)833-8331. Martin Pomerance. Weekly.

MIAMI JEWISH TRIBUNE (1986). 3550 Biscayne Blvd., Suite 600, Miami, 33137. (305)576-9500. Andrew Polin. Weekly. Jewish Media Group, Inc.

SOUTHERN JEWISH WEEKLY (1924). PO Box 3297, Jacksonville, 32206. (904)634-1469. Isadore Moscovitz. Weekly. Southern Independent Operators, Inc.

### GEORGIA

ATLANTA JEWISH TIMES (formerly SOUTHERN ISRAELITE). 1575 Northside Dr., NW, #365, Atlanta, 30318. (404)355-6139. Vida Goldgar. Weekly.

JEWISH CIVIC PRESS (1972). 3330 Peachtree Rd. NE, Atlanta, Suite 560, 30326. (404)-231-2194. Abner L. Tritt. Monthly.

### ILLINOIS

CHICAGO JUF NEWS (1972). One S. Franklin St., Chicago, 60606. (312)444-2853. Joseph Aaron. Monthly. Jewish Federation of Metropolitan Chicago.

JEWISH COMMUNITY NEWS (1941). 6464 W. Main, Suite 7A, Belleville, 62223. (618)-398-6100. Rabbi Zalman Stein. Bimonthly. Jewish Federation of Southern Illinois.

THE SENTINEL (1911). 175 W. Jackson Blvd., Suite 1927, Chicago, 60604. (312)-663-1101. J. I. Fishbein. Weekly.

### INDIANA

ILLIANA NEWS (1975). 2939 Jewett St., Highland, 46322. (219)972-2250. Barnett Labowitz. Ten times a year. Jewish Federation, Inc./Northwest Indiana.

INDIANA JEWISH POST AND OPINION (1935). PO Box 449097, Indianapolis, 46202. (317)927-7800. Ed Stattmann. Weekly.

NATIONAL JEWISH POST AND OPINION. PO Box 449097, Indianapolis, 46202. (317)-927-7800. Gabriel Cohen. Weekly.

### KANSAS

KANSAS CITY JEWISH CHRONICLE. See under MISSOURI.

### KENTUCKY

KENTUCKY JEWISH POST AND OPINION (1931). 1551 Bardstown Rd., Louisville, 40205. (502)459-1914. Gabriel Cohen. Weekly.

### LOUISIANA

JEWISH CIVIC PRESS (1965). PO Box 15500, 924 Valmont St., New Orleans, 70115. (504)895-8784. Abner Tritt. Monthly.

JEWISH TIMES (1974). 1539 Jackson Ave., Suite 323, New Orleans, 70130. (504)524-3147. Fred Shochet, Roberta Brunstetter. Fortnightly.

### MARYLAND

BALTIMORE JEWISH TIMES (1919). 2104 N. Charles St., Baltimore, 21218. (301)752-3504. Gary Rosenblatt. Weekly.

### MASSACHUSETTS

AMERICAN JEWISH HISTORY (1893). 2 Thornton Rd., Waltham, 02154. (617)891-

8110. Marc Lee Raphael. Quarterly. American Jewish Historical Society.

BOSTON JEWISH TIMES (1945). Box 18427, Boston, 02118. (617)357–8635. Sten Lukin. Semiweekly.

GENESIS 2 (1970). 99 Bishop Allen Dr., Cambridge, 02139. (617)576–1801. Lawrence Bush. Quarterly.

JEWISH ADVOCATE (1902). 1168–70 Commonwealth Ave., Boston, 02134. (617)-277–8988. Bernard M. Hyatt. Weekly.

JEWISH REPORTER (1970). 76 Salem End Rd., Framingham, 01776. (508)879–3300. Sheila Abrahams, Jodie Holzwasser. Monthly. Metro West Jewish Federation.

JEWISH WEEKLY NEWS (1945). PO Box 1569, Springfield, 01101. (413)739–4771. Leslie B. Kahn. Weekly.

JOURNAL OF THE NORTH SHORE JEWISH COMMUNITY (1977). 564 Loring Ave., Salem, 01970. (508)741–1558. Barbara Wolf. Biweekly (one issue in July). Jewish Federation of the North Shore.

## MICHIGAN

DETROIT JEWISH NEWS (1942). 20300 Civic Center Dr., Suite 240, Southfield, 48076. (313)354–6060. Gary Rosenblatt. Weekly.

HUMANISTIC JUDAISM (1968). 28611 W. Twelve Mile Rd., Farmington Hills, 48018. (313)478–7610. M. Bonnie Cousens, Ruth D. Feldman. Quarterly. Society for Humanistic Judaism.

## MINNESOTA

AMERICAN JEWISH WORLD (1912). 4509 Minnetonka Blvd., Minneapolis, 55416. (612)920–7000. Bob Epstein. Weekly.

## MISSOURI

KANSAS CITY JEWISH CHRONICLE (1920). 7373 W. 107 St., Overland Park, 66212. (913)648–4620. Ruth Baum Bigus. Weekly.

MISSOURI JEWISH POST (1948). 9531 Lackland, Suite 207, St. Louis, 63114. (314)-423–3088. Kathie Sutin. Weekly.

ST. LOUIS JEWISH LIGHT (1947). 12 Millstone Campus Dr., St. Louis, 63146. (314)-432–3353. Robert A. Cohn. Semiweekly. Jewish Federation of St. Louis.

## NEBRASKA

JEWISH PRESS (1921). 333 S. 132 St., Omaha, 68154. (402)334–8200. Morris Maline. Weekly. Jewish Federation of Omaha.

## NEVADA

JEWISH REPORTER (1976). 1030 E. Twain Ave., Las Vegas, 89109. (702)732–0556. Marla Gerecht. Monthly. Jewish Federation of Las Vegas.

LAS VEGAS ISRAELITE (1965). PO Box 14096, Las Vegas, 89114. (702)876–1255. Michael Tell. Biweekly.

## NEW JERSEY

AVOTAYNU (1985). 1485 Teaneck Rd., Teaneck, 07666. (201)837–2701. Sallyann Amdur Sack. Quarterly.

JEWISH COMMUNITY VOICE (1941). 2393 W. Marlton Pike, Cherry Hill, 08002. (609)-665–6100. Harriet Kessler. Biweekly. Jewish Federation of Southern NJ.

JEWISH HORIZON (1981). 1391 Martine Ave., Scotch Plains, 07076. (201)889–9200. Fran Gold. Weekly. Jewish Federation of Central NJ.

JEWISH NEWS (1947). 60 Glenwood Ave., E. Orange, 07017. (201)678–3900. David Frank. Weekly. United Jewish Federation of MetroWest.

JEWISH RECORD (1939). 1525 S. Main St., Pleasantville, 08232. (609)383–0999. Martin Korik. Weekly.

JEWISH STANDARD (1931). 385 Prospect Ave. Hackensack, 07601. (201)342–1115. Rebecca Kaplan Boroson. Weekly.

JEWISH STAR (1975). 100 Metroplex Dr., Edison, 08820. (201)985–1234. Mindy Belfer. Bimonthly. Jewish Federation of Greater Middlesex County.

JOURNAL OF JEWISH COMMUNAL SERVICE (1899). 3084 State Hwy. 27, Suite 1, Kendall Pk, NJ 08824–1657. (201)821–1871. Sanford N. Sherman. Quarterly. Conference of Jewish Communal Service.

## NEW YORK

AFN SHVEL (1941). 200 W. 72 St., Suite 40, NYC, 10023. (212)787–6675. Mordkhe Schaechter. Quarterly. Yiddish. League for Yiddish, Inc.

ALGEMEINER JOURNAL (1972). 404 Park Ave. S., NYC, 10016. (212)689–3390. Gershon Jacobson. Weekly. Yiddish.

AMERICAN JEWISH YEAR BOOK (1899). 165 E. 56 St., NYC, 10022. (212)751–4000. David Singer. Annually. American Jewish Committee and Jewish Publication Society.

AMERICAN ZIONIST (1910). 4 E. 34 St., NYC, 10016. (212)481–1500. Paul Flacks. Quarterly. Zionist Organization of America.

AMIT WOMAN (1925). 817 Broadway, NYC, 10003. (212)477–4720. Micheline Ratzersdorfer. Five times a year. AMIT Women (formerly American Mizrachi Women).

AUFBAU (1934). 2121 Broadway, NYC, 10023. (212)873–7400. Gert Niers, Henry Marx. Fortnightly. German. New World Club, Inc.

BITZARON (1939). PO Box 623, Cooper Station, NYC, 10003. (212)998–8985. Hayim Leaf. Bimonthly. Hebrew. Hebrew Literary Foundation.

BUFFALO JEWISH REVIEW (1918). 15 E. Mohawk St., Buffalo, 14203. (716)854–2192. Harlan C. Abbey. Weekly. Kahaal Nahalot Israel.

COMMENTARY (1945). 165 E. 56 St., NYC, 10022. (212)751–4000. Norman Podhoretz. Monthly. American Jewish Committee.

CONGRESS MONTHLY (1933). 15 E. 84 St., NYC, 10028. (212)879–4500. Maier Deshell. Seven times a year. American Jewish Congress.

CONSERVATIVE JUDAISM (1945). 3080 Broadway, NYC, 10027. (212)678–8049. Rabbi David Silverman. Quarterly. Rabbinical Assembly.

CONTEMPORARY JEWRY (1974 under the name JEWISH SOCIOLOGY AND SOCIAL RESEARCH). Center for Jewish Studies, CUNY Graduate School and University Center, 33 W. 42 St., NYC, 10036. (212)-790–4404. Paul Ritterband. Semiannually. Association for the Social Scientific Study of Jewry.

ECONOMIC HORIZONS (1953). 500 Fifth Ave., 5416, NYC, 10110–0380. (212)354–6510. Ronny Bassan. Quarterly. American-Israel Chamber of Commerce and Industry, Inc.

HADAROM (1957). 275 Seventh Ave., NYC, 10001. (212)807–7888. Rabbi Gedalia Schwartz. Annually. Hebrew. Rabbinical Council of America.

HADASSAH MAGAZINE (1921). 50 W. 58 St., NYC, 10019. (212)355–7900. Alan M. Tigay. Monthly (except for combined issues of June–July and Aug.–Sept.). Hadassah, the Women's Zionist Organization of America.

HADOAR (1921). 1841 Broadway, Rm. 510, NYC, 10023. (212)581–5151. Shlomo Shamir, Yael Feldman. Weekly. Hebrew. Hadoar Association, Inc.

ISRAEL HORIZONS (1952). 150 Fifth Ave., Suite 911, NYC, 10011. (212)753–8760. Arieh Lebowitz. Quarterly. Americans for Progressive Israel.

ISRAEL QUALITY (1976). 230 W. 41 St., Suite 1700, NYC 10036. (212)244–2011. Beth Belkin. Quarterly. American-Israel Chamber of Commerce and Industry, Inc. and Government of Israel Trade Center.

JEWISH ACTION (1950). 45 W. 36 St., NYC, 10018. (212)244–2011. Heidi Tenzer. Quarterly. Union of Orthodox Jewish Congregations of America.

JEWISH BOOK ANNUAL (1942). 15 E. 26 St., NYC, 10010–1579. (212)532–4949. Jacob Kabakoff. English-Hebrew-Yiddish. JWB Jewish Book Council.

JEWISH BOOK WORLD (1945). 15 E. 26 St., NYC, 10010–1579. (212)532–4949. William Wollheim. Quarterly. JWB Jewish Book Council.

JEWISH BRAILLE INSTITUTE VOICE (1978). 110 E. 30 St., NYC, 10016. (212)889–2525. Jacob Freid. Monthly, except May–June, July–August (audio cassettes). Jewish Braille Institute of America, Inc.

JEWISH BRAILLE REVIEW (1931). 110 E. 30 St., NYC, 10016. (212)889–2525. Jacob Freid. Monthly, except May–June, July–August. English braille. Jewish Braille Institute of America, Inc.

JEWISH CURRENT EVENTS (1959). 430 Keller Ave., Elmont, 11003. Samuel Deutsch. Biweekly.

JEWISH CURRENTS (1946). 22 E. 17 St., Suite 601, NYC, 10003. (212)924–5740. Morris U. Schappes. Monthly. Association for Promotion of Jewish Secularism, Inc.

JEWISH EDUCATION (1929). 426 W. 58 St., NYC, 10019. (212)245-8200. Alvin I. Schiff. Quarterly. Council for Jewish Education.

JEWISH FORWARD (1897). 45 E. 33 St., NYC, 10016. (212)889-8200. Mordecai Strigler. Weekly. Yiddish and English. Forward Association, Inc.

JEWISH FRONTIER (1934). 275 Seventh Ave., 17th fl., NYC, 10001. (212)645-8121. David Twersky, Nahum Guttman. Bimonthly. Labor Zionist Letters, Inc.

JEWISH GUARDIAN (1974). GPO Box 2143, Brooklyn, 11202. (718)384-4661. S. Schwartz. Irregularly. English-Hebrew. Neturei Karta of U.S.A.

JEWISH JOURNAL (1969). 8723 Third Ave., Brooklyn, 11209. (718)238-6600. Levi Kahane. Weekly.

JEWISH LEDGER (1924). 3385 Brighton-Henrietta T.L. Rd., Rochester, 14623. (716)-427-2434. Barbara Morgenstern. Weekly.

JEWISH MUSIC NOTES (1945). 15 E. 26 St., NYC, 10010-1579. (212)532-4949. Paula Gottlieb. Quarterly. JWB Jewish Music Council.

JEWISH OBSERVER (1963). 84 William St., NYC, 10038. (212)797-9000. Rabbi Nisson Wolpin. Monthly (except July and Aug.). Agudath Israel of America.

JEWISH OBSERVER (1978). PO Box 510, DeWitt, 13214. (315)445-0161. Mollie Leitzes Collins. Biweekly. Syracuse Jewish Federation, Inc.

JEWISH POST AND RENAISSANCE (1977). 57 E. 11 St., NYC, 10003. (212)420-0042. Charles Roth. Bimonthly.

JEWISH PRESS (1950). 338 Third Ave., Brooklyn, 11215-1897. (718)330-1100. Rabbi Sholom Klass. Weekly.

JEWISH SOCIAL STUDIES (1939). 2112 Broadway, Rm. 206, NYC, 10023. (212)-724-5336. Tobey B. Gitelle. Quarterly. Conference on Jewish Social Studies, Inc.

JEWISH TELEGRAPHIC AGENCY COMMUNITY NEWS REPORTER (1962). 330 Seventh Ave., 11th fl., NYC 10001-5010. (212)643-1890. Elli Wohlgelernter. Weekly.

JEWISH TELEGRAPHIC AGENCY DAILY NEWS BULLETIN (1917). 330 Seventh Ave., 11th fl., NYC 10001-5010. (212)-643-1890. Mark Joffe. Daily.

JEWISH TELEGRAPHIC AGENCY WEEKLY NEWS DIGEST (1933). 330 Seventh Ave., 11th fl., NYC 10001-5010. (212)643-1890. Mark Joffe. Weekly.

JEWISH WEEK (1876; reorg. 1970). 1457 Broadway, NYC, 10036. (212)921-7822. Sheldon Engelmayer. Weekly.

JEWISH WORLD (1965). 1104 Central Ave., Albany, 12205. (518)459-8455. Laurie J. Clevenson. Weekly.

JOURNAL OF REFORM JUDAISM (1953). 192 Lexington Ave., NYC, 10016. (212)684-4990. Samuel Stahl. Quarterly. Central Conference of American Rabbis.

JUDAISM (1952). 15 E. 84 St., NYC, 10028. (212)879-4500. Robert Gordis. Quarterly. American Jewish Congress.

JWB CIRCLE (1946). 15 E. 26 St., NYC, 10010. (212)532-4949. Shirley Frank. Bimonthly. JWB.

KIBBUTZ JOURNAL (1984). 27 W. 20 St., 9th fl., NYC, 10011. (212)255-1338. Michele Becker. Annually. Kibbutz Aliya Desk.

KOL HAT'NUA (1943). 50 W. 58 St., NYC, 10019. (212)355-7900. Lisa Primus. Irregularly. Young Judaea.

KOSHER DIRECTORY (1925). 45 W. 36 St., NYC, 10018. (212)563-4000. Tziporah Spear. Irregularly. Union of Orthodox Jewish Congregations of America.

KOSHER DIRECTORY, PASSOVER EDITION (1923). 45 W. 36 St., NYC, 10018. (212)-563-4000. Tziporah Spear. Annually. Union of Orthodox Jewish Congregations of America.

KULTUR UN LEBN—CULTURE AND LIFE (1967). 45 E. 33 St., NYC, 10016. (212)-889-6800. Joseph Mlotek. Quarterly. Yiddish. Workmen's Circle.

LAMISHPAHA. (1963). 1841 Broadway, Rm. 510, NYC, 10023-7650. (212)581-5151. Hanita Brand. Monthly (except July and Aug.). Hebrew. Histadruth Ivrith of America.

LIKUTIM (1981). 110 E. 30 St., NYC, 10016. (212)889-2525. Joanne Jahr. Two to four times a year (audio cassettes). Hebrew. Jewish Braille Institute of America, Inc.

LILITH—THE JEWISH WOMEN'S MAGAZINE (1976). 250 W. 57 St., NYC, 10107. (212)-757-0818. Susan Weidman Schneider. Quarterly.

LONG ISLAND JEWISH WORLD (1971). 115 Middle Neck Rd., Great Neck, 11021. (516)829-4000. Jerome W. Lippman. Weekly.

MARTYRDOM AND RESISTANCE (1974). 48 W. 37 St., 9th fl., NYC 10018-4708. (212)-564-1865. Eli Zborowski. Bimonthly.

MELTON JOURNAL (1982). 3080 Broadway, NYC, 10027. (212)678-8031. Eduardo Rauch, Barry W. Holtz. Biannually. Melton Research Center for Jewish Education.

MIDSTREAM (1954). 515 Park Ave., NYC, 10022. (212)752-0600. Murray Zuckoff. Nine issues a year. Theodor Herzl Foundation, Inc.

MODERN JEWISH STUDIES ANNUAL (1977). Queens College, Kiely 802, 65-30 Kissena Blvd., Flushing, 11367. (718)520-7067. Joseph C. Landis. Annually. American Association of Professors of Yiddish.

NA'AMAT WOMAN (1926). 200 Madison Ave., Suite 1808, NYC, 10016. (212)725-8010. Judith A. Sokoloff. Five times a year. English-Yiddish-Hebrew. NA'AMAT USA, the Women's Labor Zionist Organization of America.

OLOMEINU—OUR WORLD (1945). 160 Broadway, NYC, 10038. (212)227-1000. Rabbi Yaakov Fruchter, Rabbi Nosson Scherman. Monthly. English-Hebrew. Torah Umesorah-National Society for Hebrew Day Schools.

PEDAGOGIC REPORTER (1949). 730 Broadway, NYC, 10003-9540. (212)529-2000. Mordecai H. Lewittes. Quarterly. Jewish Education Service of North America, Inc.

PRESENT TENSE (1973). 165 E. 56 St., NYC, 10022. (212)751-4000. Murray Polner. Bimonthly. American Jewish Committee.

PROCEEDINGS OF THE AMERICAN ACADEMY FOR JEWISH RESEARCH (1920). 3080 Broadway, NYC, 10027. (212)678-8864. Isaac E. Barzilay. Annually. Hebrew-Arabic-English. American Academy for Jewish Research.

RABBINICAL COUNCIL RECORD (1953). 275 Seventh Ave. NYC, 10001. (212)807-7888. Rabbi Louis Bernstein. Quarterly. Rabbinical Council of America.

JEWISH PERIODICALS / 511

REFORM JUDAISM (1972; formerly DIMENSIONS IN AMERICAN JUDAISM). 838 Fifth Ave., NYC, 10021. (212)249-0100. Aron Hirt-Manheimer. Quarterly. Union of American Hebrew Congregations.

REPORTER. 500 Clubhouse Rd., Binghamton, 13903. (607)724-2360. Marc Goldberg. Weekly. Jewish Federation of Broome County.

RESPONSE (1967). 27 W. 20 St., 9th fl., NYC, 10011. (212)675-1168. Cindy Rubin. Quarterly. Jewish Educational Ventures, Inc.

SHEVILEY HA-HINNUKH (1939). 426 W. 58 St., NYC, 10019. (212)713-0290. Zvulun Ravid. Quarterly. Hebrew. Council for Jewish Education.

SH'MA (1970). Box 567, 23 Murray Ave., Port Washington, 11050. (516)944-9791. Eugene B. Borowitz. Biweekly (except June, July, Aug.).

SHMUESSEN MIT KINDER UN YUGENT (1942). 770 Eastern Pkwy., Brooklyn, 11213. (718)493-9250. Nissan Mindel. Monthly. Yiddish. Merkos L'Inyonei Chinuch, Inc.

SYNAGOGUE LIGHT (1933). 47 Beekman St., NYC, 10038. (212)227-7800. Rabbi Meyer Hager. Semiannually. Union of Chasidic Rabbis.

TALKS AND TALES (1942). 770 Eastern Pkwy., Brooklyn, 11213. (718)774-4000 or 6000. Nissan Mindel. Monthly (also Hebrew, French, and Spanish editions). Merkos L'Inyonei Chinuch, Inc.

TRADITION (1958). 275 Seventh Ave., NYC, 10001. (212)807-7888. Rabbi Emanuel Feldman. Quarterly. Rabbinical Council of America.

TRENDS (1982). 730 Broadway, NYC, 10003-9540. (212)529-2000. Leora W. Isaacs. Semiannually. Jewish Education Service of North America, Inc.

UNITED SYNAGOGUE REVIEW (1943). 155 Fifth Ave., NYC, 10010. (212)533-7800. Rochel Berman. Biannually. United Synagogue of America.

UNSER TSAIT (1941). 25 E. 21 St., 3d fl., NYC, 10010. (212)475-0059. Editorial committee. Monthly. Yiddish. Jewish Labor Bund.

512 / AMERICAN JEWISH YEAR BOOK, 1989

WOMEN'S AMERICAN ORT REPORTER (1966). 315 Park Ave. S., NYC, 10010. (212)505-7700. Elie Faust-Levy. Quarterly. Women's American ORT, Inc.

WOMEN'S LEAGUE OUTLOOK (1930). 48 E. 74 St., NYC, 10021. (212)628-1600. Lynne Heller. Quarterly. Women's League for Conservative Judaism.

WORKMEN'S CIRCLE CALL (1933). 45 E. 33 St., NYC, 10016. (212)889-6800. Walter L. Kirschenbaum. Bimonthly. Workmen's Circle.

YEARBOOK OF THE CENTRAL CONFERENCE OF AMERICAN RABBIS (1890). 192 Lexington Ave., NYC, 10016. (212)684-4990. Elliot L. Stevens. Annually. Central Conference of American Rabbis.

YIDDISH (1973). Queens College, Kiely 802, 65-30 Kissena Blvd., Flushing, 11367-0904. (718)520-7067. Joseph C. Landis. Quarterly. Queens College Press.

DI YIDDISHE HEIM (1958). 770 Eastern Pkwy., Brooklyn, 11213. (718)493-9250. Rachel Altein. Quarterly. English-Yiddish. Neshei Ub'nos Chabad.

YIDDISHE KULTUR (1938). 1123 Broadway, Rm. 305, NYC, 10010. (212)243-1304. Itche Goldberg. Monthly (except June-July, Aug.-Sept.). Yiddish. Yiddishe Kultur Farband, Inc.—YKUF.

DOS YIDDISHE VORT (1953). 5 Beekman St., NYC, 10038. (212)797-9000. Joseph Friedenson. Monthly. Yiddish. Agudath Israel of America.

YIDDISHER KEMFER (1906). 275 Seventh Ave., 17th fl., NYC, 10001. (212)675-7808. Mordechai Strigler. Weekly. Yiddish. Labor Zionist Letters, Inc.

YIDISHE SHPRAKH (1941). 1048 Fifth Ave., NYC, 10028. (212)231-7905. Mordkhe Schaechter. Irregularly. Yiddish. Yivo Institute for Jewish Research, Inc.

YIVO ANNUAL OF JEWISH SOCIAL SCIENCE (1946). 1048 Fifth Ave., NYC, 10028. (212)535-6700. Deborah Dash Moore. Irregularly. Yivo Institute for Jewish Research, Inc.

YIVO BLETER (1931). 1048 Fifth Ave., NYC, 10028. (212)535-6700. Editorial board. Irregularly. Yiddish. Yivo Institute for Jewish Research, Inc.

YOUNG ISRAEL VIEWPOINT (1952). 3 W. 16 St., NYC, 10011. (212)929-1525. Rabbi Leonard B. Guttman. Bimonthly. National Council of Young Israel.

YOUNG JUDAEAN (1910). 50 W. 58 St., NYC, 10019. (212)303-8271. Mordecai Newman. Four times a year between Sept. and June. Hadassah Zionist Youth Commission.

YUGNTRUF (1964). 200 W. 72 St., Suite 40, NYC, 10023. (212)787-6675. Hershl Glasser. Quarterly. Yiddish. Yugntruf Youth for Yiddish.

NORTH CAROLINA

AMERICAN JEWISH TIMES—OUTLOOK (1934; reorg. 1950). PO Box 33218, Charlotte, 28233-3218. (704)372-3296. Ruth Goldberg. Monthly. The Blumenthal Foundation.

OHIO

THE AMERICAN ISRAELITE (1854). 906 Main St., Rm. 508, Cincinnati, 45202. (513)621-3145. Phyllis R. Singer. Weekly.

AMERICAN JEWISH ARCHIVES (1947). 3101 Clifton Ave., Cincinnati, 45220. (513)221-1875. Jacob R. Marcus, Abraham J. Peck. Semiannually. American Jewish Archives of Hebrew Union College—Jewish Institute of Religion.

CLEVELAND JEWISH NEWS (1964). 13910 Cedar Rd., University Hts., 44118. (216)-371-0800. Cynthia Dettelbach. Weekly. Cleveland Jewish Publication Co.

DAYTON JEWISH CHRONICLE (1961). 118 Salem Ave., Dayton, 45406. (513)222-0783. Leslie Cohen Zukowsky. Weekly.

INDEX TO JEWISH PERIODICALS (1963). PO Box 18570, Cleveland Hts., 44118. (216)-321-7296. Miriam Leikind, Jean H. Foxman. Semiannually.

OHIO JEWISH CHRONICLE (1922). 1600 Brice Rd., Reynoldsburg, 43068. (614)-860-9060. Judith Franklin. Weekly.

STARK JEWISH NEWS (1920). 2631 Harvard Ave. NW, Canton, 44709. (216)452-6444. Adele Gelb. Monthly. Canton Jewish Community Federation.

STUDIES IN BIBLIOGRAPHY AND BOOKLORE (1953). 3101 Clifton Ave., Cincinnati, 45220. (513)221-1875. Herbert C. Zafren. Irregularly. English-Hebrew-German. Library of Hebrew Union College—Jewish Institute of Religion.

TOLEDO JEWISH NEWS (1987). 6505 Sylvania Ave., Sylvania, 43560. (419)885-4461. Fred Flox. Monthly. Jewish Federation of Greater Toledo.

## OKLAHOMA

SOUTHWEST JEWISH CHRONICLE (1929). 314-B N. Robinson St., Oklahoma City, 73102. (405)236-4226. E. F. Friedman. Quarterly.

TULSA JEWISH REVIEW (1930). 2021 E. 71 St., Tulsa, 74136. (918)495-1100. Dianna Aaronson. Bimonthly. Jewish Federation of Tulsa.

## PENNSYLVANIA

JEWISH CHRONICLE OF PITTSBURGH (1962). 5600 Baum Blvd., Pittsburgh, 15243-5206. (412)687-1000. Joel Roteman. Weekly. Pittsburgh Jewish Publication and Education Foundation.

JEWISH EXPONENT (1887). 226 S. 16 St., Philadelphia, 19102. (215)893-5700. Albert Erlick. Weekly. Federation of Jewish Agencies of Greater Philadelphia.

JEWISH QUARTERLY REVIEW (1910). 250 N. Highland Ave., Merion, 19149. (215)-667-1830. Leon Nemoy, Bernard Lewis, David M. Goldenberg. Quarterly.

JEWISH TIMES OF THE GREATER NORTHEAST (1925). 103A Tomlinson Rd., Huntingdon Valley, 19006. (215)938-1177. Leon E. Brown. Weekly. Federation of Jewish Agencies of Greater Philadelphia.

NEW MENORAH (1979). c/o P'nai Or Religious Fellowship, 6723 Emlen St., Philadelphia, 19119. (215)849-5385. Arthur Waskow, Shana Margolin. Quarterly. P'nai Or Religious Fellowship.

RECONSTRUCTIONIST (1935). Church Rd. and Greenwood Ave., Wyncote, 19095. (215)887-1988. Jacob J. Staub. Eight times a year. Federation of Reconstructionist Congregations and Havurot.

## RHODE ISLAND

RHODE ISLAND JEWISH HISTORICAL NOTES (1954). 130 Sessions St., Providence, 02906. (401)331-1360. Michael Fink. Annually. Rhode Island Jewish Historical Association.

## TENNESSEE

HEBREW WATCHMAN (1925) 4646 Poplar Ave., Suite 232, Memphis, 38117. (901)-763-2215. Herman I. Goldberger. Weekly.

## TEXAS

JEWISH CIVIC PRESS (1965). PO Box 35656, Houston, 77235. (713)491-1512. Abner Tritt. Monthly.

JEWISH HERALD-VOICE (1908). PO Box 153, Houston, 77001. (713)630-0391. Joseph W. and Jeanne F. Samuels. Weekly.

JEWISH JOURNAL OF SAN ANTONIO (1973). 8434 Ahern, San Antonio, 78216. (512)-341-8234. Gaylon Finklea. Monthly. Jewish Federation of San Antonio.

TEXAS JEWISH POST (1947). PO Box 742, Fort Worth, 76101. (817)927-2831. 11333 N. Central Expressway, Dallas, 75243. (214)692-7283. Jimmy Wisch. Weekly.

## VIRGINIA

RENEWAL MAGAZINE (1984). 7300 Newport Ave., Norfolk, 23505. (804)489-8040. Reba Karp. Bimonthly. United Jewish Federation of Tidewater.

UJF NEWS (1959). 7300 Newport Ave., Norfolk, 23505. (804)489-8040. Reba Karp. 18 issues yearly. United Jewish Federation of Tidewater.

## WASHINGTON

JEWISH TRANSCRIPT (1924). 1904 3rd St., Suite 510, Seattle, 98101. (206)624-0136. Craig Degginger. Bimonthly. Jewish Federation of Greater Seattle.

M'GODOLIM: THE JEWISH QUARTERLY (1979). 2921 E. Madison St., #7, Seattle, 98112-4237. (206)322-1431. Keith S. Gormezano. Quarterly. Hebrew-English.

## WISCONSIN

WISCONSIN JEWISH CHRONICLE (1921). 1360 N. Prospect Ave., Milwaukee, 53202. (414)271-2992. Andrew Muchin. Weekly. Milwaukee Jewish Federation.

## INDEXES

INDEX TO JEWISH PERIODICALS (1963). PO Box 18570, Cleveland Hts., 44118. (216)-321-7296. Miriam Leikind, Jean H. Foxman. Semiannually.

## NEWS SYNDICATES

JEWISH TELEGRAPHIC AGENCY, INC. (1917). 330 Seventh Ave., 11th fl., NYC, 10001-5010. (212)643-1890. Mark Joffe, Elli Wohlgelernter. Daily.

## CANADA

BULLETIN DU CONGRES JUIF CANADIEN (Région du Québec) (1952). 1590 Dr. Penfield Ave., Montreal, PQ H3G 1C5. (514)-931-7531. Irregularly. French. Canadian Jewish Congress.

CANADIAN JEWISH HERALD (1977). 17 Anselme Lavigne Blvd., Dollard des Ormeaux, PQ H9A 1N3. (514)684-7667. Dan Nimrod. Irregularly. Dawn Publishing Co., Ltd.

CANADIAN JEWISH NEWS (1960). 10 Gateway Blvd., Don Mills, ONT. M3C 3A1. (416)422-2331. Maurice Lucow. Weekly.

CANADIAN JEWISH OUTLOOK (1963). 6184 Ash St., #3, Vancouver, BC V5Z 3G9. (604)324-5101. Ben Chud, Henry Rosenthal. Monthly.

CANADIAN ZIONIST (1934). 5250 Decarie Blvd., Suite 550, Montreal, PQ H3X 2H9. (514)486-9526. Rabbi Meyer Krentzman. Five times a year. Canadian Zionist Federation.

JEWISH EAGLE (1907). 4180 De Courtrai, Rm. 218, Montreal, PQ H3S 1C3. (514)-735-6577. B. Hirshtal. Weekly. Yiddish-Hebrew-French.

JEWISH POST & NEWS (1987). 117 Hutchings St., Winnipeg, MAN R2X 2V4. (204)694-3332. Matt Bellan. Weekly.

JEWISH STANDARD (1929). 77 Mowat Ave., Toronto, ONT M6K 3E3. (416)537-2696. Julius Hayman. Semimonthly.

JEWISH WESTERN BULLETIN (1930). 3268 Heather St., Vancouver, BC V5Z 3K5. (604)879-6575. Samuel Kaplan. Weekly.

JOURNAL OF PSYCHOLOGY AND JUDAISM (1976). 1747 Featherston Dr., Ottawa, ONT K1H 6P4. (613)731-9119. Reuven P. Bulka. Quarterly. Center for the Study of Psychology and Judaism.

OTTAWA JEWISH BULLETIN & REVIEW (1954). 151 Chapel St., Ottawa, ONT K1N 7Y2. (613)232-7306. Cynthia Engel. Biweekly. Jewish Community Council of Ottawa.

UNDZER VEG (1932). 272 Codsell Ave., Downsview, ONT M3H 3X2. (416)636-4024. Joseph Kage. Irregularly. Yiddish-English. Achdut HaAvoda-Poale Zion of Canada.

WINDSOR JEWISH COMMUNITY BULLETIN (1938). 1641 Ouellette Ave., Windsor, ONT N8X 1K9. (519)973-1772. Joseph Eisenberg. Irregularly. Windsor Jewish Community Council.

# Obituaries: United States[1]

ALTMANN, ALEXANDER, professor, rabbi; b. Kassa, Czechoslovakia (Austria-Hungary), Apr. 16, 1906; d. Boston, Mass., June 6, 1987; in U.S. since 1959. Educ.: Hildesheimer Rabbinical Sem.; U. Berlin (PhD). Served as a communal rabbi, Manchester, England, 1938–58, where he founded and directed the Inst. of Jewish Studies and edited the *Journal of Jewish Studies*; prof., Jewish philosophy, Brandeis U., 1959–76, founder and dir. of its Lown Inst. for Advanced Jewish Studies. A scholar of broad-ranging interests, he made significant contributions to three distinct fields: Judeo-Arabic philosophy, Jewish mysticism, and German-Jewish intellectual history. He wrote seminal works on Saadya Gaon, Isaac Israeli, and Maimonides and a definitive biography of Moses Mendelssohn. Transl.: *Saadya Gaon: The Book of Doctrines and Beliefs* (1946). Author: *Isaac Israeli* (with S.M. Stern) (1958); *Studies in Religious Philosophy and Mysticism* (1969); *Moses Mendelssohn: A Biographical Study* (1973); *Essays in Jewish Intellectual History* (1981); and other works. Recipient: hon. doctorates, Hebrew University of Jerusalem, and others; fellow: Amer. Acad. for Jewish Research; Medieval Acad. of Amer.

ARONSON, JOSEPH H., rabbi; b. Kovno, Lithuania, July 1, 1891; d. Monsey, NY, Aug. 8, 1987; in U.S. since 1920. Educ.: Slobodka Yeshivah, Kovno. Rabbi: Cong. Tifereth Israel, New Britain, Conn., 1923– 47; Cong. Mogen David, Brooklyn, NY, 1950–78. V.-pres., Union of Orthodox Rabbis, 1945–55. Author: commentaries on the Jerusalem Talmud (*Shiklei Yosef, Zarei Yosef*).

BARRON, HARRY I., communal worker; b. Chicago, Ill., Dec. 9, 1909; d. NYC, Oct. 10, 1987. Educ.: Hebrew Union Coll.; U. Chicago; Graduate School for Jewish Social Work. Asst. principal, Gridley Jr. High School, Erie, Pa., 1930; medical social worker, Cincinnati Genl. Hosp., 1930–31; dir. of activities, YM/YWHA, Elizabeth, NJ, 1932–33; dir., Home Camp, Jacob H. Schiff Center, NYC, 1933; exec. dir., JCC, Bridgeport, Conn., 1933–34; research assoc. and faculty mem., Graduate School for Jewish Social Work, 1934–40; dir.: U.S. Fair Employment Practices Comm., Washington, DC, 1941–43; Jewish Community Council of Cleveland, 1943–55; New Orleans Jewish Fed., 1955–65; exec. dir., Natl. Found. for Jewish Culture, 1965–80; dir. emer., 1980–87.

BASS, RALPH, communal worker, author; b. NYC, Oct. 19, 1907; d. Woodmere, NY, Nov. 13, 1987. Public relations writer, Amer. J. Com., 40 years. Mem.: Amer. Soc. Journalists and Authors; NY Business Press; World Trade Writers Assn.; Silurians; and other orgs. Author: books and articles on a wide range of popular subjects, in *Esquire*, *Coronet*, and other magazines.

---

[1] Including Jewish residents of the United States who died between January 1 and December 31, 1987.

BEN-ZION (WEINMAN), artist, poet; b. Starokonstantinov, Ukraine, July 8, 1897; d. NYC, Jan. 23, 1987; in U.S. since 1920. Founding mem. of the Expressionist group "the Ten"; works in collections of Metropolitan Museum of Art, NYC; Whitney Museum, NYC; Art Inst., Chicago; Tel Aviv Museum, and others; one-man shows and retrospectives in major U.S. and Israeli museums. Art instr., Cooper Union, 1946–53; visiting artist: Ball State U.; Iowa U.; Omaha U. Published a number of collections of etchings on biblical and Jewish themes. Author: vols. of poetry, in Hebrew; essays on art, in English.

BERNSTEIN, ROBERT M., attorney, communal worker; b. Philadelphia, Pa., Oct. 1, 1894; d. Philadelphia, Pa., Oct. 22, 1987. Educ.: U. Pa. Law School. Sr. partner, Bernstein, Bernstein and Harrison, since 1916. Fellow: Amer. Coll. of Trial Lawyers; Internatl. Acad. of Trial Lawyers. In behalf of U. Pa. Law School: chmn., capital needs com.; v.-chmn., development fund; mem. bd. of managers. An original organizer of the Phila. Allied Jewish Appeal and its genl. chmn., 1952; lifetime hon. trustee, Fed. of Jewish Agencies. Pres., Phila. branch, ZOA; treas., Phila. branch, Amer. Friends of Hebrew U.; hon. bd. mem., Cong. Adath Jeshurun. Recipient: U. Pa. Alumni Award of Merit; Scopus Award, Amer. Friends of Hebrew U.; Cyrus Adler Community Award, Jewish Theol. Sem.; Community Service Award, Amer. J. Cong.; and other honors.

BIELSKY (Bell), TUVIA, businessman, WWII partisan; b. Stankiewicze, Poland (Byelorussia), May 8, 1906; d. NYC, June 12, 1987; in U.S. since 1956. Founder and leader of a large armed band of Jewish partisans, known as Bielsky's Brigade, that operated against the Nazis from the Naliboki forests near Novogrudok, 1941–44. Emigrated to Israel after the war. In U.S., operated a trucking business.

BIENSTOCK, VICTOR, journalist; b. Hartford, Conn., May 21, 1908; d. Boca Raton, Fla., Aug. 28, 1987. Educ.: NYU. Reporter, *NY World*, 1929–31; ed., NY Herald Tribune News Service, 1931–33; corresp., *London Morning Post*, 1933; managing ed., Jewish Telegraphic Agency, 1933–35; JTA foreign service, London, 1935–40; chief foreign ed., Overseas News Agency, JTA, 1940–50; genl. mgr., ed., and v.-pres., JTA, 1950–70; after retirement, exec. ed., *NY Jewish Week*, 1970-73; editorial page columnist, *Boca Raton Daily News*, since 1975. Sec., Amer. War Corresps. Assn., 1944–52; mem., Natl. Press Club, Washington, DC. Recipient: U.S. War Dept. citation for services as war correspondent.

BRAM, MORRIS, businessman; b. NYC, May 7, 1909; d. Tamarac, Fla., July 14, 1987. One of the founders of the American Israel Numismatic Assoc. in 1967, its founding pres. and bd. chmn.

BURNS, ARTHUR F., economist, government official; b. Stanislau, Austria, Apr. 27, 1904; d. Baltimore, Md., June 26, 1987; in U.S. since 1914. Educ.: Columbia U. (BA, MA, PhD). Instr., asst. prof., assoc. prof., prof., Rutgers U., 1927–44; visiting prof., Columbia U., 1942–44, prof. 1944–69. Asssociated with Natl. Bureau of Econ. Rsch. since 1930, as rsch. dir. 1945–53, and chmn., 1967–68. Chmn., Council of Economic Advisers, 1953–56, under Pres. Dwight Eisenhower; adviser to Pres. Richard Nixon, 1968–70; chmn., Fed. Reserve Bd., 1970–78; disting. scholar in residence, Amer. Enterprise Inst., 1978–81 and 1985–87; U.S. ambassador to W. Germany, 1981–85. Author: *Prosperity Without Inflation* and other works. Recipient: Jefferson Award, Amer. Inst. of Public Service; Hamilton Award, U.S. Treasury Dept.; Amer. Democratic Legacy Award, ADL; Grand Cross of Order of Merit, W. Germany; Gold Medal, Inst. of Social Sciences; numerous honorary doctorates and other awards.

BURTON, SALA GALANT, politician; b. Bialystok, Poland, Apr. 1, 1925; d. Washington, DC, Feb. 1, 1987; in U.S. since 1939. Educ.: U. San Francisco. Assoc. dir., Calif. Public Affairs Inst., 1948–50; v.-pres., Calif. Democratic Council, 1951–54; mem.: Calif. Democratic Steering Com.; San Francisco Democratic Women's Forum, 1957–59; Democratic Wives of House and Senate, 1972–74; legislative chmn., Women's Natl. Democratic Club; delegate, Democratic natl. conventions, 1956, 1976, 1980, 1984. Mem. adv. com., Council on Soviet Jewry. Elected to Congress from San Francisco in 1983 to complete the term of her husband, Phillip Burton, when he died, she was reelected in 1984 and 1986. Mem., House Rules Com.; an advocate for poor people, education, the environment and arms reduction.

OBITUARIES / 517

CASHDAN, LOUIS JOSEPH, rabbi; b. (?), Russia, Sept. 18, 1905; d. Silver Spring, Md., July 28, 1987; in U.S. since 1909. Educ.: U. Mich.; Hebrew Union Coll. (ordination and DD). Rabbi: West London Syn., England, 1936–42; Des Moines, Iowa, 1942–45; Charleston, W. Va., 1945–52; Kansas City, Mo., 1952–59; Toronto, Canada, 1959–66; Temple Solel, Bowie, Md., 1967–81; rabbi emer. since 1981. Taught philosophy, logic, and theology at Bowie State Coll., Johns Hopkins U., and American U. Pres. welfare councils in W. Va. and Mo.; del. to White House Conf. on Children and Youth, 1950; financial sec., treas., and exec. com. mem., Central Conf. of Amer. Rabbis; pres., rabbinical assoc.'s of Greater Kansas City, Toronto, and Washington, DC.

CEDARBAUM, DAVID I., rabbi, educator; b. NYC, Apr. 27, 1903; d. Laguna Hills, Calif., July 30, 1987. Educ.: CCNY; Teachers Coll., Columbia; Hebrew Union Coll. Chaplain, USAF,1943–46; rabbi and dir. of Jewish educ., Educational Alliance, NYC, 1936–43; supervisor, Bd. of Jewish Educ., Chicago, 1946–68; prof., Coll. of Jewish Studies, Chicago; dir. of educ., Chicago Fed. of the Union of Amer. Hebrew Congs. Author: *Teach Me to Pray*.

COHEN, WILBUR J., government official; b. Milwaukee, Wis., June 10, 1913; d. Seoul, S. Korea, May 18, 1987. Educ.: U. Wis. Went to Washington in 1934 as a researcher; in 1935 became first employee of the Social Security Admin., where he remained until 1956. Helped draft New Deal's Social Security Act and worked on various proposals for a natl. health insurance plan. Returned to Washington in Kennedy admin.: asst. sec., dept. of Health, Educ., and Welfare, 1961–65; under sec., 1965–68; sec., 1968–69. Chief architect of the 1965 Medicare Act and influential in shaping all the social welfare legislation of the 1960s. Prof., public welfare admin., U. Mich., 1956–69, 1972–83; prof. educ., U. Mich., 1969–80, and dean, School of Educ., 1969–78; prof. public affairs, U. Tex., 1980–83.

COMAY, AMOS, businessman, communal worker; b. NYC, Mar. 4, 1915; d. Pittsburgh, Pa., Nov. 12, 1987. Chmn., Action Industries, Pittsburgh, Pa. Pres., Natl. Found. for Jewish Culture, 1978–82; natl. bd. mem.: Jewish Educ. Service of N. Amer.; Council of Jewish Federations;

Amer. Jewish Joint Distribution Com.; bd. mem., v.-pres., treas., chmn., Jewish educ. com., United Jewish Fed. of Pittsburgh; pres., School of Advanced Jewish Studies; bd. mem., v.-pres., Hebrew Inst. of Pittsburgh; bd. mem., Zionist Org. of Amer., Pittsburgh dist.

DANE, OSCAR, businessman, communal worker; b. Vilna, Russia, Feb. 22, 1903; d. NYC, Dec. 22, 1987; in U.S. since 1917. Educ.: NYU (BS, LLB). Practiced law, 1928–38; founder, pres., Templetone Radio Mfg. Corp., 1939–50; founder, pres., Inland Credit Corp., 1949–83. Founder, pres., Beth-El Syn., New London, Conn., 1947–51; founder, pres., Conservative Syn. Adath Israel of Riverdale, NY, 1954–66, and hon. pres. thereafter; trustee, Fifth Ave. Syn., NYC, 1966–78. Bd. mem.: Jewish Theol. Sem. of Amer.; Beth Israel Med. Center; Hebrew Home for the Aged; Riverdale YM/YWHA; mem. adv. council, NY Bd. of Rabbis; active supporter of Boys Town Jerusalem; Amer. Com. for Shaare Zedek Hosp.; Albert Einstein Coll. of Medicine; UJA-Fed.; Israel Bonds. Recipient: Louis Marshall Medal, JTS; Outstanding Service Award, Fed. of Jewish Philanthropies, and many other honors.

DAROFF, JOSEPH A., businessman, philanthropist; b. Philadelphia, Pa., Dec. 18, 1899; d. Philadelphia, Pa., Jan. 12, 1987. Pres., H. Daroff & Sons, clothing manufs.; v.-pres. and dir., Botany Industries. Bd. mem.: Clothing Manufs. of Amer.; Phila. City Trusts; Phila. Fellowship Comm.; Moss Rehabilitation Hosp. Founder, Joseph A. Daroff Campus of Adult Studies of the JCCs of Phila.; in a long career of national and local communal activity, served in many capacities, including: v.-pres., Amer. Assoc. for Jewish Educ.; mem., bd. of overseers, Jewish Theol. Sem. of Amer.; bd. mem., Phila. Fed. of Jewish Charities and exec. com. mem. its successor, Fed. of Jewish Agencies; bd. mem., YM/YWHA; hon. v.-pres., JCCs of Greater Phila.; v.-pres., Amer. J. Cong., Phila. chap.; treas., JWB Middle Atlantic Section; v.-pres., Beth Jacob Schools; pres. and bd. chmn., Cong. Adath Jeshurun. Recipient: Stephen Wise Award, Amer. J. Cong.; Herbert Lehman Award, State of Israel Bonds; Brotherhood Award, Natl. Conf. of Christians and Jews; several awards from the JTS; Scopus Award, Amer. Friends of Hebrew U.; and many other honors.

DUKER, ABRAHAM G., professor; b. Rypin, Poland, Sept. 27, 1907; d. Kfar Saba, Israel, Nov. 18, 1987; in U.S. since 1924. Educ.: Polish gymnasium; evening high school, NYC; CCNY; Columbia U. (PhD). Served U.S. Army, 1943–45. Librarian, Jewish Theol. Sem., 1927–33; rsch. librarian, Graduate School for Jewish Social Work, 1934–38; researcher, Amer. Jewish Com., 1938–43, where he edited the *Contemporary Jewish Record* (forerunner of *Commentary*), 1938–41; instr., JTS, 1941–43, 1946–48; instr., Hebrew Union Coll., 1946–56; prof. and pres., Spertus Coll. of Jewish Studies, Chicago, 1956–62; dir. of libraries and prof. of Jewish hist., Yeshiva U., 1962–72; founder, prof., and chmn., Jewish studies dept., Brooklyn Coll., 1972–77; visiting prof., Columbia U., 1966–67; fellow, Amer. Acad. for Jewish Rsch., 1973–75. Ed.: *Universal Jewish Encyclopedia* (1939–43); *Reconstructionist*; managing ed., *Jewish Social Studies*. Author: *The Impact of Zionism on American Jewry*; *The Great Polish Emigration and the Jews*; and other works, chiefly in the areas of Polish-Jewish relations and Amer. Jewish sociology.

ETRA, MAX J., attorney, communal worker; b. Rymanov, Poland, Apr. 24, 1903; d. NYC, Apr. 8, 1987; in U.S. since 1907. Educ.: CCNY; Fordham U. Law School. Began practicing law in 1929; at the time of his death was sr. partner, Etra & Etra. V.-chmn., Beth Israel Hosp.; mem.: Natl. Council, Boy Scouts of Amer.; NYC Bar Assoc.; NY County Lawyers Assoc.; Grand St. Boys Club; Elks; Friars. Pres., Cong. Kehilath Jeshurun, NYC, for 29 years; benefactor and leader of Yeshiva U. for over 40 years: bd. chmn., 1953–77, the period of the university's greatest expansion; bd. mem.: Albert Einstein Coll. of Medicine; Benjamin Cardozo School of Law; Rabbi Isaac Elchanan Theol. Sem.; Wurzweiler School of Social Work. Chmn., Amer. Jewish Tercentenary Comm.; pres., Union of Orthodox Jewish Congs. Recipient: hon. doctorate, Yeshiva U.; 125th Anniversary Medal, CCNY; Shofar Award, Boy Scouts of Amer.; and many other honors.

GELB, MAX, rabbi; b. (?), Austria-Poland, Mar. 7, 1907; d. Boca Raton, Fla., Feb. 1, 1987; in U.S. since 1914. Educ.: CCNY; Jewish Theol. Sem. of Amer. Rabbi: Temple Beth-El, Harrisburg, Pa., 1932–39; Temple Israel Center, White Plains, NY, 1939–72. Founder and dean, Solomon Schechter School of Westchester, 1966–87. Pres.: Westchester Zionist Org.; Westchester Bd. of Rabbis. Recipient: hon. doctorate, JTS.

GOLUB, MOLLIE F., lawyer, communal worker; b. NYC, Sept. 11, 1902; d. NYC, July 14, 1987. Educ.: Brooklyn Law School. Active in Amer. Mizrachi Women (now AMIT Women) for over 40 years; served as natl. pres. 1949–51 and 1956. Mem., Actions Com., World Zionist Org. Recipient: Silver Medallion Award, Amer. Mizrachi Women.

GOULD, BERNARD S., professor, communal worker; b. Boston, Mass., Oct. 15, 1911; d. Cambridge, Mass., Feb. 11, 1987. Educ.: MIT; U. London (PhD). Assoc. prof., biochemistry, MIT, 1943–69; prof., 1969–86. Chmn.: MIT com. on the use of humans as experimental subjects; premedical advisory com.; mem., safety council. Bd. mem. and chmn., Boston Hebrew Coll.; chmn., subcom. on Jewish educ., Combined Jewish Philanthropies; v.-pres., Bureau of Jewish Educ.; bd. mem. and chmn., school com., Cong. Kehillath Israel; v.-pres., Amer. Friends of Hebrew U.; mem., gov. council, Amer. Assoc. for Jewish Educ. Served as treas. of MIT Hillel and unofficial ombudsman of Jewish affairs at MIT.

GRUSS, CAROLINE, lawyer, philanthropist; b. (?), Poland, (?), 1911; d. NYC, Jan. 14, 1987; in U.S. since 1939. Educ.: U. of Lvov. An active partner with her husband, Joseph, an investment banker, and a benefactor in her own name in a major philanthropic effort to support, improve, and expand Jewish education. Among the many recipients of Gruss endowments were Yeshiva U.; the UJA-Federation Fund for Jewish Educ., Lubavitcher and other yeshivahs.

GUTTMAN, LOUIS, professor; b. NYC, Feb. 10, 1916; d. Minneapolis, Minn., Oct. 25, 1987. Educ.: U. Minn. (BA, MA, PhD). Instr., asst. prof., assoc. prof., sociology, Cornell U., 1941–50; rsch. consultant, U.S. War Dept., 1941–45. Member of a Labor Zionist movement from youth, he went to Israel in 1947, where he founded and served for many years as dir. of the Israel Inst. of Applied Social Rsch. Prof., social and psychol. assessment, Hebrew U. of Jerusalem, 1955–87; consultant to various Israeli agencies and commissions. Visiting prof.: Howard U., Mich. State U., U. Mich., MIT, Harvard U., U. Tex., U. Minn.; prof.-at-large, Cornell U., 1972–78. Acclaimed for his many contributions to social scientific rsch., notably the "Guttman scale" for measuring and analyzing public opinion. Author: numerous works on psychometrics. Recipient: Rothschild Prize for Social Rsch. (1963); Outstanding Achievement Award, U. Minn. (1974); Israel Prize in the Social Sciences (1978); foreign hon. mem., Amer. Acad. of Arts & Sciences; Educl. Testing Service Award (1984); Helen Diverman Award, World Assoc. for Public Opinion Rsch (1988, posthumous).

HEIFETZ, JASCHA, violinist; b. Vilna, Russia, Feb. 2, 1901; d. Los Angeles, Calif., Dec. 10, 1987; in U.S. since 1917. Gave first concert at age six in Vilna; made U.S. debut at Carnegie Hall in 1917; last public performance was in 1972; thereafter devoted himself to teaching. Regarded as the greatest violin virtuoso of his time, his name was synonymous with perfection of technique and musicianship.

HORNSTEIN, BENJAMIN S., businessman, philanthropist; b. NYC, Aug. 12, 1891; d. Palm Beach, Fla., Mar. 20, 1987. Educ.: CCNY. Pres., Charles Stores Co., a chain of small dept. stores in the South. Major benefactor, Brandeis U., long-time mem. its bd. of fellows, founder of its Hornstein Program in Jewish Communal Service; founder and overseer, Jewish Theol. Sem. of Amer.; founder and bd. mem., Albert Einstein Coll. of Medicine; founder, UJA of Greater NY; mem., bd. of trustees: NY Fed. of Jewish Philanthropies for 25 years; Amer. Jewish Com.; hon. v.-pres., Assoc. Ys of Greater NY; benefactor, Jewish Community Day School of Palm Beach County, Fla. Recipient: hon. doctorate, Brandeis U., and many other honors.

IVRY, ITZHAK, journalist, editor; b. Bialystok, Poland, Nov. 12, 1908; d. NYC, July 31, 1987; in U.S. since 1951. Educ.: Rabbinical Sem., Warsaw; Berlin U.; Basel U.; Hebrew U. of Jerusalem. Emigrated to Palestine, 1935; reporter, critic, columnist, *Davar*, Tel Aviv, 1936–51; U.S. corresp., 1951–54; ed., *Hadoar* Hebrew weekly, 1970–85. Mem.: Jewish Acad. of Arts and Sciences; Hebrew Writers Assn., Israeli Journalists Assn., NY Foreign Press Assn.; v.-pres., Hebrew P.E.N. Club of NY. Author: numerous original articles and transls. in various publications; Hebrew version of Arthur Miller's *Death of a Salesman*, staged by Habimah Theater, Tel Aviv.

JUNG, LEO, rabbi, communal leader; b. Brod, Moravia (Czechoslovakia), June 20, 1892; d. NYC, Dec. 19, 1987; in U.S. since 1920. Educ.: Vienna U.; Berlin U.; Marburg-Giessen U.; Cambridge U. (BA, MA); London U. (PhD); Berlin Hildesheimer Rabbinical Sem. (ordination, 1920). Rabbi: Knesset Israel Cong., Cleveland, Ohio, 1920–22; The Jewish Center, NYC, 1922–81, emer. thereafter. Prof. of ethics, Yeshiva U., 1931–68; emer. thereafter; founding mem., Touro Coll. faculty; pres., Rabbinical Council of Amer., 1928–34; bd. mem., NY Bd. of Rabbis; chmn., cultural-religious com., Amer. Jewish Joint Distribution Com., 1941–81; named first chmn., NY State Kosher Food Advisory Bd., 1940, serving in that post for several decades; founding trustee, Jewish Braille Inst., 1931, where he helped guide publication of a Braille edition of the Hebrew Bible in 1950; hon. pres., Poale Agudath Israel; pres., Beth Jacob Movement for Educ. of Girls, 1927–84. Regarded as a senior statesman of modern Orthodoxy; described as "a fighter for kashrut, milah, mikvah, tzedakah, and rescue" and "an articulate and brilliant author, preacher, teacher, spokesman, and lover of man." Author: 37 volumes as author or editor, on Jewish religion, ethics, educ.; only Amer. contributor to Soncino transl. of the Talmud (Yoma and Arakhim). Recipient: hon. doctorates, Yeshiva U.; NYU; Congressional Medal. In Israel, Kibbutz Kfar Eliyahu and a JNF forest in Safad are named in his honor.

KADUSHIN, EVELYN GARFIEL, teacher, author, b. NYC, June 10, 1900; d. NYC, Sept. 6, 1987. Educ.: Barnard Coll.; Columbia U. (PhD). Instr. in psych., U. Chicago; U. Wis. Med. School; lect. on Jewish subjects, Jewish Theol. Sem. Women's Inst. and to groups throughout the country. Bd. mem.: Natl. Women's League; Hadassah. Author: *Service of the Heart: A Guide to the Jewish Prayerbook*, a widely used text in adult education; several numbers in the *Jewish Tract Series*.

KAPLAN, JACOB M., businessman, philanthropist; b. Lowell, Mass., Dec. 23, 1891; d. NYC, July 18, 1987. After two decades in the molasses trade in Latin Amer. and the U.S., organized and headed Natl. Grape Corp., 1934–45, and Welch Grape Juice Co., 1945–56; pres.: J. M. Kaplan & Bros., 1926–30; Kaplan Holding Corp. and various successor orgs., after 1930. Founder, J. M. Kaplan Fund, 1947, a foundation known for diversity and inventiveness, whose projects included the NAACP Legal Defense and Education Fund, the Carnegie Hall restoration, NYC's Municipal Art Soc. and Parks Council, the Coalition for the Homeless, the Eldridge St. Syn., and programs to promote cooperative housing for the elderly. Benefactor, Yeshiva U., Park East Syn., Assoc. YM/YWHAs of Greater NY. Hon. trustee, bd. chmn., New School for Social Rsch.; mem., bd. of govs., Amer. Jewish Com.

KATZNER, J. BENJAMIN, businessman, communal worker; b. Baltimore, Md., June 23, 1903; d. Baltimore, Md., Aug. 6, 1987. Educ.: Baltimore City Coll. V.-pres., Comfy Manuf. Co., a family business producing slipcovers for natl. distribution. Chmn.: fund-raising and planning coms., Sinai Hosp., 1948–60; fund-raising campaign, Baltimore Museum of Art, 1975–85. Pres., Associated Jewish Charities, 1948–50; chmn.: AJC and Welfare Fund first combined campaign, 1950; AJC's legacy and endowment fund, 1965–71; pres., v.-pres., and treas., Chizuk Amuno Cong., and a key figure in the planning and construction of its facilities; bd. mem.: Amer. Jewish Joint Distrib. Com.; Jewish Theol. Sem. of Amer. Recipient: awards from Natl. Conf. of Christians and Jews, JTS, JNF, and others; named to Hall of Fame, Baltimore City Coll.

KAYE, DANNY (Daniel Kaminsky), entertainer; b. NYC, Jan. 18, 1913; d. Los Angeles, Calif., Mar. 3, 1987. Starting out as a comedian in nightclubs and "Borscht Belt" hotels, he went on to Broadway success (notably in the 1941 musical *Lady in the Dark*) and then to Hollywood, where he starred in such hit films as *Up in Arms* (1944), *Wonder Man* (1945), *The Secret Life of Walter Mitty* (1947), *The Inspector General* (1949), *Hans Christian Anderson* (1952), and *White Christmas* (1954). Starred in his own TV series (1963–67) and in various specials. His final TV appearance, in 1981, was as a Holocaust survivor in a drama about a proposed Nazi march in Skokie, Ill. As official ambassador-at-large for UNICEF, he traveled throughout the world entertaining young audiences. He visited Israel many times and often performed for Israeli soldiers. Known and loved for his clowning, exaggerated dancing, singing, mimicry, pantomime, rapid patter, and comic symphony-orchestra conducting. Recipient: Special Oscar for service to the movie industry; Emmy and Peabody Awards for TV shows; Jean Hersholt Humanitarian Award; Kennedy Center Honors for lifetime achievement in the arts.

KEYSERLING, LEON, economist, lawyer; b. Charleston, S.C., Jan. 22, 1908; d. Washington, DC, Aug. 9, 1987. Educ.: Columbia U.; Harvard Law School. Serving in various capacities in the Roosevelt and Truman admins., was instrumental in drafting major New Deal legislation, including the Natl. Industrial Recovery Act, the Social Security Act, and the Natl. Labor Relations Act. With U.S. Housing Authority, 1933–46, in various capacities. Instrumental in passage of the Employment Act of 1946 and establishment of the Council of Econ. Advisers. Mem., Council of Econ. Advisers, 1946–49, and chmn., 1949–53. Private consultant and lawyer, 1953–71; among his clients, labor unions and the govts. of France, India, and Israel. Helped draft 1978 Full Employment and Balanced Growth Act (Humphrey-Hawkins). Founder, pres., Conf. on Econ. Progress, a nonprofit public-interest org., 1954 on; pres., Natl. Com. for Labor Israel, 1969–73; adviser, Israel Bond Org.; mem., Amer. J. Com.'s Natl. Advisory Panel. Author: numerous books and articles.

KLEINBERG, MAURICE S., rabbi, chaplain; b. Louisville, Ky., Dec. 1, 1907; d. Santa Monica, Calif., Jan. 31, 1987. Educ.: Hebrew Union Coll. Rabbi: congs. in Benton Harbor, Mich.; Ventnor, NJ; Liverpool, England; and Santa Monica, Calif. Served as U.S. Army chaplain 25 years; at retirement in 1967 was ranking Jewish chaplain in the armed services; served as Jewish chaplain at Natl. Inst. of Health, 1967–77. Recipient: Bronze Star, Legion of Merit Medal, Army Commendation Medal; named Chaplain of the Year, 1963, by Natl. Reserve Officers Assoc.

KOSAKOFF, REUVEN, pianist, composer; b. New Haven, Conn., Jan. 8, 1898; d. NYC, May 6, 1987. Educ.: Yale U. School of Music (graduated at age 15); Inst. of Musical Art (Juilliard). Performing artist, accompanist, teacher of piano and composition, composer of chamber and orchestral music, song settings, and Jewish liturgical music, his works were performed by the NY Philharmonic and the Pittsburgh, Detroit, and New Haven Symphony Orchs. Accompanied leading cantors in concert; organist at Genesis Hebrew Center, Tuckahoe, NY, and Forest Hills Jewish Center, Queens, NY. Composed three full-length synagogue services, including Friday-night services commissioned by Central Syn., NYC, and Park Ave. Syn., NYC. Among many works on Jewish themes were a chamber opera, *The Cabbalists*, settings for Yiddish poems, and cantatas on biblical subjects. Mem. and pres., the Jewish Musical Forum.

LEVICH, BENJAMIN G., physical chemist; b. (?), Russia, (?) 1918; d. Fort Lee, NJ, Jan. 19, 1987; in U.S. since 1978. Educ.: Kharkov State U. Founded the field of physicochemical hydrodynamics; head, dept. of electrochemistry, Inst. of Hydrodynamics, and prof., Moscow U. Expelled from both positions in 1972, after applying to emigrate. Following an outcry from the internatl. scientific community, was granted exit permit in Dec. 1978, becoming the only mem. of the Soviet Acad. of Sciences ever allowed to emigrate. Settled in Israel but divided his time between teaching positions at Tel Aviv U. and the City College of NY. Author: more than 150 scientific papers; a 4-vol. textbook on theoretical physics that was translated into English, German, Spanish, Czech, Portuguese, and Chinese.

LEVITAS, IRVING, professor; b. Kiev, Russia, Aug. 10, 1910; d. Hawthorne, NY, Nov. 24, 1987; in U.S. since 1914. Educ.: U. Chicago; NYU (PhD). Educ. dir., JCC and Temple B'nai Jehudah, Kansas City, Mo.; lect., Semitic studies, U. Kans., 1948–62; scholar in residence, Temple Emmanuel, Yonkers, NY, 1975–87; lect., philosophy, Judaica, and history, Sullivan County Community Coll., NY.

LICHTEN, JOSEPH I., attorney, communal worker; b. Warsaw, Poland, June 6, 1906; d. Rome, Italy, Dec. 14, 1987; in U.S. since 1941. Educ.: U. Warsaw (JD). Practicing lawyer, Warsaw, 1934–39; consultant, Polish govt. in exile, Washington, DC, 1941–45. Became U.S. citizen after Communists took control of Poland. Joined staff of Anti-Defamation League in 1945 as dir. of intercultural affairs; headed ADL's liaison office to the Vatican, 1971–86. A leader in the development of Catholic-Jewish dialogue and interfaith activity, he participated in the deliberations of Vatican Council II that led to the Declaration on the Jews in "Nostra Aetate" in 1965. Recipient: designated "Knight Commander of the Order of St. Gregory the Great" by Pope John Paul II (1986). Author: *A Question of Judgement—Pope Pius XII and the Jews*, and many articles in Catholic and Jewish publications.

LIST, ALBERT A., businessman, philanthropist; b. Fall River, Mass., May 18, 1901; d. NYC, Sept. 11, 1987. Left school at age 14 to work in family grocery; branched out into other businesses, earning a million dollars by age 36. Retired, then reentered business, eventually gaining control of the Glen Alden and later Hudson Coal Co., leading U.S. hard-coal producers, and turning them into a conglomerate that included the RKO theater chain. An early supporter of the New School for Social Rsch. in NYC; an art collector, established art centers at Kirkland Coll., Brown U., and MIT; benefactor: Lincoln Center; Museum of Contemporary Art; Metropolitan Opera. Bd. mem. and v.- chmn., Mt. Sinai Medical Center, NYC. Established chair in Jewish studies at Harvard U. Divinity School in 1982; life bd. mem. and mem. exec. com., Jewish Theol. Sem. of Amer., and benefactor, its Jewish Museum. Recipient: Solomon Schechter Medal and Citation, JTS; hon. doctorates: Brown U., Wilberforce U., Long Island U., JTS, New School.

MANN, FREDRIC R., businessman, philanthropist; b. Gomel, Russia, Sept. 13, 1903; d. Miami, Fla., Feb. 26, 1987; in U.S. since 1905. Educ.: Wharton School, U. Pa. An aspiring pianist whose career was curtailed at age 16 by an accident, he made his fortune while still in his 20s in paper-box manuf. Active in a broad range of civic and philanthropic activity, his principal interest was in classical music. In Phila., his home, established the Mann Music Center, Fairmount Park, in 1979, for free performances by the Phila. Orchestra. Mem.,

Phila. Council on the Arts; bd. mem.: Phila. Orch. Assoc.; Carnegie Hall Soc.; Ballet Theater Found.; Phila. Lyric Opera; and other musical orgs.; trustee: Villanova U.; Phila. Acad. of Natural Sciences; United Fund; Natl. Recreation Assoc.; Pa. Acad. of Fine Arts, and many other orgs. Genl. chmn.: Allied Jewish Appeal of Phila. (1953); Phila. com., Israel Bonds (1955–56); chmn., Amer. Friends of the Israel Philharmonic Orch. (he helped erect Mann Auditorium in Tel Aviv); pres., bd. chmn., hon. v.-pres., America-Israel Cultural Found.; bd. mem.: Dropsie U.; Amer. Com. for Weizmann Inst. of Science; Amer. Jewish Joint Distrib. Com.; HIAS; fellow, Brandeis U. First U.S. ambassador to Barbados, 1967–69. Recipient: Order of Merit, Republic of Italy; Govt. of Brazil Award; hon. doctorates: Phila. Musical Acad., Springfield Coll., Widener U., Dropsie U.

MATT, HERSHEL J., rabbi, professor; b. Minneapolis, Minn., July 11, 1922; d. Highland Park, NJ, Dec. 26, 1987. Educ.: U. Pa.; Gratz Coll.; Jewish Theol. Sem. of Amer. Rabbi: Beth Abraham Cong., Nashua, NH, 1947–50; Temple Beth El, Troy, NY, 1950–59; Temple Neve Shalom, Metuchen, NJ, 1959–70; Jewish Center, Princeton, NJ, 1970–75. Faculty, Reconstructionist Rabbinical Coll.; Acad. of Jewish Learning (NYC). Chmn., com. on home and syn. practice, Rabbinical Assembly; mem., RA exec. council and prayer book, ethics, and convention coms.; natl. sec., Jewish Peace Fellowship. Author: dozens of articles on prayer, liturgy, intergroup relations, world peace.

MINKOFF, BEVERLY, communal worker; b. NYC, Nov. (?), 1926; d. Rockville Centre, NY, Feb. 14, 1987. Educ.: Ohio U. Joined Women's Amer. ORT in early 1950s; v.-pres., L.I. region, 1965; mem., natl. exec. com., 1967 on, serving in a variety of positions; natl. pres., 1979–83. Natl. chmn., Leadership Conf. of Major Jewish Women's Orgs.; v.-chmn., Natl. Jewish Community Relations Advisory Council; mem., exec. com., Natl. Conf. on Soviet Jewry; v.-pres. and mem. exec. com., Amer. ORT Fed.; hon. v.-pres. and mem. exec. com., World ORT Union; trustee, Bramson ORT Technical Inst., NYC; chmn., bd. of trustees, Los Angeles ORT Technical Inst.; NGO rep. to UN, Women's Amer. ORT.

NADEL, JACK, communal worker; b. NYC, Jan. 10, 1893; d. Surfside, Fla., Jan. 26, 1987. Educ.: CCNY; NYU. Starting as a pin boy in the bowling alley of the 92nd St. YM/YWHA in 1906, rose through the ranks to become exec. dir. in 1922; retired in 1957 and thereafter served on the Y's bd. of dirs. Helped found Fed. Employment and Guidance Service in 1934. Pres., Natl. Assoc. of Center Workers; bd. mem.: Fed. of Jewish Philanthropies of NY; natl. JWB; faculty mem., Yeshiva U. Recipient: Frank L. Weil Award, JWB (1956).

NATHAN, OTTO, professor; b. Bingen/Rhine, Germany, July 15, 1893; d. NYC, Jan. 27, 1987; in U.S. since 1933. Educ.: U.'s of Brussels, London, Freiburg, Munich, Wurzburg (PhD). Faculty, Hochshule für Politik, Berlin, 1928–33; Econ. Ministry, Weimar Republic, 1920–33, representing Germany on econ. comm.'s of League of Nations. During WWII worked in various U.S. govt. agencies, incl. the Div. of Monetary Rsch. of the U.S. Treasury. Taught at Princeton, NYU, Vassar, Howard U., and others. Mem.: Amer. Econ. Assn., Royal Econ. Soc., War Resisters League, Women's Internatl. League for Peace and Freedom. Close friend of Albert Einstein, he was executor of the scientist's estate and co-trustee of the Einstein archive, to which he devoted the last three decades of his life, considerably enriching the collection of correspondence and other papers before turning it over to the Hebrew University of Jerusalem in 1982. Author: *The Nazi Economic System* and other books and articles; coed., *Einstein on Peace* (1960). Recipient: hon. fellow, Hebrew U.; hon. doctorate, Yeshiva U.

NUSSBAUM, PERRY, rabbi; b. Toronto, Canada, Feb. 16, 1908; d. San Diego, Calif., Mar. 30, 1987; in U.S. since 1926. Educ.: U. Cincinnati; U. Colo.; Hebrew Union Coll. Chaplain, U.S. Army, 1943–68, active and reserve, retiring with rank of col. Rabbi: Melbourne, Aust., 1933–34; Amarillo, Tex., 1934–35; Pueblo, Colo., 1935–41; Wichita, Kans., 1941–43; Long Beach, NY, 1947–50; Pittsfield, Mass., 1950–54; Beth Israel Cong., Jackson, Miss., 1954–73. Helped found and lead the Miss. Religious Leadership Conf. and Greater Jackson Clergy Alliance, the first ecumenical and interracial orgs. in the state, and the Miss. Council of Concern for Rebuilding Churches. Served as chaplain to civil-rights activists in Miss. jails, even after his own home and syn. were dynamited by segregationists in 1967. Off. and/or bd. mem: Jackson Urban League, Masons, Rotary, and other civic orgs. Founder and first pres., Miss. Assembly of Jewish Congs.; pres.: B'nai B'rith Lodge; Jackson Jewish Welfare Fund; state chmn., ADL; mem. exec. bd. and pres. of two regions, Central Conf. Amer. Rabbis; alumni overseer, HUC. Recipient: Miss. Governor's Award; Special Citation, Miss. Relig. Leadership Conf.; hon. doctorates: HUC.; Burton Coll.

PERLMUTTER, NATHAN, communal worker, author; b. NYC, Mar. 2, 1923; d. NYC, July 12, 1987. Educ.: Georgetown U.; Villanova Coll.; NYU School of Law. Served U.S. Marine Corps, WWII. Joined staff of Anti-Defamation League in 1949; through 1964 served as dir. of three regional offices (Detroit; Miami; NYC); assoc. natl. dir., Amer. Jewish Com., 1965–69; v.-pres., Brandeis U., 1969–73; asst. natl. dir., ADL, 1973–79, and natl. dir. thereafter. Regarded as one of Amer. Jewry's most articulate spokesmen, especially on anti-Semitism and support for Israel, he was known for his independence of viewpoint, warmth and wit, and a unique literary style. Author: *How to Win at the Races* (1964); *A Bias of Reflections* (1972); coauthor, *The Real Anti-Semitism* (1982), and numerous articles on social and political issues. Recipient: 1987 Presidential Medal of Freedom; hon. doctorate, Hebrew Union Coll.; Gold Medallion for Humanitarianism, B'nai B'rith Internatl.; Eleanor Roosevelt Human Rights Award, City of NY, and other honors.

POLIER, JUSTINE WISE, judge, communal worker; b. Portland, Ore., Apr. 12, 1903; d. NYC, July 31, 1987. Educ.: Barnard Coll.; Yale U. (LLB). Referee, NY State Labor Dept., 1929–34; asst. corp. counsel, NYC, 1934–35; counsel and sec., Mayor's Com. on Relief, 1934–35; justice, Domestic Relations Ct., 1935–62; judge, NY State Family Ct., 1962–73; dir., program for juvenile justice, Childrens Defense Fund, after 1973. Daughter of Rabbi Stephen S. Wise and Louise Waterman Wise; the first woman to hold a judicial office above magistrate in NY state; a recognized authority on juvenile justice and children's rights. Bd. mem., Citizens Com. for Children; NY del., White House Conf. on Children (1960); with Eleanor Roosevelt, helped found the Wiltwyck School in NYC, for disturbed delinquent children; served on many civic boards and commissions. Pres. and bd. mem., Louise Wise Services, adoption and child-care agency (founded by her mother); v.-pres., chmn. exec. com., Amer. Jewish Cong. (founded by her father); pres. of its Women's Div. and other key posts; mem. exec. com., World Jewish Cong. Author: *Everyone's Children, Nobody's Child*; *Back to What Woodshed*; *The Need for Law and Social Action*; *A View from the Bench*; *Parental Rights*; *The Rule of Law and the Role of Psychiatry*; coed., *Personal Letters of Stephen Wise*. Recipient: Awards from many bodies, incl. Amer. Psychiatric Assn.; NY Fed. of Jewish Philanthropies; City of NY.

RAPOPORT, NATHAN, sculptor; b. Warsaw, Poland, (?), 1911; d. NYC, June 4, 1987; in U.S. since 1959. Educ.: Warsaw Acad. of Arts and schools in Italy and France. Spent WWII years in the Soviet Union; settled in Israel in 1948. Among his works: monument to the Warsaw Ghetto Uprising, on Zamenhoff St. in the former ghetto area (1948); monument for the Jewish Fighters of WWII, Paris (1950); statue of Warsaw ghetto commander Mordecai Anielewicz, Kibbutz Yad Mordecai (1951); Monument in Commemoration of the Victims of Nazism, Philadelphia (1963); statue of Job, Yad Vashem, Jerusalem (1965); Scroll of Fire, B'nai B'rith Internatl. Martyrs Forest, near Jerusalem (1969). Created portrait busts of many notables, incl. one of pianist Artur Rubinstein selected for placement in Carnegie Hall. Recipient: Polish govt.'s Polonia Restituta Medal; named Officer of the Academy by French govt.; Handleman Prize, Jewish Acad. of Arts and Sciences; Herbert Adams Memorial Medal, National Sculpture Society.

ROSENMAN, YEHUDA J., communal worker; b. Brest Litovsk, Poland, Nov. 18, 1918; d. NYC, Aug. 4, 1987; in U.S. since 1939. Educ.: Gymnasium Tarbut and yeshivah, Brest Litovsk; U. Pittsburgh. Exec. dir., JCC, Baltimore, Md., 1949–63; consultant, Joint Distribution Com., Israel and Geneva, 1963–67; natl. dir., dept. of Jewish communal affairs, Amer. Jewish Com., 1967–87. At AJCom., initiated a wide range of ground-breaking programs aimed at enhancing Jewish family life and Jewish identity, among them the William Petschek Natl. Jewish Family Center and the Acad. for Jewish Studies Without Walls, as well as rsch. and a variety of publications. Faculty mem.: Wayne State U., Catholic U., U. Md. Mem.: Natl. Assn. Jewish Communal Relations Workers; Natl. Conf. Jewish Communal Svcs.; Assn. for Jewish Studies. Author: essays and articles in various publications.

ROUTTENBERG, MAX J., rabbi, author; b. Montreal, Canada, Mar. 22, 1909; d. Yorktown Heights, NY, Jan. 19, 1987; in U.S. since 1927. Educ.: McGill U.; NYU; Jewish Theol. Sem. of Amer. (ord. and DHL). Chaplain, U.S. Army, WWII. Rabbi, Kesher Zion Syn., Reading, Pa., 1932–48; exec. v.-pres., Rabbinical Assembly, 1949–51; exec. v.-pres., JTS, and founding dean, Cantors Inst. and Sem. Coll. of Jewish Music, 1951–54; rabbi, Temple B'nai Sholom, Rockville Center, NY, 1954–72. Pres., RA, 1964–66; mem. and chmn.: com. on Jewish law and standards; com. on chaplaincy; publications com. (1972–82); and liturgical com. (1982–87). Chmn., Natl. Acad. of Adult Jewish Studies, 1955–60; mem.: JTS-RA-United Syn. liaison com.; JTS-RA joint law conf.; United Syn. com. on syn. standards; program ed., NBC-TV's "The Eternal Light," and ABC-TV's "Directions." Mem., Comm. on Jewish Chaplaincy, Natl. JWB, and one of the three eds. of its prayer book for Jewish military personnel. Author: *Seedtime and Harvest*; *Decades of Decision*; *One in a Minyan*, and numerous articles.

RUDERMAN, YAAKOV Y., rabbi, Talmud scholar; b. Dohlinov, Lithuania, (?), 1900; d., Baltimore, Md., July 11, 1987; in U.S. since 1933. Educ.: Slobodka Yeshivah. Settled in Baltimore, where he founded Ner Israel Rabbinical Coll., which he served as *rosh yeshivah* (pres. and dean) over 50 years, ordaining more than 1,000 rabbis. Last survivor of the *roshei yeshivah* who came to the U.S. from Lithuania early in the century; sr. mem., Council of Torah Sages, Agudath Israel; chmn., rabbinic advisory bd., Torah Umesorah.

SACKLER, ARTHUR M., psychiatrist, philanthropist; b. NYC, Aug. 22, 1913; d. NYC, May 26, 1987. Educ.: NYU (BA, MD); Cooper Union. Principal owner, William Douglas MacAdams, a medical ad agency which he joined while still a medical student; pub., *Medical Tribune*, beginning 1960. Known as a pioneer in biological psychiatry; founder, rsch. dir., Creedmoor Inst. Psychobiol. Studies, 1949–54; founder, 1957, and dir., Laboratories for Therapeutic Rsch., a nonprofit basic rsch. center at Brooklyn Coll. of Pharmacy, Long Island U.; resch. prof., psychiatry, NY Medical Coll., since 1972. Benefactor (for medical/scientific purposes): NYU and NYU Medical Center, NYC; Long Island U.; Tel Aviv U. (Sackler School of Medicine); Clark U., Tufts U. A leading collector of Asian, Near Eastern, and Western art, he was a major benefactor of Harvard U. (Sackler Museum); Metropolitan Museum of Art (Sackler Wing); Beijing U. (Sackler Museum); Smithsonian Inst. (Sackler Gallery). Mem., advisory council, dept. art hist and archaeol., Columbia U.; fellow: Amer. Psychiat. Assn., Amer. Geriatrics Soc., Royal Anthropol. Inst.; mem. and chmn.: Internatl. Assn. Social Psychiatry; NY Acad. of Sciences; Chinese Art Soc.; a founder, Amer. Friends of the Israel Philharmonic Orch.

SCHLOSS, EZEKIEL, editor, artist; b. Riga, Latvia, July (?), 1912; d. NYC, Mar. 30, 1987; in U.S. since 1940. Educ.: art studies in Riga and Paris. Ed., *World Over*, a magazine for Jewish children, published by the Bd. of Jewish Educ. of NY, 1942–77. A painter, book illustrator, and political cartoonist whose work appeared in the *New York Times*, *New Republic*, *France Amérique*, the *Nation*, and various Jewish publications; illustrator, the "Silverman Haggadah." Leading collector and authority on Chinese tomb sculpture. Author: *Ancient Chinese Ceramic Sculpture* (1977).

SOYER, RAPHAEL, artist; b. Borisoglebsk, Russia, Dec. 25, 1899; d. NYC, Nov. 4, 1987; in U.S. since 1912. Educ.: Cooper Union; Natl. Acad. Design; Art Students League. One of three brothers (Moses, died 1974, and Isaac, died 1981) who achieved artistic fame, he was a leading painter of the social-realist school and a foe of abstract painting. Known for his tender portraits of New York artists and dancers and the city's lonely and dispossessed, as well as for book illustrations, incl. works by I. B. Singer.

STEINBERG, MOSHE, rabbi, Talmud scholar; b. Premyslany, Poland, Dec. 27, 1901; d. NYC, July 20, 1987; in U.S. since 1947. Chief rabbi, Brody, Poland, 1934–39; during WWII helped to rescue Jewish children and place them in monasteries; chief rabbi, Krakow, 1945–47. In U.S., served as head of the Beth Din of the Rabbinical Council of Amer. for 30 years and rabbi, Cong. Machzeh Avraham, NYC. Regarded as a world authority on Jewish matrimonial law.

TAUBES, JACOB, professor; b. Vienna, Austria, Feb. 25, 1924; d. Berlin, W. Germany, (?), 1987; in U.S. since 1948. Educ.: U.'s of Paris, Basel, Zurich (PhD). Fellow: Jewish Theol. Sem. of Amer., 1948–49; Hebrew U. of Jerusalem, 1950–52. Taught at Harvard U., Columbia U., Princeton U., Free U. of Berlin (1966–87). Author: *Studien an Geschichte und System der Abendländischen Eschatologie; Logos und Tolos; Abenländische Eschatologie; On the Ontological Interpretation of Theology; The Nature of the Theological Method; Theodicy and Theology*.

UNTERBERG, CLARENCE, businessman, philanthropist; b. NYC, May 8, 1901; d. Tinton Falls, NJ, Nov. 28, 1987. Educ.: Phila. Coll. Textile Engineering; Columbia U. (MBA). Founded C. E. Unterberg, investment banking and brokerage firm, 1932. Chmn., Bella and Israel Unterberg Found.; benefactor, Beth Israel Medical Center, NYC; bd. mem., UJA-Fed.; trustee and hon. trustee, Cong. Shearith Israel, the Spanish and Portuguese Syn., NYC. Recipient: Herbert H. Lehman Award, Amer. Jewish Com. (1971).

WEBER, SIMON, journalist; b. Stashev, Poland, May 4, 1911; d. NYC, Dec. 2, 1987; in U.S. since 1929. Writer for Yiddish papers in Poland; reporter, the *Freiheit* (NY) and *Yiddishe Welt* (Phila.), in 1930s; joined the NY *Forward* staff in 1939, where he remained until his retirement in July 1987. Served as news ed., managing ed., and from 1970, ed. in chief. Editor and friend of I.B. Singer, whom he accompanied to Stockholm in 1978, when the writer received the Nobel Prize. Transl. of Upton Sinclair's *No Passaran!* into Yiddish. Recipient: Atran Literature Prize (1981).

WISE, GEORGE S., businessman, philanthropist; b. Pinsk, Poland, Apr. 7, 1906; d. Miami Beach, Fla., July 2, 1987; in U.S. since 1926. Educ.: Furman U.; Columbia U. (PhD). Lect., sociol., Columbia U., 1951–52; visiting prof., U. Mexico, 1956–57. Pres., George S. Wise Co. and Inter-American Paper Corp., manufs. and distribs. of newsprint. Chmn., bd of govs., Hebrew U., Jerusalem, 1953–62; pres., Tel Aviv U., 1963–71, and chancellor thereafter. Chmn., CLAL Investment Co.; pres., Isr.-Amer. Chamber of Commerce; dir., Hadera Paper Mills and other Israeli companies; bd. mem.: U. of Miami; Mt. Sinai Medical Center (Miami); Greater Miami Jewish Fed.; Amer. Bd. of Overseers, Bar-Ilan U. Recipient: hon. doctorates: Hebrew U., Ben-Gurion U.

ZORINSKY, EDWARD, politician, businessman; b. Omaha, Neb., Nov. 11, 1928; d. Omaha, Neb., Mar. 6, 1987. Educ.: U. Neb.; Harvard U. Joined family wholesale candy and tobacco bus.; mayor, Omaha, 1973–77; U.S. senator, 1977–87. A lifelong Republican, he switched to the Democratic party in 1975, when denied a Senate nomination by his own party. Scoring upset victories in both the primary and general elections in 1976, he became the first Jew ever to win a statewide election in Neb.; he was reelected in 1982. Mem.: Senate Foreign Relations Com.; Senate Agriculture, Nutrition, and Forestry Com.

ZUCKER, MOSES, professor; b. Kopeczowka, Poland, Jan. 14, 1902; d. Miami, Fla., Aug. 7, 1987; in U.S. since 1937. Educ.: U. Vienna; Jewish Theol. Sem. of Vienna (ord.); Dropsie Coll. (PhD). Rabbi: Avenue N Jewish Comm. Center, Brooklyn, NY, 1938–46; prof., Jewish Theol. Sem. of Amer., 1947–80; prof. emer. in Rabbinics since 1980. An expert in Arabic and Hebrew and noted researcher of the Cairo Geniza documents. Author: two-vols. in Hebrew on the works of Saadia Gaon; articles in scholarly journals, incl. *Proceedings of the Amer. Acad. for Jewish Rsch.*.

# Calendars

## SUMMARY JEWISH CALENDAR, 5749–5753 (Sept. 1988-Aug. 1993)

| HOLIDAY | 5749 1988 | | | 5750 1989 | | | 5751 1990 | | | 5752 1991 | | | 5753 1992 | | |
|---|---|---|---|---|---|---|---|---|---|---|---|---|---|---|---|
| Rosh Ha-shanah, 1st day | M | Sept. | 12 | Sa | Sept. | 30 | Th | Sept. | 20 | M | Sept. | 9 | M | Sept. | 28 |
| Rosh Ha-shanah, 2nd day | T | Sept. | 13 | S | Oct. | 1 | F | Sept. | 21 | T | Sept. | 10 | T | Sept. | 29 |
| Fast of Gedaliah | W | Sept. | 14 | M | Oct. | 2 | S | Sept. | 23 | W | Sept. | 11 | W | Sept. | 30 |
| Yom Kippur | W | Sept. | 21 | M | Oct. | 9 | Sa | Sept. | 29 | W | Sept. | 18 | W. | Oct. | 7 |
| Sukkot, 1st day | M | Sept. | 26 | Sa | Oct. | 14 | Th | Oct. | 4 | M | Sept. | 23 | M | Oct. | 12 |
| Sukkot, 2nd day | T | Sept. | 27 | S | Oct. | 15 | F | Oct. | 5 | T | Sept. | 24 | T | Oct. | 13 |
| Hosha'na' Rabbah | S | Oct. | 2 | F | Oct. | 20 | W | Oct. | 10 | S | Sept. | 29 | S | Oct. | 18 |
| Shemini 'Azeret | M | Oct. | 3 | Sa | Oct. | 21 | Th | Oct. | 11 | M | Sept. | 30 | M | Oct. | 19 |
| Simhat Torah | T | Oct. | 4 | S | Oct. | 22 | F | Oct. | 12 | T | Oct. | 1 | T. | Oct. | 20 |
| New Moon, Heshwan, 1st day | T | Oct. | 11 | S | Oct. | 29 | F | Oct. | 19 | T | Oct. | 8 | T | Oct. | 27 |
| New Moon, Heshwan, 2nd day | W | Oct. | 12 | M | Oct. | 30 | Sa | Oct. | 20 | W | Oct. | 9 | W. | Oct. | 28 |
| New Moon, Kislew, 1st day | Th | Nov. | 10 | T | Nov. | 28 | S | Nov. | 18 | Th | Nov. | 7 | Th. | Nov. | 26 |
| New Moon, Kislew, 2nd day | | | | W | Nov. | 29 | | | | F | Nov. | 8 | | | |
| Hanukkah, 1st day | S | Dec. | 4 | Sa | Dec. | 23 | W | Dec. | 12 | M | Dec. | 2 | s | Dec. | 20 |
| New Moon, Tevet, 1st day | F | Dec. | 9 | Th | Dec. | 28 | M | Dec. | 17 | Sa | Dec. | 7 | F | Dec. | 25 |
| New Moon, Tevet, 2nd day | | | | F | Dec. | 29 | T | Dec. | 18 | S | Dec. | 8 | | | |
| Fast of 10th of Tevet | S | Dec. | 18 | S | 1990 Jan. | 7 | Th | Dec. | 27 | T | Dec. | 17 | S | 1993 Jan. | 3 |

|  | 1989 |  |  | 1990 |  |  | 1991 |  |  | 1992 |  |  | 1993 |  |
|---|---|---|---|---|---|---|---|---|---|---|---|---|---|---|
| New Moon, Shevat | Sa | Jan. | 7 | Sa | Jan. | 27 | W | Jan. | 16 | M | Jan. | 6 | Sa | Jan. | 23 |
| Hamishshah-'asar bi-Shevat | Sa | Jan. | 21 | Sa | Feb. | 10 | W | Jan. | 30 | M | Jan. | 20 | Sa | Feb. | 6 |
| New Moon, Adar I, 1st day | S | Feb. | 5 | S | Feb. | 25 | Th | Feb. | 14 | T | Feb. | 4 | S | Feb. | 21 |
| New Moon, Adar I, 2nd day | M | Feb. | 6 | M | Feb. | 26 | F | Feb. | 15 | W | Feb. | 5 | M | Feb. | 22 |
| New Moon, Adar II, 1st day | T | Mar. | 7 |  |  |  |  |  |  | Th | Mar. | 5 |  |  |  |
| New Moon, Adar II, 2nd day | W | Mar. | 8 |  |  |  |  |  |  | F | Mar. | 6 |  |  |  |
| Fast of Esther | M | Mar. | 20 | Th | Mar. | 8 | W | Feb. | 27 | W | Mar. | 18 | Th | Mar. | 4 |
| Purim | T | Mar. | 21 | S | Mar. | 11 | Th | Feb. | 28 | Th | Mar. | 19 | S | Mar. | 7 |
| Shushan Purim | W | Mar. | 22 | M | Mar. | 12 | F | Mar. | 1 | F | Mar. | 20 | M | Mar. | 8 |
| New Moon, Nisan | Th | Apr. | 6 | T | Mar. | 27 | Sa | Mar. | 16 | Sa | Apr. | 4 | T | Mar. | 23 |
| Passover, 1st day | Th | Apr. | 20 | T | Apr. | 10 | Sa | Mar. | 30 | Sa | Apr. | 18 | T | Apr. | 6 |
| Passover, 2nd day | F | Apr. | 21 | W | Apr. | 11 | S | Mar. | 31 | S | Apr. | 19 | W | Apr. | 7 |
| Passover, 7th day | W | Apr. | 26 | M | Apr. | 16 | F | Apr. | 5 | F | Apr. | 24 | M | Apr. | 12 |
| Passover, 8th day | Th | Apr. | 27 | T | Apr. | 17 | Sa | Apr. | 6 | Sa | Apr. | 25 | T | Apr. | 13 |
| Holocaust Memorial Day | T | May | 2 | S | Apr. | 22 | Th | Apr. | 11 | Th | Apr. | 30 | T | Apr. | 18 |
| New Moon, Iyar, 1st day | F | May | 5 | W | Apr. | 25 | S | Apr. | 14 | S | May | 3 | W | Apr. | 21 |
| New Moon, Iyar, 2nd day | Sa | May | 6 | Th | Apr. | 26 | M | Apr. | 15 | M | May | 4 | Th | Apr. | 22 |
| Israel Independence Day | W | May | 10 | M | Apr. | 30 | F | Apr. | 19* | F | May | 8* | M | Apr. | 26 |
| Lag Ba-'omer | T | May | 23 | S | May | 13 | Th | May | 2 | Th | May | 21 | S | May | 9 |
| Jerusalem Day | F | May | 2* | W | May | 23 | S | May | 12 | S | May | 31 | W | May | 19 |
| New Moon, Siwan | S | June | 4 | F | May | 25 | T | May | 14 | T | Jun | 2 | F | May | 21 |
| Shavu'ot, 1st day | F | June | 9 | W | May | 30 | S | May | 19 | S | Jun | 7 | W | May | 26 |
| Shavu'ot, 2nd day | Sa | June | 10 | Th | May | 31 | M | May | 20 | M | Jun | 8 | Th | May | 27 |
| New Moon, Tammuz, 1st day | M | June | 3 | Sa | June | 23 | W | June | 12 | W | July | 1 | Sa | June | 19 |
| New Moon, Tammuz, 2nd day | T | July | 4 | S | June | 24 | Th | June | 13 | Th | July | 2 | S | June | 20 |
| Fast of 17th of Tammuz | Th | July | 20 | T | July | 10 | S | June | 30 | S | July | 19 | T | July | 6 |
| New Moon, Av | W | Aug. | 2 | M | July | 23 | F | July | 12 | F | July | 31 | M | July | 19 |
| Fast of 9th of Av | Th | Aug. | 10 | T | July | 31 | S | July | 21 | S | Aug. | 9 | T | July | 27 |
| New Moon, Elul, 1st day | Th | Aug. | 31 | T | Aug. | 21 | Sa | Aug. | 10 | Sa | Aug. | 29 | T | Aug. | 17 |
| New Moon, Elul, 2nd day | F | Sept. | 1 | W | Aug. | 22 | S | Aug. | 11 | S | Aug. | 30 | W | Aug. | 18 |

*Observed Thursday, a day earlier, to avoid conflict with the Sabbath.

## CONDENSED MONTHLY CALENDAR
## (1988–1990)

1987, Dec. 22–Jan. 19, 1988] ṬEVET (29 DAYS) [5748

| Civil Date | Day of the Week | Jewish Date | SABBATHS, FESTIVALS, FASTS | PENTATEUCHAL READING | PROPHETICAL READING |
|---|---|---|---|---|---|
| Dec. 22 | T | Tevet 1 | New Moon, second day; Hanukkah, seventh day | Num. 28:1–15<br>Num. 7:48–53 | |
| 23 | W | 2 | Hanukkah, eighth day | Num. 7:54–8:4 | |
| 26 | Sa | 5 | Wa-yiggash | Gen. 44:18–47:27 | Ezekiel 37:15–28 |
| 31 | Th | 10 | Fast of 10th of Tevet | Exod. 32:11–14<br>34:1–10<br>(morning and afternoon) | Isaiah 55:6–56:8 (afternoon only) |
| Jan. 2 | Sa | 12 | Wa-yeḥi | Gen. 47:28–50:26 | I Kings 2:1–12 |
| 9 | Sa | 19 | Shemot | Exod. 1:1–6:1 | Isaiah 27:6–28:13<br>29:22–23<br>*Jeremiah 1:1–2:3* |
| 16 | Sa | 26 | Wa-'era' | Exod. 6:2–9:35 | Ezekiel 28:25–29:21 |

*Italics are for Sephardi Minhag.*

1988, Jan. 20–Feb. 18]  SHEVAṬ (30 DAYS)  [5748

| Civil Date | Day of the Week | Jewish Date | SABBATHS, FESTIVALS, FASTS | PENTATEUCHAL READING | PROPHETICAL READING |
|---|---|---|---|---|---|
| Jan. 20 | W | Shevaṭ 1 | New Moon | Num. 28:1–15 | |
| 23 | Sa | 4 | Bo' | Exod. 10:1–13:16 | Jeremiah 46:13–28 |
| 30 | Sa | 11 | Be-shallah (Shabbat Shirah) | Exod. 13:17–17:16 | Judges 4:4–5:31 *Judges 5:1–31* |
| Feb. 3 | W | 15 | Hamishshah-'asar bi-Shevaṭ | | |
| 6 | Sa | 18 | Yitro | Exod. 18:1–20:23 | Isaiah 6:1–7:6 9:5–6 *Isaiah 6:1–13* |
| 13 | Sa | 25 | Mishpaṭim (Shabbat Sheḳalim) | Exod. 21:1–24:18 Exod. 30:11–16 | II Kings 12:1–17 *II Kings 11:17–12:17* |
| 18 | Th | 30 | New Moon, first day | Num. 28:1–15 | |

*Italics are for Sephardi Minhag.*

1988, Feb. 19–Mar. 18]  ADAR (29 DAYS)  [5748

| Civil Date | Day of the Week | Jewish Date | SABBATHS, FESTIVALS, FASTS | PENTATEUCHAL READING | PROPHETICAL READING |
|---|---|---|---|---|---|
| Feb. 19 | F | Adar 1 | New Moon, second day | Num. 28:1–15 | |
| 20 | Sa | 2 | Terumah | Exod. 25:1–27:19 | I Kings 5:26–6:13 |
| 27 | Sa | 9 | Tezawweh (Shabbat Zakhor) | Exod. 27:20–30:10 Deut. 25:17–19 | I Samuel 15:2–34 *I Samuel 15:1–34* |
| Mar. 2 | W | 13 | Fast of Esther | Exod. 32:11–14 34:1–10 (morning and afternoon) | Isaiah 55:6–56:8 (afternoon only) |
| 3 | Th | 14 | Purim | Exod. 17:8–16 | Book of Esther (night before and in the morning) |
| 4 | F | 15 | Shushan Purim | | |
| 5 | Sa | 16 | Ki tissa' | Exod. 30:11–34:35 | I Kings 18:1–39 *I Kings 18:20–39* |
| 12 | Sa | 23 | Wa-yakhel, Pekude (Shabbat Parah) | Exod. 35:1–40:38 Num. 19:1–22 | Ezekiel 36:16–38 *Ezekiel 36:16–36* |

*Italics are for Sephardi Minhag.*

## 1988, Mar. 19–Apr. 17] NISAN (30 DAYS) [5748

| Civil Date | Day of the Week | Jewish Date | SABBATHS, FESTIVALS, FASTS | PENTATEUCHAL READING | PROPHETICAL READING |
|---|---|---|---|---|---|
| Mar. 19 | Sa | Nisan 1 | Wa-yikra' (Shabbat Ha-ḥodesh); New Moon | Levit. 1:1–5:26<br>Exod. 12:1–20<br>Num. 28:9–15 | Ezekiel 45:16–46:18<br>*Ezekiel 45:18–46:15*<br>*Isaiah 66:1, 23* |
| 26 | Sa | 8 | Ẓaw (Shabbat Ha-gadol) | Levit. 6:1–8:36 | Malachi 3:4–24 |
| Apr. 1 | F | 14 | Fast of Firstborn | | |
| 2 | Sa | 15 | Passover, first day | Exod. 12:21–51<br>Num. 28:16–25 | Joshua 5:2–6:1, 27 |
| 3 | S | 16 | Passover, second day | Levit. 22:26–23:44<br>Num. 28:16–25 | II Kings 23: 1–9, 21–25 |
| 4 | M | 17 | Ḥol Ha-mo'ed, first day | Exod. 13:1–16<br>Num. 28:19–25 | |
| 5 | T | 18 | Ḥol Ha-mo'ed, second day | Exod. 22:24–23:19<br>Num. 28:19–25 | |
| 6 | W | 19 | Ḥol Ha-mo'ed, third day | Exod. 34:1–26<br>Num. 28:19–25 | |
| 7 | Th | 20 | Ḥol Ha-mo'ed, fourth day | Num. 9:1–14<br>Num. 28:19–25 | |
| 8 | F | 21 | Passover, seventh day | Exod. 13:17–15:26<br>Num. 28:19–25 | II Samuel 22:1–51 |
| 9 | Sa | 22 | Passover, eighth day | Deut. 15:19–16:17<br>Num. 28:19–25 | Isaiah 10:32–12:6 |
| 14 | Th | 27 | Holocaust Memorial Day | | |
| 16 | Sa | 29 | Shemini | Levit. 9:1–11:47 | I Samuel 20:18–42 |
| 17 | S | 30 | New Moon, first day | Num. 28:1–15 | |

*Italics are for Sephardi Minhag.*

1988, Apr. 18–May 16] IYAR (29 DAYS) [5748

| Civil Date | Day of the Week | Jewish Date | SABBATHS, FESTIVALS, FASTS | PENTATEUCHAL READING | PROPHETICAL READING |
|---|---|---|---|---|---|
| Apr. 18 | M | Iyar 1 | New Moon, second day | Num. 28:1–15 | |
| 22 | F* | 5 | Israel Independence Day | | |
| 23 | Sa | 6 | Tazria', Mezora' | Levit. 12:1–15:33 | II Kings 7:3–20 |
| 30 | Sa | 13 | Ahare mot, Kedoshim | Levit. 16:1–20:27 | Amos 9:7–15 *Ezekiel 20:2–20* |
| May 5 | Th | 18 | Lag Ba-'omer | | |
| 7 | Sa | 20 | Emor | Levit. 21:1–24:23 | Ezekiel 44:15–31 |
| 14 | Sa | 27 | Be-har, Be-hukkotai | Levit. 25:1–27:34 | Jeremiah 16:19–17:14 |
| 15 | S | 28 | Jerusalem Day | | |

*Observed Thursday, a day earlier, to avoid conflict with the Sabbath.

1988, May 17–June 15] SIWAN (30 DAYS) [5748

| Civil Date | Day of the Week | Jewish Date | SABBATHS, FESTIVALS, FASTS | PENTATEUCHAL READING | PROPHETICAL READING |
|---|---|---|---|---|---|
| May 17 | T | Siwan 1 | New Moon | Num. 28:1–15 | |
| 21 | Sa | 5 | Be-midbar | Num. 1:1–4:20 | Hosea 2:1–22 |
| 22 | S | 6 | Shavu'ot, first day | Exod. 19:1–20:23 Num. 28:26–31 | Ezekiel 1:1–28 3:12 |
| 23 | M | 7 | Shavu'ot, second day | Deut. 15:19–16:17 Num. 28:26–31 | Habbakuk 3:1–19 *Habbakuk 2:20–3:19* |
| 28 | Sa | 12 | Naso' | Num. 4:21–7:89 | Judges 13:2–25 |
| June 4 | Sa | 19 | Be-ha'alotekha | Num. 8:1–12:16 | Zechariah 2:14–4:7 |
| 11 | Sa | 26 | Shelah lekha | Num. 13:1–15:41 | Joshua 2:1–24 |
| 15 | W | 30 | New Moon, first day | Num. 28:1–15 | |

*Italics are for Sephardi Minhag.*

1988, June 16–July 14]  TAMMUZ (29 DAYS)  [5748

| Civil Date | Day of the Week | Jewish Date | SABBATHS, FESTIVALS, FASTS | PENTATEUCHAL READING | PROPHETICAL READING |
|---|---|---|---|---|---|
| June 16 | Th | Tammuz 1 | New Moon, second day | Num. 28:1–15 | |
| 18 | Sa | 3 | Koraḥ | Num. 16:1–18:32 | I Samuel 11:14–12:22 |
| 25 | Sa | 10 | Ḥukkat | Num. 19:1–22:1 | Judges 11:1–33 |
| July 2 | Sa | 17 | Balak | Num. 22:2–25:9 | Micah 5:6–6:8 |
| 3 | S | 18 | Fast of 17th of Tammuz | Exod. 32:11–14 34:1–10 (morning and afternoon) | Isaiah 55:6–56:8 (afternoon only) |
| 9 | Sa | 24 | Pineḥas | Num. 25:10–30:1 | Jeremiah 1:1–2:3 |

536 / AMERICAN JEWISH YEAR BOOK, 1989

1988, July 15–Aug. 13]    AV (30 DAYS)    [5748

| Civil Date | Day of the Week | Jewish Date | SABBATHS, FESTIVALS, FASTS | PENTATEUCHAL READING | PROPHETICAL READING |
|---|---|---|---|---|---|
| July 15 | F | Av 1 | New Moon | Num. 28:1–15 | |
| 16 | Sa | 2 | Mattot, Mas'e | Num. 30:2–36:13 | Jeremiah 2:4–28 3:4 *Jeremiah 2:4–28 4:1–2* |
| 23 | Sa | 9 | Devarim (Shabbat Ḥazon) | Deut. 1:1–3:22 | Isaiah 1:1–27 |
| 24 | S | 10 | Fast of 9th of Av | Morning: Deut. 4:25–40 Afternoon: Exod. 32:11–14 34:1–10 | (Lamentations is read the night before.) Jeremiah 8:13–9:23 (morning) Isaiah 55:6–56:8 (afternoon) |
| 30 | Sa | 16 | Wa-etḥannan (Shabbat Naḥamu) | Deut. 3:23–7:11 | Isaiah 40:1–26 |
| Aug. 6 | Sa | 23 | 'Ekev | Deut. 7:12–11:25 | Isaiah 49:14–51:3 |
| 13 | Sa | 30 | Re'eh; New Moon, first day | Deut. 11:26–16:17 Num. 28:9–15 | Isaiah 66:1–24 *Isaiah 66:1–24 I Samuel 20:18, 42* |

1988, Aug. 14–Sept. 11]    ELUL (29 DAYS)    [5748

| Civil Date | Day of the Week | Jewish Date | SABBATHS, FESTIVALS, FASTS | PENTATEUCHAL READING | PROPHETICAL READING |
|---|---|---|---|---|---|
| Aug. 14 | S | Elul 1 | New Moon, second day | Num. 28:1–15 | |
| 20 | Sa | 7 | Shofeṭim | Deut. 16:18–21:9 | Isaiah 51:12–52:12 |
| 27 | Sa | 14 | Ki teze' | Deut. 21:10–25:19 | Isaiah 54:1–55:5 |
| Sept. 3 | Sa | 21 | Ki tavo' | Deut. 26:1–29:8 | Isaiah 60:1–22 |
| 10 | Sa | 28 | Niẓẓavim | Deut. 29:9–30:20 | Isaiah 61:10–63:9 |

*Italics are for Sephardi Minhag.*

# 1988, Sept. 12–Oct. 11]    TISHRI (30 DAYS)    [5749

| Civil Date | Day of the Week | Jewish Date | SABBATHS, FESTIVALS, FASTS | PENTATEUCHAL READING | PROPHETICAL READING |
|---|---|---|---|---|---|
| Sept. 12 | M | Tishri 1 | Rosh Ha-shanah, first day | Gen. 21:1–34<br>Num. 29:1–6 | I Samuel 1:1–2:10 |
| 13 | T | 2 | Rosh Ha-shanah, second day | Gen. 22:1–24<br>Num. 29:1–6 | Jeremiah 31:2–20 |
| 14 | W | 3 | Fast of Gedaliah | Exod. 32:11–14<br>34:1–10<br>(morning and afternoon) | Isaiah 55:6–56:8<br>(afternoon only) |
| 17 | Sa | 6 | Wa-yelekh<br>(Shabbat Shuvah) | Deut. 31:1–30 | Hosea 14:2–10<br>Micah 7:18–20<br>Joel 2:15–27<br>*Hosea 14:2–10*<br>*Micah 7:18–20* |
| 21 | W | 10 | Yom Kippur | Morning:<br>Levit. 16:1–34<br>Num. 29:7–11<br>Afternoon:<br>Levit. 18:1–30 | Isaiah 57:14–58:14<br><br>Jonah 1:1–4:11<br>Micah 7:18–20 |
| 24 | Sa | 13 | Ha'azinu | Deut. 32:1–52 | II Samuel 22:1–51 |
| 26 | M | 15 | Sukkot, first day | Levit. 22:26–23:44<br>Num. 29:12–16 | Zechariah 14:1–21 |
| 27 | T | 16 | Sukkot, second day | Levit. 22:26–23:44<br>Num. 29:12–16 | I Kings 8:2–21 |
| 28–30 | W-F | 17–19 | Hol Ha-mo'ed, first to third days | W  Num. 29:17–25<br>Th Num. 29:20–28<br>F  Num. 29:23–31 | |
| Oct. 1 | Sa | 20 | Hol Ha-mo'ed, fourth day | Exod. 33:12–34:26<br>Num. 29:26–31 | Ezekiel 38:18–39:16 |
| 2 | S | 21 | Hosha'na' Rabbah | Num. 29:26–34 | |
| 3 | M | 22 | Shemini 'Azeret | Deut. 14:22–16:17<br>Num. 29:35–30:1 | I Kings 8:54–66 |
| 4 | T | 23 | Simhat Torah | Deut. 33:1–34:12<br>Gen.  1:1–2:3<br>Num. 29:35–30:1 | Joshua 1:1–18<br>*Joshua 1:1–9* |
| 8 | Sa | 27 | Be-re'shit | Gen.  1:1–6:8 | Isaiah 42:5–43:10<br>*Isaiah 42:5–21* |
| 11 | T | 30 | New Moon, first day | Num. 28:1–15 | |

*Italics are for*
*Sephardi Minhag.*

538 / AMERICAN JEWISH YEAR BOOK, 1989

1988, Oct. 12–Nov. 9]  HESHWAN (30 DAYS)  [5749

| Civil Date | Day of the Week | Jewish Date | SABBATHS, FESTIVALS, FASTS | PENTATEUCHAL READING | PROPHETICAL READING |
|---|---|---|---|---|---|
| Oct. 12 | W | Heshwan 1 | New Moon, second day | Num. 28:1–15 | |
| 15 | Sa | 4 | Noah | Gen. 6:9–11:32 | Isaiah 54:1–55:5<br>*Isaiah 54:1–10* |
| 22 | Sa | 11 | Lekh lekha | Gen. 12:1–17:27 | Isaiah 40:27–41:16 |
| 29 | Sa | 18 | Wa-yera' | Gen. 18:1–22:24 | II Kings 4:1–37<br>*II Kings 4:1–23* |
| Nov. 5 | Sa | 25 | Hayye Sarah | Gen. 23:1–25:18 | I Kings 1:1–31 |

1988, Nov. 10–Dec. 8]  KISLEW (29 DAYS)  [5749

| Civil Date | Day of the Week | Jewish Date | SABBATHS, FESTIVALS, FASTS | PENTATEUCHAL READING | PROPHETICAL READING |
|---|---|---|---|---|---|
| Nov. 10 | Th | Kislew 1 | New Moon | Num. 28:1–15 | |
| 12 | Sa | 3 | Toledot | Gen. 25:19–28:9 | Malachi 1:1–2:7 |
| 19 | Sa | 10 | Wa-yeze' | Gen. 28:10–32:3 | Hosea 12:13–14:10<br>*Hosea 11:7–12:12* |
| 26 | Sa | 17 | Wa-yishlah | Gen. 32:4–36:43 | Hosea 11:7–12:12<br>*Obadiah 1:1–21* |
| Dec. 3 | Sa | 24 | Wa-yeshev | Gen. 37:1–40:23 | Amos 2:6–3:8 |
| 4–8 | S-Th | 25–29 | Hanukkah, first to fifth days | S Num. 7:1–17<br>M Num. 7:18–29<br>T Num. 7:24–35<br>W Num. 7:30–41<br>Th Num. 7:36–47 | |

*Italics are for Sephardi Minhag.*

**1988, Dec. 9–Jan. 6, 1989]　ṬEVET (29 DAYS)　[5749**

| Civil Date | Day of the Week | Jewish Date | SABBATHS, FESTIVALS, FASTS | PENTATEUCHAL READING | PROPHETICAL READING |
|---|---|---|---|---|---|
| Dec. 9 | F | Ṭevet 1 | New Moon; Hanukkah, sixth day | Num. 28:1–15 Num. 7:42–47 | |
| 10 | Sa | 2 | Mi-keẓ; Hanukkah, seventh day | Gen. 41:1–44:17 Num. 7:48–53 | Zechariah 2:14–4:7 |
| 11 | S | 3 | Hanukkah, eighth day | Num. 7:54–8:4 | |
| 17 | Sa | 9 | Wa-yiggash | Gen. 44:18–47:27 | Ezekiel 37:15–28 |
| 18 | S | 10 | Fast of 10th of Ṭevet (morning and afternoon) | Exod. 32:11–14 34:1–10 | Isaiah 55:6–56:8 (afternoon only) |
| 24 | Sa | 16 | Wa-yeḥi | Gen. 47:28–50:26 | I Kings 2:1–12 |
| 31 | Sa | 23 | Shemot | Exod. 1:1–6:1 | Isaiah 27:6–28:13 29:22–23 *Jeremiah 1:1–2:3* |

**1989, Jan. 7–Feb. 5]　SHEVAṬ (30 DAYS)　[5749**

| Civil Date | Day of the Week | Jewish Date | SABBATHS, FESTIVALS, FASTS | PENTATEUCHAL READING | PROPHETICAL READING |
|---|---|---|---|---|---|
| Jan. 7 | Sa | Shevat 1 | Wa-'era'; New Moon | Exod. 6:2–9:35 Num. 28:9–15 | Isaiah 66:1–24 |
| 14 | Sa | 8 | Bo' | Exod. 10:1–13:16 | Jeremiah 46:13–28 |
| 21 | Sa | 15 | Be-shallaḥ (Shabbat Shirah); Hamishshah-'asar bi-Shevaṭ | Exod. 13:17–17:16 | Judges 4:4–5:31 *Judges 5:1–31* |
| 28 | Sa | 22 | Yitro | Exod. 18:1–20:23 | Isaiah 6:1–7:6 9:5–6 *Isaiah 6:1–13* |
| Feb. 4 | Sa | 29 | Mishpaṭim | Exod. 21:1–24:18 | I Samuel 20:18–42 |
| 5 | S | 30 | New Moon, first day | Num. 28:1–15 | |

*Italics are for Sephardi Minhag.*

1989, Feb. 6–Mar. 7]    ADAR I (30 DAYS)    [5749

| Civil Date | Day of the Week | Jewish Date | SABBATHS, FESTIVALS, FASTS | PENTATEUCHAL READING | PROPHETICAL READING |
|---|---|---|---|---|---|
| Feb. 6 | M | I Adar 1 | New Moon, second day | Num. 28:1–15 | |
| 11 | Sa | 6 | Terumah | Exod. 25:1–27:19 | I Kings 5:26–6:13 |
| 18 | Sa | 13 | Tezawweh | Exod. 27:20–30:10 | Ezekiel 43:10–27 |
| 25 | Sa | 20 | Ki tissa' | Exod. 30:11–34:35 | I Kings 18:1–39<br>*I Kings 18:20–39* |
| Mar. 4 | Sa | 27 | Wa-yakhel (Shabbat Shekalim) | Exod. 35:1–38:20<br>Exod. 30:11–16 | II Kings 12:1–17<br>*II Kings 11:17–12:17* |
| 7 | T | 30 | New Moon, first day | Num. 28:1–15 | |

1989, Mar. 8–Apr. 5]    ADAR II (29 DAYS)    [5749

| Civil Date | Day of the Week | Jewish Date | SABBATHS, FESTIVALS, FASTS | PENTATEUCHAL READING | PROPHETICAL READING |
|---|---|---|---|---|---|
| Mar. 8 | W | II Adar 1 | New Moon, second day | Num. 28:1–15 | |
| 11 | Sa | 4 | Pekude | Exod. 38:21–40:38 | I Kings 7:51–8:21<br>*I Kings 7:40–50* |
| 18 | Sa | 11 | Wa-yikra' (Shabbat Zakhor) | Levit. 1:1–5:26<br>Deut. 25:17–19 | I Samuel 15:2–34<br>*I Samuel 15:1–34* |
| 20 | M | 13 | Fast of Esther | Exod. 32:11–14<br>34:1–10<br>(morning and afternoon) | Isaiah 55:6–56:8 (afternoon only) |
| 21 | T | 14 | Purim | Exod. 17:8–16 | Book of Esther (night before and in the morning) |
| 22 | W | 15 | Shushan Purim | | |
| 25 | Sa | 18 | Zaw (Shabbat Parah) | Levit. 6:1–8:36<br>Num. 19:1–22 | Ezekiel 36:16–38<br>*Ezekiel 36:16–36* |
| Apr. 1 | Sa | 25 | Shemini (Shabbat Ha-hodesh) | Levit. 9:1–11:47<br>Exod. 12:1–20 | Ezekiel 45:16–46:18<br>*Ezekiel 45:18–46:15* |

*Italics are for Sephardi Minhag.*

1989, Apr. 6–May 5] NISAN (30 DAYS) [5749

| Civil Date | Day of the Week | Jewish Date | SABBATHS, FESTIVALS, FASTS | PENTATEUCHAL READING | PROPHETICAL READING |
|---|---|---|---|---|---|
| Apr. 6 | Th | Nisan 1 | New Moon | Num. 28:1–15 | |
| 8 | Sa | 3 | Tazria' | Levit. 12:1–13:59 | II Kings 4:42–5:19 |
| 15 | Sa | 10 | Mezora' (Shabbat Ha-gadol) | Levit. 14:1–15:33 | Malachi 3:4–24 |
| 19 | W | 14 | Fast of Firstborn | | |
| 20 | Th | 15 | Passover, first day | Exod. 12:21–51<br>Num. 28:16–25 | Joshua 5:2–6:1, 27 |
| 21 | F | 16 | Passover, second day | Levit. 22:26–23:44<br>Num. 28:16–25 | II Kings 23:1–9, 21–25 |
| 22 | Sa | 17 | Hol Ha-mo'ed, first day | Exod. 33:12–34:26<br>Num. 28:19–25 | Ezekiel 37:1–14 |
| 23 | S | 18 | Hol Ha-mo'ed, second day | Exod. 13:1–16<br>Num. 28:19–25 | |
| 24 | M | 19 | Hol Ha-mo'ed, third day | Exod. 22:24–23:19<br>Num. 28:19–25 | |
| 25 | T | 20 | Hol Ha-mo'ed, fourth day | Num. 9:1–14<br>Num. 28:19–25 | |
| 26 | W | 21 | Passover, seventh day | Exod. 13:17–15:26<br>Num. 28:19–25 | II Samuel 22:1–51 |
| 27 | Th | 22 | Passover, eighth day | Deut. 15:19–16:17<br>Num. 28:19–25 | Isaiah 10:32–12:6 |
| 29 | Sa | 24 | Aḥare mot | Levit. 16:1–18:30 | Amos 9:7–15 |
| May 2 | T | 27 | Holocaust Memorial Day | | |
| 5 | F | 30 | New Moon, first day | Num. 28:1–15 | |

## 1989, May 6–June 3] IYAR (29 DAYS) [5749

| Civil Date | Day of the Week | Jewish Date | SABBATHS, FESTIVALS, FASTS | PENTATEUCHAL READING | PROPHETICAL READING |
|---|---|---|---|---|---|
| May 6 | Sa | Iyar 1 | Kedoshim; New Moon, second day | Levit. 19:1–20:27 Num. 28:9–15 | Isaiah 66:1–24 |
| 10 | W | 5 | Israel Independence Day | | |
| 13 | Sa | 8 | Emor | Levit. 21:1–24:23 | Ezekiel 44:15–31 |
| 20 | Sa | 15 | Be-har | Levit. 25:1–26:2 | Jeremiah 32:6–27 |
| 23 | T | 18 | Lag Ba-'omer | | |
| 27 | Sa | 22 | Be-ḥukkotai | Levit. 26:3–27:34 | Jeremiah 16:19–17:14 |
| June 2 | F* | 28 | Jerusalem Day | | |
| 3 | Sa | 29 | Be-midbar | Num. 1:1–4:20 | I Samuel 20:18–42 |

*Observed Thursday, a day earlier, to avoid conflict with the Sabbath.

## 1989, June 4–July 3] SIWAN (30 DAYS) [5749

| Civil Date | Day of the Week | Jewish Date | SABBATHS, FESTIVALS, FASTS | PENTATEUCHAL READING | PROPHETICAL READING |
|---|---|---|---|---|---|
| June 4 | S | Siwan 1 | New Moon | Num. 28:1–15 | |
| 9 | F | 6 | Shavu'ot, first day | Exod. 19:1–20:23 Num. 28:26–31 | Ezekiel 1:1–28 3:12 |
| 10 | Sa | 7 | Shavu'ot, second day | Deut. 15:19–16:17 Num. 28:26–31 | Habbakuk 3:1–19 *Habbakuk 2:20–3:19* |
| 17 | Sa | 14 | Naso' | Num. 4:21–7:89 | Judges 13:2–25 |
| 24 | Sa | 21 | Be-ha'alotekha | Num. 8:1–12:16 | Zechariah 2:14–4:7 |
| July 1 | Sa | 28 | Shelaḥ lekha | Num. 13:1–15:41 | Joshua 2:1–24 |
| 3 | M | 30 | New Moon, first day | Num. 28:1–15 | |

*Italics are for Sephardi Minhag.*

1989, July 4–Aug. 1]  TAMMUZ (29 DAYS)  [5749

| Civil Date | Day of the Week | Jewish Date | SABBATHS, FESTIVALS, FASTS | PENTATEUCHAL READING | PROPHETICAL READING |
|---|---|---|---|---|---|
| July 4 | T | Tammuz 1 | New Moon, second day | Num. 28:1–15 | |
| 8 | Sa | 5 | Korah | Num. 16:1–18:32 | I Samuel 11:14–12:22 |
| 15 | Sa | 12 | Hukkat, Balak | Num. 19:1–25:9 | Micah 5:6–6:8 |
| 20 | Th | 17 | Fast of 17th of Tammuz | Exod. 32:11–14 34:1–10 (morning and afternoon) | Isaiah 55:6–56:8 (afternoon only) |
| 22 | Sa | 19 | Pinehas | Num. 25:10–30:1 | Jeremiah 1:1–2:3 |
| 29 | Sa | 26 | Mattot, Mas'e | Num. 30:2–36:13 | Jeremiah 2:4–28 3:4 *Jeremiah 2:4–28 4:1–2* |

*Italics are for Sephardi Minhag.*

1989, Aug. 2–Aug. 31]      AV (30 DAYS)      [5749

| Civil Date | Day of the Week | Jewish Date | SABBATHS, FESTIVALS, FASTS | PENTATEUCHAL READING | PROPHETICAL READING |
|---|---|---|---|---|---|
| Aug. 2 | W | Av 1 | New Moon | Num. 28:1–15 | |
| 5 | Sa | 4 | Devarim (Shabbat Ḥazon) | Deut. 1:1–3:22 | Isaiah 1:1–27 |
| 10 | Th | 9 | Fast of 9th of Av | Morning: Deut. 4:25–40 Afternoon: Exod. 32:11–14 34:1–10 | (Lamentations is read the night before.) Jeremiah 8:13–9:23 (morning) Isaiah 55:6–56:8 (afternoon) |
| 12 | Sa | 11 | Wa-etḥannan (Shabbat Naḥamu) | Deut. 3:23–7:11 | Isaiah 40:1–26 |
| 19 | Sa | 18 | 'Eḳev | Deut. 7:12–11:25 | Isaiah 49:14–51:3 |
| 26 | Sa | 25 | Re'eh | Deut. 11:26–16:17 | Isaiah 54:11–55:5 |
| 31 | Th | 30 | New Moon, first day | Num. 28:1–15 | |

1989, Sept. 1–Sept. 29]      ELUL (29 DAYS)      [5749

| Civil Date | Day of the Week | Jewish Date | SABBATHS, FESTIVALS, FASTS | PENTATEUCHAL READING | PROPHETICAL READING |
|---|---|---|---|---|---|
| Sept. 1 | F | Elul 1 | New Moon, second day | Num. 28:1–15 | |
| 2 | Sa | 2 | Shofeṭim | Deut. 16:18–21:9 | Isaiah 51:12–52:12 |
| 9 | Sa | 9 | Ki teẓe' | Deut. 21:10–25:19 | Isaiah 54:1–10 |
| 16 | Sa | 16 | Ki tavo' | Deut. 26:1–29:8 | Isaiah 60:1–22 |
| 23 | Sa | 23 | Niẓẓavim, Wa-yelekh | Deut. 29:9–31:30 | Isaiah 61:10–63:9 |

1989, Sept. 30–Oct. 29]  TISHRI (30 DAYS)  [5750

| Civil Date | Day of the Week | Jewish Date | SABBATHS, FESTIVALS, FASTS | PENTATEUCHAL READING | PROPHETICAL READING |
|---|---|---|---|---|---|
| Sept. 30 | Sa | Tishri 1 | Rosh Ha-shanah, first day | Gen. 21:1–34<br>Num. 29:1–6 | I Samuel 1:1–2:10 |
| Oct. 1 | S | 2 | Rosh Ha-shanah, second day | Gen. 22:1–24<br>Num. 29:1–6 | Jeremiah 31:2–20 |
| 2 | M | 3 | Fast of Gedaliah | Exod. 32:11–14<br>34:1–10<br>(morning and afternoon) | Isaiah 55:6–56:8<br>(afternoon only) |
| 7 | Sa | 8 | Ha'azinu (Shabbat Shuvah) | Deut. 32:1–52 | Hosea 14:2–10<br>Micah 7:18–20<br>Joel 2:15–27<br>*Hosea 14:2–10*<br>*Micah 7:18–20* |
| 9 | M | 10 | Yom Kippur | Morning:<br>Levit. 16:1–34<br>Num. 29:7–11<br>Afternoon:<br>Levit. 18:1–30 | Isaiah 57:14–58:14<br><br>Jonah 1:1–4:11<br>Micah 7:18–20 |
| 14 | Sa | 15 | Sukkot, first day | Levit. 22:26–23:44<br>Num. 29:12–16 | Zechariah 14:1–21 |
| 15 | S | 16 | Sukkot, second day | Levit. 22:26–23:44<br>Num. 29:12–16 | I Kings 8:2–21 |
| 16–19 | M–Th | 17–20 | Hol Ha-mo'ed, first to fourth days | M Num. 29:17–25<br>T Num. 29:20–28<br>W Num. 29:23–31<br>Th Num. 29:26–34 | |
| 20 | F | 21 | Hosha'na' Rabbah | Num. 29:26–34 | |
| 21 | Sa | 22 | Shemini 'Azeret | Deut. 14:22–16:17<br>Num. 29:35–30:1 | I Kings 8:54–66 |
| 22 | S | 23 | Simḥat Torah | Deut. 33:1–34:12<br>Gen. 1:1–2:3<br>Num. 29:35–30:1 | Joshua 1:1–18<br>*Joshua 1:1–9* |
| 28 | Sa | 29 | Be-re'shit | Gen. 1:1–6:8 | I Samuel 20:18–42 |
| 29 | S | 30 | New Moon, first day | Num. 28:1–15 | |

*Italics are for*
*Sephardi Minhag.*

1989, Oct. 30–Nov. 28]  HESHWAN (30 DAYS)  [5750

| Civil Date | Day of the Week | Jewish Date | SABBATHS, FESTIVALS, FASTS | PENTATEUCHAL READING | PROPHETICAL READING |
|---|---|---|---|---|---|
| Oct. 30 | M | Heshwan 1 | New Moon, second day | Num. 28:1–15 | |
| Nov. 4 | Sa | 6 | Noah | Gen. 6:9–11:32 | Isaiah 54:1–55:5 *Isaiah 54:1–10* |
| 11 | Sa | 13 | Lekh lekha | Gen. 12:1–17:27 | Isaiah 40:27–41:16 |
| 18 | Sa | 20 | Wa-yera' | Gen. 18:1–22:24 | II Kings 4:1–37 *II Kings 4:1–23* |
| 25 | Sa | 27 | Hayye Sarah | Gen. 23:1–25:18 | I Kings 1:1–31 |
| 28 | T | 30 | New Moon, first day | Num. 28:1–15 | |

1989, Nov. 29–Dec. 28]  KISLEW (30 DAYS)  [5750

| Civil Date | Day of the Week | Jewish Date | SABBATHS, FESTIVALS, FASTS | PENTATEUCHAL READING | PROPHETICAL READING |
|---|---|---|---|---|---|
| Nov. 29 | W | Kislew 1 | New Moon, second day | Num. 28:1–15 | |
| Dec. 2 | Sa | 4 | Toledot | Gen. 25:19–28:9 | Malachi 1:1–2:7 |
| 9 | Sa | 11 | Wa-yeze' | Gen. 28:10–32:3 | Hosea 12:13–14:10 *Hosea 11:7–12:12* |
| 16 | Sa | 18 | Wa-yishlah | Gen. 32:4–36:43 | Hosea 11:7–12:12 *Obadiah 1:1–21* |
| 23 | Sa | 25 | Wa-yeshev; Hanukkah, first day | Gen. 37:1–40:23 Num. 7:1–17 | Zechariah 2:14–4:7 |
| 24–27 | S–W | 26–29 | Hanukkah, second to fifth days | S Num. 7:18–29 M Num. 7:24–35 T Num. 7:30–41 W Num. 7:36–47 | |
| 28 | Th | 30 | New Moon, first day; Hanukkah, sixth day | Num. 28:1–15 Num. 7:42–47 | |

*Italics are for Sephardi Minhag.*

1989, Dec. 29–Jan. 26, 1990] TEVET (29 DAYS) [5750

| Civil Date | Day of the Week | Jewish Date | SABBATHS, FESTIVALS, FASTS | PENTATEUCHAL READING | PROPHETICAL READING |
|---|---|---|---|---|---|
| Dec. 29 | F | Tevet 1 | New Moon, second day; Hanukkah, seventh day | Num. 28:1–15 Num. 7:48–53 | |
| 30 | Sa | 2 | Mi-kez; Hanukkah, eighth day | Gen. 41:1–44:17 Num. 7:54–8:4 | I Kings 7:40–50 |
| Jan. 6 | Sa | 9 | Wa-yiggash | Gen. 44:18–47:27 | Ezekiel 37:15–28 |
| 7 | S | 10 | Fast of 10th of Tevet | Exod. 32:11–14 34:1–10 (morning and afternoon) | Isaiah 55:6–56:8 (afternoon only) |
| 13 | Sa | 16 | Wa-yehi | Gen. 47:28–50:26 | I Kings 2:1–12 |
| 20 | Sa | 23 | Shemot | Exod. 1:1–6:1 | Isaiah 27:6–28:13 29:22–23 *Jeremiah 1:1–2:3* |

*Italics are for Sephardi Minhag.*

1990, Jan. 27–Feb. 25] SHEVAṬ (30 DAYS) [5750

| Civil Date | Day of the Week | Jewish Date | SABBATHS, FESTIVALS, FASTS | PENTATEUCHAL READING | PROPHETICAL READING |
|---|---|---|---|---|---|
| Jan. 27 | Sa | Shevaṭ 1 | Wa-'era'; New Moon | Exod. 6:2–9:35 Num. 28:9–15 | Isaiah 66:1–24 |
| Feb. 3 | Sa | 8 | Bo' | Exod. 10:1–13:16 | Jeremiah 46:13–28 |
| 10 | Sa | 15 | Be-shallah (Shabbat Shirah); Hamishshah-'asar bi-Shevaṭ | Exod. 13:17–17:16 | Judges 4:4–5:31 *Judges 5:1–31* |
| 17 | Sa | 22 | Yitro | Exod. 18:1–20:23 | Isaiah 6:1–7:6 9:5–6 *Isaiah 6:1–13* |
| 24 | Sa | 29 | Mishpaṭim (Shabbat Shekalim) | Exod. 21:1–24:18 30:11–16 | II Kings 12:1–17 *II Kings 11:17–12:17* I Samuel 20:18,42 |
| 25 | S | 30 | New Moon, first day | Num. 28:1–15 | |

*Italics are for Sephardi Minhag.*

1990, Feb. 26–Mar. 26] ADAR (29 DAYS) [5750

| Civil Date | Day of the Week | Jewish Date | SABBATHS, FESTIVALS, FASTS | PENTATEUCHAL READING | PROPHETICAL READING |
|---|---|---|---|---|---|
| Feb. 26 | M | Adar 1 | New Moon, second day | Num. 28:1–15 | |
| Mar. 3 | Sa | 6 | Terumah | Exod. 25:1–27:19 | I Kings 5:26–6:13 |
| 8 | Th | 11 | Fast of Esther | Exod. 32:11–14 34:1–10 (morning and afternoon) | Isaiah 55:6–56:8 (afternoon only) |
| 10 | Sa | 13 | Tezawweh (Shabbat Zakhor) | Exod. 27:20–30:10 Deut. 25:17–19 | I Samuel 15:2–34 *I Samuel 15:1–34* |
| 11 | S | 14 | Purim | Exod. 17:8–16 | Book of Esther (night before and in the morning) |
| 12 | M | 15 | Shushan Purim | | |
| 17 | Sa | 20 | Ki tissa' (Shabbat Parah) | Exod. 30:11–34:35 Num. 19:1–22 | Ezekiel 36:16–38 *Ezekiel 36:16–36* |
| 24 | Sa | 27 | Wa-yakhel, Pekude (Shabbat Ha-hodesh) | Exod. 35:1–40:38 12:1–20 | Ezekiel 45:16–46:18 *Ezekiel 45:18–46:15* |

*Italics are for Sephardi Minhag.*

550 / AMERICAN JEWISH YEAR BOOK, 1989

1990, Mar. 27–Apr. 25]  NISAN (30 DAYS)  [5750

| Civil Date | Day of the Week | Jewish Date | SABBATHS, FESTIVALS, FASTS | PENTATEUCHAL READING | PROPHETICAL READING |
|---|---|---|---|---|---|
| Mar. 27 | T | Nisan 1 | New Moon | Num. 28:1–15 | |
| 31 | Sa | 5 | Wa-yikra' | Levit. 1:1–5:26 | Isaiah 43:21–44:24 |
| Apr. 7 | Sa | 12 | Zaw (Shabbat Ha-gadol) | Levit. 6:1–8:36 | Malachi 3:4–24 |
| 9 | M | 14 | Fast of Firstborn | | |
| 10 | T | 15 | Passover, first day | Exod. 12:21–51<br>Num. 28:16–25 | Joshua 5:2–6:1, 27 |
| 11 | W | 16 | Passover, second day | Levit. 22:26–23:44<br>Num. 28:16–25 | II Kings 23:1–9, 21–25 |
| 12 | Th | 17 | Hol Ha-mo'ed, first day | Exod. 13:1–16<br>Num. 28:19–25 | |
| 13 | F | 18 | Hol Ha-mo'ed, second day | Exod. 22:24–23:19<br>Num. 28:19–25 | |
| 14 | Sa | 19 | Hol Ha-mo'ed, third day | Exod. 33:12–34:26<br>Num. 28:19–25 | Ezekiel 37:1–14 |
| 15 | S | 20 | Hol Ha-mo'ed, fourth day | Num. 9:1–14<br>Num. 28:19–25 | |
| 16 | M | 21 | Passover, seventh day | Exod. 13:17–15:26<br>Num. 28:19–25 | II Samuel 22:1–51 |
| 17 | T | 22 | Passover, eigth day | Deut. 15:19–16:17<br>Num. 28:19–25 | Isaiah 10:32–12:6 |
| 21 | Sa | 26 | Shemini | Levit. 9:1–11:47 | II Samuel 6:1–7:17<br>*II Samuel 6:1–19* |
| 22 | S | 27 | Holocaust Memorial Day | | |
| 25 | W | 30 | New Moon, first day | Num. 28:1–15 | |

*Italics are for Sephardi Minhag.*

1990, Apr. 26–May 24] IYAR (29 DAYS) [5750

| Civil Date | Day of the Week | Jewish Date | SABBATHS, FESTIVALS, FASTS | PENTATEUCHAL READING | PROPHETICAL READING |
|---|---|---|---|---|---|
| Apr. 26 | Th | Iyar 1 | New Moon, second day | Num. 28:1–15 | |
| 28 | Sa | 3 | Tazria', Mezora' | Levit. 12:1–15:33 | II Kings 7:3–20 |
| 30 | M | 5 | Israel Independence Day | | |
| May 5 | Sa | 10 | Ahare mot, Kedoshim | Levit. 16:1–20:27 | Amos 9:7–15 *Ezekiel 20:2–20* |
| 12 | Sa | 17 | Emor | Levit. 21:1–24:23 | Ezekiel 44:15–31 |
| 13 | S | 18 | Lag Ba-'omer | | |
| 19 | Sa | 24 | Be-har, Be-hukkotai | Levit. 25:1–27:34 | Jeremiah 16:19–17:14 |
| 23 | W | 28 | Jerusalem Day | | |

1990, May 25–June 23] SIWAN (30 DAYS) [5750

| Civil Date | Day of the Week | Jewish Date | SABBATHS, FESTIVALS, FASTS | PENTATEUCHAL READING | PROPHETICAL READING |
|---|---|---|---|---|---|
| May 25 | F | Siwan 1 | New Moon | Num. 28:1–15 | |
| 26 | Sa | 2 | Be-midbar | Num. 1:1–4:20 | Hosea 2:1–22 |
| 30 | W | 6 | Shavu'ot, first day | Exod. 19:1–20:23 Num. 28:26–31 | Ezekiel 1:1–28 3:12 |
| 31 | Th | 7 | Shavu'ot, second day | Deut. 15:19–16:17 Num. 28:26–31 | Habbakuk 3:1–19 *Habbakuk 2:20–3:19* |
| June 2 | Sa | 9 | Naso' | Num. 4:21–7:89 | Judges 13:2–25 |
| 9 | Sa | 16 | Be-ha'alotekha | Num. 8:1–12:16 | Zechariah 2:14–4:7 |
| 16 | Sa | 23 | Shelah lekha | Num. 13:1–15:41 | Joshua 2:1–24 |
| 23 | Sa | 30 | Korah; New Moon, first day | Num. 16:1–18:32 Num. 28:9–15 | Isaiah 66:1–24 *Isaiah 66:1–24 I Samuel 20:18, 42* |

*Italics are for Sephardi Minhag.*

1990, June 24–July 22]   TAMMUZ (29 DAYS)   [5750

| Civil Date | Day of the Week | Jewish Date | SABBATHS, FESTIVALS, FASTS | PENTATEUCHAL READING | PROPHETICAL READING |
|---|---|---|---|---|---|
| June 24 | S | Tammuz 1 | New Moon, second day | Num. 28:1–15 | |
| 30 | Sa | 7 | Hukkat | Num. 19:1–22:1 | Judges 11:1–33 |
| July 7 | Sa | 14 | Balak | Num. 22:2–25:9 | Micah 5:6–6:8 |
| 10 | T | 17 | Fast of 17th of Tammuz | Exod. 32:11–14 34:1–10 (morning and afternoon) | Isaiah 55:6–56:8 (afternoon only) |
| 21 | Sa | 21 | Pinehas | Num. 25:10–30:1 | Jeremiah 1:1–2:3 |
| 28 | Sa | 28 | Mattot, Mas'e | Num. 30:2–36:13 | Jeremiah 2:4–28 3:4 *Jeremiah 2:4–28 4:1–2* |

*Italics are for Sephardi Minhag.*

MONTHLY CALENDAR / 553

1990, July 23–Aug. 21]  AV (30 DAYS)  [5750

| Civil Date | Day of the Week | Jewish Date | SABBATHS, FESTIVALS, FASTS | PENTATEUCHAL READING | PROPHETICAL READING |
|---|---|---|---|---|---|
| July 23 | M | Av 1 | New Moon | Num. 28:1–15 | |
| 28 | Sa | 6 | Devarim (Shabbat Hazon) | Deut. 1:1–3:22 | Isaiah 1:1–27 |
| 31 | T | 9 | Fast of 9th of Av | Morning: Deut. 4:25–40 Afternoon: Exod. 32:11–14 34:1–10 | (Lamentations is read the night before.) Jeremiah 8:13–9:23 (morning) Isaiah 55:6–56:8 (afternoon) |
| Aug. 4 | Sa | 13 | Wa-ethannan (Shabbat Nahamu) | Deut. 3:23–7:11 | Isaiah 40:1–26 |
| 11 | Sa | 20 | 'Ekev | Deut. 7:12–11:25 | Isaiah 49:14–51:3 |
| 18 | Sa | 27 | Re'eh | Deut. 11:26–16:17 | Isaiah 54:11–55:5 |
| 21 | T | 30 | New Moon, first day | Num. 28:1–15 | |

1990, Aug. 22–Sept. 19]  ELUL (29 DAYS)  [5750

| Civil Date | Day of the Week | Jewish Date | SABBATHS, FESTIVALS, FASTS | PENTATEUCHAL READING | PROPHETICAL READING |
|---|---|---|---|---|---|
| Aug. 22 | W | Elul 1 | New Moon, second day | Num. 28:1–15 | |
| 25 | Sa | 4 | Shofetim | Deut. 16:18–21:9 | Isaiah 51:12–52:12 |
| Sept. 1 | Sa | 11 | Ki teze' | Deut. 21:10–25:19 | Isaiah 54:1–10 |
| 8 | Sa | 18 | Ki tavo' | Deut. 26:1–29:8 | Isaiah 60:1–22 |
| 15 | Sa | 25 | Nizzavim, Wa-yelekh | Deut. 29:9–31:30 | Isaiah 61:10–63:9 |

**1990, Sept. 20–Oct. 19]**     **TISHRI (30 DAYS)**     **[5751**

| Civil Date | Day of the Week | Jewish Date | SABBATHS, FESTIVALS, FASTS | PENTATEUCHAL READING | PROPHETICAL READING |
|---|---|---|---|---|---|
| Sept. 20 | Th | Tishri 1 | Rosh Ha-shanah, first day | Gen. 21:1–34<br>Num. 29:1–6 | I Samuel 1:1–2:10 |
| 21 | F | 2 | Rosh Ha-shanah, second day | Gen. 22:1–24<br>Num. 29:1–6 | Jeremiah 31:2–20 |
| 22 | Sa | 3 | Ha'azinu (Shabbat Shuvah) | Deut. 32:1–52 | Hosea 14:2–10<br>Micah 7:18–20<br>Joel 2:15–27<br>*Hosea 14:2–10*<br>*Micah 7:18–20* |
| 23 | S | 4 | Fast of Gedaliah | Exod. 32:11–14<br>34:1–10<br>(morning and afternoon) | Isaiah 55:6–56:8<br>(afternoon only) |
| 29 | Sa | 10 | Yom Kippur | Morning:<br>Levit. 16:1–34<br>Num. 29:7–11<br>Afternoon:<br>Levit. 18:1–30 | Isaiah 57:14–58:14<br><br>Jonah 1:1–4:11<br>Micah 7:18–20 |
| Oct. 4 | Th | 15 | Sukkot, first day | Levit. 22:26–23:44<br>Num. 29:12–16 | Zechariah 14:1–21 |
| 5 | F | 16 | Sukkot, second day | Levit. 22:26–23:44<br>Num. 29:12–16 | I Kings 8:2–21 |
| Oct. 6 | Sa | Tishri 17 | Hol Ha-mo'ed, first day | Exod. 33:12–34:26<br>Num. 29:17–22 | Ezekiel 38:18–39:16 |
| 7–9 | S–T | 18–20 | Hol Ha-mo'ed, second to fourth days | S Num. 29:20–28<br>M Num. 29:23–31<br>T Num. 29:26–34 | |
| 10 | W | 21 | Hosha'na' Rabbah | Num. 29:26–34 | |
| 11 | Th | 22 | Shemini 'Azeret | Deut. 14:22–16:17<br>Num. 29:35–30:1 | I Kings 8:54–66 |
| 12 | F | 23 | Simhat Torah | Deut. 33:1–34:12<br>Gen. 1:1–2:3<br>Num. 29:35–30:1 | Joshua 1:1–18<br>*Joshua 1:1–9* |
| 13 | Sa | 24 | Be-re'shit | Gen. 1:1–6:8 | Isaiah 42:5–43:10<br>*Isaiah 42:5–21* |
| 19 | F | 30 | New Moon, first day | Num. 28:1–15 | |

*Italics are for Sephardi Minhag.*

## 1990, Oct. 20–Nov. 17] ḤESHWAN (29 DAYS) [5751

| Civil Date | Day of the Week | Jewish Date | SABBATHS, FESTIVALS, FASTS | PENTATEUCHAL READING | PROPHETICAL READING |
|---|---|---|---|---|---|
| Oct. 20 | Sa | Ḥeshwan 1 | Noaḥ; New Moon, second day | Gen. 6:9–11:32 Num. 28:9–15 | Isaiah 66:1–24 |
| 27 | Sa | 8 | Lekh lekha | Gen. 12:1–17:27 | Isaiah 40:27–41:16 |
| Nov. 3 | Sa | 15 | Wa-yera' | Gen. 18:1–22:24 | II Kings 4:1–37 *II Kings 4:1–23* |
| 10 | Sa | 22 | Ḥayye Sarah | Gen. 23:1–25:18 | I Kings 1:1–31 |
| 17 | Sa | 29 | Toledot | Gen. 25:19–28:9 | I Samuel 20:18–42 |

## 1990, Nov. 18–Dec. 17] KISLEW (30 DAYS) [5751

| Civil Date | Day of the Week | Jewish Date | SABBATHS, FESTIVALS, FASTS | PENTATEUCHAL READING | PROPHETICAL READING |
|---|---|---|---|---|---|
| Nov. 18 | S | Kislew 1 | New Moon | Num. 28:1–15 | |
| 24 | Sa | 7 | Wa-yeẓe' | Gen. 28:10–32:3 | Hosea 12:13–14:10 *Hosea 11:7–12:12* |
| Dec. 1 | Sa | 14 | Wa-yishlaḥ | Gen. 32:4–36:43 | Hosea 11:7–12:12 *Obadiah 1:1–21* |
| 8 | Sa | 21 | Wa-yeshev | Gen. 37:1–40:23 | Amos 2:6–3:8 |
| 12–14 | W–F | 25–27 | Hanukkah, first to third days | W Num. 7:1–17 Th Num. 7:18–29 F Num. 7:24–35 | |
| 15 | Sa | 28 | Mi-keẓ; Hanukkah, fourth day | Gen. 41:1–44:17 Num. 7:30–35 | Zechariah 2:14–4:7 |
| 16 | S | 29 | Hanukkah, fifth day | Num. 7:36–47 | |
| 17 | M | 30 | New Moon, first day; Hanukkah, sixth day | Num. 28:1–15 Num. 7:42–47 | |

*Italics are for Sephardi Minhag.*

1990, Dec. 18–Jan. 15, 1991] TEVET (29 DAYS) [5751

| Civil Date | Day of the Week | Jewish Date | SABBATHS, FESTIVALS, FASTS | PENTATEUCHAL READING | PROPHETICAL READING |
|---|---|---|---|---|---|
| Dec. 18 | T | Tevet 1 | New Moon, second day; Hanukkah, seventh day | Num. 28:1–15 Num. 7:48–53 | |
| 19 | W | 2 | Hanukkah, eighth day | Num. 7:54–8:4 | |
| 22 | Sa | 5 | Wa-yiggash | Gen. 44:18–47:27 | Ezekiel 37:15–28 |
| 27 | Th | 10 | Fast of 10th of Tevet | Exod. 32:11–14 43:1–10 (morning and afternoon) | Isaiah 55:6–56:8 (afternoon only) |
| 29 | Sa | 12 | Wa-yehi | Gen. 47:28–50:26 | I Kings 2:1–12 |
| Jan. 5 | Sa | 19 | Shemot | Exod. 1:1–6:1 | Isaiah 27:6–28:13 29:22–23 *Jeremiah 1:1–2:3* |
| 12 | Sa | 26 | Wa-'era' | Exod. 6:2–9:35 | Ezekiel 28:25–29:21 |

*Italics are for Sephardi Minhag.*

# SELECTED ARTICLES OF INTEREST IN RECENT VOLUMES OF THE AMERICAN JEWISH YEAR BOOK

| | |
|---|---|
| The American Jewish Family Today | Steven Martin Cohen 82:136–154 |
| Attitudes of American Jews Toward Israel: Trends Over Time | Eytan Gilboa 86:110–125 |
| The Bitburg Controversy | Deborah E. Lipstadt 87:21–37 |
| California Jews: Data from the Field Polls | Alan M. Fisher and Curtis K. Tanaka 86:196–218 |
| A Century of Conservative Judaism in the United States | Abraham J. Karp 86:3–61 |
| A Century of Jewish History, 1881–1981: The View from America | Lucy S. Dawidowicz 82:3–98 |
| The "Civil Judaism" of Communal Leaders | Jonathan S. Woocher 81:149–169 |
| The Demographic Consequences of U.S. Jewish Population Trends | U.O. Schmelz and Sergio DellaPergola 83:141–187 |
| The Demography of Latin American Jewry | U.O. Schmelz and Sergio DellaPergola 85:51–102 |
| Israelis in the United States: Motives, Attitudes, and Intentions | Dov Elizur 80:53–67 |
| Jewish Education Today | Walter I. Ackerman 80:130–148 |
| Jewish Survival: The Demographic Factors | U.O. Schmelz 81:61–117 |
| Jews in the United States: Perspectives from Demography | Sidney Goldstein 81:3–59 |
| The Labor Market Status of American Jews: Patterns and Determinants | Barry R. Chiswick 85:131–153 |
| Latin American Jewry Today | Judith Laikin Elkin 85:3–49 |

| | |
|---|---|
| Leadership and Decision-making in a Jewish Federation: The New York Federation of Jewish Philanthropies | Charles S. Liebman 79:3–76 |
| Los Angeles Jewry: A Demographic Portrait | Bruce A. Phillips 86:126–195 |
| The National Gallup Polls and American Jewish Demography | Alan M. Fisher 83:111–126 |
| New Perspectives in American Jewish Sociology | Nathan Glazer 87:3–19 |
| The 1981–1982 National Survey of American Jews | Steven Martin Cohen 83:89–110 |
| The Population of Reunited Jerusalem, 1967–1985 | U.O. Schmelz 87:39–113 |
| Recent Jewish Community Population Studies: A Roundup | Gary A. Tobin and Alvin Chenkin 85:154–178 |
| Reform and Conservative Judaism in Israel: A Social and Religious Profile | Ephraim Tabory 83:41–61 |
| Religiosity Patterns in Israel | Calvin Goldscheider and Dov Friedlander 83:3–39 |
| The Social Characteristics of the New York Area Jewish Community, 1981 | Paul Ritterband and Steven M. Cohen 84:128–161 |
| South African Jewry: A Sociodemographic Profile | Sergio DellaPergola and Allie A. Dubb 88:59–140 |
| South African Jews and the Apartheid Crisis | Gideon Shimoni 88:3–58 |
| Soviet Jewry Since the Death of Stalin: A Twenty-five Year Perspective | Leon Shapiro 79:77–103 |
| Trends in Jewish Philanthropy | Steven Martin Cohen 80:29–51 |

## OBITUARIES

| | |
|---|---|
| Leo Baeck | By Max Gruenewald 59:478–82 |
| Jacob Blaustein | By John Slawson 72:547–57 |
| Martin Buber | By Seymour Siegel 67:37–43 |
| Abraham Cahan | By Mendel Osherowitch 53:527–29 |
| Albert Einstein | By Jacob Bronowski 58:480–85 |
| Felix Frankfurter | By Paul A. Freund 67:31–36 |
| Louis Ginzberg | By Louis Finkelstein 56:573–79 |
| Jacob Glatstein | By Shmuel Lapin 73:611–17 |
| Sidney Goldmann | By Milton R. Konvitz 85:401–03 |
| Hayim Greenberg | By Marie Syrkin 56:589–94 |
| Abraham Joshua Heschel | By Fritz A. Rothschild 74:533–44 |
| Horace Meyer Kallen | By Milton R. Konvitz 75:55–80 |
| Mordecai Kaplan | By Ludwig Nadelmann 85:404–11 |
| Herbert H. Lehman | By Louis Finkelstein 66:3–20 |
| Judah L. Magnes | By James Marshall 51:512–15 |
| Alexander Marx | By Abraham S. Halkin 56:580–88 |
| Reinhold Niebuhr | By Seymour Siegel 73:605–10 |
| Joseph Proskauer | By David Sher 73:618–28 |
| Maurice Samuel | By Milton H. Hindus 74:545–53 |
| Leo Strauss | By Ralph Lerner 76:91–97 |
| Max Weinreich | By Lucy S. Dawidowicz 70:59–68 |
| Chaim Weizmann | By Harry Sacher 55:462–69 |
| Stephen S. Wise | By Philip S. Bernstein 51:515–18 |
| Harry Austryn Wolfson | By Isadore Twersky 76:99–111 |

# Index

Abdallah, George Ibrahim, 305, 307
Abécassis, André, 312
Abella, Irving, 256, 264
Abelson, Kassel, 138, 138n
Abileah, Benjamin, 258
Abram, Morris, 194, 205, 213, 224, 225, 226, 227, 228, 357, 358, 364, 424, 425
Abuhatzeira, Aharon, 411
Abzug, Bella, 3
Ackelsberg, Martha, 10, 10n, 13, 14, 14n
Ackerman, Walter, 66n, 68n
Adelman, Howard, 256
Adelman, Penina V., 156n
Adler, Rachel, 3, 9, 9n, 10, 55, 57n
*Afn Shvel,* 508
Aganbegyan, Abel, 355
Agudath Ha'Admorim, 109n
Agudath HaRabbonim, 109n, 123
Agudath Israel of America, 117, 176, 220, 456
  Agudah Women of America-N'Shei Agudath Israel, 456
  Children's Division—Pirchei Agudath Israel, 456
  Girls' Division—Bnos Agudath Israel, 456
  Young Men's Division—Zeirei Agudath Israel, 456
Agudath Israel World Organization, 456
Aguinis, Marcos, 272
Agus, Arlene, 5n, 10, 51, 51n, 55, 55n, 56, 157n
Ahituv, Avraham, 389
Ajzensztadt, Amnon, 268
al-Akliq, Ibrahim, 378

Alderman, Geoffrey, 291
Alfonsín, Raúl, 270, 271, 272, 273, 275
*Algemeiner Journal,* 509
Allen, Jim, 294
Allen, Wayne, 137n
Allied Jewish Federation of Denver, 17n
Allis, Sam, 159n
Alpert, Rebecca T., 142n, 144n
Alpha Epsilon Pi Fraternity, 474
Alternative Information Center, 376
Altmann, Alexander, 515
Alvarez, Abel Ramon Caballero, 404
ALYN—American Society for Handicapped Children in Israel, 479
AMC Cancer Research Center, 476
America-Israel Cultural Foundation, 480
America-Israel Friendship League, 480
American Academy for Jewish Research, 449
American Associates, Ben-Gurion University of the Negev, 480
American Association for Ethiopian Jews, 454
American Association of Rabbis, 456
American Biblical Encyclopedia Society, 449
American Civil Liberties Union (ACLU), 176
American Committee for Israel Peace Center, 225
American Committee for Shaare Zedek Hospital in Jerusalem, 480
American Committee for Shenkar College in Israel, 480
American Committee for the Weizmann Institute of Science, 480

561

American Council for Judaism, 445
American Federation of Jews from Central Europe, 474
American Friends of Haifa University, 480
American Friends of Ramat Hanegev College, 480
American Friends of the Alliance Israélite Universelle, 454
American Friends of the Haifa Maritime Museum, 480
American Friends of the Hebrew University, 480
American Friends of the Israel Museum, 487
American Friends of the Jerusalem Mental Health Center—Ezrath Nashim, 481
American Friends of the Shalom Hartman Institute, 481
American Friends of the Tel Aviv Museum, 481
American Friends of the Tel Aviv University, 481
American Israel Public Affairs Committee (AIPAC), 481
American-Israeli Lighthouse, 481
*The American Israelite,* 512
American Jewish Alternatives to Zionism, 445
*American Jewish Archives,* 512
American Jewish Committee, 40, 167, 173, 212, 223, 226, 351, 445
American Jewish Congress, 37, 167, 168, 173, 223, 224, 226, 424, 425, 446
American Jewish Correctional Chaplains Association, 476
American Jewish Historical Society, 449
*American Jewish History,* 507
American Jewish Joint Distribution Committee—JDC, 454
American Jewish League for Israel, 481
American Jewish Philanthropic Fund, 454
American Jewish Press Association, 449
American Jewish Public Relations Society, 489
American Jewish Society for Service, 476
*American Jewish Times—Outlook,* 512
*American Jewish World,* 508
*American Jewish Year Book* (AJYB), 11, 388, 397, 400, 414, 419, 430, 509
American ORT Federation, 454
American and European Friends of ORT, 454
American Labor ORT, 454
Business and Professional ORT, 454
National ORT League, 455
Women's American ORT, 455
American Physicians Fellowship, 481
American Red Magen David for Israel, 482
American Sephardi Federation, 474
American Society for Jewish Music, 449
American Society for Technion-Israel Institute of Technology, 482
American Society for the Protection of Nature in Israel, 482
American Veterans of Israel, 475
*American Zionist,* 509
American Zionist Federation, 216, 482
American Zionist Youth Foundation, 482
Americans for a Safe Israel, 482
Americans for Progressive Israel, 482
Améry, Jean, 332
Amirav, Moshe, 372
*Amit Woman,* 509
Amit Women, 483
Ampal—American Israel Corporation, 483
Amsellem, Armand, 313
Andrade, Joaquim do Santos, 284
Andreotti, Giulio, 325, 405
Angel, Marc, 148, 149n
Annenberg Research Institute, 456
Anti-Defamation League of B'nai B'rith, 40, 167, 173, 179, 180, 214, 223, 225, 446
Antipov, Yevgeny, 355, 406, 407
Appelfeld, Aharon, 300
Apterman, Zalman, 296
Arad, Alexander, 377
Arad, Moshe, 412

Arafat, Yasir, 197, 203, 204, 368, 372, 377
Arbelli-Almoslino, Shoshana, 395, 396, 413
Arden, Harvey, 114n
Arens, Moshe, 194, 199, 206, 220, 368, 396, 399, 410
Argentina, 270–281
*Arizona Post,* 506
Arjuan, Victor, 377
Aron, Melanie W., 105n
Aron, Minna, 348
Aron, Raymond, 305
Aron, William S., 17n, 76n
Aronin, Douglas, 137n
Aronson, Joseph H., 515
Aryan Nations, 178
ARZA—Association of Reform Zionists of America, 218, 483
Arzt, Edya, 136, 136n
Ascot, Roger, 313
Asher, Samuel H., 17n
Ashour, Khalil, 373
Askoldov, Alexander, 359
al-Assad, Hafez, 183, 355, 407
Association for Jewish Studies, 456
Association for the Social Scientific Study of Jewry, 449
Association of Hillel/Jewish Campus Professionals, 456
Association of Jewish Book Publishers, 450
Association of Jewish Center Workers, 446
Association of Jewish Community Organization Personnel, 476
Association of Jewish Community Relations Workers, 446
Association of Jewish Family and Children's Agencies, 476
Association of Jewish Family and Children's Agency Professionals, 476
Association of Jewish Genealogical Societies, 450
Association of Jewish Libraries, 450
Association of Orthodox Jewish Scientists, 457
Association of Yugoslav Jews in the United States, 475
*Atlanta Jewish Times,* 507
Atlas, Yedidyah, 220
Aubron, Joëlle, 305
*Aufbau,* 509
Auque, Roger, 305
Auschwitz, 178, 311, 332, 333, 334, 363
Avineri, Shlomo, 166, 215, 424
*Avotaynu,* 508
Axelrod, Nathan, 431
Ayyash, Radwan Abu, 373
Azrieli, David, 269

Bachman, Mrs. Seymour, 77n
Bailey, Sidney D., 301
Bain, Harry, 268
Bais Rochel schools, 49
Baldridge, Malcolm, 226
Baltimore Hebrew University, 457
  Baltimore Institute for Jewish Communal Service, 457
  Bernard Manekin School of Undergraduate Studies, 457
  Peggy Meyerhoff Pearlstone School of Graduate Studies, 457
*Baltimore Jewish Times,* 507
Bank Leumi, 414
Barak, Ehud, 431
Barbie, Klaus, 178, 303, 307, 308, 309
Barghouti, Marwan, 373
Bar-Ilan University in Israel, 483
Barilko, J., 281
Barkin, Martin, 255
Baron De Hirsch Fund, 476
Barrett, Stanley, 268
Barron, Harry I., 515
Barschel, Uwe, 336, 346
Bass, Alfie, 302
Bass, Ralph, 515
Bassiouny, Muhammad, 380
Batzdorff, Susanne, 344
Baum, Charlotte, 10, 11n
Bauman, Batya, 16n
el-Baz, Ibrahim, 318
el-Baz, Osama, 291
Beatrix, Queen of the Netherlands, 322
Beck, Evelyn Torton, 16, 16n

Becker, Jurek, 352
Beckermann, Ruth, 346
Beckmann, Max, 345
Beem, Hartog, 323
Be'er, Haim, 427
Begun, Yosif, 357, 358
Beilin, Yossi, 367, 368, 380, 407, 408
Beltran, Carlos, 274
Belzberg, William, 269
Benattar, Albert, 313
Bendor, Avraham, 388
Ben-Horin, Eliashiv, 258
Benn, Nathan, 114n
Ben-Ner, Yitzhak, 427
Benvenisti, Meron, 371
Benz, Wolfgang, 347
Ben-Zion (Weinman), 516
Berenshtain, Yosif, 358
Berg, Alan, 179
Berg, Jack, 301
Berger, David, 256
Berger, Gabriel, 5n, 26n
Berger, Joseph, 123n
Berkey, Jane, 17n
Berkovits, Eliezer, 72n
Berkowitz, Joshua, 119n
Bermant, Chaim, 301
Bernstein, Ellen, 84n
Bernstein, Irving, 41
Bernstein, Louis, 47, 48, 72n, 218, 220
Bernstein, Philip, 68n
Bernstein, Robert M., 516
Berri, Nabih, 208
Beta Yisrael, 424
Betar Zionist Youth Organization, 483
Beth Chayim Chadashim, 158
Beth Medrosh Elyon (Academy of Higher Learning and Research), 457
Beuys, Barbara, 347
Bezek Telecommunications, 414
Biale, Rachel, 43, 43n
Bielsky (Bell), Tuvia, 516
Bienstock, Victor, 516
Bin-Nun, Avihu, 431
Birk, Ellis, 300
Bitkin, Vladimir, 359
*Bitzaron,* 509

Blatman, Yona, 419
Blau, Zena Smith, 38, 39n
Blitt, Pinchas, 269
Bloemendal, Hans, 323
Blumenthal, Aaron H., 131n
B'nai Brith Canada, 491
  Institute for International and Governmental Affairs, 491
  League for Human Rights, 491
B'nai B'rith Hillel Foundations, 457
B'nai B'rith International, 477
  Anti-Defamation League of (see p. 446)
  Career and Counseling Services, 477
  Hillel Foundations, (see p. 457)
  Klutznick Museum (see p. 450)
  Youth Organization (see p. 457)
*B'nai B'rith International Jewish Monthly,* 506
B'nai B'rith Klutznick Museum, 450
*B'nai B'rith Messenger,* 506
B'nai B'rith Women, 477
B'nai B'rith Youth Organization, 457
Bnai Zion—The American Fraternal Zionist Organization, 475
Board of Deputies of British Jews, 293, 294, 295
Boas, Henriette, 323
Bodenheimer, Aron Ronald, 347
Boesky, Ivan, 180
Bohm-Duchen, Monica, 301
Bono, Richard, 84n, 158n
Bookbinder, Hyman, 213, 223
Borowitz, Eugene, 99, 107n
Borowski, Elie, 428
Borwicz, Michel, 314
Boschwitz, Rudy, 210
*Boston Globe,* 368
*Boston Jewish Times,* 508
Bourassa, Robert, 268
Boys Town Jerusalem Foundation of America, 483
Brailovsky, Mikhail, 423
Brailovsky, Viktor, 297, 358, 423
Bram, Morris, 516
Bramson ORT Technical Institute, 457
Brandeis-Bardin Institute, 458

Brandeis University National Women's Committee, 489
Brandt, Willy, 336
Braverman, Jay, 269
Brayer, Menachem M., 49n
Brazil, 282–289
Brenner, Sydney, 302
Brichto, Sidney, 297
Brinkman, Elco, 317, 322
Brith Abraham, 475
Brith Sholom, 475
British Jewish Educational Development, 299
Broadbent, Edward, 265
Broder, Henryk M., 347
Brodsky, Vladimir, 297
Brokaw, Tom, 357
Broner, E. M., 54
Bronfman, Edgar, 226, 227, 272, 357, 358, 364
Bronkhorst, Bernhard, 323
Bronshtain, Shaye, 360
Brott, Alexander, 268
Brott, Boris, 268
Brown, Michael, 268
Brozan, Nadine, 29n
Brucker, Robert, 321
Brutents, Karen, 198
Bubis, Gerald B., 152n
Bubis, Ignatz, 347
Buchanan, Patrick J., 177
Buchris, Albert, 376
*Buffalo Jewish Review,* 509
Bulka, Reuven, 268
*Bulletin Du Congrès Juif Canadien,* 514
The Bund (Argentina), 281
Bunim, Sarah, 58, 58n
Burg, Yosef, 349
Burns, Arthur F., 516
Burton, Sala Galant, 516
Bush, George, 363
Büttner, Ursula, 347

Cafiero, Antonio, 276
Cahn, Judah, 101n
Camp Ramah, 128
Canada, 255–269
Canada-Israel Committee (CIC), 257

Canada-Israel Securities, Ltd., State of Israel Bonds, 491
Canadian Association for Labor Israel (Histadrut), 491
Canadian Foundation for Jewish Culture, 491
Canadian Friends of the Alliance Israélite Universelle, 491
Canadian Friends of the Hebrew University, 491
Canadian Jewish Congress (CJC), 256, 259, 264, 492
*Canadian Jewish Herald,* 514
*Canadian Jewish News,* 514
*Canadian Jewish Outlook,* 514
Canadian ORT Organization, 492
Women's Canadian ORT, 492
Canadian Red Cross Society, 257
Canadian Sephardi Federation, 264, 492
Canadian Young Judaea, 492
*Canadian Zionist,* 514
Canadian Zionist Federation, 263, 492
Bureau of Education and Culture, 492
Cantor, Aviva, 3, 8n, 10, 34, 34n, 41n, 56, 56n
Cantor, Debra S., 53n, 155n
Cantors Assembly, 458
Cantu, Antonio, 421
Caplan, Elinor, 255
Cardin, Nina Beth, 53n, 129n
Cardin, Shoshana, 35, 148, 148n, 220
Carlucci, Frank, 186, 393
Carmi, Daniella, 427
Caro, Anthony, 301
Carpey, Sissy, 144n
Carr, Donald, 264
Carter, Jimmy, 282
Casaroli, Agostino Cardinal, 168
Cashdan, Louis, 269, 517
Cassidy, Bryan, 296
Cassin, René, 313
da Cave, Mosè, 330
*CCAR Journal,* 99
Ceausescu, Nicolae, 201, 365, 370
Cedarbaum, David I., 517
Center for Holocaust Studies, Documentation & Research, 450

Center for Jewish Community Studies, 446
Central Conference of American Rabbis (CCAR), 97n, 99, 100, 101, 102, 104, 106, 146, 223, 229, 231, 458
Central Jewish Welfare Agency of Jews in Germany, 342
Central Sephardic Jewish Community of America, 475
Central Yiddish Culture Organization (CYCO), 450
Chadli, Bendjedid, 307
Chagall, Marc, 359
Chalandon, Albin, 305
Chazan, Robert, 130n
Chenkin, Alvin, 18n
Chernick, Michael, 47n
Chernin, Albert, 224
*Chicago JUF News,* 507
Chirac, Jacques, 303, 306, 307, 310, 404
Chistyakov, Alexei, 355
Chiswick, Barry, 25, 25n
Chouraqui, Nicole, 313
Christian Democrats (Fed. Republic of Germany), 336
Christian Social Union (Fed. Rep. of Germany), 336
Chutzpah (Canada), 265
Cipriani, Georges, 305
Citizens in Support of the Pollards, 214
Citron, Sabina, 260
City of Hope National Medical Center and Beckman Research Institute, 477
CLAL (*see* National Jewish Center for Learning and Leadership)
Claramount, A. Castillo, 409
Clark, Joe, 265
Cleveland College of Jewish Studies, 458
*Cleveland Jewish News,* 512
Cluverius, Wat, 199, 200
Coalition for the Advancement of Jewish Education (CAJE), 458
Coetzee, J.M., 426
Cohen, Burton I., 129n
Cohen, Gerson D., 50, 52n, 53, 129, 132, 133
Cohen, Judith Loeb, 268
Cohen, Percy, 302
Cohen, Saul, 268
Cohen, Sheldon, 269
Cohen, Steven Martin, 9n, 13, 13n, 17n, 41n, 44n, 47, 47n, 63, 76n, 80n, 81n, 87n, 108n, 110, 110n, 115n, 147n, 149n, 153n, 161n, 212
Cohen, Wilbur J., 517
Cohler, Larry, 48n
Cohon, George, 268
Collins, Kenneth, 300
Comay, Amos, 517
Comay, Michael, 432
*Commentary,* 509
Commission on Law and Public Action (COLPA), 111
Commission on Social Action of Reform Judaism, 446
*The Complete Artscroll Siddur,* 119
Conference of Jewish Communal Service (CJCS), 40, 477
Conference of Presidents of Major American Jewish Organizations, 213, 214, 224, 446
Conference on Jewish Material Claims Against Germany, 455
Conference on Jewish Social Studies, 450
Congregation Beth Simchat Torah, 158n
Congregation Bina, 450
Congregation Sha'ar Zahav, 159
Congregation Shaare Tefila, 181
*Congress Monthly,* 509
*Connecticut Jewish Ledger,* 506
*Conservative Judaism,* 10, 509
Consultative Council of Jewish Organizations—CCJO, 446
*Contemporary Jewry,* 509
Conway, Jeremy, 298
Cooper, Abraham, 293
Coordinating Board of Jewish Organizations, 447
Corbett, Robin, 295
Cordes, Rudolf, 207
Corry, John, 39n
Cossiga, Francesco, 325, 405
Cotler, Ariela, 265

INDEX / 567

Cotler, Irwin, 259, 266, 269
Cotterell, Paul, 301
Council for a Beautiful Israel Environmental Education Foundation, 483
Council for Jewish Education, 458
Council of Jewish Federations (CJF), 35, 37, 40, 219, 220, 477
Council of Jewish Organizations in Civil Service, 447
Courtois, Stéphane, 312
Craig, Jean, 179
Craxi, Bettino, 324, 328
Crewe, Ivor, 290, 291
CRIF, the Representative Council of French Jewry, 310
Croiset, Jules, 320
Crown, Richard, 302
Curtis, Tony, 363
Cussins, Manny, 302
Cutler, Phil, 269
Czechoslovakia, 361
Czyrek, Jozef, 364

Dahlan, Mohammad, 373
Dane, Oscar, 517
Danziger, Herbert, 113, 113n
Danziger, Yitzhak, 427
Daroff, Joseph A., 517
Darousha, Abdel Wahab, 411
Daum, Annette, 12n
Davidman, Lynn, 57, 57n, 58
Davidson, Aryeh, 129
d'Avigdor-Goldsmid, James, 302
Davis, Moshe, 69, 302
Dawidowicz, Lucy, 14, 15n
*Dayton Jewish Chronicle,* 512
De Benedetti, Carlo, 326
Decourtray, Albert Cardinal, 311
Decter, Midge, 30, 30n
Dekel, Michael, 371
DellaPergola, Sergio, 18n, 95n, 285, 433n
Delvalle, Eric Arturo, 409
Demjanjuk, John, 178, 317, 419–422
Democratic Front for the Liberation of Palestine (DFLP), 204
Deneman, Hanoch Steve, 377
Denmark, 404

Deri, Arye, 418
de Rijke, Marinus, 316
de Rothschild, Edmund, 326, 363
Dershowitz, Alan M., 215
Derzinskas, Antas, 293
Descelescu, Constantine, 407
Deschenes, Jules, 259, 260
De Sola Pool, David, 119
Dessel, Susan, 41n
d'Estaing, Giscard, 303
*Detroit Jewish News,* 508
Dickson, Brian, 268
Dickstein, Louis, 5n
Dickstein, Stephanie, 53n
Diepgen, Lord Mayor, 338, 345
Diner, Dan, 347
Diner, Hasia, 28n
Dinitz, Simcha, 218, 425
Distel, Barbara, 347
Dobkin, Monty, 301
Dobrin, Mel, 269
Dobrin, Mitzi, 268
Dobrinsky, Herbert, 268
Dobrynin, Anatoly, 357
Doesburg, Johan, 319
Dohanyi Street Temple, 363
Dole, Robert, 210
Dolman, Dick, 320
Donald, Beulah Mae, 179
Donald, Michael, 179
Dorff, Elliot N., 125n
Dorner, Dalia, 419
Dotan, Amira, 3n
Dresel, Alfred S., 302
Dresner, Samuel, 69
Dropsie College for Hebrew and Cognate Learning (*see* Annenberg Research Institute)
Dror, Nathan, 294
Dror—Young Kibbutz Movement—Habonim
    Chavurat Hagalil, 483
    Garin Yarden, Young Kibbutz Movement, 483
Druckman, Haim, 430
Dubinin, Yuri, 355
Duker, Abraham, 65n, 73n, 518

Dulzin, Arye, 217, 414, 425
Dunsing, Marilyn M., 36n

Eban, Abba, 193, 285, 392, 398, 399, 401
Ebbinghaus, Angelika, 347
Ebreo, Guglielmo, 331
*Economic Horizons,* 509
Edelheit, Joseph A., 105n
Edelshtein, Yuli, 265, 368, 423
Edwards, Ruth Dudley, 301
Efron, Benjamin, 70n
Efros, Anatoly, 360
Egozi, Akiva, 268
Egypt, 367, 368, 369, 380, 402, 403
Ehrenberg, Henry, 348
Eilberg, Amy, 11, 49, 53, 133
Eisendrath, Maurice, 70, 70n
Eisenstein, Ira, 139, 139n
Eitan, Rafael, 193, 194, 213, 397
Elazar, Daniel, 45, 45n, 104n, 136n, 152n
Elberg, Shaindele, 269
Eliahu, Mordechai, 219
Elizabeth, Queen of England, 291, 339
Elkann, Jean-Paul, 311
Elkerbout, Ben, 323
Ellenoff, Theodore, 168
Ellenson, David, 123n
Elton, Arnold, 301
Emunah Women of America, 484
Endres, Elisabeth, 346
Engell, Hans, 404
Engelman, Uriah Z., 66n
Epelbaum, Renee, 277
Erb, Irit, 193
Erez, Shaike, 381, 382
Erlick, Steve, 300
Etra, Max J., 518
Eylon, Pinhas, 431
Ezra, E. D., 300
Ezrat Nashim, 9, 130

Fackenheim, Emil, 267
Fahd, King of Saudi Arabia, 202, 292, 307
Fainlight, Harry, 301
Fainlight, Ruth, 301
Falk, Marcia, 10
Faris, Jamil, 376
Farrakhan, Louis, 182, 183
Fassbinder, Rainer Werner, 319
Federal Republic of Germany, 336–348, 404
Federated Council of Israel Institutions—FCII, 484
Federation of Jewish Men's Clubs, 458
Fedorenko, Feodor S., 177
Fein, Leonard, 225
Feinstein, Elaine, 301
Feinstein, Moses, 108n, 123n
Feinstein, Nina Bieber, 53n
Feirstein, Ricardo, 273
Feldman, Avigdor, 391
Finestone, Rita, 268
Fini, Massimo, 326
Fink, Reuven, 124n
Finkielkraut, Alain, 312
Finta, Imre, 260
Firestone, Shulamith, 7, 7n
Fishbein, Irwin, 101, 105n
Fisher, Eugene, 171
Fishman, Sylvia Barack, 3, 17n, 36n, 49n, 77n, 84n
Fiterman, Jacobo, 272
Fitzwater, Marlin, 208, 393, 400
Flapan, Simha, 431
Flerova, Inessa, 423
Fliss, Sharon, 53n
Fonda, Jane, 422
Foxman, Abraham, 214, 215, 224
Fraenkel, Josef, 302
France, 303–314, 404
Frank, Leonard, 319
Frank, Shirley, 31, 31n
Frankenburg, Naomi, 269
Free Democrats (Fed. Republic of Germany), 336
Free Sons of Israel, 475
Freedman, Julius, 302
Freehof, Solomon, 105
Freeson, Reg, 300
Freiman, Lawrence, 269
Frérot, Max, 305
Friderichs, Hans, 336

INDEX / 569

Fridman, Elena, 422
Fried, Sylvia Fuks, 5n
Friedan, Betty, 3, 4, 4n, 6, 6n, 11, 12n
Friedland, Eric, 98n
Friedlander, Moses, 302
Friedman, Debra, 77n
Friedman, Peter, 76n, 82n
Friedman, Reena Sigman, 35n, 40n, 156n
Friedman, Rosemary, 301
Friedman, Theodore, 143n
Friends of the Israel Defense Forces, 484
Friends of Labor Israel, 484
Friends of Pioneering Israel, 492
Friss, Debby, 40n
Fuchs-Kreimer, Nancy, 142n
Fund for Higher Education, 484
Fürst, Michael, 341
Fuss, Alisa Ilse, 348

Gainsborough, J. R., 301
Galinski, Heinz, 347
Gallob, Ben, 30n
Gans, Ileana, 38n
Gans, Moses (Max), 323
Garfiel, Evelyn, 69
Gary, Dorit Phyllis, 114n
*Gates of Mitzvah,* 102
*Gates of Prayer,* 98, 99
Gaza Strip, 377–386
Gecas, Antanas, 293
Geer, Lois, 17n, 76n
Gelb, Max, 518
Geller, Victor B., 75n
Gemayel, Amin, 307
*Genesis 2,* 508
Genscher, Hans-Dietrich, 336, 338, 339, 403
Gerlis, Daphne, 301
Gerlis, Leon, 301
German Democratic Republic, 338, 349–352
Germani, Gino, 274
Gerol, Ilya, 257
Gerold-Tucholsky, Mary, 348
Gershon, Karen, 301
GET (Getting Equitable Treatment), 59

Ghah, Boutros, 291
Gierowski, Jozef, 364
Gillman, Neil, 125, 125n
Gilman, Susan, 45n
Giordano, Ralph, 347
Girard, Patrick, 312
Gittelson, Natalie, 111n
Givat Haviva Educational Foundation, 484
Glanz, David, 151n
Glaser, Joseph, 107
Glass, Carol, 53n, 157n
Glucksman, André, 313
Godefroy-Waxman, Phyllis, 268
Godfrey, Naomi, 158n
Goeree, Jenny, 323
Goeree, Lucas, 323
Gold, Aaron, 134n
Gold, Alan B., 268
Gold, Alison Lesly, 323
Gold, Bert, 224
Gold, Doris B., 8n, 34, 34n
Golda Meir Association, 484
Goldberg, David, 273
Goldberg, Julian, 302
Goldbloom, Richard, 268
Goldbloom, Victor, 268, 269
Goldenberg, Judith Plaskow (*see* Plaskow)
Golditch, Yitzchak, 302
Goldman, Ari L., 143n
Goldscheider, Calvin, 18n, 25n, 67n, 86n, 161n
Goldsmith, James, 326
Goldstein, David, 302
Goldstein, Ira, 17n, 76n
Goldstein, Sidney, 67n, 86n
Golub, Mollie F., 518
Gomlevsky, Ronaldo, 286, 287
Gomulka, Wladyslaw, 364
Goodblatt, Morris S., 69n
Goodhill, Victor, 52n
Gorbachev, Mikhail, 198, 227, 296, 338, 339, 353, 354, 355, 357, 358, 361, 363, 406, 407
Gordimer, Nadine, 301
Gordis, Robert, 69n, 135, 138, 138n, 143n

Gordji, Wahid, 306
Gordon, Albert, 64n, 65n, 68n
Gordon, Marion Siner, 52n
Goren, Shmuel, 378, 379, 382
Goria, Giovanni, 324
Gornick, Vivian, 7, 8n
Gotlieb, Allan, 268
Gottlieb, Lynn, 156n
Gottschalk, Alfred, 107
Gould, Bernard S., 518
Graetz, Roberto, 288
Graham, Edward, 98n
Grant, Julius, 422
Grassley, Charles, 210
Gratz College, 459
Great Britain, 290–302, 405
*Greater Phoenix Jewish News*, 506
Greece, 405
Green, Arthur, 11, 11n, 128, 141, 141n, 157n, 231
Greenbat, Alan, 294
Greenberg, Blu, 10, 29, 29n, 42n, 54, 54n
Greenberg, Irving, 63n, 147, 147n, 149, 149n
Greenberg, Simon, 132n
Greenblatt, Janet, 17n, 77n
Greenblum, Joseph, 65n, 86n
Greene, Lorne, 269
Greenfeld, William, 126n
Greenfield, Libby, 268
Grinspun, Bernardo, 272
Groeneman, Sid, 15, 15n, 28n, 36n
Gromyko, Anatoly, 356
Gross, Rita M., 157n
Grossman, David, 427
Grossman, Ethel, 269
Grossman, Larry, 255
Grossman, Vassili, 311
Gruss, Caroline, 518
Gur-Arieli, Israel, 258
Gurock, Jeffrey, 117n, 118n
Gutkin, Harry, 268
Gutkin, Mildred, 268
Guttman, Louis, 518
Gyorke, Jozsef, 362

*Ha'aretz*, 195, 367, 372, 376, 384, 386, 399, 414

Habash, George, 204
Habich, Jakob, 177
Habonim-Dror North America, 484
*Hadarom*, 509
*Hadassah Magazine*, 57, 509
Hadassah, The Women's Zionist Organization of America, 484
Hashachar, 485
Hadassah—WIZO Organization of Canada, 264, 492
*Hadoar*, 509
Hall, Monty, 268
Halperin, Irving, 269
Hamadei, Mohammed Ali, 207
Hammer, Zevulun, 396, 406, 417
Hanani, Ahmed, 376
Hand, W. Brevard, 173
Handelman, Susan, 14, 14n
Hannoun, Michel, 305
Harding, John, 301
Harish, Yosef, 415, 430
Harmelim, Yosef, 389
Harris, Cyril, 298
Harris, David, 228
Harris, Helen, 301
Harris, Lis, 114n
Harris, Rivkah, 52n
Harris, Rosemary, 301
Hashomer Hatzair, Socialist Zionist Youth Movement, 485
Hassan, King of Morocco, 291, 307
Hassan, Lamia Maraf, 285
Hassin, Mahmed Abdel-Rahman, 377
Hauptman, Judith, 10, 11
Haut, Rivkeh, 47, 47n, 122n
Havurat Shalom, 150
Hawatmeh, Naif, 204
Hawke, Bob, 409
Hayoun, Maurice-Ruben, 312
Hebrew Arts School, 450
Hebrew College, 459
Hebrew Culture Foundation, 451
Hebrew Theological College, 459
Hebrew Union College-Jewish Institute of Religion, 50, 70, 70n, 103, 104, 459
    American Jewish Archives, 459
    American Jewish Periodical Center, 459

INDEX / 571

Edgar F. Magnin School of Graduate Studies, 459
Jerome H. Louchheim School of Judaic Studies, 459
Nelson Glueck School of Biblical Archaeology, 460
Rhea Hirsch School of Education, 460
School of Education, 460
School of Graduate Studies, 460
School of Jewish Communal Service, 460
School of Jewish Studies, 460
School of Sacred Music, 460
Skirball Museum, 460
*Hebrew Watchman,* 513
Heenen-Wolff, Susann, 347
Heifetz, Jascha, 519
Heilman, Samuel, 110, 110n, 115n
Heimowitz, Joseph, 115n
Heinrich, Eich, 275
Heintz, Aryeh L., 321
Heitmeyer, Wilhelm, 340
Helfgott, Esther Altshul, 136n
Hellner, Frank, 300
Helmreich, William, 108n, 109n, 110, 110n, 117n, 118n
Hendrix, Nancy, 76n
Herberg, Will, 74, 75n
*Heritage-Southwest Jewish Press,* 506
Hertz, Miriam, 5n
Hertzberg, Arthur, 67n, 213
Herut party (Israel), 426
Herut Zionists of America, 224, 485
Herzliah-Jewish Teachers Seminary, 460
Graduate School of Jewish Studies, 460
Jewish People's University of the Air, 460
Herzog, Chaim, 170, 291, 325, 339, 393, 403, 404, 405, 406, 409, 416
Heschel, Susannah, 11, 11n, 12n, 128, 128n, 156n
Hess, Walter, 264
Heth, Meir, 414
HIAS, 455
Hibey, Richard, 192
Hier, Marvin, 293

Hill, Charles, 201
Hillel, Edward, 268
Hillel, Shlomo, 325, 415, 416
Himmelfarb, Milton, 52n
Hirsch, John, 105n
Hirsch, Rudolf, 352
Hirsch, Samson Raphael, 49
Histadrut (Federation of Labor—Israel), 412, 413
Histadruth Ivrith of America, 451
Hitachduth HaRabbonim HaHaredim, 109n
Hnatyshyn, Ray, 259, 260
Hoffman, Jan, 114n
Hofi, Yitzhak, 389
Holocaust Center of the United Jewish Federation of Greater Pittsburgh, 451
Holocaust Memorial Resource & Education Center of Florida, 451
Holocaust-related groups:
American Federation of Jews from Central Europe, Inc., 474
Center for Holocaust Studies, Documentation & Research, 450
Conference on Jewish Material Claims Against Germany, Inc., 455
Holocaust Center of Greater Pittsburgh, 451
Holocaust Memorial Center of Florida, 451
Jewish Restitution Successor Organization, 455
Martyrs Memorial & Museum of the Holocaust, 452
New York Holocaust Memorial Commission, 453
Research Foundation for Jewish Immigration, Inc., 453
St. Louis Center for Holocaust Studies, 453
Simon Wiesenthal Center, 474
Thanks to Scandinavia, Inc., 455
U.S. Holocaust Memorial Council, 453
Holy Blossom Temple (Canada), 266
Honecker, Erich, 338, 342, 349
Hope Center for the Developmentally Disabled, 477

Hornstein, Benjamin S., 519
Horodisch, Abraham, 323
Horovitz, Michael, 301
Horowitz, Stanley, 216
Hosek, Chaviva, 255
Houseknecht, Sharon K., 20n
Howe, Geoffrey, 291, 296
Hoyo, José Azcona, 409
Huberman, Steven, 76n
*Humanistic Judaism,* 508
Hungary, 361, 362, 407
Hurd, Douglas, 293
Hurvitz, Yigael, 411
Hussein, King of Jordan, 197, 198, 199, 200, 202, 203, 204, 291, 292, 307, 367, 368, 374, 377, 392, 405, 410
al-Husseini, Faisal, 372
Hyams, Cecil, 302
Hyman, Paula, 3, 8n, 10, 11, 11n, 30

Iancu, O., 359
*Illiana News,* 507
Imrey, Freda, 67n
*Index to Jewish Periodicals,* 512, 513
*Indiana Jewish Post and Opinion,* 507
Inouye, Daniel, 215
Institute for Computers in Jewish Life, 461
*Intermountain Jewish News,* 506
International Conference of Jewish Communal Service (*see* World Conference of Jewish Communal Service)
International Council on Jewish Social and Welfare Services, 477
Ioffe, Alex, 265
Ioffee, Dima, 297
Iran-*Contra* affair, 188–192, 222, 392, 400–402
Ish-Kassit, Moshe, 431
Iskowitz, Gershon, 269
Israel, 170, 171, 183, 184, 185, 186–211, 212–226, 283, 292, 318, 325, 339, 349, 355, 356, 366–432
Israel Aircraft Industries, 394
Israel Chemicals, 414
*Israel Horizons,* 509
Israel Museum, 427

*Israel Quality,* 509
Israel, Sherry, 17n, 76n
Israeli, Julius, 258
Italy, 324–335
Ivry, Itzhak, 519
*Izvestiia,* 353, 355

Jackson, Jesse, 182, 183
Jackson-Vanik Amendment, 227, 358
Jacob, François, 312
Jacob, Walter, 106n
Jacobs, Julian G., 300
Jacobs, Louis, 299
Jacobson, Dan, 301
Jaffe, Mitchell, 262
Jahnke, Jutta, 352
Jakobovits, Immanuel, 294, 297, 301
Janowitz, Naomi, 156n, 157n
Japhet, Ernest, 414
Jaroslavsky, Cesar, 272
Jaruzelski, Wojciech, 363
Jean, Grand Duke of Luxembourg, 405
*Jerusalem Post,* 215, 369, 370, 410, 412, 424
Jewish Academy of Arts and Sciences, 451
*Jewish Action,* 509
*Jewish Advocate,* 508
Jewish Agency, 216, 217, 280, 414, 425
*Jewish and Female,* 12
Jewish Blind Society (Gr. Britain), 295
*Jewish Book Annual,* 509
*Jewish Book World,* 509
Jewish Braille Institute of America, 478
*Jewish Braille Institute Voice,* 509
*Jewish Braille Review,* 509
*The Jewish Catalog,* 57, 128, 157
Jewish Chautauqua Society, 461
*Jewish Chronicle* (London), 291, 292, 294
*Jewish Chronicle of Pittsburgh,* 513
*Jewish Civic Press* (Ga.), 507
*Jewish Civic Press* (La.), 507
*Jewish Civic Press* (Tex.), 513
*Jewish Community News,* 507
*Jewish Community Voice,* 508
Jewish Conciliation Board of America, 478

*Jewish Current Events,* 509
*Jewish Currents,* 509
*Jewish Eagle* (Canada), 514
*Jewish Education,* 510
Jewish Education in Media, 461
Jewish Education Service of North America, 461
*Jewish Exponent,* 513
Jewish Feminist Organization, 10
Jewish Floridian Group, 507
*Jewish Forward,* 510
*Jewish Frontier,* 510
Jewish Fund for Justice, 478
*Jewish Guardian,* 510
*Jewish Herald-Voice,* 513
*Jewish Horizon,* 508
Jewish Immigrant Aid Services, 256
Jewish Immigrant Aid Services of Canada (JIAS), 492
*Jewish Journal* (Calif.), 506
*Jewish Journal* (Fla.), 507
*Jewish Journal* (N.Y.), 510
*Jewish Journal of San Antonio,* 513
Jewish Labor Bund, 475
Jewish Labor Committee, 447
National Trade Union Council for Human Rights, 447
*Jewish Ledger,* 510
Jewish Ministers Cantors Association of America, 461
Jewish Museum, 451
*Jewish Music Notes,* 510
Jewish National Fund of America, 485
Jewish National Fund of Canada (Keren Kayemeth Le'Israel), 492
*Jewish News* (Calif.), 506
*Jewish News* (N.J.), 508
*Jewish Observer* (N.Y.C.), 146, 147, 510
*Jewish Observer* (Syracuse), 510
Jewish Peace Fellowship, 447
*Jewish Post & News* (Canada), 514
*Jewish Post and Renaissance,* 510
*Jewish Press* (Nebraska), 508
*Jewish Press* (N.Y.), 510
Jewish Publication Society, 451
*Jewish Quarterly Review,* 513
Jewish Reconstructionist Foundation, 461

Federation of Reconstructionist Congregations and Havurot, 461
Reconstructionist Rabbinical Association, 461
Reconstructionist Rabbinical College (*see* p. 465)
*Jewish Record,* 508
*Jewish Reporter* (Mass.), 508
*Jewish Reporter* (Nev.), 508
Jewish Restitution Successor Organization, 455
*Jewish Social Studies,* 510
*Jewish Spectator,* 506
*Jewish Standard,* 508
*Jewish Standard* (Canada), 514
*Jewish Star* (Calif.), 506
*Jewish Star* (N.J.), 508
Jewish Teachers Association—Morim, 462
*Jewish Telegraphic Agency Community News Reporter,* 510
*Jewish Telegraphic Agency Daily News Bulletin,* 510
Jewish Telegraphic Agency, 513
*Jewish Telegraphic Agency Weekly News Digest,* 510
Jewish Theological Seminary of America, 50, 52, 52n, 53, 68, 69, 74, 230, 462
Albert A. List College of Jewish Studies, 462
Cantors Institute and Seminary College of Jewish Music, 462
Department of Radio and Television, 462
Graduate School, 462
Jerusalem Campus, JTS, 462
Jewish Museum (*see* p. 451)
Louis Finkelstein Institute for Religious and Social Studies, 462
Melton Research Center for Jewish Education, 462
National Ramah Commission, 462
Prozdor, 463
Rabbinical School, 463
Saul Lieberman Institute of Jewish Research, 463

Schocken Institute for Jewish Research, 463
University of Judaism, 463
*Jewish Times,* 507
*Jewish Times of the Greater Northeast,* 513
*Jewish Transcript,* 513
*Jewish Veteran,* 507
Jewish War Veterans of the United States of America, 447
National Memorial, 447
*Jewish Week* (N.Y.), 510
*Jewish Weekly News,* 508
Jewish Welfare Board (Gr. Britain), 295
*Jewish Western Bulletin* (Canada), 514
*Jewish World* (Fla.), 507
*Jewish World* (N.Y.), 510
Jibril, Ahmed, 204, 385, 387
Jick, Leon A., 69n, 70n
John Paul II, Pope, 165, 166, 169, 170, 183, 230, 260, 295, 311, 330, 343, 363, 406
Johnson, Paul, 300
Joint Distribution Committee, 362
Jonas, Hans, 348
Jordan, 366, 367, 368, 369, 370, 371
Josephine-Charlotte, Grand Duchess of Luxembourg, 405
*Journal of Jewish Communal Service,* 508
*Journal of Psychology and Judaism* (Canada), 514
*Journal of Reform Judaism,* 510
*Journal of the North Shore Jewish Community,* 508
Judah L. Magnes Museum—Jewish Museum of the West, 451
Judaica Captioned Film Center, 451
*Judaism,* 510
Jung, Leo, 519
JWB, 478
   Jewish Book Council (*see* p. 452)
   Jewish Chaplains Council, 478
   Jewish Music Council (*see* p. 452)
   Lecture Bureau (*see* p. 452)
JWB Chaplaincy Board, 147
*JWB Circle,* 510
JWB Jewish Book Council, 452

JWB Jewish Music Council, 452
JWB Lecture Bureau, 452

Kach party (Israel), 384
Kadar, Janos, 361
Kadima (Canada), 264
Kadushin, Evelyn Garfiel, 519
Kagedan, Allan, 222
Kagen, Edward, 35n
Kahane, Meir, 415, 416
Kahn, Jean, 313
Kamenszain, Tamara, 273
Kamerman, Sheila, 30, 31n
Kamil, Oren, 387
Kaniuk, Yoram, 427
*Kansas City Jewish Chronicle,* 508
Kanter, Ron, 255
Kaplan, Jacob M., 520
Kaplan, Lawrence, 121, 121n
Kaplan, Mendel, 425
Kaplan, Mordecai, 44, 71, 74, 135n, 139, 140, 141, 142, 143n, 144
Karchmer, Esther, 360
Karp, Abraham, 134n
Katchen, Rosalie, 5n
Katz, Dovid, 300
Katzin, Ephraim, 275
Katzin, Olga, 302
Katzner, J. Benjamin, 520
Kaufman, Debra Renee, 5n, 57, 57n
Kaufman, Gerald, 292
Kaufman, Mark, 359–360
Kaye, Danny, 520
Kaye, David, 269
Keegstra, James, 255, 258
Keller, Jacqueline, 313
Kelman, Wolfe, 50, 114n
Kemp, Jack, 210
Kenaz, Yehoshua, 427
*Kentucky Jewish Post and Opinion,* 507
Keren Or, 485
Kertzer, Morris N., 70n, 72n, 73n
Kessler, David, 300
Kessner, Carole, 44n
Keyserling, Leon, 520
Al-Khazraji, Majid, 181
*Kibbutz Journal,* 510
Kimche, David, 188, 190, 191, 401

INDEX / 575

Kinnock, Neil, 292
Kirchmann, Karl, 275
Kirshblum, I. Usher, 131n
Klagsbrun, Francine, 52n, 134n
Klaperman, Gilbert, 230
Klarsfeld, Serge, 178
Klatzkin, Raphael, 431
Klein, Isaac, 135
Klein, Shmuel Yaakov, 268
Kleinberg, Maurice S., 520
Kligsburg, Moses, 65n
Klutznick, Philip M., 225
Koch, Edward, 182, 362
Koch, Gertrud, 347
Koenigsberg, Gary, 159n
Koffler, Murray, 269
Kohl, Helmut, 166, 336, 338, 403, 404
*Kol Hat'nua,* 510
Kollek, Teddy, 257, 404, 406, 417
Koltun, Elizabeth, 10, 10n, 52n, 155n, 157n
Kopelowitz, Lionel, 295
Korn, Bertram W., 66n, 97n
Korsunsky, Boris, 360
Kosakoff, Reuven, 521
*Kosher Directory,* 510
*Kosher Directory, Passover Edition,* 510
Kosmin, Barry, 80, 80n
Kovner, Abba, 431
Kramer, Lotte, 301
Kranzler, Gershon, 116n, 117n, 120n
Krauthammer, Charles, 215
Kreitman, Benjamin, 219, 222
Kreutzer, Franklin, 230
Krivorutskii, Peisakh (Piotr Moiseevich), 360
Kubert, Joe, 112n
Kugelmann, Cilly, 347
Ku Klux Klan, 178, 179, 182
*Kultur un Lebn—Culture and Life,* 510
Kupovetskii, Mark, 356
Kutschmann, Walter, 275
Kuzmack, Linda Gordon, 32, 32n
Kwinter, Monte, 255

Labor Alignment party (Israel), 223, 369, 410, 411, 413
Labor Zionist Alliance, 485
Labor Zionist Alliance (Canada), 264
Labor Zionist Movement of Canada, 493
Lafontaine, Oskar, 336
Lahad, Antoine, 209
Lambsdorff, Count, 336
*Lamishpaha,* 510
Lamm, Norman, 72n, 123n
Landau, Dennis, 301
Landau, Moshe, 389, 398
Landau Commission, 389, 390
Landy, David, 269
Lane, David, 179
Lanzmann, Claude, 317
Lapidot, Amos, 431
Larouche, Lyndon H., Jr., 179
*Las Vegas Israelite,* 508
Lautenberg, Frank, 210, 368
Lavendar, Abraham D., 32n
Lavi Project, 195, 196, 392, 394–396
Layton, Irving, 268
Lazar, Gyorgy, 362
Lazare, Lucien, 312
Leader, Harry, 302
League for Labor Israel, 485
League for Yiddish, 452
Lebanon, 172, 367, 373, 386, 387
Lebeau, William, 126n
Leff, Bertram, 116n
Lehmann, William, 351
Leifer, Daniel, 155n
Leifer, Myra, 155n
Lenzon, Viktor, 360
Leo Baeck Institute, 452
Léotard, François, 303
Le Pen, Jean-Marie, 295, 303, 304, 309
Lerner, Alexander, 296, 357, 358
Lerner, Anne Lapidus, 11, 16, 16n, 136n
Lerner, Motti, 426
Lerner, Stephen C., 126, 136n
Lessing, Theodore, 352
Levi, Primo, 332, 333, 334
Levi Arthritis Hospital, 478
Levich, Benjamin G., 521
Levin, Dov, 419, 420
Levin, Monty, 302
Levin, Yakov, 358
Levinas, Emmanuel, 312

Levine, Jacqueline K., 10, 35, 35n, 40, 40n
Levine, Naomi, 41
Levinson, Nathan Peter, 348
Levitas, Irving, 521
Levitt, Cyril, 267
Levy, A. B., 302
Levy, B. Barry, 112n
Lévy, Bernard-Henri, 312
Levy, David, 396, 410
Levy, Harold, 302
Levy, Moshe, 431
Levy, Robert C., 17n
Lew, Myer, 302
Lewis, Shalom, 126
Libai, David, 390
Lichten, Joseph I., 521
Liebman, Charles, 52, 52n, 53, 65n, 71n, 73n, 74n, 81n, 108, 108n, 109, 109n, 110, 116n, 117, 117n, 121n, 127, 127n, 161n
Lieff, Miriam, 269
Lifshitz, Uri, 427
Lifshitz, Vladimir, 358, 423
Ligachev, Yegor, 354
Likud party (Israel), 223, 367, 369, 410, 411, 412, 413
*Likutim,* 510
Lilienthal, David, 322
*Lilith—The Jewish Women's Magazine,* 11, 511
Lind, Jacov, 301
Lindwer, Willy, 323
Linnas, Karl, 176, 177, 355
Linzer, Norman, 32n
Lipman, Eugene, 231
Lipman, Sonia, 302
Lipsker, Eliyahu Akiva, 269
List, Albert A., 521
Litman, Jane, 54, 55n
Littman, Louis, 302
Litvin, Bernard, 72n
Livni, Menahem, 416
*Long Island Jewish World,* 511
Lookstein, Haskel, 220, 229, 230
Lorscheiter, Ivo, 284, 289
Losonci, Andras, 362
Losonczi, Pal, 362

Löw-Beer, Martin, 347
Lowbury, Edward, 301
Lozinski, Ezra, 269
Lubavitch movement, 57, 72, 112, 113, 114, 120, 220, 463
Lubbers, Ruud (Rudolf), 315
Lubeck, Jackie, 427
Lucas, Lawrence, 182
Luckner, Gertrud, 344
Lustiger, Jean, 289
Luye, Li, 408
*La Luz* (Argentina), 281

*Ma'ariv,* 371
MacGregor, John, 298
Machne Israel, 463
Macke, Anne S., 20n
al-Maganda, Mahmed Alian, 377
Magarik, Alexei, 358
Magen David Adom, 257
Magida, Arthur J., 148n
Magidson, Beverly, 133n, 134
Mai, Arkady, 358
Maimonides School, 49
Malle, Louis, 311
Malz, Yaakov, 389, 431
Mancroft, Lord, 302
Mandel, Arnold, 313
Mann, Fredric R., 521
Mann, Theodore, 224, 424
Manos, David, 375
Marcan, Peter, 301
Marder, Janet R., 159n
Margrethe II, Queen of Denmark, 404
Mariasin, Alexander, 265
Mariasin, Lea, 265
Markowitz, Yaakov, 429
Marmur, Dow, 266
Marrus, Michael, 267
Marsh, John, 399
Marshall, John, 296
Martin, Bernard, 66n, 71n
*Martyrdom and Resistance,* 511
Martyrs Memorial & Museum of the Holocaust, 452
Maslin, Simeon, 103n
al-Masri, Zafr, 376
Massarwa, Mohammed, 431

Matas, Carol, 268
Matas, David, 268
Matt, Hershel, 126, 522
Matthews, Robert T., 179
May, Archbishop John L., 168
Mayer, Daniel, 361
Mayer, Egon, 5n, 93n, 95, 95n, 96, 115n, 117n, 119n
Mayer Museum of Islamic Art, 427
McCann, James, 77n
Mechtersheimer, A., 338
Meese, Edwin, 177
Meguid, Esmat Abdel, 198, 366, 369, 402
Mehler, Barry Alan, 159n
Meiman, Inna, 357
Mellor, David, 291
*Melton Journal,* 511
Memorial Foundation for Jewish Culture, 452
Menco, Frieda Brommet, 321
Mendelevich, Yosef, 227
Menem, Carlos, 271
Ménigon, Nathalie, 305
Menuhin, Yehudi, 302
Mercaz, 218, 485
Mercaz Canada, 264
Merkos L'inyonei Chinuch, 463
Meroz, Yohanan, 347
Mesivta Yeshiva Rabbi Chaim Berlin Rabbinical Academy, 463
Mesorah Publications, 112
Meth, Arthur, 105n
Metzenbaum, Howard, 210
Metzner, Ralph, 160n
Meyer, Marshall, 277, 286
*M'Godolim: The Jewish Quarterly,* 513
*Miami Jewish Tribune,* 507
Miarri, Muhammad, 416
Michael, Sammy, 427
Michel, Sonya, 10, 11n
*Midstream,* 511
Mikardo, Ian, 300
Mikes, George, 302
Milgrom, Ida, 265
Miller, Israel, 349
Miller, Shoshana, 219, 411, 417, 418

Millet, Juan Carlos, 276
Milo, Ronnie, 417, 418
Mindlin, Murray, 302
Minkoff, Beverly, 522
Mintz, Alan, 128, 151, 151n
Mintz, Louis, 302
Mirsky, Norman, 103n
Mirvish, Ed, 268
*Missouri Jewish Post,* 508
Mitin, Mark, 360
Mitterrand, François, 303, 306, 307, 339, 368, 404, 430
Mitzna, Avraham, 375, 431
Mizrachi-Hapoel Hamizrachi Organization of Canada, 493
Modai, Yitzhak, 396
*Modern Jewish Studies Annual,* 511
*Moment,* 219, 507
Momigliano, Arnaldo Dante, 302, 332, 334
Mond, Zvi, 268
*Le Monde,* 310
Monson, Rela Geffen, 31, 31n, 45, 45n, 104n, 127n, 136n, 152n
Moonman, Eric, 300
Moonman, Jane, 300
Moore, Deborah Dash, 64n
Moran, Barbara K., 8n
Morgan, Michael, 268
Mormons' Jerusalem Center for Near Eastern Studies, 419
Moses, Avraham, 374
Moses, Ofra, 374
*Moshiach Times,* 112
Mubarak, Hosni, 197, 198, 202, 366, 369, 370, 402
Mulroney, Brian, 255, 260, 265
*Mundo Israelita* (Argentina), 281
Murphy, Richard, 197, 201, 393
Musa, Saeed, 204
Musaph, Herman, 321
Muskie, Edmund, 190

Na-amat Pioneer Women (Canada), 264
Na'amat USA, The Women's Labor Zionist Organization of America, 486
*Na'amat Woman,* 511

Nabati, Galina, 297
Nachmann, Werner, 341, 342
Nadel, Jack, 522
Nadgorny, Boris, 297
Nafsu, Izat, 388, 390
Nagy, Gabor, 362
Nakash, William, 430, 431
Nathan, Joan, 111n
Nathan, Otto, 522
National Association of Jewish Family, Children's and Health Professionals, 478
National Association of Jewish Vocational Services, 478
National Committee for Furtherance of Jewish Education, 463
National Committee for Labor Israel—Histadrut, 486
National Conference on Soviet Jewry, 226, 447
  Soviet Jewry Research Bureau, 448
National Congress of Jewish Deaf, 478
National Council for Soviet Jewry, 228
National Council of Jewish Prison Chaplains (see American Jewish Correctional Chaplains Association)
National Council of Jewish Women, 479
National Council of Jewish Women of Canada, 493
National Council of Young Israel, 109n, 464
  American Friends of Young Israel Synagogues in Israel, 464
  Armed Forces Bureau, 464
  Employment Bureau, 464
  Institute for Jewish Studies, 464
  Young Israel Collegiates and Young Adults, 464
  Young Israel Youth, 464
National Democratic party (Fed. Rep. of Germany), 336
National Foundation for Jewish Culture, 452
National Front (France), 303, 304
National Front (Gr. Britain), 295
National Hebrew Culture Council, 452
National Institute for Jewish Hospice, 479
National Jewish Center for Immunology and Respiratory Medicine, 479
National Jewish Center for Learning and Leadership—CLAL, 464
National Jewish Coalition, 448
National Jewish Commission on Law and Public Affairs (COLPA), 448
National Jewish Committee on Scouting, 479
National Jewish Community Relations Advisory Council, 40, 167, 169, 448
National Jewish Girl Scout Committee, 479
National Jewish Hospitality Committee, 464
National Jewish Information Service for the Propagation of Judaism, 465
National Jewish Population Study, 17, 77, 83
*National Jewish Post and Opinion,* 507
National Joint Community Relations Committee of Canadian Jewish Congress, 493
National Organization of Labor Students (NOLS), 292
National Organization of Women (NOW), 7
National Union of Students (NUS), 293
National Yiddish Book Center, 453
Navon, Yitzhak, 413
*Near East Report,* 507
Neher, André, 312
Ner Israel Rabbinical College, 465
The Netherlands, 315–323
Netherlands Zionist Organization, 321
Neuman, Elias, 275
Neuman, Isaac, 351
Neusner, Jacob, 69n, 70n, 128, 128n, 212
Neves, Tancredo, 282
New Israel Fund, 60, 486
New Jewish Agenda, 448
*New Menorah,* 160, 513
New York Board of Rabbis, 229

INDEX / 579

New York Holocaust Memorial Commission, 453
*New York Times*, 147, 168, 173, 185, 188, 189, 190, 192, 199, 200, 203, 213, 215, 224, 402
*New Yorker,* 114
*Nice Jewish Girls,* 16
Niepomniashchy, Mark, 358
Nimrodi, Yaacov, 190, 401
Nir, Amiram, 189, 190, 400, 401
Nir, Shaul, 416
Nissim, Moshe, 196, 395, 413
North, Oliver, 185, 188, 191, 401
North American Association of Jewish Homes and Housing for the Aging, 479
North American Conference on Ethiopian Jewry (NACOEJ), 455
North American Jewish Students Appeal, 490
North American Jewish Students' Network, 9, 491
*Northern California Jewish Bulletin,* 506
Norwood Childcare (Gr. Britain), 295
Novak, David, 134n
Novak, William, 127n, 151, 151n, 152n, 154n
Novik, Nimrod, 407
Nudel, Ida, 358, 422
*Nueva Presencia* (Argentina), 281
*Nueva Sion* (Argentina), 281
Nussbaum, Perry, 522
Nusseibeh, Sari, 372

Oakley, Phyllis, 194, 200
Obey, David, 194
Oboler, Jeffrey, 153n
O'Brien, Conor Cruise, 300
O'Connor, John Cardinal, 169, 170, 405
O'Connor, Mark, 419, 421
Offenberg, Mario, 346
Offer, Steve, 255
Ofir, Shaike, 431
*Ohio Jewish Chronicle,* 512
Okun, Herbert, 205
*Olomeinu—Our World,* 511
The Order, 178
ORT, 281

Ostow, Mortimer, 10, 10n
Ostrich, David, 105n
*Ottawa Jewish Bulletin & Review* (Canada), 514
Oury, Gérard, 311
Ovad, Uri, 376
Ovadia, Asher, 402
Ovsishcher, Lev, 358
Oz, Amos, 427
Ozar Hatorah, 465
Ozick, Cynthia, 156, 156n
Oziel, Leon, 269
Oziel, Salomon, 269

Palestine Liberation Organization (PLO), 199, 200, 203, 204, 206, 209, 210, 211, 283, 285, 285, 318, 368, 370, 372, 378, 382, 383, 387, 404
Palestine National Council (PNC), 203, 368
Paltzur, Mordechai, 365
Panama, 177
Pandraud, Robert, 306
Panerai, Paolo, 326
Papoulias, Karolos, 405
Parents of North American Israelis, 256
Parfitt, Tudor, 300
Pasqua, Charles, 306
Pasztor, Laszlo, 321
Patt, Gideon, 425
Peace Now, 286
Pearson, Lester B., 257
PEC Israel Economic Corporation, 486
*Pedagogic Reporter,* 511
PEF Israel Endowment Funds, 486
Pelavin, Michael, 41n
Penzer, Barbara Rosman, 57n
Peres, Shimon, 170, 189, 196, 197, 198, 199, 200, 201, 202, 203, 208, 224, 225, 226, 276, 284, 290, 325, 339, 335, 366–370, 392, 393, 395, 396, 397, 398, 399, 400, 402, 404, 405–411, 412, 417, 422, 423, 425
Peretz, Yitzhak, 219, 396, 411, 412, 417
Perlmutter, Fishel A., 52n
Perlmutter, Nathan, 194, 523
Peterson, David, 255

Petit, Phillipe, 426
Petuchowski, Jakob, 106n
P'eylim—American Yeshiva Student Union, 465
Phillips, Bernard, 139n
Phillips, Bruce A., 17n, 76n
Phillips, Lazarus, 269
Pickering, Thomas, 189, 194, 367, 368
Pierce, Bruce Carroll, 179
Pinkhof, Miriam Waterman, 318
Pioneer Women/Na'amat (see Na'amat USA)
Plaskow, Judith, 10, 12n, 43, 43n, 157n
Plaut, W. Gunther, 256
Plotkin, Harry M., 52n
P'nai Or Religious Fellowship, 159, 160
Poale Agudath Israel of America, 486
 Women's Division of, 486
Pogrebrin, Letty Cottin, 4, 4n, 225
Poindexter, John M., 189, 191
Poland, 363–365, 407
Polebaum, Beth, 53n
Poliakov, Léon, 308
Policy Research Corporation, 17n
Polier, Justine Wise, 523
Polish, David, 98n, 100n, 101n
Pollard, Anne-Henderson, 184, 192, 193, 212, 213, 396
Pollard, Jonathan, 184, 187, 192, 193, 194, 195, 212, 213, 214, 215, 392, 396–400, 424
Popkin, Ruth, 426
Popular Front for the Liberation of Palestine (PFLP), 204, 379, 387
Population Research Committee, 17n
Portnoi, Leopoldo, 272
Poupko, Chana, 61, 62n
*Pravda*, 353
Prell, Riv-Ellen, 150, 150n, 154n
Prendergast, Simone Ruth, 302
*Present Tense*, 511
*Di Presse* (Argentina), 281
Price, Ronald, 137n
Priesand, Sally, 11, 50
Procaccia, Ayala, 417
*Proceedings of the American Academy for Jewish Research*, 511
Progressive Zionist Caucus, 486

Prud'homme, Marcel, 257
Pryce-Jones, David, 300
Pyadeshev, Boris, 201

Rabbinical Alliance of America (Igud Harabonim), 109n, 465
Rabbinical Assembly, 50, 52, 53, 69, 69n, 74, 131, 133, 138, 229, 465
Rabbinical College of Telshe, 465
Rabbinical Council of America, 72, 109, 122, 148, 229, 230, 465
*Rabbinical Council Record*, 511
Rabin, Yitzhak, 186, 193, 194, 195, 196, 206, 208, 339, 367, 372, 373, 378, 382, 384, 391, 393, 394, 395, 397, 398, 399, 400, 403, 404, 405, 429
Rabinovitch, Joseph, 263
Rabinowitz, Henry, 159n
Rabinowitz, Mayer, 131n
Rackman, Emanuel, 72n
Rackman, Honey, 59, 59n
Rahman, Hassan, 211
Raikin, Arkady, 360
Raimond, Jean-Bernard, 306, 307, 404
Ramaz School, 49
Rankin, Michael, 159n
Raphael, Chaim, 300
Raphael, Marc Lee, 65n, 69n, 70n, 98n, 104n, 109n, 112n
Rapoport, Nathan, 523
Rappaport, Michael, 17n, 76n
Rasky, Harry, 267
Ratzinger, Joseph Cardinal, 171, 331
Rau, Johannes, 336
Ravel, Aviva, 266
Ravenswood Foundation (Gr. Britain), 295
Rayner, John, 298
Rayski, Adam, 312
Reagan, Ronald, 173, 187, 188, 190, 191, 198, 199, 207, 210, 211, 221, 338, 339, 354, 363, 383, 400, 401
Rebling, Jalda, 352
Recher, H., 347
*Reconstructionist*, 57, 74, 143, 513
Reconstructionist Rabbinical College, 139, 140, 141, 142, 144, 465
Redlich, Norman, 52n

Redman, Charles, 196
Reents, Jürgen, 337
Rees, Merlyn, 293
*Reform Judaism,* 511
Reform Synagogues of Great Britain, 297
Reich, Seymour, 225, 364
Reines, Alvin, 98n
Reinhards, Paul, 293
Reinhardt, Max, 345
Reisman, David, 27, 27n
Reitman, Dorothy, 256
Religious Zionist Movement, 218
Religious Zionists of America, 219, 486
  Bnei Akiva of North America, 486
  Mizrachi-Hapoel Hamizrachi, 487
  Mizrachi Palestine Fund, 487
  National Council for Torah Education of Mizrachi-Hapoel Hamizrachi, 487
  Noam-Mizrachi New Leadership Council, 487
*Renewal Magazine,* 573
Rennert, Jurgen, 352
Renton, Timothy, 296
*Reporter,* 511
Research Foundation for Jewish Immigration, 453
Research Institute of Religious Jewry, 466
*Response,* 10, 128, 511
RE'UTH Women's Social Service, 455
*Rhode Island Jewish Historical Notes,* 513
Rhodes, Paula, 5n
Ribak, Marcos, 273
Richey, Charles, 210
Richter, Alan, 148n
Richter, Glenn, 228
Rico, Aldo, 271, 276
Rieger, Jürgen, 340
Riese, Sylvia, 5n
al-Rifai, Zaid, 199
Rimalt, Eliahu, 431
Rimor, Mordecai, 5n
Riskin, Shlomo, 120, 120n
Ritterband, Paul, 17n, 76n, 80n
Robert, Marthe, 312
Robertson, Nan, 29n
Robinson, Aubrey E., Jr., 191, 192, 193, 212
Robinson, Ira, 108n
Rodal, Alti, 260
Röder, Werner, 347
Rogosnitsky, Mordechai Dov, 302
Roitman, Paul, 313
Romania, 365, 370, 407, 423
Rome, David, 268
Rose, Norman, 301
Rosen, Gladys, 31, 31n
Rosenberg, Eliahu, 420
Rosenberg, Louis, 269
Rosenblatt, Gary, 144n, 147n
Rosenman, Yehuda J., 523
Rosenne, Meir, 412
Rosensweig, Bernard, 119n
Rosenthal, Gilbert, 137, 138n
Rosenthal, Hans, 348
Rosenthal, Harold, 302
Rosove, John L., 158n
Ross, Malcolm, 258
Rotenstreich, Yehoshua, 194, 398
Roth, Ari, 349
Roth, Joel, 135
Roth, Shmuel J., 321
Rouillan, Jean-Marc, 305
Routtenberg, Max, 126, 126n, 524
Rubens, Bernice, 301
Rubin, Alban D., 70n
Rubin, Gary, 155n
Rubin, Rivke, 360
Rubin, Sam, 269
Rubin, Saul, 152
Rubin, Sheila, 155n
Rubinstein, Amnon, 390, 412, 415
Ruby, Walter, 148n
Ruderman, Yaakov Y., 524
Rudin, A. James, 172
Runcie, Robert, 301
Ryzhkov, Nikolai V., 166

Sachter, Robert, 268
Sackler, Arthur M., 524
Sacks, Jonathan, 300
St. Louis Center for Holocaust Studies, 453

St. Louis Jewish Light, 508
Sakal, Shlomo, 378
Salem, Wahid Abu, 378
Salgo, Nicolas, 362
Salomon, George, 32, 32n
Samad, Muayid Abdel, 376
*San Diego Jewish Times,* 506
Sarna, Jonathan, 5n
Sarna, Nahum, 5n, 48, 48n
Sarney, José, 282, 283
Sassler, Sharon, 17n
Sasson, Moshe, 380
Saudi Arabia, 292, 339
Sawan, Farid, 284
Schachter-Shalomi, Zalman, 159, 160
Schacter, Hershel, 47, 47n, 122n
Schembs, Hans Otto, 346
Schiff, Alvin I., 115n
Schiller, Herman, 277, 281
Schily, Otto, 337
Schindler, Alexander, 104, 106, 107, 107n, 183, 206, 224, 225, 226, 231
Schirman, Chalom, 258
Schlafke, Jakob, 343, 344
Schlesinger, Benjamin, 261
Schloss, Ezekiel, 524
Schmelz, U.O., 18n, 95n, 285, 433n
Schmidt, Alfred, 207
Schmidt, Henry, 349
Schmidt, Wolfgang, 207
Schnapper, Dominique, 305
Schneerson, Menachem M., 112, 148
Schneider, Susan Weidman, 3n, 11, 12n, 39n, 44n, 155n, 156n
Schneiderman, Jonathan, 268
Schnirer, Sara, 49, 49n
Schochet, Immanuel, 268
Schoenfeld, Stuart, 262
Schönberg, Arnold, 352
Schorr, Ann, 76n, 77n
Schorsch, Ismar, 124, 124n, 129, 135, 135n, 138, 138n
Schram, Vicki R., 36n
Schuder, Rosemarie, 352
Schultz, Ray, 114n
Schulweis, Harold, 127n, 143, 152, 152n
Schwager, Steven, 94n

Schwamm, Jeffrey Becker, 37n
Schwammberger, Josef Franz Leo, 275
Schwartz, Shuly Rubin, 68n
Schwarz, Sidney, 69n, 74n, 142n, 143n
Schwimmer, Al, 190, 401
Scott, Ian, 258
Scowcroft, Brent, 190
Scutari, Richard, 179
*Searchlight* (Gr. Britain), 293
Sebag-Montefiore, Ruth, 301
Segall, Alfred, 269
Segre, Dan Vittorio, 300
Seidel, Gill, 301
Seldin, Ruth R., 136n
Sella, Aviem, 193, 194, 213, 214, 397, 398
Seltzer, Sanford, 5n, 50, 94
Semi, Emanuela Trevisan, 332
Seminario Rabinico Latinoamericano, 281
*The Sentinel,* 507
Senz, Laurie S., 104n
Sephardic House, 453
Sephardic Jewish Brotherhood of America, 475
Shaffir, William, 267
Shahaf, Yigal, 377
Shahak, Amnon, 392, 400
Shakdiel, Leah, 418
Shaked, Michael, 422
Shalom, Avraham, 389
Shalom Center, 448
Shalvi, Alice, 3n
Shamgar, Meir, 388, 389, 420
Shamir, Yitzhak, 188, 190, 191, 192, 193, 195, 196, 197, 198, 199, 200, 201, 202, 203, 208, 214, 221, 224, 307, 325, 339, 366–370, 374, 379–382, 390, 393, 395, 397, 399, 401, 402, 404, 405–10, 412, 417, 418, 422, 423, 425, 429
Shankman, Jacob K., 66n
Shanks, Hershel, 105n
Shapira, Yosef, 371
Shapiro, Avraham, 219
Shapiro, Edward S., 108n
Shapiro, Lev Borisovich, 360

INDEX / 583

Shapiro, Saul, 52, 52n, 53, 81n, 120n, 127, 127n
Sharabaf, Uzi, 416
Sharansky, Natan, 226, 227, 265, 310, 423
Sharir, Avraham, 395, 430
Sharon, Ariel, 381, 396, 397, 410
Sharot, Stephen, 70n, 84n
Shas party (Israel), 411, 412
ash-Shawwa, Rashad, 386
Shazar, Michlelet, 280
Sheftel, Yoram, 419, 421
Shepherd, Naomi, 301
Sher, Neal M., 177
Sherer, Moshe, 219
Sheriff, Noam, 322
Sherman, Alfred, 295
Sheskin, Ira M., 17n, 76
Shevardnadze, Eduard, 202, 296, 407
*Sheviley Ha-Hinnukh,* 511
Shilo, Yigal, 432
Shimon, Tova, 269
Shin Bet, 375, 376, 388, 389
Shipler, David K., 301
Shipton, Sidney, 300
Shirman, Michael, 357, 423
Shizgal, Peter, 265
*Sh'ma,* 511
*Shmuessen Mit Kinder Un Yugent,* 511
Shnirman, Simon, 423
Sholem Aleichem Folk Institute, 466
Shomron, Dan, 379, 380, 394, 431
Shpeizman, Yuri, 357
Shultz, George, 184, 186, 193, 196, 197, 198, 199, 201, 202, 203, 208, 210, 221, 358, 367, 368, 369, 370, 377, 392, 395, 411, 422, 429
Sichrovsky, Peter, 347
Sieff, Marcus, 301
Sieff, Michael, 302
Siegel, Richard, 57n, 128, 128n
Siegel, Seymour, 52n, 69
Siegman, Henry, 168, 224, 225
Sifford, Darrell, 29n
Sila-Nowicki, Wladyslaw, 364
Silberman, Charles, 21, 22n, 92n, 120n
Silberman, Lou H., 97n

Silkin, John, 302
Silkin, Jon, 301
Silver, Samuel M., 99n
Silverman, David W., 129n
Silverman, Hillel, 126n
Silverman, Ira, 143n
Silverman, Morris, 69n
Silverstein, Alan, 130n
Simon Wiesenthal Center, 474
Sinclair, Clive, 301
Singer, Alexander, 387
Singer, David, 47n, 109n, 119n, 123n
Singer, Simeon, 298
Sirat, René Samuel, 310, 311, 313
al-Sissi, Hatham, 378
Sitruk, Joseph (Jo), 310
Skirball Museum, 460
Sklare, Marshall, 5n, 27n, 44n, 64n, 65n, 67n, 68n, 73, 74n, 86, 86n, 87n, 125, 125n, 126, 127, 127n, 130, 152n
Slepak, Masha, 296
Slepak, Vladimir, 296, 357, 358, 423
Sloan, Jacob, 72n, 74n
Slonim, Reuben, 268
Smith, Bailey, 172
Smith, David, 301
Sneh, Ephraim, 381
Snow, Ralph, 269
Snyder, Herman, 103n
Sobel, Bernard, 311
Sobel, Henry, 284, 286, 288
Sobol, Yehoshua, 427
Social Democrats (Fed. Republic of Germany), 336, 337
Society for Humanistic Judaism, 158, 466
Society for the History of Czechoslovak Jews, 453
Society of Friends of the Touro Synagogue, National Historical Site, 466
Society of Israel Philatelists, 487
Soetendorp, Avraham, 319
Sofer, Barbara, 112n
Sokol, Yuri, 358
Solender, Stephen, 228

Soloveitchik, Aaron, 230
Soloveitchik, Joseph B., 72, 119, 123n
Sonke, Paul, 319
Sosnow, Eric, 302
South, Hendon, 296
South Africa, 222, 223, 408
*Southern Jewish Weekly*, 507
*Southwest Jewish Chronicle*, 513
*Sovetish haimland*, 356, 359, 360
Soviet Jewry, 220, 226–228
Soviet Union, 353–360
Soyer, Raphael, 524
Spadolini, Giovanni, 405
Spain, 404
Spero, Shubert, 71n, 73n, 120n
Spertus College of Judaica, 466
Spire, Thérèse, 314
*Stark Jewish News*, 512
State of Israel Bonds, 487
Staub, Jacob J., 142n
Stavitsky, Arkady, 359
Stefanak, Michal, 361
Stein, Edith, 170, 171, 330, 343, 344
Steinbach, Peter, 347
Steinberg, Elan, 169, 177
Steinberg, Moshe, 524
Steinem, Gloria, 3, 7, 7n
Steiner, Harry, 269
Steinsaltz, Adin, 312
Stern, Fritz, 348
Stern, Hans, 269
Stern, Jack, 219
Sternberg, Lawrence, 5n, 26n
Stethem, Robert Dean, 207
Stieglitz, Joseph, 427
Stilman, Eduardo, 273
Stolar, Abe, 358
Stoleru, Lionel, 313
Stoltzman, Lou, 302
Stone, Amy, 8n, 34n
Storani, Federico, 272
Stourdze, Yves, 313
Strassfeld, Michael, 57n, 128n, 153n
Strassfeld, Sharon, 57n, 128n
Strauss, Franz-Josef, 339
Strauss, Herbert A., 347
Stroff, Michael, 269
Student Struggle for Soviet Jewry, 226, 448
*Studies in Bibliography and Booklore*, 512
Sud, Lev, 358
Suddarth, Roscoe, 187
*Sunday Times* (London), 390, 391, 392
Sunshine, Joshua, 302
Superstein, Jake, 268
*Survey of the Conservative Movement and Some of Its Religious Attitudes*, 52
Syme, Daniel, 219
Synagogue Council of America, 72, 167, 168, 466
*Synagogue Light*, 511
Syrkin, Marie, 14, 14n
Szonyi, David, 133n

Taba, 367, 402
Tack, David, 302
Taffler, Rae, 302
Tal, Josef, 347
Tal, Ron, 377
Tal, Zvi, 392, 419, 422
*Talks and Tales*, 511
TaMami, Haim, 376
Tamir, Avraham, 408
Tamir, Shmuel, 431
Tanenbaum, Marc, 68n, 72n, 183
Tannenbaum, Jacob, 177
Taratuta, Misha, 297
Tass, 177
Taubes, Jacob, 348, 525
Taubman, Philip, 359
Tebbit, Norman, 295
Tehiya party (Israel), 384
Temple Emanu-El-Beth Shalom (Canada), 266
Terasov, Vladimir, 407
Teutsch, David, 141n, 143n
*Texas Jewish Post*, 513
Thanks to Scandinavia, 455
Thatcher, Margaret, 290, 291, 292, 296, 297, 405
Theodor Herzl Foundation, 487
    Herzl Press, 487
    Theodor Herzl Institute, 487

Thorn, Gaston, 405
Thurlow, Richard, 300
*Ties and Tensions,* 212
*Tikkun,* 183, 506
Tindemans, Leo, 198, 368
Toaff, Elio, 332
Tobias, Juan Alejandro, 276
Tobin, Gary, 5n, 17n, 18n, 36n, 76n, 77n, 84n
Todres, Elaine, 255
*Toledo Jewish News,* 513
Tomasi, Giuseppe, 330
Topiol, Michel, 313
Torah Schools for Israel—Chinuch Atzmai, 466
Torah Umesorah—National Society for Hebrew Day Schools, 466
   Institute for Professional Enrichment, 466
   National Association of Hebrew Day School Administrators, 467
   National Association of Hebrew Day School Parent-Teacher Associations, 467
   National Conference of Yeshiva Principals, 467
   National Yeshiva Teachers Board of License, 467
Touro College, 467
   Barry Z. Levine School of Health Sciences and Center for Biomedical Education, 467
   College of Liberal Arts and Sciences, 467
   Graduate School of Jewish Studies, 467
   Institute of Jewish Law, 467
   Jacob D. Fuchsberg Law Center, 467
   Jewish People's University of the Air, 467
   School of General Studies, 468
   Shulamith School, 468
Tower, John, 188, 190, 400
Trachtenberg, Joshua, 71n
*Tradition,* 72, 118, 119, 511
*Tradition and Change,* 69
*Trends,* 511
Treumann, Otto, 323

Truche, Pierre, 308
Trudeau, Pierre Elliott, 260
Tsaban, Yair, 418
Tsur, Tsvi (Zvi), 194, 398
Tucker, Gordon, 52n, 132n
*Tulsa Jewish Review,* 513
Tunik, Yitzhak, 431
Turner, John, 265
Twerski, Aaron, 117n
Tyndall, Gillian, 301
Tzur, Yaacov, 221

Ubaldini, Saul, 271, 274
*UCSJ Quarterly Report,* 507
*UJF News,* 513
Umansky, Ellen, 5n, 12n, 13, 13n, 55, 55n
*Undzer Veg* (Canada), 514
Union for Traditional Conservative Judaism (UTCJ), 136, 137, 230, 266
Union of American Hebrew Congregations, 65, 69, 70, 70n, 94; 105, 182, 223, 224, 468
   American Conference of Cantors, 468
   Commission on Jewish Education, 468
   Commission on Social Action of Reform Judaism (*see* p. 446)
   Commission on Synagogue Management (with CCAR), 468
   National Association of Temple Administrators (NATA), 468
   National Association of Temple Educators (NATE), 468
   National Federation of Temple Brotherhoods, 468
   National Federation of Temple Sisterhoods, 468
   North American Federation of Temple Youth, 469
Union of Councils for Soviet Jews, 226, 228, 448
Union of Jewish Students (UJS), 293, 295
Union of Liberal and Progressive Synagogues (Gr. Britain), 297

Union of Orthodox Jewish Congregations of America, 174, 469
National Conference of Synagogue Youth, 469
Women's Branch, 469
Union of Orthodox Rabbis of the United States and Canada, 469
Union of Sephardic Congregations, 469
*Union Prayer Book,* 97
United Charity Institutions of Jerusalem, 487
United Israel Appeal, 487
United Jewish Appeal, 455
United Klans, 179
United Lubavitcher Yeshivoth, 469
United Nations, Resolutions *242* and *338,* 367, 368
United Nations, Security Council, 205
United Order True Sisters, (UOTS), 475
United States Committee Sports for Israel, 488
United Synagogue (Gr. Britain), 295, 297
United Synagogue of America, 69n, 470
 Commission on Jewish Education, 470
 Committee on Social Action and Public Policy, 470
 Jewish Educators Assembly, 470
 Kadima, 470
 National Association of Synagogue Administrators, 470
 United Synagogue Youth of, 470
*United Synagogue Review,* 511
United Torah Coalition (Canada), 264
*Unser Tsait,* 511
Unterberg, Clarence, 525
U.S. Holocaust Memorial Council, 453

Vaad Mishmereth Stam, 470
van den Broek, Hans, 319
van Thijn, Eduard, 322
van Tonningen, Flora Rost, 316
Vanunu, Mordechai, 390–392
Vardi, Rafael, 401
Varkonyi, Peter, 362
Vaughan, Suzanne, 20n

*Vechernaya Moskva,* 357
Veld, Nanno K.C.A. in't, 317
Vergès, Jacques, 307, 308
Vidal-Naquet, Pierre, 312
Vineberg, Philip, 269
Vlasov, Aleksandr, 357
Volvosky, Leonid, 358
von Brauchitsch, Eberhard, 336
von Weizsäcker, Richard, 338, 339, 403
Vorspan, Albert, 222, 223
Vosk, Marc, 74n
Vranitzky, Franz, 322

Waddington, Miriam, 269
Wagenaar, Willem A., 317
Waksberg, Joseph, 17n, 77n
Waldheim, Kurt, 165, 166, 167, 168, 169, 170, 183, 260, 295, 311, 326, 330, 406
Walesa, Lech, 363
Walsh, Lawrence, 188, 191, 401
Warschawsky, Michael, 376
Warshawski, Max, 310
*Washington Jewish Week,* 507
*Washington Post,* 189, 196, 212, 214, 215
Waskow, Arthur, 144n, 160, 160n
Wasserman, Dora, 266
Wasserman, Harry, 152n
Waxman, Chaim, 35, 35n, 115n, 119n
Waxman, Mordechai, 69
Webber, Harvey, 268
Weber, Simon, 525
Weinberg, Aubrey, 301
Weinberg, Eve, 76n
Weinberg, Henry, 267
Weinberg, Mark, 301
Weinberger, Caspar, 186, 193, 213
Weinberger, Moshe, 120n
Weiner, Gerry, 256
Weiner, Greta, 46, 46n
Weinreb, Haim, 299
Weinstein, Herb, 269
Weir, Benjamin, 171
Weisberg, Saul, 17n
Weiss, Avraham, 54
Weiss, Daniella, 375
Weissbort, Daniel, 301

Weissenberg-Akselrod, Pearl, 269
Weissler, Chava (Lenore Eve), 153n, 155, 155n
Weissman, Deborah R., 48n
Weissman, Ronen, 387
Weiss-Rosmarin, Trude, 9, 9n
Weitzman, David, 302
Weizman, Ezer, 380, 381, 403
Wenig, Maggie, 156n, 157n
Wertheimer, Jack, 63, 68n, 69n, 117n, 129n
Wertheimer, Stef, 427
Wesly, Jenny, 323
West Coast Talmudical Seminary, 471
*Western Jewish News (Canada),* 265
*Western States Jewish History,* 506
Wheeler, Ray, 77n
Whitehead, John, 351
Wiener, Carolyn L., 67n
Wiesel, Elie, 308, 313
Wiesenthal, Simon, 275
Willner, Max, 341
*Windsor Jewish Community Bulletin (Canada),* 514
Wine, Sherwin, 158
Winer, Mark L., 94n, 105n, 106n, 107n
*Winnipeg Jewish Post,* 265
Winston, Milton, 265
*Wisconsin Jewish Chronicle,* 513
Wise, George S., 525
Wisse, Ruth, 30, 30n, 268
Wohlgelernter, Devora, 61, 62n
Wolf, Bernard, 269
Wolf, Sylvin L., 101n
Wolfe, Anne, 41
Wolfe, Max, 269
Wolofsky, Jack, 265
Wolpin, Nisson, 146n
Women Against Pornography, 7
*Women's American ORT Reporter,* 512
Women's League for Conservative Judaism, 471
Women's League for Israel, 488
*Women's League Outlook,* 512
Woocher, Jonathan, 114n
Workmen's Circle, 476
    Division of Jewish Labor Committee (*see* p. 447)

*Workmen's Circle Call,* 512
World Confederation of Jewish Community Centers, 479
World Confederation of United Zionists, 488
World Conference of Jewish Communal Service, 448
World Council of Synagogues, 471
World Jewish Congress (WJC), 166, 449
World Union for Progressive Judaism, 471
World Zionist Congress, 216, 263, 299
World Zionist Organization, 217, 280, 299
World Zionist Organization—American Section, 488
    Department of Education and Culture, 488
    North American Aliyah Movement, 488
    Zionist Archives and Library of the, 488
Wörner, Manfred, 339
Wurzburger, Walter, 72n, 118, 118n, 123n

Xueqian, Wu, 409

Yaakobi, Gad, 196, 395, 412
Ya'ari, Meir, 431
Yagur, Yosef, 193
Yakir, Yevgeny, 358
Yakovlev, Alexander, 357
Yancey, William A., 17n, 76n
Yantovsky, Simon, 358
Yaron, Amos, 256
Yavne Hebrew Theological Seminary, 471
*Yearbook of the Central Conference of American Rabbis,* 512
*Yediot Aharonot,* 214
Yehoshua, A. B., 332, 427
Yelistratov, Batsheva, 296
Yelistratov, Victor, 296
Yeshiva University, 471
    Albert Einstein College of Medicine, 472
    Alumni Office, 472

Belfer Institute for Advanced Biomedical Studies, 472
Benjamin N. Cardozo School of Law, 472
Bernard Revel Graduate School, 472
Brookdale Institute for the Study of Gerontology (Wurzweiler School of Social Work), 472
David J. Azrieli Graduate Institute of Jewish Education and Administration, 472
Ferkauf Graduate School of Psychology,
Harry Fischel School for Higher Jewish Studies, 473
Rabbi Isaac Elchanan Theological Seminary, 473
Women's Organization, 473
Wurzweiler School of Social Work, 473
Yeshiva University of Los Angeles, 474
Simon Wiesenthal Center, 474
Yeshiva University Museum, 453
Yeshivath Torah Vodaath and Mesivta Rabbinical Seminary, 474
Alumni Association, 474
Yeutter, Clayton, 365
*Yiddish,* 512
*Di Yiddishe Heim,* 512
*Yiddishe Kultur,* 512
*Dos Yiddishe Vort,* 512
*Yiddisher Kemfer,* 512
Yiddisher Kultur Farband—YKUF, 453
*Yidishe Shprakh,* 512
*YIVO Annual of Jewish Social Science,* 512
*YIVO Bleter,* 512
Yivo Institute for Jewish Research, 454
Max Weinreich Center for Advanced Jewish Studies, 454
Yotam, Danny, 431

*Young Israel Viewpoint,* 124, 512
*Young Judaean,* 512
Yudkin, Leon, 300
*Yugntruf,* 512
Yugntruf Youth for Yiddish, 491
Yuter, Alan J., 137n
Yvane, Jean, 311

Zakheim, Dov, 195, 394
Zangwill, Oliver, 302
Zborowski, Mark, 74n
Zeldin, Michael, 104n
Zeldovich, Yakov Borisovich, 360
Zelichonok, Roald, 358
Zemans, Fred, 256
Zemer, Moshe, 101n
Zevi, Bruno, 334
Zevi, Tullia, 328, 329
Zichroni, Amnon, 391
Zimmer, Guido, 275
Zimmermann, Friedrich, 340
Zimmet, Judy, 391
Zion, Joel, 101
Zion Cables Ltd., 414
Zionist Federation, 299, 300
Zionist Organization of America, 488
Zionist Organization of Canada, 264, 493
Zlotowitz, Bernard, 231
Zober, Mark A., 76n, 82n
Zogby, James, 183
Zonneveld, Louk, 319
Zorinsky, Edward, 525
Zotov, Aleksandr, 198
Zuccotti, Susan, 301, 332
Zucker, David Jeremy, 105n
Zucker, Moses, 525
Zuckerman, Alan, 161n
Zuhaikah, Salah, 372
Zundel, Ernst, 255, 258
Zunshine, Tatiana, 423
Zunshine, Zachar, 297, 423
Zweiback-Levenson, Amy, 57n
Zweig, Arnold, 352

3 1542 00147 1659

296.05 A512
1989
American Jewish year book.

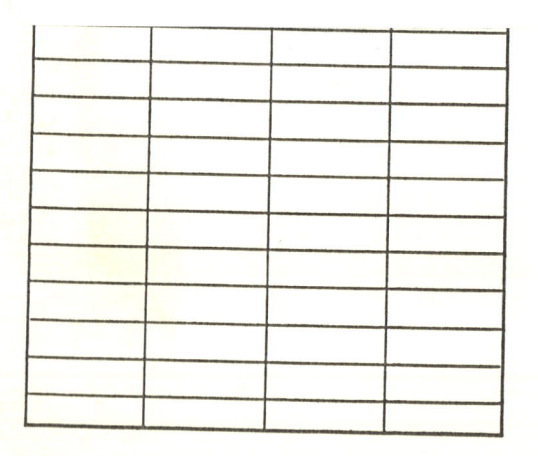

WITHDRAWN

**Trexler Library**
Muhlenberg College
Allentown, PA 18104

DEMCO